Viking Tales of Old Iceland 5

Original Texts, Translations, and Word Lists

Translated by
Matthew Leigh Embleton

Viking Tales of Old Iceland 5

The Tale of Bolli Bollason (*Old Norse*) 3
The Tale of Bolli Bollason (*Old Icelandic*) 68
The Tale of Thorsteinn House-Power (*Old Norse*) 140
The Tale of Thorsteinn House-Power (*Old Icelandic*) 216
The Tale of Sarcastic Halli (*Old Norse*) 294
The Tale of Sarcastic Halli (*Old Icelandic*) 377

Cover: Old Norse text over an outline of Iceland. Author's design.

The original Old Norse and Old Icelandic texts are in the public domain.
These translations ©2022 Matthew Leigh Embleton
©2025 Matthew Leigh Embleton (This Edition)

Acknowledgments

I have long been fascinated by languages and history, and I am very grateful to the special people in my life who have supported and encouraged me in my work. Thank you for believing in me. You know who you are.

Introduction

Old Norse is a North Germanic language spoken by inhabitants of Scandinavia from about the 7th to the 15th centuries. Old Icelandic is a variety of Old West Norse that emerged during the Norse settlement of Iceland in the second half of the 9th century. The rich tradition of Icelandic story telling survived by oral tradition over several centuries before being written down in the 13th Century. The Tales of Icelanders are known as Íslendingaþættir. The word 'þáttr' (plural: 'þættir') translates as a strand of rope or a yarn, comparable to the word 'yarn' in English sometimes used to refer to a story.

The texts are presented in Old Norse and Old Icelandic, in their original form, with a literal word-for-word line-by-line translation, and a Modern English translation, all side-by-side. In this way, it is possible to see and feel how the worked and how it has evolved. This book is designed to be of use and interest to anyone with a passion for the Old Norse or Old Icelandic language, Norse history, or languages and history in general.

The Tale of Bolli Bollason (*Old Norse*)

Old Norse	Literal	English
1	**1**	**1**
Í þann tíma, er Bolli Bollason bjó í Tungu ok nú var áðr frá sagt, þá bjó norðr í Skagafirði á Miklabæ Arnórr kerlingarnef, sonr Bjarnar Þórðarsonar frá Höfða.	At the time, that Bolli Bollason lived at Tunga also now was earlier from told, then lived north in Skagafjord in Miklabaer Arnor Crone's-Nose, son-of Bjarni Son-of-Thord from Hofdi.	At the same time that Bolli Bollason lived at Tunga, as was spoken of earlier, Arnor Crone's-Nose lived north at Skagafjord in Miklabaer, he was the son of Bjarni Thordarson from Hofdi.
Þórðr hét maðr, er bjó á Marbæli.	Thord named a-man, who lived at Marbaeli.	There was a man named Thord who lived at Marbaeli.
Guðrún hét kona hans.	Gudrun named wife his.	His wife was named Gudrun.
Þau váru vel at sér ok höfðu gnótt fjár.	They were well of themselves and had an-abundance of-wealth.	They were fine people and had an abundance of wealth.
Sonr þeira hét Óláfr, ok var hann ungr at aldri ok allra manna efniligastr.	Son theirs named Olaf, and was he young in age and of-all men promising.	Their son was named Olaf, and he was young and the most promising of all men.
Guðrún, kona Þórðar, var náskyld Bolla Bollasyni.	Gudrun, wife-of Thord, was closely-related Bolli Bollason.	Gudrun, Thord's wife, was closely related to Bolli Bollason.
Var hon systrungr hans.	Was she mother's-sister's-son his.	She was his cousin.
Óláfr, sonr þeira Þórðar, var heitinn eftir Óláfi þá í Hjarðarholti.	Olaf, son theirs Thord, was named after Olaf Peacock in Hjardarholt.	Their son Olaf was named after Olaf Peacock in Hjardarholt.
Þórðr ok Þorvaldr Hjaltasynir bjuggu at Hofi í Hjaltadal.	Thord and Thorvald Sons-of-Hjalti lived at Hof in Hjaltadal.	Thord and Thorvald Hjaltason lived at Hof in Hjaltadal.
Þeir váru höfðingjar miklir.	They were chieftains great.	They were great chieftains.
Maðr hét Þórólfr ok var kallaðr stertimaðr.	A-man was-named Thorolf and was called Stately-man.	There was a man named Thorolf and he was called Stuck-up.
Hann bjó í Þúfum.	He lived in Thufur.	He lived at Thufur.

The Tale of Bolli Bollason (Old Norse)

Old Norse	Literal	English
Hann var óvinveittr í skapi ok æðimaðr mikill.	He was unfriendly in mood and frenzy-man much.	He was unfriendly in nature and a very angry man.
Hann átti graðung grán, ólman.	He had a-bull grey, wild.	He had a wild grey bull.
Þórðr af Marbæli var í förum með Arnóri.	Thord of Marbaeli was on a-journey with Arnor.	Thord of Marbaeli was travelling with Arnor.
Þórólfr stærimaðr átti frændkonu Arnórs, en hann var þingmaðr Hjaltasona.	Thorolf Stately-man married kinswoman Arnor's, and he was assembly-man Hjaltasons.	Thorolf Stuck-up married one of Arnor's kinswomen, and was one of the assembly men of the Hjaltasons.
Hann átti illt við búa sína ok lagði þat í vanða sinn.	He had bad-terms with settlers his and became that in custom his.	He was on bad terms with his neighbours and that became the custom.
Kom þat mest til þeira Marbælinga.	Came that most to they-of Marbaeli.	And most of this came to the people of Marbaeli.
Graðungr hans gerði mönnum margt mein, þá er hann kom ór afréttum.	Bull his made people many harm, then as he came back-from the-pastures.	His bull did many people harm, when he came back from the pastures.
Meiddi hann fé manna, en gekk eigi undan grjóti.	Wounded he cattle people's, and went not away-from rocks.	He wounded people's cattle, and could not be made to go away with rocks.
Hann braut ok andvirki ok gerði margt illt.	He broke also haystacks and did much ill.	He also damaged haystacks and did much harm.
Þórðr af Marbæli hitti Þórólf at máli ok bað hann varðveita graðung sinn.	Thord of Marbaeli met Thorolf to discuss and asked him ward-knowing bull his.	Thord of Marbaeli met Thorolf to discuss this with him, and asked him to watch guard over his bull.
"Viljum vér eigi þola honum ofríki".	"Will we not endure his rampages".	"Will we not endure his rampages".
Þórólfr lézt eigi mundu sitja at fé sínu.	Thorolf said not would sit at cattle his.	Thorold said that he would not sit by his cattle.
Ferr Þórðr heim við svá búit.	Travelled Thord home with so prepared.	Thord travelled home with this reply.
Eigi miklu síðar getr Þórðr at líta, hvar graðungrinn hefir brotit niðr torfstakka hans.	Not much afterwards got Thord that look, where the-bull had broken down turf-stacks his.	Not long afterwards Thord noticed that the bull had torn apart his stacks of turf.

The Tale of Bolli Bollason (Old Norse)

Old Norse	Literal	English
Þórðr hleypr þá til ok hefir spjót í hendi, ok er boli sér þat, veðr hann jörð, svá at upp tekr um klaufir.	Thord ran then to and had spear in hand, and when the-bull saw that, weathered he earth, so that up took about hooves.	Thord then ran over with a spear in his hand, and when he saw it, the bull beat the ground and took up on his hooves.
Þórðr leggr til hans, svá at hann fellr dauðr á jörð.	Thord lunged to him, so that he fell dead to the-earth.	Thord lunged at him so that he fell dead on the ground.
Þórðr hittir Þórólf ok sagði honum, at boli var dauðr.	Thord met Thorolf and told him, that the-bull was dead.	Thord met Thorolf and told him, that the-bull was dead.
"Þetta var lítit frægðarverk", svarar Þórólfr, "en gera mynda ek þat vilja, er þér þætti eigi betr".	"This was little famous-work", answered Thorolf, "and do should I that will, that to-you seems not better".	"This deed is of little honour", answered Thorolf, "and I should wish to do to you something that is no better".
Þórólfr var málóði ok heitaðist í hverju orði.	Thorolf was of-violent-language and called at every word.	Thorolf called on violent language with every word.
Þórðr átti heimanferð fyrir höndum.	Thord had from-home-travel before his-hands.	Thord had to leave his farm.
Óláfr, sonr hans, var þá sjau vetra eða átta.	Olaf, son his, was then seven winters or eight.	His son Olaf was then seven or eight winters.
Hann fór af bænum með leik sínum ok gerði sér hús, sem börnum er títt, en Þórólfr kom þar at honum.	He went off the-farm with game his and made himself a-house, which children are reported, then Thorolf came there at him.	He went away from the farm and played a game of making himself a house, which children often do, and then Thorolf came at him.
Hann lagði sveininn í gegnum með spjóti.	He lunged the-boy in through with spear.	He lunged through the boy with a spear.
Síðan fór hann heim ok sagði konu sinni.	Afterwards travelled he home and told wife his.	Afterwards he travelled home and told his wife.
Hon svarar:	She answered:	She answered:
"Þetta er illt verk ok ómannligt.	"This is ill work and inhumane.	"This is an evil and inhumane deed.
Mun þér þetta illu reifa".	Shall you this evil account-for".	You shall account for this evil".

The Tale of Bolli Bollason (Old Norse)

Old Norse	Literal	English
En er hon tók á honum þungt, þá fór hann í brott þaðan ok létti eigi fyrr en hann kom á Miklabæ til Arnórs.	Since that she took of him negatively, then travelled he to away from-there and relieved not before that he came to Miklabaer to Arnor's.	Since she responded so negatively, he then travelled away and did not rest until he came to Miklabaer to Arnor.
Fréttust þeir tíðenda.	Reported they news.	They exchanged news.
Þórólfr segir honum víg Óláfs.	Thorolf told him slaying-of Olaf's.	Thorolf told him of the killing of Olaf.
"Sé ek þar nú til trausts, sem þér eruð, sakar mágsemðar".	"See I here now to trust, that you are, sake as-in-laws".	"I look here to trust in you, for my sake, as we are in-laws".
"Eigi ferr þú sjándi eftir um þenna hlut", sagði Arnórr, "at ek muna virða meira mágsemð við þik en virðing mína ok sæmð, ok ásjá áttu hér engrar ván af mér".	"Not going you seeing after about this lot", said Arnor, "that I should worth more in-laws with you than worth my and honour, and assistance have-you here none to-expect of me".	"You will not see it after this", said Arnor, "as I do not value my in-laws more than my honour, and you have no assistance to expect from me".
Fór Þórólfr upp eftir Hjaltadal til Hofs ok fann þá Hjaltasonu ok sagði þeim, hvar komit var hans máli, "ok sé ek hér nú til ásjá, sem þit eruð".	Travelled Thorolf up after Hjaltadal to Hof and found then Hjaltasons and told them, what came was his matter, "and being I here now to assistance, as you-two are".	Thorolf travelled for Hof in Hjaltadal and found the Hjaltasons and told them what had happened, "and I am here now to ask for your assistance, as you are".
Þórðr svarar:	Thord answered:	Thord answered:
"Slíkt eru níðingsverk, ok mun ek enga ásjá veita þér um þetta efni".	"Such is lowly-deed, and should I none assistance grant to-you about this matter".	"This is such a lowly deed, and I should grant you no assistance in this matter".
Þorvaldr varð um fár.	Thorvald was about few.	Thorvald was of few words.
Fær Þórólfr ekki af þeim at sinni.	Got Thorolf nothing from them in his.	Thorolf got nothing from them in this matter.
Reið hann í brott ok upp eftir Hjaltadal til Reykja, fór þar í laug.	Rode he to away and up after Hjaltadal to Reykir, went there to bathe.	He rode away for Hjaltadal to Reykir, where he went to bathe.

The Tale of Bolli Bollason (Old Norse)

Old Norse	Literal	English
En um kveldit reið hann ofan aftr ok undir virkit at Hofi ok ræddist við einn saman, svá sem annarr maðr væri fyrir ok kveddi hann ok frétti, hverr þar væri kominn.	Then about evening rode he down back and near the-compound at Hof and discussed with alone together, so as another man was before and greeting him and asking, who there was come.	Then in the evening he rode back down near the farmhouse at Hof where he spoke to himself, as if someone was standing there, who greeted him and asked who was there.
"Ek heiti Þórólfr", kvað hann.	"I am-named Thorolf", said he.	"I am named Thorolf", he said.
"Hvert vartu farinn, eða hvat er þér á höndum?" spyrr launmaðrinn.	"Which where travelling, and what is your in hand?" asked the-unseen-man.	"Where are you travelling, and what is your problem?" asked the unseen man.
Þórólfr segir tilfelli þessi öll, eftir því sem váru.	Thorolf told occurrence this all, after accordingly as was.	Thorolf told him all that had occurred.
"Bað ek Hjaltasonu ásjá", segir hann, "sakar nauðsynja minna".	"Asked I Hjaltasons assistance", said he, "for-the-sake-of deed-refuse mine".	"I asked for the Hjaltasons assistance", he said, "for the sake of my assistance".
Þessi svarar, er fyrir skyldi vera:	This answered, who before should be:	The man who should be before him answered:
"Gengit er nú þaðan, er þeir gerðu erfit þat it fjölmenna, er tólf hundruð manna sátu at, ok ganga slíkir höfðingjar mjök saman, er nú vilja eigi veita einum manni nökkura ásjá".	"Gone are now from-there, that they made difficulty that the many-men, were twelve hundred men sitting about, and went such chieftains many together, are now willing not grant any man any assistance".	"They are now gone, they who made the difficulty with many men, there were twelve hundred sitting about, and many such chieftains went together, who are not willing to grant any man assistance".
Þorvaldr var úti staddr ok heyrði talit.	Thorvald was outside standing and heard conversation.	Thorvald was standing outside and heard the conversation.
Hann gengr þangat til ok tók í tauma hestsins ok bað hann af baki stíga, "en þó er eigi virðingarvænligt við þik at eiga fyrir sakar fólsku þinnar".	He went there to and took the reins horse's and asked him off horseback step, "but though is not respect-kindly with you to have before conviction false yours".	He went over and took the reins of the horse and asked him to step off horseback, "but it is not with honour to help a man before me with a conviction as false as yours".

2

Nú er at segja frá Þórði, er hann kom heim ok frá víg sonar síns ok harmaði þat mjök.	Now is to say from Thord, that he came home and from the-slaying-of son his and mourned that much.	Now the story turns to Thord, who came home and learned of the killing of his sun, and mourned it very much.

The Tale of Bolli Bollason (Old Norse)

Old Norse	Literal	English
Guðrún, kona hans, mælti:	Gudrun, wife his, spoke:	His wife Gudrun spoke:
"Þat er þér ráð at lýsa vígi sveinsins á hönd Þórólfi, en ek mun ríða suðr til Tungu ok finna Bolla, frænda minn, ok vita, hvern styrk hann vill veita okkr til eftirmáls".	"It is to-you declare that describe the-slaying son-yours in hand Thorolf, and I should ride south to Tunga and find Bolli, kinsman mine, and know, what strength he wished grant us to after-matter".	"It is for you to declare Thorolf responsible for the slaying of your son, and I shall ride south to Tunga and find Bolli my kinsman, and know what help he is willing to grant us to gain redress".
Þau gerðu svá.	They did so.	This they did.
Ok er Guðrún kom í Tungu, fær hon þar viðtökur góðar.	And was Gudrun come to Tunga, travelled she there with-taking good.	And when Gudrun came to Tunga, she was given a good welcome.
Hon segir Bolla víg Óláfs, sonar síns, ok beiddi, at hann tæki við eftirmálinu.	She said Bolli killing Olaf's, son her, and asked, that he take with the-after-matter.	She told Bolli about the killing of her son Olaf, and asked that he take over the prosecution of the case.
Hann svarar:	He answered:	He answered:
"Eigi þykkir mér þetta svá hægligt, at seilast til sæmðar í hendr þeim Norðlendingum.	"Not seems to-me this so easily, to obtain to honour in hand they Northerners.	"It does not seem to me to be so easy, to obtain honour from those northerners.
Fréttist mér ok svá til sem maðrinn muni þar niðr kominn, at ekki muni hægt eftir at leita".	Reported me and so to that the-man should there down come, that not should possible after to seek".	It has been reported to me that this man has gone down somewhere that it will not be possible to seek him out.
Bolli tók þó við málinu um síðir, ok fór Guðrún norðr ok kom heim.	Bolli took though with the-case about eventually, and travelled Gudrun north and came home.	Bolli agreed to take on the case, and Gudrun travelled north and came home.
Hon sagði Þórði, bónda sínum, svá sem nú var komit, ok líðr svá fram um hríð.	She told Thord, husband hers, so as now was come, and passed so from about awhile.	When she arrived home, she told her husband Thord what had happened, and so it passed for a while.
Eftir jól um vetrinn var lagðr fundr í Skagafirði at Þverá, ok stefndi Þorvaldr þangat Guðdala-Starra.	After Yule about winter was laid a-meeting in Skagafjord at Thvera, and summoned Thorvald from-there Starri-of-Guddalir.	After Yule in winter there was a meeting held in Skagafjord at Thvera, and Thorvald summoned Starri of Guddalir.

The Tale of Bolli Bollason (Old Norse)

Old Norse	Literal	English
Hann var vinr þeira bræðra.	He was a-friend of-they the-brothers.	He was a friend of the (Hjaltason) brothers.
Þorvaldr fór til þingsins við sína menn, ok er þeir kómu fyrir Urðskriðuhóla, þá hljóp ór hlíðinni ofan at þeim maðr.	Thorvald travelled to the-assembly with his men, and when they came before Urdskriduholar, then ran from the-slope down at them a-man.	Thorvald travelled to the assembly with his men, and when they came to Urdskriduholar, a man came running down the slope towards them.
Var þar Þórólfr.	Was it Thorolf.	It was Thorolf.
Réðst hann í ferð með þeim Þorvaldi.	Rode he in travelling with them Thorvald.	He joined and rode with Thorvald (and his men).
Ok er þeir áttu skammt til Þverár, þá mælti Þorvaldr við Þórólf:	And when they had a-short-distance to Thvera, then spoke Thorvald with Thorolf:	When they had a short distance remaining to Thvera, Thorvald spoke to Thorolf:
"Nú skaltu hafa með þér þrjár merkr silfrs ok sitja hér upp frá bænum at Þverá.	"Now shall have with you three marks of-silver and sit here up from farmhouse at Thvera.	"Take three marks of silver and stay here above the farmhouse at Thvera.
Haf þat at marki, at ek mun snúa skildi mínum ok at þér holinu, ef þér er fritt, ok máttu þá fram ganga.	Have this as a-sign, that I shall turn shield mine and that you hollow, if you are safe, and may then from go.	Have this as a sign, that I will turn the inside of my shield if you are safe and can come from there.
Skjöldrinn er hvítr innan".	The-shield is white inside".	The shield is white on the inside".
Ok er Þorvaldr kom til þingsins, hittust þeir Starri ok tóku tal saman.	And when Thorvald came to the-assembly, met they Starri and took-to talking together.	And when Thorvald came to the assembly, they met Starri and talked together.
Þorvaldr mælti:	Thorvald spoke:	Thorvald spoke:
"Svá er mál með vexti, at ek vil þess beiða, at þú takir við Þórólfi stærimanni til varðveizlu ok trausts.	"So is the-matter with grown, that I will this offer, that you take with Thorolf Stately-man to hospitality and trust.	"So is the matter has come, I will offer this, that I wish you to take Thorolf Stuck-up into your hospitality and support.
Mun ek fá þér þrjár merkr silfrs ok vináttu mína".	Should I fee to-you three marks of-silver and friendship mine".	I shall pay you three marks of silver and give you my friendship.

The Tale of Bolli Bollason (Old Norse)

Old Norse	Literal	English
"Þar er sá maðr", svarar Starri, *"er mér þykkir ekki vinsæll, ok óvíst, at honum fylgi hamingja.*	"There is so a-man", answered Starri, "that to-me seems not popular, and uncertain, that he follows luck.	"There is such a man", answered Starri, "that is not popular in my eyes, and not likely to bring much luck.
En sakar okkars vinskapar þá vil ek við honum taka".	But for-the-sake-of our friendship then will I with him take".	But for the sake of our friendship I will take him with me".
"Þá gerir þú vel", segir Þorvaldr.	"The do you well", said Thorvald.	"You do well in that case", said Thorvald.
Sneri hann þá skildinum ok frá sér hválfinu, ok er Þórólfr sér þat, gengr hann fram, ok tók Starri við honum.	Turned he then the-shield and from himself half, and when Thorolf saw that, went he from, and took Starri with him.	He then turned his shield from himself half way, and when Thorolf saw that, he went from where he was and received him.
Starri átti jarðhús í Guðdölum, því at jafnan váru með honum skógarmenn.	Starri had earth-house in Guddalir, because that usually were with him forest-men.	Starri had an earth house in Guddalir because he usually had outlaws with him.
Átti hann ok nökkut sökótt.	Had he also some accusations.	He had also had some charges against him.

3

Bolli Bollason býr til vígsmálit Óláfs.	Bolli Son-of-Bolli prepared to fight-the-case Olaf's.	Bolli Bollason prepared to prosecute Olaf's case.
Hann býst heiman ok ferr norðr til Skagafjarðar með þrjá tigu manna.	He prepared at-home and set-out north to Skagafjord with three ten men.	He made preparations and set out north to Skagafjord with thirty men.
Hann kemr á Miklabæ, ok er honum þar vel fagnat.	He came to Miklabaer, and was he there well welcomed.	He came to Miklabaer and was well welcomed there.
Segir hann, hversu af stóð um ferðir hans.	Said he, how-so of stood about journey his.	He told them the reasons for his journey.
"Ætla ek at hafa fram vígsmálit nú á Hegranessþingi á hendr Þórólfi stærimanni.	"Intend I to have from fight-the-case now to Hegranes-Assembly in hand Thorolf Stately-man.	"I intend to prosecute the case at Hegranes Assembly for Thorolf Stuck-up.
Vilda ek, at þú værir mér um þetta mál liðsinnaðr".	Wish I, that you would-be to-me about this matter team-minded".	I would like you to assist and cooperate with me in this matter".

The Tale of Bolli Bollason (Old Norse)

Old Norse	Literal	English
Arnórr svarar:	Arnor answered:	Arnor answered:
"Ekki þykkir mér þú, Bolli, vænt stefna út, er þú sækir norðr hingat, við slíka ójafnaðarmenn sem hér er at eiga.	"Not seems to-me you, Bolli, expect agreement from, that you seek north here, with such un-equal-men which here are to in.	"It doesn't seems to me, Bolli, that you can expect an agreement that you seek here in the north, with such unjust men that are here".
Munu þeir þetta mál meir verja með kappi en réttendum.	Should they this matter more protect with warriors whether right.	They would defend this matter as warriors whether just or unjust.
En ærin nauðsyn þykkir mér þér á vera.	But considerable necessity seems to-me to-you to be.	But it seems that you have a considerable necessity.
Munum vér ok freista, at þetta mál gangi fram".	Should we also try, that this matter going from".	So we should try to do what we can in this matter.
Arnórr dregr at sér fjölmenni mikit.	Arnor drew to himself followers-many much.	Arnor collected a large number of men.
Ríða þeir Bolli til þingsins.	Rode they Bolli to the-assembly.	They rode with Bolli to the assembly.
Þeir bræðr fjölmenna mjök til Hegranessþings.	The brothers following-men much to Hegranes-Assembly.	The brothers also came with many followers to Hegranes Assembly.
Þeir hafa frétt um ferðir Bolla.	They had news about journey Bolli's.	They had news about Bolli's journey.
Ætla þeir at verja málit.	Intended they to defend the-case.	They intended to defend the case.
Ok er menn koma til þingsins, hefir Bolli fram sakar á hendr Þórólfi,	And when people came to the-assembly, had Bolli from the-charges in hand Thorolf,	And when people came to the assembly, Bolli presented the charges against Thorolf,
ok er til varna var boðit, gengu þeir til Þorvaldr ok Starri við sveit sína ok hugðu at eyða málinu fyrir Bolla með styrk ok ofríki.	and was to defence was bid, went they to Thorvald and Starri with company theirs and thought that devastate the-case before Bolli with strength and un-rule.	and then the defence was made, and Thorvald and Starri came forward with their company, they intended to block Bolli's prosecution with strength and unruliness.
En er þetta sér Arnórr, gengr hann í milli með sína sveit ok mælti:	Then when this saw Arnor, went he in between with his company and spoke:	Then when Arnor saw this, he went in-between with his company and spoke:

The Tale of Bolli Bollason (Old Norse)

Old Norse	Literal	English
"Þat er mönnum einsætt at færa hér eigi svá marga góða menn í vandræði sem á horfist, at menn skyli eigi ná lögum um mál sín.	"It is to-people one-agreement that bringing here not so many good men in dispute as to looks, that people shall not obtain law about the-matter this.	"It is clear that so many good men should not be here in the dispute as now looks likely, that people shall not get justice in this matter.
Er ok ófallit at fylgja Þórólfi um þetta mál.	It-is also misguided to follow Thorolf about this case.	It is also misguided to support Thorolf in this case.
Muntu, Þorvaldr, ok óliðdrjúgr verða, ef reyna skal".	Should-you, Thorvald, also un-substantial-company become, if tested shall-be".	And you, Thorvald, will have little backing if it comes to a show of force.
Þeir Þorvaldr ok Starri sá nú, at málit myndi fram ganga, því at þeir höfðu ekki liðsafla við þeim Arnóri ok léttu þeir frá.	They Thorvald and Starri saw now, that the-case should from go, since that they had not company-provided with them Arnor and relieved they from.	Thorvald and Starri now saw that the case would be concluded, since they did not have the same number of men with them to match Arnor, so they withdrew.
Bolli sekði Þórólf stærimann þar á Hegranessþingi um víg Óláfs, frænda síns, ok fór við þat heim.	Bolli convicted Thorolf Stately-man there at Hegranes-Assembly about the-killing-of Olaf's, kinsman his, and travelled with that home.	Bolli convicted Thorolf Stuck-up there at Hegranes Assembly for the killing of his kinsman Olaf, and then went home.
Skilðust þeir Arnórr með kærleik.	Separated they Arnor with friendship.	He separated from Arnor with friendship.
Sat Bolli í búi sínu.	Sat Bolli in farm his.	Bolli stayed on his farm.
4	4	4
Þorgrímr hét maðr.	Thorgrim was-named a-man.	There was a man named Thorgrim.
Hann átti skip uppi standanda í Hrútafirði.	He had a-ship up stood in Hrutafjord.	He had a ship which stood at Hrutafjord.
Þangat reið Starri ok Þórólfr við honum.	There rode Starri and Thorolf to him.	Starri and Thorolf rode there to be with him.
Starri mælti við stýrimann:	Starri spoke with the-captain:	Starri spoke with the captain:

The Tale of Bolli Bollason (Old Norse)

Old Norse	Literal	English
"Hér er maðr, at ek vil, at þú takir við ok flytir útan, ok hér eru þrjár merkr silfrs, er þú skalt hafa ok þar með vináttu mína".	"Here is a-man, that I wish, that you take with and with-fleetness abroad, and here are three marks of-silver, and you shall have also there with friendship mine".	"Here is a man that I wish you to take abroad quickly, and here are three marks of silver, and you shall also have my friendship".
Þorgrímr mælti:	Thorgrim spoke:	Thorgrim spoke:
"Á þessu þykkir mér nökkurr vandi, hversu af hendi verðr leyst.	"About this seems to-me somewhat difficulty, how-so of hand becomes solved.	"It seems to me that it will be somewhat difficult to be able to solve.
En við áskorun þína mun ek við honum taka,	But with challenge yours should I with him take,	But with your challenge I shall take him,
en þó þykkir mér þessi maðr vera ekki giftuvænligr".	but though seems to-me this a-man becomes not luck-promised".	though it seems to me that this man promises much luck".
Þórólfr réðst nú í sveit með kaupmönnum, en Starri ríðr heim við svá búit.	Thorolf rode now in company with trading-men, and Starri rode home with so prepared.	Thorolf then rode in company with the merchants, and Starri rode home so prepared.
Nú er at segja frá Bolla.	Now is to say from Bolli.	Now the story turns to Bolli.
Hann hugsar nú efni þeira Þórólfs ok þykkir eigi verða mjök með öllu fylgt, ef Þórólfr skal sleppa.	He thought now the-matter theirs Thorolf's and thought not would-be much with all followed, if Thorolf should escape.	He thought about their matter with Thorolf and thought it would not be much if it followed that Thorolf should escape.
Frétti hann nú, at hann er til skips riðinn.	Learned he now, that he was to ships riding.	He now learned that he was riding to the ships.
Bolli býst heiman.	Bolli prepared from-home.	Bolli prepared to leave home.
Setr hann hjálm á höfuð sér, skjöld á hlið,	Set he helmet on head his, shield about side,	He put his helmet on his head, his shield by his side,
spjót hafði hann í hendi, en gyrðr sverðinu Fótbít.	spear had he in hand, in buckled the-sword Leg-Biter.	his spear in his hand, and buckled the sword Leg Biter.
Hann ríðr norðr til Hrútafjarðar ok kom í þat mund, er kaupmenn váru albúnir.	He rode north to Hrutafjord and came in so about-that-time, as trading-men were all-prepared.	He rode north to Hrutafjord and arrived at about the time that the merchants were all prepared.

The Tale of Bolli Bollason (Old Norse)

Old Norse	Literal	English
Var þá ok vindr á kominn.	Then when also the-wind up came.	Then the wind also came up.
Ok er Bolli reið at búðardurunum, gekk Þórólfr út í því ok hafði húðfat í fangi sér.	And as Bolli rode to the-booth-doors, went Thorolf out about because also had bed-roll in arms his.	And as Bolli rode up to the camp doors, Thorolf came out carrying his bed roll in his arms.
Bolli bregðr Fótbít ok leggr í gegnum hann.	Bolli drew Leg-Biter and lunged at through him.	Bolli drew Leg Biter and lunged through him.
Fellr Þórólfr á bak aftr í búðina inn, en Bolli hleypr á hest sinn.	Fell Thorolf on back down in the-booth inside, and Bolli ran to horse his.	Thorolf fell back into the camp, and Bolli ran to his horse.
Kaupmenn hljópu saman ok at honum.	Trading-men ran together and at him.	The merchants ran together towards him.
Bolli mælti:	Bolli spoke:	Bolli spoke:
"Hitt er yðr ráðligast at láta nú vera kyrrt, því at yðr mun ofstýri verða at leggja mik við velli,	"Find is you advisable that leave now being peace, because that you should unmanageable being to lay me with the-fields,	"It is advisable that you leave now in peace, because you shall not manage to bring me down in the fields,
en vera má, at ek kvista einhvern yðvarn eða alla tvá, áðr ek em felldr".	but being may, that I trim one of-you or all two, before I am falling".	and it may be, that I trim one or two of you before I fall".
Þorgrímr segir:	Thorgrim said:	Thorgrim said:
"Ek hygg, at þetta sé satt".	"I think, that this is true".	"I think that this is true".
Létu þeir vera kyrrt, en Bolli reið heim ok hefir sótt mikinn frama í þessi ferð.	Let they be still, and Bolli rode home and had attended much honour in this journey.	They remained still, and Bolli rode home and earned a great deal of honour from this journey.
Færr hann af þessu virðing mikla, ok þótti mönnum farit sköruliga, hefir sekðan manninn í öðrum fjórðungi, en síðan riðit einn saman í hendr óvinum sínum ok drepit hann þar.	Accomplished he of this honour much, and thought people travelled boldly, had outlawed person in another district, and then ride alone together in hand un-friends his and kill him there.	He accomplished much honour in this, and people thought he travelled boldly, to have the man outlawed in another district, and then riding alone into the hands of his enemies and killing him there.

The Tale of Bolli Bollason (Old Norse)

Old Norse	Literal	English
# 5	# 5	# 5
Um sumarit á alþingi fundust þeir Bolli ok Guðmundr inn ríki ok töluðu margt.	About summer at the-assembly met they Bolli and Gudmund the powerful and talked much.	About summer at the assembly Bolli and Gudmund the Powerful met and talked much.
Þá mælti Guðmundr;	Then spoke Gudmund;	Then Gudmund spoke:
"Því vil ek lýsa, Bolli, at ek vil við slíka menn vingast sem þér eruð.	"Because wish I show, Bolli, that I wish with such people make-friends as you are.	"I wish to say to you, Bolli, that I wish to make friends with people like you.
Ek vil bjóða þér norðr til mín til hálfsmánaðar veizlu, ok þykkir mér betr, at þú komir".	I wish to-invite you north to mine to half-month's feast, and consider me better, that you come".	I wish to invite you north to mine for a half month's feast, and I would think the best of it if you came".
Bolli svarar, at vísu vill hann þiggja sæmðir at slíkum manni, ok hét hann ferðinni.	Bolli answered, that certainly wished he accept honour from such a-man, and promised he the-journey.	Bolli answered that he certainly wished to accept this honour from such a man, and promised that he would make the journey.
Þá urðu ok fleiri menn til at veita honum þessi vinganarmál.	Then became also more men to that grant him this friendship-matter.	Then others also came to grant him friendship.
Arnórr kerlingarnef bauð Bolla ok til veizlu á Miklabæ.	Arnor Crone's-nose invited Bolli also to feast at Miklabaer.	Arnor Crone's-Nose also invited Bolli to a feast at Miklabaer.
Maðr hét Þorsteinn.	A-man named Thorstein.	There was a man named Thorstein.
Hann bjó at Hálsi.	He lived at Hals.	He lived at Hals.
Hann var sonr Hellu-Narfa.	He was the-son-of Hellu-Narfi.	He was the son of Hellu-Narfi.
Hann bauð Bolla til sín, er hann færi norðan, ok Þórðr á Marbæli bauð Bolla.	He invited Bolli to his, that he travel north, and Thord at Marbaeli invited Bolli.	He invited Bolli to travel north to his, and so did Thord at Marbaeli.
Fóru menn af þinginu, ok reið Bolli heim.	Travelled people to the-assembly, and rode Bolli home.	People travelled to the assembly, and Bolli rode home.
Þetta sumar kom skip í Dögurðarnes ok settist þar upp.	That summer came a-ship in Dagverdarnes and set there up.	That summer a ship came in at Dagverdarnes and set up there.
Bolli tók til vistar í Tungu tólf kaupmenn.	Bolli took to lodging at Tunga twelve trading-men.	Bolli took lodging for twelve trading men.

The Tale of Bolli Bollason (Old Norse)

Old Norse	Literal	English
Váru þeir þar um vetrinn, ok veitti Bolli þeim allstórmannliga.	Were they there about winter, and granted Bolli home all-great-man-like.	They were there about winter, and Bolli provided from them generously.
Sátu þeir um kyrrt fram yfir jól.	Sat they about still from over Yule.	They stayed there for Yule.
En eftir jól ætlar Bolli at vitja heimboðanna norðr, ok lætr hann þá járna hesta ok býr ferð sína.	Then after Yule intended Bolli to visit home-invitation north, and had he then iron-shod horses and prepared travel his.	Then after Yule, Bolli intended to visit the north as invited, and he had horses shod and prepared to travel.
Váru þeir átján í reið.	Were they eighteen in riding.	There were eighteen of them riding.
Váru kaupmenn allir vápnaðir.	Were trading-men all weaponed.	All the merchants were armed.
Bolli reið í blári kápu ok hafði í hendi spjótit konungsnaut, it góða.	Bolli rode in black cape and had in hand spear king's-gift, the good.	Bolli rode in a black cape and in his hand the spear, King's Gift, the good.
Þeir ríða nú norðr ok koma á Marbæli til Þórðar.	They rode now north and came to Marbaeli to Thord.	They now rode north and came to Marbaeli to Thord.
Var þar allvel við þeim tekit, sátu þrjár nætr í miklum fagnaði.	Were there all-well with them taken, sat three nights in much celebration.	They were all well received and stayed three nights in celebration.
Þaðan riðu þeir á Miklabæ til Arnórs, ok tók hann ágætliga vel við þeim.	From-there rode they to Miklabaer to Arnor's, and took him greatly well with them.	From there they rode to Miklabaer to Arnor, and he received them well.
Var þar veizla in bezta.	Was there the-feast the best.	There was the best feast.
Þá mælti Arnórr:	Then spoke Arnor:	Then Arnor spoke:
"Vel hefir þú gert, Bolli, er þú hefir mik heimsótt.	"Well have you done, Bolli, that you have my home-sought.	"You have done well, Bolli, for seeking my home.
Þykkir mér þú hafa lýst í því við mik mikinn félagsskap.	Think I you have shown it therefore with me much comradeship.	I think you have therefore shown me much comradeship.
Skulu eigi eftir betri gjafar með mér en þú skalt þiggja mega.	Shall not after better gifts with me than you shall accept may.	And no better gifts will remain here with me that the ones you accept at parting.

The Tale of Bolli Bollason (Old Norse)

Old Norse	Literal	English
Mín vinátta skal þér ok heimul vera.	My friendship shall to-you also have-right be.	My friendship is also yours for the asking.
En nökkurr grunr er mér á, at þér sé eigi allir menn hliðhollir í þessu heraði, þykkjast sviptir vera sæmðum.	But somewhat suspect that for-me about, that you being not all men open-whole in this district, think loss being honour.	But I suspect that around me, not everyone in this district is inclined towards you, thinking that they have lost their honour.
Kemr þat mest til þeira Hjaltasona.	Coming that most to they Hjaltasons.	Most of that coming to the Hjaltasons.
Mun ek nú ráðast til ferðar með þér norðr á Heljardalsheiði, þá er þér farið heðan".	Should I now arrange to travel with you north to Heljardal Heath, then when you travel from-here".	I shall now arrange to travel north with you to Herjardal Heath when you leave here".
Bolli svarar:	Bolli answered:	Bolli answered:
"Þakka vil ek yðr, Arnórr bóndi, alla sæmð, er þér gerið til mín nú ok fyrrum.	"Thanks wish I you, Arnor host, all honour, that you do about mine now and before-us.	"I wish to thank you, Arnor my host, for all the honour, that you have shown me now before us.
Þykkir mér ok þat bæta várn flokk, at þér ríðið með oss.	Seems to-me also that better our flock, that you ride with us.	It seems to me better for our flock, if you ride with us.
En allt hugðum vér at fara með spekð um þessi heruð,	Then all think we that travel with wisdom about this district,	Then we think we will travel with wisdom through this district,
en ef aðrir leita á oss, þá má vera, at vér leikim þá enn nökkut í mót".	that if others look for us, then may be, that we sport then but somewhat in meeting".	so that if others look for us, as they may, then we will give them some sport in meeting us".
Síðan ræðst Arnórr til ferðar með þeim, ok ríða nú veg sinn.	Afterwards rode Arnor to travel with them, and rode now way theirs.	Afterwards Arnor prepared to ride with them, and they set out on their way.

6

Nú er at segja frá Þorvaldi, at hann tekr til orða við Þórð, bróður sinn:	Now is to say from Thorvald, that he took to words with Thord, brother his:	Now the story turns to Thorvald, that he spoke to his brother Thord:
"Vita muntu, at Bolli ferr heðra at heimboðum.	"Know shall-you, that Bolli travels district at home-invitations.	"You know that Bolli travels in this district going to home invitations.

The Tale of Bolli Bollason (Old Norse)

Old Norse	Literal	English
Eru þeir nú at Arnórs átján saman ok ætla norðr Heljardalsheiði".	Are they now at Arnor's eighteen together and intend north Heljardal Heath".	There are eighteen of then together, and they intend north to Herjardal Heath.
"Veit ek þat", svarar Þórðr.	"Know I that", answered Thord.	"I know that", answered Thord.
Þorvaldr mælti:	Thorvald spoke:	Thorvald said:
"Ekki er mér þó um þat, at Bolli hlaupi hér svá um horn oss, at vér finnim hann eigi, því at ek veit eigi, hverr minni sæmð hefir meir niðr drepit en hann".	"Not am I though about that, that Bolli running here so about horn ours, that we find him not, such that I know none, who diminish honour has more down killing than him".	"I am not happy with the idea that Bolli is running around here under our noses, and we don't go to meet him, because I know no one, who has diminished my honour more than him".
Þórðr mælti:	Thord spoke:	Thord spoke:
"Mjök ertu íhlutunarsamr ok meir en ek vilda, ok ófarin myndi þessi, ef ek réða.	"Great are-you in-sharing-together also more than I wish, and un-faring should this, if I decide.	"You are great at sharing in things more than I wish, and this should not go, if I am the one to decide.
Þykkir mér óvíst, at Bolli sé ráðlauss fyrir þér".	Seems to-me uncertain, that Bolli so ill-advised for you".	It seems uncertain to me, that Bolli would be so ill-advised about you".
"Eigi mun ek letjast láta", svarar Þorvaldr, "en þú munt ráða ferð þinni".	"Not should I dissuaded allow", answered Thorvald, "but you should decide travel yours".	"I should not allow that to dissuade me", answered Thorvald, "but you should decide your course".
Þórðr mælti:	Thord spoke:	Third spoke:
"Eigi mun ek eftir sitja, ef þú ferr, bróðir, en þér munum vér eigna alla virðing, þá er vér hljótum í þessi ferð, ok svá, ef öðruvís berr til".	"Not should I after sitting, if you travel, brother, but you shall we own all worthiness, then as we we-get in this journey, and so, if other-knowing bear to".	"I shall not stay, if you travel, brother, but you shall own all the honour we may get from this journey, or any other consequences".
Þorvaldr safnar at sér mönnum, ok verða þeir átján saman ok ríða á leið fyrir þá Bolla ok ætla at sitja fyrir þeim.	Thorvald collected for his men, and became they eighteen together and rode to journey for then Bolli and intended to sit before them.	Thorvald collected together his men to become a party of eighteen and together they rode on the journey that Bolli made and intended to sit in ambush before them.
Þeir Arnórr ok Bolli ríða nú með sína menn.	They Arnor and Bolli rode now with their men.	Arnor and Bolli rode with their men.

The Tale of Bolli Bollason (Old Norse)

Old Norse	Literal	English
Ok er skammt var í milli þeira ok Hjaltasona, þá mælti Bolli til Arnórs:	And when short-distance were in between them and Hjaltasons, then spoke Bolli to Arnor's:	And when there was a short distance between them and the Hjaltasons, Bolli said to Arnor:
"Mun eigi þat nú ráð, at þér hverfið aftr? Hafið þér þó fylgt oss it drengiligsta.	"Should not is now advised, that you turn back?" Have you though followed us the bravely.	"Should it not now be advised that you turn back? Though you have followed us bravely.
Munu þeir Hjaltasynir ekki sæta fláráðum við mik".	Should they Hjaltasons not sit-in-ambush treacherous with me".	The Hjaltasons should not sit in ambush for me in treachery".
Arnórr mælti:	Arnor spoke:	Arnor spoke:
"Eigi mun ek enn aftr hverfa, því at svá er sem annarr segi mér, at Þorvaldr muni til þess ætla at hafa fund þinn,	"Not should I then back turn, because that so is that another say me, that Thorvald should to this intend to have meet you,	"I shall not turn back, because something tells me that Thorvald intends to meet you,
eða hvat sé ek þar upp koma? Blika þar eigi skildir við? Ok munu þar vera Hjaltasynir.	and what see I there up coming? Shining there not shields with?" And should there be Hjaltasons.	and what is that I see moving there? Is that not the glimmer of shields? That will be the Hjaltasons.
En þó mætti nú svá um búast, at þessi þeira ferð yrði þeim til engrar virðingar, en megi metast fjörráð við þik".	But though may now so about prepare, that this they travel with them to no honour, but may meet plotting against you".	But now shall we be prepared, that they will travel with no honour, that they are plotting against you".
Nú sjá þeir Þorvaldr bræðr, at þeir Bolli eru hvergi liðfæri en þeir, ok þykkjast sjá, ef þeir sýna nökkura óhæfu af sér, at þeira kostr myndi mikit versna.	Now saw they Thorvald brothers, that they Bolli were neither company-less than they, and realised saw, if they seemed somewhat unqualified of themselves, that they chose would much worse.	Thorvald and his brother saw that Bolli and his company were no less in numbers than they were, and when they saw this they realised, that if they were unqualified themselves, that the choice of aggression would be much worse.
Sýnist þeim þat ráðligast at snúa aftr, alls þeir máttu ekki sínum vilja fram koma.	Seemed to-them that advice that return back, all they may not theirs will from coming.	It seemed to them that the best advice was now to turn back, since they were not able to carry out their will.
Þá mælti Þórðr:	Then spoke Thord:	Then Thord spoke:

The Tale of Bolli Bollason (Old Norse)

Old Norse	Literal	English
"Nú fór sem mik varði, at þessi ferð myndi verða hæðilig, ok þætti mér enn betra heima setit,	"Now goes as much expect, that this journey would become mockery, and seems to-me the better home stay,	"Now it goes as I expected, that this journey would make a mockery of us, and it seems better if we had stayed at home,
höfum sýnt oss í fjandskap við menn, en komit engu á leið".	has shown us in fiendship with people, but come nothing from passed".	we have shown hostility with people, but achieved nothing".
Þeir Bolli ríða leið sína.	They Bolli rode way theirs.	Bolli and his men rode their way.
Fylgir Arnórr þeim upp á heiðina, ok skilði hann eigi fyrr við þá en hallaði af norðr.	Followed Arnor them up to the-heath, and separated he not before with then but turned of north.	Arnor followed them up to the heath, and did not leave them until they turned north.
Þá hvarf hann aftr, en þeir riðu ofan eftir Svarfaðardal ok kómu á bæ þann, er á Skeiði heitir.	Then broke-away he back, but they rode down along Svarfadardal and came to a-farm then, which was Skeid named.	Then he broke away and returned home while they rode down through Svarfadardal until they reached a farm called Skeid.
Þar bjó sá maðr, er Helgi hét.	There lived so a-man, who Helgi named.	There lived a man there who was named Helgi.
Hann var ættsmár ok illa í skapi, auðigr at fé.	He was of-family-small and bad in mood, rich in wealth.	He was not from a good family, ill-tempered, but wealthy.
Hann átti þá konu, er Sigríðr hét.	He had then wife, who Sigrid named.	He had a wife named Sigrid.
Hon var frændkona Þorsteins Hellu-Narfasonar.	She was kinswoman Thorstein's Hellu-Narfason.	The was a kinswoman of Thorstein Hellu-Narfason.
Hon var þeira skörungr meiri.	She was of-them noble the-more.	She was the more outstanding of them.
Þeir Bolli litu heygarð hjá sér.	There Bolli looked hay-stacks beside them.	Bolli looked and saw hay stacks nearby.
Stigu þeir þar af baki, ok kasta þeir fyrir hesta sína ok verja til heldr litlu, en þó helt Bolli þeim aftr at heygjöfinni.	Dismounted they there off horseback, and cast there before horses theirs and guarding to rather little, but though held Bolli they back the hay-giving.	They dismounted their horses, and cast them before the horses, taking rather little, and Bolli restrained them even more.

The Tale of Bolli Bollason (Old Norse)

Old Norse	Literal	English
"Veit ek eigi", segir hann, *"hvert skaplyndi bóndi hefir".*	"Know I not", said he, "what nature the-farmer has".	"I don't know", he said, "what sort of nature this farmer has".
Þeir gáfu heyvöndul ok létu hestana grípa í.	They gave hay-bundle and led the-horses grab to.	They took handfuls of hay and let the horses eat them.
Á bænum heima gekk út maðr ok þegar inn aftr ok mælti:	About the-farm home went out a-man and from-there inside returned and spoke:	About the farm came out a man from inside who went back inside and spoke:
"Menn eru við heygarð þinn, bóndi, ok reyna desjarnar".	"Men are with hay-stacks yours, farmer, and trying the-hay".	"Men are at your haystacks, master, trying the hay".
Sigríðr húsfreyja svarar:	Sigrid housewife answered:	Sigrid the housewife answered,
"Þeir einir munu þar menn vera, at þat mun ráð at spara eigi hey við".	"They only would there men be, that it would decide to spare not hey with".	"The only men who will be there, are those that it will be a good idea not to spare hay".
Helgi hljóp upp í óðafári ok kvað aldri hana skyldu þessu ráða, at hann léti stela heyjum sínum.	Helgi leapt up in a-hurry and said never he should this allow, that he let steal hay his.	Helgi leapt up in a hurry and said that he would never allow others to steal his hay.
Hann hleypr þegar, sem hann sé vitlauss, ok kemr þar at, sem þeir áðu.	He ran immediately, as-if he was wit-less, and came there to, as they to.	He ran out immediately as if he were crazed, and came up to where the men were.
Bolli stóð upp, er hann leit ferðina mannsins, ok studdist við spjótit konungsnaut.	Bolli stood up, as he saw going the-man, and stood with the-spear king's-gift.	Bolli stood up as he saw the man coming, and stood up with the help of the spear, King's Gift.
Ok þegar Helgi kom at honum, mælti hann:	And as-soon-as Helgi came to him, spoke he:	As soon as Helgi reached him, he spoke:
"Hverir eru þessir þjófarnir, er mér bjóða ofríki ok stela mik eign minni ok rífa í sundr hey mitt fyrir fararskjóta sína?"	"Who are these thieves, that me offer unruly and stealing my own less and tearing to asunder hay mine for horses theirs?"	"Who are these thieves, that harass me and steal what is mine and tearing apart my hay for their horses?".
Bolli segir nafn sitt.	Bolli said name his.	Bolli told him his name.
Helgi svarar:	Helgi answered:	Helgi answered:
"Þat er óliðligt nafn, ok muntu vera óréttvíss".	"That is unsuitable name, and should-you be un-right-knowing".	"That is an unsuitable name, and you must be an unjust man".

The Tale of Bolli Bollason (Old Norse)

Old Norse	Literal	English
"Vera má, at svá sé", segir Bolli, "en hinu skaltu mæta, er réttvísi er í".	"Be-it may, that so this", said Bolli, "but the shall-you meet, which right-knowing that is".	"It may be that it is", said Bolli, "but you shall have your justice".
Bolli keyrði þá hestana frá heyinu ok bað þá eigi æja lengr.	Bolli spurred then horses from the-hay and ordered then none rest any-longer.	Bolli then spurred the horses away from the hay, and ordered that none would rest there any longer.
Helgi mælti:	Helgi spoke:	Helgi spoke:
"Ek kalla yðr hafa stolit mik þessu, sem þér hafið haft, ok gert á hendr yðr skóggangssök".	"I declare you have stolen mine this, as you have had, and done in hand your forest-seeking".	"I declare you have stolen what is mine, which you have, and you have committed an offence to outlawry".
"Þú munt vilja, bóndi", sagði Bolli, "at vér komim fyrir oss fébótum við þik, ok hafir þú eigi sakar á oss.	"You should wish, farmer", said Bolli, "that we come before us compensation with you, and have you no conviction of us.	"You will want, farmer", said Bolli, "that we bring forth compensation with you, so that you will have no conviction with us.
Mun ek gjalda tvenn verð fyrir hey þitt".	Shall I pay twice the-worth for hay yours".	I shall pay twice the worth of your hay".
"Þat ferr heldr fjarri", svarar hann, "mun ek framar á hyggja um þat, er vér skiljum".	"That goes behind far-away", answered he, "should I honour to think about that, which our understanding".	"That is nowhere near enough", he answered, "I should think about my honour, what understanding we shall have".
Bolli mælti:	Bolli spoke:	Bolli spoke:
"Eru nökkurir hlutir þeir, bóndi, er þú vilir hafa í sætt af oss?"	"Are-there some things they, farmer, that you wish to-have to settle of us?"	"Are there any objects, farmer, that you wish to have to settle with us?".
"Þat þykkir mér vera mega", svarar Helgi, "at ek vilja spjót þat it gullrekna, er þú hefir í hendi".	"That think I be may", answered Helgi, "that I wish spear that the gold-inlaid, that you have in hand".	"I think it might be", answered Helgi, "that I wish to have the spear that is inlaid with gold, that you have in your hand".
"Eigi veit ek", sagði Bolli, "hvárt ek nenni þat til at láta.	"Not know I", said Bolli, "whether I care that to have allow.	"I do not know", said Bolli, "whether I care to allow that.
Hefi ek annat nökkut heldr fyrir því ætlat.	Have I another something rather for therefore intended.	I have some other intentions with it.

The Tale of Bolli Bollason (Old Norse)

Old Norse	Literal	English
Máttu þat ok varla tala at beiðast vápns ór hendi mér.	May that also barely speak to ask weapons from-out-of hand mine.	You could hardly speak to ask for a weapon from my hand.
Tak heldr annat fé svá mikit, at þú þykkist vel haldinn af".	Take rather another fee so much, that you think well holds of".	Take instead as much money as you consider that you are well off".
"Fjarri ferr þat", svarar Helgi, "er þat ok bezt, at þér svarið slíku fyrir sem þér hafið til gert".	"Far-away goes that", answered Helgi, "is it also best, that you answer such for as you have to done".	"Far be it from me", answered Helgi, "it is best that you answer for what you have done".
Síðan hóf Helgi upp stefnu ok stefndi Bolla um þjófnað ok lét varða skóggang.	Then began Helgi upped summons and charged Bolli with theft and had warranted outlawry.	Then Helgi started a lawsuit and sued Bolli for theft and had a warranted outlawry.
Bolli stóð ok heyrði til ok brosti við lítinn þann.	Bolli stood and heard to and laughed against a-little then.	Bolli stood and listened and laughed a little.
En er Helgi hafði lokit stefnunni, mælti hann:	Then when Helgi had finished the-summons, spoke he:	But when Helgi had finished the summons, he said:
"Nær fórtu heiman?"	"When travelled-you from-home?"	"When did you leave home?".
Bolli sagði honum.	Bolli told him.	Bolli told him.
Þá mælti bóndi:	Then spoke the-farmer:	Then the farmer said:
"Þá tel ek þik hafa á öðrum alizt meir en hálfan mánuð".	"Then say I you have of others homes more than half a-month".	"Then I think you have been living off others for more than half a month".
Helgi hefr þá upp aðra stefnu ok stefnir Bolla um verðgang.	Helgi had then upped another summons and charged Bolli with vagrancy.	Helgi had then brought up another summons and charged Bolli with vagrancy.
Ok er því var lokit, þá mælti Bolli:	And when that was finished, then spoke Bolli:	And when it was over, Bolli said:
"Þú hefir mikit við, Helgi, ok mun betr fallit at leika nökkut í móti við þik".	"You have much with, Helgi, and should better make that sport somewhat in meeting with you".	"You are making a lot of it, Helgi, and it would be better to play something against you".

The Tale of Bolli Bollason (Old Norse)

Old Norse	Literal	English
Þá hefr Bolli upp stefnu ok stefndi Helga um illmæli við sik ok annarri stefnu um brekráð til fjár síns.	Then had Bolli upped summons and charged Helgi about slander with him and another summons about treachery to wealth his.	Then Bolli instituted a summons, and sued Helgi for a slander against him, and another summons for accusations of treachery to his property.
Þeir mæltu, förunautar hans, at drepa skyldi skelmi þann.	There spoke, companions his, that kill should devilish-man then.	They, his companions, said that the scoundrel should be killed.
Bolli kvað þat eigi skyldu.	Bolli said that not should.	Bolli said it was not his duty.
Bolli lét varða skóggang.	Bolli had warranted outlawry.	Bolli had warranted outlawry.
Hann mælti eftir stefnuna:	He spoke after the-summons:	He said after the summons:
"Þér skuluð færa heim húsfreyju Helga kníf ok belti, er ek sendi henni, því at mér er sagt, at hon hafi gott eina lagt til várra haga".	"You should bring home housewife Helgi knife and belt, that I send her, because to me is said, that she had benefit one had to ours fairly".	"You should bring home this knife and belt for your housewife that I send her, because I am told that she spoke up fairly for us".
Bolli ríðr nú í brott, en Helgi er þar eftir.	Bolli rode now to away, then Helgi was there afterwards.	Bolli now rode away, and Helgi was left behind.
Þeir Bolli koma til Þorsteins á Hálsi ok fá þar góðar viðtökur.	They Bolli came to Thorstein's at Hals and got there good with-taken.	Bolli and his men came to Thorstein at Hals and were well received there.
Er þar búin veizla fríð.	As there prepared feast peaceful.	There was a beautiful feast there.

7

Nú er at segja frá Helga, at hann kemr heim á Skeið ok segir húsfreyju sinni, hvat þeir Bolli höfðu við átzt.	Now is it to-say from Helgi, that he came home at Skeid and told housewife his, what they Bolli had with to.	Now it is said of Helgi that he came home to Skeid and told his housewife what Bolli and they had done.
"Þykkjumst ek eigi vita", segir hann, "hvat mér verðr til ráðs at eiga við slíkan mann sem Bolli er, ne ek em málamaðr engi.	"Think I not know", said he, "what to-me becomes to advice that have with such men as Bolli is, nor I am man-of-law none.	"I do not think I know", he said, "what I can do with such a man as Bolli is, nor am I a lawyer.
Á ek ok ekki marga, þá er mér muni at málum veita".	As I also not many, then that me would to the-matter grant".	I also do not have many who will help me".

The Tale of Bolli Bollason (Old Norse)

Old Norse	Literal	English
Sigríðr húsfreyja svarar:	Sigrid housewife answered:	Sigrid the housewife answered:
"Þú ert orðinn mannfóli mikill, hefir átt við ina göfgustu menn ok gert þik at undri.	"You have become an-idiot much, have had with these noblest men and made you a fool-of-yourself.	"You have been very foolish, you have dealt with these noblest men, and you have made a fool of yourself.
Mun þér ok fara sem makligt er, at þú munt hér fyrir upp gefa allt fé þitt ok sjálfan þik".	Should you also go as deserve then, that you should here because-of up give all wealth yours and yourself you".	It will be as you deserve, that you shall lose your wealth and your life".
Helgi heyrði á orð hennar ok þóttu ill vera, en grunaði þó, at satt myndi vera, því at honum var svá farit, at íhann var vesalmenni ok þó skapillr ok heimskr.	Helgi heard the words hers and thought ill were, but suspected though, that true would be, because that he was so fared, that cowardly was wretch and though bad-temper and foolishness.	Helgi heard her words, and thought they were evil, but still suspected that it would be true, for he had done so, that he was a poor man, and yet temperamental and foolish.
Sá hann sik engi færi hafa til leiðréttu, en mælt sik í ófæru.	Saw he such no way-out had to rectify, what talked himself into impassable.	He saw that he had no opportunity to correct himself, the impasse he had talked himself into.
Barst hann heldr illa af fyrir þetta allt jafnsaman.	Overcome he rather ill of for this all together.	He was overcome badly for all of it all at once.
Sigríðr lét taka sér hest ok reið at finna Þorstein, frænda sinn, Narfason, ok váru þeir Bolli þá komnir.	Sigrid had taken her horse and rode to find Thorstein, kinsman hers, Narfason, and were they Bolli then come.	Sigrid had a horse taken, and rode to find Thorstein, her kinsman, Narfason, and Bolli and his men had arrived.
Hon heimti Þorstein á mál ok sagði honum, í hvert efni komit var.	She asked-for Thorstein to speak-to and told him, about how the-matter come was.	She called Thorstein to speak to and told him what had happened.
"Þó hefir slíkt illa til tekizt", svarar Þorsteinn.	"Though has such ill to taken", answered Thorstein.	This has turned out very badly", answered Thorstein.
Hon sagði ok, hversu vel Bolli hafði boðit eða hversu heimskliga Helga fór.	She told also, how well Bolli had offered an how-so foolishly Helgi did.	She also said how well Bolli had offered and how stupid Helgi was.
Bað hon Þorstein eiga í allan hlut, at þetta mál greiddist.	Asked she Thorstein to-have it all lot, that this matter resolved.	She asked Thorstein to have everything to do with this matter being settled.

The Tale of Bolli Bollason (Old Norse)

Old Norse	Literal	English
Eftir þat fór hon heim, en Þorsteinn kom at máli við Bolla:	After that went she home, and Thorstein came to speak with Bolli:	After that she went home, then Thorstein spoke to Bolli:
"Hvat er um, vinr", segir hann, "hvárt hefir Helgi af Skeiði sýnt fólsku mikla við þik? Vil ek biðja, at þér leggið niðr fyrir mín orð ok virðið þat engis, því at ómæt eru þar afglapa orð".	"What is about, friend", said he, "how has Helgi of Skeid shown falsehood much with you?" Wish I offer, that you lay down for my words and honour that none, therefore that un-good are there foolish words".	"What is the matter, friend?" he said, "has Helgi of Skeid shown great falsehood to you? I want to ask you to lay down those words and do not honour them, because they are foolish words there".
Bolli svarar:	Bolli answered:	Bolli answers:
"Þat er víst, at þetta er engis vert.	"That is certainly, that this is none worthy.	"It is certain that this is of no value.
Mun ek mér ok ekki um þetta gefa".	Should I to-me also not about this give".	I will not worry about this".
"Þá vil ek", sagði Þorsteinn, "at þér gefið honum upp þetta fyrir mína skyld ok hafið þar fyrir mína vináttu".	"Then wish I", said Thorstein, "that you give him up this for my guilt and have there for my friendship".	"Then I wish", said Thorstein, "that you give him this for my sake, and have it there for my friendship".
"Ekki mun þetta til neins váða horfa", sagði Bolli,	"Not would this to any risk turn", said Bolli,	"This will not look to any risk", said Bolli,
"lét ek mér fátt um finnast, ok bíðr þat várdaga".	"let I me few about encounter, and wait to spring-days".	"I did not care much for it, and it will wait for spring days".
Þorsteinn mælti:	Thorstein spoke:	Thorstein said:
"Þat mun ek sýna, at mér þykkir máli skipta, at þetta gangi eftir mínum vilja.	"That would I show, that to-me thought the-matter exchange, that this going after my will.	"I will show that it is important to me that this goes according to my will.
Ek vil gefa þér hest þann, er beztr er hér í sveitum, ok eru tólf saman hrossin".	I will give you horse then, the best is here in the-district, and there twelve together herd".	I want to give you the horse that is the best here in the countryside, and there are twelve horses together".
Bolli svarar:	Bolli answered:	Bolli answers:
"Slíkt er allvel boðit, en eigi þarftu at leggja hér svá mikla stund á.	"Such is all-well offered, but not need-you to have here so much while to.	"Such a thing is very well offered, but you do not have to spend so much time here.
Ek gaf mér lítit um slíkt.	I gave me little about such.	I gave myself little of that.

The Tale of Bolli Bollason (Old Norse)

Old Norse	Literal	English
Mun ok lítit af verða, þá er í dóm kemr".	Should also little of be, then that in self-judgement come".	There will be little of it when it comes to judgment".
"Þat er sannast", sagði Þorsteinn, "at ek vil selja þér sjálfdæmi fyrir málit"	"That is the-truest", said Thorstein, "that I wish repay you self-judgement for the-matter"	"It is true", said Thorstein, "that I wish to grant you self-judgement in this matter".
Bolli svarar:	Bolli answered:	Bolli answered:
"Þat ætla ek sannast, at ekki þurfi um at leitast, því at ek vil ekki sættast á þetta mál".	"That expect I truly, that no need about to seek, because that I wish not reconcile to this case".	"I think it is true that there is no need to seek it, because I do not want to accept a settlement in this matter".
"Þá kýstu þat, er öllum oss gegnir verst", sagði Þorsteinn.	"Then choosing that, which all us serves the-worst", said Thorstein.	"Then you are choosing what is worst for all of us" said Thorstein.
"Þótt Helgi sé lítils verðr, þá er hann þó í venzlum bundinn við oss.	"Though Helgi is little worth, then is he though in marriage bound with us.	"Although Helgi is of little value, he is still bound to us.
Þá munum vér hann eigi upp gefa undir vápn yðvar, síðan þú vill engis mín orð virða.	Then should we him not up give into weapons yours, after you wish none my words value.	Then we will not give him up under your weapons, since you do not want to honour my words.
En at þeim atkvæðum, at Helgi hafði í stefnu við þik, lízt mér þat engi sæmðarauki, þó at þat sé á þing borit".	But that them charges, that Helgi has in summoned with you, appears to-me that none honour, though that it is at the-assembly carried".	But with the charges that Helgi had in summons with you, I do not think it is an honour, even though it has been presented to the assembly".
Skilðu þeir Þorsteinn ok Bolli heldr fáliga.	Separated they Thorstein and Bolli rather poorly.	Thorstein and Bolli parted rather poorly.
Ríðr hann í brott ok hans félagar, ok er ekki getit, at hann sé með gjöfum í brott leystr.	Rode he to away and his comrades, and was not got, that he being with gifts in away releasing.	He and his companions rode away, and it is not mentioned that he was released with gifts.

8

Bolli ok hans förunautar kómu á Möðruvöllu til Guðmundar ins ríka.	Bolli and his companions came to Modruvellir to Gudmund the Powerful.	Bolli and his companions came to Modruvellir to Gudmund the Powerful.

The Tale of Bolli Bollason (Old Norse)

Old Norse	Literal	English
Hann gengr í móti þeim með allri blíðu ok var inn glaðasti.	He came to meet them with all joyfulness and was the gladdest.	He came to meet them with all joyfulness and was the gladdest.
Þar sátu þeir hálfan mánuð í góðum fagnaði.	There stayed they half a-month in good celebration.	They stayed there half a-month in good celebration.
Þá mælti Guðmundr til Bolla:	Then spoke Gudmund to Bolli:	Then Gudmund said to Bolli:
"Hvat er til haft um þat, hefir sundrþykki orðit með yðr Þorsteini?"	"What is to have about that, have discord words with your Thorstein?"	"What is that matter, has there been discord with you and Thorstein?"
Bolli kvað lítit til haft um þat ok tók annat mál.	Bolli spoke little to have about that and took another matter.	Bolli said he had little to say about it and took another matter.
Guðmundr mælti:	Gudmund spoke:	Gudmund said:
"Hverja leið ætlar þú aftr at ríða?"	"What way intend you return to ride?"	"Which way are you going to ride back?"
"Ina sömu", svarar Bolli.	"The same", answered Bolli.	"The same", answered Bolli.
Guðmundr mælti:	Gudmund spoke:	Gudmund said:
"Letja vil ek yðr þess, því at mér er svá sagt, at þit Þorsteinn hafið skilit fáliga.	"Discourage wish I you this, because that to-me is so said, that you Thorstein have separated coldly.	"I wish to discourage you, for I am told that Thorstein has separated with you poorly.
Ver heldr hér með mér ok ríð suðr í vár, ok látum þá þessi mál ganga til vegar".	Be rather here with me and ride south in spring, and let then this matter go its way".	Stay here with me and ride south in the spring, and then let these matters go".
Bolli lézt eigi mundu bregða ferðinni fyrir hót þeira, "en þat hugða ek, þá er Helgi fólit lét sem heimskligast ok mælti hvert óorðan at öðru við oss ok vildi hafa spjótit konungsnaut ór hendi mér fyrir einn heyvöndul, at ek skylda freista, at hann fengi ombun orða sinna.	Bolli said not would break travel for threat theirs, "but that think I, then that Helgi foolishly had as foolishly and speaking each slanderous to another with us and willing to-have spear king's-gift out-of hand mine for only a-haystack, that I should test, that he gets return words his.	Bolli said that he would not break from his travel plans because of their threat, "but I think that Helgi was stupid, and spoke foolishly with one slanderous charge after another to us, and wanting to take the spear King's Gift out of my hand for only a haystack, I should see to it that he gets what he deserves for his words.

The Tale of Bolli Bollason (Old Norse)

Old Norse	Literal	English
Hefi ek ok annat ætlat fyrir spjótinu, at ek mynda heldr gefa þér ok þar með gullhringinn, þann er stólkonungrinn gaf mér.	Have I also other plans for spear, that I should rather give to-you and there with gold-ring, then that the-emperor gave me.	I also have other plans for my spear, as I intend to give it to you, along with the gold arm ring that the emperor gave me.
Hygg ek nú, at gripirnir sé betr niðr komnir en þá, at Helgi hefði þá".	Think I now, that treasures are better kinsman coming than then, that Helgi has then".	I think now, that the treasures are better coming to a kinsman than Helgi having them".
Guðmundr þakkaði honum gjafar þessar ok mælti:	Gudmund thanked him the-gift these and spoke:	Gudmund thanked him for these gifts, and said,
"Hér munu smæri gjafar í móti koma en verðugt er".	"Here shall smaller gifts in return coming than worth are".	"Here smaller gifts will come in return than are worthy".
Guðmundr gaf Bolla skjöld gulllagðan ok gullhring ok skikkju.	Gudmund gave Bolli shield gold-laid and gold-ring and cloak.	Gudmund gave Bolli a gold-plated shield and a gold ring and a cloak.
Var í henni it dýrsta klæði ok búin öll, þar er bæta þótti.	Were about her the dearest clothing and prepared all, there was better thought.	And about it was prepared all the most precious material that made it better.
Allir váru gripirnir mjök ágætir.	All were treasures much renowned.	All the treasures were very good.
Þá mælti Guðmundr:	Then spoke Gudmund:	Then Gudmund said:
"Illa þykkir mér þú gera, Bolli, er þú vill ríða um Svarfaðardal".	"Bad think I you doing, Bolli, that you wish to-ride about Svarfadardal".	"I think you do badly, Bolli, when you want to ride through Svarfadardal".
Bolli segir þat ekki skaða munu.	Bolli said that not scathed would-be.	Bolli said that he would not be scathed.
Riðu þeir í brott, ok skilja þeir Guðmundr við inum mestum kærleikum.	Rode they to away, and separated they Gudmund with the most friendship.	They rode away, and Gudmund parted with the greatest friendship.
Þeir Bolli ríða nú veg sinn út um Galmarströnd.	Then Bolli rode now way his out about Galmarstrond.	Then Bolli and his men rode their way out over Galmarstrond.
Um kveldit kómu þeir á þann bæ, er at Krossum heitir.	About evening came they to the farm, which that Krossar named.	In the evening they came to a town called Krossar.
Þar bjó sá maðr, er Óttarr hét.	There lived so a-man, who Ottar named.	There lived a man named Ottar.

The Tale of Bolli Bollason (Old Norse)

Old Norse	Literal	English
Hann stóð úti.	He stood outside.	He stood outside.
Hann var sköllóttr ok í skinnstakki	He was bald and in skin-cloak.	He was bald, and wearing a fur coat.
Óttarr kvaddi þá vel ok bauð þeim þar at vera.	Ottar greeted then well and invited them there to be.	Ottar greeted them well and invited them to stay there.
Þat þiggja þeir.	That accepted they.	They accepted.
Var þar góðr beini ok bóndi inn kátasti.	Were there good benefit and farmer the merriest.	There was a good benefit and the farmer was merry.
Váru þeir þar um nóttina.	Were they there about the-night.	They were there that night.
Um morgininn, er þeir Bolli váru ferðar búnir, þá mælti Óttarr:	About morning, when they Bolli were travel preparing, then spoke Ottar:	In the morning, when Bolli and his men were ready to go, Ottar said:
"Vel hefir þú gert, Bolli, er þú hefir sótt heim bæ minn.	"Well have you done, Bolli, that you have sought home farm mine.	"You have done well, Bolli, when you have visited my farm.
Vil ek ok sýna þér lítit tillæti, gefa þér gullhring ok kunna þökk, at þú þiggir.	Wish I also show you little deference, give you gold-ring and know thanks, that you accept.	I also want to show you a little favour, and give you a gold ring and I would be thankful if you accept.
Hér er ok fingrgull, er fylgja skal".	Here is also gold-ring, that follow shall".	Here is also a gold ring to go with it".
Bolli þiggr gjafarnar ok þakkar bónda.	Bolli accepted the-gifts and thanks the-farmer.	Bolli accepted the gifts and thanked the farmer.
Óttarr var á hesti sínum því næst ok reið fyrir þeim leiðina, því at fallit hafði snjór lítill um nóttina.	Ottar was about horse his as nearest and rode ahead them the-way, because that fallen had snow little about the-night.	Ottar was then on his horse, and rode in front of them, for little snow had fallen that night.
Þeir ríða nú veg sinn út til Svarfaðardals,	They rode now way theirs out to Svarfadardal,	They now rode their way out to Svarfadardal,
ok er þeir hafa eigi lengi riðit, snerist hann við Óttarr ok mælti til Bolla:	and when they had not long ridden, turned he with Ottar and spoke to Bolli:	and when they had not ridden long, Ottar turned to Bolli and said:

The Tale of Bolli Bollason (Old Norse)

Old Norse	Literal	English
"Þat mun ek sýna, at ek vilda, at þú værir vin minn.	"That should I show, that I wish, that you be friend mine.	"I will show that I wish you to be my friend.
Er hér annarr gullhringr, er ek vil þér gefa.	Is here another gold-ring, that I wish to-you to-give.	Here's another gold ring I want to give you.
Væra ek yðr velviljaðr í því, er ek mætta.	Be I your well-willing for accordingly, as I might.	I wish to help you in any way that I might.
Munuð þér ok þess þurfa".	Shall you also this need".	If you shall need it".
Bolli kvað bónda fara stórmannliga til sín, "en þó vil ek þiggja hringinn".	Bolli thanked the-farmer going great-man-ness to him, "but though wish I to-accept the-ring".	Bolli thanked the farmer for being so generous, "but still I want to accept the ring".
"Þá gerir þú vel", segir bóndi.	"Then doing you well", said the-farmer.	"Then you do well", said the farmer.

9   9   9

Old Norse	Literal	English
Nú er at segja frá Þorsteini af Hálsi.	Now is to say from Thorstein of Hals.	Now the story turns to Thorstein of Hals.
Þegar honum þykkir ván, at Bolli muni norðan ríða, þá safnar hann mönnum ok ætlar at sitja fyrir Bolla ok vill nú, at verði umskipti um mál þeira Helga.	When he thought expected, that Bolli would north ride, then collected he men and intended to sit-in-ambush before Bolli and wishing now, to become about-exchanged about the-matter theirs Helgi.	When he expected Bolli to ride north, he gathered men and intended to sit in ambush before Bolli, and now wished to alter the matter between him and Helgi.
Þeir Þorsteinn hafa þrjá tigu manna ok ríða fram til Svarfaðardalsár ok setjast þar.	They Thorstein had three ten men and rode from to Svarfadardal and stayed there.	Thorstein and his men had thirty men, and rode up to Svarfadardal, and settled there.
Ljótr hét maðr, er bjó á Völlum í Svarfaðardal.	Ljot was-named a-man, who lived at Vellir in Svarfadardal.	There was a man named Ljot, who lived at Vellir in Svarfadardal.
Hann var höfðingi mikill ok vinsæll ok málamaðr mikill.	He was chieftain great and popular and law-man great.	He was a great chieftain, popular, and a great man of law.

The Tale of Bolli Bollason (Old Norse)

Old Norse	Literal	English
Þat var búningr hans hversdagliga, at hann hafði svartan kyrtil ok refði í hendi, en ef hann bjóst til víga, þá hafði hann blán kyrtil ok öxi snaghyrnda.	It was costume his everyday, that he had a-black tunic and poleaxe in hand, but if he prepared to fight, then had he a-blue tunic and axe snag-cornered.	It was his everyday costume that he had a black tunic and a poleaxe in his hand, but if he was preparing for battle, he had a blue tunic and a sharp-edged axe.
Var hann þá heldr ófrýnligr.	Was he then rather inconspicuous.	He was then rather inconspicuous.
Þeir Bolli ríða út eftir Svarfaðardal.	They Bolli rode out along Svarfadardal.	Bolli and his men rode out along Svarfadardal.
Fylgir Óttarr þeim út um bæinn at Hálsi ok at ánni út.	Followed Ottar them out about the-farm at Hals and to-the-river from.	Ottar followed them out of the town at Hals and out to the river.
Þar sat fyrir þeim Þorsteinn við sína menn, ok þegar er Óttarr sér fyrirsátina, bregðr hann við ok keyrir hest sinn þvers í brott.	There sat before them Thorstein with his men, and when that Ottar saw for-the-ambush, broke he with and spurred horse his across to away.	There Thorstein sat before them with his men, and when Ottar saw the ambush, he responded and drove his horse across.
Þeir Bolli ríða at djarfliga, ok er þeir Þorsteinn sjá þat ok hans menn, spretta þeir upp.	They Bolli rode to boldly, and when they Thorstein saw that and his men, sprang they up.	Bolli and his men rode boldly, and when Thorstein and his men saw it, they sprang up.
Þeir váru sínum megin ár hvárir, en áin var leyst með löndum, en íss flaut á miðri.	There were they sides the-river opposite, about the-river was down with land, was ice floating in the-middle.	They were on either side of the river, but the river flowed with land, and ice floated in the middle.
Hleypa þeir Þorsteinn út á ísinn.	Ran they Thorstein out into the-ice.	Thorstein and his men ran out onto the ice.
Helgi af Skeiði var ok þar ok eggjar þá fast ok kvað nú vel, at þeir Bolli reyndi, hvárt honum væri kapp sitt ok metnaðr einhlítt eða hvárt nökkurir menn norðr þar myndi þora at halda til móts við hann.	Helgi of Skeid was also there and encouraged then closely and said now well, that they Bolli test, whether he was eager his and pride unanimously or whether some men north there would dare to hold to meet with him.	Helgi of Skeid was also there and encouraged them, and said that Bolli and his men would be tested as to whether he was eagerness and pride would be unanimous, or whether there were men of the north who would dare to meet him.
"Þarf nú ok eigi at spara at drepa þá alla.	"Need now and not that spare to kill then all.	"We do not need to spare from killing them all.

The Tale of Bolli Bollason (Old Norse)

Old Norse	Literal	English
Mun þat ok leiða öðrum", sagði Helgi, "at veita oss ágang".	Would it also loath others", said Helgi, "that giving us aggression".	As it would also deter others", said Helgi, "from attacking us".
Bolli heyrir orð Helga ok sér, hvar hann er kominn út á ísinn.	Bolli heard words Helgi's and saw, where he had come out on the-ice.	Bolli heard Helgi's words and saw where he had come out on the ice.
Bolli skýtr at honum spjóti, ok kemr á hann miðjan.	Bolli shot at him spear, and came it his middle.	Bolli shot at him with a spear, and struck him in the middle.
Fellr hann á bak aftr í ána, en spjótit flýgr í bakkann öðrum megum, svá at fast var, ok hekk Helgi þar á niðr í ána.	Fell he on back back in river, but the-spear followed the bank other may, so that fastened was, and hung Helgi there at down in the-river.	He fell backwards into the river, but the spear flew into the bank the other way, so that it was stuck, and Helgi hung down there in the river.
Eftir þat tókst þar bardagi inn skarpasti.	After that took there battle the hardest.	After that, the battle became the hardest.
Bolli gengr at svá fast, at þeir hrökkva undan, er nær váru.	Bolli went to so fast, that they recoiled away-from, who near were.	Bolli went so fast that those who were near him recoiled.
Þá sótti fram Þorsteinn í móti Bolla, ok þegar þeir fundust, höggr Bolli til Þorsteins á öxlina, ok varð þat mikit sár.	Then sought from Thorstein to meet Bolli, and then they found, striking Bolli to Thorstein's with an-axe, and became that much wounding.	Then Thorstein went out to meet Bolli, and when they met, Bolli struck Thorstein on the shoulder, and it was a great wound.
Annat sár fekk Þorsteinn á fæti.	Another wound got Thorstein about the-leg.	Thorstein received another wound on his leg.
Sóknin var in harðasta.	The-struggle was the hardest.	The attack was the hardest.
Bolli varð ok sárr nökkut ok þó ekki mjök.	Bolli became also wounded somewhat and though not much.	Bolli was also slightly injured, but not very badly.
Nú er at segja frá Óttari.	Now is to say from Ottar.	Now the story turns to Ottar.
Hann ríðr upp á Völlu til Ljóts, ok þegar þeir finnast, mælti Óttarr:	He rode up to Vellir to Ljot, and then they met, spoke Ottar:	He rode up to Vellir, to Ljot, and when they met Ottar spoke:
"Eigi er nú setuefni, Ljótr", sagði hann, "ok fylg þú nú virðing þinni, er þér liggr laus fyrir".	"Not is now sitting, Ljot", said he, "and follows you now honour yours, that you lay less for".	"No cause to sit about, Ljot", he said, "what follows now is your honour to prove".

The Tale of Bolli Bollason (Old Norse)

Old Norse	Literal	English
"Hvat er nú helzt í því, Óttarr?"	"What is now rather that according, Ottar?"	"What would that involve, Ottar?"
"Ek hygg, at þeir berist hér niðri við ána Þorsteinn á Hálsi ok Bolli, ok er þat in mesta hamingja at skirra vandræðum þeira".	"I think, that they fight here down by the-river Thorstein of Hals and Bolli, and is that the most fortunate that prevent trouble theirs".	"I expect that they will be fighting here down by the river, Thorstein of Hals and Bolli, and it would be most fortunate to prevent their hostilities".
Ljótr mælti:	Ljot spoke:	Ljot spoke:
"Oft sýnir þú af þér mikinn drengskap".	"Often showed you of your great honour".	"You have often showed great honour".
Ljótr brá við skjótt ok við nökkura menn ok þeir Óttarr báðir.	Ljot startled with quickly and with several men and they Ottar both.	He reacted quickly and with several others hurried back to Ottar.
Ok er þeir koma til árinnar, berjast þeir Bolli sem óðast.	And when they came to the-river, fought they Bolli as furious.	And when they came to the river, Bolli and the others were fighting furiously.
Váru þá fallnir þrír menn af Þorsteini.	Were they fallen three men of Thorstein's.	There were three of Thorstein's men that had fallen.
Þeir Ljótr ganga fram í meðal þeira snarliga, svá at þeir máttu nær ekki at hafast.	Then Ljot went from to between them quickly, so that they may close not to have.	Ljot and his men quickly ran between the fighters so that they could not get close.
Þá mælti Ljótr:	Then spoke Ljot:	Then Ljot spoke:
"Þér skuluð skilja þegar í stað", segir hann, "ok er þó nú ærit at orðit.	"You should separate immediately this place", said he, "and is though now plenty-of has become.	"You should separate immediately from this place", he said, "and now more than enough has been done.
Vil ek einn gera milli yðvar um þessi mál, en ef því níta aðrir hvárir, þá skulum vér veita þeim atgöngu".	Wish I alone to-do between you about this matter, that if therefore refuse others each, then should we grant them to-going".	I alone wish to decide to settle this matter, and if either of you refuses, then they shall be granted an attack".
En með því at Ljótr gekk at svá fast, þá hættu þeir at berjast, ok því játtu hvárirtveggju, at Ljótr skyldi gera um þetta þeira í milli.	Then with because that Ljot went that so close, then stop they the fight, and therefore agreed either-side, that Ljot should do about that their in between.	Then because Ljot went so close, they stopped fighting, and either side agreed, that Ljot should handle the matter between them.

The Tale of Bolli Bollason (Old Norse)

Old Norse	Literal	English
Skilðust þeir við svá búit.	Separated they with so prepared.	They parted ways so prepared.
Fór Þorsteinn heim, en Ljótr býðr þeim Bolla heim með sér, ok þat þiggr hann.	Went Thorstein home, and Ljot invited them Bolli home with him, and that accepted he.	Thorstein went home, but Ljot invited Bolli and his men home with him, and he accepted.
Fóru þeir Bolli á Völlu til Ljóts.	Went they Bolli to Vellir to Ljot's.	Bolli and his men went to Vellir to Ljot's.
Þar heitir í Hestanesi, sem þeir höfðu barizt.	There named is Hestanes, which they had bears.	There is named Hestanes, which bears today.
Óttarr bóndi skilðist eigi fyrri við þá Bolla en þeir kómu heim með Ljóti.	Ottar the-farmer separated not before with then Bolli then they came home with Ljot.	Farmer Ottar did not part with Bolli until they came home with Ljot.
Gaf Bolli honum stórmannligar gjafar at skilnaði ok þakkaði honum vel sitt liðsinni.	Gave Bolli him great-man-like gifts as parted and thanked him well this assistance.	Bolli gave him great gifts at parting, and thanked him well for his help.
Hét Bolli Óttari sinni vináttu.	Pledged Bolli Ottar his friendship.	Bolli pledged Ottar his friendship.
Fór hann heim til Krossa ok sat í búi sínu.	Travelled he home to Krossar and stayed in farm his.	He went home to Krossar and stayed at his farm.

10

Eftir bardagann í Hestanesi fór Bolli heim með Ljóti á Völlu við alla sína menn, en Ljótr bindr sár þeira, ok greru þau skjótt, því at gaumr var at gefinn.	After the-battle at Hestanes travelled Bolli home with Ljot to Vellir with all his men, then Ljot bound wounds theirs, and healed they quickly, because that attention were for given.	After the battle in Hestanes, Bolli went home with Ljot at Vellir with all his men, where Ljot bound up their wounds, and they healed quickly, for the attention was paid to them.
En er þeir váru heilir sára sinna, þá stefndi Ljótr þing fjölmennt.	Then when they were safe wounds theirs, then summoned Ljot assembly full-of-people.	Then when they were healed of their wounds, Ljot convened a great assembly.
Riðu þeir Bolli á þingit.	Rode they Bolli to the-assembly.	Bolli and his men rode to the assembly.
Þar kom ok Þorsteinn af Hálsi við sína menn.	There came also Thorstein of Hals with his men.	Thorstein of Hals also came there with his men.

The Tale of Bolli Bollason (Old Norse)

Old Norse	Literal	English
Ok er þingit var sett, mælti Ljótr:	And when the-assembly was set, spoke Ljot:	And when the Thing was set, Ljot said,
"Nú skal ekki fresta uppsögn um gerð þá, er ek hefi samit milli þeira Þorsteins af Hálsi ok Bolla.	"Now shall not postpone up-saying about made then, but I have agreement between they Thorstein's of Hals and Bolli.	"Now the conclusion of the agreement which I have brought up between Thorstein of Hals and Bolli shall not be postponed.
Hefi ek þat upphaf at gerðinni, at Helgi skal hafa fallit óheilagr fyrir illyrði sín ok tiltekju við Bolla.	Have I that begun to make, that Helgi shall have failed unholy for ill-words his and exchange with Bolli.	I have the beginning of the deed, that Helgi has fallen without right for compensation for his wickedness and betrayal of Bolli.
Sárum þeira Þorsteins ok Bolla jafna ek saman,	The-wounds they Thorstein's and Bolli equal I the-same,	I will make amends for the wounds of Thorstein and Bolli,
en þeir þrír menn, er fellu af Þorsteini, skal Bolli bæta.	But they three men who fell of Thorstein shall Bolli compensate.	but the three men who fell from Thorstein shall be compensated by Bolli.
En fyrir fjörráð við Bolla ok fyrirsát skal Þorsteinn greiða honum fimmtán hundruð þriggja alna aura.	But for plotting-against with Bolli and ambush shall Thorstein assist him fifteen hundred three ells pay.	But for the conspiracy and plotting-against Bolli, Thorstein shall pay him fifteen hundred three cubit lengths of homespun cloth.
Skulu þeir at þessu alsáttir".	Shall they at this all-settle".	They shall all settle at this".
Eftir þat var slitit þinginu.	After it was dissolved the-assembly.	After that the assembly was dissolved.
Segir Bolli Ljóti, at hann mun ríða heimleiðis, ok þakkar honum vel alla sína liðveizlu, ok skiptust þeir fögrum gjöfum við ok skilðu við góðum vinskap.	Told Bolli Ljot, that he would ride home-ways, and thanked him well all his assistance, and exchanged they fair gifts with and separated with good friendship.	Bolli told Ljot that he would ride home, and thanked him well for all his help, and they exchanged beautiful gifts and parted with good friendship.
Bolli tók upp bú Sigríðar á Skeiði, því at hon vildi fara vestr með honum.	Bolli took up the-farm Sigrid of Skeid, because that she wished to-travel west with him.	Bolli took up Sigrid's estate at Skeid, because she wanted to go west with him.
Ríða þau veg sinn, þar til er þau koma á Miklabæ til Arnórs.	Rode they way theirs, there until that they came to Miklabaer to Arnor's.	They rode their way, until they came to Miklabær to Arnor.
Tók hann harðla vel við þeim,	Took he greatly well with them,	He received them very kindly,

The Tale of Bolli Bollason (Old Norse)

Old Norse	Literal	English
dvölðust þar um hríð, ok sagði Bolli Arnóri allt um skipti þeira Svarfdæla, hversu farit hafði.	dwelled there about awhile, and told Bolli Arnor all about exchanged theirs Svarfadardal, how-so gone had.	they stayed there for a while, and Bolli told Arnor all about the exchange of the Svarfadardal, and how things had gone.
Arnórr mælti:	Arnor spoke:	Arnor said:
"Mikla heill hefir þú til borit um ferð þessa, við slíkan mann sem þú áttir, þar er Þorsteinn var.	"Much luck have you to bear about journey this, with such a-man as you have, there as Thorstein was.	"You have been very lucky in this journey, and in your dealings with such a man as Thorstein.
Er þat sannast um at tala, at fáir eða engir höfðingjar munu sótt hafa meira frama ór öðrum heruðum norðr hingat en þú, þeir sem jafnmarga öfundarmenn áttu hér fyrir".	Is it true about that said, that few or none chieftains should attend have more honour of other provinces north here than you, they who equal-many slanderous-men had here for".	Is it true to say that few or no chiefs will have sought more fame from other provinces north here than you, those who had so many envious people here before".
Bolli ríðr nú í brott af Miklabæ við sína menn ok heim suðr.	Bolli rode now to away from Miklabaer with his men and home south.	Bolli now rode away from Miklabær with his men and home south.
Tala þeir Arnórr til vináttu með sér af nýju at skilnaði.	Spoke they Arnor to friendship with them of anew at parting.	Bolli and Arnor spoke of friendship anew before parting.
En er Bolli kom heim í Tungu, varð Þórdís, húsfreyja hans, honum fegin.	Then when Bolli came home to Tunga, was Thordis, housewife his, to-him relieved.	But when Bolli came home to Tunga, Thordis, his housewife, was glad to see him.
Hafði hon frétt áðr nökkut af róstum þeira Norðlendinga ok þótti mikit í hættu, at honum tækist vel til.	Had she news before some of unruliness theirs The-northerners and thought much at danger, that he took well to.	She had heard something before about the skirmishes of the Northerners, and thought it was very dangerous for him to succeed.
Sitr Bolli nú í búi sínu með mikilli virðingu.	Stayed Bolli now at farm his with much honour.	Bolli now stayed in his estate with great honour.
Þessi ferð Bolla var ger at nýjum sögum um allar sveitir, ok töluðu allir einn veg um, at slík þótti varla farin hafa verit náliga.	This journey Bolli's was made to new sagas about all areas, and told all one way about, that such thought barely gone had been near-to.	This journey of Bolli was the subject of new stories about all the districts, and everyone agreed that such a thing was scarcely thought to have been equalled.
Óx virðing hans af slíku ok mörgu öðru.	Grew respect his of such and many others.	His respect from this and many other things grew.

The Tale of Bolli Bollason (Old Norse)

Old Norse	Literal	English
Bolli fekk Sigríði gjaforð göfugt ok lauk vel við hana,	Bolli found Sigrid married worthy and concluded well with her,	Bolli gave Sigrid a noble marriage match and it concluded well,
ok höfum vér eigi heyrt þessa sögu lengri.	and have we none heard this saga longer.	and we have not heard any more of this story.

Word List (Old Norse to English)

Word List (Old Norse to English)

Old Norse	English	*Old Norse*	English
		á	about, as, at, for, from, in, into, it, of, on, the, to, up, was, with

A, a

Old Norse	English
aðra	another
aðrir	others
af	from, from, of, of, off, to
afglapa	foolish
afréttum	the-pastures
aftr	back, down, return, returned
albúnir	all-prepared
aldri	age, never
alizt	homes
alla	all, all
allan	all
allar	all
allir	all, all
allra	of-all
allri	all
alls	all
allstórmannliga	all-great-man-like
allt	all, all
allvel	all-well, all-well
alna	ells
alsáttir	all-settle
alþingi	the-assembly
andvirki	haystacks
annarr	another
annarri	another
annat	another, other
Arnóri	Arnor (name)
Arnórr	Arnor (name)
Arnórs	Arnor's (name)
at	a, about, as, at, for, from, has, have, in, it, of, that, the, to
atgöngu	to-going
atkvæðum	charges
auðigr	rich
aura	pay

Á, á

Old Norse	English
áðr	before, earlier
áðu	to
ágætir	renowned
ágætliga	greatly
ágang	aggression
áin	the-river
ána	river, the-river, the-river
ánni	the-river
ár	the-river
árinnar	the-river
ásjá	assistance
áskorun	challenge
átján	eighteen
átt	had
átta	eight
átti	had, married
áttir	have
áttu	had, have-you
átzt	to

Æ, æ

Old Norse	English
æðimaðr	frenzy-man
æja	rest
ærin	considerable
ærit	plenty-of
ætla	expect, intend, intended
ætlar	intend, intended
ætlat	intended, plans
ættsmár	of-family-small

B, b

Old Norse	English
bað	asked, ordered

Word List (Old Norse to English)

Old Norse	English
báðir	both
bæ	a-farm, farm
bæinn	the-farm
bænum	farmhouse, the-farm
bæta	better, compensate
bak	back
baki	horseback
bakkann	bank
bardagann	the-battle
bardagi	battle
barizt	bears
barst	overcome
bauð	invited
beiða	offer
beiðast	ask
beiddi	asked
beini	benefit
belti	belt
berist	fight
berjast	fight, fought
berr	bear
betr	better
betra	better
betri	better
bezt	best
bezta	best
beztr	best
biðja	offer
bíðr	wait
bindr	bound
Bjarnar	Bjarni (name)
bjó	lived
bjóða	offer, to-invite
bjóst	prepared
bjuggu	lived
blán	a-blue
blári	black
blíðu	joyfulness
blika	shining
boðit	bid, offered
boli	the-bull
Bolla	Bolli (name), Bolli's (name)
Bollason	Bollason (name), Son-of-Bolli (name)
Bollasyni	Bollason (name)
Bolli	Bolli (name)
bónda	husband, the-farmer
bóndi	farmer, host, the-farmer
borit	bear, carried
börnum	children
brá	startled
bræðr	brothers
bræðra	the-brothers
braut	broke
bregða	break
bregðr	broke, drew
brekráð	treachery
bróðir	brother
bróður	brother
brosti	laughed
brotit	broken
brott	away
bú	the-farm
búa	settlers
búast	prepare
búðardurunum	the-booth-doors
búðina	the-booth
búi	farm
búin	prepared
búit	prepared
bundinn	bound
búningr	costume
búnir	preparing
býðr	invited
býr	prepared
býst	prepared

D, d

Old Norse	English
dauðr	dead
desjarnar	the-hay
djarfliga	boldly
Dögurðarnes	Dagverdarnes (place)
dóm	self-judgement
dregr	drew
drengiligsta	bravely
drengskap	honour
drepa	kill
drepit	kill, killing

Word List (Old Norse to English)

Old Norse	English
dvölðust	dwelled
dýrsta	dearest

E, e

Old Norse	English
eða	an, and, or
ef	if
efni	matter, the-matter
efniligastr	promising
eftir	after, afterwards, along
eftirmálinu	the-after-matter
eftirmáls	after-matter
eggjar	encouraged
eiga	have, in, to-have
eigi	no, none, not
eign	own
eigna	own
eina	one
einhlítt	unanimously
einhvern	one
einir	only
einn	alone, one, only
einsætt	one-agreement
einum	any
ek	I
ekki	no, not, nothing
em	am
en	about, and, but, in, since, than, that, then, was, what, whether
enga	none
engi	no, none
engir	none
engis	none
engrar	no, none
engu	nothing
enn	but, the, then
er	am, and, are, as, but, had, is, it-is, that, the, then, was, were, when, which, who
erfit	difficulty
ert	have
ertu	are-you
eru	are, are-there, is, there, were
eruð	are
eyða	devastate

F, f

Old Norse	English
fá	fee, got
fær	accomplished, got, travelled
færa	bring, bringing
færi	travel, way-out
fæti	the-leg
fagnaði	celebration
fagnat	welcomed
fáir	few
fáliga	coldly, poorly
fallit	failed, fallen, make
fallnir	fallen
fangi	arms
fann	found
fár	few
fara	go, going, to-travel, travel
fararskjóta	horses
farið	travel
farin	gone
farinn	travelling
farit	fared, gone, travelled
fast	close, closely, fast, fastened
fátt	few
fé	cattle, fee, wealth
fébótum	compensation
fegin	relieved
fekk	found, got
félagar	comrades
félagsskap	comradeship
felldr	falling
fellr	fell
fellu	well
fengi	gets
ferð	journey, travel, travelling
ferðar	travel
ferðina	going

Word List (Old Norse to English)

Old Norse	English
ferðinni	the-journey, travel
ferðir	journey
ferr	goes, going, set-out, travel, travelled, travels
fimmtán	fifteen
fingrgull	gold-ring
finna	find
finnast	encounter, met
finnim	find
fjandskap	fiendship
fjár	of-wealth, wealth
fjarri	far-away
fjölmenna	following-men, many-men
fjölmenni	followers-many
fjölmennt	full-of-people
fjórðungi	district
fjörráð	plotting, plotting-against
fláráðum	treacherous
flaut	floating
fleiri	more
flokk	flock
flýgr	followed
flytir	with-fleetness
fögrum	fair
fólit	foolishly
fólsku	false, falsehood
fór	did, goes, travelled, went
fórtu	travelled-you
fóru	travelled, went
förum	a-journey
förunautar	companions, companions
Fótbít	Leg-Biter (name)
frá	from
frægðarverk	famous-work
frænda	kinsman
frændkona	kinswoman
frændkonu	kinswoman
fram	from
frama	honour, honour
framar	honour
freista	test, try
fresta	postpone
frétt	news
frétti	asking, learned
fréttist	reported
fréttust	reported
frið	peaceful
fritt	safe
fund	meet
fundr	a-meeting
fundust	found, met
fylg	follows
fylgi	follows
fylgir	followed
fylgja	follow
fylgt	followed
fyrir	ahead, because-of, before, for
fyrirsát	ambush
fyrirsátina	for-the-ambush
fyrr	before
fyrri	before
fyrrum	before-us

G, g

Old Norse	English
gaf	gave
gáfu	gave
Galmarströnd	Galmarstrond (place)
ganga	go, went
gangi	going
gaumr	attention
gefa	give, to-give
gefið	give
gefinn	given
gegnir	serves
gegnum	through
gekk	went
gengit	gone
gengr	came, went
gengu	went
ger	made
gera	do, doing, to-do
gerð	made
gerði	did, made
gerðinni	make

Word List (Old Norse to English)

Old Norse	English
gerðu	did, made
gerið	do
gerir	do, doing
gert	done, made
getit	got
getr	got
giftuvænligr	luck-promised
gjafar	gifts, the-gift
gjafarnar	the-gifts
gjaforð	married
gjalda	pay
gjöfum	gifts
glaðasti	gladdest
gnótt	an-abundance
góða	good
góðar	good
góðr	good
góðum	good
göfgustu	noblest
göfugt	worthy
gott	benefit
graðung	a-bull, bull
graðungr	bull
graðungrinn	the-bull
grán	grey
greiða	assist
greiddist	resolved
greru	healed
grípa	grab
gripirnir	treasures
grjóti	rocks
grunaði	suspected
grunr	suspect
guðdala-starra	Starri-of-Guddalir
Guðdölum	Guddalir (place)
Guðmundar	Gudmund (name)
Guðmundr	Gudmund (name)
Guðrún	Gudrun (name)
gullhring	gold-ring
gullhringinn	gold-ring
gullhringr	gold-ring
gulllagðan	gold-laid
gullrekna	gold-inlaid
gyrðr	buckled

H, h

Old Norse	English
hæðilig	mockery
hægligt	easily
hægt	possible
hættu	danger, stop
haf	have
hafa	had, have, to-have
hafast	have
hafði	had, has
hafi	had
hafið	have
hafir	have
haft	had, have
haga	fairly
halda	hold
haldinn	holds
hálfan	half
hálfsmánaðar	half-month's
hallaði	turned
Háls	Hals (place)
Hálsi	Hals (place)
hamingja	fortunate, luck
hana	he, her
hann	he, him, his
hans	him, his
harðasta	hardest
harðla	greatly
harmaði	mourned
heðan	from-here
heðra	district
hefði	has
hefi	have
hefir	had, has, have
hefr	had
Hegranessþingi	Hegranes (place)-Assembly
Hegranessþings	Hegranes (place)-Assembly
heiðina	the-heath
heilir	safe
heill	luck
heim	home
heima	home
heiman	at-home, from-home

Word List (Old Norse to English)

Old Norse	English
heimanferð	from-home-travel
heimboðanna	home-invitation
heimboðum	home-invitations
heimleiðis	home-ways
heimskliga	foolishly
heimskligast	foolishly
heimskr	foolishness
heimsótt	home-sought
heimti	asked-for
heimul	have-right
heitaðist	called
heiti	am-named
heitinn	named
heitir	named
hekk	hung
heldr	behind, rather
Helga	Helgi (name), Helgi's (name)
Helgi	Helgi (name)
Heljardalsheiði	Heljardal Heath (place)
Hellu-Narfa	Hellu-Narfi (name)
Hellu-Narfasonar	Hellu-Narfason (name)
helt	held
helzt	rather
hendi	hand
hendr	hand
hennar	hers
henni	her
hér	here
heraði	district
heruð	district
heruðum	provinces
hest	horse
hesta	horses
hestana	horses, the-horses
Hestanesi	Hestanes (place)
hesti	horse
hestsins	horse's
hét	named, pledged, promised, was-named
hey	hay, hey
heygarð	hay-stacks
heygjöfinni	hay-giving
heyinu	the-hay

Old Norse	English
heyjum	hay
heyrði	heard
heyrir	heard
heyrt	heard
heyvöndul	a-haystack, hay-bundle
hingat	here
hinu	the
hitt	find
hitti	met
hittir	met
hittust	met
hjá	beside
hjálm	helmet
Hjaltadal	Hjaltadal (place)
Hjaltasona	Hjaltasons (name)
Hjaltasonu	Hjaltasons (name)
Hjaltasynir	Hjaltasons (name), Sons-of-Hjalti (name)
Hjarðarholti	Hjardarholt (place)
hlaupi	running
hleypa	ran
hleypr	ran
hlið	side
hliðhollir	open-whole
hlíðinni	the-slope
hljóp	leapt, ran
hljópu	ran
hljótum	we-get
hlut	lot
hlutir	things
hóf	began
Höfða	Hofdi (place)
höfðingi	chieftain
höfðingjar	chieftains
höfðu	had
Hofi	Hof (place)
Hofs	Hof (place)
höfuð	head
höfum	has, have
höggr	striking
holinu	hollow
hon	she
hönd	hand
höndum	hand, his-hands
honum	he, him, his, to-him

Word List (Old Norse to English)

Old Norse	English
horfa	turn
horfist	looks
horn	horn
hót	threat
hríð	awhile
hringinn	the-ring
hrökkva	recoiled
hrossin	herd
Hrútafirði	Hrutafjord (place)
Hrútafjarðar	Hrutafjord (place)
húðfat	bed-roll
hugða	think
hugðu	thought
hugðum	think
hugsar	thought
hundruð	hundred
hús	a-house
húsfreyja	housewife
húsfreyju	housewife
hválfinu	half
hvar	what, where
hvarf	broke-away
hvárir	each, opposite
hvárirtveggju	either-side
hvárt	how, whether
hvat	what
hverfa	turn
hverfið	turn
hvergi	neither
hverir	who
hverja	what
hverju	every
hvern	what
hverr	who
hversdagliga	everyday
hversu	how, how-so
hvert	each, how, what, which
hvítr	white
hygg	think
hyggja	think

I, i

ill	ill
illa	bad, ill
illmæli	slander
illt	bad-terms, ill
illu	evil
illyrði	ill-words
in	the
ina	the, these
inn	inside, the
innan	inside
ins	the
inum	the
it	the

Í, í

í	about, at, for, in, into, is, it, on, that, the, this, to
íhann	cowardly
íhlutunarsamr	in-sharing-together
ísinn	the-ice
íss	ice

J, j

jafna	equal
jafnan	usually
jafnmarga	equal-many
jafnsaman	together
jarðhús	earth-house
járna	iron-shod
játtu	agreed
Jól	Yule (name)
jörð	earth, the-earth

K, k

kærleik	friendship
kalla	declare
kallaðr	called
kapp	eager
kappi	warriors
kápu	cape

Word List (Old Norse to English)

Old Norse	English
kasta	cast
kátasti	merriest
kaupmenn	trading-men
kaupmönnum	trading-men
kemr	came, come, coming
Kerlingarnef	Crone's-Nose (name)
keyrði	spurred
keyrir	spurred
klæði	clothing
klaufir	hooves
kníf	knife
kom	came, come
koma	came, coming
komim	come
kominn	came, come
komir	come
komit	came, come
komnir	come, coming
kómu	came
kona	wife, wife-of
konu	wife
konungsnaut	king's-gift
kostr	chose
Krossa	Krossar (place)
Krossum	Krossar (place)
kunna	know
kvað	said, spoke, thanked
kvaddi	greeted
kveddi	greeting
kveldit	evening
kvista	trim
kyrrt	peace, still
kyrtil	tunic
kýstu	choosing

L, l

Old Norse	English
lætr	had
lagði	became, lunged
lagðr	laid
lagt	had
láta	allow, leave
látum	let
laug	bathe
lauk	concluded
launmaðrinn	the-unseen-man
laus	less
leggið	lay
leggja	have, lay
leggr	lunged
leið	journey, passed, way
leiða	loath
leiðina	the-way
leiðréttu	rectify
leik	game
leika	sport
leikim	sport
leit	saw
leita	look, seek
leitast	seek
lengi	long
lengr	any-longer
lengri	longer
lét	had, let
léti	let
letja	discourage
letjast	dissuaded
létti	relieved
léttu	relieved
létu	led, let
leyst	down, solved
leystr	releasing
lézt	said
liðfæri	company-less
líðr	passed
liðsafla	company-provided
liðsinnaðr	team-minded
liðsinni	assistance
liðveizlu	assistance
liggr	lay
líta	look
lítill	little
lítils	little
lítinn	a-little
lítit	little
litlu	little
litu	looked
lízt	appears
Ljóti	Ljot (name), Ljot (place)

Word List (Old Norse to English)

Old Norse	English
Ljótr	Ljot (name)
Ljóts	Ljot (place), Ljot's (name)
lögum	law
lokit	finished
löndum	land
lýsa	describe, show
lýst	shown

M, m

Old Norse	English
má	may
maðr	a-man, man
maðrinn	the-man
mælt	talked
mælti	speaking, spoke
mæltu	spoke
mæta	meet
mætta	might
mætti	may
mágsemð	in-laws
mágsemðar	as-in-laws
makligt	deserve
mál	case, matter, speak-to, the-matter
málamaðr	law-man, man-of-law
máli	discuss, matter, speak, the-matter
málinu	the-case
málit	the-case, the-matter
málóði	of-violent-language
málum	the-matter
mann	a-man, men
manna	men, people's
mannfóli	an-idiot
manni	a-man, man
manninn	person
mannsins	the-man
mánuð	a-month
Marbæli	Marbaeli (place)
Marbælinga	Marbaeli (place)
marga	many
margt	many, much
marki	a-sign
máttu	may
með	with
meðal	between
mega	may
megi	may
megin	sides
megum	may
meiddi	wounded
mein	harm
meir	more
meira	more
meiri	the-more
menn	men, people
mér	for-me, I, me, mine, to-me
merkr	marks
mest	most
mesta	most
mestum	most
metast	meet
metnaðr	pride
miðjan	middle
miðri	the-middle
mik	me, mine, much, my
mikill	great, much
mikilli	much
mikinn	great, much
mikit	much
mikla	much
Miklabæ	Miklabaer (place)
miklir	great
miklu	much
miklum	much
milli	between
mín	mine, my
mína	mine, my
minn	mine
minna	mine
minni	diminish, less
mínum	mine, my
mitt	mine
mjök	great, many, much
Möðruvöllu	Modruvellir (place)
mönnum	men, people, to-people
morgininn	morning
mörgu	many

Word List (Old Norse to English)

Old Norse	English
mót	meeting
móti	meet, return
móts	meet
mun	shall, should, would
muna	should
mund	about-that-time
mundu	would
muni	should, would
munt	should
muntu	shall-you, should-you
munu	shall, should, would, would-be
munuð	shall
munum	shall, should
mynda	should
myndi	should, would

N, n

Old Norse	English
ná	obtain
nær	close, near, when
næst	nearest
nætr	nights
nafn	name, name
náliga	near-to
Narfason	Narfason (name)
náskyld	closely-related
nauðsyn	necessity
nauðsynja	deed-refuse
ne	nor
neins	any
nenni	care
níðingsverk	lowly-deed
niðr	down, kinsman
niðri	down
níta	refuse
nökkura	any, several, somewhat
nökkurir	some
nökkurr	somewhat
nökkut	some, something, somewhat
norðan	north
norðlendinga	the-northerners
norðlendingum	northerners
norðr	north
nóttina	the-night
nú	now
nýju	anew
nýjum	new

O, o

Old Norse	English
ofan	down
ofríki	rampages, un-rule, unruly
ofstýri	unmanageable
oft	often
ok	also, and
okkars	our
okkr	us
ombun	return
orð	words
orða	words
orði	word
orðinn	become
orðit	become, words
oss	ours, us

Ó, ó

Old Norse	English
óðafári	a-hurry
óðast	furious
ófæru	impassable
ófallit	misguided
ófarin	un-faring
ófrýnligr	inconspicuous
óhæfu	unqualified
óheilagr	unholy
ójafnaðarmenn	un-equal-men
Óláfi	Olaf (name)
Óláfr	Olaf (name)
Óláfs	Olaf's (name)
óliðdrjúgr	un-substantial-company
óliðligt	unsuitable
ólman	wild
ómæt	un-good
ómannligt	inhumane

Word List (Old Norse to English)

Old Norse	English
óorðan	slanderous
ór	back-from, from, from-out-of, of, out-of
óréttvíss	un-right-knowing
Óttari	Ottar (name)
Óttarr	Ottar (name)
óvinum	un-friends
óvinveittr	unfriendly
óvíst	uncertain
óx	grew

Ö, ö

Old Norse	English
öðru	another, others
öðrum	another, other, others
öðruvís	other-knowing
öfundarmenn	slanderous-men
öll	all
öllu	all
öllum	all
öxi	axe
öxlina	an-axe

P, p

Old Norse	English
Pá	Peacock (name)

R, r

Old Norse	English
ráð	advised, decide, declare
ráða	allow, decide
ráðast	arrange
ráðlauss	ill-advised
ráðligast	advice, advisable
ráðs	advice
ræddist	discussed
ræðst	rode
réða	decide
réðst	rode
refði	poleaxe
reið	riding, rode
reifa	account-for
réttendum	right
réttvísi	right-knowing
Reykja	Reykir (place)
reyna	tested, trying
reyndi	test
ríð	ride
ríða	ride, rode, to-ride
ríðið	ride
riðinn	riding
riðit	ridden, ride
ríðr	rode
riðu	rode
rífa	tearing
Ríka	Powerful (name)
ríki	powerful
róstum	unruliness

S, s

Old Norse	English
sá	saw, so
sækir	seek
sæmð	honour
sæmðar	honour
sæmðarauki	honour
sæmðir	honour
sæmðum	honour
sæta	sit-in-ambush
sætt	settle
sættast	reconcile
safnar	collected
sagði	said, told
sagt	said, told
sakar	conviction, for-the-sake-of, for-the-sake-of, sake, the-charges
saman	the-same, together
samit	agreement
sannast	the-truest, true, truly
sár	wound, wounding, wounds
sára	wounds
sárr	wounded
sárum	the-wounds
sat	sat, stayed
satt	TRUE

Word List (Old Norse to English)

Old Norse	English
sátu	sat, sitting, stayed
sé	are, being, is, see, so, this, was
segi	say
segir	said, told
segja	say, to-say
seilast	obtain
sekðan	outlawed
sekði	convicted
selja	repay
sem	as, as-if, that, which, who
sendi	send
sér	her, him, himself, his, saw, them, themselves
setit	stay
setjast	stayed
setr	set
sett	set
settist	set
setuefni	sitting
síðan	after, afterwards, then
síðar	afterwards
síðir	eventually
Sigríðar	Sigrid (name)
Sigríði	Sigrid (name)
Sigríðr	Sigrid (name)
sik	him, himself, such
silfrs	of-silver
sín	him, his, this
sína	his, their, theirs
sinn	hers, his, theirs
sinna	his, theirs
sinni	his
síns	her, his
sínu	his
sínum	hers, his, theirs, they
sitja	sit, sit-in-ambush, sitting
sitr	stayed
sitt	his, this
sjá	saw
sjálfan	yourself
sjálfdæmi	self-judgement
sjándi	seeing
sjau	seven
skaða	scathed
Skagafirði	Skagafjord (place)
Skagafjarðar	Skagafjord (place)
skal	shall, shall-be, should
skalt	shall
skaltu	shall, shall-you
skammt	a-short-distance, short-distance
skapi	mood
skapillr	bad-temper
skaplyndi	nature
skarpasti	hardest
Skeið	Skeid (place)
Skeiði	Skeid (place)
skelmi	devilish-man
skikkju	cloak
skildi	shield
skilði	separated
skildinum	the-shield
skildir	shields
skilðist	separated
skilðu	separated
skilðust	separated
skilit	separated
skilja	separate, separated
skiljum	understanding
skilnaði	parted, parting
skinnstakki	skin-cloak
skip	a-ship
skips	ships
skipta	exchange
skipti	exchanged
skiptust	exchanged
skirra	prevent
skjöld	shield
skjöldrinn	the-shield
skjótt	quickly
skógarmenn	forest-men
skóggang	outlawry
skóggangssök	forest-seeking
sköllóttr	bald
sköruliga	boldly
skörungr	noble
skulu	shall
skuluð	should

Word List (Old Norse to English)

Old Norse	English
skulum	should
skyld	guilt
skylda	should
skyldi	should
skyldu	should
skyli	shall
skýtr	shot
sleppa	escape
slík	such
slitit	dissolved
smæri	smaller
snaghyrnda	snag-cornered
snarliga	quickly
sneri	turned
snerist	turned
snjór	snow
snúa	return, turn
sögu	saga
sögum	sagas
sóknin	the-struggle
sökótt	accusations
sömu	same
sonar	son
sonr	son, son-of, the-son-of
sótt	attend, attended, sought
sótti	sought
spara	spare
spekð	wisdom
spjót	spear
spjóti	spear
spjótinu	spear
spjótit	spear, the-spear
spretta	sprang
spyrr	asked
stað	place
staddr	standing
Stærimaðr	Stately-man (name)
Stærimann	Stately-man (name)
Stærimanni	Stately-man (name)
standanda	stood
Starri	Starri (name)
stefna	agreement
stefndi	charged, summoned
stefnir	charged
stefnu	summoned, summons
stefnuna	the-summons
stefnunni	the-summons
stela	steal, stealing
Stertimaðr	Stately-man (name)
stíga	step
stigu	dismounted
stóð	stood
stolit	stolen
stólkonungrinn	the-emperor
stórmannliga	great-man-ness
stórmannligar	great-man-like
studdist	stood
stund	while
stýrimann	the-captain
styrk	strength
suðr	south
sumar	summer
sumarit	summer
sundr	asunder
sundrþykki	discord
svá	so
svarar	answered
Svarfaðardal	Svarfadardal (place)
Svarfaðardals	Svarfadardal (place)
Svarfaðardalsár	Svarfadardal (place)
Svarfdæla	Svarfadardal (place)
svarið	answer
svartan	a-black
sveininn	the-boy
sveinsins	son-yours
sveit	company
sveitir	areas
sveitum	the-district
sverðinu	the-sword
sviptir	loss
sýna	seemed, show
sýnir	showed
sýnist	seemed
sýnt	shown
systrungr	mother's-sister's-son

T, t

Old Norse	English
tæki	take

Word List (Old Norse to English)

Old Norse	English
tækist	took
tak	take
taka	take, taken
takir	take
tal	talking
tala	said, speak, spoke
talit	conversation
tauma	reins
tekit	taken
tekizt	taken
tekr	took
tel	say
tíðenda	news
tigu	ten
til	about, its, to, until
tilfelli	occurrence
tillæti	deference
tiltekju	exchange
tíma	time
títt	reported
tók	took
tókst	took
tóku	took-to
tólf	twelve
töluðu	talked, told
torfstakka	turf-stacks
trausts	trust
Tungu	Tunga (place)
tvá	two
tvenn	twice

Þ, þ

Old Norse	English
þá	the, then, they, when
þaðan	from-there
þætti	seems
þakka	thanks
þakkaði	thanked
þakkar	thanked, thanks
þangat	from-there, there, there
þann	the, then
þar	here, it, there, there
þarf	need
þarftu	need-you
þat	is, it, so, that, this, to
þau	they
þegar	as-soon-as, from-there, immediately, then, when
þeim	home, them, they, to-them
þeir	the, then, there, they
þeira	of-them, of-they, their, theirs, them, they, they-of
þenna	this
þér	to-you, you, your
þess	this
þessa	this
þessar	these
þessi	this
þessir	these
þessu	this
þetta	that, this
þiggir	accept
þiggja	accept, accepted, to-accept
þiggr	accepted
þik	you
þína	yours
þing	assembly, the-assembly
þinginu	the-assembly
þingit	the-assembly
þingmaðr	assembly-man
þingsins	the-assembly
þinn	you, yours
þinnar	yours
þinni	yours
þit	you, you-two
þitt	yours
þjófarnir	thieves
þjófnað	theft
þó	though
þökk	thanks
þola	endure
þora	dare
Þórð	Thord (name)
Þórðar	Thord (name)
Þórðarsonar	Son-of-Thord (name)
Þórði	Thord (name)

Word List (Old Norse to English)

Old Norse	English
Þórdís	Thordis (name)
Þórðr	Thord (name)
Þorgrímr	Thorgrim (name)
Þórólf	Thorolf (name)
Þórólfi	Thorolf (name)
Þórólfr	Thorolf (name)
Þórólfs	Thorolf's (name)
Þorstein	Thorstein (name), Thorstein (name)
Þorsteini	Thorstein (name), Thorstein's (name)
Þorsteinn	Thorstein (name)
Þorsteins	Thorstein's (name)
Þorvaldi	Thorvald (name)
Þorvaldr	Thorvald (name)
þótt	though
þótti	thought
þóttu	thought
þriggja	three
þrír	three
þrjá	three
þrjár	three
þú	you
Þúfum	Thufur (place)
þungt	negatively
þurfa	need
þurfi	need
Þverá	Thvera (place)
Þverár	Thvera (place)
þvers	across
því	according, accordingly, as, because, since, such, that, therefore
þykkir	consider, seems, think, thought
þykkist	think
þykkjast	realised, think
þykkjumst	think

U, u

Old Norse	English
um	about, with
umskipti	about-exchanged
undan	away-from
undir	into, near
undri	fool-of-yourself
ungr	young
upp	up, upped
upphaf	begun
uppi	up
uppsögn	up-saying
Urðskriðuhóla	Urdskriduholar (place)
urðu	became

Ú, ú

Old Norse	English
út	from, out
útan	abroad
úti	outside

V, v

Old Norse	English
váða	risk
vænt	expect
væra	be
væri	was
værir	be, would-be
ván	expected, to-expect
vanða	custom
vandi	difficulty
vandræði	dispute
vandræðum	trouble
vápn	weapons
vápnaðir	weaponed
vápns	weapons
var	then, was, were
vár	spring
varð	became, was
varða	warranted
várdaga	spring-days
varði	expect
varðveita	ward-knowing
varðveizlu	hospitality
varla	barely
várn	our
varna	defence
várra	ours
vartu	where
váru	was, were

Word List (Old Norse to English)

Old Norse	English
veðr	weathered
veg	way
vegar	way
veit	know
veita	giving, grant
veitti	granted
veizla	feast, the-feast
veizlu	feast
vel	well
velli	the-fields
velviljaðr	well-willing
venzlum	marriage
ver	be
vér	our, we
vera	be, becomes, being, be-it, were
verð	the-worth
verða	be, became, become, being, would-be
verðgang	vagrancy
verði	become
verðr	becomes, worth
verðugt	worth
verit	been
verja	defend, guarding, protect
verk	work
versna	worse
verst	the-worst
vert	worthy
vesalmenni	wretch
vestr	west
vetra	winters
vetrinn	winter
vexti	grown
við	against, by, to, with
viðtökur	with-taken, with-taking
víg	killing, slaying-of, the-killing-of, the-slaying-of
víga	fight
vígi	the-slaying
vígsmálit	fight-the-case
vil	will, wish
vilda	wish
vildi	willing, wished
vilir	wish
vilja	will, willing, wish
viljum	will
vill	wish, wished, wishing
vin	friend
vinátta	friendship
vináttu	friendship
vindr	the-wind
vinganarmál	friendship-matter
vingast	make-friends
vinr	a-friend, friend
vinsæll	popular
vinskap	friendship
vinskapar	friendship
virða	value, worth
virðið	honour
virðing	honour, respect, worth, worthiness
virðingar	honour
virðingarvænligt	respect-kindly
virðingu	honour
virkit	the-compound
víst	certainly
vistar	lodging
vísu	certainly
vita	know
vitja	visit
vitlauss	wit-less
Völlu	Vellir (place)
Völlum	Vellir (place)

Y, y

Old Norse	English
yðr	you, your
yður	yours
yðvar	you
yðvarn	of-you
yfir	over
yrði	with

Word List (English to Old Norse)

Word List (English to Old Norse)

English	Old Norse

A, a

English	Old Norse
a	*at*
a-black	*svartan*
a-blue	*blán*
about	*á, at, en, í, til, um*
about-exchanged	*umskipti*
about-that-time	*mund*
abroad	*útan*
a-bull	*graðung*
accept	*þiggir, þiggja*
accepted	*þiggja, þiggr*
accomplished	*fær*
according	*því*
accordingly	*því*
account-for	*reifa*
accusations	*sökótt*
across	*þvers*
advice	*ráðligast, ráðs*
advisable	*ráðligast*
advised	*ráð*
a-farm	*bæ*
a-friend	*vinr*
after	*eftir, síðan*
after-matter	*eftirmáls*
afterwards	*eftir, síðan, síðar*
against	*við*
age	*aldri*
aggression	*ágang*
agreed	*játtu*
agreement	*samit, stefna*
a-haystack	*heyvöndul*
ahead	*fyrir*
a-house	*hús*
a-hurry	*óðafári*
a-journey	*förum*
a-little	*lítinn*
all	*alla, alla, allan, allar, allir, allir, allri, alls, allt, allt, öll, öllu, öllum*
all-great-man-like	*allstórmannliga*
allow	*láta, ráða*
all-prepared	*albúnir*
all-settle	*alsáttir*
all-well	*allvel, allvel*
alone	*einn*
along	*eftir*
also	*ok*
am	*em, er*
a-man	*maðr, mann, manni*
ambush	*fyrirsát*
a-meeting	*fundr*
am-named	*heiti*
a-month	*mánuð*
an	*eða*
an-abundance	*gnótt*
an-axe	*öxlina*
and	*eða, en, er, ok*
anew	*nýju*
an-idiot	*mannfóli*
another	*aðra, annarr, annarri, annat, öðru, öðrum*
answer	*svarið*
answered	*svarar*
any	*einum, neins, nökkura*
any-longer	*lengr*
appears	*lízt*
are	*er, eru, eruð, sé*
areas	*sveitir*
are-there	*eru*
are-you	*ertu*
arms	*fangi*
Arnor (name)	*Arnóri, Arnórr*
Arnor's (name)	*Arnórs*
arrange	*ráðast*
as	*á, at, er, sem, því*
a-ship	*skip*
a-short-distance	*skammt*
as-if	*sem*
a-sign	*marki*
as-in-laws	*mágsemðar*
ask	*beiðast*
asked	*bað, beiddi, spyrr*
asked-for	*heimti*
asking	*frétti*
assembly	*þing*
assembly-man	*þingmaðr*

Word List (English to Old Norse)

English	Old Norse	English	Old Norse
assist	*greiða*	belt	*belti*
assistance	*ásjá, liðsinni, liðveizlu*	benefit	*beini, gott*
as-soon-as	*þegar*	beside	*hjá*
asunder	*sundr*	best	*bezt, bezta, beztr*
at	*á, at, í*	better	*bæta, betr, betra, betri*
at-home	*heiman*	between	*meðal, milli*
attend	*sótt*	bid	*boðit*
attended	*sótt*	Bjarni (name)	*Bjarnar*
attention	*gaumr*	black	*blári*
away	*brott*	boldly	*djarfliga, sköruliga*
away-from	*undan*	Bollason (name)	*Bollason, Bollasyni*
awhile	*hríð*	Bolli (name)	*Bolla, Bolli*
axe	*öxi*	Bolli's (name)	*Bolla*
		both	*báðir*
		bound	*bindr, bundinn*
		bravely	*drengiligsta*
		break	*bregða*

B, b

English	Old Norse	English	Old Norse
back	*aftr, bak*	bring	*færa*
back-from	*ór*	bringing	*færa*
bad	*illa*	broke	*braut, bregðr*
bad-temper	*skapillr*	broke-away	*hvarf*
bad-terms	*illt*	broken	*brotit*
bald	*sköllóttr*	brother	*bróðir, bróður*
bank	*bakkann*	brothers	*bræðr*
barely	*varla*	buckled	*gyrðr*
bathe	*laug*	bull	*graðung, graðungr*
battle	*bardagi*	but	*en, enn, er*
be	*væra, værir, ver, vera, verða*	by	*við*
bear	*berr, borit*		
bears	*barizt*		

C, c

English	Old Norse
became	*lagði, urðu, varð, verða*
because	*því*
because-of	*fyrir*
become	*orðinn, orðit, verða, verði*
becomes	*vera, verðr*
bed-roll	*húðfat*
been	*verit*
before	*áðr, fyrir, fyrr, fyrri*
before-us	*fyrrum*
began	*hóf*
begun	*upphaf*
behind	*heldr*
being	*sé, vera, verða*
be-it	*vera*

English	Old Norse
called	*heitaðist, kallaðr*
came	*gengr, kemr, kom, koma, kominn, komit, kómu*
cape	*kápu*
care	*nenni*
carried	*borit*
case	*mál*
cast	*kasta*
cattle	*fé*
celebration	*fagnaði*
certainly	*víst, vísu*
challenge	*áskorun*
charged	*stefndi, stefnir*

Word List (English to Old Norse)

English	Old Norse	English	Old Norse
charges	*atkvæðum*	deed-refuse	*nauðsynja*
chieftain	*höfðingi*	defence	*varna*
chieftains	*höfðingjar*	defend	*verja*
children	*börnum*	deference	*tillæti*
choosing	*kýstu*	describe	*lýsa*
chose	*kostr*	deserve	*makligt*
cloak	*skikkju*	devastate	*eyða*
close	*fast, nær*	devilish-man	*skelmi*
closely	*fast*	did	*fór, gerði, gerðu*
closely-related	*náskyld*	difficulty	*erfit, vandi*
clothing	*klæði*	diminish	*minni*
coldly	*fáliga*	discord	*sundrþykki*
collected	*safnar*	discourage	*letja*
come	*kemr, kom, komim, kominn, komir, komit, komnir*	discuss	*máli*
		discussed	*ræddist*
		dismounted	*stigu*
coming	*kemr, koma, komnir*	dispute	*vandræði*
companions	*förunautar, förunautar*	dissolved	*slitit*
company	*sveit*	dissuaded	*letjast*
company-less	*liðfæri*	district	*fjórðungi, heðra, heraði, heruð*
company-provided	*liðsafla*		
compensate	*bæta*	do	*gera, gerið, gerir*
compensation	*fébótum*	doing	*gera, gerir*
comrades	*félagar*	done	*gert*
comradeship	*félagsskap*	down	*aftr, leyst, niðr, niðri, ofan*
concluded	*lauk*		
consider	*þykkir*	drew	*bregðr, dregr*
considerable	*ærin*	dwelled	*dvölðust*
conversation	*talit*		
convicted	*sekði*		
conviction	*sakar*		

E, e

English	Old Norse
costume	*búningr*
cowardly	*íhann*
Crone's-Nose (name)	*Kerlingarnef*
custom	*vanða*

each	*hvárir, hvert*
eager	*kapp*
earlier	*áðr*
earth	*jörð*

D, d

earth-house	*jarðhús*
easily	*hægligt*
eight	*átta*
eighteen	*átján*
Dagverdarnes (place)	*Dögurðarnes*
either-side	*hvárirtveggju*
danger	*hættu*
ells	*alna*
dare	*þora*
encounter	*finnast*
dead	*dauðr*
encouraged	*eggjar*
dearest	*dýrsta*
endure	*þola*
decide	*ráð, ráða, réða*
equal	*jafna*
declare	*kalla, ráð*		

Word List (English to Old Norse)

English	Old Norse	English	Old Norse
equal-many	*jafnmarga*	follows	*fylg, fylgi*
escape	*sleppa*	foolish	*afglapa*
evening	*kveldit*	foolishly	*fólit, heimskliga, heimskligast*
eventually	*síðir*		
every	*hverju*	foolishness	*heimskr*
everyday	*hversdagliga*	fool-of-yourself	*undri*
evil	*illu*	for	*á, at, fyrir, í*
exchange	*skipta, tiltekju*	forest-men	*skógarmenn*
exchanged	*skipti, skiptust*	forest-seeking	*skóggangssök*
expect	*ætla, vænt, varði*	for-me	*mér*
expected	*ván*	for-the-ambush	*fyrirsátina*
		for-the-sake-of	*sakar, sakar*
		fortunate	*hamingja*
		fought	*berjast*
		found	*fann, fekk, fundust*

F, f

		frenzy-man	*æðimaðr*
failed	*fallit*	friend	*vin, vinr*
fair	*fögrum*	friendship	*kærleik, vinátta, vináttu, vinskap, vinskapar*
fairly	*haga*		
fallen	*fallit, fallnir*	friendship-matter	*vinganarmál*
falling	*felldr*	from	*á, af, af, at, frá, fram, ór, út*
false			
falsehood	*fólsku*	from-here	*heðan*
famous-work	*frægðarverk*	from-home	*heiman*
far-away	*fjarri*	from-home-travel	*heimanferð*
fared	*farit*	from-out-of	*ór*
farm	*bæ, búi*	from-there	*þaðan, þangat, þegar*
farmer	*bóndi*	full-of-people	*fjölmennt*
farmhouse	*bænum*	furious	*óðast*
fast	*fast*		
fastened	*fast*		

G, g

feast	*veizla, veizlu*		
fee	*fá, fé*		
fell	*fellr*	Galmarstrond (place)	*Galmarströnd*
few	*fáir, fár, fátt*	game	*leik*
fiendship	*fjandskap*	gave	*gaf, gáfu*
fifteen	*fimmtán*	gets	*fengi*
fight	*berist, berjast, víga*	gifts	*gjafar, gjöfum*
fight-the-case	*vígsmálit*	give	*gefa, gefið*
find	*finna, finnim, hitt*	given	*gefinn*
finished	*lokit*	giving	*veita*
floating	*flaut*	gladdest	*glaðasti*
flock	*flokk*	go	*fara, ganga*
follow	*fylgja*	goes	*ferr, fór*
followed	*flýgr, fylgir, fylgt*	going	*fara, ferðina, ferr, gangi*
followers-many	*fjölmenni*	gold-inlaid	*gullrekna*
following-men	*fjölmenna*		

Word List (English to Old Norse)

English	Old Norse
gold-laid	*gulllagðan*
gold-ring	*fingrgull, gullhring, gullhringinn, gullhringr*
gone	*farin, farit, gengit*
good	*góða, góðar, góðr, góðum*
got	*fá, fær, fekk, getit, getr*
grab	*grípa*
grant	*veita*
granted	*veitti*
great	*mikill, mikinn, miklir, mjök*
greatly	*ágætliga, harðla*
great-man-like	*stórmannligar*
great-man-ness	*stórmannliga*
greeted	*kvaddi*
greeting	*kveddi*
grew	*óx*
grey	*grán*
grown	*vexti*
guarding	*verja*
Guddalir (place)	*Guðdölum*
Gudmund (name)	*Guðmundar, Guðmundr*
Gudrun (name)	*Guðrún*
guilt	*skyld*

H, h

English	Old Norse
had	*átt, átti, áttu, er, hafa, hafði, hafi, haft, hefir, hefr, höfðu, lætr, lagt, lét*
half	*hálfan, hválfinu*
half-month's	*hálfsmánaðar*
Hals (place)	*Háls, Hálsi*
hand	*hendi, hendr, hönd, höndum*
hardest	*harðasta, skarpasti*
harm	*mein*
has	*at, hafði, hefði, hefir, höfum*
have	*at, áttir, eiga, ert, haf, hafa, hafast, hafið, hafir, haft, hefi, hefir, höfum, leggja*
have-right	*heimul*
have-you	*áttu*
hay	*hey, heyjum*
hay-bundle	*heyvöndul*
hay-giving	*heygjöfinni*
haystacks	*andvirki*
hay-stacks	*heygarð*
he	*hana, hann, honum*
head	*höfuð*
healed	*greru*
heard	*heyrði, heyrir, heyrt*
Hegranes (place)-Assembly	*Hegranessþingi, Hegranessþings*
held	*helt*
Helgi (name)	*Helga, Helgi*
Helgi's (name)	*Helga*
Heljardal Heath (place)	*Heljardalsheiði*
Hellu-Narfason (name)	*Hellu-Narfasonar*
Hellu-Narfi (name)	*Hellu-Narfa*
helmet	*hjálm*
her	*hana, henni, sér, síns*
herd	*hrossin*
here	*hér, hingat, þar*
hers	*hennar, sinn, sínum*
Hestanes (place)	*Hestanesi*
hey	*hey*
him	*hann, hans, honum, sér, sik, sín*
himself	*sér, sik*
his	*hann, hans, honum, sér, sín, sína, sinn, sinna, sinni, síns, sínu, sínum, sitt*
his-hands	*höndum*
Hjaltadal (place)	*Hjaltadal*
Hjaltasons (name)	*Hjaltasona, Hjaltasonu, Hjaltasynir*
Hjardarholt (place)	*Hjarðarholti*
Hof (place)	*Hofi, Hofs*
Hofdi (place)	*Höfða*
hold	*halda*
holds	*haldinn*
hollow	*holinu*
home	*heim, heima, þeim*
home-invitation	*heimboðanna*
home-invitations	*heimboðum*
homes	*alizt*

Word List (English to Old Norse)

English	Old Norse	English	Old Norse
home-sought	heimsótt	iron-shod	járna
home-ways	heimleiðis	is	er, eru, í, sé, þat
honour	drengskap, frama, frama, framar, sæmð, sæmðar, sæmðarauki, sæmðir, sæmðum, virðið, virðing, virðingar, virðingu	it	á, at, í, þar, þat
		it-is	er
		its	til
hooves	klaufir		

J, j

hooves	klaufir	journey	ferð, ferðir, leið
horn	horn	joyfulness	blíðu
horse	hest, hesti		
horseback	baki		

K, k

horses	fararskjóta, hesta, hestana		
horse's	hestsins	kill	drepa, drepit
hospitality	varðveizlu	killing	drepit, víg
host	bóndi	king's-gift	konungsnaut
housewife	húsfreyja, húsfreyju	kinsman	frænda, niðr
how	hvárt, hversu, hvert	kinswoman	frændkona, frændkonu
how-so	hversu	knife	kníf
Hrutafjord (place)	Hrútafirði, Hrútafjarðar	know	kunna, veit, vita
hundred	hundruð	Krossar (place)	Krossa, Krossum
hung	hekk		
husband	bónda		

L, l

I, i

English	Old Norse	English	Old Norse
		laid	lagðr
I	ek, mér	land	löndum
ice	íss	laughed	brosti
if	ef	law	lögum
ill	ill, illa, illt	law-man	málamaðr
ill-advised	ráðlauss	lay	leggið, leggja, liggr
ill-words	illyrði	leapt	hljóp
immediately	þegar	learned	frétti
impassable	ófæru	leave	láta
in	á, at, eiga, en, í	led	létu
inconspicuous	ófrýnligr	Leg-Biter (name)	Fótbít
inhumane	ómannligt	less	laus, minni
in-laws	mágsemð	let	látum, lét, léti, létu
in-sharing-together	íhlutunarsamr	little	lítill, lítils, lítit, litlu
inside	inn, innan	lived	bjó, bjuggu
intend	ætla, ætlar	Ljot (name)	Ljóti, Ljótr
intended	ætla, ætlar, ætlat	Ljot (place)	Ljóti, Ljóts
into	á, í, undir	Ljot's (name)	Ljóts
invited	bauð, býðr	loath	leiða

Word List (English to Old Norse)

English	*Old Norse*
lodging	*vistar*
long	*lengi*
longer	*lengri*
look	*leita, líta*
looked	*litu*
looks	*horfist*
loss	*sviptir*
lot	*hlut*
lowly-deed	*níðingsverk*
luck	*hamingja, heill*
luck-promised	*giftuvænligr*
lunged	*lagði, leggr*

M, m

made	*ger, gerð, gerði, gerðu, gert*
make	*fallit, gerðinni*
make-friends	*vingast*
man	*maðr, manni*
man-of-law	*málamaðr*
many	*marga, margt, mjök, mörgu*
many-men	*fjölmenna*
Marbaeli (place)	*Marbæli, Marbælinga*
marks	*merkr*
marriage	*venzlum*
married	*átti, gjaforð*
matter	*efni, mál, máli*
may	*má, mætti, máttu, mega, megi, megum*
me	*mér, mik*
meet	*fund, mæta, metast, móti, móts*
meeting	*mót*
men	*mann, manna, menn, mönnum*
merriest	*kátasti*
met	*finnast, fundust, hitti, hittir, hittust*
middle	*miðjan*
might	*mætta*
Miklabaer (place)	*Miklabæ*
mine	*mér, mik, mín, mína, minn, minna, mínum, mitt*

English	*Old Norse*
misguided	*ófallit*
mockery	*hæðilig*
Modruvellir (place)	*Möðruvöllu*
mood	*skapi*
more	*fleiri, meir, meira*
morning	*morgininn*
most	*mest, mesta, mestum*
mother's-sister's-son	*systrungr*
mourned	*harmaði*
much	*margt, mik, mikill, mikilli, mikinn, mikit, mikla, miklu, miklum, mjök*
my	*mik, mín, mína, mínum*

N, n

name	*nafn, nafn*
named	*heitinn, heitir, hét*
Narfason (name)	*Narfason*
nature	*skaplyndi*
near	*nær, undir*
nearest	*næst*
near-to	*náliga*
necessity	*nauðsyn*
need	*þarf, þurfa, þurfi*
need-you	*þarftu*
negatively	*þungt*
neither	*hvergi*
never	*aldri*
new	*nýjum*
news	*frétt, tíðenda*
nights	*nætr*
no	*eigi, ekki, engi, engrar*
noble	*skörungr*
noblest	*göfgustu*
none	*eigi, enga, engi, engir, engis, engrar*
nor	*ne*
north	*norðan, norðr*
northerners	*norðlendingum*
not	*eigi, ekki*
nothing	*ekki, engu*
now	*nú*

Word List (English to Old Norse)

English	Old Norse

O, o

English	Old Norse
obtain	ná, seilast
occurrence	tilfelli
of	á, af, af, at, ór
of-all	allra
off	af
of-family-small	ættsmár
offer	beiða, biðja, bjóða
offered	boðit
of-silver	silfrs
often	oft
of-them	þeira
of-they	þeira
of-violent-language	málóði
of-wealth	fjár
of-you	yðvarn
Olaf (name)	Óláfi, Óláfr
Olaf's (name)	Óláfs
on	á, í
one	eina, einhvern, einn
one-agreement	einsætt
only	einir, einn
open-whole	hliðhollir
opposite	hvárir
or	eða
ordered	bað
other	annat, öðrum
other-knowing	öðruvís
others	aðrir, öðru, öðrum
Ottar (name)	Óttari, Óttarr
our	okkars, várn, vér
ours	oss, várra
out	út
outlawed	sekðan
outlawry	skóggang
out-of	ór
outside	úti
over	yfir
overcome	barst
own	eign, eigna

P, p

English	Old Norse
parted	skilnaði
parting	skilnaði
passed	leið, líðr
pay	aura, gjalda
peace	kyrrt
peaceful	fríð
Peacock (name)	Pá
people	menn, mönnum
people's	manna
person	manninn
place	stað
plans	ætlat
pledged	hét
plenty-of	ærit
plotting	fjörráð
plotting-against	fjörráð
poleaxe	refði
poorly	fáliga
popular	vinsæll
possible	hægt
postpone	fresta
powerful	ríki
Powerful (name)	Ríka
prepare	búast
prepared	bjóst, búin, búit, býr, býst
preparing	búnir
prevent	skirra
pride	metnaðr
promised	hét
promising	efniligastr
protect	verja
provinces	heruðum

Q, q

English	Old Norse
quickly	skjótt, snarliga

R, r

English	Old Norse
rampages	ofríki
ran	hleypa, hleypr, hljóp, hljópu
rather	heldr, helzt

Word List (English to Old Norse)

English	*Old Norse*	English	*Old Norse*
realised	*þykkjast*	seeing	*sjándi*
recoiled	*hrökkva*	seek	*leita, leitast, sækir*
reconcile	*sættast*	seemed	*sýna, sýnist*
rectify	*leiðréttu*	seems	*þætti, þykkir*
refuse	*níta*	self-judgement	*dóm, sjálfdæmi*
reins	*tauma*	send	*sendi*
releasing	*leystr*	separate	*skilja*
relieved	*fegin, létti, léttu*	separated	*skilði, skilðist, skilðu, skilðust, skilit, skilja*
renowned	*ágætir*		
repay	*selja*	serves	*gegnir*
reported	*fréttist, fréttust, títt*	set	*setr, sett, settist*
resolved	*greiddist*	set-out	*ferr*
respect	*virðing*	settle	*sætt*
respect-kindly	*virðingarvænligt*	settlers	*búa*
rest	*æja*	seven	*sjau*
return	*aftr, móti, ombun, snúa*	several	*nökkura*
returned	*aftr*	shall	*mun, munu, munuð, munum, skal, skalt, skaltu, skulu, skyli*
Reykir (place)	*Reykja*		
rich	*auðigr*		
ridden	*riðit*	shall-be	*skal*
ride	*ríð, ríða, ríðið, riðit*	shall-you	*muntu, skaltu*
riding	*reið, riðinn*	she	*hon*
right	*réttendum*	shield	*skildi, skjöld*
right-knowing	*réttvísi*	shields	*skildir*
risk	*váða*	shining	*blika*
river	*ána*	ships	*skips*
rocks	*grjóti*	short-distance	*skammt*
rode	*ræðst, réðst, reið, ríða, ríðr, riðu*	shot	*skýtr*
		should	*mun, muna, muni, munt, munu, munum, mynda, myndi, skal, skuluð, skulum, skylda, skyldi, skyldu*
running	*hlaupi*		

S, s

English	*Old Norse*	English	*Old Norse*
		should-you	*muntu*
safe	*fritt, heilir*	show	*lýsa, sýna*
saga	*sögu*	showed	*sýnir*
sagas	*sögum*	shown	*lýst, sýnt*
said	*kvað, lézt, sagði, sagt, segir, tala*	side	*hlið*
		sides	*megin*
sake	*sakar*	Sigrid (name)	*Sigríðar, Sigríði, Sigríðr*
same	*sömu*	since	*en, því*
sat	*sat, sátu*	sit	*sitja*
saw	*leit, sá, sér, sjá*	sit-in-ambush	*sæta, sitja*
say	*segi, segja, tel*	sitting	*sátu, setuefni, sitja*
scathed	*skaða*	Skagafjord (place)	*Skagafirði, Skagafjarðar*
see	*sé*	Skeid (place)	*Skeið, Skeiði*

Word List (English to Old Norse)

English	Old Norse	English	Old Norse
skin-cloak	skinnstakki	stolen	stolit
slander	illmæli	stood	standanda, stóð, studdist
slanderous	óorðan		
slanderous-men	öfundarmenn	stop	hættu
slaying-of	víg	strength	styrk
smaller	smæri	striking	höggr
snag-cornered	snaghyrnda	such	sik, slík, því
snow	snjór	summer	sumar, sumarit
so	sá, sé, svá, þat	summoned	stefndi, stefnu
solved	leyst	summons	stefnu
some	nökkurir, nökkut	suspect	grunr
something	nökkut	suspected	grunaði
somewhat	nökkura, nökkurr, nökkut	Svarfadardal (place)	Svarfaðardal, Svarfaðardals, Svarfaðardalsár, Svarfdæla
son	sonar, sonr		
son-of	sonr		
Son-of-Bolli (name)	Bollason		
Son-of-Thord (name)	Þórðarsonar		
Sons-of-Hjalti (name)	Hjaltasynir		

T, t

English	Old Norse
son-yours	sveinsins
sought	sótt, sótti	take	tæki, tak, taka, takir
south	suðr	taken	taka, tekit, tekizt
spare	spara	talked	mælt, töluðu
speak	máli, tala	talking	tal
speaking	mælti	team-minded	liðsinnaðr
speak-to	mál	tearing	rífa
spear	spjót, spjóti, spjótinu, spjótit	ten	tigu
		test	freista, reyndi
spoke	kvað, mælti, mæltu, tala	tested	reyna
sport	leika, leikim	than	en
sprang	spretta	thanked	kvað, þakkaði, þakkar
spring	vár	thanks	þakka, þakkar, þökk
spring-days	várdaga	that	at, en, er, í, sem, þat, þetta, því
spurred	keyrði, keyrir		
standing	staddr	the	á, at, enn, er, hinu, í, in, ina, inn, ins, inum, it, þá, þann, þeir
Starri (name)	Starri		
Starri-of-Guddalir	guðdala-starra		
startled	brá	the-after-matter	eftirmálinu
Stately-man (name)	Stærimaðr, Stærimann, Stærimanni, Stertimaðr	the-assembly	alþingi, þing, þinginu, þingit, þingsins
		the-battle	bardagann
stay	setit	the-booth	búðina
stayed	sat, sátu, setjast, sitr	the-booth-doors	búðardurunum
steal	stela	the-boy	sveininn
stealing	stela	the-brothers	bræðra
step	stíga	the-bull	boli, graðungrinn
still	kyrrt	the-captain	stýrimann

Word List (English to Old Norse)

English	*Old Norse*	English	*Old Norse*
the-case	*málinu, málit*	the-slope	*hlíðinni*
the-charges	*sakar*	the-son-of	*sonr*
the-compound	*virkit*	the-spear	*spjótit*
the-district	*sveitum*	the-struggle	*sóknin*
the-earth	*jörð*	the-summons	*stefnuna, stefnunni*
the-emperor	*stólkonungrinn*	the-sword	*sverðinu*
the-farm	*bæinn, bænum, bú*	the-truest	*sannast*
the-farmer	*bónda, bóndi*	the-unseen-man	*launmaðrinn*
the-feast	*veizla*	the-way	*leiðina*
the-fields	*velli*	the-wind	*vindr*
theft	*þjófnað*	the-worst	*verst*
the-gift	*gjafar*	the-worth	*verð*
the-gifts	*gjafarnar*	the-wounds	*sárum*
the-hay	*desjarnar, heyinu*	they	*sínum, þá, þau, þeim, þeir, þeira*
the-heath	*heiðina*		
the-horses	*hestana*	they-of	*þeira*
the-ice	*ísinn*	thieves	*þjófarnir*
their	*sína, þeira*	things	*hlutir*
theirs	*sína, sinn, sinna, sínum, þeira*	think	*hugða, hugðum, hygg, hyggja, þykkir, þykkist, þykkjast, þykkjumst*
the-journey	*ferðinni*		
the-killing-of	*víg*	this	*í, sé, sín, sitt, þat, þenna, þess, þessa, þessi, þessu, þetta*
the-leg	*fæti*		
them	*sér, þeim, þeira*		
the-man	*maðrinn, mannsins*	Thord (name)	*Þórð, Þórðar, Þórði, Þórðr*
the-matter	*efni, mál, máli, málit, málum*	Thordis (name)	*Þórdís*
the-middle	*miðri*	Thorgrim (name)	*Þorgrímr*
the-more	*meiri*	Thorolf (name)	*Þórólf, Þórólfi, Þórólfr*
themselves	*sér*	Thorolf's (name)	*Þórólfs*
then	*en, enn, er, síðan, þá, þann, þegar, þeir, var*	Thorstein (name)	*Þorstein, Þorstein, Þorsteini, Þorsteinn*
the-night	*nóttina*	Thorstein's (name)	*Þorsteini, Þorsteins*
the-northerners	*norðlendinga*	Thorvald (name)	*Þorvaldi, Þorvaldr*
the-pastures	*afréttum*	though	*þó, þótt*
there	*eru, þangat, þangat, þar, þar, þeir*	thought	*hugðu, hugsar, þótti, þóttu, þykkir*
therefore	*því*	threat	*hót*
the-ring	*hringinn*	three	*þriggja, þrír, þrjá, þrjár*
the-river	*áin, ána, ána, ánni, ár, árinnar*	through	*gegnum*
		Thufur (place)	*Þúfum*
the-same	*saman*	Thvera (place)	*Þverá, Þverár*
these	*ina, þessar, þessir*	time	*tíma*
the-shield	*skildinum, skjöldrinn*	to	*á, áðu, af, at, átzt, í, þat, til, við*
the-slaying	*vígi*	to-accept	*þiggja*
the-slaying-of	*víg*	to-do	*gera*

Word List (English to Old Norse)

English	Old Norse	English	Old Norse
to-expect	ván		
together	jafnsaman, saman		
to-give	gefa	## U, u	
to-going	atgöngu		
to-have	eiga, hafa	unanimously	einhlítt
to-him	honum	uncertain	óvíst
to-invite	bjóða	understanding	skiljum
told	sagði, sagt, segir, töluðu	un-equal-men	ójafnaðarmenn
		un-faring	ófarin
to-me	mér	unfriendly	óvinveittr
took	tækist, tekr, tók, tókst	un-friends	óvinum
took-to	tóku	un-good	ómæt
to-people	mönnum	unholy	óheilagr
to-ride	ríða	unmanageable	ofstýri
to-say	segja	unqualified	óhæfu
to-them	þeim	un-right-knowing	óréttvíss
to-travel	fara	un-rule	ofríki
to-you	þér	unruliness	róstum
trading-men	kaupmenn, kaupmönnum	unruly	ofríki
		un-substantial-company	óliðdrjúgr
travel	færi, fara, farið, ferð, ferðar, ferðinni, ferr	unsuitable	óliðligt
		until	til
travelled	fær, farit, ferr, fór, fóru	up	á, upp, uppi
travelled-you	fórtu	upped	upp
travelling	farinn, ferð	up-saying	uppsögn
travels	ferr	Urdskriduholar (place)	Urðskriðuhóla
treacherous	fláráðum	us	okkr, oss
treachery	brekráð	usually	jafnan
treasures	gripirnir		
trim	kvista	## V, v	
trouble	vandræðum		
true			
true		vagrancy	verðgang
truly	sannast	value	virða
trust	trausts	Vellir (place)	Völlu, Völlum
try	freista	visit	vitja
trying	reyna		
Tunga (place)	Tungu	## W, w	
tunic	kyrtil		
turf-stacks	torfstakka		
turn	horfa, hverfa, hverfið, snúa	wait	bíðr
		ward-knowing	varðveita
turned	hallaði, sneri, snerist	warranted	varða
twelve	tólf	warriors	kappi
twice	tvenn	was	á, en, er, sé, væri, var, varð, váru
two	tvá		

Word List (English to Old Norse)

English	*Old Norse*	English	*Old Norse*
was-named	*hét*	worth	*verðr, verðugt, virða, virðing*
way	*leið, veg, vegar*	worthiness	*virðing*
way-out	*færi*	worthy	*göfugt, vert*
we	*vér*	would	*mun, mundu, muni, munu, myndi*
wealth	*fé, fjár*	would-be	*munu, værir, verða*
weaponed	*vápnaðir*	wound	*sár*
weapons	*vápn, vápns*	wounded	*meiddi, sárr*
weathered	*veðr*	wounding	*sár*
we-get	*hljótum*	wounds	*sár, sára*
welcomed	*fagnat*	wretch	*vesalmenni*
well	*fellu, vel*		
well-willing	*velviljaðr*		
went	*fór, fóru, ganga, gekk, gengr, gengu*		
were	*er, eru, var, váru, vera*		
west	*vestr*		

Y, y

English	*Old Norse*
what	*en, hvar, hvat, hverja, hvern, hvert*
when	*er, nær, þá, þegar*
where	*hvar, vartu*
whether	*en, hvárt*
which	*er, hvert, sem*
while	*stund*
white	*hvítr*
who	*er, hverir, hverr, sem*
wife	*kona, konu*
wife-of	*kona*
wild	*ólman*
will	*vil, vilja, viljum*
willing	*vildi, vilja*
winter	*vetrinn*
winters	*vetra*
wisdom	*spekð*
wish	*vil, vilda, vilir, vilja, vill*
wished	*vildi, vill*
wishing	*vill*
with	*á, með, um, við, yrði*
with-fleetness	*flytir*
with-taken	*viðtökur*
with-taking	*viðtökur*
wit-less	*vitlauss*
word	*orði*
words	*orð, orða, orðit*
work	*verk*
worse	*versna*

English	*Old Norse*
you	*þér, þik, þinn, þit, þú, yðr, yðvar*
young	*ungr*
your	*þér, yðr*
yours	*þína, þinn, þinnar, þinni, þitt, yður*
yourself	*sjálfan*
you-two	*þit*
Yule (name)	*Jól*

The Tale of Bolli Bollason (*Old Icelandic*)

Old Icelandic	Literal	English
1	**1**	**1**
Í þann tíma er Bolli Bollason bjó í Tungu og nú var áður frá sagt þá bjó norður í Skagafirði á Miklabæ Arnór kerlingarnef son Bjarnar Þórðarsonar frá Höfða.	At the time that Bolli Bollason lived at Tunga also now was earlier from told then lived north in Skagafjord in Miklabaer Arnor Crone's-Nose son-of Bjarni Son-of-Thord from Hofdi.	At the same time that Bolli Bollason lived at Tunga, as was spoken of earlier, Arnor Crone's-Nose lived north at Skagafjord in Miklabaer, he was the son of Bjarni Thordarson from Hofdi.
Þórður hét maður er bjó á Marbæli.	Thord named a-man who lived at Marbaeli.	There was a man named Thord who lived at Marbaeli.
Guðrún hét kona hans.	Gudrun named wife his.	His wife was named Gudrun.
Þau voru vel að sér og höfðu gnótt fjár.	They were well of themselves and had an-abundance of-wealth.	They were fine people and had an abundance of wealth.
Son þeirra hét Ólafur og var hann ungur að aldri og allra manna efnilegastur.	Son theirs named Olaf and was he young in age and of-all men promising.	Their son was named Olaf, and he was young and the most promising of all men.
Guðrún kona Þórðar var náskyld Bolla Bollasyni.	Gudrun wife-of Thord was closely-related Bolli Bollason.	Gudrun, Thord's wife, was closely related to Bolli Bollason.
Var hún systrungur hans.	Was she mother's-sister's-son his.	She was his cousin.
Ólafur son þeirra Þórðar var heitinn eftir Ólafi pá í Hjarðarholti.	Olaf son theirs Thord was named after Olaf Peacock in Hjardarholt.	Their son Olaf was named after Olaf Peacock in Hjardarholt.
Þórður og Þorvaldur Hjaltasynir bjuggu að Hofi í Hjaltadal.	Thord and Thorvald Sons-of-Hjalti lived at Hof in Hjaltadal.	Thord and Thorvald Hjaltason lived at Hof in Hjaltadal.
Þeir voru höfðingjar miklir.	They were chieftains great.	They were great chieftains.
Maður hét Þórólfur og var kallaður stertimaður.	A-man was-named Thorolf and was called Stately-man.	There was a man named Thorolf and he was called Stuck-up.
Hann bjó í Þúfum.	He lived in Thufur.	He lived at Thufur.

The Tale of Bolli Bollason (Old Icelandic)

Old Icelandic	Literal	English
Hann var óvinveittur í skapi og æðimaður mikill.	He was unfriendly in mood and frenzy-man much.	He was unfriendly in nature and a very angry man.
Hann átti griðung grán, ólman.	He had a-bull grey, wild.	He had a wild grey bull.
Þórður af Marbæli var í förum með Arnóri.	Thord of Marbaeli was on a-journey with Arnor.	Thord of Marbaeli was travelling with Arnor.
Þórólfur stærimaður átti frændkonu Arnórs en hann var þingmaður Hjaltasona.	Thorolf Stately-man married kinswoman Arnor's and he was assembly-man Hjaltasons.	Thorolf Stuck-up married one of Arnor's kinswomen, and was one of the assembly men of the Hjaltasons.
Hann átti illt við búa sína og lagði það í vanda sinn.	He had bad-terms with settlers his and became that in custom his.	He was on bad terms with his neighbours and that became the custom.
Kom það mest til þeirra Marbælinga.	Came that most to they-of Marbaeli.	And most of this came to the people of Marbaeli.
Graðungur hans gerði mönnum margt mein þá er hann kom úr afréttum.	Bull his made people many harm then as he came back-from the-pastures.	His bull did many people harm, when he came back from the pastures.
Meiddi hann fé manna en gekk eigi undan grjóti.	Wounded he cattle people's and went not away-from rocks.	He wounded people's cattle, and could not be made to go away with rocks.
Hann braut og andvirki og gerði margt illt.	He broke also haystacks and did much ill.	He also damaged haystacks and did much harm.
Þórður af Marbæli hitti Þórólf að máli og bað hann varðveita graðung sinn:	Thord of Marbaeli met Thorolf to discuss and asked him ward-knowing bull his.	Thord of Marbaeli met Thorolf to discuss this with him, and asked him to watch guard over his bull.
"Viljum vér eigi þola honum ofríki".	"Will we not endure his rampages".	"Will we not endure his rampages".
Þórólfur lést eigi mundu sitja að fé sínu.	Thorolf said not would sit at cattle his.	Thorold said that he would not sit by his cattle.
Fer Þórður heim við svo búið.	Travelled Thord home with so prepared.	Thord travelled home with this reply.
Eigi miklu síðar getur Þórður að líta hvar graðungurinn hefir brotið niður torfstakka hans.	Not much afterwards got Thord that look where the-bull had broken down turf-stacks his.	Not long afterwards Thord noticed that the bull had torn apart his stacks of turf.

The Tale of Bolli Bollason (Old Icelandic)

Old Icelandic	Literal	English
Þórður hleypur þá til og hefir spjót í hendi og er boli sér það veður hann jörð svo að upp tekur um klaufir.	Thord ran then to and had spear in hand and when the-bull saw that weathered he earth so that up took about hooves.	Thord then ran over with a spear in his hand, and when he saw it, the bull beat the ground and took up on his hooves.
Þórður leggur til hans svo að hann fellur dauður á jörð.	Thord lunged to him so that he fell dead to the-earth.	Thord lunged at him so that he fell dead on the ground.
Þórður hitti Þórólf og sagði honum að boli var dauður.	Thord met Thorolf and told him that the-bull was dead.	Thord met Thorolf and told him, that the-bull was dead.
"Þetta var lítið frægðarverk", svarar Þórólfur, "en gera mundi eg það vilja er þér þætti eigi betur".	"This was little famous-work", answered Thorolf, "and do should I that will that to-you seems not better".	"This deed is of little honour", answered Thorolf, "and I should wish to do to you something that is no better".
Þórólfur var málóði og heitaðist í hverju orði.	Thorolf was of-violent-language and called at every word.	Thorolf called on violent language with every word.
Þórður átti heimanferð fyrir höndum.	Thord had from-home-travel before his-hands.	Thord had to leave his farm.
Ólafur sonur hans var þá sjö vetra eða átta.	Olaf son his was then seven winters or eight.	His son Olaf was then seven or eight winters.
Hann fór af bænum með leik sínum og gerði sér hús sem börnum er títt en Þórólfur kom þar að honum.	He went off the-farm with game his and made himself a-house which children are reported then Thorolf came there at him.	He went away from the farm and played a game of making himself a house, which children often do, and then Thorolf came at him.
Hann lagði sveininn í gegnum með spjóti.	He lunged the-boy in through with spear.	He lunged through the boy with a spear.
Síðan fór hann heim og sagði konu sinni.	Afterwards travelled he home and told wife his.	Afterwards he travelled home and told his wife.
Hún svarar:	She answered.	She answered:
"Þetta er illt verk og ómannlegt.	"This is ill work and inhumane.	"This is an evil and inhumane deed.
Mun þér þetta illu reifa".	Shall you this evil account-for".	You shall account for this evil".
En er hún tók á honum þungt þá fór hann í brott þaðan og létti eigi fyrr en hann kom á Miklabæ til Arnórs.	Since that she took of him negatively then travelled he to away from-there and relieved not before that he came to Miklabaer to Arnor's.	Since she responded so negatively, he then travelled away and did not rest until he came to Miklabaer to Arnor.

The Tale of Bolli Bollason (Old Icelandic)

Old Icelandic	Literal	English
Fréttust þeir tíðinda.	Reported they news.	They exchanged news.
Þórólfur segir honum víg Ólafs:	Thorolf told him slaying-of Olaf's.	Thorolf told him of the killing of Olaf.
"Sé eg þar nú til trausts sem þér eruð sakir mágsemdar".	"See I here now to trust that you are sake as-in-laws".	"I look here to trust in you, for my sake, as we are in-laws".
"Eigi ferð þú sjáandi eftir um þenna hlut", sagði Arnór, "að eg muni virða meira mágsemd við þig en virðing mína og sæmd, og ásjá áttu hér engrar von af mér".	"Not going you seeing after about this lot", said Arnor, "that I should worth more in-laws with you than worth my and honour, and assistance have-you here none to-expect of me".	"You will not see it after this", said Arnor, "as I do not value my in-laws more than my honour, and you have no assistance to expect from me".
Fór Þórólfur upp eftir Hjaltadal til Hofs og fann þá Hjaltasonu og sagði þeim hvar komið var hans máli "og sé eg hér nú til ásjá sem þið eruð".	Travelled Thorolf up after Hjaltadal to Hof and found then Hjaltasons and told them what came was his matter "and being I here now to assistance as you-two are".	Thorolf travelled for Hof in Hjaltadal and found the Hjaltasons and told them what had happened, "and I am here now to ask for your assistance, as you are".
Þórður svarar:	Thord answered.	Thord answered:
"Slíkt eru níðingsverk og mun eg enga ásjá veita þér um þetta efni".	"Such is lowly-deed and should I none assistance grant to-you about this matter".	"This is such a lowly deed, and I should grant you no assistance in this matter".
Þorvaldur varð um fár.	Thorvald was about few.	Thorvald was of few words.
Fær Þórólfur ekki af þeim að sinni.	Got Thorolf nothing from them in his.	Thorolf got nothing from them in this matter.
Reið hann í brott og upp eftir Hjaltadal til Reykja, fór þar í laug.	Rode he to away and up after Hjaltadal to Reykir, went there to bathe.	He rode away for Hjaltadal to Reykir, where he went to bathe.
En um kveldið reið hann ofan aftur og undir virkið að Hofi og ræddist við einn saman svo sem annar maður væri fyrir og kveddi hann og frétti hver þar væri kominn.	Then about evening rode he down back and near the-compound at Hof and discussed with alone together so as another man was before and greeting him and asking who there was come.	Then in the evening he rode back down near the farmhouse at Hof where he spoke to himself, as if someone was standing there, who greeted him and asked who was there.
"Eg heiti Þórólfur", kvað hann.	"I am-named Thorolf", said he.	"I am named Thorolf", he said.

The Tale of Bolli Bollason (Old Icelandic)

Old Icelandic	Literal	English
"Hvert varstu farinn eða hvað er þér á höndum?" spyr launmaðurinn.	"Which where travelling and what is your in hand?" asked the-unseen-man.	"Where are you travelling, and what is your problem?" asked the unseen man.
Þórólfur segir tilfelli þessi öll eftir því sem voru:	Thorolf told occurrence this all after accordingly as was.	Thorolf told him all that had occurred.
"Bað eg Hjaltasonu ásjár", segir hann, "sakir nauðsynja minna".	"Asked I Hjaltasons assistance", said he, "for-the-sake-of deed-refuse mine".	"I asked for the Hjaltasons assistance", he said, "for the sake of my assistance".
Þessi svarar er fyrir skyldi vera:	This answered who before should be.	The man who should be before him answered:
"Gengið er nú þaðan er þeir gerðu erfið það hið fjölmenna er tólf hundruð manna sátu að og ganga slíkir höfðingjar mjög saman er nú vilja eigi veita einum manni nokkura ásjá".	"Gone are now from-there that they made difficulty that the many-men were twelve hundred men sitting about and went such chieftains many together are now willing not grant any man any assistance".	"They are now gone, they who made the difficulty with many men, there were twelve hundred sitting about, and many such chieftains went together, who are not willing to grant any man assistance".
Þorvaldur var úti staddur og heyrði talið.	Thorvald was outside standing and heard conversation.	Thorvald was standing outside and heard the conversation.
Hann gengur þangað til og tók í tauma hestsins og bað hann af baki stíga "en þó er eigi virðingarvænlegt við þig að eiga fyrir sakir fólsku þinnar".	He went there to and took the reins horse's and asked him off horseback step "but though is not respect-kindly with you to have before conviction false yours".	He went over and took the reins of the horse and asked him to step off horseback, "but it is not with honour to help a man before me with a conviction as false as yours".

2

Old Icelandic	Literal	English
Nú er að segja frá Þórði er hann kom heim og frá víg sonar síns og harmaði það mjög.	Now is to say from Thord that he came home and from the-slaying-of son his and mourned that much.	Now the story turns to Thord, who came home and learned of the killing of his sun, and mourned it very much.
Guðrún kona hans mælti:	Gudrun wife his spoke.	His wife Gudrun spoke:
"Það er þér ráð að lýsa vígi sveinsins á hönd Þórólfi en eg mun ríða suður til Tungu og finna Bolla frænda minn og vita hvern styrk hann vill veita okkur til eftirmáls".	"It is to-you declare that describe the-slaying son-yours in hand Thorolf and I should ride south to Tunga and find Bolli kinsman mine and know what strength he wished grant us to after-matter".	"It is for you to declare Thorolf responsible for the slaying of your son, and I shall ride south to Tunga and find Bolli my kinsman, and know what help he is willing to grant us to gain redress".

The Tale of Bolli Bollason (Old Icelandic)

Old Icelandic	Literal	English
Þau gerðu svo.	They did so.	This they did.
Og er Guðrún kom í Tungu fær hún þar viðtökur góðar.	And was Gudrun come to Tunga travelled she there with-taking good.	And when Gudrun came to Tunga, she was given a good welcome.
Hún segir Bolla víg Ólafs sonar síns og beiddi að hann tæki við eftirmálinu.	She said Bolli killing Olaf's son her and asked that he take with the-after-matter.	She told Bolli about the killing of her son Olaf, and asked that he take over the prosecution of the case.
Hann svarar:	He answered.	He answered:
"Eigi þykir mér þetta svo hæglegt að seilast til sæmdar í hendur þeim Norðlendingum.	"Not seems to-me this so easily to obtain to honour in hand they Northerners.	"It does not seem to me to be so easy, to obtain honour from those northerners.
Fréttist mér og svo til sem maðurinn muni þar niður kominn að ekki muni hægt eftir að leita".	Reported me and so to that the-man should there down come that not should possible after to seek".	It has been reported to me that this man has gone down somewhere that it will not be possible to seek him out.
Bolli tók þó við málinu um síðir og fór Guðrún norður og kom heim.	Bolli took though with the-case about eventually and travelled Gudrun north and came home.	Bolli agreed to take on the case, and Gudrun travelled north and came home.
Hún sagði Þórði bónda sínum svo sem nú var komið og líður nú svo fram um hríð.	She told Thord husband hers so as now was come and passed so from about awhile.	When she arrived home, she told her husband Thord what had happened, and so it passed for a while.
Eftir jól um veturinn var lagður fundur í Skagafirði að Þverá og stefndi Þorvaldur þangað Guðdala-Starra.	After Yule about winter was laid a-meeting in Skagafjord at Thvera and summoned Thorvald from-there Starri-of-Guddalir.	After Yule in winter there was a meeting held in Skagafjord at Thvera, and Thorvald summoned Starri of Guddalir.
Hann var vinur þeirra bræðra.	He was a-friend of-they the-brothers.	He was a friend of the (Hjaltason) brothers.
Þorvaldur fór til þingsins við sína menn og er þeir komu fyrir Urðskriðuhóla þá hljóp úr hlíðinni ofan að þeim maður.	Thorvald travelled to the-assembly with his men and when they came before Urdskriduholar then ran from the-slope down at them a-man.	Thorvald travelled to the assembly with his men, and when they came to Urdskriduholar, a man came running down the slope towards them.
Var þar Þórólfur.	Was it Thorolf.	It was Thorolf.

The Tale of Bolli Bollason (Old Icelandic)

Old Icelandic	Literal	English
Réðst hann í ferð með þeim Þorvaldi.	Rode he in travelling with them Thorvald.	He joined and rode with Thorvald (and his men).
Og er þeir áttu skammt til Þverár þá mælti Þorvaldur við Þórólf:	And when they had a-short-distance to Thvera then spoke Thorvald with Thorolf.	When they had a short distance remaining to Thvera, Thorvald spoke to Thorolf:
"Nú skaltu hafa með þér þrjár merkur silfurs og sitja hér upp frá bænum að Þverá.	"Now shall have with you three marks of-silver and sit here up from farmhouse at Thvera.	"Take three marks of silver and stay here above the farmhouse at Thvera.
Haf það að marki að eg mun snúa skildi mínum og að þér holinu ef þér er fritt og máttu þá fram ganga.	Have this as a-sign that I shall turn shield mine and that you hollow if you are safe and may then from go.	Have this as a sign, that I will turn the inside of my shield if you are safe and can come from there.
Skjöldurinn er hvítur innan".	The-shield is white inside".	The shield is white on the inside".
Og er Þorvaldur kom til þingsins hittust þeir Starri og tóku tal saman.	And when Thorvald came to the-assembly met they Starri and took-to talking together.	And when Thorvald came to the assembly, they met Starri and talked together.
Þorvaldur mælti:	Thorvald spoke.	Thorvald spoke:
"Svo er mál með vexti að eg vil þess beiða að þú takir við Þórólfi stærimanni til varðveislu og trausts.	"So is the-matter with grown that I will this offer that you take with Thorolf Stately-man to hospitality and trust.	"So is the matter has come, I will offer this, that I wish you to take Thorolf Stuck-up into your hospitality and support.
Mun eg fá þér þrjár merkur silfurs og vináttu mína".	Should I fee to-you three marks of-silver and friendship mine".	I shall pay you three marks of silver and give you my friendship.
"Þar er sá maður", svarar Starri, "er mér þykir ekki vinsæll og óvíst að honum fylgi hamingja.	"There is so a-man", answered Starri, "that to-me seems not popular and uncertain that he follows luck.	"There is such a man", answered Starri, "that is not popular in my eyes, and not likely to bring much luck.
En sakir okkars vinskapar þá vil eg við honum taka".	But for-the-sake-of our friendship then will I with him take".	But for the sake of our friendship I will take him with me".
"Þá gerir þú vel", segir Þorvaldur.	"The do you well", said Thorvald.	"You do well in that case", said Thorvald.

The Tale of Bolli Bollason (Old Icelandic)

Old Icelandic	Literal	English
Sneri hann þá skildinum og frá sér hvolfinu og er Þórólfur sér það gengur hann fram og tók Starri við honum.	Turned he then the-shield and from himself half and when Thorolf saw that went he from and took Starri with him.	He then turned his shield from himself half way, and when Thorolf saw that, he went from where he was and received him.
Starri átti jarðhús í Guðdölum því að jafnan voru með honum skógarmenn.	Starri had earth-house in Guddalir because that usually were with him forest-men.	Starri had an earth house in Guddalir because he usually had outlaws with him.
Átti hann og nokkuð sökótt.	Had he also some accusations.	He had also had some charges against him.

3

Old Icelandic	Literal	English
Bolli Bollason býr til vígsmálið Ólafs.	Bolli Son-of-Bolli prepared to fight-the-case Olaf's.	Bolli Bollason prepared to prosecute Olaf's case.
Hann býst heiman og fer norður til Skagafjarðar við þrjá tigi manna.	He prepared at-home and set-out north to Skagafjord with three ten men.	He made preparations and set out north to Skagafjord with thirty men.
Hann kemur á Miklabæ og er honum þar vel fagnað.	He came to Miklabaer and was he there well welcomed.	He came to Miklabaer and was well welcomed there.
Segir hann hversu af stóð um ferðir hans:	Said he how-so of stood about journey his.	He told them the reasons for his journey.
"Ætla eg að hafa fram vígsmálið nú á Hegranessþingi á hendur Þórólfi stærimanni.	"Intend I to have from fight-the-case now to Hegranes-Assembly in hand Thorolf Stately-man.	"I intend to prosecute the case at Hegranes Assembly for Thorolf Stuck-up.
Vildi eg að þú værir mér um þetta mál liðsinnaður".	Wish I that you would-be to-me about this matter team-minded".	I would like you to assist and cooperate with me in this matter".
Arnór svarar:	Arnor answered.	Arnor answered:
"Ekki þykir mér þú Bolli vænt stefna út er þú sækir norður hingað, við slíka ójafnaðarmenn sem hér er að eiga.	"Not seems to-me you Bolli expect agreement from that you seek north here, with such un-equal-men which here are to in.	"It doesn't seems to me, Bolli, that you can expect an agreement that you seek here in the north, with such unjust men that are here".
Munu þeir þetta mál meir verja með kappi en réttindum.	Should they this matter more protect with warriors whether right.	They would defend this matter as warriors whether just or unjust.

The Tale of Bolli Bollason (Old Icelandic)

Old Icelandic	Literal	English
En ærin nauðsyn þykir mér þér á vera.	But considerable necessity seems to-me to-you to be.	But it seems that you have a considerable necessity.
Munum vér og freista að þetta mál gangi fram".	Should we also try that this matter going from".	So we should try to do what we can in this matter.
Arnór dregur að sér fjölmenni mikið.	Arnor drew to himself followers-many much.	Arnor collected a large number of men.
Ríða þeir Bolli til þingsins.	Rode they Bolli to the-assembly.	They rode with Bolli to the assembly.
Þeir bræður fjölmenna mjög til Hegranessþings.	The brothers following-men much to Hegranes-Assembly.	The brothers also came with many followers to Hegranes Assembly.
Þeir hafa frétt um ferðir Bolla.	They had news about journey Bolli's.	They had news about Bolli's journey.
Ætla þeir að verja málið.	Intended they to defend the-case.	They intended to defend the case.
Og er menn koma til þingsins hefir Bolli fram sakir á hendur Þórólfi.	And when people came to the-assembly had Bolli from the-charges in hand Thorolf.	And when people came to the assembly, Bolli presented the charges against Thorolf,
Og er til varna var boðið gengu þeir til Þorvaldur og Starri við sveit sína og hugðu að eyða málinu fyrir Bolla með styrk og ofríki.	And was to defence was bid went they to Thorvald and Starri with company theirs and thought that devastate the-case before Bolli with strength and un-rule.	and then the defence was made, and Thorvald and Starri came forward with their company, they intended to block Bolli's prosecution with strength and unruliness.
En er þetta sér Arnór gengur hann í milli með sína sveit og mælti:	Then when this saw Arnor went he in between with his company and spoke.	Then when Arnor saw this, he went in-between with his company and spoke:
"Það er mönnum einsætt að færa hér eigi svo marga góða menn í vandræði sem á horfist að menn skuli eigi ná lögum um mál sín.	"It is to-people one-agreement that bringing here not so many good men in dispute as to looks that people shall not obtain law about the-matter this.	"It is clear that so many good men should not be here in the dispute as now looks likely, that people shall not get justice in this matter.
Er og ófallið að fylgja Þórólfi um þetta mál.	It-is also misguided to follow Thorolf about this case.	It is also misguided to support Thorolf in this case.

The Tale of Bolli Bollason (Old Icelandic)

Old Icelandic	Literal	English
Muntu Þorvaldur og óliðdrjúgur verða ef reyna skal".	Should-you Thorvald also un-substantial-company become if tested shall-be".	And you, Thorvald, will have little backing if it comes to a show of force.
Þeir Þorvaldur og Starri sáu nú að málið mundi fram ganga því að þeir höfðu ekki liðsafla við þeim Arnóri og léttu þeir frá.	They Thorvald and Starri saw now that the-case should from go since that they had not company-provided with them Arnor and relieved they from.	Thorvald and Starri now saw that the case would be concluded, since they did not have the same number of men with them to match Arnor, so they withdrew.
Bolli sekti Þórólf stærimann þar á Hegranessþingi um víg Ólafs frænda síns og fór við það heim.	Bolli convicted Thorolf Stately-man there at Hegranes-Assembly about the-killing-of Olaf's kinsman his and travelled with that home.	Bolli convicted Thorolf Stuck-up there at Hegranes Assembly for the killing of his kinsman Olaf, and then went home.
Skildust þeir Arnór með kærleikum.	Separated they Arnor with friendship.	He separated from Arnor with friendship.
Sat Bolli í búi sínu.	Sat Bolli in farm his.	Bolli stayed on his farm.

4

Old Icelandic	Literal	English
Þorgrímur hét maður.	Thorgrim was-named a-man.	There was a man named Thorgrim.
Hann átti skip uppi standanda í Hrútafirði.	He had a-ship up stood in Hrutafjord.	He had a ship which stood at Hrutafjord.
Þangað reið Starri og Þórólfur við honum.	There rode Starri and Thorolf to him.	Starri and Thorolf rode there to be with him.
Starri mælti við stýrimann:	Starri spoke with the-captain.	Starri spoke with the captain:
"Hér er maður að eg vil að þú takir við og flytjir utan og hér eru þrjár merkur silfurs er þú skalt hafa og þar með vináttu mína".	"Here is a-man that I wish that you take with and with-fleetness abroad and here are three marks of-silver and you shall have also there with friendship mine".	"Here is a man that I wish you to take abroad quickly, and here are three marks of silver, and you shall also have my friendship".
Þorgrímur mælti:	Thorgrim spoke.	Thorgrim spoke:
"Á þessu þykir mér nokkur vandi hversu af hendi verður leyst.	"About this seems to-me somewhat difficulty how-so of hand becomes solved.	"It seems to me that it will be somewhat difficult to be able to solve.

The Tale of Bolli Bollason (Old Icelandic)

Old Icelandic	Literal	English
En við áskoran þína mun eg við honum taka.	But with challenge yours should I with him take.	But with your challenge I shall take him,
En þó þykir mér þessi maður vera ekki giftuvænlegur".	But though seems to-me this a-man becomes not luck-promised".	though it seems to me that this man promises much luck".
Þórólfur réðst nú í sveit með kaupmönnum en Starri ríður heim við svo búið.	Thorolf rode now in company with trading-men and Starri rode home with so prepared.	Thorolf then rode in company with the merchants, and Starri rode home so prepared.
Nú er að segja frá Bolla.	Now is to say from Bolli.	Now the story turns to Bolli.
Hann hugsar nú efni þeirra Þórólfs og þykir eigi verða mjög með öllu fylgt ef Þórólfur skal sleppa.	He thought now the-matter theirs Thorolf's and thought not would-be much with all followed if Thorolf should escape.	He thought about their matter with Thorolf and thought it would not be much if it followed that Thorolf should escape.
Frétti hann nú að hann er til skips ráðinn.	Learned he now that he was to ships riding.	He now learned that he was riding to the ships.
Bolli býst heiman.	Bolli prepared from-home.	Bolli prepared to leave home.
Setur hann hjálm á höfuð sér, skjöld á hlið.	Set he helmet on head his, shield about side.	He put his helmet on his head, his shield by his side,
Spjót hafði hann í hendi en gyrður sverðinu Fótbít.	Spear had he in hand in buckled the-sword Leg-Biter.	his spear in his hand, and buckled the sword Leg Biter.
Hann ríður norður til Hrútafjarðar og kom í það mund er kaupmenn voru albúnir.	He rode north to Hrutafjord and came in so about-that-time as trading-men were all-prepared.	He rode north to Hrutafjord and arrived at about the time that the merchants were all prepared.
Var þá og vindur á kominn.	Then when also the-wind up came.	Then the wind also came up.
Og er Bolli reið að búðardyrunum gekk Þórólfur út í því og hafði húðfat í fangi sér.	And as Bolli rode to the-booth-doors went Thorolf out about because also had bed-roll in arms his.	And as Bolli rode up to the camp doors, Thorolf came out carrying his bed roll in his arms.
Bolli bregður Fótbít og leggur í gegnum hann.	Bolli drew Leg-Biter and lunged at through him.	Bolli drew Leg Biter and lunged through him.
Fellur Þórólfur á bak aftur í búðina inn en Bolli hleypur á hest sinn.	Fell Thorolf on back down in the-booth inside and Bolli ran to horse his.	Thorolf fell back into the camp, and Bolli ran to his horse.

The Tale of Bolli Bollason (Old Icelandic)

Old Icelandic	Literal	English
Kaupmenn hljópu saman og að honum.	Trading-men ran together and at him.	The merchants ran together towards him.
Bolli mælti:	Bolli spoke.	Bolli spoke:
"Hitt er yður ráðlegast að láta nú vera kyrrt því að yður mun ofstýri verða að leggja mig við velli.	"Find is you advisable that leave now being peace because that you should unmanageable being to lay me with the-fields.	"It is advisable that you leave now in peace, because you shall not manage to bring me down in the fields,
En vera má að eg kvisti einnhvern yðvarn eða alla tvo áður eg er felldur".	But being may that I trim one of-you or all two before I am falling".	and it may be, that I trim one or two of you before I fall".
Þorgrímur svarar:	Thorgrim said.	Thorgrim said:
"Eg hygg að þetta sé satt".	"I think that this is true".	"I think that this is true".
Létu þeir vera kyrrt en Bolli reið heim og hefir sótt mikinn frama í þessi ferð.	Let they be still and Bolli rode home and had attended much honour in this journey.	They remained still, and Bolli rode home and earned a great deal of honour from this journey.
Fær hann af þessu virðing mikla og þótti mönnum farið skörulega, hefir sektan manninn í öðrum fjórðungi en síðan riðið einn saman í hendur óvinum sínum og drepið hann þar.	Accomplished he of this honour much and thought people travelled boldly, had outlawed person in another district and then ride alone together in hand un-friends his and kill him there.	He accomplished much honour in this, and people thought he travelled boldly, to have the man outlawed in another district, and then riding alone into the hands of his enemies and killing him there.

5   5   5

Old Icelandic	Literal	English
Um sumarið á alþingi fundust þeir Bolli og Guðmundur hinn ríki og töluðu margt.	About summer at the-assembly met they Bolli and Gudmund the powerful and talked much.	About summer at the assembly Bolli and Gudmund the Powerful met and talked much.
Þá mælti Guðmundur:	Then spoke Gudmund.	Then Gudmund spoke:
"Því vil eg lýsa Bolli að eg vil við slíka menn vingast sem þér eruð.	"Because wish I show Bolli that I wish with such people make-friends as you are.	"I wish to say to you, Bolli, that I wish to make friends with people like you.
Eg vil bjóða þér norður til mín til hálfs mánaðar veislu og þykir mér betur að þú komir".	I wish to-invite you north to mine to half-month's a-month's feast and consider me better that you come".	I wish to invite you north to mine for a half month's feast, and I would think the best of it if you came".

The Tale of Bolli Bollason (Old Icelandic)

Old Icelandic	Literal	English
Bolli svarar, að vísu vill hann þiggja sæmdir að slíkum manni og hét hann ferðinni.	Bolli answered, that certainly wished he accept honour from such a-man and promised he the-journey.	Bolli answered that he certainly wished to accept this honour from such a man, and promised that he would make the journey.
Þá urðu og fleiri menn til að veita honum þessi vinganarmál.	Then became also more men to that grant him this friendship-matter.	Then others also came to grant him friendship.
Arnór kerlingarnef bauð Bolla og til veislu á Miklabæ.	Arnor Crone's-nose invited Bolli also to feast at Miklabaer.	Arnor Crone's-Nose also invited Bolli to a feast at Miklabaer.
Maður hét Þorsteinn.	A-man named Thorstein.	There was a man named Thorstein.
Hann bjó að Hálsi.	He lived at Hals.	He lived at Hals.
Hann var sonur Hellu-Narfa.	He was the-son-of Hellu-Narfi.	He was the son of Hellu-Narfi.
Hann bauð Bolla til sín er hann færi norðan og Þórður af Marbæli bauð Bolla.	He invited Bolli to his that he travel north and Thord at Marbaeli invited Bolli.	He invited Bolli to travel north to his, and so did Thord at Marbaeli.
Fóru menn af þinginu og reið Bolli heim.	Travelled people to the-assembly and rode Bolli home.	People travelled to the assembly, and Bolli rode home.
Þetta sumar kom skip í Dögurðarnes og settist þar upp.	That summer came a-ship in Dagverdarnes and set there up.	That summer a ship came in at Dagverdarnes and set up there.
Bolli tók til vistar í Tungu tólf kaupmenn.	Bolli took to lodging at Tunga twelve trading-men.	Bolli took lodging for twelve trading men.
Voru þeir þar um veturinn og veitti Bolli þeim allstórmannlega.	Were they there about winter and granted Bolli home all-great-man-like.	They were there about winter, and Bolli provided from them generously.
Sátu þeir um kyrrt fram yfir jól.	Sat they about still from over Yule.	They stayed there for Yule.
En eftir jól ætlar Bolli að vitja heimboðanna norður og lætur hann þá járna hesta og býr ferð sína.	Then after Yule intended Bolli to visit home-invitation north and had he then iron-shod horses and prepared travel his.	Then after Yule, Bolli intended to visit the north as invited, and he had horses shod and prepared to travel.
Voru þeir átján í reið.	Were they eighteen in riding.	There were eighteen of them riding.

The Tale of Bolli Bollason (Old Icelandic)

Old Icelandic	Literal	English
Voru kaupmenn allir vopnaðir.	Were trading-men all weaponed.	All the merchants were armed.
Bolli reið í blárri kápu og hafði í hendi spjótið konungsnaut hið góða.	Bolli rode in black cape and had in hand spear king's-gift the good.	Bolli rode in a black cape and in his hand the spear, King's Gift, the good.
Þeir ríða nú norður og koma á Marbæli til Þórðar.	They rode now north and came to Marbaeli to Thord.	They now rode north and came to Marbaeli to Thord.
Var þar allvel við þeim tekið, sátu þrjár nætur í miklum fagnaði.	Were there all-well with them taken, sat three nights in much celebration.	They were all well received and stayed three nights in celebration.
Þaðan riðu þeir á Miklabæ til Arnórs og tók hann ágætlega vel við þeim.	From-there rode they to Miklabaer to Arnor's and took him greatly well with them.	From there they rode to Miklabaer to Arnor, and he received them well.
Var þar veisla hin besta.	Was there the-feast the best.	There was the best feast.
Þá mælti Arnór:	Then spoke Arnor.	Then Arnor spoke:
"Vel hefir þú gert Bolli er þú hefir mig heimsótt.	"Well have you done Bolli that you have my home-sought.	"You have done well, Bolli, for seeking my home.
Þykir mér þú hafa lýst í því við mig mikinn félagsskap.	Think I you have shown it therefore with me much comradeship.	I think you have therefore shown me much comradeship.
Skulu eigi eftir betri gjafir með mér en þú skalt þiggja mega.	Shall not after better gifts with me than you shall accept may.	And no better gifts will remain here with me that the ones you accept at parting.
Mín vinátta skal þér og heimul vera.	My friendship shall to-you also have-right be.	My friendship is also yours for the asking.
En nokkur grunur er mér á að þér séu eigi allir menn vinhollir í þessu héraði, þykjast sviptir vera sæmdum.	But somewhat suspect that for-me about that you being not all men open-whole in this district, think loss being honour.	But I suspect that around me, not everyone in this district is inclined towards you, thinking that they have lost their honour.
Kemur það mest til þeirra Hjaltasona.	Coming that most to they Hjaltasons.	Most of that coming to the Hjaltasons.
Mun eg nú ráðast til ferðar með þér norður á Heljardalsheiði þá er þér farið héðan".	Should I now arrange to travel with you north to Heljardal Heath then when you travel from-here".	I shall now arrange to travel north with you to Herjardal Heath when you leave here".

The Tale of Bolli Bollason (Old Icelandic)

Old Icelandic	Literal	English
Bolli svarar:	Bolli answered.	Bolli answered:
"Þakka vil eg yður Arnór bóndi alla sæmd er þér gerið til mín nú og fyrrum.	"Thanks wish I you Arnor host all honour that you do about mine now and before-us.	"I wish to thank you, Arnor my host, for all the honour, that you have shown me now before us.
Þykir mér og það bæta vorn flokk að þér ríðið með oss.	Seems to-me also that better our flock that you ride with us.	It seems to me better for our flock, if you ride with us.
En allt hugðum vér að fara með spekt um þessi héruð.	Then all think we that travel with wisdom about this district.	Then we think we will travel with wisdom through this district,
En ef aðrir leita á oss þá má vera að vér leikum þá enn nokkuð í mót".	That if others look for us then may be that we sport then but somewhat in meeting".	so that if others look for us, as they may, then we will give them some sport in meeting us".
Síðan ræðst Arnór til ferðar með þeim og ríða nú veg sinn.	Afterwards rode Arnor to travel with them and rode now way theirs.	Afterwards Arnor prepared to ride with them, and they set out on their way.

6

Nú er að segja frá Þorvaldi að hann tekur til orða við Þórð bróður sinn:	Now is to say from Thorvald that he took to words with Thord brother his.	Now the story turns to Thorvald, that he spoke to his brother Thord:
"Vita muntu að Bolli fer héðra að heimboðum.	"Know shall-you that Bolli travels district at home-invitations.	"You know that Bolli travels in this district going to home invitations.
Eru þeir nú að Arnórs átján saman og ætla norður Heljardalsheiði".	Are they now at Arnor's eighteen together and intend north Heljardal Heath".	There are eighteen of then together, and they intend north to Herjardal Heath.
"Veit eg það", svarar Þórður.	"Know I that", answered Thord.	"I know that", answered Thord.
Þorvaldur mælti:	Thorvald spoke.	Thorvald said:
"Ekki er mér þó um það að Bolli hlaupi hér svo um horn oss að vér finnum hann eigi því að eg veit eigi hver minni sæmd hefir meir niður drepið en hann".	"Not am I though about that that Bolli running here so about horn ours that we find him not such that I know none who diminish honour has more down killing than him".	"I am not happy with the idea that Bolli is running around here under our noses, and we don't go to meet him, because I know no one, who has diminished my honour more than him".
Þórður mælti:	Thord spoke.	Thord spoke:

The Tale of Bolli Bollason (Old Icelandic)

Old Icelandic	Literal	English
"Mjög ertu íhlutunarsamur og meir en eg vildi og ófarin mundi þessi ef eg réði.	"Great are-you in-sharing-together also more than I wish and un-faring should this if I decide.	"You are great at sharing in things more than I wish, and this should not go, if I am the one to decide.
Þykir mér óvíst að Bolli sé ráðlaus fyrir þér".	Seems to-me uncertain that Bolli so ill-advised for you".	It seems uncertain to me, that Bolli would be so ill-advised about you".
"Eigi mun eg letjast láta", svarar Þorvaldur, "en þú munt ráða ferð þinni".	"Not should I dissuaded allow", answered Thorvald, "but you should decide travel yours".	"I should not allow that to dissuade me", answered Thorvald, "but you should decide your course".
Þórður mælti:	Thord spoke.	Third spoke:
"Eigi mun eg eftir sitja ef þú ferð bróðir en þér munum vér eigna alla virðing þá er vér hljótum í þessi ferð, og svo ef öðruvís ber til".	"Not should I after sitting if you travel brother but you shall we own all worthiness then as we we-get in this journey, and so if other-knowing bear to".	"I shall not stay, if you travel, brother, but you shall own all the honour we may get from this journey, or any other consequences".
Þorvaldur safnar að sér mönnum og verða þeir átján saman og ríða á leið fyrir þá Bolla og ætla að sitja fyrir þeim.	Thorvald collected for his men and became they eighteen together and rode to journey for then Bolli and intended to sit before them.	Thorvald collected together his men to become a party of eighteen and together they rode on the journey that Bolli made and intended to sit in ambush before them.
Þeir Arnór og Bolli ríða nú með sína menn	They Arnor and Bolli rode now with their men	Arnor and Bolli rode with their men.
og er skammt var í milli þeirra og Hjaltasona þá mælti Bolli til Arnórs:	and when short-distance were in between them and Hjaltasons then spoke Bolli to Arnor's.	And when there was a short distance between them and the Hjaltasons, Bolli said to Arnor:
"Mun eigi það nú ráð að þér hverfið aftur? Hafið þér þó fylgt oss hið drengilegsta.	"Should not is now advised that you turn back?" Have you though followed us the bravely.	"Should it not now be advised that you turn back? Though you have followed us bravely.
Munu þeir Hjaltasynir ekki sæta fláráðum við mig".	Should they Hjaltasons not sit-in-ambush treacherous with me".	The Hjaltasons should not sit in ambush for me in treachery".
Arnór mælti:	Arnor spoke.	Arnor spoke:

The Tale of Bolli Bollason (Old Icelandic)

Old Icelandic	Literal	English
"Eigi mun eg enn aftur hverfa því að svo er sem annar segi mér að Þorvaldur muni til þess ætla að hafa fund þinn.	"Not should I then back turn because that so is that another say me that Thorvald should to this intend to have meet you.	"I shall not turn back, because something tells me that Thorvald intends to meet you,
Eða hvað sé eg þar upp koma, blika þar eigi skildir við? Og munu þar vera Hjaltasynir.	And what see I there up coming, shining there not shields with?" And should there be Hjaltasons.	and what is that I see moving there? Is that not the glimmer of shields? That will be the Hjaltasons.
En þó mætti nú svo um búast að þessi þeirra ferð yrði þeim til engrar virðingar en megi metast fjörráð við þig".	But though may now so about prepare that this they travel with them to no honour but may meet plotting against you".	But now shall we be prepared, that they will travel with no honour, that they are plotting against you".
Nú sjá þeir Þorvaldur bræður að þeir Bolli eru hvergi liðfærri en þeir og þykjast sjá ef þeir sýna nokkura óhæfu af sér að þeirra kostur mundi mikið versna.	Now saw they Thorvald brothers that they Bolli were neither company-less than they and realised saw if they seemed somewhat unqualified of themselves that they chose would much worse.	Thorvald and his brother saw that Bolli and his company were no less in numbers than they were, and when they saw this they realised, that if they were unqualified themselves, that the choice of aggression would be much worse.
Sýnist þeim það ráðlegast að snúa aftur alls þeir máttu ekki sínum vilja fram koma.	Seemed to-them that advice that return back all they may not theirs will from coming.	It seemed to them that the best advice was now to turn back, since they were not able to carry out their will.
Þá mælti Þórður:	Then spoke Thord.	Then Thord spoke:
"Nú fór sem mig varði að þessi ferð mundi verða hæðileg og þætti mér enn betra heima setið.	"Now goes as much expect that this journey would become mockery and seems to-me the better home stay.	"Now it goes as I expected, that this journey would make a mockery of us, and it seems better if we had stayed at home,
Höfum sýnt oss í fjandskap við menn en komið engu á leið".	Has shown us in fiendship with people but come nothing from passed".	we have shown hostility with people, but achieved nothing".
Þeir Bolli ríða leið sína.	They Bolli rode way theirs.	Bolli and his men rode their way.
Fylgir Arnór þeim upp á heiðina og skildi hann eigi fyrr við þá en hallaði af norður.	Followed Arnor them up to the-heath and separated he not before with then but turned of north.	Arnor followed them up to the heath, and did not leave them until they turned north.

The Tale of Bolli Bollason (Old Icelandic)

Old Icelandic	Literal	English
Þá hvarf hann aftur en þeir riðu ofan eftir Svarfaðardal og komu á bæ þann er á Skeiði heitir.	Then broke-away he back but they rode down along Svarfadardal and came to a-farm then which was Skeid named.	Then he broke away and returned home while they rode down through Svarfadardal until they reached a farm called Skeid.
Þar bjó sá maður er Helgi hét.	There lived so a-man who Helgi named.	There lived a man there who was named Helgi.
Hann var ættsmár og illa í skapi, auðigur að fé.	He was of-family-small and bad in mood, rich in wealth.	He was not from a good family, ill-tempered, but wealthy.
Hann átti þá konu er Sigríður hét.	He had then wife who Sigrid named.	He had a wife named Sigrid.
Hún var frændkona Þorsteins Hellu-Narfasonar.	She was kinswoman Thorstein's Hellu-Narfason.	The was a kinswoman of Thorstein Hellu-Narfason.
Hún var þeirra skörungur meiri.	She was of-them noble the-more.	She was the more outstanding of them.
Þeir Bolli litu heygarð hjá sér.	There Bolli looked hay-stacks beside them.	Bolli looked and saw hay stacks nearby.
Stigu þeir þar af baki og kasta þeir fyrir hesta sína og verja til heldur litlu en þó hélt Bolli þeim aftur að heygjöfinni.	Dismounted they there off horseback and cast there before horses theirs and guarding to rather little but though held Bolli they back the hay-giving.	They dismounted their horses, and cast them before the horses, taking rather little, and Bolli restrained them even more.
"Veit eg eigi", segir hann, "hvert skaplyndi bóndi hefir".	"Know I not", said he, "what nature the-farmer has".	"I don't know", he said, "what sort of nature this farmer has".
Þeir gáfu heyvöndul og létu hestana grípa í.	They gave hay-bundle and led the-horses grab to.	They took handfuls of hay and let the horses eat them.
Á bænum heima gekk út maður og þegar inn aftur og mælti:	About the-farm home went out a-man and from-there inside returned and spoke.	About the farm came out a man from inside who went back inside and spoke:
"Menn eru við heygarð þinn bóndi og reyna desjarnar".	"Men are with hay-stacks yours farmer and trying the-hay".	"Men are at your haystacks, master, trying the hay".
Sigríður húsfreyja svarar:	Sigrid housewife answered.	Sigrid the housewife answered,
"Þeir einir munu þar menn vera að það mun ráð að spara eigi hey við".	"They only would there men be that it would decide to spare not hey with".	"The only men who will be there, are those that it will be a good idea not to spare hay".

The Tale of Bolli Bollason (Old Icelandic)

Old Icelandic	Literal	English
Helgi hljóp upp í óðafári og kvað aldrei hana skyldu þessu ráða að hann léti stela heyjum sínum.	Helgi leapt up in a-hurry and said never he should this allow that he let steal hay his.	Helgi leapt up in a hurry and said that he would never allow others to steal his hay.
Hann hleypur þegar sem hann sé vitlaus og kemur þar að sem þeir áðu.	He ran immediately as-if he was wit-less and came there to as they to.	He ran out immediately as if he were crazed, and came up to where the men were.
Bolli stóð upp er hann leit ferðina mannsins og studdist við spjótið konungsnaut.	Bolli stood up as he saw going the-man and stood with the-spear king's-gift.	Bolli stood up as he saw the man coming, and stood up with the help of the spear, King's Gift.
Og þegar Helgi kom að honum mælti hann:	And as-soon-as Helgi came to him spoke he.	As soon as Helgi reached him, he spoke:
"Hverjir eru þessir þjófarnir er mér bjóða ofríki og stela mig eign minni og rífa í sundur hey mitt fyrir faraskjóta sína?"	"Who are these thieves that me offer unruly and stealing my own less and tearing to asunder hay mine for horses theirs?"	"Who are these thieves, that harass me and steal what is mine and tearing apart my hay for their horses?".
Bolli segir nafn sitt.	Bolli said name his.	Bolli told him his name.
Helgi svarar:	Helgi answered.	Helgi answered:
"Það er óliðlegt nafn og muntu vera óréttvís".	"That is unsuitable name and should-you be un-right-knowing".	"That is an unsuitable name, and you must be an unjust man".
"Vera má að svo sé", segir Bolli, "en hinu skaltu mæta er réttvísi er í".	"Be-it may that so this", said Bolli, "but the shall-you meet which right-knowing that is".	"It may be that it is", said Bolli, "but you shall have your justice".
Bolli keyrði þá hestana frá heyinu og bað þá eigi æja lengur.	Bolli spurred then horses from the-hay and ordered then none rest any-longer.	Bolli then spurred the horses away from the hay, and ordered that none would rest there any longer.
Helgi mælti:	Helgi spoke.	Helgi spoke:
"Eg kalla yður hafa stolið mig þessu sem þér hafið haft og gert á hendur yður skóggangssök".	"I declare you have stolen mine this as you have had and done in hand your forest-seeking".	"I declare you have stolen what is mine, which you have, and you have committed an offence to outlawry".

The Tale of Bolli Bollason (Old Icelandic)

Old Icelandic	Literal	English
"Þú munt vilja bóndi", sagði Bolli, "að vér komum fyrir oss fébótum við þig og hafir þú eigi sakir á oss.	"You should wish farmer", said Bolli, "that we come before us compensation with you and have you no conviction of us.	"You will want, farmer", said Bolli, "that we bring forth compensation with you, so that you will have no conviction with us.
Mun eg gjalda tvenn verð fyrir hey þitt".	Shall I pay twice the-worth for hay yours".	I shall pay twice the worth of your hay".
"Það fer heldur fjarri", svarar hann, "mun eg framar á hyggja um það er vér skiljum".	"That goes behind far-away", answered he, "should I honour to think about that which our understanding".	"That is nowhere near enough", he answered, "I should think about my honour, what understanding we shall have".
Bolli mælti:	Bolli spoke.	Bolli spoke:
"Eru nokkurir hlutir þeir bóndi er þú viljir hafa í sætt af oss?"	"Are-there some things they farmer that you wish to-have to settle of us?"	"Are there any objects, farmer, that you wish to have to settle with us?".
"Það þykir mér vera mega", svarar Helgi, "að eg vilji spjót það hið gullrekna er þú hefir í hendi".	"That think I be may", answered Helgi, "that I wish spear that the gold-inlaid that you have in hand".	"I think it might be", answered Helgi, "that I wish to have the spear that is inlaid with gold, that you have in your hand".
"Eigi veit eg", sagði Bolli, "hvort eg nenni það til að láta.	"Not know I", said Bolli, "whether I care that to have allow.	"I do not know", said Bolli, "whether I care to allow that.
Hefi eg annað nokkuð heldur fyrir því ætlað.	Have I another something rather for therefore intended.	I have some other intentions with it.
Máttu það og varla tala að beiðast vopns úr hendi mér.	May that also barely speak to ask weapons from-out-of hand mine.	You could hardly speak to ask for a weapon from my hand.
Tak heldur annað fé svo mikið að þú þykist vel haldinn af".	Take rather another fee so much that you think well holds of".	Take instead as much money as you consider that you are well off".
"Fjarri fer það", svarar Helgi, "er það og best að þér svarið slíku fyrir sem þér hafið til gert".	"Far-away goes that", answered Helgi, "is it also best that you answer such for as you have to done".	"Far be it from me", answered Helgi, "it is best that you answer for what you have done".
Síðan hóf Helgi upp stefnu og stefndi Bolla um þjófnað og lét varða skóggang.	Then began Helgi upped summons and charged Bolli with theft and had warranted outlawry.	Then Helgi started a lawsuit and sued Bolli for theft and had a warranted outlawry.

The Tale of Bolli Bollason (Old Icelandic)

Old Icelandic	Literal	English
Bolli stóð og heyrði til og brosti við lítinn þann.	Bolli stood and heard to and laughed against a-little then.	Bolli stood and listened and laughed a little.
En er Helgi hafði lokið stefnunni mælti hann:	Then when Helgi had finished the-summons spoke he.	But when Helgi had finished the summons, he said:
"Nær fórstu heiman?"	"When travelled-you from-home?"	"When did you leave home?".
Bolli sagði honum.	Bolli told him.	Bolli told him.
Þá mælti bóndi:	Then spoke the-farmer.	Then the farmer said:
"Þá tel eg þig hafa á öðrum alist meir en hálfan mánuð".	"Then say I you have of others homes more than half a-month".	"Then I think you have been living off others for more than half a month".
Helgi hefur þá upp aðra stefnu og stefnir Bolla um verðgang.	Helgi had then upped another summons and charged Bolli with vagrancy.	Helgi had then brought up another summons and charged Bolli with vagrancy.
Og er því var lokið þá mælti Bolli:	And when that was finished then spoke Bolli.	And when it was over, Bolli said:
"Þú hefir mikið við Helgi og mun betur fallið að leika nokkuð í móti við þig".	"You have much with Helgi and should better make that sport somewhat in meeting with you".	"You are making a lot of it, Helgi, and it would be better to play something against you".
Þá hefur Bolli upp stefnu og stefndi Helga um illmæli við sig og annarri stefnu um brekráð til fjár síns.	Then had Bolli upped summons and charged Helgi about slander with him and another summons about treachery to wealth his.	Then Bolli instituted a summons, and sued Helgi for a slander against him, and another summons for accusations of treachery to his property.
Þeir mæltu förunautar hans að drepa skyldi skelmi þann.	There spoke companions his that kill should devilish-man then.	They, his companions, said that the scoundrel should be killed.
Bolli kvað það eigi skyldu.	Bolli said that not should.	Bolli said it was not his duty.
Bolli lét varða skóggang.	Bolli had warranted outlawry.	Bolli had warranted outlawry.
Hann mælti eftir stefnuna:	He spoke after the-summons.	He said after the summons:

The Tale of Bolli Bollason (Old Icelandic)

Old Icelandic	Literal	English
"Þér skuluð færa heim húsfreyju Helga hníf og belti er eg sendi henni því að mér er sagt að hún hafi gott eina lagt til vorra haga".	"You should bring home housewife Helgi knife and belt that I send her because to me is said that she had benefit one had to ours fairly".	"You should bring home this knife and belt for your housewife that I send her, because I am told that she spoke up fairly for us".
Bolli ríður nú í brott en Helgi er þar eftir.	Bolli rode now to away then Helgi was there afterwards.	Bolli now rode away, and Helgi was left behind.
Þeir Bolli koma til Þorsteins á Háls og fá þar góðar viðtökur.	They Bolli came to Thorstein's at Hals and got there good with-taken.	Bolli and his men came to Thorstein at Hals and were well received there.
Er þar búin veisla fríð.	As there prepared feast peaceful.	There was a beautiful feast there.

7

Nú er að segja frá Helga að hann kemur heim á Skeið og segir húsfreyju sinni hvað þeir Bolli höfðu við ást.	Now is it to-say from Helgi that he came home at Skeid and told housewife his what they Bolli had with to.	Now it is said of Helgi that he came home to Skeid and told his housewife what Bolli and they had done.
"Þykist eg eigi vita", segir hann, "hvað mér verður til ráðs að eiga við slíkan mann sem Bolli er en eg er málamaður engi.	"Think I not know", said he, "what to-me becomes to advice that have with such men as Bolli is nor I am man-of-law none.	"I do not think I know", he said, "what I can do with such a man as Bolli is, nor am I a lawyer.
Á eg og ekki marga þá er mér muni að málum veita".	As I also not many then that me would to the-matter grant".	I also do not have many who will help me".
Sigríður húsfreyja svarar:	Sigrid housewife answered.	Sigrid the housewife answered:
"Þú ert orðinn mannfóli mikill, hefir átt við hina göfgustu menn og gert þig að undri.	"You have become an-idiot much, have had with these noblest men and made you a fool-of-yourself.	"You have been very foolish, you have dealt with these noblest men, and you have made a fool of yourself.
Mun þér og fara sem maklegt er að þú munt hér fyrir upp gefa allt fé þitt og sjálfan þig".	Should you also go as deserve then that you should here because-of up give all wealth yours and yourself you".	It will be as you deserve, that you shall lose your wealth and your life".

The Tale of Bolli Bollason (Old Icelandic)

Old Icelandic	Literal	English
Helgi heyrði á orð hennar og þóttu ill vera en grunaði þó að satt mundi vera því að honum var svo farið að hann var vesalmenni og þó skapillur og heimskur.	Helgi heard the words hers and thought ill were but suspected though that true would be because that he was so fared that cowardly was wretch and though bad-temper and foolishness.	Helgi heard her words, and thought they were evil, but still suspected that it would be true, for he had done so, that he was a poor man, and yet temperamental and foolish.
Sá hann sig engi færi hafa til leiðréttu en mælt sig í ófæru.	Saw he such no way-out had to rectify what talked himself into impassable.	He saw that he had no opportunity to correct himself, the impasse he had talked himself into.
Barst hann heldur illa af fyrir þetta allt jafnsaman.	Overcome he rather ill of for this all together.	He was overcome badly for all of it all at once.
Sigríður lét taka sér hest og reið að finna Þorstein frænda sinn Narfason og voru þeir Bolli þá komnir.	Sigrid had taken her horse and rode to find Thorstein kinsman hers Narfason and were they Bolli then come.	Sigrid had a horse taken, and rode to find Thorstein, her kinsman, Narfason, and Bolli and his men had arrived.
Hún heimti Þorstein á mál og sagði honum í hvert efni komið var.	She asked-for Thorstein to speak-to and told him about how the-matter come was.	She called Thorstein to speak to and told him what had happened.
"Þó hefir slíkt illa til tekist", svarar Þorsteinn.	"Though has such ill to taken", answered Thorstein.	This has turned out very badly", answered Thorstein.
Hún sagði og hversu vel Bolli hafði boðið eða hversu heimsklega Helga fór.	She told also how well Bolli had offered an how-so foolishly Helgi did.	She also said how well Bolli had offered and how stupid Helgi was.
Bað hún Þorstein eiga í allan hlut að þetta mál greiddist.	Asked she Thorstein to-have it all lot that this matter resolved.	She asked Thorstein to have everything to do with this matter being settled.
Eftir það fór hún heim en Þorsteinn kom að máli við Bolla.	After that went she home and Thorstein came to speak with Bolli.	After that she went home, then Thorstein spoke to Bolli:
"Hvað er um vinur", segir hann, "hvort hefir Helgi af Skeiði sýnt fólsku mikla við þig? Vil eg biðja að þér leggið niður fyrir mín orð og virðið það engis því að ómæt eru þar afglapa orð".	"What is about friend", said he, "how has Helgi of Skeid shown falsehood much with you?" Wish I offer that you lay down for my words and honour that none therefore that un-good are there foolish words".	"What is the matter, friend?" he said, "has Helgi of Skeid shown great falsehood to you? I want to ask you to lay down those words and do not honour them, because they are foolish words there".
Bolli svarar:	Bolli answered.	Bolli answers:

The Tale of Bolli Bollason (Old Icelandic)

Old Icelandic	Literal	English
"Það er víst að þetta er engis vert.	"That is certainly that this is none worthy.	"It is certain that this is of no value.
Mun eg mér og ekki um þetta gefa".	Should I to-me also not about this give".	I will not worry about this".
"Þá vil eg", sagði Þorsteinn, "að þér gefið honum upp þetta fyrir mína skyld og hafið þar fyrir mína vináttu".	"Then wish I", said Thorstein, "that you give him up this for my guilt and have there for my friendship".	"Then I wish", said Thorstein, "that you give him this for my sake, and have it there for my friendship".
"Ekki mun þetta til neins voða horfa", sagði Bolli.	"Not would this to any risk turn", said Bolli.	"This will not look to any risk", said Bolli,
"Lét eg mér fátt um finnast og bíður það vordaga".	"Let I me few about encounter and wait to spring-days".	"I did not care much for it, and it will wait for spring days".
Þorsteinn mælti:	Thorstein spoke.	Thorstein said:
"Það mun eg sýna að mér þykir máli skipta að þetta gangi eftir mínum vilja.	"That would I show that to-me thought the-matter exchange that this going after my will.	"I will show that it is important to me that this goes according to my will.
Eg vil gefa þér hest þann er bestur er hér í sveitum og eru tólf saman hrossin".	I will give you horse then the best is here in the-district and there twelve together herd".	I want to give you the horse that is the best here in the countryside, and there are twelve horses together".
Bolli svarar:	Bolli answered.	Bolli answers:
"Slíkt er allvel boðið en eigi þarftu að leggja hér svo mikla stund á.	"Such is all-well offered but not need-you to have here so much while to.	"Such a thing is very well offered, but you do not have to spend so much time here.
Eg gaf mér lítið um slíkt.	I gave me little about such.	I gave myself little of that.
Mun og lítið af verða þá er í dóm kemur".	Should also little of be then that in self-judgement come".	There will be little of it when it comes to judgment".
"Það er sannast", sagði Þorsteinn, "að eg vil selja þér sjálfdæmi fyrir málið".	"That is the-truest", said Thorstein, "that I wish repay you self-judgement for the-matter".	"It is true", said Thorstein, "that I wish to grant you self-judgement in this matter".
Bolli svarar:	Bolli answered.	Bolli answered:

The Tale of Bolli Bollason (Old Icelandic)

Old Icelandic	Literal	English
"Það ætla eg sannast að ekki þurfi um að leitast því að eg vil ekki sættast á þetta mál".	"That expect I truly that no need about to seek because that I wish not reconcile to this case".	"I think it is true that there is no need to seek it, because I do not want to accept a settlement in this matter".
"Þá kýstu það er öllum oss gegnir verst", sagði Þorsteinn,	"Then choosing that which all us serves the-worst", said Thorstein,	"Then you are choosing what is worst for all of us" said Thorstein.
"þótt Helgi sé lítils verður þá er hann þó í venslum bundinn við oss.	"though Helgi is little worth then is he though in marriage bound with us.	"Although Helgi is of little value, he is still bound to us.
Þá munum vér hann eigi upp gefa undir vopn yður síðan þú vilt engis mín orð virða.	Then should we him not up give into weapons yours after you wish none my words value.	Then we will not give him up under your weapons, since you do not want to honour my words.
En að þeim atkvæðum að Helgi hafði í stefnu við þig líst mér það engi sæmdarauki þó að það sé á þing borið".	But that them charges that Helgi has in summoned with you appears to-me that none honour though that it is at the-assembly carried".	But with the charges that Helgi had in summons with you, I do not think it is an honour, even though it has been presented to the assembly".
Skildu þeir Þorsteinn og Bolli heldur fálega.	Separated they Thorstein and Bolli rather poorly.	Thorstein and Bolli parted rather poorly.
Ríður hann í brott og hans félagar og er ekki getið að hann sé með gjöfum í brott leystur.	Rode he to away and his comrades and was not got that he being with gifts in away releasing.	He and his companions rode away, and it is not mentioned that he was released with gifts.

8

Bolli og hans förunautar komu á Möðruvöllu til Guðmundar hins ríka.	Bolli and his companions came to Modruvellir to Gudmund the Powerful.	Bolli and his companions came to Modruvellir to Gudmund the Powerful.
Hann gengur í móti þeim með allri blíðu og var hinn glaðasti.	He came to meet them with all joyfulness and was the gladdest.	He came to meet them with all joyfulness and was the gladdest.
Þar sátu þeir hálfan mánuð í góðum fagnaði.	There stayed they half a-month in good celebration.	They stayed there half a-month in good celebration.
Þá mælti Guðmundur til Bolla:	Then spoke Gudmund to Bolli.	Then Gudmund said to Bolli:

The Tale of Bolli Bollason (Old Icelandic)

Old Icelandic	Literal	English
"Hvað er til haft um það, hefir sundurþykki orðið með yður Þorsteini?"	"What is to have about that, have discord words with your Thorstein?"	"What is that matter, has there been discord with you and Thorstein?"
Bolli kvað lítið til haft um það og tók annað mál.	Bolli spoke little to have about that and took another matter.	Bolli said he had little to say about it and took another matter.
Guðmundur mælti:	Gudmund spoke.	Gudmund said:
"Hverja leið ætlar þú aftur að ríða?"	"What way intend you return to ride?"	"Which way are you going to ride back?"
"Hina sömu", svarar Bolli.	"The same", answered Bolli.	"The same", answered Bolli.
Guðmundur mælti:	Gudmund spoke.	Gudmund said:
"Letja vil eg yður þess því að mér er svo sagt að þið Þorsteinn hafið skilið fálega.	"Discourage wish I you this because that to-me is so said that you Thorstein have separated coldly.	"I wish to discourage you, for I am told that Thorstein has separated with you poorly.
Ver heldur hér með mér og ríð suður í vor og látum þá þessi mál ganga til vegar".	Be rather here with me and ride south in spring and let then this matter go its way".	Stay here with me and ride south in the spring, and then let these matters go".
Bolli lést eigi mundu bregða ferðinni fyrir hót þeirra "en það hugði eg þá er Helgi fólið lét sem heimsklegast og mælti hvert óorðan að öðru við oss og vildi hafa spjótið konungsnaut úr hendi mér fyrir einn heyvöndul að eg skyldi freista að hann fengi ömbun orða sinna.	Bolli said not would break travel for threat theirs "but that think I then that Helgi foolishly had as foolishly and speaking each slanderous to another with us and willing to-have spear king's-gift out-of hand mine for only a-haystack that I should test that he gets return words his.	Bolli said that he would not break from his travel plans because of their threat, "but I think that Helgi was stupid, and spoke foolishly with one slanderous charge after another to us, and wanting to take the spear King's Gift out of my hand for only a haystack, I should see to it that he gets what he deserves for his words.
Hefi eg og annað ætlað fyrir spjótinu að eg mundi heldur gefa þér og þar með gullhringinn þann er stólkonungurinn gaf mér.	Have I also other plans for spear that I should rather give to-you and there with gold-ring then that the-emperor gave me.	I also have other plans for my spear, as I intend to give it to you, along with the gold arm ring that the emperor gave me.
Hygg eg nú að gripirnir séu betur niður komnir en þá að Helgi hefði þá".	Think I now that treasures are better kinsman coming than then that Helgi has then".	I think now, that the treasures are better coming to a kinsman than Helgi having them".

The Tale of Bolli Bollason (Old Icelandic)

Old Icelandic	Literal	English
Guðmundur þakkaði honum gjafir þessar og mælti:	Gudmund thanked him the-gift these and spoke.	Gudmund thanked him for these gifts, and said,
"Hér munu smærri gjafir í móti koma en verðugt er".	"Here shall smaller gifts in return coming than worth are".	"Here smaller gifts will come in return than are worthy".
Guðmundur gaf Bolla skjöld gulllagðan og gullhring og skikkju.	Gudmund gave Bolli shield gold-laid and gold-ring and cloak.	Gudmund gave Bolli a gold-plated shield and a gold ring and a cloak.
Var í henni hið dýrsta klæði og búin öll þar er bæta þótti.	Were about her the dearest clothing and prepared all there was better thought.	And about it was prepared all the most precious material that made it better.
Allir voru gripirnir mjög ágætir.	All were treasures much renowned.	All the treasures were very good.
Þá mælti Guðmundur:	Then spoke Gudmund.	Then Gudmund said:
"Illa þykir mér þú gera Bolli er þú vilt ríða um Svarfaðardal".	"Bad think I you doing Bolli that you wish to-ride about Svarfadardal".	"I think you do badly, Bolli, when you want to ride through Svarfadardal".
Bolli segir það ekki skaða munu.	Bolli said that not scathed would-be.	Bolli said that he would not be scathed.
Riðu þeir í brott og skilja þeir Guðmundur við hinum mestum kærleikum.	Rode they to away and separated they Gudmund with the most friendship.	They rode away, and Gudmund parted with the greatest friendship.
Þeir Bolli ríða nú veg sinn út um Galmarströnd.	Then Bolli rode now way his out about Galmarstrond.	Then Bolli and his men rode their way out over Galmarstrond.
Um kveldið komu þeir á þann bæ er að Krossum heitir.	About evening came they to the farm which that Krossar named.	In the evening they came to a town called Krossar.
Þar bjó sá maður er Óttar hét.	There lived so a-man who Ottar named.	There lived a man named Ottar.
Hann stóð úti.	He stood outside.	He stood outside.
Hann var sköllóttur og í skinnstakki.	He was bald and in skin-cloak.	He was bald, and wearing a fur coat.
Óttar kvaddi þá vel og bauð þeim þar að vera.	Ottar greeted then well and invited them there to be.	Ottar greeted them well and invited them to stay there.
Það þiggja þeir.	That accepted they.	They accepted.

The Tale of Bolli Bollason (Old Icelandic)

Old Icelandic	Literal	English
Var þar góður beini og bóndi hinn kátasti.	Were there good benefit and farmer the merriest.	There was a good benefit and the farmer was merry.
Voru þeir þar um nóttina.	Were they there about the-night.	They were there that night.
Um morguninn er þeir Bolli voru ferðar búnir þá mælti Óttar:	About morning when they Bolli were travel preparing then spoke Ottar.	In the morning, when Bolli and his men were ready to go, Ottar said:
"Vel hefir þú gert Bolli er þú hefir sótt heim bæ minn.	"Well have you done Bolli that you have sought home farm mine.	"You have done well, Bolli, when you have visited my farm.
Vil eg og sýna þér lítið tillæti, gefa þér gullhring og kunna þökk að þú þiggir.	Wish I also show you little deference, give you gold-ring and know thanks that you accept.	I also want to show you a little favour, and give you a gold ring and I would be thankful if you accept.
Hér er og fingurgull er fylgja skal".	Here is also gold-ring that follow shall".	Here is also a gold ring to go with it".
Bolli þiggur gjafirnar og þakkar bónda.	Bolli accepted the-gifts and thanks the-farmer.	Bolli accepted the gifts and thanked the farmer.
Óttar var á hesti sínum því næst og reið fyrir þeim leiðina því að fallið hafði snjór lítill um nóttina.	Ottar was about horse his as nearest and rode ahead them the-way because that fallen had snow little about the-night.	Ottar was then on his horse, and rode in front of them, for little snow had fallen that night.
Þeir ríða nú veg sinn út til Svarfaðardals.	They rode now way theirs out to Svarfadardal.	They now rode their way out to Svarfadardal,
Og er þeir hafa eigi lengi riðið snerist hann við Óttar og mælti til Bolla:	And when they had not long ridden turned he with Ottar and spoke to Bolli.	and when they had not ridden long, Ottar turned to Bolli and said:
"Það mun eg sýna að eg vildi að þú værir vin minn.	"That should I show that I wish that you be friend mine.	"I will show that I wish you to be my friend.
Er hér annar gullhringur er eg vil þér gefa.	Is here another gold-ring that I wish to-you to-give.	Here's another gold ring I want to give you.
Væri eg yður vel viljaður í því er eg mætti.	Be I your well-willing willing for accordingly as I might.	I wish to help you in any way that I might.
Munuð þér og þess þurfa".	Shall you also this need".	If you shall need it".

The Tale of Bolli Bollason (Old Icelandic)

Old Icelandic	Literal	English
Bolli kvað bónda fara stórmannlega til sín "en þó vil eg þiggja hringinn".	Bolli thanked the-farmer going great-man-ness to him "but though wish I to-accept the-ring".	Bolli thanked the farmer for being so generous, "but still I want to accept the ring".
"Þá gerir þú vel", segir bóndi.	"Then doing you well", said the-farmer.	"Then you do well", said the farmer.

9

Nú er að segja frá Þorsteini af Hálsi.	Now is to say from Thorstein of Hals.	Now the story turns to Thorstein of Hals.
Þegar honum þykir von að Bolli muni norðan ríða þá safnar hann mönnum og ætlar að sitja fyrir Bolla og vill nú að verði umskipti um mál þeirra Helga.	When he thought expected that Bolli would north ride then collected he men and intended to sit-in-ambush before Bolli and wishing now to become about-exchanged about the-matter theirs Helgi.	When he expected Bolli to ride north, he gathered men and intended to sit in ambush before Bolli, and now wished to alter the matter between him and Helgi.
Þeir Þorsteinn hafa þrjá tigi manna og ríða fram til Svarfaðardalsár og setjast þar.	They Thorstein had three ten men and rode from to Svarfadardal and stayed there.	Thorstein and his men had thirty men, and rode up to Svarfadardal, and settled there.
Ljótur hét maður er bjó á Völlum í Svarfaðardal.	Ljot was-named a-man who lived at Vellir in Svarfadardal.	There was a man named Ljot, who lived at Vellir in Svarfadardal.
Hann var höfðingi mikill og vinsæll og málamaður mikill.	He was chieftain great and popular and law-man great.	He was a great chieftain, popular, and a great man of law.
Það var búningur hans hversdaglega að hann hafði svartan kyrtil og refði í hendi en ef hann bjóst til víga þá hafði hann blán kyrtil og öxi snaghyrnda.	It was costume his everyday that he had a-black tunic and poleaxe in hand but if he prepared to fight then had he a-blue tunic and axe snag-cornered.	It was his everyday costume that he had a black tunic and a poleaxe in his hand, but if he was preparing for battle, he had a blue tunic and a sharp-edged axe.
Var hann þá heldur ófrýnlegur.	Was he then rather inconspicuous.	He was then rather inconspicuous.
Þeir Bolli ríða út eftir Svarfaðardal.	They Bolli rode out along Svarfadardal.	Bolli and his men rode out along Svarfadardal.
Fylgir Óttar þeim út um bæinn að Hálsi og að ánni út.	Followed Ottar them out about the-farm at Hals and to-the-river from.	Ottar followed them out of the town at Hals and out to the river.

The Tale of Bolli Bollason (Old Icelandic)

Old Icelandic	Literal	English
Þar sat fyrir þeim Þorsteinn við sína menn og þegar er Óttar sér fyrirsátina bregður hann við og keyrir hest sinn þvers í brott.	There sat before them Thorstein with his men and when that Ottar saw for-the-ambush broke he with and spurred horse his across to away.	There Thorstein sat before them with his men, and when Ottar saw the ambush, he responded and drove his horse across.
Þeir Bolli ríða að djarflega og er þeir Þorsteinn sjá það og hans menn spretta þeir upp.	They Bolli rode to boldly and when they Thorstein saw that and his men sprang they up.	Bolli and his men rode boldly, and when Thorstein and his men saw it, they sprang up.
Þeir voru sínum megin ár hvorir en áin var leyst með löndum en ís flaut á miðri.	There were they sides the-river opposite about the-river was down with land was ice floating in the-middle.	They were on either side of the river, but the river flowed with land, and ice floated in the middle.
Hleypa þeir Þorsteinn út á ísinn.	Ran they Thorstein out into the-ice.	Thorstein and his men ran out onto the ice.
Helgi af Skeiði var og þar og eggjar þá fast og kvað nú vel að þeir Bolli reyndu hvort honum væri kapp sitt og metnaður einhlítt eða hvort nokkurir menn norður þar mundu þora að halda til móts við hann.	Helgi of Skeid was also there and encouraged then closely and said now well that they Bolli test whether he was eager his and pride unanimously or whether some men north there would dare to hold to meet with him.	Helgi of Skeid was also there and encouraged them, and said that Bolli and his men would be tested as to whether he was eagerness and pride would be unanimous, or whether there were men of the north who would dare to meet him.
"Þarf nú og eigi að spara að drepa þá alla.	"Need now and not that spare to kill then all.	"We do not need to spare from killing them all.
Mun það og leiða öðrum", sagði Helgi, "að veita oss ágang".	Would it also loath others", said Helgi, "that giving us aggression".	As it would also deter others", said Helgi, "from attacking us".
Bolli heyrir orð Helga og sér hvar hann er kominn út á ísinn.	Bolli heard words Helgi's and saw where he had come out on the-ice.	Bolli heard Helgi's words and saw where he had come out on the ice.
Bolli skýtur að honum spjóti og kemur á hann miðjan.	Bolli shot at him spear and came it his middle.	Bolli shot at him with a spear, and struck him in the middle.
Fellur hann á bak aftur í ána en spjótið flýgur í bakkann öðrum megum svo að fast var og hékk Helgi þar á niður í ána.	Fell he on back back in river but the-spear followed the bank other may so that fastened was and hung Helgi there at down in the-river.	He fell backwards into the river, but the spear flew into the bank the other way, so that it was stuck, and Helgi hung down there in the river.

The Tale of Bolli Bollason (Old Icelandic)

Old Icelandic	Literal	English
Eftir það tókst þar bardagi hinn skarpasti.	After that took there battle the hardest.	After that, the battle became the hardest.
Bolli gengur að svo fast að þeir hrökkva undan er nær voru.	Bolli went to so fast that they recoiled away-from who near were.	Bolli went so fast that those who were near him recoiled.
Þá sótti fram Þorsteinn í móti Bolla og þegar þeir fundust höggur Bolli til Þorsteins á öxlina og varð það mikið sár.	Then sought from Thorstein to meet Bolli and then they found striking Bolli to Thorstein's with an-axe and became that much wounding.	Then Thorstein went out to meet Bolli, and when they met, Bolli struck Thorstein on the shoulder, and it was a great wound.
Annað sár fékk Þorsteinn á fæti.	Another wound got Thorstein about the-leg.	Thorstein received another wound on his leg.
Sóknin var hin harðasta.	The-struggle was the hardest.	The attack was the hardest.
Bolli varð og sár nokkuð og þó ekki mjög.	Bolli became also wounded somewhat and though not much.	Bolli was also slightly injured, but not very badly.
Nú er að segja frá Óttari.	Now is to say from Ottar.	Now the story turns to Ottar.
Hann ríður upp á Völlu til Ljóts og þegar þeir finnast mælti Óttar:	He rode up to Vellir to Ljot and then they met spoke Ottar.	He rode up to Vellir, to Ljot, and when they met Ottar spoke:
"Eigi er nú setuefni Ljótur", sagði hann, "og fylg þú nú virðing þinni er þér liggur laus fyrir".	"Not is now sitting Ljot", said he, "and follows you now honour yours that you lay less for".	"No cause to sit about, Ljot", he said, "what follows now is your honour to prove".
"Hvað er nú helst í því Óttar?"	"What is now rather that according Ottar?"	"What would that involve, Ottar?"
"Eg hygg að þeir berjist hér niðri við ána Þorsteinn af Hálsi og Bolli og er það hin mesta hamingja að skirra vandræðum þeirra".	"I think that they fight here down by the-river Thorstein of Hals and Bolli and is that the most fortunate that prevent trouble theirs".	"I expect that they will be fighting here down by the river, Thorstein of Hals and Bolli, and it would be most fortunate to prevent their hostilities".
Ljótur mælti:	Ljot spoke.	Ljot spoke:
"Oft sýnir þú af þér mikinn drengskap".	"Often showed you of your great honour".	"You have often showed great honour".

The Tale of Bolli Bollason (Old Icelandic)

Old Icelandic	Literal	English
Ljótur brá við skjótt og við nokkura menn og þeir Óttar báðir.	Ljot startled with quickly and with several men and they Ottar both.	He reacted quickly and with several others hurried back to Ottar.
Og er þeir koma til árinnar berjast þeir Bolli sem óðast.	And when they came to the river fought they Bolli as furious.	And when they came to the river, Bolli and the others were fighting furiously.
Voru þá fallnir þrír menn af Þorsteini.	Were they fallen three men of Thorstein's.	There were three of Thorstein's men that had fallen.
Þeir Ljótur ganga fram í meðal þeirra snarlega svo að þeir máttu nær ekki að hafast.	Then Ljot went from to between them quickly so that they may close not to have.	Ljot and his men quickly ran between the fighters so that they could not get close.
Þá mælti Ljótur:	Then spoke Ljot.	Then Ljot spoke:
"Þér skuluð skilja þegar í stað", segir hann, "og er þó nú ærið að orðið.	"You should separate immediately this place", said he, "and is though now plenty-of has become.	"You should separate immediately from this place", he said, "and now more than enough has been done.
Vil eg einn gera milli yðvar um þessi mál en ef því níta aðrir hvorir þá skulum vér veita þeim atgöngu".	Wish I alone to-do between you about this matter that if therefore refuse others each then should we grant them to-going".	I alone wish to decide to settle this matter, and if either of you refuses, then they shall be granted an attack".
En með því að Ljótur gekk að svo fast þá hættu þeir að berjast og því játtu hvorirtveggju að Ljótur skyldi gera um þetta þeirra í milli.	Then with because that Ljot went that so close then stop they the fight and therefore agreed either-side that Ljot should do about that their in between.	Then because Ljot went so close, they stopped fighting, and either side agreed, that Ljot should handle the matter between them.
Skildust þeir við svo búið.	Separated they with so prepared.	They parted ways so prepared.
Fór Þorsteinn heim en Ljótur býður þeim Bolla heim með sér og það þiggur hann.	Went Thorstein home and Ljot invited them Bolli home with him and that accepted he.	Thorstein went home, but Ljot invited Bolli and his men home with him, and he accepted.
Fóru þeir Bolli á Völlu til Ljóts.	Went they Bolli to Vellir to Ljot's.	Bolli and his men went to Vellir to Ljot's.
Þar heitir í Hestanesi sem þeir höfðu barist.	There named is Hestanes which they had bears.	There is named Hestanes, which bears today.

The Tale of Bolli Bollason (Old Icelandic)

Old Icelandic	Literal	English
Óttar bóndi skildist eigi fyrri við þá Bolla en þeir komu heim með Ljóti.	Ottar the-farmer separated not before with then Bolli then they came home with Ljot.	Farmer Ottar did not part with Bolli until they came home with Ljot.
Gaf Bolli honum stórmannlegar gjafar að skilnaði og þakkaði honum vel sitt liðsinni.	Gave Bolli him great-man-like gifts as parted and thanked him well this assistance.	Bolli gave him great gifts at parting, and thanked him well for his help.
Hét Bolli Óttari sinni vináttu.	Pledged Bolli Ottar his friendship.	Bolli pledged Ottar his friendship.
Fór hann heim til Krossa og sat í búi sínu.	Travelled he home to Krossar and stayed in farm his.	He went home to Krossar and stayed at his farm.

10

Old Icelandic	Literal	English
Eftir bardagann í Hestanesi fór Bolli heim með Ljóti á Völlu við alla sína menn en Ljótur bindur sár þeirra og greru þau skjótt því að gaumur var að gefinn.	After the-battle at Hestanes travelled Bolli home with Ljot to Vellir with all his men then Ljot bound wounds theirs and healed they quickly because that attention were for given.	After the battle in Hestanes, Bolli went home with Ljot at Vellir with all his men, where Ljot bound up their wounds, and they healed quickly, for the attention was paid to them.
En er þeir voru heilir sára sinna þá stefndi Ljótur þing fjölmennt.	Then when they were safe wounds theirs then summoned Ljot assembly full-of-people.	Then when they were healed of their wounds, Ljot convened a great assembly.
Riðu þeir Bolli á þingið.	Rode they Bolli to the-assembly.	Bolli and his men rode to the assembly.
Þar kom og Þorsteinn af Hálsi við sína menn.	There came also Thorstein of Hals with his men.	Thorstein of Hals also came there with his men.
Og er þingið var sett mælti Ljótur:	And when the-assembly was set spoke Ljot.	And when the Thing was set, Ljot said,
"Nú skal ekki fresta uppsögn um gerð þá er eg hefi samið milli þeirra Þorsteins af Hálsi og Bolla.	"Now shall not postpone up-saying about made then but I have agreement between they Thorstein's of Hals and Bolli.	"Now the conclusion of the agreement which I have brought up between Thorstein of Hals and Bolli shall not be postponed.
Hefi eg það upphaf að gerðinni að Helgi skal hafa fallið óheilagur fyrir illyrði sín og tiltekju við Bolla.	Have I that begun to make that Helgi shall have failed unholy for ill-words his and exchange with Bolli.	I have the beginning of the deed, that Helgi has fallen without right for compensation for his wickedness and betrayal of Bolli.

The Tale of Bolli Bollason (Old Icelandic)

Old Icelandic	Literal	English
Sárum þeirra Þorsteins og Bolla jafna eg saman.	The-wounds they Thorstein's and Bolli equal I the-same.	I will make amends for the wounds of Thorstein and Bolli,
En þá þrjá menn er féllu af Þorsteini skal Bolli bæta.	But they three men who fell of Thorstein shall Bolli compensate.	but the three men who fell from Thorstein shall be compensated by Bolli.
En fyrir fjörráð við Bolla og fyrirsát skal Þorsteinn greiða honum fimmtán hundruð þriggja alna aura.	But for plotting-against with Bolli and ambush shall Thorstein assist him fifteen hundred three ells pay.	But for the conspiracy and plotting-against Bolli, Thorstein shall pay him fifteen hundred three cubit lengths of homespun cloth.
Skulu þeir að þessu alsáttir".	Shall they at this all-settle".	They shall all settle at this".
Eftir þetta var slitið þinginu.	After it was dissolved the-assembly.	After that the assembly was dissolved.
Segir Bolli Ljóti að hann mun ríða heimleiðis og þakkar honum vel alla sína liðveislu og skiptust þeir fögrum gjöfum við og skildu við góðum vinskap.	Told Bolli Ljot that he would ride home-ways and thanked him well all his assistance and exchanged they fair gifts with and separated with good friendship.	Bolli told Ljot that he would ride home, and thanked him well for all his help, and they exchanged beautiful gifts and parted with good friendship.
Bolli tók upp bú Sigríðar á Skeiði því að hún vildi fara vestur með honum.	Bolli took up the-farm Sigrid of Skeid because that she wished to-travel west with him.	Bolli took up Sigrid's estate at Skeid, because she wanted to go west with him.
Ríða þau veg sinn þar til er þau koma á Miklabæ til Arnórs.	Rode they way theirs there until that they came to Miklabaer to Arnor's.	They rode their way, until they came to Miklabær to Arnor.
Tók hann harðla vel við þeim.	Took he greatly well with them.	He received them very kindly,
Dvöldust þar um hríð og sagði Bolli Arnóri allt um skipti þeirra Svarfdæla hversu farið hafði.	Dwelled there about awhile and told Bolli Arnor all about exchanged theirs Svarfadardal how-so gone had.	they stayed there for a while, and Bolli told Arnor all about the exchange of the Svarfadardal, and how things had gone.
Arnór mælti:	Arnor spoke.	Arnor said:
"Mikla heill hefir þú til borið um ferð þessa við slíkan mann sem þú áttir þar er Þorsteinn var.	"Much luck have you to bear about journey this with such a-man as you have there as Thorstein was.	"You have been very lucky in this journey, and in your dealings with such a man as Thorstein.

The Tale of Bolli Bollason (Old Icelandic)

Old Icelandic	Literal	English
Er það sannast um að tala að fáir eða öngvir höfðingjar munu sótt hafa meira frama úr öðrum héruðum norður hingað en þú, þeir sem jafnmarga öfundarmenn áttu hér fyrir".	Is it true about that said that few or none chieftains should attend have more honour of other provinces north here than you, they who equal-many slanderous-men had here for".	Is it true to say that few or no chiefs will have sought more fame from other provinces north here than you, those who had so many envious people here before".
Bolli ríður nú í brott af Miklabæ við sína menn og heim suður.	Bolli rode now to away from Miklabaer with his men and home south.	Bolli now rode away from Miklabær with his men and home south.
Tala þeir Arnór til vináttu með sér af nýju að skilnaði.	Spoke they Arnor to friendship with them of anew at parting.	Bolli and Arnor spoke of friendship anew before parting.
En er Bolli kom heim í Tungu varð Þórdís húsfreyja hans honum fegin.	Then when Bolli came home to Tunga was Thordis housewife his to-him relieved.	But when Bolli came home to Tunga, Thordis, his housewife, was glad to see him.
Hafði hún frétt áður nokkuð af róstum þeirra Norðlendinga og þótti mikið í hættu að honum tækist vel til.	Had she news before some of unruliness theirs The-northerners and thought much at danger that he took well to.	She had heard something before about the skirmishes of the Northerners, and thought it was very dangerous for him to succeed.
Situr Bolli nú í búi sínu með mikilli virðingu.	Stayed Bolli now at farm his with much honour.	Bolli now stayed in his estate with great honour.
Þessi ferð Bolla var ger að nýjum sögum um allar sveitir og töluðu allir einn veg um að slík þótti varla farin hafa verið nálega.	This journey Bolli's was made to new sagas about all areas and told all one way about that such thought barely gone had been near-to.	This journey of Bolli was the subject of new stories about all the districts, and everyone agreed that such a thing was scarcely thought to have been equalled.
Óx virðing hans af slíku og mörgu öðru.	Grew respect his of such and many others.	His respect from this and many other things grew.
Bolli fékk Sigríði gjaforð göfugt og lauk vel við hana.	Bolli found Sigrid married worthy and concluded well with her.	Bolli gave Sigrid a noble marriage match and it concluded well,
Og höfum vér eigi heyrt þessa sögu lengri.	And have we none heard this saga longer.	and we have not heard any more of this story.

Word List (Old Icelandic to English)

Word List (Old Icelandic to English)

Old Icelandic	English

A, a

að	a, about, as, at, for, from, has, have, in, it, of, that, the, to
aðra	another
aðrir	others
af	at, from, from, of, of, off, to
afglapa	foolish
afréttum	the-pastures
aftur	back, down, return, returned
albúnir	all-prepared
aldrei	never
aldri	age
alist	homes
alla	all, all
allan	all
allar	all
allir	all, all
allra	of-all
allri	all
alls	all
allstórmannlega	all-great-man-like
allt	all, all
allvel	all-well, all-well
alna	ells
alsáttir	all-settle
alþingi	the-assembly
andvirki	haystacks
annað	another, another, other
annar	another, another
annarri	another
Arnór	Arnor (name)
Arnóri	Arnor (name)
Arnórs	Arnor's (name)
atgöngu	to-going
atkvæðum	charges
auðigur	rich
aura	pay

Á, á

Á	about, as, at, for, from, in, into, it, of, on, the, to, up, was, with
áðu	to
áður	before, earlier
ágætir	renowned
ágætlega	greatly
ágang	aggression
áin	the-river
ána	river, the-river, the-river
ánni	the-river
ár	the-river
árinnar	the-river
ásjá	assistance, assistance
ásjár	assistance
áskoran	challenge
ást	to
átján	eighteen, eighteen
átt	had
átta	eight
átti	had, married
áttir	have
áttu	had, have-you

Æ, æ

æðimaður	frenzy-man
æja	rest
ærið	plenty-of
ærin	considerable
ætla	expect, intend, intended
ætlað	intended, plans
ætlar	intend, intended
ættsmár	of-family-small

B, b

Word List (Old Icelandic to English)

Old Icelandic	English
bað	asked, ordered
báðir	both
bæ	a-farm, farm
bæinn	the-farm
bænum	farmhouse, the-farm
bæta	better, compensate
bak	back
baki	horseback
bakkann	bank
bardagann	the-battle
bardagi	battle
barist	bears
Barst	overcome
bauð	invited
beiða	offer
beiðast	ask
beiddi	asked
beini	benefit
belti	belt
ber	bear
berjast	fight, fought
berjist	fight
best	best
besta	best
bestur	best
betra	better
betri	better
betur	better
biðja	offer
bíður	wait
bindur	bound
Bjarnar	Bjarni (name)
bjó	lived
bjóða	offer, to-invite
bjóst	prepared
bjuggu	lived
blán	a-blue
blárri	black
blíðu	joyfulness
blika	shining
boðið	bid, offered
boli	the-bull
Bolla	Bolli (name), Bolli's (name)
Bollason	Bollason (name), Son-of-Bolli (name)
Bollasyni	Bollason (name)
Bolli	Bolli (name)
bónda	husband, the-farmer
bóndi	farmer, host, the-farmer
borið	bear, carried
börnum	children
brá	startled
bræðra	the-brothers
bræður	brothers
braut	broke
bregða	break
bregður	broke, drew
brekráð	treachery
bróðir	brother
bróður	brother
brosti	laughed
brotið	broken
brott	away
bú	the-farm
búa	settlers
búast	prepare
búðardyrunum	the-booth-doors
búðina	the-booth
búi	farm
búið	prepared
búin	prepared
bundinn	bound
búningur	costume
búnir	preparing
býður	invited
býr	prepared
býst	prepared

D, d

Old Icelandic	English
dauður	dead
desjarnar	the-hay
djarflega	boldly
Dögurðarnes	Dagverdarnes (place)
dóm	self-judgement
dregur	drew
drengilegsta	bravely

Word List (Old Icelandic to English)

Old Icelandic	English
drengskap	honour
drepa	kill
drepið	kill, killing
Dvöldust	dwelled
dýrsta	dearest

E, e

Old Icelandic	English
eða	an, and, or
ef	if
efni	matter, the-matter
efnilegastur	promising
eftir	after, afterwards, along
eftirmálinu	the-after-matter
eftirmáls	after-matter
eg	I
eggjar	encouraged
eiga	have, in, to-have
eigi	no, none, not
eign	own
eigna	own
eina	one
einhlítt	unanimously
einir	only
einn	alone, one, only
einnhvern	one
einsætt	one-agreement
einum	any
ekki	no, not, nothing
en	about, and, but, in, nor, since, than, that, then, was, what, whether
enga	none
engi	no, none
engis	none
engrar	no, none
engu	nothing
enn	but, the, then
er	am, and, are, as, but, had, is, it-is, that, the, then, was, were, when, which, who
erfið	difficulty
ert	have
ertu	are-you
eru	are, are-there, is, there, were
eruð	are
eyða	devastate

F, f

Old Icelandic	English
fá	fee, got
Fær	accomplished, got, travelled
færa	bring, bringing
færi	travel, way-out
fæti	the-leg
fagnað	welcomed
fagnaði	celebration
fáir	few
fálega	coldly, poorly
fallið	failed, fallen, make
fallnir	fallen
fangi	arms
fann	found
fár	few
fara	go, going, to-travel, travel
faraskjóta	horses
farið	fared, gone, travel, travelled
farin	gone
farinn	travelling
fast	close, closely, fast, fastened
fátt	few
fé	cattle, fee, wealth
fébótum	compensation
fegin	relieved
fékk	found, got
félagar	comrades
félagsskap	comradeship
felldur	falling
féllu	well
fellur	fell
fengi	gets
fer	goes, set-out, travelled, travels

Word List (Old Icelandic to English)

Old Icelandic	English
ferð	going, journey, travel, travelling
ferðar	travel
ferðina	going
ferðinni	the-journey, travel
ferðir	journey
fimmtán	fifteen
fingurgull	gold-ring
finna	find
finnast	encounter, met
finnum	find
fjandskap	fiendship
fjár	of-wealth, wealth
fjarri	far-away
fjölmenna	following-men, many-men
fjölmenni	followers-many
fjölmennt	full-of-people
fjórðungi	district
fjörráð	plotting, plotting-against
fláráðum	treacherous
flaut	floating
fleiri	more
flokk	flock
flýgur	followed
flytjir	with-fleetness
fögrum	fair
fólið	foolishly
fólsku	false, falsehood
fór	did, goes, travelled, went
fórstu	travelled-you
Fóru	travelled, went
förum	a-journey
förunautar	companions, companions
Fótbít	Leg-Biter (name)
frá	from
frægðarverk	famous-work
frænda	kinsman
frændkona	kinswoman
frændkonu	kinswoman
fram	from
frama	honour, honour
framar	honour
freista	test, try
fresta	postpone
frétt	news
frétti	asking, learned
Fréttist	reported
Fréttust	reported
fríð	peaceful
fritt	safe
fund	meet
fundur	a-meeting
fundust	found, met
fylg	follows
fylgi	follows
Fylgir	followed
fylgja	follow
fylgt	followed
fyrir	ahead, because-of, before, for
fyrirsát	ambush
fyrirsátina	for-the-ambush
fyrr	before
fyrri	before
fyrrum	before-us

G, g

Old Icelandic	English
gaf	gave
gáfu	gave
Galmarströnd	Galmarstrond (place)
ganga	go, went
gangi	going
gaumur	attention
gefa	give, to-give
gefið	give
gefinn	given
gegnir	serves
gegnum	through
gekk	went
Gengið	gone
gengu	went
gengur	came, went
ger	made
gera	do, doing, to-do
gerð	made
gerði	did, made

Word List (Old Icelandic to English)

Old Icelandic	English
gerðinni	make
gerðu	did, made
gerið	do
gerir	do, doing
gert	done, made
getið	got
getur	got
giftuvænlegur	luck-promised
gjafar	gifts
gjafir	gifts, the-gift
gjafirnar	the-gifts
gjaforð	married
gjalda	pay
gjöfum	gifts
glaðasti	gladdest
gnótt	an-abundance
góða	good
góðar	good
góðum	good
góður	good
göfgustu	noblest
göfugt	worthy
gott	benefit
graðung	bull
Graðungur	bull
graðungurinn	the-bull
grán	grey
greiða	assist
greiddist	resolved
greru	healed
griðung	a-bull
grípa	grab
gripirnir	treasures
grjóti	rocks
grunaði	suspected
grunur	suspect
Guðdala-Starra	Starri-of-Guddalir
Guðdölum	Guddalir (place)
Guðmundar	Gudmund (name)
Guðmundur	Gudmund (name)
Guðrún	Gudrun (name)
gullhring	gold-ring
gullhringinn	gold-ring
gullhringur	gold-ring
gulllagðan	gold-laid
gullrekna	gold-inlaid
gyrður	buckled

H, h

Old Icelandic	English
hæðileg	mockery
hæglegt	easily
hægt	possible
hættu	danger, stop
Haf	have
hafa	had, have, to-have
hafast	have
hafði	had, has
hafi	had
Hafið	have
hafir	have
haft	had, have
haga	fairly
halda	hold
haldinn	holds
hálfan	half
hálfs	half-month's
hallaði	turned
Háls	Hals (place)
Hálsi	Hals (place)
hamingja	fortunate, luck
hana	he, her
hann	cowardly, he, him, his
hans	him, his
harðasta	hardest
harðla	greatly
harmaði	mourned
héðan	from-here
héðra	district
hefði	has
Hefi	have
hefir	had, has, have
hefur	had
Hegranessþingi	Hegranes (place)-Assembly
Hegranessþings	Hegranes (place)-Assembly
heiðina	the-heath
heilir	safe
heill	luck

Word List (Old Icelandic to English)

Old Icelandic	English
heim	home
heima	home
heiman	at-home, from-home
heimanferð	from-home-travel
heimboðanna	home-invitation
heimboðum	home-invitations
heimleiðis	home-ways
heimsklega	foolishly
heimsklegast	foolishly
heimskur	foolishness
heimsótt	home-sought
heimti	asked-for
heimul	have-right
heitaðist	called
heiti	am-named
heitinn	named
heitir	named
hékk	hung
heldur	behind, rather
Helga	Helgi (name), Helgi's (name)
Helgi	Helgi (name)
Heljardalsheiði	Heljardal Heath (place)
Hellu-Narfa	Hellu-Narfi (name)
Hellu-Narfasonar	Hellu-Narfason (name)
helst	rather
hélt	held
hendi	hand
hendur	hand
hennar	hers
henni	her
hér	here
héraði	district
héruð	district
héruðum	provinces
hest	horse
hesta	horses
hestana	horses, the-horses
Hestanesi	Hestanes (place)
hesti	horse
hestsins	horse's
hét	named, pledged, promised, was-named
hey	hay, hey
heygarð	hay-stacks
heygjöfinni	hay-giving
heyinu	the-hay
heyjum	hay
heyrði	heard
heyrir	heard
heyrt	heard
heyvöndul	a-haystack, hay-bundle
hið	the
hin	the
Hina	the, these
hingað	here
hinn	the
hins	the
hinu	the
hinum	the
Hitt	find
hitti	met
hittust	met
hjá	beside
hjálm	helmet
Hjaltadal	Hjaltadal (place)
Hjaltasona	Hjaltasons (name)
Hjaltasonu	Hjaltasons (name)
Hjaltasynir	Hjaltasons (name), Sons-of-Hjalti (name)
Hjarðarholti	Hjardarholt (place)
hlaupi	running
Hleypa	ran
hleypur	ran
hlið	side
hlíðinni	the-slope
hljóp	leapt, ran
hljópu	ran
hljótum	we-get
hlut	lot
hlutir	things
hníf	knife
hóf	began
Höfða	Hofdi (place)
höfðingi	chieftain
höfðingjar	chieftains
höfðu	had
Hofi	Hof (place)

Word List (Old Icelandic to English)

Old Icelandic	English
Hofs	Hof (place)
höfuð	head
Höfum	has, have
höggur	striking
holinu	hollow
hönd	hand
höndum	hand, his-hands
honum	he, him, his, to-him
horfa	turn
horfist	looks
horn	horn
hót	threat
hríð	awhile
hringinn	the-ring
hrökkva	recoiled
hrossin	herd
Hrútafirði	Hrutafjord (place)
Hrútafjarðar	Hrutafjord (place)
húðfat	bed-roll
hugði	think
hugðu	thought
hugðum	think
hugsar	thought
hún	she
hundruð	hundred
hús	a-house
húsfreyja	housewife
húsfreyju	housewife
hvað	what
hvar	what, where
hvarf	broke-away
hver	who
hverfa	turn
hverfið	turn
hvergi	neither
Hverja	what
Hverjir	who
hverju	every
hvern	what
hversdaglega	everyday
hversu	how, how-so
hvert	each, how, what, which
hvítur	white
hvolfinu	half
hvorir	each, opposite
hvorirtveggju	either-side
hvort	how, whether
hygg	think
hyggja	think

I, i

ill	ill
illa	bad, ill
illmæli	slander
illt	bad-terms, ill
illu	evil
illyrði	ill-words
inn	inside
innan	inside

Í, í

í	about, at, for, in, into, is, it, on, that, the, this, to
íhlutunarsamur	in-sharing-together
ís	ice
ísinn	the-ice

J, j

jafna	equal
jafnan	usually
jafnmarga	equal-many
jafnsaman	together
jarðhús	earth-house
járna	iron-shod
játtu	agreed
jól	Yule (name)
jörð	earth, the-earth

K, k

kærleikum	friendship
kalla	declare
kallaður	called

Word List (Old Icelandic to English)

Old Icelandic	English	Old Icelandic	English
kapp	eager	láta	allow, leave
kappi	warriors	látum	let
kápu	cape	laug	bathe
kasta	cast	lauk	concluded
kátasti	merriest	launmaðurinn	the-unseen-man
kaupmenn	trading-men	laus	less
kaupmönnum	trading-men	leggið	lay
kemur	came, come, coming	leggja	have, lay
kerlingarnef	Crone's-Nose (name)	leggur	lunged
keyrði	spurred	leið	journey, passed, way
keyrir	spurred	leiða	loath
klæði	clothing	leiðina	the-way
klaufir	hooves	leiðréttu	rectify
Kom	came, come	leik	game
koma	came, coming	leika	sport
komið	came, come	leikum	sport
kominn	came, come	leit	saw
komir	come	leita	look, seek
komnir	come, coming	leitast	seek
komu	came	lengi	long
komum	come	lengri	longer
kona	wife, wife-of	lengur	any-longer
konu	wife	lést	said
konungsnaut	king's-gift	lét	had, let
kostur	chose	léti	let
Krossa	Krossar (place)	Letja	discourage
Krossum	Krossar (place)	letjast	dissuaded
kunna	know	létti	relieved
kvað	said, spoke, thanked	léttu	relieved
kvaddi	greeted	létu	led, let
kveddi	greeting	leyst	down, solved
kveldið	evening	leystur	releasing
kvisti	trim	liðfærri	company-less
kyrrt	peace, still	liðsafla	company-provided
kyrtil	tunic	liðsinnaður	team-minded
kýstu	choosing	liðsinni	assistance
		líður	passed
		liðveislu	assistance
		liggur	lay
		líst	appears

L, l

Old Icelandic	English	Old Icelandic	English
lætur	had	líta	look
lagði	became, lunged	lítið	little
lagður	laid	lítill	little
lagt	had	lítils	little
		lítinn	a-little

Word List (Old Icelandic to English)

Old Icelandic	English
litlu	little
litu	looked
Ljóti	Ljot (name), Ljot (place)
Ljóts	Ljot (place), Ljot's (name)
Ljótur	Ljot (name)
lögum	law
lokið	finished
löndum	land
lýsa	describe, show
lýst	shown

M, m

Old Icelandic	English
má	may
maður	a-man, man
maðurinn	the-man
mælt	talked
mælti	speaking, spoke
mæltu	spoke
mæta	meet
mætti	may, might
mágsemd	in-laws
mágsemdar	as-in-laws
maklegt	deserve
mál	case, matter, speak-to, the-matter
málamaður	law-man, man-of-law
máli	discuss, matter, speak, the-matter
málið	the-case, the-matter
málinu	the-case
málóði	of-violent-language
málum	the-matter
mánaðar	a-month's
mann	a-man, men
manna	men, people's
mannfóli	an-idiot
manni	a-man, man
manninn	person
mannsins	the-man
mánuð	a-month
Marbæli	Marbaeli (place)
Marbælinga	Marbaeli (place)
marga	many
margt	many, much
marki	a-sign
máttu	may
með	with
meðal	between
mega	may
megi	may
megin	sides
megum	may
Meiddi	wounded
mein	harm
meir	more
meira	more
meiri	the-more
menn	men, people
mér	for-me, I, me, mine, to-me
merkur	marks
mest	most
mesta	most
mestum	most
metast	meet
metnaður	pride
miðjan	middle
miðri	the-middle
mig	me, mine, much, my
mikið	much
mikill	great, much
mikilli	much
mikinn	great, much
mikla	much
Miklabæ	Miklabaer (place)
miklir	great
miklu	much
miklum	much
milli	between
mín	mine, my
mína	mine, my
minn	mine
minna	mine
minni	diminish, less
mínum	mine, my
mitt	mine
Mjög	great, many, much
Möðruvöllu	Modruvellir (place)

Word List (Old Icelandic to English)

Old Icelandic	English
mönnum	men, people, to-people
mörgu	many
morguninn	morning
mót	meeting
móti	meet, return
móts	meet
Mun	shall, should, would
mund	about-that-time
mundi	should, would
mundu	would
muni	should, would
munt	should
muntu	shall-you, should-you
munu	shall, should, would, would-be
Munuð	shall
munum	shall, should

N, n

Old Icelandic	English
ná	obtain
nær	close, near, when
næst	nearest
nætur	nights
nafn	name, name
nálega	near-to
Narfason	Narfason (name)
náskyld	closely-related
nauðsyn	necessity
nauðsynja	deed-refuse
neins	any
nenni	care
níðingsverk	lowly-deed
niðri	down
niður	down, kinsman
níta	refuse
nokkuð	some, something, somewhat
nokkur	somewhat
nokkura	any, several, somewhat
nokkurir	some
norðan	north
Norðlendinga	the-northerners
Norðlendingum	northerners
norður	north
nóttina	the-night
nú	now, so
nýju	anew
nýjum	new

O, o

Old Icelandic	English
ofan	down
ofríki	rampages, un-rule, unruly
ofstýri	unmanageable
Oft	often
og	also, and
okkars	our
okkur	us
orð	words
orða	words
orði	word
orðið	become, words
orðinn	become
oss	ours, us

Ó, ó

Old Icelandic	English
óðafári	a-hurry
óðast	furious
ófæru	impassable
ófallið	misguided
ófarin	un-faring
ófrýnlegur	inconspicuous
óhæfu	unqualified
óheilagur	unholy
ójafnaðarmenn	un-equal-men
Ólafi	Olaf (name)
Ólafs	Olaf's (name)
Ólafur	Olaf (name)
óliðdrjúgur	un-substantial-company
óliðlegt	unsuitable
ólman	wild
ómæt	un-good
ómannlegt	inhumane

Word List (Old Icelandic to English)

Old Icelandic	English
óorðan	slanderous
óréttvís	un-right-knowing
Óttar	Ottar (name)
Óttari	Ottar (name)
óvinum	un-friends
óvinveittur	unfriendly
óvíst	uncertain
Óx	grew

Ö, ö

öðru	another, others
öðrum	another, other, others
öðruvís	other-knowing
öfundarmenn	slanderous-men
öll	all
öllu	all
öllum	all
ömbun	return
öngvir	none
öxi	axe
öxlina	an-axe

P, p

pá	Peacock (name)

R, r

ráð	advised, decide, declare
ráða	allow, decide
ráðast	arrange
ráðinn	riding
ráðlaus	ill-advised
ráðlegast	advice, advisable
ráðs	advice
ræddist	discussed
ræðst	rode
réði	decide
Réðst	rode
refði	poleaxe
reið	riding, rode
reifa	account-for
réttindum	right
réttvísi	right-knowing
Reykja	Reykir (place)
reyna	tested, trying
reyndu	test
ríð	ride
ríða	ride, rode, to-ride
riðið	ridden, ride
ríðið	ride
riðu	rode
ríður	rode
rífa	tearing
ríka	Powerful (name)
ríki	powerful
róstum	unruliness

S, s

Sá	saw, so
sækir	seek
sæmd	honour
sæmdar	honour
sæmdarauki	honour
sæmdir	honour
sæmdum	honour
sæta	sit-in-ambush
sætt	settle
sættast	reconcile
safnar	collected
sagði	said, said, told, told
sagt	said, told
sakir	conviction, for-the-sake-of, sake, the-charges
saman	the-same, together, together
samið	agreement
sannast	the-truest, true, truly
sár	wound, wounded, wounding, wounds
sára	wounds
Sárum	the-wounds
Sat	sat, stayed
satt	TRUE

Word List (Old Icelandic to English)

Old Icelandic	English
Sátu	sat, sitting, stayed
sáu	saw
sé	being, is, see, so, this, was
segi	say
segir	said, told
segja	say, to-say
seilast	obtain
sektan	outlawed
sekti	convicted
selja	repay
sem	as, as-if, that, which, who
sendi	send
sér	her, him, himself, his, saw, them, themselves
setið	stay
setjast	stayed
sett	set
settist	set
setuefni	sitting
Setur	set
séu	are, being
síðan	after, afterwards, then
síðar	afterwards
síðir	eventually
sig	him, himself, such
Sigríðar	Sigrid (name)
Sigríði	Sigrid (name)
Sigríður	Sigrid (name)
silfurs	of-silver
sín	him, his, this
sína	his, their, theirs
sinn	hers, his, theirs
sinna	his, theirs
sinni	his
síns	her, his
sínu	his
sínum	hers, his, theirs, they
sitja	sit, sit-in-ambush, sitting
sitt	his, this
Situr	stayed
sjá	saw
sjáandi	seeing
sjálfan	yourself
sjálfdæmi	self-judgement
sjö	seven
skaða	scathed
Skagafirði	Skagafjord (place)
Skagafjarðar	Skagafjord (place)
skal	shall, shall-be, should
skalt	shall
skaltu	shall, shall-you
skammt	a-short-distance, short-distance
skapi	mood
skapillur	bad-temper
skaplyndi	nature
skarpasti	hardest
Skeið	Skeid (place)
Skeiði	Skeid (place)
skelmi	devilish-man
skikkju	cloak
skildi	separated, shield
skildinum	the-shield
skildir	shields
skildist	separated
Skildu	separated
Skildust	separated
skilið	separated
skilja	separate, separated
skiljum	understanding
skilnaði	parted, parting
skinnstakki	skin-cloak
skip	a-ship
skips	ships
skipta	exchange
skipti	exchanged
skiptust	exchanged
skirra	prevent
skjöld	shield
Skjöldurinn	the-shield
skjótt	quickly
skógarmenn	forest-men
skóggang	outlawry
skóggangssök	forest-seeking
sköllóttur	bald
skörulega	boldly
skörungur	noble
skuli	shall

Word List (Old Icelandic to English)

Old Icelandic	English
Skulu	shall
skuluð	should
skulum	should
skyld	guilt
skyldi	should
skyldu	should
skýtur	shot
sleppa	escape
slík	such
slitið	dissolved
smærri	smaller
snaghyrnda	snag-cornered
snarlega	quickly
Sneri	turned
snerist	turned
snjór	snow
snúa	return, turn
sögu	saga
sögum	sagas
Sóknin	the-struggle
sökótt	accusations
sömu	same
Son	son, son-of
sonar	son
sonur	son, the-son-of
sótt	attend, attended, sought
sótti	sought
spara	spare
spekt	wisdom
spjót	spear
spjóti	spear
spjótið	spear, the-spear
spjótinu	spear
spretta	sprang
spyr	asked
stað	place
staddur	standing
stærimaður	Stately-man (name)
stærimann	Stately-man (name)
stærimanni	Stately-man (name)
standanda	stood
Starri	Starri (name)
stefna	agreement
stefndi	charged, summoned
stefnir	charged
stefnu	summoned, summons
stefnuna	the-summons
stefnunni	the-summons
stela	steal, stealing
stertimaður	Stately-man (name)
stíga	step
Stigu	dismounted
stóð	stood
stolið	stolen
stólkonungurinn	the-emperor
stórmannlega	great-man-ness
stórmannlegar	great-man-like
studdist	stood
stund	while
stýrimann	the-captain
styrk	strength
suður	south
sumar	summer
sumarið	summer
sundur	asunder
sundurþykki	discord
svarar	answered, said
Svarfaðardal	Svarfadardal (place)
Svarfaðardals	Svarfadardal (place)
Svarfaðardalsár	Svarfadardal (place)
Svarfdæla	Svarfadardal (place)
svarið	answer
svartan	a-black
sveininn	the-boy
sveinsins	son-yours
sveit	company
sveitir	areas
sveitum	the-district
sverðinu	the-sword
sviptir	loss
svo	so, 0
sýna	seemed, show
sýnir	showed
Sýnist	seemed
sýnt	shown
systrungur	mother's-sister's-son

T, t

Word List (Old Icelandic to English)

Old Icelandic	English
tæki	take
tækist	took
Tak	take
taka	take, taken
takir	take
tal	talking
tala	said, speak, spoke
talið	conversation
tauma	reins
tekið	taken
tekist	taken
tekur	took
tel	say
tíðinda	news
tigi	ten
til	about, its, to, until
tilfelli	occurrence
tillæti	deference
tiltekju	exchange
tíma	time
títt	reported
tók	took
tókst	took
tóku	took-to
tólf	twelve
töluðu	talked, told
torfstakka	turf-stacks
trausts	trust
Tungu	Tunga (place)
tvenn	twice
tvo	two

Þ, þ

Old Icelandic	English
Þá	the, then, they, when
það	is, it, so, that, this, to
þaðan	from-there
þætti	seems
Þakka	thanks
þakkaði	thanked
þakkar	thanked, thanks
þangað	from-there, there, there
þann	the, then
þar	here, it, there, there
Þarf	need
þarftu	need-you
Þau	they, they
þegar	as-soon-as, from-there, immediately, then, when
þeim	home, them, they, to-them
Þeir	the, then, there, they
þeirra	of-them, of-they, their, theirs, them, they, they-of
þenna	this
þér	to-you, you, your
þess	this
þessa	this
þessar	these
þessi	this
þessir	these
þessu	this
þetta	it, that, this
þið	you, you-two
þig	you
þiggir	accept
þiggja	accept, accepted, to-accept
þiggur	accepted
þína	yours
þing	assembly, the-assembly
þingið	the-assembly
þinginu	the-assembly
þingmaður	assembly-man
þingsins	the-assembly
þinn	you, yours
þinnar	yours
þinni	yours
þitt	yours
þjófarnir	thieves
þjófnað	theft
þó	though
þökk	thanks
þola	endure
þora	dare
Þórð	Thord (name)
Þórðar	Thord (name)

Word List (Old Icelandic to English)

Old Icelandic	English
Þórðarsonar	Son-of-Thord (name)
Þórði	Thord (name)
Þórdís	Thordis (name)
Þórður	Thord (name)
Þorgrímur	Thorgrim (name)
Þórólf	Thorolf (name)
Þórólfi	Thorolf (name)
Þórólfs	Thorolf's (name)
Þórólfur	Thorolf (name)
Þorstein	Thorstein (name), Thorstein (name)
Þorsteini	Thorstein (name), Thorstein's (name)
Þorsteinn	Thorstein (name)
Þorsteins	Thorstein's (name)
Þorvaldi	Thorvald (name), Thorvald (name)
Þorvaldur	Thorvald (name)
þótt	though
þótti	thought
þóttu	thought
þriggja	three
þrír	three
þrjá	three
þrjár	three
þú	you
Þúfum	Thufur (place)
þungt	negatively
þurfa	need
þurfi	need
Þverá	Thvera (place)
Þverár	Thvera (place)
þvers	across
því	according, accordingly, as, because, since, such, that, therefore
þykir	consider, seems, think, thought
þykist	think
þykjast	realised, think

U, u

um	about, with
umskipti	about-exchanged
undan	away-from
undir	into, near
undri	fool-of-yourself
ungur	young
upp	up, upped
upphaf	begun
uppi	up
uppsögn	up-saying
Urðskriðuhóla	Urdskriduholar (place)
urðu	became
utan	abroad

Ú, ú

úr	back-from, from, from-out-of, of, out-of
út	from, out
úti	outside

V, v

vænt	expect
Væri	be, was
værir	be, would-be
vanda	custom
vandi	difficulty
vandræði	dispute
vandræðum	trouble
Var	then, was, were
varð	became, was
varða	warranted
varði	expect
varðveislu	hospitality
varðveita	ward-knowing
varla	barely
varna	defence
varstu	where
veður	weathered
veg	way
vegar	way
veisla	feast, the-feast
veislu	feast

Word List (Old Icelandic to English)

Old Icelandic	English
Veit	know
veita	giving, grant
veitti	granted
vel	well, well-willing
velli	the-fields
venslum	marriage
Ver	be
vér	our, we
vera	be, becomes, being, be-it, were
verð	the-worth
verða	be, became, become, being, would-be
verðgang	vagrancy
verði	become
verðugt	worth
verður	becomes, worth
verið	been
verja	defend, guarding, protect
verk	work
versna	worse
verst	the-worst
vert	worthy
vesalmenni	wretch
vestur	west
vetra	winters
veturinn	winter
vexti	grown
við	against, by, to, with
viðtökur	with-taken, with-taking
víg	killing, slaying-of, the-killing-of, the-slaying-of
víga	fight
vígi	the-slaying
vígsmálið	fight-the-case
vil	will, wish
vildi	willing, wish, wished
vilja	will, willing, wish
viljaður	willing
vilji	wish
viljir	wish
Viljum	will
vill	wished, wishing
vilt	wish
vin	friend
vinátta	friendship
vináttu	friendship
vindur	the-wind
vinganarmál	friendship-matter
vingast	make-friends
vinhollir	open-whole
vinsæll	popular
vinskap	friendship
vinskapar	friendship
vinur	a-friend, friend
virða	value, worth
virðið	honour
virðing	honour, respect, worth, worthiness
virðingar	honour
virðingarvænlegt	respect-kindly
virðingu	honour
virkið	the-compound
víst	certainly
vistar	lodging
vísu	certainly
vita	know
vitja	visit
vitlaus	wit-less
voða	risk
Völlu	Vellir (place)
Völlum	Vellir (place)
von	expected, to-expect
vopn	weapons
vopnaðir	weaponed
vopns	weapons
vor	spring
vordaga	spring-days
vorn	our
vorra	ours
voru	was, were

Y, y

Old Icelandic	English
yður	you, your, yours
yðvar	you

Word List (Old Icelandic to English)

Old Icelandic	English
yðvarn	of-you
yfir	over
yrði	with

Word List (English to Old Icelandic)

English	Old Icelandic

A, a

English	Old Icelandic
a	að
a-black	svartan
a-blue	blán
about	Á, að, en, í, til, um
about-exchanged	umskipti
about-that-time	mund
abroad	utan
a-bull	griðung
accept	þiggir, þiggja
accepted	þiggja, þiggur
accomplished	Fær
according	því
accordingly	því
account-for	reifa
accusations	sökótt
across	þvers
advice	ráðlegast, ráðs
advisable	ráðlegast
advised	ráð
a-farm	bæ
a-friend	vinur
after	eftir, síðan
after-matter	eftirmáls
afterwards	eftir, Síðan, síðar
against	við
age	aldri
aggression	ágang
agreed	játtu
agreement	samið, stefna
a-haystack	heyvöndul
ahead	fyrir
a-house	hús
a-hurry	óðafári
a-journey	förum
a-little	lítinn
all	alla, alla, allan, allar, allir, allir, allri, alls, allt, allt, öll, öllu, öllum
all-great-man-like	allstórmannlega
allow	láta, ráða
all-prepared	albúnir
all-settle	alsáttir
all-well	allvel, allvel
alone	einn
along	eftir
also	og
am	er
a-man	maður, mann, manni
ambush	fyrirsát
a-meeting	fundur
am-named	heiti
a-month	mánuð
a-month's	mánaðar
an	eða
an-abundance	gnótt
an-axe	öxlina
and	eða, en, er, og
anew	nýju
an-idiot	mannfóli
another	aðra, annað, annað, annar, annar, annarri, öðru, öðrum
answer	svarið
answered	svarar
any	einum, neins, nokkura
any-longer	lengur
appears	líst
are	er, eru, eruð, séu
areas	sveitir
are-there	Eru
are-you	ertu
arms	fangi
Arnor (name)	Arnór, Arnóri
Arnor's (name)	Arnórs
arrange	ráðast
as	Á, að, er, sem, því
a-ship	skip
a-short-distance	skammt
as-if	sem
a-sign	marki
as-in-laws	mágsemdar
ask	beiðast
asked	bað, beiddi, spyr
asked-for	heimti
asking	frétti

120

Word List (English to Old Icelandic)

English	*Old Icelandic*
assembly	þing
assembly-man	þingmaður
assist	greiða
assistance	ásjá, ásjá, ásjár, liðsinni, liðveislu
as-soon-as	þegar
asunder	sundur
at	á, að, af, Í
at-home	heiman
attend	sótt
attended	sótt
attention	gaumur
away	brott
away-from	undan
awhile	hríð
axe	öxi

B, b

English	*Old Icelandic*
back	aftur, bak
back-from	úr
bad	illa
bad-temper	skapillur
bad-terms	illt
bald	sköllóttur
bank	bakkann
barely	varla
bathe	laug
battle	bardagi
be	Væri, værir, Ver, vera, verða
bear	ber, borið
bears	barist
became	lagði, urðu, varð, verða
because	því
because-of	fyrir
become	orðið, orðinn, verða, verði
becomes	vera, verður
bed-roll	húðfat
been	verið
before	áður, fyrir, fyrr, fyrri
before-us	fyrrum
began	hóf

English	*Old Icelandic*
begun	upphaf
behind	heldur
being	sé, séu, vera, verða
be-it	Vera
belt	belti
benefit	beini, gott
beside	hjá
best	best, besta, bestur
better	bæta, betra, betri, betur
between	meðal, milli
bid	boðið
Bjarni (name)	Bjarnar
black	blárri
boldly	djarflega, skörulega
Bollason (name)	Bollason, Bollasyni
Bolli (name)	Bolla, Bolli
Bolli's (name)	Bolla
both	báðir
bound	bindur, bundinn
bravely	drengilegsta
break	bregða
bring	færa
bringing	færa
broke	braut, bregður
broke-away	hvarf
broken	brotið
brother	bróðir, bróður
brothers	bræður
buckled	gyrður
bull	graðung, Graðungur
but	en, enn, er
by	við

C, c

English	*Old Icelandic*
called	heitaðist, kallaður
came	gengur, kemur, Kom, koma, komið, kominn, komu
cape	kápu
care	nenni
carried	borið
case	mál
cast	kasta

Word List (English to Old Icelandic)

English	Old Icelandic
cattle	*fé*
celebration	*fagnaði*
certainly	*víst, vísu*
challenge	*áskoran*
charged	*stefndi, stefnir*
charges	*atkvæðum*
chieftain	*höfðingi*
chieftains	*höfðingjar*
children	*börnum*
choosing	*kýstu*
chose	*kostur*
cloak	*skikkju*
close	*fast, nær*
closely	*fast*
closely-related	*náskyld*
clothing	*klæði*
coldly	*fálega*
collected	*safnar*
come	*kemur, kom, komið, kominn, komir, komnir, komum*
coming	*Kemur, koma, komnir*
companions	*förunautar, förunautar*
company	*sveit*
company-less	*liðfærri*
company-provided	*liðsafla*
compensate	*bæta*
compensation	*fébótum*
comrades	*félagar*
comradeship	*félagsskap*
concluded	*lauk*
consider	*þykir*
considerable	*ærin*
conversation	*talið*
convicted	*sekti*
conviction	*sakir*
costume	*búningur*
cowardly	*hann*
Crone's-Nose (name)	*kerlingarnef*
custom	*vanda*

D, d

English	Old Icelandic
Dagverdarnes (place)	*Dögurðarnes*
danger	*hættu*
dare	*þora*
dead	*dauður*
dearest	*dýrsta*
decide	*ráð, ráða, réði*
declare	*kalla, ráð*
deed-refuse	*nauðsynja*
defence	*varna*
defend	*verja*
deference	*tillæti*
describe	*lýsa*
deserve	*maklegt*
devastate	*eyða*
devilish-man	*skelmi*
did	*fór, gerði, gerðu*
difficulty	*erfið, vandi*
diminish	*minni*
discord	*sundurþykki*
discourage	*Letja*
discuss	*máli*
discussed	*ræddist*
dismounted	*Stigu*
dispute	*vandræði*
dissolved	*slitið*
dissuaded	*letjast*
district	*fjórðungi, héðra, héraði, héruð*
do	*gera, gerið, gerir*
doing	*gera, gerir*
done	*gert*
down	*aftur, leyst, niðri, niður, ofan*
drew	*bregður, dregur*
dwelled	*Dvöldust*

E, e

English	Old Icelandic
each	*hvert, hvorir*
eager	*kapp*
earlier	*áður*
earth	*jörð*
earth-house	*jarðhús*
easily	*hæglegt*
eight	*átta*

Word List (English to Old Icelandic)

English	*Old Icelandic*
eighteen	*átján, átján*
either-side	*hvorirtveggju*
ells	*alna*
encounter	*finnast*
encouraged	*eggjar*
endure	*þola*
equal	*jafna*
equal-many	*jafnmarga*
escape	*sleppa*
evening	*kveldið*
eventually	*síðir*
every	*hverju*
everyday	*hversdaglega*
evil	*illu*
exchange	*skipta, tiltekju*
exchanged	*skipti, skiptust*
expect	*ætla, vænt, varði*
expected	*von*

F, f

English	*Old Icelandic*
failed	*fallið*
fair	*fögrum*
fairly	*haga*
fallen	*fallið, fallnir*
falling	*felldur*
false	
falsehood	*fólsku*
famous-work	*frægðarverk*
far-away	*fjarri*
fared	*farið*
farm	*bæ, búi*
farmer	*bóndi*
farmhouse	*bænum*
fast	*fast*
fastened	*fast*
feast	*veisla, veislu*
fee	*fá, fé*
fell	*fellur*
few	*fáir, fár, fátt*
fiendship	*fjandskap*
fifteen	*fimmtán*
fight	*berjast, berjist, víga*
fight-the-case	*vígsmálið*
find	*finna, finnum, Hitt*

English	*Old Icelandic*
finished	*lokið*
floating	*flaut*
flock	*flokk*
follow	*fylgja*
followed	*flýgur, Fylgir, fylgt*
followers-many	*fjölmenni*
following-men	*fjölmenna*
follows	*fylg, fylgi*
foolish	*afglapa*
foolishly	*fólið, heimsklega, heimsklegast*
foolishness	*heimskur*
fool-of-yourself	*undri*
for	*á, að, fyrir, í*
forest-men	*skógarmenn*
forest-seeking	*skóggangssök*
for-me	*mér*
for-the-ambush	*fyrirsátina*
for-the-sake-of	*sakir*
fortunate	*hamingja*
fought	*berjast*
found	*fann, fékk, fundust*
frenzy-man	*æðimaður*
friend	*vin, vinur*
friendship	*kærleikum, vinátta, vináttu, vinskap, vinskapar*
friendship-matter	*vinganarmál*
from	*á, að, af, af, frá, fram, úr, út*
from-here	*héðan*
from-home	*heiman*
from-home-travel	*heimanferð*
from-out-of	*úr*
from-there	*þaðan, þangað, þegar*
full-of-people	*fjölmennt*
furious	*óðast*

G, g

English	*Old Icelandic*
Galmarstrond (place)	*Galmarströnd*
game	*leik*
gave	*gaf, gáfu*
gets	*fengi*
gifts	*gjafar, gjafir, gjöfum*

Word List (English to Old Icelandic)

English	Old Icelandic	English	Old Icelandic
give	*gefa, gefið*	Hals (place)	*Háls, Hálsi*
given	*gefinn*	hand	*hendi, hendur, hönd, höndum*
giving	*veita*	hardest	*harðasta, skarpasti*
gladdest	*glaðasti*	harm	*mein*
go	*fara, ganga*	has	*að, hafði, hefði, hefir, Höfum*
goes	*fer, fór*	have	*að, áttir, eiga, ert, Haf, hafa, hafast, Hafið, hafir, haft, Hefi, hefir, höfum, leggja*
going	*fara, ferð, ferðina, gangi*		
gold-inlaid	*gullrekna*		
gold-laid	*gulllagðan*	have-right	*heimul*
gold-ring	*fingurgull, gullhring, gullhringinn, gullhringur*	have-you	*áttu*
		hay	*hey, heyjum*
gone	*farið, farin, Gengið*	hay-bundle	*heyvöndul*
good	*góða, góðar, góðum, góður*	hay-giving	*heygjöfinni*
		haystacks	*andvirki*
got	*fá, Fær, fékk, getið, getur*	hay-stacks	*heygarð*
		he	*hana, hann, honum*
grab	*grípa*	head	*höfuð*
grant	*veita*	healed	*greru*
granted	*veitti*	heard	*heyrði, heyrir, heyrt*
great	*mikill, mikinn, miklir, Mjög*	Hegranes (place)-Assembly	*Hegranessþingi, Hegranessþings*
greatly	*ágætlega, harðla*	held	*hélt*
great-man-like	*stórmannlegar*	Helgi (name)	*Helga, Helgi*
great-man-ness	*stórmannlega*	Helgi's (name)	*Helga*
greeted	*kvaddi*	Heljardal Heath (place)	*Heljardalsheiði*
greeting	*kveddi*		
grew	*Óx*	Hellu-Narfason (name)	*Hellu-Narfasonar*
grey	*grán*		
grown	*vexti*	Hellu-Narfi (name)	*Hellu-Narfa*
guarding	*verja*	helmet	*hjálm*
Guddalir (place)	*Guðdölum*	her	*hana, henni, sér, síns*
Gudmund (name)	*Guðmundar, Guðmundur*	herd	*hrossin*
		here	*hér, hingað, þar*
Gudrun (name)	*Guðrún*	hers	*hennar, sinn, sínum*
guilt	*skyld*	Hestanes (place)	*Hestanesi*
		hey	*hey*
		him	*hann, hans, honum, sér, sig, sín*

H, h

English	Old Icelandic	English	Old Icelandic
had	*átt, átti, áttu, er, hafa, hafði, hafi, haft, hefir, hefur, höfðu, lætur, lagt, lét*	himself	*sér, sig*
		his	*hann, hans, honum, sér, sín, sína, sinn, sinna, sinni, síns, sínu, sínum, sitt*
half	*hálfan, hvolfinu*		
half-month's	*hálfs*	his-hands	*höndum*

124

Word List (English to Old Icelandic)

English	*Old Icelandic*
Hjaltadal (place)	*Hjaltadal*
Hjaltasons (name)	*Hjaltasona, Hjaltasonu, Hjaltasynir*
Hjardarholt (place)	*Hjarðarholti*
Hof (place)	*Hofi, Hofs*
Hofdi (place)	*Höfða*
hold	*halda*
holds	*haldinn*
hollow	*holinu*
home	*heim, heima, þeim*
home-invitation	*heimboðanna*
home-invitations	*heimboðum*
homes	*alist*
home-sought	*heimsótt*
home-ways	*heimleiðis*
honour	*drengskap, frama, frama, framar, sæmd, sæmdar, sæmdarauki, sæmdir, sæmdum, virðið, virðing, virðingar, virðingu*
hooves	*klaufir*
horn	*horn*
horse	*hest, hesti*
horseback	*baki*
horses	*faraskjóta, hesta, hestana*
horse's	*hestsins*
hospitality	*varðveislu*
host	*bóndi*
housewife	*húsfreyja, húsfreyju*
how	*hversu, hvert, hvort*
how-so	*hversu*
Hrutafjord (place)	*Hrútafirði, Hrútafjarðar*
hundred	*hundruð*
hung	*hékk*
husband	*bónda*

I, i

English	*Old Icelandic*
I	*eg, mér*
ice	*ís*
if	*ef*
ill	*ill, illa, illt*
ill-advised	*ráðlaus*
ill-words	*illyrði*
immediately	*þegar*
impassable	*ófæru*
in	*á, að, eiga, en, í*
inconspicuous	*ófrýnlegur*
inhumane	*ómannlegt*
in-laws	*mágsemd*
in-sharing-together	*íhlutunarsamur*
inside	*inn, innan*
intend	*Ætla, ætlar*
intended	*Ætla, ætlað, ætlar*
into	*á, í, undir*
invited	*bauð, býður*
iron-shod	*járna*
is	*er, eru, í, sé, það*
it	*á, að, í, Það, þar, þetta*
it-is	*Er*
its	*til*

J, j

English	*Old Icelandic*
journey	*ferð, ferðir, leið*
joyfulness	*blíðu*

K, k

English	*Old Icelandic*
kill	*drepa, drepið*
killing	*drepið, víg*
king's-gift	*konungsnaut*
kinsman	*frænda, niður*
kinswoman	*frændkona, frændkonu*
knife	*hníf*
know	*kunna, Veit, vita*
Krossar (place)	*Krossa, Krossum*

L, l

English	*Old Icelandic*
laid	*lagður*
land	*löndum*

Word List (English to Old Icelandic)

English	Old Icelandic	English	Old Icelandic
laughed	*brosti*	matter	*efni, mál, máli*
law	*lögum*	may	*má, mætti, máttu, mega, megi, megum*
law-man	*málamaður*	me	*mér, mig*
lay	*leggið, leggja, liggur*	meet	*fund, mæta, metast, móti, móts*
leapt	*hljóp*	meeting	*mót*
learned	*Frétti*	men	*mann, manna, menn, mönnum*
leave	*láta*	merriest	*kátasti*
led	*létu*	met	*finnast, fundust, hitti, hittust*
Leg-Biter (name)	*Fótbít*	middle	*miðjan*
less	*laus, minni*	might	*mætti*
let	*látum, Lét, léti, Létu*	Miklabaer (place)	*Miklabæ*
little	*lítið, lítill, lítils, litlu*	mine	*mér, mig, mín, mína, minn, minna, mínum, mitt*
lived	*bjó, bjuggu*	misguided	*ófallið*
Ljot (name)	*Ljóti, Ljótur*	mockery	*hæðileg*
Ljot (place)	*Ljóti, Ljóts*	Modruvellir (place)	*Möðruvöllu*
Ljot's (name)	*Ljóts*	mood	*skapi*
loath	*leiða*	more	*fleiri, meir, meira*
lodging	*vistar*	morning	*morguninn*
long	*lengi*	most	*mest, mesta, mestum*
longer	*lengri*	mother's-sister's-son	*systrungur*
look	*leita, líta*	mourned	*harmaði*
looked	*litu*	much	*margt, mig, mikið, mikill, mikilli, mikinn, mikla, miklu, miklum, mjög*
looks	*horfist*	my	*mig, Mín, mína, mínum*
loss	*sviptir*		
lot	*hlut*		
lowly-deed	*níðingsverk*		
luck	*hamingja, heill*		
luck-promised	*giftuvænlegur*		
lunged	*lagði, leggur*		

M, m

English	Old Icelandic
made	*ger, gerð, gerði, gerðu, gert*
make	*fallið, gerðinni*
make-friends	*vingast*
man	*maður, manni*
man-of-law	*málamaður*
many	*marga, margt, mjög, mörgu*
many-men	*fjölmenna*
Marbaeli (place)	*Marbæli, Marbælinga*
marks	*merkur*
marriage	*venslum*
married	*átti, gjaforð*

N, n

English	Old Icelandic
name	*nafn, nafn*
named	*heitinn, heitir, hét*
Narfason (name)	*Narfason*
nature	*skaplyndi*
near	*nær, undir*
nearest	*næst*
near-to	*nálega*
necessity	*nauðsyn*
need	*Þarf, þurfa, þurfi*
need-you	*þarftu*

Word List (English to Old Icelandic)

English	Old Icelandic
negatively	*þungt*
neither	*hvergi*
never	*aldrei*
new	*nýjum*
news	*frétt, tíðinda*
nights	*nætur*
no	*eigi, ekki, engi, engrar*
noble	*skörungur*
noblest	*göfgustu*
none	*eigi, enga, engi, engis, engrar, öngvir*
nor	*en*
north	*norðan, norður*
northerners	*Norðlendingum*
not	*eigi, ekki*
nothing	*ekki, engu*
now	*nú*

O, o

English	Old Icelandic
obtain	*ná, seilast*
occurrence	*tilfelli*
of	*á, að, af, af, úr*
of-all	*allra*
off	*af*
of-family-small	*ættsmár*
offer	*beiða, biðja, bjóða*
offered	*boðið*
of-silver	*silfurs*
often	*Oft*
of-them	*þeirra*
of-they	*þeirra*
of-violent-language	*málóði*
of-wealth	*fjár*
of-you	*yðvarn*
Olaf (name)	*Ólafi, Ólafur*
Olaf's (name)	*Ólafs*
on	*á, í*
one	*eina, einn, einnhvern*
one-agreement	*einsætt*
only	*einir, einn*
open-whole	*vinhollir*
opposite	*hvorir*
or	*eða*
ordered	*bað*

English	Old Icelandic
other	*annað, öðrum*
other-knowing	*öðruvís*
others	*aðrir, öðru, öðrum*
Ottar (name)	*Óttar, Óttari*
our	*okkars, vér, vorn*
ours	*oss, vorra*
out	*út*
outlawed	*sektan*
outlawry	*skóggang*
out-of	*úr*
outside	*úti*
over	*yfir*
overcome	*Barst*
own	*eign, eigna*

P, p

English	Old Icelandic
parted	*skilnaði*
parting	*skilnaði*
passed	*leið, líður*
pay	*aura, gjalda*
peace	*kyrrt*
peaceful	*frið*
Peacock (name)	*pá*
people	*menn, mönnum*
people's	*manna*
person	*manninn*
place	*stað*
plans	*ætlað*
pledged	*Hét*
plenty-of	*ærið*
plotting	*fjörráð*
plotting-against	*fjörráð*
poleaxe	*refði*
poorly	*fálega*
popular	*vinsæll*
possible	*hægt*
postpone	*fresta*
powerful	*ríki*
Powerful (name)	*ríka*
prepare	*búast*
prepared	*bjóst, búið, búin, býr, býst*
preparing	*búnir*
prevent	*skirra*

Word List (English to Old Icelandic)

English	*Old Icelandic*
pride	*metnaður*
promised	*hét*
promising	*efnilegastur*
protect	*verja*
provinces	*héruðum*

Q, q

quickly	*skjótt, snarlega*

R, r

rampages	*ofríki*
ran	*Hleypa, hleypur, hljóp, hljópu*
rather	*heldur, helst*
realised	*þykjast*
recoiled	*hrökkva*
reconcile	*sættast*
rectify	*leiðréttu*
refuse	*níta*
reins	*tauma*
releasing	*leystur*
relieved	*fegin, létti, léttu*
renowned	*ágætir*
repay	*selja*
reported	*Fréttist, Fréttust, títt*
resolved	*greiddist*
respect	*virðing*
respect-kindly	*virðingarvænlegt*
rest	*æja*
return	*aftur, móti, ömbun, snúa*
returned	*aftur*
Reykir (place)	*Reykja*
rich	*auðigur*
ridden	*riðið*
ride	*ríð, ríða, riðið, ríðið*
riding	*ráðinn, reið*
right	*réttindum*
right-knowing	*réttvísi*
risk	*voða*
river	*ána*
rocks	*grjóti*

English	*Old Icelandic*
rode	*ræðst, Réðst, Reið, Ríða, riðu, ríður*
running	*hlaupi*

S, s

safe	*fritt, heilir*
saga	*sögu*
sagas	*sögum*
said	*kvað, lést, sagði, sagði, sagt, segir, svarar, tala*
sake	*sakir*
same	*sömu*
sat	*Sat, Sátu*
saw	*leit, Sá, sáu, sér, sjá*
say	*segi, segja, tel*
scathed	*skaða*
see	*Sé*
seeing	*sjáandi*
seek	*leita, leitast, sækir*
seemed	*sýna, Sýnist*
seems	*þætti, þykir*
self-judgement	*dóm, sjálfdæmi*
send	*sendi*
separate	*skilja*
separated	*skildi, skildist, Skildu, Skildust, skilið, skilja*
serves	*gegnir*
set	*sett, settist, Setur*
set-out	*fer*
settle	*sætt*
settlers	*búa*
seven	*sjö*
several	*nokkura*
shall	*Mun, munu, Munuð, munum, skal, skalt, skaltu, skuli, Skulu*
shall-be	*skal*
shall-you	*muntu, skaltu*
she	*hún*
shield	*skildi, skjöld*
shields	*skildir*
shining	*blika*
ships	*skips*
short-distance	*skammt*

Word List (English to Old Icelandic)

English	*Old Icelandic*
shot	*skýtur*
should	*mun, mundi, muni, munt, Munu, Munum, skal, skuluð, skulum, skyldi, skyldu*
should-you	*Muntu*
show	*lýsa, sýna*
showed	*sýnir*
shown	*lýst, sýnt*
side	*hlið*
sides	*megin*
Sigrid (name)	*Sigríðar, Sigríði, Sigríður*
since	*En, því*
sit	*sitja*
sit-in-ambush	*sæta, sitja*
sitting	*sátu, setuefni, sitja*
Skagafjord (place)	*Skagafirði, Skagafjarðar*
Skeid (place)	*Skeið, Skeiði*
skin-cloak	*skinnstakki*
slander	*illmæli*
slanderous	*óorðan*
slanderous-men	*öfundarmenn*
slaying-of	*víg*
smaller	*smærri*
snag-cornered	*snaghyrnda*
snow	*snjór*
so	*nú, sá, sé, svo, það*
solved	*leyst*
some	*nokkuð, nokkurir*
something	*nokkuð*
somewhat	*nokkuð, nokkur, nokkura*
son	*Son, sonar, sonur*
son-of	*son*
Son-of-Bolli (name)	*Bollason*
Son-of-Thord (name)	*Þórðarsonar*
Sons-of-Hjalti (name)	*Hjaltasynir*
son-yours	*sveinsins*
sought	*sótt, sótti*
south	*suður*
spare	*spara*
speak	*máli, tala*
speaking	*mælti*
speak-to	*mál*
spear	*spjót, spjóti, spjótið, spjótinu*
spoke	*kvað, mælti, mæltu, Tala*
sport	*leika, leikum*
sprang	*spretta*
spring	*vor*
spring-days	*vordaga*
spurred	*keyrði, keyrir*
standing	*staddur*
Starri (name)	*Starri*
Starri-of-Guddalir	*Guðdala-Starra*
startled	*brá*
Stately-man (name)	*stærimaður, stærimann, stærimanni, stertimaður*
stay	*setið*
stayed	*sat, sátu, setjast, Situr*
steal	*stela*
stealing	*stela*
step	*stíga*
still	*kyrrt*
stolen	*stolið*
stood	*standanda, stóð, studdist*
stop	*hættu*
strength	*styrk*
striking	*höggur*
such	*sig, slík, því*
summer	*sumar, sumarið*
summoned	*stefndi, stefnu*
summons	*stefnu*
suspect	*grunur*
suspected	*grunaði*
Svarfadardal (place)	*Svarfaðardal, Svarfaðardals, Svarfaðardalsár, Svarfdæla*

T, t

take	*tæki, Tak, taka, takir*
taken	*taka, tekið, tekist*
talked	*mælt, töluðu*
talking	*tal*

Word List (English to Old Icelandic)

English	Old Icelandic
team-minded	liðsinnaður
tearing	rífa
ten	tigi
test	freista, reyndu
tested	reyna
than	en
thanked	kvað, þakkaði, þakkar
thanks	Þakka, þakkar, þökk
that	að, en, er, í, sem, það, Þetta, því
the	á, að, enn, er, hið, hin, Hina, hinn, hins, hinu, hinum, í, Þá, þann, Þeir
the-after-matter	eftirmálinu
the-assembly	alþingi, þing, þingið, þinginu, þingsins
the-battle	bardagann
the-booth	búðina
the-booth-doors	búðardyrunum
the-boy	sveininn
the-brothers	bræðra
the-bull	boli, graðungurinn
the-captain	stýrimann
the-case	málið, málinu
the-charges	sakir
the-compound	virkið
the-district	sveitum
the-earth	jörð
the-emperor	stólkonungurinn
the-farm	bæinn, bænum, bú
the-farmer	bónda, bóndi
the-feast	veisla
the-fields	velli
theft	þjófnað
the-gift	gjafir
the-gifts	gjafirnar
the-hay	desjarnar, heyinu
the-heath	heiðina
the-horses	hestana
the-ice	ísinn
their	sína, þeirra
theirs	sína, sinn, sinna, sínum, þeirra
the-journey	ferðinni
the-killing-of	víg
the-leg	fæti
them	sér, þeim, þeirra
the-man	maðurinn, mannsins
the-matter	efni, mál, máli, málið, málum
the-middle	miðri
the-more	meiri
themselves	sér
then	en, enn, er, síðan, þá, þann, þegar, Þeir, Var
the-night	nóttina
the-northerners	Norðlendinga
the-pastures	afréttum
there	eru, þangað, Þangað, þar, þar, Þeir
therefore	því
the-ring	hringinn
the-river	áin, ána, ána, ánni, ár, árinnar
the-same	saman
these	hina, þessar, þessir
the-shield	skildinum, Skjöldurinn
the-slaying	vígi
the-slaying-of	víg
the-slope	hlíðinni
the-son-of	sonur
the-spear	spjótið
the-struggle	Sóknin
the-summons	stefnuna, stefnunni
the-sword	sverðinu
the-truest	sannast
the-unseen-man	launmaðurinn
the-way	leiðina
the-wind	vindur
the-worst	verst
the-worth	verð
the-wounds	Sárum
they	sínum, þá, Þau, Þau, þeim, Þeir, þeirra
they-of	þeirra
thieves	þjófarnir
things	hlutir
think	hugði, hugðum, hygg, hyggja, Þykir, þykist, þykjast

Word List (English to Old Icelandic)

English	Old Icelandic
this	í, sé, sín, sitt, það, þenna, þess, þessa, þessi, þessu, Þetta
Thord (name)	Þórð, Þórðar, Þórði, Þórður
Thordis (name)	Þórdís
Thorgrim (name)	Þorgrímur
Thorolf (name)	Þórólf, Þórólfi, Þórólfur
Thorolf's (name)	Þórólfs
Thorstein (name)	Þorstein, Þorstein, Þorsteini, Þorsteinn
Thorstein's (name)	Þorsteini, Þorsteins
Thorvald (name)	Þorvaldi, Þorvaldi, Þorvaldur
though	þó, þótt
thought	hugðu, hugsar, þótti, þóttu, þykir
threat	hót
three	þriggja, þrír, þrjá, þrjár
through	gegnum
Thufur (place)	Þúfum
Thvera (place)	Þverá, Þverár
time	tíma
to	á, að, áðu, af, ást, í, það, til, við
to-accept	þiggja
to-do	gera
to-expect	von
together	jafnsaman, saman, saman
to-give	gefa
to-going	atgöngu
to-have	eiga, hafa
to-him	honum
to-invite	bjóða
told	sagði, sagði, sagt, segir, töluðu
to-me	mér
took	tækist, tekur, tók, tókst
took-to	tóku
to-people	mönnum
to-ride	ríða
to-say	segja
to-them	þeim
to-travel	fara
to-you	þér

English	Old Icelandic
trading-men	kaupmenn, kaupmönnum
travel	færi, fara, farið, ferð, ferðar, ferðinni
travelled	fær, farið, Fer, fór, Fóru
travelled-you	fórstu
travelling	farinn, ferð
travels	fer
treacherous	fláráðum
treachery	brekráð
treasures	gripirnir
trim	kvisti
trouble	vandræðum
true	
true	
truly	sannast
trust	trausts
try	freista
trying	reyna
Tunga (place)	Tungu
tunic	kyrtil
turf-stacks	torfstakka
turn	horfa, hverfa, hverfið, snúa
turned	hallaði, Sneri, snerist
twelve	tólf
twice	tvenn
two	tvo

U, u

English	Old Icelandic
unanimously	einhlítt
uncertain	óvíst
understanding	skiljum
un-equal-men	ójafnaðarmenn
un-faring	ófarin
unfriendly	óvinveittur
un-friends	óvinum
un-good	ómæt
unholy	óheilagur
unmanageable	ofstýri
unqualified	óhæfu
un-right-knowing	óréttvís
un-rule	ofríki

Word List (English to Old Icelandic)

English	Old Icelandic
unruliness	róstum
unruly	ofríki
un-substantial-company	óliðdrjúgur
unsuitable	óliðlegt
until	til
up	á, upp, uppi
upped	upp
up-saying	uppsögn
Urdskriduholar (place)	Urðskriðuhóla
us	okkur, oss
usually	jafnan

V, v

vagrancy	verðgang
value	virða
Vellir (place)	Völlu, Völlum
visit	vitja

W, w

wait	bíður
ward-knowing	varðveita
warranted	varða
warriors	kappi
was	á, en, er, sé, væri, var, varð, voru
was-named	hét
way	leið, veg, vegar
way-out	færi
we	vér
wealth	fé, fjár
weaponed	vopnaðir
weapons	vopn, vopns
weathered	veður
we-get	hljótum
welcomed	fagnað
well	féllu, vel
well-willing	vel
went	fór, Fóru, ganga, gekk, gengu, gengur
were	er, eru, Var, vera, voru
west	vestur

English	Old Icelandic
what	en, hvað, hvar, Hverja, hvern, hvert
when	er, Nær, þá, Þegar
where	hvar, varstu
whether	en, hvort
which	er, Hvert, sem
while	stund
white	hvítur
who	er, hver, Hverjir, sem
wife	kona, konu
wife-of	kona
wild	ólman
will	vil, vilja, Viljum
willing	vildi, vilja, viljaður
winter	veturinn
winters	vetra
wisdom	spekt
wish	vil, Vildi, vilja, vilji, viljir, vilt
wished	vildi, vill
wishing	vill
with	á, með, um, við, yrði
with-fleetness	flytjir
with-taken	viðtökur
with-taking	viðtökur
wit-less	vitlaus
word	orði
words	orð, orða, orðið
work	verk
worse	versna
worth	verðugt, verður, virða, virðing
worthiness	virðing
worthy	göfugt, vert
would	mun, mundi, mundu, muni, munu
would-be	munu, værir, verða
wound	sár
wounded	Meiddi, sár
wounding	sár
wounds	sár, sára
wretch	vesalmenni

Y, y

132

Word List (English to Old Icelandic)

English	*Old Icelandic*
you	*þér, þið, þig, þinn, þú, yður, yðvar*
young	*ungur*
your	*þér, yður*
yours	*þína, þinn, þinnar, þinni, þitt, yður*
yourself	*sjálfan*
you-two	*þið*
Yule (name)	*jól*

A Word Comparison of Old Norse and Old Icelandic Words

A Word Comparison of Old Norse and Old Icelandic Words

Old Norse	Old Icelandic	English	Old Norse	Old Icelandic	English
á	af	at	berr	ber	bear
á	af	of	betr	betur	better
áðr	áður	before	bezt	best	best
áðr	áður	earlier	bezta	besta	best
æðimaðr	æðimaður	frenzy-man	beztr	bestur	best
ærit	ærið	plenty-of	bíðr	bíður	wait
ætlat	ætlað	intended	bindr	bindur	bound
ætlat	ætlað	plans	blári	blárri	black
aftr	aftur	back	boðit	boðið	bid
aftr	aftur	down	boðit	boðið	offered
aftr	aftur	return	borit	borið	bear
aftr	aftur	returned	borit	borið	carried
ágætliga	ágætlega	greatly	bræðr	bræður	brothers
aldri	aldrei	never	bregðr	bregður	broke
alizt	alist	homes	bregðr	bregður	drew
allstórmannliga	allstórmannlega	all-great-man-like	brotit	brotið	broken
			búðardurunum	búðardyrunum	the-booth-doors
annarr	annar	another			
annat	annað	another	búit	búið	prepared
annat	annað	other	búningr	búningur	costume
Arnórr	Arnór	Arnor (name)	býðr	býður	invited
ásjá	ásjár	assistance	dauðr	dauður	dead
áskorun	áskoran	challenge	djarfliga	djarflega	boldly
at	að	a	dregr	dregur	drew
at	að	about	drengiligsta	drengilegsta	bravely
at	að	as	drepit	drepið	kill
at	að	at	drepit	drepið	killing
at	að	for	dvölðust	Dvöldust	dwelled
at	að	from	efniligastr	efnilegastur	promising
at	að	has	einhvern	einnhvern	one
at	að	have	ek	eg	I
at	að	in	em	er	am
at	að	it	engir	öngvir	none
at	að	of	erfit	erfið	difficulty
at	að	that	fagnat	fagnað	welcomed
at	að	the	fáliga	fálega	coldly
at	að	to	fáliga	fálega	poorly
átzt	ást	to	fallit	fallið	failed
auðigr	auðigur	rich	fallit	fallið	fallen
barizt	barist	bears	fallit	fallið	make
berist	berjist	fight	fararskjóta	faraskjóta	horses

134

A Word Comparison of Old Norse and Old Icelandic Words

Old Norse	Old Icelandic	English	Old Norse	Old Icelandic	English
farit	farið	fared	heðan	héðan	from-here
farit	farið	gone	heðra	héðra	district
farit	farið	travelled	hefr	hefur	had
fekk	fékk	found	heimskliga	heimsklega	foolishly
fekk	fékk	got	heimskligast	heimsklegast	foolishly
felldr	felldur	falling	heimskr	heimskur	foolishness
fellr	fellur	fell	hekk	hékk	hung
fellu	féllu	well	heldr	heldur	behind
ferr	fer	goes	heldr	heldur	rather
ferr	fer	set-out	helt	hélt	held
ferr	Fer	travelled	helzt	helst	rather
ferr	fer	travels	hendr	hendur	hand
ferr	ferð	going	heraði	héraði	district
ferr	ferð	travel	heruð	héruð	district
fingrgull	fingurgull	gold-ring	heruðum	héruðum	provinces
finnim	finnum	find	hingat	hingað	here
flýgr	flýgur	followed	hittir	hitti	met
flytir	flytjir	with-fleetness	hleypr	hleypur	ran
fólit	fólið	foolishly	hliðhollir	vinhollir	open-whole
fórtu	fórstu	travelled-you	höggr	höggur	striking
fundr	fundur	a-meeting	hon	hún	she
gaumr	gaumur	attention	hugða	hugði	think
gengit	Gengið	gone	hválfinu	hvolfinu	half
gengr	gengur	came	hvárir	hvorir	each
gengr	gengur	went	hvárir	hvorir	opposite
getit	getið	got	hvárirtveggju	hvorirtveggju	either-side
getr	getur	got	hvárt	hvort	how
giftuvænligr	giftuvænlegur	luck-promised	hvárt	hvort	whether
gjafar	gjafir	gifts	hvat	hvað	what
gjafar	gjafir	the-gift	hverir	Hverjir	who
gjafarnar	gjafirnar	the-gifts	hverr	hver	who
góðr	góður	good	hversdagliga	hversdaglega	everyday
graðung	griðung	a-bull	hvítr	hvítur	white
graðungr	Graðungur	bull	íhann	hann	cowardly
graðungrinn	graðungurinn	the-bull	íhlutunarsamr	íhlutunarsamur	in-sharing-together
grunr	grunur	suspect	in	hin	the
Guðmundr	Guðmundur	Gudmund (name)	ina	Hina	the
gullhringr	gullhringur	gold-ring	ina	hina	these
gyrðr	gyrður	buckled	inn	hinn	the
hæðilig	hæðileg	mockery	ins	hins	the
hægligt	hæglegt	easily	inum	hinum	the
hálfsmánaðar	hálfs	half-month's	íss	ís	ice

A Word Comparison of Old Norse and Old Icelandic Words

Old Norse	Old Icelandic	English	Old Norse	Old Icelandic	English
it	*hið*	the	*með*	*við*	with
kærleik	*kærleikum*	friendship	*merkr*	*merkur*	marks
kallaðr	*kallaður*	called	*metnaðr*	*metnaður*	pride
kemr	*kemur*	came	*mik*	*mig*	me
kemr	*kemur*	come	*mik*	*mig*	mine
kemr	*Kemur*	coming	*mik*	*mig*	much
kníf	*hníf*	knife	*mik*	*mig*	my
komim	*komum*	come	*mikit*	*mikið*	much
komit	*komið*	came	*mjök*	*Mjög*	great
komit	*komið*	come	*mjök*	*mjög*	many
kómu	*komu*	came	*mjök*	*mjög*	much
kostr	*kostur*	chose	*morgininn*	*morguninn*	morning
kveldit	*kveldið*	evening	*muna*	*muni*	should
kvista	*kvisti*	trim	*mynda*	*mundi*	should
lætr	*lætur*	had	*myndi*	*mundi*	should
lagðr	*lagður*	laid	*myndi*	*mundi*	would
launmaðrinn	*launmaðurinn*	the-unseen-man	*myndi*	*mundu*	would
			nætr	*nætur*	nights
leggr	*leggur*	lunged	*náliga*	*nálega*	near-to
leikim	*leikum*	sport	*ne*	*en*	nor
lengr	*lengur*	any-longer	*niðr*	*niður*	down
leystr	*leystur*	releasing	*niðr*	*niður*	kinsman
lézt	*lést*	said	*nökkura*	*nokkura*	any
liðfæri	*liðfærri*	company-less	*nökkura*	*nokkura*	several
líðr	*líður*	passed	*nökkura*	*nokkura*	somewhat
liðsinnaðr	*liðsinnaður*	team-minded	*nökkurir*	*nokkurir*	some
liðveizlu	*liðveislu*	assistance	*nökkurr*	*nokkur*	somewhat
liggr	*liggur*	lay	*nökkut*	*nokkuð*	some
lítit	*lítið*	little	*nökkut*	*nokkuð*	something
lízt	*líst*	appears	*nökkut*	*nokkuð*	somewhat
Ljótr	*Ljótur*	Ljot (name)	*norðr*	*norður*	north
lokit	*lokið*	finished	*ófallit*	*ófallið*	misguided
maðr	*maður*	a-man	*ófrýnligr*	*ófrýnlegur*	inconspicuous
maðr	*maður*	man			
maðrinn	*maðurinn*	the-man	*óheilagr*	*óheilagur*	unholy
mætta	*mætti*	might	*ok*	*og*	also
mágsemð	*mágsemd*	in-laws	*ok*	*og*	and
mágsemðar	*mágsemdar*	as-in-laws	*okkr*	*okkur*	us
makligt	*maklegt*	deserve	*Óláfi*	*Ólafi*	Olaf (name)
málamaðr	*málamaður*	law-man	*Óláfr*	*Ólafur*	Olaf (name)
málamaðr	*málamaður*	man-of-law	*Óláfs*	*Ólafs*	Olaf's (name)
málit	*málið*	the-case	*óliðdrjúgr*	*óliðdrjúgur*	un-substantial-company
málit	*málið*	the-matter			

A Word Comparison of Old Norse and Old Icelandic Words

Old Norse	Old Icelandic	English
óliðligt	óliðlegt	unsuitable
ómannligt	ómannlegt	inhumane
ombun	ömbun	return
ór	úr	back-from
ór	úr	from
ór	úr	from-out-of
ór	úr	of
ór	úr	out-of
orðit	orðið	become
orðit	orðið	words
óréttvíss	óréttvís	un-right-knowing
Óttarr	Óttar	Ottar (name)
óvinveittr	óvinveittur	unfriendly
ráðlauss	ráðlaus	ill-advised
ráðligast	ráðlegast	advice
ráðligast	ráðlegast	advisable
réða	réði	decide
réttendum	réttindum	right
reyndi	reyndu	test
riðinn	ráðinn	riding
riðit	riðið	ridden
riðit	riðið	ride
ríðr	ríður	rode
sá	sáu	saw
sæmð	sæmd	honour
sæmðar	sæmdar	honour
sæmðarauki	sæmdarauki	honour
sæmðir	sæmdir	honour
sæmðum	sæmdum	honour
sakar	sakir	conviction
sakar	sakir	for-the-sake-of
sakar	sakir	for-the-sake-of
sakar	sakir	sake
sakar	sakir	the-charges
samit	samið	agreement
sárr	sár	wounded
sé	séu	are
sé	séu	being
segir	svarar	said
sekðan	sektan	outlawed
sekði	sekti	convicted
setit	setið	stay
setr	Setur	set
Sigríðr	Sigríður	Sigrid (name)
sik	sig	him
sik	sig	himself
sik	sig	such
silfrs	silfurs	of-silver
sitr	Situr	stayed
sjándi	sjáandi	seeing
sjau	sjö	seven
skapillr	skapillur	bad-temper
skilði	skildi	separated
skilðist	skildist	separated
skilðu	Skildu	separated
skilðust	Skildust	separated
skilit	skilið	separated
skjöldrinn	Skjöldurinn	the-shield
sköllóttr	sköllóttur	bald
sköruliga	skörulega	boldly
skörungr	skörungur	noble
skylda	skyldi	should
skyli	skuli	shall
skýtr	skýtur	shot
slitit	slitið	dissolved
smæri	smærri	smaller
snarliga	snarlega	quickly
sonr	Son	son
sonr	son	son-of
sonr	sonur	son
sonr	sonur	the-son-of
spekð	spekt	wisdom
spjótit	spjótið	spear
spjótit	spjótið	the-spear
spyrr	spyr	asked
staddr	staddur	standing
Stærimaðr	stærimaður	Stately-man (name)
Stertimaðr	stertimaður	Stately-man (name)
stolit	stolið	stolen
stólkonungrinn	stólkonungurinn	the-emperor
stórmannliga	stórmannlega	great-man-ness

A Word Comparison of Old Norse and Old Icelandic Words

Old Norse	Old Icelandic	English	Old Norse	Old Icelandic	English
stórmannligar	stórmannlegar	great-man-like	þrír	þrjá	three
			þykkir	þykir	consider
suðr	suður	south	þykkir	þykir	seems
sumarit	sumarið	summer	þykkir	Þykir	think
sundr	sundur	asunder	þykkir	þykir	thought
sundrþykki	sundurþykki	discord	þykkist	þykist	think
svá	nú	so	þykkjast	þykjast	realised
svá	svo	so	þykkjast	þykjast	think
systrungr	systrungur	mother's-sister's-son	þykkjumst	Þykist	think
		conversation	tíðenda	tíðinda	news
talit	talið		tigu	tigi	ten
tekit	tekið	taken	tvá	tvo	two
tekizt	tekist	taken	ungr	ungur	young
tekr	tekur	took	útan	utan	abroad
þangat	þangað	from-there	váða	voða	risk
þangat	þangað	there	væra	Væri	be
þat	það	is	ván	von	expected
þat	Það	it	ván	von	to-expect
þat	það	so	vanða	vanda	custom
þat	það	that	vápn	vopn	weapons
þat	það	this	vápnaðir	vopnaðir	weaponed
þat	það	to	vápns	vopns	weapons
þat	þetta	it	vár	vor	spring
þeir	þá	they	várdaga	vordaga	spring-days
þeira	þeirra	of-them	varðveizlu	varðveislu	hospitality
þeira	þeirra	of-they	várn	vorn	our
þeira	þeirra	their	várra	vorra	ours
þeira	þeirra	theirs	vartu	varstu	where
þeira	þeirra	them	váru	voru	was
þeira	þeirra	they	váru	voru	were
þeira	þeirra	they-of	veðr	veður	weathered
þiggr	þiggur	accepted	veizla	veisla	feast
þik	þig	you	veizla	veisla	the-feast
þingit	þingið	the-assembly	veizlu	veislu	feast
þingmaðr	þingmaður	assembly-man	velviljaðr	vel	well-willing
			venzlum	venslum	marriage
þit	þið	you	verðr	verður	becomes
þit	þið	you-two	verðr	verður	worth
Þórðr	Þórður	Thord (name)	verit	verið	been
Þorgrímr	Þorgrímur	Thorgrim (name)	vestr	vestur	west
Þórólfr	Þórólfur	Thorolf (name)	vetrinn	veturinn	winter
			vígsmálit	vígsmálið	fight-the-case
Þorvaldr	Þorvaldur	Thorvald (name)	vilda	Vildi	wish

A Word Comparison of Old Norse and Old Icelandic Words

Old Norse	Old Icelandic	English
vilir	*viljir*	wish
vilja	*vilji*	wish
vill	*vilt*	wish
vindr	*vindur*	the-wind
vinr	*vinur*	a-friend
vinr	*vinur*	friend
virðingarvænligt	*virðingarvænlegt*	respect-kindly
virkit	*virkið*	the-compound
vitlauss	*vitlaus*	wit-less
yðr	*yður*	you
yðr	*yður*	your

The Tale of Thorsteinn House-Power (Old Norse)

The Tale of Thorsteinn House-Power (*Old Norse*)

Old Norse	Literal	English
1	**1**	**1**
Í þann tíma, er Hákon jarl Sigurðarson réð fyrir Noregi, bjó sá bóndi í Gaulardal, er Brynjólfr hét.	At that time, was Hakon earl Son-of-Sigurd ruled over Norway, lived there farmer in Gaulardale, was Brynjolf named.	About the time when Earl Hakon Sigurdson was ruler of Norway, there lived a farmer in Gaulardale, named Brynjolf.
Hann var kallaðr úlfaldi.	He was called Camel.	He was called Brynjolf Camel.
Hann var lendr maðr ok mikil kempa.	He was landed man and great warrior.	He was a landed man and a great warrior.
Kona hans hét Dagný; hún var dóttir Járnskeggja af Yrjum.	Wife his named Dagny she was daughter Iron-Beard of Yrjar.	His wife was named Dagny and she was the daughter of Iron-Beard of Yrjar.
Þau áttu einn son, er Þorsteinn hét.	They had one son, who Thorstein named.	They had one son who was named Thorstein.
Hann var mikill ok sterkr, harðúðigr ok óaflátssamr við hvern, sem eiga var.	He was great and strong, hard-minded and un-indulgent with everyone, as said-of was.	He was large and strong, strong-minded and unflinching with everyone that he spoke with.
Engi var jafnstórr í Noregi, ok trautt fengust þær dyrr, at honum væri hægt um at ganga, ok því var hann kallaðr bæjarmagn, því at hann þótti ofmagni bera flestum húsum.	None were equally-big in Norway, and scarcely got-they there door, that he would possible about to walk, and because was he called House-Power, because that he seemed to-overpower bear most houses.	No one was as big in all Norway, and there was scarcely a door that he could walk through, and he was called House-Power, because he seemed to overpower most houses.
Hann var óþýðr, ok fekk faðir hans honum því skip ok menn, ok var Þorsteinn þá ýmist í hernaði eða í kaupferðum, ok tókst honum hvárttveggja vel.	He was unfriendly, and got father his him therefore a-ship and men, and was Thorstein then either in raiding or in trading-journeys, and took he either well.	He was so unfriendly that his father gave him a ship with some men, and Thorstein was either raiding or trading, and he took to both well.

The Tale of Thorsteinn House-Power (Old Norse)

Old Norse	Literal	English
Í þenna tíma tók ríki í Noregi Óláfr konungr Tryggvason, en Hákon jarl var skorinn á háls af þræli sínum, þeim sem Þormóðr karkr hét.	In that time took kingdom in Norway Olaf the-king Tryggvason, when Hakon earl was cut in the-neck of servant his, then as Thormod Kark named.	It was about this time that King Olaf Tryggvason ruled the kingdom of Norway, when Earl Hakon had his throat slit by one of his servants, who was named Thormod Kark.
Þorsteinn bæjarmagn gerðist hirðmaðr Óláfs konungs.	Thorstein House-Power became court-man Olaf's the-king's.	Thorstein House-Power became a court man of King Olaf's.
Þótti konungi hann röskr maðr ok helt mikit til hans, en ekki var hann mjök kenndr af hirðmönnum.	Thought the-king he brave man and held much to him, but not was he much recognised of court-men.	The king thought he was a brave man and thought highly of him, but he was not liked by the other court-men.
Þótti þeim hann stríðlyndr ok óvæginn, ok hafði konungr hann mjök til þess at fara sendiferðir þær, sem aðrir töldust undan at fara.	Thought they he obstinate and ruthless, and had the-king he great for this to travel missions those, that others considered away from travelling.	They found him obstinate and ruthless, and the king had him going on great missions, that others were reluctant to travel on.
En stundum fór hann kaupferðir at afla konungnum gersema.	About awhile travelled he trading-voyages to provide the-king precious-things.	For a while he went on trading voyages to bring the king treasures.

2

Eitt sinn lá Þorsteinn austr fyrir Bálagarðssíðu, ok gaf honum eigi at sigla.	One occasion lay Thorstein east before Balagardsida, and gave him not to sail.	On one occasion Thorstein lay east near Balagardsida, and he was not given wind to sail.
Gekk hann á land einn morgin, ok er sól var í landsuðri, var Þorsteinn kominn í eitt rjóðr.	Went he to land one morning, and when the-sun was in South-East, was Thorstein coming to a clearing.	He went to land one morning, and when the sun was in the South-East, Thorstein came to a clearing.
Hóll fagr var í rjóðrinu.	Mound beautiful was in the-clearing.	There was a beautiful mound in the clearing.
Hann sá einn kollóttan pilt uppi á hólnum, ok mælti:	He saw a bald-headed boy up on the-mound, and spoke:	He saw a bald-headed boy up on the mound, and he spoke:
"Móðir mín",	"Mother mine",	"Mother mine",

The Tale of Thorsteinn House-Power (Old Norse)

Old Norse	Literal	English
segir hann, "fá þú mér út krókstaf minn ok bandvettlinga, því at ek vil á gandreið fara.	said he, "get you me out crooked-staff mine and mittens, because that I wish to witch-ride go.	he said, "get me my crooked staff and mittens, because I wish to go on a witch ride.
Er nú hátíð í heiminum neðra".	Is now festival in the-world under".	There is now a festival in the underworld".
Þá var snarat út ór hólnum einum krókstaf, sem eldsskara væri.	Then was twisted out from the-mound a crooked-staff, as fire-poker was.	Then a crooked staff was thrown out from the mound, shaped like a poker.
Hann stígr á stafinn ok dregr á sik vettlingana ok keyrir, sem börn eru vön at gera.	He climbed on the-staff and drew of his mitten and the-stick, as children are want to do.	He climbed on the staff and drew on his mittens and began riding the stick, as children often do.
Þorsteinn gengr á hólinn ok mælti slikum orðum sem piltrinn, ok var þegar út kastat staf ok vöttum ok mælt þetta:	Thorstein went to the-mound and spoke such words as the-boy, and was then out cast staff and gloves and spoke this:	Thorstein went to the mound and spoke the same words that the boy had, and then a staff and gloves were cast out and a voice asked:
"Hverr tekr nú við?"	"Who takes now with?"	"Who wants these now?".
"Bjálfi, sonr þinn",	"Bjalfi, son yours",	"Bjalfi, your son",
sagði Þorsteinn.	said Thorstein.	said Thorstein.
Síðan stígr hann á stafinn ok ríðr þar eptir, sem piltrinn fór undan.	Afterwards climbed he on the-staff and rode there after, as the-boy travelled away-from.	Afterwards he climbed on the staff and rode away after the boy.
Þeir kómu at einni móðu ok steyptu sér ofan í hana, ok var því líkast sem þeir væði reyk.	They came to a large-river and cast he down in it, and was it like as they waded-through smoke.	They came to a large river and cast down into it, and it was like they were wading through smoke.
Því næst birti þeim fyrir augum, ok kómu þeir at, sem á fell fram af hömrum.	Then near revealed they before eyes, and came they to, as a-river falling from off a-steep-cliff.	Then revealed before their eyes, they came to where a river was falling from a steep cliff.
Sér Þorsteinn þá byggð mikla ok borg stóra.	Saw Thorstein then settlements great and a-city great.	Thorstein then saw large settlements and a great city.
Þeir stefna til borgarinnar, ok sitr þar fólk yfir borðum.	They directed to the-city, and sat there folk across a-table.	They turned to the city, and there people were sat across a table.

The Tale of Thorsteinn House-Power (Old Norse)

Old Norse	Literal	English
Þeir gengu í höllina, ok var höll skipuð af fólki, ok var þar af engu drukkit utan af silfrkerum.	They went in the-hall, and was the-hall equipped of folk, and were they of nothing drinking except-for of silver.	They walked into the hall, and there were people filling the hall, and they were drinking from nothing but silver cups.
Trapiza stóð á gólfi.	Table stood on the-floor.	A table stood on the floor.
Allt sýndist þeim þar gullligt ok ekki drukkit nema vín.	All seemed they there gold and nothing drunk but wine.	Everything seemed to be gold, and everyone drunk nothing but wine.
Þat þóttist Þorsteinn skilja, at engi maðr sá þá.	That thought Thorstein such, that no man see then.	Then Thorstein realised that no man could see them.
Félagi hans fór með borðum ok henti allt þat, sem niðr fell.	Companion his went along the-tables and caught all that, as down fell.	His companion went along the tables and caught all that fell down from them.
Konungr sat þar í hásæti ok drottning.	The-king sat there in high-seat and the-queen.	The king sat there in the high seat with the queen.
Menn váru glaðir um höllina.	Men were glad about the-hall.	The men about the hall were glad.
Þessu næst sér Þorsteinn, at maðr kom í höllina ok kvaddi konung ok kveðst vera sendr til hans utan af Indíalandi ór fjalli því, er Lúkanus heitir, frá jarli þeim, er þar réð fyrir, ok segir konungi, at hann var huldumaðr.	This next saw Thorstein, that a-man came into the-hall and called the-king and greetings were sent to him out of India from mountains because, that Lucanus named, from the-earl they, that was advised for, and said the-king, that he was a-hidden-man.	Then Thorstein saw that a man had come into the hall and greeted the king, and he sent greetings from the mountains of India because the earl Lucanus ruled there, and he advised the king that he was an elf-man.
Hann færði honum einn gullhring.	He took to-him a gold-ring.	He presented him with a gold ring.
Eigi þóttist konungr betri hring sét hafa, ok fór hringrinn um höllina til sýnis, ok lofuðu hann allir.	Not thought the-king better ring seen had, and went the-ring about the-hall to his, and praised it all.	The king thought that he had not seen a better ring, and it was shown around the hall, and praised by all.
Hann var sundr tekinn í fjórum stöðum.	It was apart taken in four places.	This ring could be taken apart in four sections.
Annan grip sá Þorsteinn, er honum þótti mikils um vert.	Another-thing grabbed seeing Thorstein, that to-him thought much about worth.	Another thing grabbed Thorstein's sight, that he thought might be worth a lot.

The Tale of Thorsteinn House-Power (Old Norse)

Old Norse	Literal	English
Þat var dúkr sá, er lá á konungs borðinu.	It was table-cloth saw, that laid at the-king's table.	It was the table cloth that he saw, which was laid at the king's table.
Hann var með gullligum röndum ok í festir þeir tólf gimsteinar, sem beztir eru.	It was with gold stripes and on fastened there twelve precious-stones, that best were.	It had stripes of gold and was fastened with twelve of the best precious stones.
Gjarna vildi Þorsteinn dúkinn eiga.	Gladly willed Thorstein table-cloth to-own.	Thorstein gladly wished to own the table-cloth.
Kemr honum í hug at treysta á konungs hamingju ok vita, hvárt hann getr ekki nát hringnum.	Came he to think to reckon on the-king's luck and know, whether he get not get-hold-of the-ring.	He came to think about the king's luck and find out whether or not he could get hold of the ring.
Nú sér Þorsteinn, at konungrinn ætlar at draga hringinn á hönd sér.	Now saw Thorstein, that the-king intended to carry the-ring on hand his.	Now Thorstein saw that the king intended to carry the ring on his hand.
Þá greip Þorsteinn hringinn af honum, en annarri hendi tók hann dúkinn, ok fór allr matr í saur, en Þorsteinn hljóp á dyrr, en krókstafr hans varð honum eptir í höllinni.	Then grabbed Thorstein the-ring off him, then another hand took he the-table-cloth, and went all food in the-mud, then Thorstein ran to the-door, but crooked-stick his was him behind in the-hall.	Then Thorstein grabbed the ring off him, and then with his other hand he took the table cloth, and all the food fell in the mud, and then Thorstein ran to the door, but the crooked stick was behind him in the hall.
Verðr nú upphlaup mikit, hlaupa menn út síðan ok sjá, hvar Þorsteinn ferr, ok stefna eptir honum.	Became now uproar great, ran men out after and saw, where Thorstein went, and directed after him.	There now became a great uproar, and men ran out afterwards and saw where Thorstein went and started after him.
Sér hann nú, at þeir muni geta nát honum.	Saw he now, that they would get hold-of him.	He saw now that they would catch him.
Hann mælti þá:	He spoke then:	He then spoke:
"Ef þú ert svá góðr, Óláfr konungr, sem ek treysti mikit til þín, þá veittu mér lið".	"If you are so good, Olaf king, as I trust much to you, then grant me assistance".	"If you are so good king Olaf, as I trust you are, then grant me assistance".
En svá var Þorsteinn frár, at þeir kómust ekki fyrir hann, fyrr en hann kom at ánni, ok staldraði hann þá við.	Then so was Thorstein swift, that they came not for him, before that he came to the-river, and lingered he then with.	Then Thorstein was so fast, that they could not catch him before he came to the river, where he had to wait.

The Tale of Thorsteinn House-Power (Old Norse)

Old Norse	Literal	English
Þeir slógu hring um hann, en Þorsteinn varðist vel ok drap ótal marga, áðr förunautr hans kom ok færði honum stafinn, ok hurfu þeir þegar í móðuna.	They formed a-circle around him, and Thorstein defended well and killed countless many, after companion his came and brought him the-stick, and disappeared they straightaway into the-river.	They formed a circle around him, and Thorstein defended himself well killing a countless many of them, and afterwards his companion came and brought him the stick, and they disappeared straightaway into the river.
Komu þeir aptr á inn sama hól sem fyrr gátum vér, þá sól var í vestri.	Came they back to the same hill as before opening was, then the-sun was in the-west.	They came back to the same hill where the opening had been before, and then the sun was in the west.
Kastaði piltrinn þá inn stafnum ok klæðsekk þeim, sem hann hafði fylldan af góðum krásum, ok svá gerði Þorsteinn.	Cast the-boy then the stick and sack theirs, which he had filled of good food, and so did Thorstein.	The boy cast the stick and their sack, which he had filled with good food, and so did Thorstein.
Kollsveinn hljóp inn, en Þorsteinn nam staðar við glugginn.	The-boy ran in, but Thorstein took to-stand by the-skylight.	They boy ran inside, but Thorstein waited by a skylight window.
Hann sá þar tvær konur, ok vaf önnur guðvef, en önnur ruggaði barni.	He saw then two women, and wove one precious-cloth, and another rocking a-baby.	He then saw two women, and one wove precious cloth, and another was rocking a baby.
Sú mælti:	So spoke:	So they spoke:
"Hvat dvelr hann Bjálfa, bróður þinn?"	"What delays him Bjalfi, brother yours?"	"What delays your brother Bjalfi?".
"Ekki hefir hann mér fylgt í dag?"	"Not has he me followed to day?"	"Has he not followed me today?",
sagði hann.	said he.	he said.
"Hverr hefir þá farit með krókstafinn?"	"Who has then gone with the-crooked-stick?"	"Who has gone with the crooked-stick then?" she said.
segir hún.	said she.	"That was Thorstein House-Power",
"Þat var Þorsteinn bæjarmagn",	"That was Thorstein House-Power",	said Kollsvein,
segir Kollsveinn, "hirðmaðr Óláfs konungs.	said Kollsvein, "court-man Olaf's the-king's.	"a court man of King Olaf's.

The Tale of Thorsteinn House-Power (Old Norse)

Old Norse	Literal	English
Kom hann okkr í mikinn vanda, því at hann hafði ór undirheimum þau þing, at eigi munu slík í Noregi, ok var við því búit, at vit mundum drepnir, er hann kastaði stafnum í hendr þeim, ok eltu þeir hann til niðrgangs, ok þá færði ek honum stafinn, ok víst er hann hraustr maðr, því at eigi veit ek, hversu marga hann drap".	Came he us in much difficulty, because that he had away-from under-world their assembly, which not would-be such in Norway, and were with therefore prepared, to know would-be killed, when he cast stick in hand theirs, and chased they him to down-going, and then took I to-him the-stick, and certainly was he brave man, because that not know I, how-so many men killed".	He has brought us unto much difficulty by stealing from the assembly in the underworld, the like of which aren't to be found in Norway, and was nearly killed when he threw his stick into their hands, and they were chasing him to his death, and then I took the stick to him, and he certainly was a brave man, because I do not know how many men were killed".
Ok nú laukst aptr haugrinn.	And now closed back the-mound.	And now the mound closed.
Fór Þorsteinn nú til sinna manna, ok sigldu þaðan til Noregs, ok fann Óláf konung austr í Vík ok færði honum gersemi þessi ok sagði frá ferðum sínum, ok fannst mönnum mikit um.	Went Thorstein now to his men, and sailed from-there to Norway, and found Olaf the-king east in Vik and brought him treasures these and said from voyage his, and found men much about.	Thorstein now went to his men, and sailed from there to Norway, and found King Olaf at Vik in the east, and brought him the treasures and told him of his voyage, and people thought much about it.
Konungr bauð at gefa Þorsteini lén mikit, en hann kveðst enn vilja fara eina ferð í Austrveg.	The-king offered to give Thorstein a-fee great, but he said but wished travel one voyage to Eastern-Lands.	The king offered to give Thorstein a great fee but he said that he wished to travel on a voyage to the Eastern-Lands.
Var hann nú með konungi um vetrinn.	Was he now with the-king about winter.	He was now with the king over the winter.

3

At vári bjó Þorsteinn skip sitt.	In spring prepared Thorstein ship his.	In spring Thorstein prepared his ship.
Hann hafði snekkju ok fjóra menn ok tuttugu.	He had a-sailboat and four men and twenty.	He had a sailboat and twenty four men.
Ok er hann kom við Jamtaland, lá hann í höfn einn dag, ok gekk hann á land at skemmta sér.	And when he came to Jamtland, lay he in the-harbour one day, and went he to land to amuse himself.	And when he came to Jamtland, he lay in port one day, and he went ashore to amuse himself.
Hann kom í eitt rjóðr.	He came to a clearing.	He came to a clearing.

The Tale of Thorsteinn House-Power (Old Norse)

Old Norse	Literal	English
Þar var einn mikill steinn.	There was a large stone.	There was a large stone.
Skammt þaðan sá hann einn dverg furðuliga ljótan, ok grenjaði upp yfir sik.	A-short-distance from-there saw he a dwarf exceedingly hideous, and howling up over himself.	A short distance from there he saw a dwarf strangely ugly, and he was howling about himself.
Sýndist Þorsteini kjaptrinn snúinn út at eyranu, en öðrum megin nefit niðr at kjaptinum.	Thought Thorstein jaw twisted out at ears, on one side nose below the mouth.	It seemed to Thorstein that his jaw twisted up to the ear on one side and on the other side his nose overlapped his mouth.
Þorsteinn segir, hví hann léti svá heimsliga.	Thorstein said, why he made so foolishly.	Thorstein asked him why he was behaving so foolishly.
"Þú, góði maðr",	"You, good man",	"You, good man",
sagði hann, "undrast eigi.	said he, "wonder not.	he said,
Sér þú eigi þann mikla örn, er þar flýgr?	See you not that great eagle, that there flies?	"it is no wonder.
Hann hefir tekit son minn.	He had taken son mine.	Do you not see the great eagle that flies there? He's taken my son.
Ætla ek þat, at sá ófögnuðr sé sendr af Óðni, en ek spring, ef ek missi barnit".	Suppose I that, it so unhappy he-is sent of Odin, that I burst, if I lost child".	I think that the unhappy one was sent by Odin, but I will explode if I lose my child".
Þorsteinn skaut eptir erninum, ok kom undir vænginn, ok datt hann dauðr niðr, en Þorsteinn henti dvergsbarnit á lopti ok færði föðurnum, en dvergrinn varð feginn mjök ok mælti:	Thorstein shot after the-eagle, and came down the-wing, and fell he dead down, but Thorstein caught the-dwarf's-boy from-the-sky and brought to-the-father, the dwarf was relieved much and spoke:	Thorstein shot at the eagle, and it came down on the wing, and he fell down dead, but Thorstein caught the dwarf's boy as he fell from the sky, and brought it to his father, and the dwarf was relieved and spoke
"Þér á ek at launa lífgjöf ok sonr minn, ok kjós þér nú fyrir laun í gulli ok silfri".	"To-you that I to repay life-gift and son mine, and choose to-you now for to-repay in gold and silver".	"To you I owe a great debt for saving my son's life, and I choose to repay you in gold and silver".
"Græð þú fyrst son þinn",	"Tend-to you first son yours",	"Tend to your son first",
sagði Þorsteinn; "er ek eigi vanr at taka mútur á afli mínu".	said Thorstein "that I not accustomed to take payment for strength mine".	said Thorstein, "because I am not accustomed to taking payment for my strength".

The Tale of Thorsteinn House-Power (Old Norse)

Old Norse	Literal	English
"Eigi væri mér at óskyldara at launa",	"Not should-be to-me that less-should to repay",	"That should not make me repay you any less",
segir dvergrinn.	said the-dwarf.	said the dwarf.
"Mun þér ekki þykkja framboðligr serkr minn af sauða ullu, en eigi muntu á sundi mæðast ok eigi sár fá, ef þú hefir hann næst þér".	"Would you not value be-offered shirt mine of wether's wool, that not shall-you to swimming get-tired and not wound get, if you have it next to-you".	"Would you not value if I offered you my shirt of ram's wool, for you shall never get tired when swimming and never be wounded if you wear it next to your skin".
Þorsteinn fór í serkinn, ok var honum mátuligr, en honum sýndist dvergnum of lítill.	Thorstein went to-the-shirt, and was he fitting, though to-him seemed the-dwarf of small.	Thorstein tried on the shirt, and it fit him, even though it seemed too small for the dwarf.
Hann tók ok silfrhring ór pungi sínum ok gaf Þorsteini ok bað hann vel geyma ok sagði honum aldri féfátt verða mundu, meðan hann ætti hringinn.	He took also silver-ring from pouch his and gave Thorstein and asked him well retain and said he never lack-of-money become would, as-long-as he had the-ring.	He also took a silver ring from his pouch and gave it to Thorstein and asked him to keep it safe saying that he would never lack money as long as he had the ring.
Síðan tók hann einn stein svartan ok gaf Þorsteini, "ok ef þú felr hann í lófa þér, sér þik engi.	Afterwards took he a stone black and gave Thorstein, "and if you fold it in promise to-you, see you none.	Afterwards he took a black stone and gave it to Thorstein: "and if you fold it in your hand in promise, no one shall see you.
Eigi hefi ek fleira, þat þér megi gagn at vera.	Not have I more, that to-you may benefit to be.	I do not have any more that may be of benefit to you.
Hall einn vil ek gefa þér til skemmtunar".	Piece-of-marble one will I give to-you for amusement".	There is a piece of marble that I will give to you for your amusement".
Tók hann þá hallinn ór pungi sínum.	Took he then the-piece-of-marble from pouch his.	He took the piece of marble then from his pouch.
Fylgdi honum einn stálbroddr.	Following it a steel-point.	There followed a steel point.
Hallrinn var þríhyrndr.	The-piece-of-marble was three-sided.	The piece of marble was three sided.
Hann var hvítr í miðju, en rauðr öðrum megin, en gul rönd utan um.	It was white in the-middle, and red other side, and gold around outside about.	It was white in the middle, red on one side, and gold around the outside.
Dvergrinn mælti:	The-dwarf said:	The dwarf said:

The Tale of Thorsteinn House-Power (Old Norse)

Old Norse	Literal	English
"Ef þú pjakkar broddinum á hallinn, þar sem hann er hvítr, þá kemr haglhríð svá mikil, at engi þorir móti at sjá.	"If you prick the-point of the-piece-of-marble, there where it is white, then comes hailstorm so great, that none dare to-meet to see.	"If you prick the point of the piece of marble where it is white, then there will come a hailstorm so great that none will dare to look towards it.
En ef þú vilt þíða þann snjó, þá skaltu pjakka þar, sem gulr er hallrinn, ok kemr þá sólskin, svá at allt bræðir.	Then if you wish thaw then snow, then shall-you prick there, where gold is the-marble, and comes then sunshine, so that all thaws.	Then if you wish to thaw the snow, then you should prick there, where the marble is gold, and then there will come sunshine, so that everything thaws.
En ef þú pjakkar þar í, sem rautt er, þá kemr þar ór eldr ok eimyrja með gneistaflaug, svá at engi má móti at sjá.	Then if you prick there in, where red is, then comes there out-of fire and embers with a-shower-of-sparks, so that none may meet to see.	Then if you prick there, where it is red, then there will come embers of fire with a shower of sparks, so much that none will dare to look towards
Þú mátt ok hæfa þat, sem þú vilt, með broddinum ok hallinum, ok hann kemr sjálfr aptr í hönd þér, þegar þú kallar.	You may also hit that, whatever you wish, with the-point and the-marble, and it comes itself back in hand to-you, as-soon-as you call.	You may also hit, whatever you wish, with the point and the marble, and it will come back by itself into your hand, as soon as you call for them.
Get ek nú ekki launat þér fleira at sinni".	Guess I now not repay you more than this".	I guess now that I cannot repay you more than this".
Þorsteinn þakkar honum gjafirnar.	Thorstein thanked him the-gifts.	Thorstein thanked him for the gifts.
Fór hann nú til sinna manna, ok var honum þessi ferð betr farin en ófarin.	Went he now to his men, and was to-him this journey better gone than unfinished.	He now went to his men, and to him the journey had gone better than when it was unfinished.
Þessu næst gefr þeim byr ok sigla í Austrveginn.	This next given them fair-wind and sailed to Eastern-Lands.	Next they were given a favourable wind and sailed to the Eastern-Lands.
Koma nú á fyrir þeim myrkr ok hafvillur, ok vita þeir ekki, hvar þeir fara, ok var þat hálfan mánuð, at þessi villa helzt.	Came now to before them fog and open-sea, and knew they not, where they travelled, and was that half a-month, that this lost-way held.	Now a fog came before them in the open sea, and they did not know where they travelled, and this held for half a month.

4   4   4

The Tale of Thorsteinn House-Power (Old Norse)

Old Norse	Literal	English
Þat var eitt kvöld, at þeir urðu varir við land.	It was one evening, that they became aware with land.	It was one evening that they were aware that they were close to land.
Köstuðu þeir nú akkerum ok lágu þar um nóttina.	Cast they now anchor and laid there about the-night.	They cast anchor and lay there overnight.
Um morguninn var gott veðr ok sólskin fagrt.	About morning was good weather and sunshine fair.	In the morning the weather was good with fair sunshine.
Váru þeir þá komnir á einn fjörð langan, ok sjá þeir þar hlíðir fagrar ok skóga.	Were they then come to a fjord long, and saw they there slope fair and forests.	They came to a long fjord, and saw fair slopes and forests.
Engi maðr var sá innanborðs, at þetta land þekkti.	No man was saw aboard, that this land knew.	There was no man aboard that saw the land and knew this land.
Ekki sáu þeir kvikt, hvárki dýr né fugla.	Not saw they living-thing, neither wild-animals nor birds.	They saw no living thing, neither animals nor birds.
Reistu þeir nú tjald á landi ok bjuggust vel um.	Raised they now tents on the-land and settled well about.	They now raised tents on the land and settled there well.
At morgni mælti Þorsteinn til sinna manna:	At morning spoke Thorstein to his men:	At morning Thorstein spoke to his men:
"Ek vil gera yðr kunnigt um ætlan mína.	"I wish to-make you know about intentions mine.	"I wish to let you know about my intentions.
Þér skuluð bíða mín hér sex nætr.	You should await me here six nights.	You should wait for me here for six nights.
Ætla ek mér at kanna land þetta".	Intend I me to explore the-land this".	It is my intention to explore this land.
Þeim þótti mikit fyrir því ok vilja með honum fara, en Þorsteinn vill þat eigi, "ok ef ek kem eigi aptr, áðr sjau sólir eru af himni",	They thought much for therefore and wished with him to-travel, but Thorstein wished that not, "and if I come not back, after seven suns they-are of the-sky",	They thought much of this because they also wished to travel with him, but Thorstein did not wish for that, "and if I do not come back before the seventh sunset in the sky",
segir hann, "þá skuluð þér sigla heim ok segja svá Óláfi konungi, at mér mun ekki auðit verða aptr at koma".	said he, "then should you sail home and tell so Olaf the-king, that I should not fated be return to come".	he said, "then you should sail home and tell King Olaf that I am not fated to return home".

The Tale of Thorsteinn House-Power (Old Norse)

Old Norse	Literal	English
Gengu þeir þá með honum upp á skóginn.	Went they then with him up to the-forests.	They went with him up to the forests.
Því næst hvarf hann þeim, ok fóru þeir aptr til skips ok breyttu eptir því, sem Þorsteinn bauð þeim.	Then next disappeared he from-them, and went they back to the-ships and behaved after accordingly, as Thorstein asked them.	Then next he disappeared from their sight, and they went back to the ships and behaved, as Thorstein had asked them.
Nú er at segja af Þorsteini, at allan þann dag gengr hann um mörkina ok verðr við ekki varr.	Now is to say that Thorstein, about all the day went he about the-trees and came with not aware.	Now is to say of Thorstein, that all day he went through the trees and was not aware of anything.
En at áliðnum degi kemr hann á eina braut breiða.	Then that following day came he to a way broad.	Then the following day he came to a broad road.
Hann gekk eptir brautinni, þangat til at aptnaði.	He went after turned-away, from-there to the the-evening.	He turned to follow it until the evening.
Gekk hann þá brott af brautinni ok víkr at einni stórri eik ok stígr upp í hana.	Went he then away of turning and moved towards a large oak and climbed up it he.	He turned off the track and moved towards a large oak tree and he climbed up it.
Var þar nóg rúm í at liggja.	Was there enough room of to lie-down.	There was enough room for him to lie down.
Sefr hann þar um nóttina.	Slept he there about the-night.	He slept there for the night.
En er sólin kom upp, heyrir hann dunur miklar ok manna mál.	When that sunrise came up, heard he a-din great and men's conversations.	When sunrise came, he heard a great din and men talking.
Sá hann þá, hvar margir menn ríða.	Saw he then, were many men riding.	He then saw that there were many man riding.
Þeir váru tveir ok tuttugu.	They were two and twenty.	There were twenty two.
Þá bar svá skjótt um fram.	Then bore so swiftly about from.	They came so swiftly past.
Undraðist Þorsteinn mjök vöxt þeira.	Surprised Thorstein much grown they-were.	Thorstein was surprised by how large they were.
Hafði hann eigi sét jafnstóra menn fyrr.	Had he not seen equally-large men before.	He had not seen men as large before.
Þorsteinn klæðir sik.	Thorstein clothed himself.	Thorstein clothed himself.

The Tale of Thorsteinn House-Power (Old Norse)

Old Norse	Literal	English
Líðr nú morgininn til þess, at sól er komin í landsuðr.	Passed now morning to this, that the-sun was coming to the-south-east.	Now the morning passed so that the sun was coming to the South-East.

5

Old Norse	Literal	English
Nú sér Þorsteinn þrjá menn ríða vel vápnaða ok svá stóra, at enga menn sá hann fyrr jafnstóra.	Now saw Thorstein three men riding well weaponed and saw great, that none men saw him before equally-as-big.	Now Thorstein saw three men riding well armed and very large, no men had he seen equally as big.
Sá var mestr, er í miðit reið, í gullskotnum klæðum á bleikum hesti, en hinir tveir riðu á grám hestum í rauðum skarlatsklæðum.	So was the-most, then in the-middle riding, in gold-trimmed clothes a pale horse, but the-other two rode on grey horses in red scarlet-clothing.	The most large, then riding in the middle, was in gold-trimmed clothes on a pale horse, but the other two rode on grey horses in red scarlet clothing.
En er þeir kómu þar gegnt, sem Þorsteinn var, mælti sá, sem fyrir þeim var, ok nam staðar:	And when they came there opposite, where Thorstein was, spoke so, as for they were, and took standing:	And when they came opposite where Thorstein was, they spoke where they were, and stood:
"Hvat er kvikt í eikinni?"	"What is alive in the-oak?"	"What is alive in that oak?"
Þorsteinn gekk þá á veginn fyrir þá ok heilsaði þeim, en þeir ráku upp hlátr mikinn, ok mælti inn mikli maðr:	Thorstein went then to the-road before-them then and greeted them, but they drove up laughter much, and spoke the larger man:	Thorstein then went to the road before them and then greeted them, but they erupted with much laughter, and the larger man spoke:
"Sjaldsénir eru oss þvílíkir menn, eða hvert er nafn þitt, eða hvaðan ertu?"	"Rarely-seen are us the-like men, but what is name yours, and from-where are-you?"	"Rarely have we seen the like of such a man, but what is your name, and where are you from?"
Þorsteinn nefndi sik ok kveðst vera kallaðr bæjarmagn, "en kyn mitt er í Noregi.	Thorstein named himself and said being called House-Power, "and kin mine is in Norway.	Thorstein named himself and said about-being called House-Power, "and my kin is in Norway.
Er ek hirðmaðr Óláfs konungs".	Am I court-man Olaf's the-king".	I am a court man of King Olaf".
Inn mikli maðr brosti ok mælti:	The largest man burst-out-laughing and said:	The largest man burst out laughing and said:
"Mest er logit frá hirðprýði hans, ef hann hefir engan vaskligri.	"Mostly is a-lie from court his, if he has no-one braver.	"Most about his court must be lies if he has no one braver.

The Tale of Thorsteinn House-Power (Old Norse)

Old Norse	Literal	English
Þykki mér þú heldr mega heita bæjarbarn en bæjarmagn".	Think me you rather may be-named House-Child than House-Power".	I think you may rather be called House-Child than House-Power".
"Lát nokkut fylgja nafnfesti",	"Have some following naming-gift",	"Give me a naming gift then",
segir Þorsteinn.	said Thorstein.	said Thorstein.
Inn mikli maðr tók fingrgull ok gaf Þorsteini.	The largest man took finger-gold and gave Thorstein.	The largest man took a gold ring from his finger and gave it to Thorstein.
Þat vá þrjá aura.	That was three ounces.	It was three ounces.
Þorsteinn mælti:	Thorstein spoke:	Thorstein spoke:
"Hvert er þitt nafn, eða hverrar ættar ertu, eða í hvert land er ek kominn?"	"What is your name, and whose lineage are-you, and in what land have I come?"	"What is your name, and whose lineage are you, and in what land have I come?"
"Goðmundr heiti ek.	"Godmund named I.	"I am named Godmund.
Ræð er þar fyrir, sem á Glæsisvöllum heitir.	Ruler am here over, which is Glasir-Plains named.	I rule over here, which is named Glasir-Plains.
Þar þjónar til þat land, er Risaland heitir.	There serve to that land, which Giant-Land named.	There serves to that land, which is named Giant-Land.
Ek er konungsson, en mínir sveinar heitir annarr Fullsterkr, en annarr Allsterkr, eða sáttu enga menn ríða hér um í morgin?"	I am a-king's-son, and my companions named one Full-Strong, and another All-Strong, and saw-you any men riding here about in the-morning?"	I am a king's son and my companions, one is named Full-Strong, and the other All-Strong, and did you see any men riding through here in the morning?"
Þorsteinn mælti:	Thorstein spoke:	Thorstein spoke:
"Hér riðu um tveir menn ok tuttugu ok létu eigi lítinn".	"Here rode about two men and twenty and had none little".	"Twenty two men rode through here and none were little".
"Þeir eru sveinar mínir",	"They were men mine",	"They were my men",
segir Goðmundr.	said Godmund.	said Godmund.
"Þat land liggr hér næst, er Jötunheimar heitir.	"That land lying here next-to, is Giant-Land named.	"That land lying next to here is named Giant-Land.

The Tale of Thorsteinn House-Power (Old Norse)

Old Norse	Literal	English
Þar ræðr sá konungr, er Geirröðr heitir.	There rules so the-king, who Geirrod named.	So there rules the king who is named Geirrod.
Undir hann erum vér skattgildir.	Under him are we tributaries.	We are tributaries under him.
Faðir minn hét Úlfheðinn trausti.	Father mine is-named Ulfhedin Trusty.	My father is named Ulfhedin Trusty.
Hann var kallaðr Goðmundr sem allir aðrir, þeir á Glæsisvöllum búa.	He was called Godmund as all others, they who Glasir-Plains live.	He was called Godmund as are all others who live in Glasir-Plains.
En faðir minn fór í Geirröðargarða at afhenda konungi skatta sína, ok í þeiri ferð fekk hann bana.	But father mine went to Geirrod's-Town to of-hand the-king tax his, and on their journey got he death.	But my father went to Geirrod's-Town to hand taxes to the king, but on their journey they got death.
Hefir konungr gert mér boð, at ek skyldi drekka erfi eptir föður minn ok taka slíkar nafnbætr sem faðir minn hafði, en þó unum vér illa við at þjóna Jötnum".	Has the-king made me an-invite, that I should drink inheritance after father mine and take such name-titles as father mine had, but though happy we badly with that serving Giants".	The king has made me an invite, for me to drink to his honour and take such titles that my father had, but we are not happy about serving giants".
"Hví riðu yðrir menn undan?"	"Why rode your men before?",	"Why did your men ride before?",
segir Þorsteinn.	said Thorstein.	said Thorstein.
"Mikil á skilr land vort",	"Great is separating land ours",	"There is a great separation of our land",
segir Goðmundr.	said Godmund.	said Godmund.
"Sú heitir Hemra.	"So named Hemra.	"It is called Hemra.
Hún er svá djúp ok ströng, at hana vaða engir hestar nema þeir, sem vér kumpánar eigum.	She is so deep and strong, that she wades no horses except they, which we fellows own.	It is so deep and strong, that no horses can wade it, except for the three which we are on.
Skulu hinir ríða fyrir uppsprettu árinnar, ok finnumst vér í kveld".	Shall others ride before up-spring the-river, and meet we in the-evening".	The others shall ride before the river spring, and we will meet in the evening".
"Þat mundi skemmtan at fara með yðr",	"That could-be amusement to travel with you",	"It could be an amusement to travel with you",

The Tale of Thorsteinn House-Power (Old Norse)

Old Norse	Literal	English
segir Þorsteinn, "ok sjá, hvat þar verðr til tíðenda".	said Thorstein, "and see, what there becomes to news".	said Thorstein, "and see what happens".
"Eigi veit ek, hversu þat hentar",	"Not know I, how-so that suits",	"I do not know how that suits",
segir Goðmundr, "því at þú munt kristinn".	said Godmund, "because that you must-be Christian".	said Godmund", because you must be a Christian".
"Ek mun mik ábyrgjast",	"I could myself take-care-of",	"I can take care of myself",
segir Þorsteinn.	said Thorstein.	said Thorstein.
"Ekki vilda ek þú hlytir vánt af mér",	"Not wish I you to-get difficulty from me",	"I do not wish for you to get any difficulty from me",
sagði Goðmundr, "en ef Óláfr konungr vill leggja gæfu á með oss, þá mundi ek framt á treysta, at þú færir".	said Godmund, "but if Olaf the-king will grant luck then with us, then should I provide to trust, that you travel".	said Godmund", but if King Olaf will grant you luck to travel with us, then I shall trust you to travel".
Þorsteinn segist því heita vilja.	Thorstein said accordingly promised he-wished.	Thorstein gave him his word as he wished.
Goðmundr biðr hann fara á bak með sér, ok svá gerði hann.	Godmund asked him to-travel on the-back with him, and so did he.	Godmund asked him to travel back with him, and so he did.
Ríða þeir nú til árinnar.	Rode they now to the-river.	They now rode to the river.
Var þar eitt hús, ok tóku þeir þar önnur klæði ok klæddu sik ok sína hesta.	Was there a house, and took they there other clothes and dressed themselves and their horses.	There was a house, and they took their other clothes and dressed themselves and their horses.
Þau klæði váru þeirar náttúru, at ekki festi vatn á þeim, en vatnit var svá kalt, at þegar hljóp drep í, ef nokkut vöknaði.	Their clothes were there natured, that not joined the-water to them, about the-water was so cold, that there ran gangrene to, if anything became-wet.	Their clothes were of a nature that the water could not touch them, because the water was so cold, that gangrene ran if anything became wet.
Riðu þeir nú yfir ána.	Rode they now across the-river.	They now rode across the river.
Hestarnir óðu sterkliga.	The-horses waded strongly.	The horses waded strongly.
Hestr Goðmundar rasaði, ok varð Þorsteinn vátr á tánni, ok hljóp þegar drep í.	Horse Godmund's tumbled, and became Thorstein water about toe, and ran there gangrene to.	Godmund's horse tumbled, and Thorstein's toe came into the water, and there ran gangrene.

The Tale of Thorsteinn House-Power (Old Norse)

Old Norse	Literal	English
En er þeir kómu af ánni, breiddu þeir niðr klæðin til þerris.	When that they came off the-river, spread they down clothes to dry.	When they came off the river, they spread their clothes to dry.
Þorsteinn hjó af sér tána, ok fannst þeim mikit um hreysti hans.	Thorstein hewed off his toe, and found they much about bravery his.	Thorstein cut his toe off, and they thought much of his bravery.
Ríða þeir nú sinn veg.	Rode they now their way.	They now rode on their way.
Bað Þorsteinn þá eigi fela sik, "því at ek kann at gera þann hulinshjálm, at mik sér engi".	Asked Thorstein then not hide him, "because that I can to make then helm-of-invisibility, that me see none".	Thorstein asked them not to hide him, "because I have a helm of invisibility, that none see me".
Goðmundr segir þat góða kunnáttu.	Godmund said that good skills.	Godmund said that was a good skill.
Kómu þeir nú til borgarinnar, ok kómu menn Goðmundar í móti honum.	Came they now to the-town, and came men Godmund's to meet him.	They now came to the town, and Godmund's men came to meet him.
Riðu þeir nú í borgina.	Rode they now into the-town.	They now rode into the town.
Mátti þar nú heyra alls háttar hljóðfæri, en ekki þótti Þorsteini af setning slegit.	Could they now hear all kinds musical-instruments, but not thought Thorstein of the-setting struck.	They could now hear all kinds of musical instruments, but Thorstein did not think much of the settings being played.
Geirröðr konungr kom nú í mót þeim ok fagnaði þeim vel, ok var þeim skipat eitt steinhús eða höll at sofa í ok menn til fengnir at leiða hesta þeira á stall.	Geirrod the-king came now to meet them and celebrated they well, and were they directed-to a stone-house and a-hall to sleep in and men to get to led horses there to stable.	King Geirrod now came to meet them and they were well welcomed, and they were directed to a stone house and a hall to sleep in, and men led their horses to a stable.
Var Goðmundr leiddr í konungshöll.	Was Godmund led to the-king's-hall.	Godmund was led to the king's hall.
Konungr sat í hásæti ok jarl sá hjá honum, er Agði hét.	The-king sat on a-high-seat and the-earl so beside him, was Agdi named.	The king sat on a high seat and the earl so beside him, was named Agdi.
Hann réð fyrir því heraði, er Grundir heita.	He ruled over therefore district, was Grundir named.	He ruled over the district, which was named Grundir.
Þat er á millum Risalands ok Jötunheima.	It was in between Giant-Land and Giant-Home.	It was in between Giant-Land and Giant-Home.

The Tale of Thorsteinn House-Power (Old Norse)

Old Norse	Literal	English
Hann hafði atsetu at Gnípalundi.	He had a-seat at Gnipalund.	He had an estate at Gnipalund.
Hann var fjölkunnigr, ok menn hans váru tröllum líkari en mönnum.	He was skilled-in-magic, and men his were trolls like than men.	He was skilled in magic, and his men were more like trolls than men.
Goðmundr settist á skörina fyrir öndvegit gagnvart konungi.	Godmund sat beside high-seat before opposite going-from the-king.	Godmund sat beside the high seat opposite the king.
Var sá siðr þeira, at konungsson skyldi ekki í hásæti sitja, fyrr en hann hafði tekit nafnbætr eptir föður sinn ok drukkit væri it fyrsta full.	Was so the-custom theirs, that the-king's-son should not in high-seat sit, before that he had taken name-titles after father his and drink-to was the first drunk.	It was their custom, that the king's son should not sit in the high seat, before he had taken his titles and the first drink to honour his father had been drunk.
Ríss þar nú upp in vænsta veizla, ok drukku menn glaðir ok kátir ok fóru síðan at sofa.	Rose there now up the good feast, and drank men gladly and merry and went then to sleep.	They now rose up and had a good feast, and the men drank gladly and merrily, and then went to sleep.
En er Goðmundr kom í hús sitt, sýndi Þorsteinn sik.	And when Godmund came to the-house his, showed Thorstein himself.	And when Godmund came to his house, Thorstein showed himself.
Hlógu þeir at honum.	Laughed they at him.	They laughed at him.
Goðmundr sagði mönnum sínum, hverr hann var, ok bað þá ekki hafa hann at hlátri.	Godmund told the-men his, who he was, and ordered then not have he to laughter.	Godmund told his men who he was and ordered them not to laugh at him.
Ok sofa þeir af um nóttina.	And slept they of through the-night.	And they slept through the night.

6   6   6

Nú er morginn kom, váru þeir snemma á fótum.	Now when morning came, were they early about feet.	Now when morning came, they were up early and on their feet.
Var Goðmundr leiddr til konungs hallar.	Was Godmund led to the-king's hall.	Godmund was led to the king's hall.
Konungr fagnaði honum vel.	The-king celebrated him well.	The king welcomed him well.
"Viljum vér nú vita",	"Wish we now know",	"We wish to know",

The Tale of Thorsteinn House-Power (Old Norse)

Old Norse	Literal	English
segir konungr, "hvárt þú vilt veita mér slíka hlýðni sem faðir þinn, ok vil ek þá auka þínar nafnbætr.	said the-king, "whether you wish to-grant me such homage as father yours, and wish I then extra your name-titles.	said the king, "whether you wish to grant me such homage as your father, and then I wish to give you more titles.
Skaltu þá halda Risalandi ok sverja mér eiða".	Shall-you then keep Giant-Land and swear to-me oath".	You shall then keep Giant-Land and swear an oath to me".
Goðmundr svarar:	Godmund answered:	Godmund answered:
"Ekki er þat lög at krefja svá unga menn til eiða".	"Not is that law that demand so young men to oath".	"It is not lawful to demand oaths from a man as young as me".
"Þat skal vera",	"That shall be",	"So it shall be",
sagði konungr.	said the-king.	said the king.
Síðan tók konungr guðvefjarskikkju ok lagði yfir Goðmund ok gaf honum konungsnafn, tók síðan horn mikit ok drakk til Goðmundi.	Then took the-king a-precious-cloak and laid over Godmund and gave him the-king's-name, took afterwards horn great and drank to Godmund.	Then the king took a precious cloak and laid it over Godmund and gave him the title of king, and then took a great horn and drank to Godmund.
Hann tók við horninu ok þakkaði konungi.	He took with the-horn and thanked the-king.	He took the horn and thanked the king.
Síðan stóð Goðmundr upp ok sté á stokkinn fyrir sæti konungs ok strengdi þess heit, at hann skal engum konungi þjóna né hlýðni veita, meðan Geirröðr konungr lifði.	Afterwards stood Godmund up and stepped onto the-foot-board before seat the-king's and boldly this declared, that he shall no king serve nor homage grant, while Geirrod the-king lived.	Afterwards Godmund stood up and stepped onto the footboard before the king's seat and boldly declared, that he would serve no king nor grant homage, while King Geirrod lived.
Konungr þakkaði honum, sagði sér þat þykkja meira vert en þótt hann hefði eiða svarit.	The-king thanked him, told him that valued more worth that though he had oaths sworn.	The king thanked him, and told him that he would have valued more if he had sworn oaths.
Síðan drakk Goðmundr af horninu ok gekk til sætis síns.	Afterwards drank Godmund of the-horn and went to seat his.	Afterwards Godmund drank from the horn and went to his seat.
Váru menn þá glaðir ok kátir.	Were men then glad and merry.	Then the men were glad and merry.
Tveir menn eru nefndir með Agða jarli.	Two men were named with Agdi the-earl.	Two men were with Earl Agdi.

The Tale of Thorsteinn House-Power (Old Norse)

Old Norse	Literal	English
Hét annarr Jökull, en annarr Frosti.	Named one Jokul, and the-other Frosti.	One was named Jokul, and the other Frosti.
Þeir váru öfundsjúkir.	They were jealous.	They were jealous.
Jökull þreif upp uxahnútu ok kastaði í lið Goðmundar.	Jokul grabbed up ox-bone and threw at the-company-of Godmund.	Jokul grabbed an ox-bone and threw it at Godmund's company.
Þorsteinn sá þat ok henti á lopti ok sendi aptr, ok kom á nasir þeim, er Gustr hét, ok brotnaði í honum nefit ok ór honum allar tennrnar, en hann fell í óvit.	Thorstein saw that and caught in the-air and sent back, and came about nose them, was Gust named, and broke it his nose and through his all teeth, and he fell to unconscious.	Thorstein saw that, caught it in the air and sent it back, and it hit the nose of a man named Gust, and it broke his nose and all his teeth, and he fell unconscious.
Geirröðr konungr reiddist ok spurði, hverr berði beinum yfir hans borð.	Geirrod the-king rose and asked, who threw the-bone across his table.	Geirrod the king rose up and asked who threw the bone across the table.
Sagði hann, at reynt skyldi verða, hverr sterkastr væri í steinkastinu, áðr en úti væri.	Said he, that test should be, who strongest was in stone-throwing, after then out was.	He said that there should be a test to find out before it was over who was the strongest at stone throwing.
Síðan kallar konungr til tvá menn, Drött ok Hösvi:	Afterwards called the-king to two men, Drott and Hosvir:	Afterwards the king called two men, Drott and Hosvir:
"Farið þit ok sækið gullhnött minn ok berið hann hingat".	"Go you-two and seek gold-ball mine and bring it here".	"You two go and seek my gold ball and bring it here".
Þeir fóru ok kómu aptr með eitt selshöfuð, er stóð tíu fjórðunga.	They went and came back with a seal's-head, and weighed ten quarters.	They went and came back with a seal's head, which weighed ten quarters.
Þat var glóanda, svá at sindraði af svá sem ór afli, en fitan draup niðr sem glóanda bik.	It was glowing, so that sparkled of so as from a-forge, and fat dripped down as burning pitch.	It was glowing hot, so that sparks came off it as if from a forge, and fat dripped from it like burning pitch.
Konungr mælti:	The-king spoke:	The king spoke:
"Takið nú knöttinn ok kastið hverr at öðrum.	"Take now the-ball and throw each to other.	"Now take the ball and throw it to each other.

The Tale of Thorsteinn House-Power (Old Norse)

Old Norse	Literal	English
Hverr, sem niðr fellir, skal fara útlægr ok missa eignir sínar, en hverr eigi þorir at henda, skal heita níðingr".	Anyone, who down drops, shall go outlawed and lose property his, and anyone not daring to catch, shall be-named a-coward".	Anyone who drops it shall go outlawed and lose his property, and anyone who does not dare to catch, shall be named a coward.

7

Old Norse	Literal	English
Nú kastar Dröttr knettinum at Fullsterk.	Now threw Drott the-ball at Full-Strong.	Now Drott threw the ball at Full-Strong.
Hann greip á móti annarri hendi.	He gripped to meet one hand.	He gripped against it with one hand.
Þorsteinn sá, at honum varð orkufátt, ok hljóp undir knöttinn.	Thorstein saw, that he became low-energy, and ran behind the-ball.	Thorstein saw that his strength weakened, and got behind the ball.
Þeir snöruðu at Frosta, því at kapparnir stóðu fremstir við hvárntveggja bekkinn.	They threw at Frosti, because that champions stood foremost against either-side of-the-bench.	They threw it at Frosti, because the champions stood in front of the benches on either side.
Frosti tók mót sterkliga, ok kom svá nær andliti hans, at kinnbeinit rifnaði.	Frosti took against strongly, and came so near face his, that chin-bone split.	Frosti caught it strongly, and it came so near his face, that it split his chin bone.
Hann kastar knettinum at Allsterk.	He threw the-ball at All-Strong.	He threw the ball at All-Strong.
Hann tók í móti báðum höndum, ok lá við, at hann mundi kikna, áðr Þorsteinn studdi hann.	He received it against both hands, and had with, that he would-have bent-backwards, before Thorstein steadied him.	He caught it with both hands, and he would have bent backwards, before Thorstein steadied him.
Allsterkr snaraði at Agða jarli, en hann greip móti báðum höndum.	All-Strong turned-quickly at Agdi the-earl, and he grabbed against both hands.	All-Strong hurled the ball at Earl Agdi, and he caught it with both hands.
Fitan kom í skeggit á honum, ok logaði þat allt, ok var honum til þess annast at afhenda knöttinn ok fleygir at Goðmundi konungi.	Fat came to beard of his, and blazed that all, and was he to this he-took-care-of that off-handed the-ball and flew-it at Godmund the-king.	Burning fat went on to his beard, and it was all ablaze, and as he had to take care of that, he hurriedly threw the ball at King Godmund.

The Tale of Thorsteinn House-Power (Old Norse)

Old Norse	Literal	English
En Goðmundr snaraði at Geirröði konungi, en hann veik sér undan, ok urðu þeir fyrir Dröttr ok Hösvir, ok fengu þeir bana.	Then Godmund flew-it at Geirrod the-king, but he turned himself away, and came they for Drott and Hosvir, and caught them dead.	Then Godmund threw it at King Geirrod, but he turned out of the way, and it came to Drott and Hosvir, and killed them both.
En knöttrinn kom á glerglugg einn ok svá út í díki þat, sem grafit var um borgina, ok hljóp upp eldr logandi.	Then the-ball came to glass-window one and so out into the-moat that, which dug was about the-city, and ran up the-flames ablaze.	Then the ball went through a glass window and out into the moat, which was dug around the city, and the flames ran up in a blaze.
Var nú lokit þessu gamni.	Was now ended this game.	The game was now ended.
Tóku menn þá til drykkju.	Took men then to drinking.	The men took to drinking.
Sagði Agði jarl, at honum hrysi hugr við jafnan, er hann kom í flokk Goðmundar.	Said Agdi the-earl, that he trembled thought with every-time, that he came to band Godmund's.	Earl Agdi said that he thought he trembled every time he came to Godmund's company.
Um kveldit gekk Goðmundr at sofa ok hans menn.	About evening went Godmund to seep and his men.	In the evening Godmund went to sleep and so did his men.
Þökkuðu þeir Þorsteini hjástöðu, at þeim hefði slysalaust farit.	Thanked they Thorstein beside-standing, to them had accidents-without gone.	They thanked Thorstein for standing by them, so that they were without accidents.
Þorsteinn kvað lítit til reynt, "eða hvat mun til gamans haft á morgin?"	Thorstein said little to test, "but what should to games have in the-morning?"	Thorstein said it was nothing much, "but what sort of games will we have in the morning?"
"Konungr mun láta glíma",	"The-king should have wrestling",	"The king shall have wrestling",
segir Goðmundr, "ok munu þeir þá hefna sín, því at fjarstætt er um afl várt".	said Godmund, "and should they then avenge themselves, accordingly to far-away from about strength ours".	said Godmund, "and they shall avenge themselves accordingly because their strength is far more than ours".
"Konungs gæfa mun styrkja oss",	"The-king's luck should strengthen us",	"The king's luck shall strengthen us",
segir Þorsteinn.	said Thorstein.	said Thorstein.
"Hirðið eigi, þótt þér berizt þangat at, sem ek er fyrir".	"Take-care not, though you bear from-there that, which I am before".	"Take care not to bear it there, but bear towards me".

The Tale of Thorsteinn House-Power (Old Norse)

Old Norse	Literal	English
Sofa þeir af um nóttina.	Slept they of through night.	They slept through the night.
En at morgni fór hverr til sinnar skemmtunar, en matsveinar at dúka borð.	And at morning went each to his entertainment, while food-servants to tablecloths table.	And in the morning each went to his entertainment, while the food servants put the tablecloths on the table.
Geirröðr konungr spurði, hvárt menn vildu ekki glíma, en þeir sögðu, at hann skyldi ráða.	Geirrod the-king asked, which men wished not wrestling, and they said, as he should decide.	King Geirrod asked, which men wished to wrestle, and they said that he should decide.
Síðan afklæðast þeir ok tókust fangbrögðum.	Afterwards undressed they and took to-wrestling.	Then they undressed and took to wrestling.
Þorsteinn þóttist eigi sét hafa slíkan atgang, því at allt skalf, þá þeir fellu, ok lékst mjök á mönnum Agða jarls.	Thorstein thought not seen had such to-going, because that all shook, then they fell, and played much to men Agdi the-earl's.	Thorstein thought he had not seen such a clash, because everywhere shook, whenever they fell, and this happened often to Earl Agdi's men.
Frosti gekk nú fram á gólfit ok mælti:	Frosti went now to the floor and spoke:	Frosti now went to the floor and said:
"Hverr skal mér á móti?"	"Who shall me to meet?"	"Who shall oppose me?"
"Til mun verða einhverr",	"To should be someone",	"There will be someone",
sagði Fullsterkr.	said Full-Strong.	said Full-Strong.
Ráðast þeir nú á, ok váru með þeim miklar sviptingar, ok er Frosti miklu sterkari.	Arranged they now to, and were with they much tussle, and was Frosti much stronger.	They now attacked, and there were great upheavals with them, and Frosti was much stronger.
Berast þeir nú at Goðmundi.	Bore they now to Godmund.	They now arrived at Godmund.
Frosti tekr hann upp á bringu sér ok keiktist mjök.	Frosti took him up by the-chest his and bent much.	Frosti took him up by his chest and he had to bend his knees.
Þorsteinn slær fæti sínum á knésbætr honum, ok fell Frosti á bak aptr, en Fullsterkr á hann ofan.	Thorstein struck feet his about the-back-of-the-knees his, and fell Frosti on back back, but Full-Strong on him over.	Thorstein struck his foot on the back of his knees, and Frosti fell on his back, and Full-Strong fell on him.
Hnakkinn sprakk á Frosta ok olnbogarnir.	The-back-of-the-head broke of Frosti and elbows.	The back of Frosti's head was broken, and so were his elbows.

The Tale of Thorsteinn House-Power (Old Norse)

Old Norse	Literal	English
Hann stóð seint upp ok mælti:	He stood slowly up and spoke:	He slowly stood up and spoke:
"Ekki eru þér einir at gamninu, eða hví er svá fúlt í flokki yðrum?"	"Not are you alone in the-game, and what is so foul among men yours?"	"You are not alone in this game, and what is it that is so foul among your men?"
"Skammt á nefit at kenna ór kjaptinum",	"Short is nose to know from the-mouth",	"Your nose is too close to your own mouth",
sagði Fullsterkr.	said Full-Strong.	said Full-Strong.
Jökull stóð þá upp, ok Allsterkr réðst þá í móti honum, ok var þeira atgangr inn harðasti.	Jokul stood then up, and All-Strong moved then to oppose him, and were they to-going the hardest.	Jokul then stood up, and All-Strong moved to oppose him, and their clash was the hardest yet.
En þó var Jökull sterkari ok bar hann at bekk, þar sem Þorsteinn var fyrir.	But though was Jokul stronger and carried him to a-bench, there as Thorstein was before.	But Jokul was stronger and carried him to a bench, where Thorstein was.
Jökull vildi draga Allsterk frá bekknum ok togast við fast, en Þorsteinn helt honum.	Jokul wished-to drag All-Strong from the-bench and pulled against hard, but Thorstein held him.	Jokul tried had to drag All-Strong from the bench and pulled hard against him, but Thorstein held him.
Jökull tók svá fast, at hann sté í hallargólfit upp at ökkla, en Þorsteinn hratt Allsterk frá sér, ok fell Jökull á bak aptr, ok gekk ór liði á honum fótrinn.	Jokul tugged so hard, that he stepped in hall-floor up to ankles, then Thorstein pushed All-Strong away-from him, and fell Jokul on back back, and went out-of dislocated of his leg.	Jokul pulled so hard, that his feet sunk into the hall floor up to his ankles, then Thorstein pushed All-Strong away from him, and Jokul fell back and dislocated his leg.
Allsterkr gekk til bekkjar, en Jökull stóð upp seint ok mælti:	All-Strong went to bench, but Jokul stood up slowly and spoke:	All-Strong went back to his bench, but Jokul stood up slowly and spoke:
"Ekki sjáum vér alla þessa, sem á bekknum eru".	"Not see we all this, which on that-bench they-are".	"We cannot see everyone that is on that bench".
Geirröðr segir Goðmundi, hvárt hann vildi ekki glíma.	Geirrod said-to Godmund, whether he would not wrestle.	Geirrod asked Godmund if he would wrestle.
En hann kveðst aldri glímt hafa, en kveðst eigi vildu synjast.	And he said never wrestled had, but said not would refuse.	And he said that he had never wrestled, but he would not refuse.
Konungr bað Agða jarl hefna manna sinna.	The-king ordered Agdi the-earl avenge men his.	The king ordered Earl Agdi to avenge his men.

The Tale of Thorsteinn House-Power (Old Norse)

Old Norse	Literal	English
Hann kveðst löngu hafa af lagt, en segir konung ráða skyldu.	He said long had of left, but told the-king advice would.	He said that he had given up long ago, but he would do as the king decided.
Síðan afklæddust þeir.	Afterwards undressed they.	Then they undressed.
Eigi þóttist Þorsteinn sét hafa tröllsligri búk en á Agða.	Not thought Thorstein seen had troll-like thick-set than was Agdi.	Thorstein thought that he had not seen such a troll-like thick set man as Agdi.
Var hann blár sem hel.	Was he black as death.	He was black as death.
Goðmundr reis mót honum.	Godmund rose to-meet him.	Godmund rose to meet him.
Var hann hvítr á skinnslit.	Was he white in colour.	He was white in colour.
Agði jarl hösvaðist at honum ok lagði svá fast krummurnar at síðum hans, at allt gekk niðr at beini, ok bárust þeir víða um höllina.	Agdi the-earl went-for at him and had so fastened grabbed at sides his, that all went down to the-bone, and bore they widely about the-hall.	Earl Agdi went for him and grabbed at his sides so hard that it went down to the bone, and the carried widely around the hall.
Ok er þeir kómu þar, sem Þorsteinn var, þá brá Goðmundr jarli til sniðglímu ok sneri honum vakrliga.	And when they came there, where Thorstein was, then drew Godmund the-earl to hip-throw and turned him nimbly.	And when they came where Thorstein was, Godmund drew the earl into a hip throw and turned him nimbly.
Þorsteinn lagðist niðr fyrir fætr jarli, ok fell hann þá ok stakk niðr nösunum, ok brotnaði í honum þjófsnefit ok fjórar tennr.	Thorstein lay down before feet the-earl's, and fell he then and struck down on-the-nose, and broke was his thieving-nose and four teeth.	Thorstein lay down before the earl's feet, and then he fell and struck his nose, and his thieving nose was broken, and four teeth.
Jarl stóð upp ok mælti:	The-earl stood up and spoke:	The earl stood up and spoke:
"Þung verða gamalla manna föll, ok svá þyngst, at þrír gangi at einum".	"Heavy becomes the-old man falling, and so heaviest, when three go against one".	"Heavy becomes the old man falling, and heaviest, when it's three against one".
Fóru menn þá í klæði sín.	Went the-men then with-that clothed themselves.	With that the men clothed themselves.

8   8   8

Þessu næst fóru þeir konungr til borða.	This next went they the-king to the-tables.	After this the king and his guests went to the tables.

The Tale of Thorsteinn House-Power (Old Norse)

Old Norse	Literal	English
Töluðu þeir Agði jarl um, at þeir mundu einhvern prett við hafa haft, "því at mér býðr ávallt hita, er ek kem í þeira flokk".	Told they Agdi the-earl about, that they must-be some-way tricked against having had, "because that I invite always heat, when I come in their company".	Earl Agdi and the others said that they must have been tricked in some way, "because I always heat up, when I come in their company".
"Látum bíða",	"Leave-it abide",	"Let it be",
segir konungr, "sá mun koma, at okkr mun kunngera".	said the-king, "so shall come, that us should wiser".	said the king, "something will come and make us wiser".
Tóku menn þá at drekka.	Took men then to drinking.	Then the men took to drinking.
Þá váru borin inn tvau horn í höllina.	Then were brought in two horns into the-hall.	There were then two horns brought into the hall.
Þau átti Agði jarl, gersemar miklar, ok váru kölluð Hvítingar.	They had Agdi the-earl, treasured much, and were called Whitings.	They belonged to Earl Agdi, who treasured them, and they were called Whitings.
Þau váru tveggja álna há ok gulli búin.	They were two cubits high and gold prepared.	They were two cubits high and inlaid with gold.
Konungr lét sitt hornit ganga á hvárn bekk, "ok skal hverr drekka af í einu.	The-king had sat a-horn going to each bench, "and shall each drink of in one.	The king had set a horn on each bench, "and everyone shall drink from it in one.
Sá, sem því orkar eigi, skal fá byrlaranum eyri silfrs".	So, that accordingly able-to not, shall pay the-cup-bearer an-ounce-of silver".	So, therefore those not able to shall pay the cup bearer an ounce of silver".
Gekk engum af at drekka utan köppunum, en Þorsteinn gat svá til sét, at þeir, sem með Goðmundi váru, varð engi víttr.	Went none of to drink out-of the-cups, but Thorstein got so to seen, that they, which with Godmund were, became not bewitched.	No one was able to drink out of the cups, but Thorstein could see that those who were with Godmund did not become bewitched.
Drukku menn nú glaðir þat, sem eptir var dagsins, en um kveldit fóru menn at sofa.	Drank men now gladly that, as after was of-the-day, then about evening went men to sleep.	People now drank happily what was left of the day, but in the evening they went to sleep.
Goðmundr þakkaði Þorsteini fyrir góða hjástöðu.	Godmund thanked Thorstein for the-good beside-standing.	Godmund thanked Thorstein for his good help.
Þorsteinn spurði, nær endast mundi veizlan.	Thorstein asked, near ending would the-feast.	Thorstein asked, when the feast would end.

The Tale of Thorsteinn House-Power (Old Norse)

Old Norse	Literal	English
"At morgni skulu menn mínir ríða",	"At morning should men mine ride",	"In the morning my men shall ride",
segir Goðmundr.	said Godmund.	said Godmund.
"Veit ek, at nú lætr konungr allt við hafa.	"Know I, that now acts the-king all against have.	"I know that now the king will act against us with all he has.
Eru nú sýndar gersemar.	They-are now shown treasures.	When the treasures are shown.
Lætr konungr nú bera inn horn sitt it mikla.	Have the-king now brought in a-horn his this great.	Let the king now carry in his great horn.
Þat er kallat Grímr inn góði.	That is called Grim the Good.	That is called Grim the Good.
Þat er gersemi mikil ok þó galdrafullt ok búit með gull.	That is a-treasure great and though magic-full and inlaid with gold.	It is a great treasure, and magical and rich in gold.
Mannshöfuð er á stiklinum með holdi ok munni, ok þat mælir við menn ok segir fyrir óorðna hluti ok ef þat veit ófriðar ván.	A-man's-head is about the-narrow with flesh and a-mouth, and that speaks with men and said for unspoken lot and if that known un-peace is-expected.	A man's head is about the narrow end with flesh and a mouth, and it speaks to men and says unspoken things, and if war is expected.
Verðr þat bani vár, ef konungr veit, at kristinn maðr er með oss.	Becomes it the-death ours, if the-king knows, that a-Christian man is with us.	It will be the death of us if the king knows that a Christian man is with us.
Munum vér eigi þurfa at vera fésparir við hann".	Should we not need to be fee-sparing with him".	We should not need to spare wealth with him".
Þorsteinn sagði Grím eigi mæla fleira enn Óláfr konungr vildi, "en ek ætla, at Geirröðr sé feigr.	Thorstein said Grim not speak more than Olaf the-king wished, "and I suppose, that Geirrod is fated-to-die.	Thorstein said that Grim would not say to him any more than King Olaf wished, "and I suppose that Geirrod is a doomed man.
Þykki mér ráð, at þér hafið mín ráð heðan af.	Seems to-me advice, that you have my counsel from-hence of.	It seems to me to advise, that you do as I advise you from now on.
Skal ek sýna mik á morgin".	Shall I show myself in the-morning".	I shall show myself in the morning".
En þeir sögðu þat hættu ráð.	But they said that dangerous advice.	But they said that it was a dangerous decision.

The Tale of Thorsteinn House-Power (Old Norse)

Old Norse	Literal	English
Þorsteinn sagði, at Geirröðr vildi þá feiga, "eða hvat segir þú mér af Grími inum góða fleira?"	Thorstein said, that Geirrod wished then doomed, "but what say you to-me of Grim the Good more?"	Thorstein said that Geirrod wished them all doomed, "but what else can you tell me about Grim the Good"?
"Þat er frá honum at segja, at meðalmaðr má standa undir bugtinni á honum, en álnar breitt yfir beitina, ok er sá mestr drykkjumaðr í þeira liði, er drekkr beitina, en konungr drekkr af í einu.	"That is from him to say, that an-average-man may stand under the-curve of him, and a-yard broad across opening, and is so the-greatest drinking-man of their company, that drinks the-opening, but the-king drinks of all in-one.	"The first thing to say, is that an average man can stand under the curve of the horn, and it is a yard across at the opening, and the greatest drinking man in their company can drink deep into the horn, but only the king can drink it all in one.
Hverr maðr á at gefa Grími nokkura gersemi, en sú virðing þykkir honum sér mest ger, at í einu sé af drukkit.	Each man is to give Grim some treasure, but so worthy seems to-him to-see most done, that in one you of drink.	Each man has to give Grim something valuable, but most worthy honour to him is to drink it in one.
En ek veit, at mér ber fyrstum af at drekka, en þat er einskis manns þol at drekka þat í einu".	But I know, that I bear first of to drink, but that is nothing man endure than drink that in one".	But I know that I have to drink first, but it is no man's endurance to drink it at once".
Þorsteinn mælti:	Thorstein spoke:	Thorstein spoke:
"Þú skalt fara í serk minn, því at þér má þá ekki granda, þó at ólyfjan sé í drykknum.	"You shall go in shirt mine, because that you may then not to-injure, though that poison even if drink.	"You shall go in my shirt, because then you shall not come to injury, even if there is poison in the drink.
Tak kórónu af höfði þér ok gef Grími inum góða ok seg í eyra honum, at þú skalt gera honum miklu meira heiðr en Geirröðr, ok síðan skaltu láta sem þú drekkir.	Take the-crown off head yours and give Grim the Good and say in ear his, that you shall do him much more honour than Geirrod, and afterwards shall-you lay-out that you drink.	Take the crown off your head, and give it to Grim the Good, and say in his ear that you will do him much more honour than Geirrod, and afterwards shall you drink to that.
En eitr mun í horninu, ok skaltu steypa niðr næst þér, ok mun þik ekki saka.	Then poison should-be in the-horn, ad shall-you cast down near you, and shall you not injury.	Then should the poison be in the horn, you shall cast it down beside you, and you shall not be injured.
En þá er drykkjuskapr er úti, skaltu láta menn þína ríða".	But then when drinking is over, shall-you have men yours ride-away".	But when the drinking is over, have your men ride away".
Goðmundr sagði, at hann skuli ráða.	Godmund said, that he shall decide.	Godmund said, that he shall decide.

The Tale of Thorsteinn House-Power (Old Norse)

Old Norse	Literal	English
"En ef Geirröðr deyr, þá á ek alla Jötunheima, en ef hann lifir lengr, verðr þat bani vár".	"But if Geirrod dies, then with I all Giant-Home, but if he lives longer, becomes that death ours".	"But if Geirrod dies, then I own all the Giant-Home, but if he lives longer, that death will be ours".
Síðan sofa þeir af um nóttina.	Afterwards slept they of about the-night.	Afterwards they slept through the night.

9

Old Norse	Literal	English
Um morguninn eru þeir snemma á fótum ok taka sín klæði.	About morning were they soon about feet and took their clothes.	In the morning they got up early and took their clothes.
Þá kemr Geirröðr konungr til þeira ok biðr þá drekka velfaranda sinn.	Then came Geirrod the-king to them and asked them to-drink well-faring his.	Then King Geirrod came to them and asked them to drink their welfare.
Þeir gerðu svá.	They did so.	They did so.
Váru fyrst drukkin hornin Hvítingar næst máldrykkju skálum, en þá var drukkit minni Þórs ok Óðins.	Were first drunk the-horns Whitings next drinking bowls, and then were drunk in-memory Thor's and Odin's.	First the horns called Whitings were drunk from, next the drinking bowls, and they were drunk from in memory of Thor and Odin.
Því næst kómu inn margir slagir hljóðfæra, ok tveir menn, nokkuru minni en Þorsteinn, þeir báru Grím inn góða.	Then next came in many artful musical-instruments, and two men, somewhat smaller than Thorstein, they carried Grim the Good.	Then many kinds of instruments came in, and two men, somewhat smaller than Thorstein, brought in Grim the Good.
Allir stóðu upp ok fellu á kné fyrir honum.	All stood up and fell to knees before him.	Everyone stood up and fell on their knees before him.
Grímr var óhýrligr.	Grim was unfriendly-looking.	Grim was hideous.
Geirröðr mælti til Goðmundar:	Geirrod spoke to Godmund:	Geirrod said to Godmund:
"Tak við Grími inum góða, ok er þetta þín handsals skál".	"Take with Grim the Good, and be this your binding shall".	"Take Grim the Good and let this toast be your binding pledge".
Goðmundr gekk at Grími ok tók af sér gullkórónu ok setti á hann ok mælti í eyra honum, sem Þorsteinn hafði sagt honum.	Godmund went to Grim and took off himself gold-crown and set on him and spoke in ear his, as Thorstein had told him.	Godmund went to Grim, took off his gold crown, set it upon him, and spoke in his ear, as Thorstein had told him.

The Tale of Thorsteinn House-Power (Old Norse)

Old Norse	Literal	English
Síðan lét hann renna af horninu ofan í serk sér, ok var eitr í.	Then had he ran of the-horn over into shirt his, and was poison in.	Then he ran the horn over into his shirt, and poured the poisonous drink in.
Hann drakk til Geirröði konungi ok kyssti á stikilinn, ok fór Grímr hlæjandi frá honum.	He drank to Geirrod the-king and kissed the horn-point, and went Grim smiling went-from him.	He drank to King Geirrod and kissed the point of the horn, and Grim was taken away from him with a smile on his face.
Tók Geirröðr þá við fullu horninu ok bað Grím með góðri heill koma ok bað hann kunngera sér, ef nokkurr háski væri nær.	Took Geirrod then with the-full horn and asked Grim with luck whole coming and asked him to-announce to-him, if something dangerous was near.	Geirrod took the full horn and asked Grim to bring him good luck and asked him if there was anything dangerous near.
"Hefi ek opt sét þik með betra bragði".	"Have I often seen you with better looking".	"I have often seen you in a better mood".
Tók hann gullmen af sér ok gaf Grími, drakk síðan til Agða jarli, ok þótti því líkast sem boði felli á sker, er niðr rann eptir hálsinum á honum, ok drakk af allt.	Took he gold-necklace off himself and gave Grim, drank afterwards to Agdi the-earl, and seemed therefore like as breaking wave on a-rock, as down ran after throat of him, and drank of all.	He took a gold necklace off himself and gave it to Grim, and drank afterwards to Earl Agdi, and it was like a wave breaking on a rock, as the drink ran down his throat, and he drank all of it.
Grímr hristi höfuðit, ok var hann borinn Agða jarli, ok gaf hann honum tvá gullhringa ok bað sér miskunnar ok drakk síðan af í þremr ok fekk byrlaranum.	Grim shook his-head, and was he carried Agdi the-earl, and gave it to-him two gold-rings and asked his mercy and drank afterwards of in three and went the-cup-bearer.	Grim shook his head, and he was carried to Earl Agdi who gave him two gold rings and asked for his mercy, and he drank in three draughts and then returned it to the cup-bearer.
Grímr mælti:	Grim said:	Grim said:
"Svá ergist hverr sem eldist".	"The feebler each who oldest".	"The older the man, the feebler"
Þá var hornit fyllt, ok skyldu þeir drekka af tveir, Jökull ok Fullsterkr.	Then was the horn, filled and should they drink of, Jokul and Full-Strong.	The horn was filled again so that Jokul and Full-Strong would drink from it.
Fullsterkr drakk fyrr.	Full-Strong drank before.	Full-Strong drank before.
Jökull tók við ok leit í hornit ok kvað lítilmannliga drukkit ok sló Fullsterk með horninu.	Jokul took with and had in horn and said weakly drank and struck Full-Strong with the-horn.	Jokul took the horn and said that Full-Strong drank like a weakling, and struck him with the horn.

The Tale of Thorsteinn House-Power (Old Norse)

Old Norse	Literal	English
En hann rak hnefann á nasir Jökli, svá at þjófshakan brotnaði, en ór hrutu tennrnar.	But he drove fist to nose Jokul's, so that thievish-chin broken, then out-of erupted the-teeth.	But he drove his first into Jokul's nose, so that his thievish chin was broken, and then teeth erupted out of his mouth.
Var þá upphlaup mikit.	Was then uproar much.	There was much uproar.
Geirröðr bað menn eigi láta þetta spyrjast, at þeir skildi svá illa.	Geirrod asked men not have this was-heard, that they separated so ill.	Geirrod asked the men not to have it heard that they had separated on bad terms.
Váru þeir þegar sáttir, ok var Grímr inn góði burt borinn.	Were they straightaway agreed, and was Grim the Good away carried.	They were reconciled straight away and Grim the Good was carried away.

10

Old Norse	Literal	English
Litlu síðar kom maðr gangandi í höllina.	Little afterwards came a-man walking into the-hall.	A little afterwards a man came walking into the hall.
Allir undruðust, hversu lítill hann var.	All wondered, how-so little he was.	Everyone wondered at how little he was.
Þat var Þorsteinn bæjarbarn.	That was Thorstein House-Child.	It was Thorstein House-Child.
Hann veik at Goðmundi ok sagði, at hestar væru til reiðu.	He turned to Godmund and told, him horses were to ride.	He turned to Godmund and told him to prepare the horses to ride.
Geirröðr spurði, hvat barn at þat væri.	Geirrod asked, who the-child that it was.	Geirrod asked who the child was.
Goðmundr segir:	Godmund said:	Godmund said:
"Þat er smásveinn minn, er Óðinn konungr sendi mér, ok er konungs gersemi ok kann marga smáleika, ok ef yðr þætti nokkuru neytr, þá vil ek gefa yðr hann".	"That is little-boy mine, that Odin the-king sent me, and is the-king's treasure and knows many small-games, and if you seem some good-use, then will I give you him".	"This is my little boy that king Odin sent me, and is the king's treasure, and he knows many tricks, and if you think he may be of use then I will give him to you".
"Þat er svipmikill drengr",	"That is a-striking fellow",	"That is a striking fellow",
segir konungr, "ok vil ek sjá fimleika hans",	said the-king, "and wish I to-see tricks his",	said the king, "and I wish to see his tricks",

The Tale of Thorsteinn House-Power (Old Norse)

Old Norse	Literal	English
ok bað Þorstein leika nokkurn smáleik.	and asked Thorstein play some small-games.	and asked Thorstein to play some tricks.
Þorsteinn tók hall sinn ok brodd ok pjakkar þar í, sem hvítt er.	Thorstein took marble his and point and pricked there in, where white was.	Thorstein took his marble and point and pricked where it was white.
Kemr haglhríð svá mikil, at engi þorir í móti at sjá, ok varð svá mikil fönn í höllinni, at tók í ökkla.	Came hailstorm so great, that none dared to meet to see, and was so great snow in the-hall, that took at ankles.	There came a hailstorm so great, that none dared to meet it with their eyes, and the snow was so great in the hall that it was up to everyone's ankles".
Konungr hló at.	The-king laughed at.	The king laughed at this.
Nú stangaði Þorsteinn hallinn, þar sem hann var gulr.	Now stabbed Thorstein the-marble, there where it was yellow.	Now Thorstein stabbed at the marble where it was yellow.
Kom þá sólskin svá heitt, at snjórinn bráðnaði allr á lítilli stundu.	Came then sunshine so hot, that the-snow melted all in little while.	Then came sunshine so hot that the snow melted in a short while.
Þar fylgdi sætr ilmr, en Geirröðr kvað hann var listamann.	There followed mountain-pastures sweet-smell, and Geirrod said he was a-skilled-craftsman.	There followed the sweet smell of mountain pastures, and Geirrod said that he was a skilled craftsman.
En Þorsteinn segir eptir einn leikinn, er heitir svipuleikr.	Then Thorstein said after one trick, that called the-scourge.	Then Thorstein said that there remained one trick which was called the scourge.
Konungr segist hann sjá vilja.	The-king said he to-see wished.	The king said he wished to see it.
Þorsteinn stóð á miðju hallargólfi ok pjakkar þar í hallinn, sem rautt er.	Thorstein stood in the-middle hall-floor and pricked there in the-marble, where red was.	Thorstein stood in the middle of the hall floor and pricked the marble where it was red.
Stökkva þar ór gneistar.	Jumped there of sparks.	Then sparks jumped from it.
Síðan hleypr hann um höllina fyrir hvert sæti.	Afterwards ran he about the-hall before each seat.	Afterwards he ran about the hall in front of each seat.
Tókust þá at vaxa gneistaflaugin, svá at hverr maðr varð at geyma sín augu.	Took then to grow sparks-flying, so that each man was to to-mind their eyes.	Then the fling sparks grew so that every man had to mind his eyes.

The Tale of Thorsteinn House-Power (Old Norse)

Old Norse	Literal	English
En Geirröðr konungr hló at.	Then Geirrod the-king laughed at.	Then King Geirrod laughed at this.
Tók þá at vaxa eldrinn, svá at öllum þótti við of um.	Took then to grow the-fire, so that all thought against of about.	The fires grew so that all thought against it.
Þorsteinn hafði sagt Goðmundi fyrir, at hann skyldi út ganga ok fara á hest.	Thorstein had told Godmund before, that he should out go and travel with horses.	Thorstein had told Godmund before, that he should go and travel with the horses.
Þorsteinn hleypr fyrir Geirröð ok mælti:	Thorstein ran before Geirrod and said:	Thorstein ran before Geirrod and said:
"Vili þér láta auka leikinn?"	"Wish you to-have more games?"	"Do you wish to have more games?"
"Lát sjá, sveinn",	"Let see, boy",	"Let's see, boy",
sagði hann.	said he.	he said.
Pjakkar Þorsteinn þá í fastara lagi.	Pricked Thorstein then to harder thrust.	Thorstein then pricked harder.
Kemr þá í auga Geirröði konungi.	Came then in eyes Geirrod's the-king.	Then came sparks into King Geirrod's eyes.
Þorsteinn hleypr til dyranna ok snaraði hallinum ok broddinum, ok kom í sitt auga hvárt á Geirröði konungi, ok steyptist hann dauðr á gólfit, en Þorsteinn gekk út.	Thorstein ran to the-door and threw the-marble and point, and came to his eyes each that Geirrod the-king, and knocked him dead on the-floor, then Thorstein went out.	Thorstein ran to the door and threw the marble and the point, and each came to King Geirrod's eyes, and he was knocked dead on the floor, then Thorstein went out.
Var Goðmundr þá kominn á hest.	When Godmund then came to horses.	Godmund had then come on horseback.
Þorsteinn bað þá ríða, "því at nú er ekki deigum vært".	Thorstein bid then to-ride, "because that now is not weak short".	Thorstein then bid then that they ride away, "because now is not the time for weakness".
Þeir ríða til árinnar.	They rode to the-river.	They rode to the river
Var þá aptr kominn hallrinn ok broddrinn.	Was then back coming the-marble and the-point.	Then the marble and point was coming back.
Þorsteinn segir, at Geirröðr var dauðr.	Thorstein said, that Geirrod was dead.	Thorstein said that Geirrod was dead.

The Tale of Thorsteinn House-Power (Old Norse)

Old Norse	Literal	English
Ríða þeir nú yfir ána ok þangat, sem þeir höfðu fundizt.	Rode they now across the river from-there, where they had met.	They now rode across the river from there, where they had met.
Þá mælti Þorsteinn:	Then spoke Thorstein:	Then Thorstein spoke:
"Hér munum vér nú skilja, ok mun mönnum mínum mál þykkja, at ek komi til þeira".	"Forces should we now separate, and should men mine the-matter think, that I come to them".	"Our forces should now separate, and my men think that I should come to them.
"Far heim með mér",	"Travel home with me",	"Travel home with me",
sagði Goðmundr, "ok skal ek launa þér góða fylgd".	said Godmund, "and shall I repay you good following".	said Godmund, "and I shall repay you for your good help".
"Síðan mun ek þess vitja",	"Afterwards should I this visit",	"Afterwards I should visit",
segir Þorsteinn, "en aptr skalt þú fara með fjölmenni í Geirröðargarða.	said Thorstein, "but back shall you travel with following-men to Geirrod's-Town.	said Thorstein, "but you should travel back to Geirrod's-Town with a following of men.
Er nú landit í yðru valdi".	Is now the-land in your control".	Now the land is in your control".
"Þú munt ráða",	"You should reckon",	"Whatever you reckon"
sagði Goðmundr, "en Óláfi konungi skaltu færa kveðju mína".	said Godmund, "then Olaf the-king shall be-brought greetings mine".	said Godmund, "then King Olaf shall be brought my greetings".
Tók hann þá eitt gullker ok silfrdisk ok tvítugt handklæði gullofit ok sendi konungi, en bað Þorstein vitja sín, ok skildu með kærleikum.	Took he then a golden-bowl and silver-dish and twenty hand-cloths gold-woven and sent the-king, and asked Thorstein visit him, and separated with friendly-terms.	He then took a golden bowl and a silver dish and twenty gold woven towels also to send to the king, and he asked Thorstein to visit him, and they separated on friendly terms.

11

En nú sér Þorsteinn, hvar Agði jarl ferr í allmiklum jötunmóð.	And now saw Thorstein, where Agdi the-earl travelling in all-mighty giant's-wrath.	And now saw Thorstein, where Earl Agdi was travelling in an almighty giant's wrath.
Þorsteinn ferr eptir honum.	Thorstein went after him.	Thorstein went after him.
Sér hann þá mikinn húsabæ, er Agði átti.	Saw he then great farmstead, which Agdi owned.	He then saw a great farmstead, which Agdi owned.

The Tale of Thorsteinn House-Power (Old Norse)

Old Norse	Literal	English
Aldingarðr var við grindhliðit, ok stóð þar við ein jungfrú.	Orchard was with gate, and stood there with a young-woman.	There was an orchard, and at the gate there stood a young woman.
Hún var dóttir Agða ok hét Goðrún.	She was daughter Agdi's and named Gudrun.	She was Agdi's daughter and was named Gudrun.
Mikil var hún ok fríð.	Tall was she and peaceful.	She was tall and fair.
Hún heilsaði föður sínum ok spurði tíðenda.	She greeted father hers and asked of-news.	She greeted her father and asked him the news.
"Nóg eru tíðendi",	"Enough is news",	"There is news enough",
segir hann.	said he.	he said.
"Geirröðr konungr er dauðr, ok hefir Goðmundr af Glæsisvöllum svikit oss alla ok hefir leynt þar kristnum manni, ok heitir sá Þorsteinn bæjarmagn.	"Geirrod the-king is dead, and has Godmund of Glasir-Plains tricked us all and has hidden there Christian man, and named so Thorstein House-Power.	"King Geirrod is dead, and Godmund of Glasir-Plains has tricked us all and has hidden a Christian man there, and he is named Thorstein House-Power.
Hann hefir ausit eldi í augu oss.	He has thrown fire in eyes ours.	He has thrown fire in our eyes.
Skal ek nú drepa menn hans".	Shall I now kill men his".	I shall now kill his men".
Kastar hann þar niðr hornunum Hvítingum ok hljóp til skógar, sem hann væri galinn.	Threw he there down the-horn Whitings and ran to the-forest, as-if he was mad.	There he threw down the horn called Whitings and ran to the forest as if he was mad.
Þorsteinn gekk at Goðrúnu.	Thorstein went to Gudrun.	Thorstein went to Gudrun.
Hún heilsaði honum ok spurði hann at nafni.	She greeted him and asked him of name.	She greeted him and asked him his name.
Hann kvaðst Þorsteinn bæjarbarn heita, hirðmaðr Óláfs konungs.	He said Thorstein House-Child named, court-man Olaf's the-king.	He said he was named Thorstein House-Child, a court man of King Olaf.
"Stórr mun þar inn stærsti, sem þú ert barnit",	"Big must there the biggest, if you are the-child",	"His big must be the biggest, if you are the child",
sagði hún.	said she.	she said.
"Viltu fara með mér",	"Will-you travel with me",	"Will you travel with me",

174

The Tale of Thorsteinn House-Power (Old Norse)

Old Norse	Literal	English
segir Þorsteinn, "ok taka við trú?"	said Thorstein, "and take with the-faith?"	said Thorstein, "and take the faith?".
"Við lítit yndi á ek hér at skiljast",	"With little happiness that I here to separate",	"With little happiness here to separate from", she said,
segir hún, "því at móðir mín er dauð.	said she, "because that mother mine is dead.	"because my mother is dead.
Hún var dóttir Óttars jarls af Hólmgörðum, ok váru þau ólík at skapsmunum, því at faðir minn er mjök tröllaukinn, ok sé ek nú, at hann er feigr.	She was daughter Ottar's the-earl of Novgorod, and were they unlike in mood-mind, as that father mine is much troll-possessed, and see I now, that he is doomed.	She was the daughter of Earl Ottar of Novgorod, and they were unlike in temperament, as my father who is troll-possessed, and I see now that he is doomed.
En ef þú vilt fylgja mér aptr hingat, þá mun ek fara með þér".	Then if you will follow me back here, then shall I travel with you".	Then if you will follow back here with me, then I shall travel with you".
Síðan tók hún þing sín, en Þorsteinn tók hornin Hvítinga.	Afterwards took she things hers, and Thorstein took the-horn Whitings.	Afterwards she took her things, and Thorstein took the horn called Whitings.
Síðan gengu þau á skóginn ok sáu, hvar Agði fór.	Afterwards went they into the-forest and saw, where Agdi went.	Afterwards they went into the forest and saw, where Agdi went.
Hann grenjaði mjök ok helt fyrir augun.	He screamed much and held before eyes.	He screamed a lot and held his hands before his eyes.
Hafði þat saman borit, þegar hann sá skip Þorsteins, hljóp sá verkr í þjófsaugun á honum, at hann sá eigi.	Had that together borne, as-soon-as he saw ship Thorstein's, ran so pain in thief's-eyes of his, that he saw not.	That had happened together with, as soon as he saw Thorstein's ship, a pain ran in his thief's eyes, so that he could not see.
Var þá komit at sólarfalli, er þau komu til skips.	Was then coming to sunset, when they came to ships.	It was approaching sunset, when they came to the ships.
Váru menn Þorsteins þá burt búnir, en er þeir sáu Þorstein, urðu þeir fegnir.	When men Thorstein's then away prepared, then when they saw Thorstein, became they joyful.	When Thorstein's men were preparing to journey away, then they saw Thorstein and became joyful.
Sté Þorsteinn þá á skip, ok sigldu burt.	Stepped Thorstein then onto the-ship, and sailed away.	Thorstein stepped onto the ship, and they sailed away.

The Tale of Thorsteinn House-Power (Old Norse)

Old Norse	Literal	English
Er eigi getit um ferð hans, fyrr en hann kom heim í Noreg.	Is nothing told-of about the-journey his, before that he came home to Norway.	Nothing is told of his journey, before he came home to Norway.
12	**12**	**12**
Þenna vetr sat Óláfr konungr í Þrándheimi.	That winter sat Olaf the-king in Trondheim.	That winter King Olaf sat at Trondheim.
Þorsteinn fann konung at jólum ok færði honum gripi þá, sem Goðmundr sendi honum, ok hornin Hvítinga ok marga aðra gripi.	Thorstein met the-king at Yule and brought him treasure then, which Godmund sent him, and the-horn Whitings and many other treasures.	Thorstein met the king at Yule and brought him treasure, which Godmund had sent him, and the horn called Whitings, and many other treasures.
Sagði hann konungi frá ferðum sínum ok sýndi honum Goðrúnu.	Told he the-king from voyage his and showed him Gudrun.	He told the king of his voyages and showed him Gudrun.
Konungr þakkaði honum, ok lofuðu allir hans hreysti ok þótti mikils um vert.	The-king thanked him, and praised all his valour and thought much about worthy.	The king thanked him, and praised all his valour and thought much of his worthiness.
Síðan lét konungr skíra Goðrúnu ok kenna trú.	Afterwards had the-king baptised Gudrun and taught the-faith.	Afterwards the king had Gudrun baptised and taught the faith.
Þorsteinn lék svipuleik um jólin, ok þótti mönnum þat skemmtan mikil.	Thorstein played the-scourge about Yule, and thought men that amusement great.	Thorstein played the scourge through Yule, and men thought it was great amusement.
Hvítingar gengu í minnum, ok váru tveir menn um hvárt horn.	Whitings went in came, and were two men about each horn.	The Whitings were brought in, and two men shared each horn.
En ker þat, sem Goðmundr hafði sent konungi, gekk engum af at drekka utan Þorsteini bæjarbarni.	The vessel that, which Godmund had sent the-king, went none of of drinking except Thorstein House-Child.	The cup that Godmund had sent the king, was not drunk from except by Thorstein House-Child.
Handklæðit brann eigi, þótt því væri í eld kastat, ok var hreinna eptir en áðr.	Hand-cloth burned not, though that was in fire cast, and was cleaner after than before.	The hand-cloth did not burn, even though it was cast in fire, and was cleaner than before.
Þorsteinn talar um við konung, at hann vildi gera brullaup til Goðrúnar, en konungr veitti honum þat, ok var þat sæmilig veizla.	Thorstein talked through with the-king, that he wished to-make wedding-proposal to Gudrun, and the-king granted him that, and was that well feast.	Thorstein talked through with the king, that he wished to make a wedding proposal to Gudrun, and the king granted him that, and was there a splendid feast.

The Tale of Thorsteinn House-Power (Old Norse)

Old Norse	Literal	English
Ok ina fyrstu nótt, er þau kómu í eina sæng ok niðr var hleypt fortjaldinu, þá brast upp þilfjöl at höfðum Þorsteins, ok var þar kominn Agði jarl ok ætlaði at drepa hann.	And the first night, when they came to one bed and down was cast the-curtain, then burst up decks over head Thorstein's, and was then come Agdi the-earl and intended to kill him.	And on the first night, when they came to bed together, the curtain was cast down, and then the decks over Thorstein's head burst open, and there had come Earl Agdi intending to kill him.
En þar laust í móti hita svá miklum, at hann þorði eigi inn at ganga.	But then loosed in opposition heat so great, that he dared not in to go.	But then was released so great a heat against him, that he dared not go in.
Sneri hann þá í burtu.	Turned he then to away.	He turned away.
Þá kom konungr at ok sló hann með gullbúnu refði í höfuðit, en hann steyptist niðr í jörðina.	Then came the-king to and struck him with gold-plated staff about head, then he fell down to the-ground.	Then the king came and struck him with a gold plated staff on the head, then he fell face down on the ground.
Helt konungr vörð um nóttina, en um morguninn váru horfin hornin Hvítingar.	Held the-king guard about the-night, then about morning were disappeared the-horns Whitings.	The king held guard through the night, and then in the morning the horns called Whitings had disappeared.
Gekk veizlan vel fram.	Went the-feast well from-there.	The feast went well from there.
Sat Þorsteinn með konungi um vetrinn, ok unnust þau Goðrún vel.	Sat Thorstein with the-king through winter, and loved they Gudrun well.	Thorstein sat with the king through the winter, and he and Gudrun loved each other well.
Um várit beiddi Þorsteinn orlofs at sigla í Austrveginn ok finna Goðmund konung.	About spring asked Thorstein vacation to sail to Eastern-Lands and find Godmund the-king.	In the spring Thorstein asked for a vacation to sail to the Eastern-Lands to find King Godmund.
En konungr sagðist þat eigi gera, utan hann lofaði at koma aptr.	But the-king said that not to-do, without him pledging to come back.	But the king said that he should not do it without promising to come back.
Þorsteinn hét því.	Thorstein promised accordingly.	Thorstein promised accordingly.
Konungr bað hann halda trú sína vel, "ok eig meira undir þér en þeim austr þar".	The-king asked him keep faith his well, "and have more behind you than they Eastern-Lands there".	The king asked him to keep his faith well: "and have more behind you than those in the Eastern-Lands there".

The Tale of Thorsteinn House-Power (Old Norse)

Old Norse	Literal	English
Skildust þeir með kærleikum, ok báðu allir vel fyrir honum, því at Þorsteinn var orðinn vinsæll.	Separated they with friendship, and bid all well for him, because that Thorstein was became popular.	They separated with friendship, and all bid him well, for Thorstein had become popular.
Sigldi hann í Austrveg, ok er eigi getit annars en sú ferð færist vel.	Sailed he to Eastern-Lands, and was nothing told-of other than so travelled the-journey well.	He sailed to the Eastern-Lands, and nothing was told other than that he travelled the journey well.
Kom hann á Glæsisvöllu, ok fagnaði Goðmundr honum vel.	Came he to Glasir-Plains, and welcomed Godmund him well.	He came to Glasir-Plains, and Godmund welcomed him well.
Þorsteinn mælti:	Thorstein spoke:	Thorstein spoke:
"Hvat hafið þér frétt ór Geirröðargörðum?"	"What have you news of Geirrod's-Town?"	"What news do you have of Geirrod's-Town?"
"Þangat fór ek",	"There travelled I",	"I travelled there",
segir Goðmundr, "ok gáfu þeir landit í mitt vald, ok ræðr þar fyrir Heiðrekr úlfhamr, sonr minn".	said Godmund, "and gave they land to me power, and rules there over Heidrek Wolf-Skin, son mine".	said Godmund, "and they gave me power over the land, and ruling over there is Heidrek Wolf-Skin, my son".
"Hvar er Agði jarl?"	"What of Agdi the-earl?"	"What of Earl Agdi?"
segir Þorsteinn.	said Thorstein.	said Thorstein.
"Hann lét gera sér haug, þá þér fóruð",	"He had done himself a-burial-mound, when you travelled",	"He had made himself a burial mound, when you travelled",
segir Goðmundr, "ok gekk þar í með mikit fé, en þeir Jökull ok Frosti drukknuðu í ánni Hemru, er þeir fóru frá veizlunni, en ek hefi nú vald yfir heraðinu á Grundum".	said Godmund, "and went there in with much wealth, but they Jokul and Frosti drowned in the-river Hemra, as they travelled from the-feast, then I have now power across the-district of Grundir".	said Godmund", and retired there with much wealth, and Jokul and Frosti drowned in the river Hemra, as they travelled from the feast, and I now have power across the district of Grundir".
"Þar er nú mikit undir",	"There is now much under",	"There is now a lot under it",
segir Þorsteinn, "hverju þú vilt mér af skipta, því at mér þykkir Goðrún eiga arf allan eptir föður sinn, Agða jarl".	said Thorstein, "how you will me to give, because that to-me seems Gudrun my-wife inheritance all after father his, Agdi the-earl".	said Thorstein, "how much you wish to let me have, because it seems to me that my wife Gudrun is entitled to all the inheritance after he father, Earl Agdi".

The Tale of Thorsteinn House-Power (Old Norse)

Old Norse	Literal	English
"Ef þú vilt vera minn maðr",	"If you will be my man",	"If you will be my man",
sagði Goðmundr.	said Godmund.	said Godmund.
"Þá muntu ekki vanda um trú mína",	"Then should not custom about the-faith mine",	"Then you will not have any problems with my faith",
segir Þorsteinn.	said Thorstein.	said Thorstein.
"Þat vil ek",	"That will I",	"That I will",
sagði Goðmundr.	said Godmund.	said Godmund.
Síðan fóru þeir til Grunda, ok tók Þorsteinn heraðit undir sik.	Afterwards travelled they to Grundir, and took Thorstein the-district under himself.	Afterwards they travelled to Grundir, and Thorstein took the district under himself.

13

Þorsteinn reisti bú at Gnípalundi, því at Agði jarl hafði gengit aptr ok eytt bæinn.	Thorstein raised the-dwelling at Gnipalund, because that Agdi the-earl had come back and devastated the-dwelling.	Thorstein raised the house at Gnipalund, as Earl Agdi had come back and devastated the old house.
Gerðist Þorsteinn höfðingi mikill.	Became Thorstein a-chieftain great.	Thorstein became a great chieftain.
Goðrún fæddi sveinbarn mikit litlu síðar, ok hét Brynjólfr.	Gudrun raised a-baby-boy large little since, and named Brynjolf.	Gudrun gave birth to a big baby boy, and he was named Brynjolf.
Ekki var traust, at Agði jarl glettist eigi við Þorstein.	Not was trusted, that Agdi the-earl playing-tricks not against Thorstein.	There was no confidence that Earl Agdi would not play-tricks against Thorstein.
Eina nótt gekk Þorsteinn af sæng sinni ok sá, hvar at Agði fór.	One night went Thorstein to bed his and saw, where that Agdi moving.	One night Thorstein got out of his bed and saw where Agdi was moving.
Hann þorði hvergi inn í hliðin, því at kross var fyrir hverjum dyrum.	He dared neither in the the-gates, because that the-cross was before each doorway.	He dared not enter the gates, for there was a cross at every door.
Þorsteinn gekk til haugsins.	Thorstein went to burial-mound-his.	Thorstein went to the mound.

The Tale of Thorsteinn House-Power (Old Norse)

Old Norse	Literal	English
Hann var opinn, ok gekk hann inn ok tók burt hornin Hvítinga.	It was open, and went he inside and took away the-horns Whitings.	It was open, and he went inside and took away the horns called Whitings.
Þá kom Agði jarl í hauginn, en Þorsteinn hljóp út hjá honum ok setti kross í dyrrnar, ok laukst aptr haugrinn, ok hefir ekki orðit vart við Agða síðan.	Then came Agdi the-earl into the-mound, and Thorstein ran out beside him and set the-cross in the-door, and closed afterwards the-mound, and has no word was of Agdi since..	Then Earl Agdi came to the mound, but Thorstein ran out beside him and put a cross in the door, and the mound was closed, and Agdi has not been seen since.
Um sumarit eptir fór Þorsteinn til Noregs ok færði Óláfi konungi hornin Hvítinga.	About summer after went Thorstein to Norway and brought Olaf the-king the-horns Whitings.	The following summer Thorstein went to Norway, and brought King Olaf the horns called Whitings.
Síðan fekk hann orlof ok sigldi til eigna sinna.	Then got he leave to sail to possessions his.	Then he took leave and sailed to his possessions.
Bauð konungr honum halda vel trú sína.	Asked the-king him hold well faith his.	The king commanded him to keep his faith well.
Höfum vér eigi frétt síðan til Þorsteins.	Have we not news since of Thorstein's.	We have not heard from Thorstein since.
En þá Óláfr konungr hvarf af Orminum langa, hurfu hornin Hvítingar.	But when Olaf the-king disappeared from The-Serpent Long, vanished the-horns Whitings.	But when King Olaf disappeared from the Long Serpent, the horns of the Whites disappeared.
Lúkum vér þar þætti Þorsteins bæjarbarns.	End we there the-story Thorstein's House-Child.	We end there the tale of Thorstein House-Child.

Word List (Old Norse to English)

Word List (Old Norse to English)

Old Norse	English	*Old Norse*	English
A, a		at	about, against, as, at, at, from, him, in, in, it, of, of, over, than, than, that, that, the, the, to, to, towards, when, which
aðra	other		
aðrir	others		
af	drink, from, from, of, of, off, that, to, to	atgang	to-going
afhenda	off-handed, of-hand	atgangr	to-going
afklæðast	undressed	atsetu	a-seat
afklæddust	undressed	auðit	fated
afl	strength	auga	eyes, eyes
afla	provide	augu	eyes, eyes
afli	a-forge, strength	augum	eyes
agða	Agdi (name), Agdi (name), Agdi's (name)	augun	eyes
		auka	extra, more
agði	Agdi (name), Agdi (name)	aura	ounces
		ausit	thrown
akkerum	anchor	austr	east, east, Eastern-Lands (place)
aldingarðr	orchard		
aldri	never, never	austrveg	Eastern-Lands (place)
alla	all, all	austrveginn	Eastern-Lands (place)
allan	all		
allar	all	**Á, á**	
allir	all, all		
allmiklum	all-mighty	á	a, about, a-river, at, beside, by, for, from, in, into, is, of, on, onto, that, the, then, to, was, who, with
allr	all, all		
alls	all		
allsterk	All-Strong (name)		
allsterkr	All-Strong (name)	ábyrgjast	take-care-of
allt	all, all	áðr	after, before
andliti	face	áliðnum	following
annan	another-thing	álna	cubits
annarr	another, one, one, the-other	álnar	a-yard
		ána	the, the-river
annarri	another, one	ánni	the-river, the-river
annars	other	árinnar	the-river, the-river
annast	he-took-care-of	átti	had, owned
aptnaði	the-evening	áttu	had
aptr	afterwards, back, back, return	ávallt	always
arf	inheritance		
		Æ, æ	

Word List (Old Norse to English)

Old Norse	English
ætla	intend, suppose
ætlaði	intended
ætlan	intentions
ætlar	intended
ættar	lineage
ætti	had

B, b

Old Norse	English
bað	asked, bid, ordered
báðu	bid
báðum	both
bæinn	the-dwelling
bæjarbarn	House-Child (name)
bæjarbarni	House-Child (name)
bæjarbarns	House-Child (name)
bæjarmagn	House-Power (name)
bak	back, the-back
bálagarðssíðu	Balagardsida (place)
bana	dead, death
bandvettlinga	mittens
bani	death, the-death
bar	bore, carried
barn	the-child
barni	a-baby
barnit	child, the-child
báru	carried
bárust	bore
bauð	asked, offered
beiddi	asked
beini	the-bone
beinum	the-bone
beitina	opening, the-opening
bekk	a-bench, bench
bekkinn	of-the-bench
bekkjar	bench
bekknum	that-bench, the-bench
ber	bear
bera	bear, brought
berast	bore
berði	threw
berið	bring
berizt	bear
betr	better
betra	better
betri	better
beztir	best
bíða	abide, await
biðr	asked
bik	pitch
birti	revealed
bjálfa	Bjalfi
bjálfi	Bjalfi
bjó	lived, prepared
bjuggust	settled
blár	black
bleikum	pale
boð	an-invite
boði	breaking
bóndi	farmer
borð	table
borða	the-tables
borðinu	table
borðum	a-table, the-tables
borg	a-city
borgarinnar	the-city, the-town
borgina	the-city, the-town
borin	brought
borinn	carried
borit	borne
börn	children
brá	drew
bráðnaði	melted
bræðir	thaws
bragði	looking
brann	burned
brast	burst
braut	way
brautinni	turned-away, turning
breiða	broad
breiddu	spread
breitt	broad
breyttu	behaved
bringu	the-chest
brodd	point
broddinum	point, the-point
broddrinn	the-point
bróður	brother
brosti	burst-out-laughing

Word List (Old Norse to English)

Old Norse	English
brotnaði	broke, broken
brott	away
brullaup	wedding-proposal
brynjólfr	Brynjolf (name)
bú	the-dwelling
búa	live
bugtinni	the-curve
búin	prepared
búit	inlaid, prepared
búk	thick-set
búnir	prepared
burt	away
burtu	away
býðr	invite
byggð	settlements
byr	fair-wind
byrlaranum	the-cup-bearer

D, d

Old Norse	English
dag	day
dagný	Dagny (name)
dagsins	of-the-day
datt	fell
dauð	dead
dauðr	dead
degi	day
deigum	weak
deyr	dies
díki	the-moat
djúp	deep
dóttir	daughter
draga	carry, drag
drakk	drank
drap	killed
draup	dripped
dregr	drew
drekka	drink, drinking, they, to-drink
drekkir	drink
drekkr	drinks
drengr	fellow
drep	gangrene
drepa	kill
drepnir	killed
drött	Drott (name)
drottning	the-queen
dröttr	Drott (name)
drukkin	drunk
drukkit	drank, drink, drinking, drink-to, drunk
drukknuðu	drowned
drukku	drank
drykkju	drinking
drykkjumaðr	drinking-man
drykkjuskapr	drinking
drykknum	drink
dúka	tablecloths
dúkinn	table-cloth, the-table-cloth
dúkr	table-cloth
dunur	a-din
dvelr	delays
dverg	dwarf
dvergnum	the-dwarf
dvergrinn	dwarf, the-dwarf
dvergsbarnit	the-dwarf's-boy
dýr	wild-animals
dyranna	the-door
dyrr	door, the-door
dyrrnar	the-door
dyrum	doorway

E, e

Old Norse	English
eða	and, but, or
ef	if
eiða	oath, oaths
eig	have
eiga	my-wife, said-of, to-own
eigi	none, not, nothing
eigna	possessions
eignir	property
eigum	own
eik	oak
eikinni	the-oak
eimyrja	embers
ein	a
eina	a, one

Word List (Old Norse to English)

Old Norse	English
einhvern	some-way
einhverr	someone
einir	alone
einn	a, one
einni	a
einskis	nothing
einu	in-one, one
einum	a, one
eitr	poison
eitt	a, one
ek	I
ekki	no, not, nothing
eld	fire
eldi	fire
eldist	oldest
eldr	fire, the-flames
eldrinn	the-fire
eldsskara	fire-poker
eltu	chased
en	about, and, but, on, than, that, the, then, though, when, while
endast	ending
enga	any, none
engan	no-one
engi	no, none, not
engir	no
engu	nothing
engum	no, none
enn	but, than
eptir	after, behind
er	am, and, as, be, from, have, is, of, that, then, was, when, which, who
erfi	inheritance
ergist	feebler
erninum	the-eagle
ert	are
ertu	are-you
eru	are, is, they-are, were
erum	are
eyra	ear
eyranu	ears
eyri	an-ounce-of
eytt	devastated

F, f

Old Norse	English
fá	get, pay
faðir	father
fæddi	raised
færa	be-brought
færði	brought, took
færir	travel
færist	the-journey
fæti	feet
fætr	feet
fagnaði	celebrated, welcomed
fagr	beautiful
fagrar	fair
fagrt	fair
fangbrögðum	to-wrestling
fann	found, met
fannst	found
far	travel
fara	go, to-travel, travel, travelled, travelling
farið	go
farin	gone
farit	gone
fast	fastened, hard, hard
fastara	harder
fé	wealth
féfátt	lack-of-money
feginn	relieved
fegnir	joyful
feiga	doomed
feigr	doomed, fated-to-die
fekk	got, went
fela	hide
félagi	companion
fell	falling, fell
felli	wave
fellir	drops
fellu	fell
felr	fold
fengnir	get
fengu	caught
fengust	got-they

Word List (Old Norse to English)

Old Norse	English
ferð	journey, the-journey, travelled, voyage
ferðum	voyage
ferr	travelling, went
físparir	fee-sparing
festi	joined
festir	fastened
fimleika	tricks
fingrgull	finger-gold
finna	find
finnumst	meet
fitan	fat
fjalli	mountains
fjarstætt	far-away
fjölkunnigr	skilled-in-magic
fjölmenni	following-men
fjóra	four
fjórar	four
fjörð	fjord
fjórðunga	quarters
fjórum	four
fleira	more
flestum	most
fleygir	flew-it
flokk	band, company
flokki	men
flýgr	flies
föður	father
föðurnum	to-the-father
fólk	folk
fólki	folk
föll	falling
fönn	snow
fór	moving, travelled, went
fortjaldinu	the-curtain
fóru	travelled, went
fóruð	travelled
förunautr	companion
fótrinn	leg
fótum	feet
frá	away-from, from, went-from
fram	from, from-there, to
framboðligr	be-offered
framt	provide
frár	swift
fremstir	foremost
frétt	news
fríð	peaceful
frosta	Frosti (name)
frosti	Frosti, Frosti (name)
fugla	birds
full	drunk
fullsterk	Full-Strong (name)
fullsterkr	Full-Strong (name)
fullu	the-full
fúlt	foul
fundizt	met
furðuliga	exceedingly
fylgd	following
fylgdi	followed, following
fylgja	follow, following
fylgt	followed
fylldan	filled
fyllt	horn
fyrir	before, before-them, for, over
fyrr	before
fyrst	first
fyrsta	first
fyrstu	first
fyrstum	first

G, g

Old Norse	English
gæfa	luck
gæfu	luck
gaf	gave
gáfu	gave
gagn	benefit
gagnvart	going-from
galdrafullt	magic-full
galinn	mad
gamalla	the-old
gamans	games
gamni	game
gamninu	the-game
gandreið	witch-ride
ganga	go, going, walk
gangandi	walking

Word List (Old Norse to English)

Old Norse	English
gangi	go
gat	got
gátum	opening
gaulardal	Gaulardale (place)
gef	give
gefa	give
gefr	given
gegnt	opposite
geirröð	Geirrod (name)
geirröðargarða	Geirrod's-Town (place)
geirröðargörðum	Geirrod's-Town (place)
geirröði	Geirrod (name), Geirrod's (name)
geirröðr	Geirrod (name)
gekk	went
gengit	come
gengr	went
gengu	went
ger	done
gera	do, done, make, to-do, to-make
gerði	did
gerðist	became
gerðu	did
gersema	precious-things
gersemar	treasured, treasures
gersemi	a-treasure, treasure, treasures
gert	made
get	guess
geta	get
getit	told-of
getr	get
geyma	retain, to-mind
gimsteinar	precious-stones
gjafirnar	the-gifts
gjarna	gladly
glaðir	glad, gladly
glæsisvöllu	Glasir-Plains (place)
glæsisvöllum	Glasir-Plains (place)
glerglugg	glass-window
glettist	playing-tricks
glíma	wrestle, wrestling
glímt	wrestled
glóanda	burning, glowing
glugginn	the-skylight
gneistaflaug	a-shower-of-sparks
gneistaflaugin	sparks-flying
gneistar	sparks
gnípalundi	Gnipalund (place)
góða	good, Good (name), the-good
góði	good, Good (name)
goðmund	Godmund (name)
goðmundar	Godmund (name), Godmund's (name)
goðmundi	Godmund (name)
goðmundr	Godmund, Godmund (name)
góðr	good
góðri	luck
goðrún	Gudrun (name)
goðrúnar	Gudrun (name)
goðrúnu	Gudrun (name)
góðum	good
gólfi	the-floor
gólfit	floor, the-floor
gott	good
græð	tend-to
grafit	dug
grám	grey
granda	to-injure
greip	grabbed, gripped
grenjaði	howling, screamed
grím	Grim (name)
grími	Grim (name)
grímr	Grim (name)
grindhlíðit	gate
grip	grabbed
gripi	treasure, treasures
grunda	Grundir (place)
grundir	Grundir (place)
grundum	Grundir (place)
guðvef	precious-cloth
guðvefjarskikkju	a-precious-cloak
gul	gold
gull	gold
gullbúnu	gold-plated
gullhnött	gold-ball
gullhring	gold-ring

Word List (Old Norse to English)

Old Norse	English
gullhringa	gold-rings
gulli	gold
gullker	golden-bowl
gullkórónu	gold-crown
gullligt	gold
gullligum	gold
gullmen	gold-necklace
gullofit	gold-woven
gullskotnum	gold-trimmed
gulr	gold, yellow
gustr	Gust

H, h

Old Norse	English
há	high
hæfa	hit
hægt	possible
hættu	dangerous
hafa	had, had, have, having
hafði	had
hafið	have
haft	had, have
hafvillur	open-sea
haglhríð	hailstorm
hákon	Hakon (name)
halda	hold, keep
hálfan	half
hall	marble, piece-of-marble
hallar	hall
hallargólfi	hall-floor
hallargólfit	hall-floor
hallinn	the-marble, the-piece-of-marble
hallinum	the-marble
hallrinn	the-marble, the-piece-of-marble
háls	the-neck
hálsinum	throat
hamingju	luck
hana	he, it, she
handklæði	hand-cloths
handklæðit	hand-cloth
handsals	binding
hann	he, him, it, men
hans	him, his
harðasti	hardest
harðúðigr	hard-minded
hásæti	a-high-seat, high-seat
háski	dangerous
hátíð	festival
háttar	kinds
haug	a-burial-mound
hauginn	the-mound
haugrinn	the-mound, the-mound
haugsins	burial-mound-his
heðan	from-hence
hefði	had
hefi	have
hefir	had, has, have
hefna	avenge
heiðr	honour
heiðrekr	Heidrek (name)
heill	whole
heilsaði	greeted
heim	home
heiminum	the-world
heimsliga	foolishly
heit	declared
heita	be-named, named, promised
heiti	named
heitir	called, named
heitt	hot
hel	death
heldr	rather
helt	held
helzt	held
hemra	Hemra (place)
hemru	Hemra (place)
henda	catch
hendi	hand
hendr	hand
hentar	suits
henti	caught
hér	forces, here
heraði	district
heraðinu	the-district
heraðit	the-district

Word List (Old Norse to English)

Old Norse	English
hernaði	raiding
hest	horses
hesta	horses
hestar	horses
hestarnir	the-horses
hesti	horse
hestr	horse
hestum	horses
hét	is-named, named, promised
heyra	hear
heyrir	heard
himni	the-sky
hingat	here
hinir	others, the-other
hirðið	take-care
hirðmaðr	court-man
hirðmönnum	court-men
hirðprýði	court
hita	heat
hjá	beside
hjástöðu	beside-standing
hjó	hewed
hlæjandi	smiling
hlátr	laughter
hlátri	laughter
hlaupa	ran
hleypr	ran
hleypt	cast
hliðin	the-gates
hlíðir	slope
hljóðfæra	musical-instruments
hljóðfæri	musical-instruments
hljóp	ran
hló	laughed
hlógu	laughed
hluti	lot
hlýðni	homage
hlytir	to-get
hnakkinn	the-back-of-the-head
hnefann	fist
höfði	head
höfðingi	a-chieftain
höfðu	had
höfðum	head
höfn	the-harbour
höfuðit	head, his-head
höfum	have
hól	hill
holdi	flesh
hólinn	the-mound
hóll	mound
höll	a-hall, the-hall
höllina	the-hall
höllinni	the-hall
hólmgörðum	Novgorod (place)
hólnum	the-mound
hömrum	a-steep-cliff
hönd	hand
höndum	hands
honum	he, him, his, it, to-him
horfin	disappeared
horn	a-horn, horn, horns
hornin	the-horn, the-horns
horninu	horn, the-horn
hornit	a-horn, horn, the
hornunum	the-horn
hösvaðist	went-for
hösvi	Hosvir (name)
hösvir	Hosvir (name)
hratt	pushed
hraustr	brave
hreinna	cleaner
hreysti	bravery, valour
hring	a-circle, ring
hringinn	the-ring
hringnum	the-ring
hringrinn	the-ring
hristi	shook
hrutu	erupted
hrysi	trembled
hug	think
hugr	thought
huldumaðr	a-hidden-man
hulinshjálm	helm-of-invisibility
hún	she
hurfu	disappeared, vanished
hús	house, the-house
húsabæ	farmstead
húsum	houses
hvaðan	from-where

Word List (Old Norse to English)

Old Norse	English
hvar	were, what, where
hvarf	disappeared
hvárki	neither
hvárn	each
hvárntveggja	either-side
hvárt	each, whether, which
hvárttveggja	either
hvat	what, who
hvergi	neither
hverju	how
hverjum	each
hvern	everyone
hverr	anyone, each, who
hverrar	whose
hversu	how-so
hvert	each, what
hví	what, why
hvítinga	Whitings (name)
hvítingar	Whitings (name)
hvítingum	Whitings (name)
hvítr	white
hvítt	white

I, i

Old Norse	English
illa	badly, ill
ilmr	sweet-smell
in	the
ina	the
indíalandi	India
inn	in, inside, the
innanborðs	aboard
inum	the
it	the, this

Í, í

Old Norse	English
í	about, all, among, at, if, in, into, it, of, on, the, to, was, with-that

J, j

Old Norse	English
jafnan	every-time
jafnstóra	equally-as-big, equally-large
jafnstórr	equally-big
jamtaland	Jamtland (place)
jarl	earl, the-earl
jarli	the-earl, the-earl's
jarls	the-earl, the-earl's
járnskeggja	Iron-Beard (name)
jökli	Jokul's (name)
jökull	Jokul (name)
jólin	Yule (name)
jólum	Yule (name)
jörðina	the-ground
jötnum	giants
jötunheima	Giant-Home (place)
jötunheimar	Giant-Land (place)
jötunmóð	giant's-wrath
jungfrú	young-woman

K, k

Old Norse	English
kærleikum	friendly-terms, friendship
kallaðr	called
kallar	call, called
kallat	called
kalt	cold
kann	can, knows
kanna	explore
kapparnir	champions
karkr	Kark (name)
kastaði	cast, threw
kastar	threw
kastat	cast
kastið	throw
kátir	merry
kaupferðir	trading-voyages
kaupferðum	trading-journeys
keiktist	bent
kem	come
kempa	warrior
kemr	came, comes
kenna	know, taught

Word List (Old Norse to English)

Old Norse	English
kenndr	recognised
ker	vessel
keyrir	the-stick
kikna	bent-backwards
kinnbeinit	chin-bone
kjaptinum	mouth, the-mouth
kjaptrinn	jaw
kjós	choose
klæddu	dressed
klæði	clothed, clothes
klæðin	clothes
klæðir	clothed
klæðsekk	sack
klæðum	clothes
kné	knees
knésbætr	the-back-of-the-knees
knettinum	the-ball
knöttinn	the-ball
knöttrinn	the-ball
kollóttan	bald-headed
kollsveinn	Kollsvein (name), the-boy
kölluð	called
kom	came
koma	came, come, coming
komi	come
komin	coming
kominn	came, come, coming
komit	coming
komnir	come
komu	came
kómu	came
kómust	came
kona	wife
konung	the-king
konungi	king, the-king
konungnum	the-king
konungr	king, the-king
konungrinn	the-king
konungs	the-king, the-king's
konungshöll	the-king's-hall
konungsnafn	the-king's-name
konungsson	a-king's-son, the-king's-son
konur	women
köppunum	the-cups
kórónu	the-crown
köstuðu	cast
krásum	food
krefja	demand
kristinn	a-Christian, Christian
kristnum	Christian
krókstaf	crooked-staff
krókstafinn	the-crooked-stick
krókstafr	crooked-stick
kross	the-cross
krummurnar	grabbed
kumpánar	fellows
kunnáttu	skills
kunngera	to-announce, wiser
kunnigt	know
kvað	said
kvaddi	called
kvaðst	said
kveðju	greetings
kveðst	greetings, said
kveld	the-evening
kveldit	evening
kvikt	alive, living-thing
kvöld	evening
kyn	kin
kyssti	kissed

L, l

Old Norse	English
lá	had, laid, lay
lætr	acts, have
lagði	had, laid
lagðist	lay
lagi	thrust
lagt	left
lágu	laid
land	land, the-land
landi	the-land
landit	land, the-land
landsuðr	the-south-east
landsuðri	South-East
langa	Long (name)
langan	long
lát	have, let
láta	have, lay-out, to-have

Word List (Old Norse to English)

Old Norse	English
látum	leave-it
laukst	closed
laun	to-repay
launa	repay
launat	repay
laust	loosed
leggja	grant
leiða	led
leiddr	led
leika	play
leikinn	games, trick
leit	had
lék	played
lékst	played
lén	a-fee
lendr	landed
lengr	longer
lét	had
léti	made
létu	had
leynt	hidden
lið	assistance, the-company-of
liði	company, dislocated
líðr	passed
lifði	lived
lífgjöf	life-gift
lifir	lives
liggja	lie-down
liggr	lying
líkari	like
líkast	like
listamann	a-skilled-craftsman
lítill	little, small
lítilli	little
lítilmannliga	weakly
lítinn	little
lítit	little
litlu	little
ljótan	hideous
lófa	promise
lofaði	pledging
lofuðu	praised
lög	law
logaði	blazed
logandi	ablaze
logit	a-lie
lokit	ended
löngu	long
lopti	the-air, the-sky
lúkanus	Lucanus (name)
lúkum	end

M, m

Old Norse	English
má	may
maðr	a-man, man
mæðast	get-tired
mæla	speak
mælir	speaks
mælt	spoke
mælti	said, spoke
mál	conversations, the-matter
máldrykkju	drinking
manna	man, men, men, men's
manni	man
manns	man
mannshöfuð	a-man's-head
mánuð	a-month
marga	many
margir	many
matr	food
matsveinar	food-servants
mátt	may
mátti	could
mátuligr	fitting
með	along, with
meðalmaðr	an-average-man
meðan	as-long-as, while
mega	may
megi	may
megin	side
meira	more
menn	men, the-men
mér	I, me, to-me
mest	most, mostly
mestr	the-greatest, the-most
miðit	the-middle
miðju	the-middle

Word List (Old Norse to English)

Old Norse	English
mik	me, myself
mikil	great, tall
mikill	great, large
mikils	much
mikinn	great, much
mikit	great, large, much
mikla	great
miklar	great, much
mikli	larger, largest
miklu	much
miklum	great
millum	between
mín	me, mine, my
mína	mine
mínir	mine, my
minn	mine, my
minni	in-memory, smaller
minnum	came
mínu	mine
mínum	mine
miskunnar	mercy
missa	lose
missi	lost
mitt	me, mine
mjök	great, much
móðir	mother
móðu	large-river
móðuna	the-river
mönnum	men, the-men
morgin	morning, the-morning
morgininn	morning
morginn	morning
morgni	morning
morguninn	morning
mörkina	the-trees
mót	against, meet, to-meet
móti	against, meet, oppose, opposition, to-meet
mun	could, must, shall, should, should-be, would
mundi	could-be, should, would, would-have
mundu	must-be, would
mundum	would-be
muni	would
munni	a-mouth
munt	must-be, should
muntu	shall-you, should
munu	should, would-be
munum	should
mútur	payment
myrkr	fog

N, n

Old Norse	English
nær	near
næst	near, next, next-to
nætr	nights
nafn	name
nafnbætr	name-titles
nafnfesti	naming-gift
nafni	name
nam	took
nasir	nose
nát	get-hold-of, hold-of
náttúru	natured
né	nor
neðra	under
nefit	nose
nefndi	named
nefndir	named
nema	but, except
neytr	good-use
níðingr	a-coward
niðr	below, down
niðrgangs	down-going
nóg	enough
nokkura	some
nokkurn	some
nokkurr	something
nokkuru	some, somewhat
nokkut	anything, some
noreg	Norway (place)
noregi	Norway (place)
noregs	Norway (place)
nösunum	on-the-nose
nótt	night
nóttina	night, the-night

Word List (Old Norse to English)

Old Norse	English
nú	now

O, o

Old Norse	English
of	of
ofan	down, over
ofmagni	to-overpower
ok	ad, also, and, filled, river, to
okkr	us, us
olnbogarnir	elbows
opinn	open
opt	often
orðinn	became
orðit	word
orðum	words
orkar	able-to
orkufátt	low-energy
orlof	leave
orlofs	vacation
orminum	The-Serpent (name)
oss	ours, us

Ó, ó

Old Norse	English
óaflátssamr	un-indulgent
óðinn	Odin (name)
óðins	Odin's (name)
óðni	Odin (name)
óðu	waded
ófarin	unfinished
ófögnuðr	unhappy
ófriðar	un-peace
óhýrligr	unfriendly-looking
óláf	Olaf (name)
óláfi	Olaf (name)
Óláfr	Olaf (name)
óláfs	Olaf's (name)
ólík	unlike
ólyfjan	poison
óorðna	unspoken
ór	away-from, from, of, out-of, through
óskyldara	less-should

Old Norse	English
ótal	countless
óþýðr	unfriendly
óttars	Ottar's (name)
óvæginn	ruthless
óvit	unconscious

Ö, ö

Old Norse	English
öðrum	one, other
öfundsjúkir	jealous
ökkla	ankles
öllum	all
öndvegit	opposite
önnur	another, one, other
örn	eagle

P, p

Old Norse	English
pilt	boy
piltrinn	the-boy
pjakka	prick
pjakkar	prick, pricked
prett	tricked
pungi	pouch

R, r

Old Norse	English
ráð	advice, counsel
ráða	advice, decide, reckon
ráðast	arranged
ræð	ruler
ræðr	rules
rak	drove
ráku	drove
rann	ran
rasaði	tumbled
rauðr	red
rauðum	red
rautt	red
réð	advised, ruled
réðst	moved
refði	staff

Word List (Old Norse to English)

Old Norse	English
reið	riding
reiddist	rose
reiðu	ride
reis	rose
reisti	raised
reistu	raised
renna	ran
reyk	smoke
reynt	test
ríða	ride, ride-away, riding, rode, to-ride
ríðr	rode
riðu	rode
rifnaði	split
ríki	kingdom
risaland	Giant-Land (place)
risalandi	Giant-Land (place)
risalands	Giant-Land (place)
ríss	rose
rjóðr	clearing
rjóðrinu	the-clearing
rönd	around
röndum	stripes
röskr	brave
ruggaði	rocking
rúm	room

S, s

Old Norse	English
sá	saw, see, seeing, so, there
sækið	seek
sæmilig	well
sæng	bed
sæti	seat
sætis	seat
sætr	mountain-pastures
sagði	said, said, told, told
sagðist	said
sagt	told, told
saka	injury
sama	same
saman	together
sár	wound
sat	sat
sáttir	agreed
sáttu	saw-you
sáu	saw
sauða	wether's
saur	the-mud
sé	even, he-is, is, see, you
sefr	slept
seg	say
segir	said, said-to, say, told
segist	said
segja	say, tell
seint	slowly
selshöfuð	seal's-head
sem	as, as-if, if, that, whatever, where, which, who
sendi	sent
sendiferðir	missions
sendr	sent
sent	sent
sér	he, him, himself, his, saw, see, to-him, to-see
serk	shirt
serkinn	the-shirt
serkr	shirt
sét	seen
setning	the-setting
setti	set
settist	sat
sex	six
sídan	afterwards
síðan	after, afterwards, since, since., then
síðar	afterwards, since
siðr	the-custom
síðum	sides
sigla	sail, sailed
sigldi	sail, sailed
sigldu	sailed
sigurðarson	Son-of-Sigurd (name)
sik	him, himself, his, themselves
silfrdisk	silver-dish
silfrhring	silver-ring
silfri	silver

Word List (Old Norse to English)

Old Norse	English
silfrkerum	silver
silfrs	silver
sín	hers, him, their, themselves
sína	his, their
sínar	his
sindraði	sparkled
sinn	his, occasion, their
sinna	his
sinnar	his
sinni	his, this
síns	his
sínum	hers, his
sitja	sit
sitr	sat
sitt	his, sat
sjá	saw, see, to-see
sjaldsénir	rarely-seen
sjálfr	itself
sjau	seven
sjáum	see
skal	shall
skál	shall
skalf	shook
skalt	shall
skaltu	shall, shall-you
skálum	bowls
skammt	a-short-distance, short
skapsmunum	mood-mind
skarlatsklæðum	scarlet-clothing
skatta	tax
skattgildir	tributaries
skaut	shot
skeggit	beard
skemmta	amuse
skemmtan	amusement
skemmtunar	amusement, entertainment
sker	a-rock
skildi	separated
skildu	separated
skildust	separated
skilja	separate, such
skiljast	separate
skilr	separating
skinnslit	colour
skip	a-ship, ship, the-ship
skipat	directed-to
skips	ships, the-ships
skipta	give
skipuð	equipped
skíra	baptised
skjótt	swiftly
skóga	forests
skógar	the-forest
skóginn	the-forest, the-forests
skörina	high-seat
skorinn	cut
skuli	shall
skulu	shall, should
skuluð	should
skyldi	should
skyldu	and, would
slær	struck
slagir	artful
slegit	struck
slík	such
slíka	such
slíkan	such
slíkar	such
slikum	such
sló	struck
slógu	formed
slysalaust	accidents-without
smáleik	small-games
smáleika	small-games
smásveinn	little-boy
snaraði	flew-it, threw, turned-quickly
snarat	twisted
snekkju	a-sailboat
snemma	early, soon
sneri	turned
sniðglímu	hip-throw
snjó	snow
snjórinn	the-snow
snöruðu	threw
snúinn	twisted
sofa	seep, sleep, slept
sögðu	said
sól	the-sun

Word List (Old Norse to English)

Old Norse	English
sólarfalli	sunset
sólin	sunrise
sólir	suns
sólskin	sunshine
son	son
sonr	son
sprakk	broke
spring	burst
spurði	asked
spyrjast	was-heard
staðar	standing, to-stand
stærsti	biggest
staf	staff
stafinn	the-staff, the-stick
stafnum	stick
stakk	struck
stálbroddr	steel-point
staldraði	lingered
stall	stable
standa	stand
stangaði	stabbed
sté	stepped
stefna	directed
stein	stone
steinhús	stone-house
steinkastinu	stone-throwing
steinn	stone
sterkari	stronger
sterkastr	strongest
sterkliga	strongly
sterkr	strong
steypa	cast
steyptist	fell, knocked
steyptu	cast
stígr	climbed
stikilinn	horn-point
stiklinum	the-narrow
stóð	stood, weighed
stóðu	stood
stöðum	places
stokkinn	the-foot-board
stökkva	jumped
stóra	great
stórr	big
stórri	large
strengdi	boldly
stríðlyndr	obstinate
ströng	strong
studdi	steadied
stundu	while
stundum	awhile
styrkja	strengthen
sú	so
sumarit	summer
sundi	swimming
sundr	apart
svá	saw, so, the
svarar	answered
svarit	sworn
svartan	black
sveinar	companions, men
sveinbarn	a-baby-boy
sveinn	boy
sverja	swear
svikit	tricked
svipmikill	a-striking
sviptingar	tussle
svipuleik	the-scourge
svipuleikr	the-scourge
sýna	show
sýndar	shown
sýndi	showed
sýndist	seemed, thought
sýnis	his
synjast	refuse

T, t

Old Norse	English
tak	take
taka	take, took
takið	take
talar	talked
tána	toe
tánni	toe
tekinn	taken
tekit	taken
tekr	takes, took
tennr	teeth
tennrnar	teeth, the-teeth
tíðenda	news, of-news

Word List (Old Norse to English)

Old Norse	English
tíðendi	news
til	for, of, to
tíma	time
tíu	ten
tjald	tents
togast	pulled
tók	received, took, tugged
tókst	took
tóku	took
tókust	took
töldust	considered
tólf	twelve
töluðu	told
trapiza	table
traust	trusted
trausti	Trusty (name)
trautt	scarcely
treysta	reckon, trust
treysti	trust
tröllaukinn	troll-possessed
tröllsligri	troll-like
tröllum	trolls
trú	faith, the-faith
tryggvason	Tryggvason (name)
tuttugu	twenty
tvá	two
tvær	two
tvau	two
tveggja	two
tveir	of, two
tvítugt	twenty

Þ, þ

Old Norse	English
þá	them, then, when
þaðan	from-there
þær	there, those
þætti	seem, the-story
þakkaði	thanked, thanked
þakkar	thanked
þangat	from-there, there
þann	that, the, then
þar	here, then, then, there, they, was
þat	it, that
þau	their, they
þegar	as-soon-as, straightaway, then, there
þeim	from-them, theirs, them, then, they
þeir	should, them, there, they
þeira	their, theirs, them, there, they, they-were
þeirar	there
þeiri	their
þekkti	knew
þenna	that
þér	to-you, you, yours
þerris	dry
þess	this
þessa	this
þessi	these, this
þessu	this
þetta	this
þíða	thaw
þik	you
þilfjöl	decks
þín	you, your
þína	yours
þínar	your
þing	assembly, things
þinn	yours
þit	you-two
þitt	your, yours
þjófsaugun	thief's-eyes
þjófshakan	thievish-chin
þjófsnefit	thieving-nose
þjóna	serve, serving
þjónar	serve
þó	though
þökkuðu	thanked
þol	endure
þorði	dared
þorir	dare, dared, daring
þormóðr	Thormod (name)
þórs	Thor's (name)
þorstein	Thorstein (name)
þorsteini	Thorstein (name)
þorsteinn	Thorstein (name)

Word List (Old Norse to English)

Old Norse	English
þorsteins	Thorstein's (name)
þótt	though
þótti	seemed, thought
þóttist	thought
þræli	servant
þrándheimi	Trondheim (place)
þreif	grabbed
þremr	three
þríhyrndr	three-sided
þrír	three
þrjá	three
þú	you
þung	heavy
þurfa	need
því	accordingly, as, because, it, that, then, therefore
þvílíkir	the-like
þykki	seems, think
þykkir	seems
þykkja	think, value, valued
þyngst	heaviest

U, u

Old Norse	English
ullu	wool
um	about, around, through
undan	away, away-from, before
undir	behind, down, under
undirheimum	under-world
undraðist	surprised
undrast	wonder
undruðust	wondered
unga	young
unnust	loved
unum	happy
upp	up
upphlaup	uproar
uppi	up
uppsprettu	up-spring
urðu	became, came
utan	except, except-for, out, out-of, outside, without
uxahnútu	ox-bone

Ú, ú

Old Norse	English
úlfaldi	camel
úlfhamr	Wolf-Skin (name)
úlfheðinn	Ulfhedin (name)
út	out
úti	out, over
útlægr	outlawed

V, v

Old Norse	English
vá	was
vaða	wades
væði	waded-through
vænginn	the-wing
vænsta	good
væri	should-be, was, would
vært	short
væru	were
vaf	wove
vakrliga	nimbly
vald	power
valdi	control
ván	is-expected
vanda	custom, difficulty
vanr	accustomed
vánt	difficulty
vápnaða	weaponed
var	was, were, when
vár	ours
varð	became, was
varðist	defended
vári	spring
varir	aware
várit	spring
varr	aware
vart	was
várt	ours
váru	were, when
vaskligri	braver
vatn	the-water

Word List (Old Norse to English)

Old Norse	English
vatnit	the-water
vátr	water
vaxa	grow
veðr	weather
veg	way
veginn	the-road
veik	turned
veit	know, known, knows
veita	grant, to-grant
veitti	granted
veittu	grant
veizla	feast
veizlan	the-feast
veizlunni	the-feast
vel	well
velfaranda	well-faring
vér	was, we
vera	be, being, were
verða	be, become, becomes
verðr	became, becomes, came
verkr	pain
vert	worth, worthy
vestri	the-west
vetr	winter
vetrinn	winter
vettlingana	mitten
við	against, by, of, to, with
víða	widely
vík	Vik (place)
víkr	moved
vil	will, wish
vilda	wish
vildi	willed, wished, wished-to, would
vildu	wished, would
vili	wish
vilja	he-wished, wished
viljum	wish
vill	will, wished
villa	lost-way
vilt	will, wish
viltu	will-you
vín	wine
vinsæll	popular
virðing	worthy
víst	certainly
vit	know
vita	knew, know
vitja	visit
víttr	bewitched
vöknaði	became-wet
vön	want
vörð	guard
vort	ours
vöttum	gloves
vöxt	grown

Y, y

Old Norse	English
yðr	you
yðrir	your
yðru	your
yðrum	yours
yfir	across, over
yndi	happiness
yrjum	Yrjar (place)

Ý, ý

Old Norse	English
ýmist	either

Word List (English to Old Norse)

Word List (English to Old Norse)

English	Old Norse

A, a

English	Old Norse
a	á, ein, eina, einn, einni, einum, eitt
a-baby	barni
a-baby-boy	sveinbarn
a-bench	bekk
abide	bíða
ablaze	logandi
able-to	orkar
aboard	innanborðs
about	á, at, en, í, um
a-burial-mound	haug
accidents-without	slysalaust
accordingly	því
accustomed	vanr
a-chieftain	höfðingi
a-Christian	kristinn
a-circle	hring
a-city	borg
a-coward	níðingr
across	yfir
acts	lætr
ad	ok
a-din	dunur
advice	ráð, ráða
advised	réð
a-fee	lén
a-forge	afli
after	áðr, eptir, síðan
afterwards	aptr, sídan, síðan, síðar
against	at, mót, móti, við
Agdi (name)	agða, agði
Agdi's (name)	agða
agreed	sáttir
a-hall	höll
a-hidden-man	huldumaðr
a-high-seat	hásæti
a-horn	horn, hornit
a-king's-son	konungsson
a-lie	logit
alive	kvikt

English	Old Norse
all	alla, allan, allar, allir, allr, alls, allt, í, öllum
all-mighty	allmiklum
All-Strong (name)	allsterk, allsterkr
alone	einir
along	með
also	ok
always	ávallt
am	er
a-man	maðr
a-man's-head	mannshöfuð
among	í
a-month	mánuð
a-mouth	munni
amuse	skemmta
amusement	skemmtan, skemmtunar
an-average-man	meðalmaðr
anchor	akkerum
and	eða, en, er, ok, skyldu
an-invite	boð
ankles	ökkla
another	annarr, annarri, önnur
another-thing	annan
an-ounce-of	eyri
answered	svarar
any	enga
anyone	hverr
anything	nokkut
apart	sundr
a-precious-cloak	guðvefjarskikkju
are	ert, eru, erum
are-you	ertu
a-river	á
a-rock	sker
around	rönd, um
arranged	ráðast
artful	slagir
as	at, er, sem, því
a-sailboat	snekkju
a-seat	atsetu
a-ship	skip
a-short-distance	skammt
a-shower-of-sparks	gneistaflaug

Word List (English to Old Norse)

English	Old Norse	English	Old Norse
as-if	sem	behind	eptir, undir
asked	bað, bauð, beiddi, biðr, spurði	being	vera
		below	niðr
a-skilled-craftsman	listamann	be-named	heita
as-long-as	meðan	bench	bekk, bekkjar
assembly	þing	benefit	gagn
assistance	lið	bent	keiktist
as-soon-as	þegar	bent-backwards	kikna
a-steep-cliff	hömrum	be-offered	framboðligr
a-striking	svipmikill	beside	á, hjá
at	á, at, í	beside-standing	hjástöðu
a-table	borðum	best	beztir
a-treasure	gersemi	better	betr, betra, betri
avenge	hefna	between	millum
await	bíða	bewitched	víttr
aware	varir, varr	bid	bað, báðu
away	brott, burt, burtu, undan	big	stórr
		biggest	stærsti
away-from	frá, ór, undan	binding	handsals
awhile	stundum	birds	fugla
a-yard	álnar	Bjalfi	bjálfa, bjálfi
		black	blár, svartan
		blazed	logaði

B, b

English	Old Norse	English	Old Norse
		boldly	strengdi
back	aptr, bak	bore	bar, bárust, berast
badly	illa	borne	borit
Balagardsida (place)	bálagarðssíðu	both	báðum
bald-headed	kollóttan	bowls	skálum
band	flokk	boy	pilt, sveinn
baptised	skíra	brave	hraustr, röskr
be	er, vera, verða	braver	vaskligri
bear	ber, bera, berizt	bravery	hreysti
beard	skeggit	breaking	boði
beautiful	fagr	bring	berið
be-brought	færa	broad	breiða, breitt
became	gerðist, orðinn, urðu, varð, verðr	broke	brotnaði, sprakk
		broken	brotnaði
became-wet	vöknaði	brother	bróður
because	því	brought	bera, borin, færði
become	verða	Brynjolf (name)	brynjólfr
becomes	verða, verðr	burial-mound-his	haugsins
bed	sæng	burned	brann
before	áðr, fyrir, fyrr, undan	burning	glóanda
before-them	fyrir	burst	brast, spring
behaved	breyttu	burst-out-laughing	brosti

Word List (English to Old Norse)

English	Old Norse	English	Old Norse
but	eða, en, enn, nema	considered	töldust
by	á, við	control	valdi
		conversations	mál
		could	mátti, mun
		could-be	mundi
		counsel	ráð
		countless	ótal
		court	hirðprýði
		court-man	hirðmaðr
		court-men	hirðmönnum
		crooked-staff	krókstaf
		crooked-stick	krókstafr
		cubits	álna
		custom	vanda
		cut	skorinn

C, c

English	Old Norse
call	kallar
called	heitir, kallaðr, kallar, kallat, kölluð, kvaddi
came	kemr, kom, koma, kominn, komu, kómu, kómust, minnum, urðu, verðr
camel	úlfaldi
can	kann
carried	bar, báru, borinn
carry	draga
cast	hleypt, kastaði, kastat, köstuðu, steypa, steyptu
catch	henda
caught	fengu, henti
celebrated	fagnaði
certainly	víst
champions	kapparnir
chased	eltu
child	barnit
children	börn
chin-bone	kinnbeinit
choose	kjós
Christian	kristinn, kristnum
cleaner	hreinna
clearing	rjóðr
climbed	stígr
closed	laukst
clothed	klæði, klæðir
clothes	klæði, klæðin, klæðum
cold	kalt
colour	skinnslit
come	gengit, kem, koma, komi, kominn, komnir
comes	kemr
coming	koma, komin, kominn, komit
companion	félagi, förunautr
companions	sveinar
company	flokk, liði

D, d

English	Old Norse
Dagny (name)	dagný
dangerous	hættu, háski
dare	þorir
dared	þorði, þorir
daring	þorir
daughter	dóttir
day	dag, degi
dead	bana, dauð, dauðr
death	bana, bani, hel
decide	ráða
decks	þilfjöl
declared	heit
deep	djúp
defended	varðist
delays	dvelr
demand	krefja
devastated	eytt
did	gerði, gerðu
dies	deyr
difficulty	vanda, vánt
directed	stefna
directed-to	skipat
disappeared	horfin, hurfu, hvarf
dislocated	liði
district	heraði
do	gera
done	ger, gera

Word List (English to Old Norse)

English	*Old Norse*
doomed	feiga, feigr
door	dyrr
doorway	dyrum
down	niðr, ofan, undir
down-going	niðrgangs
drag	draga
drank	drakk, drukkit, drukku
dressed	klæddu
drew	brá, dregr
drink	af, drekka, drekkir, drukkit, drykknum
drinking	drekka, drukkit, drykkju, drykkjuskapr, máldrykkju
drinking-man	drykkjumaðr
drinks	drekkr
drink-to	drukkit
dripped	draup
drops	fellir
Drott (name)	drött, dröttr
drove	rak, ráku
drowned	drukknuðu
drunk	drukkin, drukkit, full
dry	þerris
dug	grafit
dwarf	dverg, dvergrinn

E, e

each	hvárn, hvárt, hverjum, hverr, hvert
eagle	örn
ear	eyra
earl	jarl
early	snemma
ears	eyranu
east	austr
Eastern-Lands (place)	austr, austrveg, austrveginn
either	hvárttveggja, ýmist
either-side	hvárntveggja
elbows	olnbogarnir
embers	eimyrja
end	lúkum
ended	lokit
ending	endast
endure	þol
enough	nóg
entertainment	skemmtunar
equally-as-big	jafnstóra
equally-big	jafnstórr
equally-large	jafnstóra
equipped	skipuð
erupted	hrutu
even	sé
evening	kveldit, kvöld
everyone	hvern
every-time	jafnan
exceedingly	furðuliga
except	nema, utan
except-for	utan
explore	kanna
extra	auka
eyes	auga, augu, augum, augun

F, f

face	andliti
fair	fagrar, fagrt
fair-wind	byr
faith	trú
falling	fell, föll
far-away	fjarstætt
farmer	bóndi
farmstead	húsabæ
fastened	fast, festir
fat	fitan
fated	auðit
fated-to-die	feigr
father	faðir, föður
feast	veizla
feebler	ergist
fee-sparing	fésparir
feet	fæti, fætr, fótum
fell	datt, fell, fellu, steyptist
fellow	drengr
fellows	kumpánar
festival	hátíð

Word List (English to Old Norse)

English	*Old Norse*
filled	fylldan, ok
find	finna
finger-gold	fingrgull
fire	eld, eldi, eldr
fire-poker	eldsskara
first	fyrst, fyrsta, fyrstu, fyrstum
fist	hnefann
fitting	mátuligr
fjord	fjörð
flesh	holdi
flew-it	fleygir, snaraði
flies	flýgr
floor	gólfit
fog	myrkr
fold	felr
folk	fólk, fólki
follow	fylgja
followed	fylgdi, fylgt
following	áliðnum, fylgd, fylgdi, fylgja
following-men	fjölmenni
food	krásum, matr
food-servants	matsveinar
foolishly	heimsliga
for	á, fyrir, til
forces	hér
foremost	fremstir
forests	skóga
formed	slógu
foul	fúlt
found	fann, fannst
four	fjóra, fjórar, fjórum
friendly-terms	kærleikum
friendship	kærleikum
from	á, af, at, er, frá, fram, ór
from-hence	heðan
from-them	þeim
from-there	fram, þaðan, þangat
from-where	hvaðan
Frosti	frosti
Frosti (name)	frosta, frosti
Full-Strong (name)	fullsterk, fullsterkr

G, g

English	*Old Norse*
game	gamni
games	gamans, leikinn
gangrene	drep
gate	grindhliðit
Gaulardale (place)	gaulardal
gave	gaf, gáfu
Geirrod (name)	geirröð, geirröði, geirröðr
Geirrod's (name)	geirröði
Geirrod's-Town (place)	geirröðargarða, geirröðargörðum
get	fá, fengnir, geta, getr
get-hold-of	nát
get-tired	mæðast
Giant-Home (place)	jötunheima
Giant-Land (place)	jötunheimar, risaland, risalandi, risalands
giants	jötnum
giant's-wrath	jötunmóð
give	gef, gefa, skipta
given	gefr
glad	glaðir
gladly	gjarna, glaðir
Glasir-Plains (place)	glæsisvöllu, glæsisvöllum
glass-window	glerglugg
gloves	vöttum
glowing	glóanda
Gnipalund (place)	gnípalundi
go	fara, farið, ganga, gangi
Godmund	goðmundr
Godmund (name)	goðmund, goðmundar, goðmundi, goðmundr
Godmund's (name)	goðmundar
going	ganga
going-from	gagnvart
gold	gul, gull, gulli, gullligt, gullligum, gulr
gold-ball	gullhnött
gold-crown	gullkórónu
golden-bowl	gullker
gold-necklace	gullmen

Word List (English to Old Norse)

English	Old Norse
gold-plated	gullbúnu
gold-ring	gullhring
gold-rings	gullhringa
gold-trimmed	gullskotnum
gold-woven	gullofit
gone	farin, farit
good	góða, góði, góðr, góðum, gott, vænsta
Good (name)	góða, góði
good-use	neytr
got	fekk, gat
got-they	fengust
grabbed	greip, grip, krummurnar, þreif
grant	leggja, veita, veittu
granted	veitti
great	mikil, mikill, mikinn, mikit, mikla, miklar, miklum, mjök, stóra
greeted	heilsaði
greetings	kveðju, kveðst
grey	grám
Grim (name)	grím, grími, grímr
gripped	greip
grow	vaxa
grown	vöxt
Grundir (place)	grunda, grundir, grundum
guard	vörð
Gudrun (name)	goðrún, goðrúnar, goðrúnu
guess	get
Gust	gustr

H, h

English	Old Norse
had	ætti, átti, áttu, hafa, hafði, haft, hefði, hefir, höfðu, lá, lagði, leit, lét, létu
hailstorm	haglhríð
Hakon (name)	hákon
half	hálfan
hall	hallar
hall-floor	hallargólfi, hallargólfit
hand	hendi, hendr, hönd
hand-cloth	handklæðit
hand-cloths	handklæði
hands	höndum
happiness	yndi
happy	unum
hard	fast
harder	fastara
hardest	harðasti
hard-minded	harðúðigr
has	hefir
have	eig, er, hafa, hafið, haft, hefi, hefir, höfum, lætr, lát, láta
having	hafa
he	hana, hann, honum, sér
head	höfði, höfðum, höfuðit
hear	heyra
heard	heyrir
heat	hita
heaviest	þyngst
heavy	þung
Heidrek (name)	heiðrekr
he-is	sé
held	helt, helzt
helm-of-invisibility	hulinshjálm
Hemra (place)	hemra, hemru
here	hér, hingat, þar
hers	sín, sínum
he-took-care-of	annast
hewed	hjó
he-wished	vilja
hidden	leynt
hide	fela
hideous	ljótan
high	há
high-seat	hásæti, skörina
hill	hól
him	at, hann, hans, honum, sér, sik, sín
himself	sér, sik
hip-throw	sniðglímu
his	hans, honum, sér, sik, sína, sínar, sinn, sinna, sinnar, sinni, síns, sínum, sitt, sýnis

Word List (English to Old Norse)

English	Old Norse
his-head	höfuðit
hit	hæfa
hold	halda
hold-of	nát
homage	hlýðni
home	heim
honour	heiðr
horn	fyllt, horn, horninu, hornit
horn-point	stikilinn
horns	horn
horse	hesti, hestr
horses	hest, hesta, hestar, hestum
Hosvir (name)	hösvi, hösvir
hot	heitt
house	hús
House-Child (name)	bæjarbarn, bæjarbarni, bæjarbarns
House-Power (name)	bæjarmagn
houses	húsum
how	hverju
howling	grenjaði
how-so	hversu

I, i

English	Old Norse
I	ek, mér
if	ef, í, sem
ill	illa
in	á, at, í, inn
India	indíalandi
inheritance	arf, erfi
injury	saka
inlaid	búit
in-memory	minni
in-one	einu
inside	inn
intend	ætla
intended	ætlaði, ætlar
intentions	ætlan
into	á, í
invite	býðr
Iron-Beard (name)	járnskeggja
is	á, er, eru, sé
is-expected	ván
is-named	hét
it	at, hana, hann, honum, í, þat, því
itself	sjálfr

J, j

English	Old Norse
Jamtland (place)	jamtaland
jaw	kjaptrinn
jealous	öfundsjúkir
joined	festi
Jokul (name)	jökull
Jokul's (name)	jökli
journey	ferð
joyful	fegnir
jumped	stökkva

K, k

English	Old Norse
Kark (name)	karkr
keep	halda
kill	drepa
killed	drap, drepnir
kin	kyn
kinds	háttar
king	konungi, konungr
kingdom	ríki
kissed	kyssti
knees	kné
knew	þekkti, vita
knocked	steyptist
know	kenna, kunnigt, veit, vit, vita
known	veit
knows	kann, veit
Kollsvein (name)	kollsveinn

L, l

English	Old Norse
lack-of-money	féfátt

Word List (English to Old Norse)

English	Old Norse
laid	lá, lagði, lágu
land	land, landit
landed	lendr
large	mikill, mikit, stórri
larger	mikli
large-river	móðu
largest	mikli
laughed	hló, hlógu
laughter	hlátr, hlátri
law	lög
lay	lá, lagðist
lay-out	láta
leave	orlof
leave-it	látum
led	leiða, leiddr
left	lagt
leg	fótrinn
less-should	óskyldara
let	lát
lie-down	liggja
life-gift	lífgjöf
like	líkari, líkast
lineage	ættar
lingered	staldraði
little	lítill, lítilli, lítinn, lítit, litlu
little-boy	smásveinn
live	búa
lived	bjó, lifði
lives	lifir
living-thing	kvikt
long	langan, löngu
Long (name)	langa
longer	lengr
looking	bragði
loosed	laust
lose	missa
lost	missi
lost-way	villa
lot	hluti
loved	unnust
low-energy	orkufátt
Lucanus (name)	lúkanus
luck	gæfa, gæfu, góðri, hamingju
lying	liggr

M, m

English	Old Norse
mad	galinn
made	gert, léti
magic-full	galdrafullt
make	gera
man	maðr, manna, manni, manns
many	marga, margir
marble	hall
may	má, mátt, mega, megi
me	mér, mik, mín, mitt
meet	finnumst, mót, móti
melted	bráðnaði
men	flokki, hann, manna, menn, mönnum, sveinar
men's	manna
mercy	miskunnar
merry	kátir
met	fann, fundizt
mine	mín, mína, mínir, minn, mínu, mínum, mitt
missions	sendiferðir
mitten	vettlingana
mittens	bandvettlinga
mood-mind	skapsmunum
more	auka, fleira, meira
morning	morgin, morgininn, morginn, morgni, morguninn
most	flestum, mest
mostly	mest
mother	móðir
mound	hóll
mountain-pastures	sætr
mountains	fjalli
mouth	kjaptinum
moved	réðst, víkr
moving	fór
much	mikils, mikinn, mikit, miklar, miklu, mjök
musical-instruments	hljóðfæra, hljóðfæri
must	mun

Word List (English to Old Norse)

English	Old Norse
must-be	mundu, munt
my	mín, mínir, minn
myself	mik
my-wife	eiga

N, n

English	Old Norse
name	nafn, nafni
named	heita, heiti, heitir, hét, nefndi, nefndir
name-titles	nafnbætr
naming-gift	nafnfesti
natured	náttúru
near	nær, næst
need	þurfa
neither	hvárki, hvergi
never	aldri
news	frétt, tíðenda, tíðendi
next	næst
next-to	næst
night	nótt, nóttina
nights	nætr
nimbly	vakrliga
no	ekki, engi, engir, engum
none	eigi, enga, engi, engum
no-one	engan
nor	né
Norway (place)	noreg, noregi, noregs
nose	nasir, nefit
not	eigi, ekki, engi
nothing	eigi, einskis, ekki, engu
Novgorod (place)	hólmgörðum
now	nú

O, o

English	Old Norse
oak	eik
oath	eiða
oaths	eiða
obstinate	stríðlyndr
occasion	sinn
Odin (name)	óðinn, óðni
Odin's (name)	óðins
of	á, af, at, er, í, of, ór, til, tveir, við
off	af
offered	bauð
off-handed	afhenda
of-hand	afhenda
of-news	tíðenda
often	opt
of-the-bench	bekkinn
of-the-day	dagsins
Olaf (name)	óláf, óláfi, Óláfr
Olaf's (name)	óláfs
oldest	eldist
on	á, en, í
one	annarr, annarri, eina, einn, einu, einum, eitt, öðrum, önnur
on-the-nose	nösunum
onto	á
open	opinn
opening	beitina, gátum
open-sea	hafvillur
oppose	móti
opposite	gegnt, öndvegit
opposition	móti
or	eða
orchard	aldingarðr
ordered	bað
other	aðra, annars, öðrum, önnur
others	aðrir, hinir
Ottar's (name)	óttars
ounces	aura
ours	oss, vár, várt, vort
out	út, utan, úti
outlawed	útlægr
out-of	ór, utan
outside	utan
over	at, fyrir, ofan, úti, yfir
own	eigum
owned	átti
ox-bone	uxahnútu

P, p

Word List (English to Old Norse)

English	Old Norse
pain	verkr
pale	bleikum
passed	líðr
pay	fá
payment	mútur
peaceful	fríð
piece-of-marble	hall
pitch	bik
places	stöðum
play	leika
played	lék, lékst
playing-tricks	glettist
pledging	lofaði
point	brodd, broddinum
poison	eitr, ólyfjan
popular	vinsæll
possessions	eigna
possible	hægt
pouch	pungi
power	vald
praised	lofuðu
precious-cloth	guðvef
precious-stones	gimsteinar
precious-things	gersema
prepared	bjó, búin, búit, búnir
prick	pjakka, pjakkar
pricked	pjakkar
promise	lófa
promised	heita, hét
property	eignir
provide	afla, framt
pulled	togast
pushed	hratt

Q, q

English	Old Norse
quarters	fjórðunga

R, r

English	Old Norse
raiding	hernaði
raised	fæddi, reisti, reistu
ran	hlaupa, hleypr, hljóp, rann, renna
rarely-seen	sjaldsénir
rather	heldr
received	tók
reckon	ráða, treysta
recognised	kenndr
red	rauðr, rauðum, rautt
refuse	synjast
relieved	feginn
repay	launa, launat
retain	geyma
return	aptr
revealed	birti
ride	reiðu, ríða
ride-away	ríða
riding	reið, ríða
ring	hring
river	ok
rocking	ruggaði
rode	ríða, ríðr, riðu
room	rúm
rose	reiddist, reis, ríss
ruled	réð
ruler	ræð
rules	ræðr
ruthless	óvæginn

S, s

English	Old Norse
sack	klæðsekk
said	kvað, kvaðst, kveðst, mælti, sagði, sagðist, segir, segist, sögðu
said-of	eiga
said-to	segir
sail	sigla, sigldi
sailed	sigla, sigldi, sigldu
same	sama
sat	sat, settist, sitr, sitt
saw	sá, sáu, sér, sjá, svá
saw-you	sáttu
say	seg, segir, segja
scarcely	trautt
scarlet-clothing	skarlatsklæðum

Word List (English to Old Norse)

English	Old Norse	English	Old Norse
screamed	grenjaði	since.	síðan
seal's-head	selshöfuð	sit	sitja
seat	sæti, sætis	six	sex
see	sá, sé, sér, sjá, sjáum	skilled-in-magic	fjölkunnigr
seeing	sá	skills	kunnáttu
seek	sækið	sleep	sofa
seem	þætti	slept	sefr, sofa
seemed	sýndist, þótti	slope	hlíðir
seems	þykki, þykkir	slowly	seint
seen	sét	small	lítill
seep	sofa	smaller	minni
sent	sendi, sendr, sent	small-games	smáleik, smáleika
separate	skilja, skiljast	smiling	hlæjandi
separated	skildi, skildu, skildust	smoke	reyk
separating	skilr	snow	fönn, snjó
servant	þræli	so	sá, sú, svá
serve	þjóna, þjónar	some	nokkura, nokkurn, nokkuru, nokkut
serving	þjóna		
set	setti	someone	einhverr
settled	bjuggust	something	nokkurr
settlements	byggð	some-way	einhvern
seven	sjau	somewhat	nokkuru
shall	mun, skal, skál, skalt, skaltu, skuli, skulu	son	son, sonr
		Son-of-Sigurd (name)	sigurðarson
shall-you	muntu, skaltu	soon	snemma
she	hana, hún	South-East	landsuðri
ship	skip	sparkled	sindraði
ships	skips	sparks	gneistar
shirt	serk, serkr	sparks-flying	gneistaflaugin
shook	hristi, skalf	speak	mæla
short	skammt, vært	speaks	mælir
shot	skaut	split	rifnaði
should	mun, mundi, munt, muntu, munu, munum, skulu, skuluð, skyldi, þeir	spoke	mælt, mælti
		spread	breiddu
		spring	vári, várit
		stabbed	stangaði
should-be	mun, væri	stable	stall
show	sýna	staff	refði, staf
showed	sýndi	stand	standa
shown	sýndar	standing	staðar
side	megin	steadied	studdi
sides	síðum	steel-point	stálbroddr
silver	silfri, silfrkerum, silfrs	stepped	sté
silver-dish	silfrdisk	stick	stafnum
silver-ring	silfrhring	stone	stein, steinn
since	síðan, síðar	stone-house	steinhús

Word List (English to Old Norse)

English	Old Norse
stone-throwing	steinkastinu
stood	stóð, stóðu
straightaway	þegar
strength	afl, afli
strengthen	styrkja
stripes	röndum
strong	sterkr, ströng
stronger	sterkari
strongest	sterkastr
strongly	sterkliga
struck	slær, slegit, sló, stakk
such	skilja, slík, slíka, slíkan, slíkar, slikum
suits	hentar
summer	sumarit
sunrise	sólin
suns	sólir
sunset	sólarfalli
sunshine	sólskin
suppose	ætla
surprised	undraðist
swear	sverja
sweet-smell	ilmr
swift	frár
swiftly	skjótt
swimming	sundi
sworn	svarit

T, t

English	Old Norse
table	borð, borðinu, trapiza
table-cloth	dúkinn, dúkr
tablecloths	dúka
take	tak, taka, takið
take-care	hirðið
take-care-of	ábyrgjast
taken	tekinn, tekit
takes	tekr
talked	talar
tall	mikil
taught	kenna
tax	skatta
teeth	tennr, tennrnar
tell	segja
ten	tíu
tend-to	græð
tents	tjald
test	reynt
than	at, en, enn
thanked	þakkaði, þakkar, þökkuðu
that	á, af, at, en, er, sem, þann, þat, þenna, því
that-bench	bekknum
thaw	þíða
thaws	bræðir
the	á, ána, at, en, hornit, í, in, ina, inn, inum, it, svá, þann
the-air	lopti
the-back	bak
the-back-of-the-head	hnakkinn
the-back-of-the-knees	knésbætr
the-ball	knettinum, knöttinn, knöttrinn
the-bench	bekknum
the-bone	beini, beinum
the-boy	kollsveinn, piltrinn
the-chest	bringu
the-child	barn, barnit
the-city	borgarinnar, borgina
the-clearing	rjóðrinu
the-company-of	lið
the-crooked-stick	krókstafinn
the-cross	kross
the-crown	kórónu
the-cup-bearer	byrlaranum
the-cups	köppunum
the-curtain	fortjaldinu
the-curve	bugtinni
the-custom	siðr
the-death	bani
the-district	heraðinu, heraðit
the-door	dyranna, dyrr, dyrrnar
the-dwarf	dvergnum, dvergrinn
the-dwarf's-boy	dvergsbarnit
the-dwelling	bæinn, bú
the-eagle	erninum
the-earl	jarl, jarli, jarls
the-earl's	jarli, jarls
the-evening	aptnaði, kveld

Word List (English to Old Norse)

English	Old Norse
the-faith	trú
the-feast	veizlan, veizlunni
the-fire	eldrinn
the-flames	eldr
the-floor	gólfi, gólfit
the-foot-board	stokkinn
the-forest	skógar, skóginn
the-forests	skóginn
the-full	fullu
the-game	gamninu
the-gates	hliðin
the-gifts	gjafirnar
the-good	góða
the-greatest	mestr
the-ground	jörðina
the-hall	höll, höllina, höllinni
the-harbour	höfn
the-horn	hornin, horninu, hornunum
the-horns	hornin
the-horses	hestarnir
the-house	hús
their	sín, sína, sinn, þau, þeira, þeiri
theirs	þeim, þeira
the-journey	færist, ferð
the-king	konung, konungi, konungnum, konungr, konungrinn, konungs
the-king's	konungs
the-king's-hall	konungshöll
the-king's-name	konungsnafn
the-king's-son	konungsson
the-land	land, landi, landit
the-like	þvílíkir
them	þá, þeim, þeir, þeira
the-marble	hallinn, hallinum, hallrinn
the-matter	mál
the-men	menn, mönnum
the-middle	miðit, miðju
the-moat	díki
the-morning	morgin
the-most	mestr
the-mound	hauginn, haugrinn, hólinn, hólnum
the-mouth	kjaptinum
themselves	sik, sín
the-mud	saur
then	á, en, er, síðan, þá, þann, þar, þegar, þeim, því
the-narrow	stiklinum
the-neck	háls
the-night	nóttina
the-oak	eikinni
the-old	gamalla
the-opening	beitina
the-other	annarr, hinir
the-piece-of-marble	hallinn, hallrinn
the-point	broddinum, broddrinn
the-queen	drottning
there	sá, þær, þangat, þar, þegar, þeir, þeira, þeirar
therefore	því
the-ring	hringinn, hringnum, hringrinn
the-river	ána, ánni, árinnar, móðuna
the-road	veginn
the-scourge	svipuleik, svipuleikr
these	þessi
The-Serpent (name)	orminum
the-setting	setning
the-ship	skip
the-ships	skips
the-shirt	serkinn
the-sky	himni, lopti
the-skylight	glugginn
the-snow	snjórinn
the-south-east	landsuðr
the-staff	stafinn
the-stick	keyrir, stafinn
the-story	þætti
the-sun	sól
the-table-cloth	dúkinn
the-tables	borða, borðum
the-teeth	tennrnar
the-town	borgarinnar, borgina
the-trees	mörkina
the-water	vatn, vatnit

Word List (English to Old Norse)

English	Old Norse
the-west	vestri
the-wing	vænginn
the-world	heiminum
they	drekka, þar, þau, þeim, þeir, þeira
they-are	eru
they-were	þeira
thick-set	búk
thief's-eyes	þjófsaugun
thieving-nose	þjófsnefit
thievish-chin	þjófshakan
things	þing
think	hug, þykki, þykkja
this	it, sinni, þess, þessa, þessi, þessu, þetta
Thormod (name)	Þormóðr
Thor's (name)	Þórs
Thorstein (name)	Þorstein, Þorsteini, Þorsteinn
Thorstein's (name)	Þorsteins
those	þær
though	en, þó, þótt
thought	hugr, sýndist, þótti, þóttist
three	þremr, þrír, þrjá
three-sided	þríhyrndr
threw	berði, kastaði, kastar, snaraði, snöruðu
throat	hálsinum
through	ór, um
throw	kastið
thrown	ausit
thrust	lagi
time	tíma
to	á, af, at, fram, í, ok, til, við
to-announce	kunngera
to-do	gera
to-drink	drekka
toe	tána, tánni
to-get	hlytir
together	saman
to-going	atgang, atgangr
to-grant	veita
to-have	láta
to-him	honum, sér
to-injure	granda

English	Old Norse
told	sagði, sagt, segir, töluðu
told-of	getit
to-make	gera
to-me	mér
to-meet	mót, móti
to-mind	geyma
took	færði, nam, taka, tekr, tók, tókst, tóku, tókust
to-overpower	ofmagni
to-own	eiga
to-repay	laun
to-ride	ríða
to-see	sér, sjá
to-stand	staðar
to-the-father	föðurnum
to-travel	fara
towards	at
to-wrestling	fangbrögðum
to-you	þér
trading-journeys	kaupferðum
trading-voyages	kaupferðir
travel	færir, far, fara
travelled	fara, ferð, fór, fóru, fóruð
travelling	fara, ferr
treasure	gersemi, gripi
treasured	gersemar
treasures	gersemar, gersemi, gripi
trembled	hrysi
tributaries	skattgildir
trick	leikinn
tricked	prett, svikit
tricks	fimleika
troll-like	tröllsligri
troll-possessed	tröllaukinn
trolls	tröllum
Trondheim (place)	Þrándheimi
trust	treysta, treysti
trusted	traust
Trusty (name)	trausti
Tryggvason (name)	tryggvason
tugged	tók
tumbled	rasaði
turned	sneri, veik

Word List (English to Old Norse)

English	Old Norse
turned-away	brautinni
turned-quickly	snaraði
turning	brautinni
tussle	sviptingar
twelve	tólf
twenty	tuttugu, tvítugt
twisted	snarat, snúinn
two	tvá, tvær, tvau, tveggja, tveir

U, u

English	Old Norse
Ulfhedin (name)	úlfheðinn
unconscious	óvit
under	neðra, undir
under-world	undirheimum
undressed	afklæðast, afklæddust
unfinished	ófarin
unfriendly	óþýðr
unfriendly-looking	óhýrligr
unhappy	ófögnuðr
un-indulgent	óaflátssamr
unlike	ólík
un-peace	ófriðar
unspoken	óorðna
up	upp, uppi
uproar	upphlaup
up-spring	uppsprettu
us	okkr, oss

V, v

English	Old Norse
vacation	orlofs
valour	hreysti
value	þykkja
valued	þykkja
vanished	hurfu
vessel	ker
Vik (place)	vík
visit	vitja
voyage	ferð, ferðum

W, w

English	Old Norse
waded	óðu
waded-through	væði
wades	vaða
walk	ganga
walking	gangandi
want	vön
warrior	kempa
was	á, er, í, þar, vá, væri, var, varð, vart, vér
was-heard	spyrjast
water	vátr
wave	felli
way	braut, veg
we	vér
weak	deigum
weakly	lítilmannliga
wealth	fé
weaponed	vápnaða
weather	veðr
wedding-proposal	brullaup
weighed	stóð
welcomed	fagnaði
well	sæmilig, vel
well-faring	velfaranda
went	fekk, ferr, fór, fóru, gekk, gengr, gengu
went-for	hösvaðist
went-from	frá
were	eru, hvar, væru, var, váru, vera
wether's	sauða
what	hvar, hvat, hvert, hví
whatever	sem
when	at, en, er, þá, var, váru
where	hvar, sem
whether	hvárt
which	at, er, hvárt, sem
while	en, meðan, stundu
white	hvítr, hvítt
Whitings (name)	hvítinga, hvítingar, hvítingum
who	á, er, hvat, hverr, sem
whole	heill
whose	hverrar

Word List (English to Old Norse)

English	Old Norse
why	hví
widely	víða
wife	kona
wild-animals	dýr
will	vil, vill, vilt
willed	vildi
will-you	viltu
wine	vín
winter	vetr, vetrinn
wiser	kunngera
wish	vil, vilda, vili, viljum, vilt
wished	vildi, vildu, vilja, vill
wished-to	vildi
witch-ride	gandreið
with	á, með, við
without	utan
with-that	í
Wolf-Skin (name)	úlfhamr
women	konur
wonder	undrast
wondered	undruðust
wool	ullu
word	orðit
words	orðum
worth	vert
worthy	vert, virðing
would	mun, mundi, mundu, muni, skyldu, væri, vildi, vildu
would-be	mundum, munu
would-have	mundi
wound	sár
wove	vaf
wrestle	glíma
wrestled	glímt
wrestling	glíma

Y, y

English	Old Norse
yellow	gulr
you	sé, þér, þik, þín, þú, yðr
young	unga
young-woman	jungfrú
your	þín, þínar, þitt, yðrir, yðru
yours	þér, þína, þinn, þitt, yðrum
you-two	þit
Yrjar (place)	yrjum
Yule (name)	jólin, jólum

The Tale of Thorsteinn House-Power (*Old Icelandic*)

Old Icelandic	Literal	English
1	**1**	**1**
Í þann tíma, er Hákon jarl Sigurðarson réð fyrir Noregi, bjó sá bóndi í Gaulardal, er Brynjólfur hét.	At that time, was Hakon earl Son-of-Sigurd ruled over Norway, lived there farmer in Gaulardale, was Brynjolf named.	About the time when Earl Hakon Sigurdson was ruler of Norway, there lived a farmer in Gaulardale, named Brynjolf.
hann var kallaður úlfaldi.	he was called Camel.	He was called Brynjolf Camel.
hann var lendur maður og mikil kempa.	he was landed man and great warrior.	He was a landed man and a great warrior.
kona hans hét Dagný hún var dóttir Járnskeggja af Yrjum.	wife his named Dagny she was daughter Iron-Beard of Yrjar.	His wife was named Dagny and she was the daughter of Iron-Beard of Yrjar.
þau áttu einn son, er Þorsteinn hét.	they had one son, who Thorstein named.	They had one son who was named Thorstein.
hann var mikill og sterkr, harðúðigr og óaflátssamr við hvern, sem eiga var.	he was great and strong, hard-minded and un-indulgent with everyone, as said-of was.	He was large and strong, strong-minded and unflinching with everyone that he spoke with.
engi var jafnstórr í Noregi, og trautt fengust þær dyrr, að honum væri hægt um að ganga, og því var hann kallaður Bæjarmagn, því að hann þótti ofmagni bera flestum húsum.	none were equally-big in Norway, and scarcely got-they there door, that he would possible about to walk, and because was he called House-Power, because that he seemed to-overpower bear most houses.	No one was as big in all Norway, and there was scarcely a door that he could walk through, and he was called House-Power, because he seemed to overpower most houses.
hann var óþýður, og fekk faðir hans honum því skip og menn, og var Þorsteinn þá ýmist í hernaði eða í kaupferðum, og tókst honum hvárttveggja vel.	he was unfriendly, and got father his him therefore a-ship and men, and was Thorstein then either in raiding or in trading-journeys, and took he either well.	He was so unfriendly that his father gave him a ship with some men, and Thorstein was either raiding or trading, and he took to both well.

The Tale of Thorsteinn House-Power (Old Icelandic)

Old Icelandic	Literal	English
Í þenna tíma tók ríki í Noregi Óláfur konungr Tryggvason, en Hákon jarl var skorinn á háls af þræli sínum, þeim sem Þormóður Karkr hét.	in that time took kingdom in Norway Olaf the-king Tryggvason, when Hakon earl was cut in the-neck of servant his, then as Thormod Kark named.	It was about this time that King Olaf Tryggvason ruled the kingdom of Norway, when Earl Hakon had his throat slit by one of his servants, who was named Thormod Kark.
Þorsteinn Bæjarmagn gerðist hirðmaður Óláfs konungs.	Thorstein House-Power became court-man Olaf's the-king's.	Thorstein House-Power became a court man of King Olaf's.
þótti konungi hann röskr maður og helt mikið til hans, en ekki var hann mjög kenndur af hirðmönnum.	thought the-king he brave man and held much to him, but not was he much recognised of court-men.	The king thought he was a brave man and thought highly of him, but he was not liked by the other court-men.
þótti þeim hann stríðlyndur og óvæginn, og hafði konungr hann mjög til þess að fara sendiferðir þær, sem aðrir töldust undan að fara.	thought they he obstinate and ruthless, and had the-king he great for this to travel missions those, that others considered away from travelling.	They found him obstinate and ruthless, and the king had him going on great missions, that others were reluctant to travel on.
en stundum fór hann kaupferðir að afla konungnum gersema.	about awhile travelled he trading-voyages to provide the-king precious-things.	For a while he went on trading voyages to bring the king treasures.

2

Old Icelandic	Literal	English
eitt sinn lá Þorsteinn austr fyrir Bálagarðssíðu, og gaf honum eigi að sigla.	one occasion lay Thorstein east before Balagardsida, and gave him not to sail.	On one occasion Thorstein lay east near Balagardsida, and he was not given wind to sail.
gekk hann á land einn morgin, og er sól var í landsuðri, var Þorsteinn kominn í eitt rjóður.	went he to land one morning, and when the-sun was in South-East, was Thorstein coming to a clearing.	He went to land one morning, and when the sun was in the South-East, Thorstein came to a clearing.
hóll fagr var í rjóðrinu.	mound beautiful was in the-clearing.	There was a beautiful mound in the clearing.
hann sá einn kollóttan pilt uppi á hólnum, og mælti:	he saw a bald-headed boy up on the-mound, and spoke:	He saw a bald-headed boy up on the mound, and he spoke:
"móðir mín",	"mother mine",	"Mother mine",

The Tale of Thorsteinn House-Power (Old Icelandic)

Old Icelandic	Literal	English
segir hann, "fá þú mér út krókstaf minn og bandvettlinga, því að ek vil á gandreið fara.	said he, "get you me out crooked-staff mine and mittens, because that I wish to witch-ride go.	he said, "get me my crooked staff and mittens, because I wish to go on a witch ride.
er nú hátíð í heiminum neðra".	is now festival in the-world under".	There is now a festival in the underworld".
þá var snarað út ór hólnum einum krókstaf, sem eldsskara væri.	then was twisted out from the-mound a crooked-staff, as fire-poker was.	Then a crooked staff was thrown out from the mound, shaped like a poker.
hann stígr á stafinn og dregr á sik vettlingana og keyrir, sem börn eru vön að gera.	he climbed on the-staff and drew of his mitten and the-stick, as children are want to do.	He climbed on the staff and drew on his mittens and began riding the stick, as children often do.
Þorsteinn gengr á hólinn og mælti slikum orðum sem piltrinn, og var þegar út kastað staf og vöttum og mælt þetta:	Thorstein went to the-mound and spoke such words as the-boy, and was then out cast staff and gloves and spoke this:	Thorstein went to the mound and spoke the same words that the boy had, and then a staff and gloves were cast out and a voice asked:
"hverr tekr nú við?"	"who takes now with?"	"Who wants these now?".
"bjálfi, sonr þinn",	"Bjalfi, son yours",	"Bjalfi, your son",
sagði Þorsteinn.	said Thorstein.	said Thorstein.
síðan stígr hann á stafinn og ríður þar eptir, sem piltrinn fór undan.	afterwards climbed he on the-staff and rode there after, as the-boy travelled away-from.	Afterwards he climbed on the staff and rode away after the boy.
þeir kómu að einni móðu og steyptu sér ofan í hana, og var því líkast sem þeir væði reyk.	they came to a large-river and cast he down in it, and was it like as they waded-through smoke.	They came to a large river and cast down into it, and it was like they were wading through smoke.
því næst birti þeim fyrir augum, og kómu þeir að, sem á fell fram af hömrum.	then near revealed they before eyes, and came they to, as a-river falling from off a-steep-cliff.	Then revealed before their eyes, they came to where a river was falling from a steep cliff.
sér Þorsteinn þá byggð mikla og borg stóra.	saw Thorstein then settlements great and a-city great.	Thorstein then saw large settlements and a great city.
þeir stefna til borgarinnar, og sitr þar fólk yfir borðum.	they directed to the-city, and sat there folk across a-table.	They turned to the city, and there people were sat across a table.

The Tale of Thorsteinn House-Power (Old Icelandic)

Old Icelandic	Literal	English
þeir gengu í höllina, og var höll skipuð af fólki, og var þar af engu drukkið utan af silfrkerum.	they went in the-hall, and was the-hall equipped of folk, and were they of nothing drinking except-for of silver.	They walked into the hall, and there were people filling the hall, and they were drinking from nothing but silver cups.
trapiza stóð á gólfi.	table stood on the-floor.	A table stood on the floor.
allt sýndist þeim þar gullligt og ekki drukkið nema vín.	all seemed they there gold and nothing drunk but wine.	Everything seemed to be gold, and everyone drunk nothing but wine.
það þóttist Þorsteinn skilja, að engi maður sá þá.	that thought Thorstein such, that no man see then.	Then Thorstein realised that no man could see them.
félagi hans fór með borðum og henti allt það, sem niður fell.	companion his went along the-tables and caught all that, as down fell.	His companion went along the tables and caught all that fell down from them.
konungr sat þar í hásæti og drottning.	the-king sat there in high-seat and the-queen.	The king sat there in the high seat with the queen.
menn váru glaðir um höllina.	men were glad about the-hall.	The men about the hall were glad.
þessu næst sér Þorsteinn, að maður kom í höllina og kvaddi konung og kveðst vera sendur til hans utan af indíalandi ór fjalli því, er Lúkanus heitir, frá jarli þeim, er þar réð fyrir, og segir konungi, að hann var huldumaður.	this next saw Thorstein, that a-man came into the-hall and called the-king and greetings were sent to him out of India from mountains because, that Lucanus named, from the-earl they, that was advised for, and said the-king, that he was a-hidden-man.	Then Thorstein saw that a man had come into the hall and greeted the king, and he sent greetings from the mountains of India because the earl Lucanus ruled there, and he advised the king that he was an elf-man.
hann færði honum einn gullhring.	he took to-him a gold-ring.	He presented him with a gold ring.
eigi þóttist konungr betri hring sét hafa, og fór hringrinn um höllina til sýnis, og lofuðu hann allir.	not thought the-king better ring seen had, and went the-ring about the-hall to his, and praised it all.	The king thought that he had not seen a better ring, and it was shown around the hall, and praised by all.
hann var sundur tekinn í fjórum stöðum.	it was apart taken in four places.	This ring could be taken apart in four sections.
annan grip sá Þorsteinn, er honum þótti mikils um vert.	another-thing grabbed seeing Thorstein, that to-him thought much about worth.	Another thing grabbed Thorstein's sight, that he thought might be worth a lot.

The Tale of Thorsteinn House-Power (Old Icelandic)

Old Icelandic	Literal	English
það var dúkr sá, er lá á konungs borðinu.	it was table-cloth saw, that laid at the-king's table.	It was the table cloth that he saw, which was laid at the king's table.
hann var með gullligum röndum og í festir þeir tólf gimsteinar, sem beztir eru.	it was with gold stripes and on fastened there twelve precious-stones, that best were.	It had stripes of gold and was fastened with twelve of the best precious stones.
gjarna vildi Þorsteinn dúkinn eiga.	gladly willed Thorstein table-cloth to-own.	Thorstein gladly wished to own the table-cloth.
kemur honum í hug að treysta á konungs hamingju og vita, hvárt hann getr ekki nát hringnum.	came he to think to reckon on the-king's luck and know, whether he get not get-hold-of the-ring.	He came to think about the king's luck and find out whether or not he could get hold of the ring.
nú sér Þorsteinn, að konungrinn ætlar að draga hringinn á hönd sér.	now saw Thorstein, that the-king intended to carry the-ring on hand his.	Now Thorstein saw that the king intended to carry the ring on his hand.
þá greip Þorsteinn hringinn af honum, en annarri hendi tók hann dúkinn, og fór allr matr í saur, en Þorsteinn hljóp á dyrr, en krókstafur hans varð honum eptir í höllinni.	then grabbed Thorstein the-ring off him, then another hand took he the-table-cloth, and went all food in the-mud, then Thorstein ran to the-door, but crooked-stick his was him behind in the-hall.	Then Thorstein grabbed the ring off him, and then with his other hand he took the table cloth, and all the food fell in the mud, and then Thorstein ran to the door, but the crooked stick was behind him in the hall.
verður nú upphlaup mikið, hlaupa menn út síðan og sjá, hvar Þorsteinn ferr, og stefna eptir honum.	became now uproar great, ran men out after and saw, where Thorstein went, and directed after him.	There now became a great uproar, and men ran out afterwards and saw where Thorstein went and started after him.
sér hann nú, að þeir muni geta nát honum.	saw he now, that they would get hold-of him.	He saw now that they would catch him.
hann mælti þá:	he spoke then:	He then spoke:
"ef þú ert svá góður, Óláfur konungr, sem ek treysti mikið til þín, þá veittu mér lið".	"if you are so good, Olaf king, as I trust much to you, then grant me assistance".	"If you are so good king Olaf, as I trust you are, then grant me assistance".
en svá var Þorsteinn frár, að þeir kómust ekki fyrir hann, fyrr en hann kom að ánni, og staldraði hann þá við.	then so was Thorstein swift, that they came not for him, before that he came to the-river, and lingered he then with.	Then Thorstein was so fast, that they could not catch him before he came to the river, where he had to wait.

The Tale of Thorsteinn House-Power (Old Icelandic)

Old Icelandic	Literal	English
þeir slógu hring um hann, en Þorsteinn varðist vel og drap ótal marga, áður förunautr hans kom og færði honum stafinn, og hurfu þeir þegar í móðuna.	they formed a-circle around him, and Thorstein defended well and killed countless many, after companion his came and brought him the-stick, and disappeared they straightaway into the-river.	They formed a circle around him, and Thorstein defended himself well killing a countless many of them, and afterwards his companion came and brought him the stick, and they disappeared straightaway into the river.
komu þeir aptr á inn sama hól sem fyrr gátum vér, þá sól var í vestri.	came they back to the same hill as before opening was, then the-sun was in the-west.	They came back to the same hill where the opening had been before, and then the sun was in the west.
kastaði piltrinn þá inn stafnum og klæðsekk þeim, sem hann hafði fylldan af góðum krásum, og svá gerði Þorsteinn.	cast the-boy then the stick and sack theirs, which he had filled of good food, and so did Thorstein.	The boy cast the stick and their sack, which he had filled with good food, and so did Thorstein.
kollsveinn hljóp inn, en Þorsteinn nam staðar við glugginn.	the-boy ran in, but Thorstein took to-stand by the-skylight.	They boy ran inside, but Thorstein waited by a skylight window.
hann sá þar tvær konur, og vaf önnur guðvef, en önnur ruggaði barni.	he saw then two women, and wove one precious-cloth, and another rocking a-baby.	He then saw two women, and one wove precious cloth, and another was rocking a baby.
sú mælti:	so spoke:	So they spoke:
"hvað dvelr hann bjálfa, bróður þinn?"	"what delays him Bjalfi, brother yours?"	"What delays your brother Bjalfi?".
"ekki hefir hann mér fylgt í dag?"	"not has he me followed to day?"	"Has he not followed me today?",
sagði hann.	said he.	he said.
"hverr hefir þá farið með krókstafinn?"	"who has then gone with the-crooked-stick?"	"Who has gone with the crooked-stick then?" she said.
segir hún.	said she.	"That was Thorstein House-Power",
"það var Þorsteinn Bæjarmagn",	"that was Thorstein House-Power",	said Kollsvein,
segir Kollsveinn, "hirðmaður Ólafs konungs.	said Kollsvein, "court-man Olaf's the-king's.	"a court man of King Olaf's.

The Tale of Thorsteinn House-Power (Old Icelandic)

Old Icelandic	Literal	English
kom hann okkr í mikinn vanda, því að hann hafði ór undirheimum þau þing, að eigi munu slík í Noregi, og var við því búið, að vit mundum drepnir, er hann kastaði stafnum í hendur þeim, og eltu þeir hann til niðrgangs, og þá færði ek honum stafinn, og víst er hann hraustr maðr, því að eigi veit ek, hversu marga hann drap".	came he us in much difficulty, because that he had away-from under-world their assembly, which not would-be such in Norway, and were with therefore prepared, to know would-be killed, when he cast stick in hand theirs, and chased they him to down-going, and then took I to-him the-stick, and certainly was he brave man, because that not know I, how-so many men killed".	He has brought us unto much difficulty by stealing from the assembly in the underworld, the like of which aren't to be found in Norway, and was nearly killed when he threw his stick into their hands, and they were chasing him to his death, and then I took the stick to him, and he certainly was a brave man, because I do not know how many men were killed".
og nú laukst aptr haugrinn.	and now closed back the-mound.	And now the mound closed.
fór Þorsteinn nú til sinna manna, og sigldu þaðan til Noregs, og fann Óláf konung austr í Vík og færði honum gersemi þessi og sagði frá ferðum sínum, og fannst mönnum mikið um.	went Thorstein now to his men, and sailed from-there to Norway, and found Olaf the-king east in Vik and brought him treasures these and said from voyage his, and found men much about.	Thorstein now went to his men, and sailed from there to Norway, and found King Olaf at Vik in the east, and brought him the treasures and told him of his voyage, and people thought much about it.
konungr bauð að gefa Þorsteini lén mikið, en hann kveðst enn vilja fara eina ferð í Austrveg.	the-king offered to give Thorstein a-fee great, but he said but wished travel one voyage to Eastern-Lands.	The king offered to give Thorstein a great fee but he said that he wished to travel on a voyage to the Eastern-Lands.
var hann nú með konungi um vetrinn.	was he now with the-king about winter.	He was now with the king over the winter.

3

Old Icelandic	Literal	English
að vári bjó Þorsteinn skip sitt.	in spring prepared Thorstein ship his.	In spring Thorstein prepared his ship.
hann hafði snekkju og fjóra menn og tuttugu.	he had a-sailboat and four men and twenty.	He had a sailboat and twenty four men.
og er hann kom við Jamtaland, lá hann í höfn einn dag, og gekk hann á land að skemmta sér.	and when he came to Jamtland, lay he in the-harbour one day, and went he to land to amuse himself.	And when he came to Jamtland, he lay in port one day, and he went ashore to amuse himself.
hann kom í eitt rjóður.	he came to a clearing.	He came to a clearing.

The Tale of Thorsteinn House-Power (Old Icelandic)

Old Icelandic	Literal	English
þar var einn mikill steinn.	there was a large stone.	There was a large stone.
skammt þaðan sá hann einn dverg furðuliga ljótan, og grenjaði upp yfir sik.	a-short-distance from-there saw he a dwarf exceedingly hideous, and howling up over himself.	A short distance from there he saw a dwarf strangely ugly, and he was howling about himself.
sýndist Þorsteini kjaptrinn snúinn út að eyranu, en öðrum megin nefit niður að kjaptinum.	thought Thorstein jaw twisted out at ears, on one side nose below the mouth.	It seemed to Thorstein that his jaw twisted up to the ear on one side and on the other side his nose overlapped his mouth.
Þorsteinn segir, hví hann léti svá heimsliga.	Thorstein said, why he made so foolishly.	Thorstein asked him why he was behaving so foolishly.
"þú, góði maður",	"you, good man",	"You, good man",
sagði hann, "undrast eigi.	said he, "wonder not.	he said,
sér þú eigi þann mikla örn, er þar flýgr?	see you not that great eagle, that there flies?	"it is no wonder.
hann hefir tekið son minn.	he had taken son mine.	Do you not see the great eagle that flies there? He's taken my son.
ætla ek það, að sá ófögnuður sé sendur af Óðni, en ek spring, ef ek missi barnit".	suppose I that, it so unhappy he-is sent of Odin, that I burst, if I lost child".	I think that the unhappy one was sent by Odin, but I will explode if I lose my child".
Þorsteinn skaut eptir erninum, og kom undir vænginn, og datt hann dauður niður, en Þorsteinn henti dvergsbarnit á lopti og færði föðurnum, en dvergrinn varð feginn mjög og mælti:	Thorstein shot after the-eagle, and came down the-wing, and fell he dead down, but Thorstein caught the-dwarf's-boy from-the-sky and brought to-the-father, the dwarf was relieved much and spoke:	Thorstein shot at the eagle, and it came down on the wing, and he fell down dead, but Thorstein caught the dwarf's boy as he fell from the sky, and brought it to his father, and the dwarf was relieved and spoke
"þér á ek að launa lífgjöf og sonr minn, og kjós þér nú fyrir laun í gulli og silfri".	"to-you that I to repay life-gift and son mine, and choose to-you now for to-repay in gold and silver".	"To you I owe a great debt for saving my son's life, and I choose to repay you in gold and silver".
"græð þú fyrst son þinn",	"tend-to you first son yours",	"Tend to your son first",
sagði Þorsteinn "er ek eigi vanr að taka mútur á afli mínu".	said Thorstein "that I not accustomed to take payment for strength mine".	said Thorstein, "because I am not accustomed to taking payment for my strength".

The Tale of Thorsteinn House-Power (Old Icelandic)

Old Icelandic	Literal	English
"eigi væri mér að óskyldara að launa",	"not should-be to-me that less-should to repay",	"That should not make me repay you any less",
segir dvergrinn.	said the-dwarf.	said the dwarf.
"mun þér ekki þykkja framboðligr serkr minn af sauða ullu, en eigi muntu á sundi mæðast og eigi sár fá, ef þú hefir hann næst þér".	"would you not value be-offered shirt mine of wether's wool, that not shall-you to swimming get-tired and not wound get, if you have it next to-you".	"Would you not value if I offered you my shirt of ram's wool, for you shall never get tired when swimming and never be wounded if you wear it next to your skin".
Þorsteinn fór í serkinn, og var honum mátuligr, en honum sýndist dvergnum of lítill.	Thorstein went to the-shirt, and was he fitting, though to-him seemed the-dwarf of small.	Thorstein tried on the shirt, and it fit him, even though it seemed too small for the dwarf.
hann tók og silfrhring ór pungi sínum og gaf Þorsteini og bað hann vel geyma og sagði honum aldri féfátt verða mundu, meðan hann ætti hringinn.	he took also silver-ring from pouch his and gave Thorstein and asked him well retain and said he never lack-of-money become would, as-long-as he had the-ring.	He also took a silver ring from his pouch and gave it to Thorstein and asked him to keep it safe saying that he would never lack money as long as he had the ring.
síðan tók hann einn stein svartan og gaf Þorsteini, "og ef þú felr hann í lófa þér, sér þik engi.	afterwards took he a stone black and gave Thorstein, "and if you fold it in promise to-you, see you none.	Afterwards he took a black stone and gave it to Thorstein: "and if you fold it in your hand in promise, no one shall see you.
eigi hefi ek fleira, það þér megi gagn að vera.	not have I more, that to-you may benefit to be.	I do not have any more that may be of benefit to you.
hall einn vil ek gefa þér til skemmtunar".	piece-of-marble one will I give to-you for amusement".	There is a piece of marble that I will give to you for your amusement".
tók hann þá hallinn ór pungi sínum.	took he then the-piece-of-marble from pouch his.	He took the piece of marble then from his pouch.
fylgdi honum einn stálbroddr.	following it a steel-point.	There followed a steel point.
hallrinn var þríhyrndr.	the-piece-of-marble was three-sided.	The piece of marble was three sided.
hann var hvítr í miðju, en rauður öðrum megin, en gul rönd utan um.	it was white in the-middle, and red other side, and gold around outside about.	It was white in the middle, red on one side, and gold around the outside.
dvergrinn mælti:	the-dwarf said:	The dwarf said:

The Tale of Thorsteinn House-Power (Old Icelandic)

Old Icelandic	Literal	English
"ef þú pjakkar broddinum á hallinn, þar sem hann er hvítr, þá kemur haglhríð svá mikil, að engi þorir móti að sjá.	"if you prick the-point of the-piece-of-marble, there where it is white, then comes hailstorm so great, that none dare to-meet to see.	"If you prick the point of the piece of marble where it is white, then there will come a hailstorm so great that none will dare to look towards it.
en ef þú vilt þíða þann snjó, þá skaltu pjakka þar, sem gulr er hallrinn, og kemur þá sólskin, svá að allt bræðir.	then if you wish thaw then snow, then shall-you prick there, where gold is the-marble, and comes then sunshine, so that all thaws.	Then if you wish to thaw the snow, then you should prick there, where the marble is gold, and then there will come sunshine, so that everything thaws.
en ef þú pjakkar þar í, sem rautt er, þá kemur þar ór eldur og eimyrja með gneistaflaug, svá að engi má móti að sjá.	then if you prick there in, where red is, then comes there out-of fire and embers with a-shower-of-sparks, so that none may meet to see.	Then if you prick there, where it is red, then there will come embers of fire with a shower of sparks, so much that none will dare to look towards
þú mátt og hæfa það, sem þú vilt, með broddinum og hallinum, og hann kemur sjálfur aptr í hönd þér, þegar þú kallar.	you may also hit that, whatever you wish, with the-point and the-marble, and it comes itself back in hand to-you, as-soon-as you call.	You may also hit, whatever you wish, with the point and the marble, and it will come back by itself into your hand, as soon as you call for them.
get ek nú ekki launað þér fleira að sinni".	guess I now not repay you more than this".	I guess now that I cannot repay you more than this".
Þorsteinn þakkar honum gjafirnar.	Thorstein thanked him the-gifts.	Thorstein thanked him for the gifts.
fór hann nú til sinna manna, og var honum þessi ferð betr farin en ófarin.	went he now to his men, and was to-him this journey better gone than unfinished.	He now went to his men, and to him the journey had gone better than when it was unfinished.
þessu næst gefur þeim byr og sigla í Austrveginn.	this next given them fair-wind and sailed to Eastern-Lands.	Next they were given a favourable wind and sailed to the Eastern-Lands.
koma nú á fyrir þeim myrkr og hafvillur, og vita þeir ekki, hvar þeir fara, og var það hálfan mánuð, að þessi villa helzt.	came now to before them fog and open-sea, and knew they not, where they travelled, and was that half a-month, that this lost-way held.	Now a fog came before them in the open sea, and they did not know where they travelled, and this held for half a month.

4   4   4

The Tale of Thorsteinn House-Power (Old Icelandic)

Old Icelandic	Literal	English
það var eitt kvöld, að þeir urðu varir við land.	it was one evening, that they became aware with land.	It was one evening that they were aware that they were close to land.
köstuðu þeir nú akkerum og lágu þar um nóttina.	cast they now anchor and laid there about the-night.	They cast anchor and lay there overnight.
um morguninn var gott veður og sólskin fagrt.	about morning was good weather and sunshine fair.	In the morning the weather was good with fair sunshine.
váru þeir þá komnir á einn fjörð langan, og sjá þeir þar hlíðir fagrar og skóga.	were they then come to a fjord long, and saw they there slope fair and forests.	They came to a long fjord, and saw fair slopes and forests.
engi maður var sá innanborðs, að þetta land þekkti.	no man was saw aboard, that this land knew.	There was no man aboard that saw the land and knew this land.
ekki sáu þeir kvikt, hvárki dýr né fugla.	not saw they living-thing, neither wild-animals nor birds.	They saw no living thing, neither animals nor birds.
reistu þeir nú tjald á landi og bjuggust vel um.	raised they now tents on the-land and settled well about.	They now raised tents on the land and settled there well.
að morgni mælti Þorsteinn til sinna manna:	at morning spoke Thorstein to his men:	At morning Thorstein spoke to his men:
"ek vil gera yðor kunnigt um ætlan mína.	"I wish to-make you know about intentions mine.	"I wish to let you know about my intentions.
þér skuluð bíða mín hér sex nætr.	you should await me here six nights.	You should wait for me here for six nights.
ætla ek mér að kanna land þetta".	intend I me to explore the-land this".	It is my intention to explore this land.
þeim þótti mikið fyrir því og vilja með honum fara, en Þorsteinn vill það eigi, "og ef ek kem eigi aptr, áður sjau sólir eru af himni",	they thought much for therefore and wished with him to-travel, but Thorstein wished that not, "and if I come not back, after seven suns they-are of the-sky",	They thought much of this because they also wished to travel with him, but Thorstein did not wish for that, "and if I do not come back before the seventh sunset in the sky",
segir hann, "þá skuluð þér sigla heim og segja svá Óláfi konungi, að mér mun ekki auðið verða aptr að koma".	said he, "then should you sail home and tell so Olaf the-king, that I should not fated be return to come".	he said, "then you should sail home and tell King Olaf that I am not fated to return home".

The Tale of Thorsteinn House-Power (Old Icelandic)

Old Icelandic	Literal	English
gengu þeir þá með honum upp á skóginn.	went they then with him up to the-forests.	They went with him up to the forests.
því næst hvarf hann þeim, og fóru þeir aptr til skips og breyttu eptir því, sem Þorsteinn bauð þeim.	then next disappeared he from-them, and went they back to the-ships and behaved after accordingly, as Thorstein asked them.	Then next he disappeared from their sight, and they went back to the ships and behaved, as Thorstein had asked them.
nú er að segja af Þorsteini, að allan þann dag gengr hann um mörkina og verður við ekki varr.	now is to say that Thorstein, about all the day went he about the-trees and came with not aware.	Now is to say of Thorstein, that all day he went through the trees and was not aware of anything.
en að áliðnum degi kemur hann á eina braut breiða.	then that following day came he to a way broad.	Then the following day he came to a broad road.
hann gekk eptir brautinni, þangað til að aptnaði.	he went after turned-away, from-there to the the-evening.	He turned to follow it until the evening.
gekk hann þá brott af brautinni og víkr að einni stórri eik og stígr upp í hana.	went he then away of turning and moved towards a large oak and climbed up it he.	He turned off the track and moved towards a large oak tree and he climbed up it.
var þar nóg rúm í að liggja.	was there enough room of to lie-down.	There was enough room for him to lie down.
sefur hann þar um nóttina.	slept he there about the-night.	He slept there for the night.
en er sólin kom upp, heyrir hann dunur miklar og manna mál.	when that sunrise came up, heard he a-din great and men's conversations.	When sunrise came, he heard a great din and men talking.
sá hann þá, hvar margir menn ríða.	saw he then, were many men riding.	He then saw that there were many man riding.
þeir váru tveir og tuttugu.	they were two and twenty.	There were twenty two.
þá bar svá skjótt um fram.	then bore so swiftly about from.	They came so swiftly past.
undraðist Þorsteinn mjög vöxt þeira.	surprised Thorstein much grown they-were.	Thorstein was surprised by how large they were.
hafði hann eigi sét jafnstóra menn fyrr.	had he not seen equally-large men before.	He had not seen men as large before.
Þorsteinn klæðir sik.	Thorstein clothed himself.	Thorstein clothed himself.

The Tale of Thorsteinn House-Power (Old Icelandic)

Old Icelandic	Literal	English
líður nú morgininn til þess, að sól er komin í landsuður.	passed now morning to this, that the-sun was coming to the-south-east.	Now the morning passed so that the sun was coming to the South-East.

5

Old Icelandic	Literal	English
nú sér Þorsteinn þrjá menn ríða vel vápnaða og svá stóra, að enga menn sá hann fyrr jafnstóra.	now saw Thorstein three men riding well weaponed and saw great, that none men saw him before equally-as-big.	Now Thorstein saw three men riding well armed and very large, no men had he seen equally as big.
sá var mestr, er í miðit reið, í gullskotnum klæðum á bleikum hesti, en hinir tveir riðu á grám hestum í rauðum skarlatsklæðum.	so was the-most, then in the-middle riding, in gold-trimmed clothes a pale horse, but the-other two rode on grey horses in red scarlet-clothing.	The most large, then riding in the middle, was in gold-trimmed clothes on a pale horse, but the other two rode on grey horses in red scarlet clothing.
en er þeir kómu þar gegnt, sem Þorsteinn var, mælti sá, sem fyrir þeim var, og nam staðar:	and when they came there opposite, where Thorstein was, spoke so, as for they were, and took standing:	And when they came opposite where Thorstein was, they spoke where they were, and stood:
"hvað er kvikt í eikinni?"	"what is alive in the-oak?"	"What is alive in that oak?"
Þorsteinn gekk þá á veginn fyrir þá og heilsaði þeim, en þeir ráku upp hlátr mikinn, og mælti inn mikli maður:	Thorstein went then to the-road before-them then and greeted them, but they drove up laughter much, and spoke the larger man:	Thorstein then went to the road before them and then greeted them, but they erupted with much laughter, and the larger man spoke:
"sjaldsénir eru oss þvílíkir menn, eða hvert er nafn þitt, eða hvaðan ertu?"	"rarely-seen are us the-like men, but what is name yours, and from-where are-you?"	"Rarely have we seen the like of such a man, but what is your name, and where are you from?"
Þorsteinn nefndi sik og kveðst vera kallaður Bæjarmagn, "en kyn mitt er í Noregi.	Thorstein named himself and said being called House-Power, "and kin mine is in Norway.	Thorstein named himself and said about-being called House-Power, "and my kin is in Norway.
er ek hirðmaður Óláfs konungs".	am I court-man Olaf's the-king".	I am a court man of King Olaf".
inn mikli maður brosti og mælti:	the largest man burst-out-laughing and said:	The largest man burst out laughing and said:
"mest er logit frá hirðprýði hans, ef hann hefir engan vaskligri.	"mostly is a-lie from court his, if he has no-one braver.	"Most about his court must be lies if he has no one braver.

The Tale of Thorsteinn House-Power (Old Icelandic)

Old Icelandic	Literal	English
þykki mér þú heldur mega heita Bæjarbarn en Bæjarmagn".	think me you rather may be-named House-Child than House-Power".	I think you may rather be called House-Child than House-Power".
"lát nokkut fylgja nafnfesti",	"have some following naming-gift",	"Give me a naming gift then",
segir Þorsteinn.	said Thorstein.	said Thorstein.
inn mikli maður tók fingrgull og gaf Þorsteini.	the largest man took finger-gold and gave Thorstein.	The largest man took a gold ring from his finger and gave it to Thorstein.
það vá þrjá aura.	that was three ounces.	It was three ounces.
Þorsteinn mælti:	Thorstein spoke:	Thorstein spoke:
"hvert er þitt nafn, eða hverrar ættar ertu, eða í hvert land er ek kominn?"	"what is your name, and whose lineage are-you, and in what land have I come?"	"What is your name, and whose lineage are you, and in what land have I come?"
"Goðmundur heiti ek.	"Godmund named I.	"I am named Godmund.
ræð er þar fyrir, sem á Glæsisvöllum heitir.	ruler am here over, which is Glasir-Plains named.	I rule over here, which is named Glasir-Plains.
þar þjónar til það land, er Risaland heitir.	there serve to that land, which Giant-Land named.	There serves to that land, which is named Giant-Land.
ek er konungsson, en mínir sveinar heitir annarr Fullsterkr, en annarr Allsterkr, eða sáttu enga menn ríða hér um í morgin?"	I am a-king's-son, and my companions named one Full-Strong, and another All-Strong, and saw-you any men riding here about in the-morning?"	I am a king's son and my companions, one is named Full-Strong, and the other All-Strong, and did you see any men riding through here in the morning?"
Þorsteinn mælti:	Thorstein spoke:	Thorstein spoke:
"hér riðu um tveir menn og tuttugu og létu eigi lítinn".	"here rode about two men and twenty and had none little".	"Twenty two men rode through here and none were little".
"þeir eru sveinar mínir",	"they were men mine",	"They were my men",
segir Goðmundr.	said Godmund.	said Godmund.
"það land liggr hér næst, er Jötunheimar heitir.	"that land lying here next-to, is Giant-Land named.	"That land lying next to here is named Giant-Land.

The Tale of Thorsteinn House-Power (Old Icelandic)

Old Icelandic	Literal	English
þar ræður sá konungr, er Geirröður heitir.	there rules so the-king, who Geirrod named.	So there rules the king who is named Geirrod.
undir hann erum vér skattgildir.	under him are we tributaries.	We are tributaries under him.
faðir minn hét Úlfheðinn Trausti.	father mine is-named Ulfhedin Trusty.	My father is named Ulfhedin Trusty.
hann var kallaður goðmundur sem allir aðrir, þeir á Glæsisvöllum búa.	he was called Godmund as all others, they who Glasir-Plains live.	He was called Godmund as are all others who live in Glasir-Plains.
en faðir minn fór í Geirröðargarða að afhenda konungi skatta sína, og í þeiri ferð fekk hann bana.	but father mine went to Geirrod's-Town to of-hand the-king tax his, and on their journey got he death.	But my father went to Geirrod's-Town to hand taxes to the king, but on their journey they got death.
hefir konungr gert mér boð, að ek skyldi drekka erfi eptir föður minn og taka slíkar nafnbætr sem faðir minn hafði, en þó unum vér illa við að þjóna jötnum".	has the-king made me an-invite, that I should drink inheritance after father mine and take such name-titles as father mine had, but though happy we badly with that serving giants".	The king has made me an invite, for me to drink to his honour and take such titles that my father had, but we are not happy about serving giants".
"hví riðu yðrir menn undan?",	"why rode your men before?",	"Why did your men ride before?",
segir Þorsteinn.	said Thorstein.	said Thorstein.
"mikil á skilr land vort",	"great is separating land ours",	"There is a great separation of our land",
segir Goðmundr.	said Godmund.	said Godmund.
"sú heitir Hemra.	"so named Hemra.	"It is called Hemra.
hún er svá djúp og ströng, að hana vaða engir hestar nema þeir, sem vér kumpánar eigum.	she is so deep and strong, that she wades no horses except they, which we fellows own.	It is so deep and strong, that no horses can wade it, except for the three which we are on.
skulu hinir ríða fyrir uppsprettu árinnar, og finnumst vér í kveld".	shall others ride before up-spring the-river, and meet we in the-evening".	The others shall ride before the river spring, and we will meet in the evening".
"það mundi skemmtan að fara með yður",	"that could-be amusement to travel with you",	"It could be an amusement to travel with you",

The Tale of Thorsteinn House-Power (Old Icelandic)

Old Icelandic	Literal	English
segir Þorsteinn, "og sjá, hvað þar verður til tíðenda".	said Thorstein, "and see, what there becomes to news".	said Thorstein, "and see what happens".
"eigi veit ek, hversu það hentar",	"not know I, how-so that suits",	"I do not know how that suits",
segir Goðmundr, "því að þú munt kristinn".	said Godmund, "because that you must-be Christian".	said Godmund", because you must be a Christian".
"ek mun mik ábyrgjast",	"I could myself take-care-of",	"I can take care of myself",
segir Þorsteinn.	said Thorstein.	said Thorstein.
"ekki vilda ek þú hlytir vánt af mér",	"not wish I you to-get difficulty from me",	"I do not wish for you to get any difficulty from me",
sagði Goðmundr, "en ef Óláfur konungr vill leggja gæfu á með oss, þá mundi ek framt á treysta, að þú færir".	said Godmund, "but if Olaf the-king will grant luck then with us, then should I provide to trust, that you travel".	said Godmund", but if King Olaf will grant you luck to travel with us, then I shall trust you to travel".
Þorsteinn segist því heita vilja.	Thorstein said accordingly promised he-wished.	Thorstein gave him his word as he wished.
Goðmundur biður hann fara á bak með sér, og svá gerði hann.	Godmund asked him to-travel on the-back with him, and so did he.	Godmund asked him to travel back with him, and so he did.
ríða þeir nú til árinnar.	rode they now to the-river.	They now rode to the river.
var þar eitt hús, og tóku þeir þar önnur klæði og klæddu sik og sína hesta.	was there a house, and took they there other clothes and dressed themselves and their horses.	There was a house, and they took their other clothes and dressed themselves and their horses.
þau klæði váru þeirar náttúru, að ekki festi vatn á þeim, en vatnið var svá kalt, að þegar hljóp drep í, ef nokkut vöknaði.	their clothes were there natured, that not joined the-water to them, about the-water was so cold, that there ran gangrene to, if anything became-wet.	Their clothes were of a nature that the water could not touch them, because the water was so cold, that gangrene ran if anything became wet.
riðu þeir nú yfir ána.	rode they now across the-river.	They now rode across the river.
hestarnir óðu sterkliga.	the-horses waded strongly.	The horses waded strongly.
hestr Goðmundar rasaði, og varð Þorsteinn vátr á tánni, og hljóp þegar drep í.	horse Godmund's tumbled, and became Thorstein water about toe, and ran there gangrene to.	Godmund's horse tumbled, and Thorstein's toe came into the water, and there ran gangrene.

The Tale of Thorsteinn House-Power (Old Icelandic)

Old Icelandic	Literal	English
en er þeir kómu af ánni, breiddu þeir niður klæðin til þerris.	when that they came off the-river, spread they down clothes to dry.	When they came off the river, they spread their clothes to dry.
Þorsteinn hjó af sér tána, og fannst þeim mikið um hreysti hans.	Thorstein hewed off his toe, and found they much about bravery his.	Thorstein cut his toe off, and they thought much of his bravery.
ríða þeir nú sinn veg.	rode they now their way.	They now rode on their way.
bað Þorsteinn þá eigi fela sik, "því að ek kann að gera þann hulinshjálm, að mik sér engi".	asked Thorstein then not hide him, "because that I can to make then helm-of-invisibility, that me see none".	Thorstein asked them not to hide him, "because I have a helm of invisibility, that none see me".
Goðmundur segir það góða kunnáttu.	Godmund said that good skills.	Godmund said that was a good skill.
kómu þeir nú til borgarinnar, og kómu menn Goðmundar í móti honum.	came they now to the-town, and came men Godmund's to meet him.	They now came to the town, and Godmund's men came to meet him.
riðu þeir nú í borgina.	rode they now into the-town.	They now rode into the town.
mátti þar nú heyra alls háttar hljóðfæri, en ekki þótti Þorsteini af setning slegit.	could they now hear all kinds musical-instruments, but not thought Thorstein of the-setting struck.	They could now hear all kinds of musical instruments, but Thorstein did not think much of the settings being played.
Geirröður konungr kom nú í mót þeim og fagnaði þeim vel, og var þeim skipað eitt steinhús eða höll að sofa í og menn til fengnir að leiða hesta þeira á stall.	Geirrod the-king came now to meet them and celebrated they well, and were they directed-to a stone-house and a-hall to sleep in and men to get to led horses there to stable.	King Geirrod now came to meet them and they were well welcomed, and they were directed to a stone house and a hall to sleep in, and men led their horses to a stable.
var Goðmundur leiddur í konungshöll.	was Godmund led to the-king's-hall.	Godmund was led to the king's hall.
konungr sat í hásæti og jarl sá hjá honum, er Agði hét.	the-king sat on a-high-seat and the-earl so beside him, was Agdi named.	The king sat on a high seat and the earl so beside him, was named Agdi.
hann réð fyrir því heraði, er Grundir heita.	he ruled over therefore district, was Grundir named.	He ruled over the district, which was named Grundir.
það er á millum Risalands og Jötunheima.	it was in between Giant-Land and Giant-Home.	It was in between Giant-Land and Giant-Home.

The Tale of Thorsteinn House-Power (Old Icelandic)

Old Icelandic	Literal	English
hann hafði atsetu að Gnípalundi.	he had a-seat at Gnipalund.	He had an estate at Gnipalund.
hann var fjölkunnigr, og menn hans váru tröllum líkari en mönnum.	he was skilled-in-magic, and men his were trolls like than men.	He was skilled in magic, and his men were more like trolls than men.
Goðmundur settist á skörina fyrir öndvegit gagnvart konungi.	Godmund sat beside high-seat before opposite going-from the-king.	Godmund sat beside the high seat opposite the king.
var sá siður þeira, að konungsson skyldi ekki í hásæti sitja, fyrr en hann hafði tekið nafnbætr eptir föður sinn og drukkið væri it fyrsta full.	was so the-custom theirs, that the-king's-son should not in high-seat sit, before that he had taken name-titles after father his and drink-to was the first drunk.	It was their custom, that the king's son should not sit in the high seat, before he had taken his titles and the first drink to honour his father had been drunk.
ríss þar nú upp in vænsta veizla, og drukku menn glaðir og kátir og fóru síðan að sofa.	rose there now up the good feast, and drank men gladly and merry and went then to sleep.	They now rose up and had a good feast, and the men drank gladly and merrily, and then went to sleep.
en er Goðmundur kom í hús sitt, sýndi Þorsteinn sik.	and when Godmund came to the-house his, showed Thorstein himself.	And when Godmund came to his house, Thorstein showed himself.
hlógu þeir að honum.	laughed they at him.	They laughed at him.
Goðmundur sagði mönnum sínum, hverr hann var, og bað þá ekki hafa hann að hlátri.	Godmund told the-men his, who he was, and ordered then not have he to laughter.	Godmund told his men who he was and ordered them not to laugh at him.
og sofa þeir af um nóttina.	and slept they of through the-night.	And they slept through the night.

6

nú er morginn kom, váru þeir snemma á fótum.	now when morning came, were they early about feet.	Now when morning came, they were up early and on their feet.
var Goðmundur leiddur til konungs hallar.	was Godmund led to the-king's hall.	Godmund was led to the king's hall.
konungr fagnaði honum vel.	the-king celebrated him well.	The king welcomed him well.

The Tale of Thorsteinn House-Power (Old Icelandic)

Old Icelandic	Literal	English
"viljum vér nú vita",	"wish we now know",	"We wish to know",
segir konungr, "hvárt þú vilt veita mér slíka hlýðni sem faðir þinn, og vil ek þá auka þínar nafnbætr.	said the-king, "whether you wish to-grant me such homage as father yours, and wish I then extra your name-titles.	said the king, "whether you wish to grant me such homage as your father, and then I wish to give you more titles.
skaltu þá halda Risalandi og sverja mér eiða".	shall-you then keep Giant-Land and swear to-me oath".	You shall then keep Giant-Land and swear an oath to me".
Goðmundur svarar:	Godmund answered:	Godmund answered:
"ekki er það lög að krefja svá unga menn til eiða".	"not is that law that demand so young men to oath".	"It is not lawful to demand oaths from a man as young as me".
"það skal vera",	"that shall be",	"So it shall be",
sagði konungr.	said the-king.	said the king.
síðan tók konungr guðvefjarskikkju og lagði yfir Goðmund og gaf honum konungsnafn, tók síðan horn mikið og drakk til Goðmundi.	then took the-king a-precious-cloak and laid over Godmund and gave him the-king's-name, took afterwards horn great and drank to Godmund.	Then the king took a precious cloak and laid it over Godmund and gave him the title of king, and then took a great horn and drank to Godmund.
hann tók við horninu og þakkaði konungi.	he took with the-horn and thanked the-king.	He took the horn and thanked the king.
síðan stóð Goðmundur upp og sté á stokkinn fyrir sæti konungs og strengdi þess heit, að hann skal engum konungi þjóna né hlýðni veita, meðan Geirröður konungr lifði.	afterwards stood Godmund up and stepped onto the-foot-board before seat the-king's and boldly this declared, that he shall no king serve nor homage grant, while Geirrod the-king lived.	Afterwards Godmund stood up and stepped onto the footboard before the king's seat and boldly declared, that he would serve no king nor grant homage, while King Geirrod lived.
konungr þakkaði honum, sagði sér það þykkja meira vert en þótt hann hefði eiða svarið.	the-king thanked him, told him that valued more worth that though he had oaths sworn.	The king thanked him, and told him that he would have valued more if he had sworn oaths.
síðan drakk Goðmundur af horninu og gekk til sætis síns.	afterwards drank Godmund of the-horn and went to seat his.	Afterwards Godmund drank from the horn and went to his seat.
váru menn þá glaðir og kátir.	were men then glad and merry.	Then the men were glad and merry.

The Tale of Thorsteinn House-Power (Old Icelandic)

Old Icelandic	Literal	English
tveir menn eru nefndir með Agða jarli.	two men were named with Agdi the-earl.	Two men were with Earl Agdi.
hét annarr Jökull, en annarr frosti.	named one Jokul, and the-other Frosti.	One was named Jokul, and the other Frosti.
þeir váru öfundsjúkir.	they were jealous.	They were jealous.
Jökull þreif upp uxahnútu og kastaði í lið Goðmundar.	Jokul grabbed up ox-bone and threw at the-company-of Godmund.	Jokul grabbed an ox-bone and threw it at Godmund's company.
Þorsteinn sá það og henti á lopti og sendi aptr, og kom á nasir þeim, er gustr hét, og brotnaði í honum nefit og ór honum allar tennrnar, en hann fell í óvit.	Thorstein saw that and caught in the-air and sent back, and came about nose them, was Gust named, and broke it his nose and through his all teeth, and he fell to unconscious.	Thorstein saw that, caught it in the air and sent it back, and it hit the nose of a man named Gust, and it broke his nose and all his teeth, and he fell unconscious.
Geirröður konungr reiddist og spurði, hverr berði beinum yfir hans borð.	Geirrod the-king rose and asked, who threw the-bone across his table.	Geirrod the king rose up and asked who threw the bone across the table.
sagði hann, að reynt skyldi verða, hverr sterkastr væri í steinkastinu, áður en úti væri.	said he, that test should be, who strongest was in stone-throwing, after then out was.	He said that there should be a test to find out before it was over who was the strongest at stone throwing.
síðan kallar konungr til tvá menn, Drött og Hösvi:	afterwards called the-king to two men, Drott and Hosvir:	Afterwards the king called two men, Drott and Hosvir:
"farið þit og sækið gullhnött minn og berið hann hingað".	"go you-two and seek gold-ball mine and bring it here".	"You two go and seek my gold ball and bring it here".
þeir fóru og kómu aptr með eitt selshöfuð, er stóð tíu fjórðunga.	they went and came back with a seal's-head, and weighed ten quarters.	They went and came back with a seal's head, which weighed ten quarters.
það var glóanda, svá að sindraði af svá sem ór afli, en fitan draup niður sem glóanda bik.	it was glowing, so that sparkled of so as from a-forge, and fat dripped down as burning pitch.	It was glowing hot, so that sparks came off it as if from a forge, and fat dripped from it like burning pitch.
konungr mælti:	the-king spoke:	The king spoke:
"takið nú knöttinn og kastið hverr að öðrum.	"take now the-ball and throw each to other.	"Now take the ball and throw it to each other.

The Tale of Thorsteinn House-Power (Old Icelandic)

Old Icelandic	Literal	English
hverr, sem niður fellir, skal fara útlægr og missa eignir sínar, en hverr eigi þorir að henda, skal heita níðingr".	anyone, who down drops, shall go outlawed and lose property his, and anyone not daring to catch, shall be-named a-coward".	Anyone who drops it shall go outlawed and lose his property, and anyone who does not dare to catch, shall be named a coward.

7

Old Icelandic	Literal	English
nú kastar Dröttr knettinum að Fullsterk.	now threw Drott the-ball at Full-Strong.	Now Drott threw the ball at Full-Strong.
hann greip á móti annarri hendi.	he gripped to meet one hand.	He gripped against it with one hand.
Þorsteinn sá, að honum varð orkufátt, og hljóp undir knöttinn.	Thorstein saw, that he became low-energy, and ran behind the-ball.	Thorstein saw that his strength weakened, and got behind the ball.
þeir snöruðu að Frosta, því að kapparnir stóðu fremstir við hvárntveggja bekkinn.	they threw at Frosti, because that champions stood foremost against either-side of-the-bench.	They threw it at Frosti, because the champions stood in front of the benches on either side.
Frosti tók mót sterkliga, og kom svá nær andliti hans, að kinnbeinit rifnaði.	Frosti took against strongly, and came so near face his, that chin-bone split.	Frosti caught it strongly, and it came so near his face, that it split his chin bone.
hann kastar knettinum að Allsterk.	he threw the-ball at All-Strong.	He threw the ball at All-Strong.
hann tók í móti báðum höndum, og lá við, að hann mundi kikna, áður Þorsteinn studdi hann.	he received it against both hands, and had with, that he would-have bent-backwards, before Thorstein steadied him.	He caught it with both hands, and he would have bent backwards, before Thorstein steadied him.
Allsterkr snaraði að Agða jarli, en hann greip móti báðum höndum.	All-Strong turned-quickly at Agdi the-earl, and he grabbed against both hands.	All-Strong hurled the ball at Earl Agdi, and he caught it with both hands.
fitan kom í skeggit á honum, og logaði það allt, og var honum til þess annast að afhenda knöttinn og fleygir að Goðmundi konungi.	fat came to beard of his, and blazed that all, and was he to this he-took-care-of that off-handed the-ball and flew-it at Godmund the-king.	Burning fat went on to his beard, and it was all ablaze, and as he had to take care of that, he hurriedly threw the ball at King Godmund.

The Tale of Thorsteinn House-Power (Old Icelandic)

Old Icelandic	Literal	English
en Goðmundur snaraði að Geirröði konungi, en hann veik sér undan, og urðu þeir fyrir Dröttr og Hösvir, og fengu þeir bana.	then Godmund flew-it at Geirrod the-king, but he turned himself away, and came they for Drott and Hosvir, and caught them dead.	Then Godmund threw it at King Geirrod, but he turned out of the way, and it came to Drott and Hosvir, and killed them both.
en knöttrinn kom á glerglugg einn og svá út í díki það, sem grafit var um borgina, og hljóp upp eldur logandi.	then the-ball came to glass-window one and so out into the-moat that, which dug was about the-city, and ran up the-flames ablaze.	Then the ball went through a glass window and out into the moat, which was dug around the city, and the flames ran up in a blaze.
var nú lokið þessu gamni.	was now ended this game.	The game was now ended.
tóku menn þá til drykkju.	took men then to drinking.	The men took to drinking.
sagði Agði jarl, að honum hrysi hugr við jafnan, er hann kom í flokk Goðmundar.	said Agdi the-earl, that he trembled thought with every-time, that he came to band Godmund's.	Earl Agdi said that he thought he trembled every time he came to Godmund's company.
um kveldið gekk Goðmundur að sofa og hans menn.	about evening went Godmund to seep and his men.	In the evening Godmund went to sleep and so did his men.
þökkuðu þeir Þorsteini hjástöðu, að þeim hefði slysalaust farið.	thanked they Thorstein beside-standing, to them had accidents-without gone.	They thanked Thorstein for standing by them, so that they were without accidents.
Þorsteinn kvað lítit til reynt, "eða hvað mun til gamans haft á morgin?"	Thorstein said little to test, "but what should to games have in the-morning?"	Thorstein said it was nothing much, "but what sort of games will we have in the morning?"
"konungr mun láta glíma",	"the-king should have wrestling",	"The king shall have wrestling",
segir Goðmundr, "og munu þeir þá hefna sín, því að fjarstætt er um afl várt".	said Godmund, "and should they then avenge themselves, accordingly to far-away from about strength ours".	said Godmund, "and they shall avenge themselves accordingly because their strength is far more than ours".
"konungs gæfa mun styrkja oss",	"the-king's luck should strengthen us",	"The king's luck shall strengthen us",
segir Þorsteinn.	said Thorstein.	said Thorstein.
"hirðið eigi, þótt þér berizt þangað að, sem ek er fyrir".	"take-care not, though you bear from-there that, which I am before".	"Take care not to bear it there, but bear towards me".

The Tale of Thorsteinn House-Power (Old Icelandic)

Old Icelandic	Literal	English
sofa þeir af um nóttina.	slept they of through night.	They slept through the night.
en að morgni fór hverr til sinnar skemmtunar, en matsveinar að dúka borð.	and at morning went each to his entertainment, while food-servants to tablecloths table.	And in the morning each went to his entertainment, while the food servants put the tablecloths on the table.
Geirröður konungr spurði, hvárt menn vildu ekki glíma, en þeir sögðu, að hann skyldi ráða.	Geirrod the-king asked, which men wished not wrestling, and they said, as he should decide.	King Geirrod asked, which men wished to wrestle, and they said that he should decide.
síðan afklæðast þeir og tókust fangbrögðum.	afterwards undressed they and took to-wrestling.	Then they undressed and took to wrestling.
Þorsteinn þóttist eigi sét hafa slíkan atgang, því að allt skalf, þá þeir fellu, og lékst mjög á mönnum Agða jarls.	Thorstein thought not seen had such to-going, because that all shook, then they fell, and played much to men Agdi the-earl's.	Thorstein thought he had not seen such a clash, because everywhere shook, whenever they fell, and this happened often to Earl Agdi's men.
frosti gekk nú fram á gólfit og mælti:	Frosti went now to the floor and spoke:	Frosti now went to the floor and said:
"hverr skal mér á móti?"	"who shall me to meet?"	"Who shall oppose me?"
"til mun verða einhverr",	"to should be someone",	"There will be someone",
sagði Fullsterkr.	said Full-Strong.	said Full-Strong.
ráðast þeir nú á, og váru með þeim miklar sviptingar, og er frosti miklu sterkari.	arranged they now to, and were with they much tussle, and was Frosti much stronger.	They now attacked, and there were great upheavals with them, and Frosti was much stronger.
berast þeir nú að Goðmundi.	bore they now to Godmund.	They now arrived at Godmund.
frosti tekr hann upp á bringu sér og keiktist mjög.	Frosti took him up by the-chest his and bent much.	Frosti took him up by his chest and he had to bend his knees.
Þorsteinn slær fæti sínum á knésbætr honum, og fell frosti á bak aptr, en Fullsterkr á hann ofan.	Thorstein struck feet his about the-back-of-the-knees his, and fell Frosti on back back, but Full-Strong on him over.	Thorstein struck his foot on the back of his knees, and Frosti fell on his back, and Full-Strong fell on him.
hnakkinn sprakk á Frosta og olnbogarnir.	the-back-of-the-head broke of Frosti and elbows.	The back of Frosti's head was broken, and so were his elbows.

The Tale of Thorsteinn House-Power (Old Icelandic)

Old Icelandic	Literal	English
hann stóð seint upp og mælti:	he stood slowly up and spoke:	He slowly stood up and spoke:
"ekki eru þér einir að gamninu, eða hví er svá fúlt í flokki yðrum?"	"not are you alone in the-game, and what is so foul among men yours?"	"You are not alone in this game, and what is it that is so foul among your men?"
"skammt á nefit að kenna ór kjaptinum",	"short is nose to know from the-mouth",	"Your nose is too close to your own mouth",
sagði Fullsterkr.	said Full-Strong.	said Full-Strong.
Jökull stóð þá upp, og Allsterkr réðst þá í móti honum, og var þeira atgangr inn harðasti.	Jokul stood then up, and All-Strong moved then to oppose him, and were they to-going the hardest.	Jokul then stood up, and All-Strong moved to oppose him, and their clash was the hardest yet.
en þó var Jökull sterkari og bar hann að bekk, þar sem Þorsteinn var fyrir.	but though was Jokul stronger and carried him to a-bench, there as Thorstein was before.	But Jokul was stronger and carried him to a bench, where Thorstein was.
Jökull vildi draga Allsterk frá bekknum og togast við fast, en Þorsteinn helt honum.	Jokul wished-to drag All-Strong from the-bench and pulled against hard, but Thorstein held him.	Jokul tried had to drag All-Strong from the bench and pulled hard against him, but Thorstein held him.
Jökull tók svá fast, að hann sté í hallargólfit upp að ökkla, en Þorsteinn hratt Allsterk frá sér, og fell Jökull á bak aptr, og gekk ór liði á honum fótrinn.	Jokul tugged so hard, that he stepped in hall-floor up to ankles, then Thorstein pushed All-Strong away-from him, and fell Jokul on back back, and went out-of dislocated of his leg.	Jokul pulled so hard, that his feet sunk into the hall floor up to his ankles, then Thorstein pushed All-Strong away from him, and Jokul fell back and dislocated his leg.
Allsterkr gekk til bekkjar, en Jökull stóð upp seint og mælti:	All-Strong went to bench, but Jokul stood up slowly and spoke:	All-Strong went back to his bench, but Jokul stood up slowly and spoke:
"ekki sjáum vér alla þessa, sem á bekknum eru".	"not see we all this, which on that-bench they-are".	"We cannot see everyone that is on that bench".
Geirröður segir Goðmundi, hvárt hann vildi ekki glíma.	Geirrod said-to Godmund, whether he would not wrestle.	Geirrod asked Godmund if he would wrestle.
en hann kveðst aldri glímt hafa, en kveðst eigi vildu synjast.	and he said never wrestled had, but said not would refuse.	And he said that he had never wrestled, but he would not refuse.
konungr bað Agða jarl hefna manna sinna.	the-king ordered Agdi the-earl avenge men his.	The king ordered Earl Agdi to avenge his men.

The Tale of Thorsteinn House-Power (Old Icelandic)

Old Icelandic	Literal	English
hann kveðst löngu hafa af lagt, en segir konung ráða skyldu.	he said long had of left, but told the-king advice would.	He said that he had given up long ago, but he would do as the king decided.
síðan afklæddust þeir.	afterwards undressed they.	Then they undressed.
eigi þóttist Þorsteinn sét hafa tröllsligri búk en á Agða.	not thought Thorstein seen had troll-like thick-set than was Agdi.	Thorstein thought that he had not seen such a troll-like thick set man as Agdi.
var hann blár sem hel.	was he black as death.	He was black as death.
Goðmundur reis mót honum.	Godmund rose to-meet him.	Godmund rose to meet him.
var hann hvítr á skinnslit.	was he white in colour.	He was white in colour.
Agði jarl hösvaðist að honum og lagði svá fast krummurnar að síðum hans, að allt gekk niður að beini, og bárust þeir víða um höllina.	Agdi the-earl went-for at him and had so fastened grabbed at sides his, that all went down to the-bone, and bore they widely about the-hall.	Earl Agdi went for him and grabbed at his sides so hard that it went down to the bone, and the carried widely around the hall.
og er þeir kómu þar, sem Þorsteinn var, þá brá Goðmundur jarli til sniðglímu og sneri honum vakrliga.	and when they came there, where Thorstein was, then drew Godmund the-earl to hip-throw and turned him nimbly.	And when they came where Thorstein was, Godmund drew the earl into a hip throw and turned him nimbly.
Þorsteinn lagðist niður fyrir fætr jarli, og fell hann þá og stakk niður nösunum, og brotnaði í honum þjófsnefit og fjórar tennr.	Thorstein lay down before feet the-earl's, and fell he then and struck down on-the-nose, and broke was his thieving-nose and four teeth.	Thorstein lay down before the earl's feet, and then he fell and struck his nose, and his thieving nose was broken, and four teeth.
jarl stóð upp og mælti:	the-earl stood up and spoke:	The earl stood up and spoke:
"þung verða gamalla manna föll, og svá þyngst, að þrír gangi að einum".	"heavy becomes the-old man falling, and so heaviest, when three go against one".	"Heavy becomes the old man falling, and heaviest, when it's three against one".
fóru menn þá í klæði sín.	went the-men then with-that clothed themselves.	With that the men clothed themselves.

8

þessu næst fóru þeir konungr til borða.	this next went they the-king to the-tables.	After this the king and his guests went to the tables.

The Tale of Thorsteinn House-Power (Old Icelandic)

Old Icelandic	Literal	English
töluðu þeir Agði jarl um, að þeir mundu einhvern prett við hafa haft, "því að mér býður ávallt hita, er ek kem í þeira flokk".	told they Agdi the-earl about, that they must-be some-way tricked against having had, "because that I invite always heat, when I come in their company".	Earl Agdi and the others said that they must have been tricked in some way, "because I always heat up, when I come in their company".
"látum bíða",	"leave-it abide",	"Let it be",
segir konungr, "sá mun koma, að okkr mun kunngera".	said the-king, "so shall come, that us should wiser".	said the king, "something will come and make us wiser".
tóku menn þá að drekka.	took men then to drinking.	Then the men took to drinking.
þá váru borin inn tvau horn í höllina.	then were brought in two horns into the-hall.	There were then two horns brought into the hall.
þau átti Agði jarl, gersemar miklar, og váru kölluð Hvítingar.	they had Agdi the-earl, treasured much, and were called Whitings.	They belonged to Earl Agdi, who treasured them, and they were called Whitings.
þau váru tveggja álna há og gulli búin.	they were two cubits high and gold prepared.	They were two cubits high and inlaid with gold.
konungr lét sitt hornit ganga á hvárn bekk, "og skal hverr drekka af í einu.	the-king had sat a-horn going to each bench, "and shall each drink of in one.	The king had set a horn on each bench, "and everyone shall drink from it in one.
sá, sem því orkar eigi, skal fá byrlaranum eyri silfrs".	so, that accordingly able-to not, shall pay the-cup-bearer an ounce-of silver".	So, therefore those not able to shall pay the cup bearer an ounce of silver".
gekk engum af að drekka utan köppunum, en Þorsteinn gað svá til sét, að þeir, sem með Goðmundi váru, varð engi víttr.	went none of to drink out-of the-cups, but Thorstein got so to seen, that they, which with Godmund were, became not bewitched.	No one was able to drink out of the cups, but Thorstein could see that those who were with Godmund did not become bewitched.
drukku menn nú glaðir það, sem eptir var dagsins, en um kveldið fóru menn að sofa.	drank men now gladly that, as after was of-the-day, then about evening went men to sleep.	People now drank happily what was left of the day, but in the evening they went to sleep.
Goðmundur þakkaði Þorsteini fyrir góða hjástöðu.	Godmund thanked Thorstein for the-good beside-standing.	Godmund thanked Thorstein for his good help.
Þorsteinn spurði, nær endast mundi veizlan.	Thorstein asked, near ending would the-feast.	Thorstein asked, when the feast would end.

The Tale of Thorsteinn House-Power (Old Icelandic)

Old Icelandic	Literal	English
"að morgni skulu menn mínir ríða",	"at morning should men mine ride",	"In the morning my men shall ride",
segir Goðmundr.	said Godmund.	said Godmund.
"veit ek, að nú lætr konungr allt við hafa.	"know I, that now acts the-king all against have.	"I know that now the king will act against us with all he has.
eru nú sýndar gersemar.	they-are now shown treasures.	When the treasures are shown.
lætr konungr nú bera inn horn sitt it mikla.	have the-king now brought in a-horn his this great.	Let the king now carry in his great horn.
það er kallað Grímr inn Góði.	that is called Grim the Good.	That is called Grim the Good.
það er gersemi mikil og þó galdrafullt og búið með gull.	that is a-treasure great and though magic-full and inlaid with gold.	It is a great treasure, and magical and rich in gold.
mannshöfuð er á stiklinum með holdi og munni, og það mælir við menn og segir fyrir óorðna hluti og ef það veit ófriðar ván.	a-man's-head is about the-narrow with flesh and a-mouth, and that speaks with men and said for unspoken lot and if that known un-peace is-expected.	A man's head is about the narrow end with flesh and a mouth, and it speaks to men and says unspoken things, and if war is expected.
verður það bani vár, ef konungr veit, að kristinn maður er með oss.	becomes it the-death ours, if the-king knows, that a-Christian man is with us.	It will be the death of us if the king knows that a Christian man is with us.
munum vér eigi þurfa að vera fésparir við hann".	should we not need to be fee-sparing with him".	We should not need to spare wealth with him".
Þorsteinn sagði Grím eigi mæla fleira enn Óláfur konungr vildi, "en ek ætla, að Geirröður sé feigr.	Thorstein said Grim not speak more than Olaf the-king wished, "and I suppose, that Geirrod is fated-to-die.	Thorstein said that Grim would not say to him any more than King Olaf wished, "and I suppose that Geirrod is a doomed man.
þykki mér ráð, að þér hafið mín ráð heðan af.	seems to-me advice, that you have my counsel from-hence of.	It seems to me to advise, that you do as I advise you from now on.
skal ek sýna mik á morgin".	shall I show myself in the-morning".	I shall show myself in the morning".
en þeir sögðu það hættu ráð.	but they said that dangerous advice.	But they said that it was a dangerous decision.

The Tale of Thorsteinn House-Power (Old Icelandic)

Old Icelandic	Literal	English
Þorsteinn sagði, að Geirröður vildi þá feiga, "eða hvað segir þú mér af Grími inum Góða fleira?"	Thorstein said, that Geirrod wished then doomed, "but what say you to-me of Grim the Good more?"	Thorstein said that Geirrod wished them all doomed, "but what else can you tell me about Grim the Good"?
"það er frá honum að segja, að meðalmaður má standa undir bugtinni á honum, en álnar breitt yfir beitina, og er sá mestr drykkjumaður í þeira liði, er drekkr beitina, en konungr drekkr af í einu.	"that is from him to say, that an-average-man may stand under the-curve of him, and a-yard broad across opening, and is so the-greatest drinking-man of their company, that drinks the-opening, but the-king drinks of all in-one.	"The first thing to say, is that an average man can stand under the curve of the horn, and it is a yard across at the opening, and the greatest drinking man in their company can drink deep into the horn, but only the king can drink it all in one.
hverr maður á að gefa Grími nokkura gersemi, en sú virðing þykkir honum sér mest ger, að í einu sé af drukkið.	each man is to give Grim some treasure, but so worthy seems to-him to-see most done, that in one you of drink.	Each man has to give Grim something valuable, but most worthy honour to him is to drink it in one.
en ek veit, að mér ber fyrstum af að drekka, en það er einskis manns þol að drekka það í einu".	but I know, that I bear first of to drink, but that is nothing man endure than drink that in one".	But I know that I have to drink first, but it is no man's endurance to drink it at once".
Þorsteinn mælti:	Thorstein spoke:	Thorstein spoke:
"þú skalt fara í serk minn, því að þér má þá ekki granda, þó að ólyfjan sé í drykknum.	"you shall go in shirt mine, because that you may then not to-injure, though that poison even if drink.	"You shall go in my shirt, because then you shall not come to injury, even if there is poison in the drink.
tak kórónu af höfði þér og gef Grími inum góða og seg í eyra honum, að þú skalt gera honum miklu meira heiður en Geirröður, og síðan skaltu láta sem þú drekkir.	take the-crown off head yours and give Grim the Good and say in ear his, that you shall do him much more honour than Geirrod, and afterwards shall-you lay-out that you drink.	Take the crown off your head, and give it to Grim the Good, and say in his ear that you will do him much more honour than Geirrod, and afterwards shall you drink to that.
en eitr mun í horninu, og skaltu steypa niður næst þér, og mun þik ekki saka.	then poison should-be in the-horn, ad shall-you cast down near you, and shall you not injury.	Then should the poison be in the horn, you shall cast it down beside you, and you shall not be injured.
en þá er drykkjuskapr er úti, skaltu láta menn þína ríða".	but then when drinking is over, shall-you have men yours ride-away".	But when the drinking is over, have your men ride away".
Goðmundur sagði, að hann skuli ráða.	Godmund said, that he shall decide.	Godmund said, that he shall decide.

The Tale of Thorsteinn House-Power (Old Icelandic)

Old Icelandic	Literal	English
"en ef Geirröður deyr, þá á ek alla Jötunheima, en ef hann lifir lengr, verður það bani vár".	"but if Geirrod dies, then with I all Giant-Home, but if he lives longer, becomes that death ours".	"But if Geirrod dies, then I own all the Giant-Home, but if he lives longer, that death will be ours".
síðan sofa þeir af um nóttina.	afterwards slept they of about the-night.	Afterwards they slept through the night.
9	**9**	**9**
um morguninn eru þeir snemma á fótum og taka sín klæði.	about morning were they soon about feet and took their clothes.	In the morning they got up early and took their clothes.
þá kemur Geirröður konungr til þeira og biður þá drekka velfaranda sinn.	then came Geirrod the-king to them and asked them to-drink well-faring his.	Then King Geirrod came to them and asked them to drink their welfare.
þeir gerðu svá.	they did so.	They did so.
váru fyrst drukkin hornin Hvítingar næst máldrykkju skálum, en þá var drukkið minni Þórs og Óðins.	were first drunk the-horns Whitings next drinking bowls, and then were drunk in-memory Thor's and Odin's.	First the horns called Whitings were drunk from, next the drinking bowls, and they were drunk from in memory of Thor and Odin.
því næst kómu inn margir slagir hljóðfæra, og tveir menn, nokkuru minni en Þorsteinn, þeir báru Grím inn Góða.	then next came in many artful musical-instruments, and two men, somewhat smaller than Thorstein, they carried Grim the Good.	Then many kinds of instruments came in, and two men, somewhat smaller than Thorstein, brought in Grim the Good.
allir stóðu upp og fellu á kné fyrir honum.	all stood up and fell to knees before him.	Everyone stood up and fell on their knees before him.
Grímr var óhýrligr.	Grim was unfriendly-looking.	Grim was hideous.
Geirröður mælti til Goðmundar:	Geirrod spoke to Godmund:	Geirrod said to Godmund:
"tak við Grími inum Góða, og er þetta þín handsals skál".	"take with Grim the Good, and be this your binding shall".	"Take Grim the Good and let this toast be your binding pledge".
Goðmundur gekk að Grími og tók af sér gullkórónu og setti á hann og mælti í eyra honum, sem Þorsteinn hafði sagt honum.	Godmund went to Grim and took off himself gold-crown and set on him and spoke in ear his, as Thorstein had told him.	Godmund went to Grim, took off his gold crown, set it upon him, and spoke in his ear, as Thorstein had told him.

The Tale of Thorsteinn House-Power (Old Icelandic)

Old Icelandic	Literal	English
síðan lét hann renna af horninu ofan í serk sér, og var eitr í.	then had he ran of the-horn over into shirt his, and was poison in.	Then he ran the horn over into his shirt, and poured the poisonous drink in.
hann drakk til Geirröði konungi og kyssti á stikilinn, og fór Grímr hlæjandi frá honum.	he drank to Geirrod the-king and kissed the horn-point, and went Grim smiling went-from him.	He drank to King Geirrod and kissed the point of the horn, and Grim was taken away from him with a smile on his face.
tók Geirröður þá við fullu horninu og bað Grím með góðri heill koma og bað hann kunngera sér, ef nokkurr háski væri nær.	took Geirrod then with the-full horn and asked Grim with luck whole coming and asked him to-announce to-him, if something dangerous was near.	Geirrod took the full horn and asked Grim to bring him good luck and asked him if there was anything dangerous near.
"hefi ek opt sét þik með betra bragði".	"have I often seen you with better looking".	"I have often seen you in a better mood".
tók hann gullmen af sér og gaf Grími, drakk síðan til Agða jarli, og þótti því líkast sem boði felli á sker, er niður rann eptir hálsinum á honum, og drakk af allt.	took he gold-necklace off himself and gave Grim, drank afterwards to Agda the-earl, and seemed therefore like as breaking wave on a-rock, as down ran after throat of him, and drank of all.	He took a gold necklace off himself and gave it to Grim, and drank afterwards to Earl Agdi, and it was like a wave breaking on a rock, as the drink ran down his throat, and he drank all of it.
Grímr hristi höfuðið, og var hann borinn Agða jarli, og gaf hann honum tvá gullhringa og bað sér miskunnar og drakk síðan af í þremr og fekk byrlaranum.	Grim shook his-head, and was he carried Agdi the-earl, and gave it to-him two gold-rings and asked his mercy and drank afterwards of in three and went the-cup-bearer.	Grim shook his head, and he was carried to Earl Agdi who gave him two gold rings and asked for his mercy, and he drank in three draughts and then returned it to the cup-bearer.
Grímr mælti:	Grim said:	Grim said:
"svá ergist hverr sem eldist".	"the feebler each who oldest".	"The older the man, the feebler"
þá var hornit fyllt, og skyldu þeir drekka af tveir, Jökull og Fullsterkr.	then was the horn, filled and should they drink of, Jokul and Full-Strong.	The horn was filled again so that Jokul and Full-Strong would drink from it.
Fullsterkr drakk fyrr.	Full-Strong drank before.	Full-Strong drank before.

The Tale of Thorsteinn House-Power (Old Icelandic)

Old Icelandic	Literal	English
Jökull tók við og leit í hornit og kvað lítilmannliga drukkið og sló Fullsterk með horninu.	Jokul took with and had in horn and said weakly drank and struck Full-Strong with the-horn.	Jokul took the horn and said that Full-Strong drank like a weakling, and struck him with the horn.
en hann rak hnefann á nasir Jökli, svá að þjófshakan brotnaði, en ór hrutu tennrnar.	but he drove fist to nose Jokul's, so that thievish-chin broken, then out-of erupted the-teeth.	But he drove his first into Jokul's nose, so that his thievish chin was broken, and then teeth erupted out of his mouth.
var þá upphlaup mikið.	was then uproar much.	There was much uproar.
Geirröður bað menn eigi láta þetta spyrjast, að þeir skildi svá illa.	Geirrod asked men not have this was-heard, that they separated so ill.	Geirrod asked the men not to have it heard that they had separated on bad terms.
váru þeir þegar sáttir, og var Grímr inn góði burt borinn.	were they straightaway agreed, and was Grim the Good away carried.	They were reconciled straight away and Grim the Good was carried away.

10

Old Icelandic	Literal	English
litlu síðar kom maður gangandi í höllina.	little afterwards came a-man walking into the-hall.	A little afterwards a man came walking into the hall.
allir undruðust, hversu lítill hann var.	all wondered, how-so little he was.	Everyone wondered at how little he was.
það var Þorsteinn Bæjarbarn.	that was Thorstein House-Child.	It was Thorstein House-Child.
hann veik að Goðmundi og sagði, að hestar væru til reiðu.	he turned to Godmund and told, him horses were to ride.	He turned to Godmund and told him to prepare the horses to ride.
Geirröður spurði, hvað barn að það væri.	Geirrod asked, who the-child that it was.	Geirrod asked who the child was.
Goðmundur segir:	Godmund said:	Godmund said:
"það er smásveinn minn, er Óðinn konungr sendi mér, og er konungs gersemi og kann marga smáleika, og ef yður þætti nokkuru neytr, þá vil ek gefa yðor hann".	"that is little-boy mine, that Odin the-king sent me, and is the-king's treasure and knows many small-games, and if you seem some good-use, then will I give you him".	"This is my little boy that king Odin sent me, and is the king's treasure, and he knows many tricks, and if you think he may be of use then I will give him to you".

The Tale of Thorsteinn House-Power (Old Icelandic)

Old Icelandic	Literal	English
"það er svipmikill drengr",	"that is a-striking fellow",	"That is a striking fellow",
segir konungr, "og vil ek sjá fimleika hans",	said the-king, "and wish I to-see tricks his",	said the king, "and I wish to see his tricks",
og bað Þorstein leika nokkurn smáleik.	and asked Thorstein play some small-games.	and asked Thorstein to play some tricks.
Þorsteinn tók hall sinn og brodd og pjakkar þar í, sem hvítt er.	Thorstein took marble his and point and pricked there in, where white was.	Thorstein took his marble and point and pricked where it was white.
kemur haglhríð svá mikil, að engi þorir í móti að sjá, og varð svá mikil fönn í höllinni, að tók í ökkla.	came hailstorm so great, that none dared to meet to see, and was so great snow in the-hall, that took at ankles.	There came a hailstorm so great, that none dared to meet it with their eyes, and the snow was so great in the hall that it was up to everyone's ankles".
konungr hló að.	the-king laughed at.	The king laughed at this.
nú stangaði Þorsteinn hallinn, þar sem hann var gulr.	now stabbed Thorstein the-marble, there where it was yellow.	Now Thorstein stabbed at the marble where it was yellow.
kom þá sólskin svá heitt, að snjórinn bráðnaði allr á lítilli stundu.	came then sunshine so hot, that the-snow melted all in little while.	Then came sunshine so hot that the snow melted in a short while.
þar fylgdi sætr ilmr, en Geirröður kvað hann var listamann.	there followed mountain-pastures sweet-smell, and Geirrod said he was a-skilled-craftsman.	There followed the sweet smell of mountain pastures, and Geirrod said that he was a skilled craftsman.
en Þorsteinn segir eptir einn leikinn, er heitir svipuleikr.	then Thorstein said after one trick, that called the-scourge.	Then Thorstein said that there remained one trick which was called the scourge.
konungr segist hann sjá vilja.	the-king said he to-see wished.	The king said he wished to see it.
Þorsteinn stóð á miðju hallargólfi og pjakkar þar í hallinn, sem rautt er.	Thorstein stood in the-middle hall-floor and pricked there in the-marble, where red was.	Thorstein stood in the middle of the hall floor and pricked the marble where it was red.
stökkva þar ór gneistar.	jumped there of sparks.	Then sparks jumped from it.
síðan hleypr hann um höllina fyrir hvert sæti.	afterwards ran he about the-hall before each seat.	Afterwards he ran about the hall in front of each seat.

The Tale of Thorsteinn House-Power (Old Icelandic)

Old Icelandic	Literal	English
tókust þá að vaxa gneistaflaugin, svá að hverr maður varð að geyma sín augu.	took then to grow sparks-flying, so that each man was to to-mind their eyes.	Then the fling sparks grew so that every man had to mind his eyes.
en Geirröður konungr hló að.	then Geirrod the-king laughed at.	Then King Geirrod laughed at this.
tók þá að vaxa eldrinn, svá að öllum þótti við of um.	took then to grow the-fire, so that all thought against of about.	The fires grew so that all thought against it.
Þorsteinn hafði sagt Goðmundi fyrir, að hann skyldi út ganga og fara á hest.	Thorstein had told Godmund before, that he should out go and travel with horses.	Thorstein had told Godmund before, that he should go and travel with the horses.
Þorsteinn hleypr fyrir Geirröð og mælti:	Thorstein ran before Geirrod and said:	Thorstein ran before Geirrod and said:
"vili þér láta auka leikinn?"	"wish you to-have more games?"	"Do you wish to have more games?"
"lát sjá, sveinn",	"let see, boy",	"Let's see, boy",
sagði hann.	said he.	he said.
þjakkar Þorsteinn þá í fastara lagi.	pricked Thorstein then to harder thrust.	Thorstein then pricked harder.
kemur þá í auga Geirröði konungi.	came then in eyes Geirrod's the-king.	Then came sparks into King Geirrod's eyes.
Þorsteinn hleypr til dyranna og snaraði hallinum og broddinum, og kom í sitt auga hvárt á Geirröði konungi, og steyptist hann dauður á gólfit, en Þorsteinn gekk út.	Thorstein ran to the-door and threw the-marble and point, and came to his eyes each that Geirrod the-king, and knocked him dead on the-floor, then Thorstein went out.	Thorstein ran to the door and threw the marble and the point, and each came to King Geirrod's eyes, and he was knocked dead on the floor, then Thorstein went out.
var Goðmundur þá kominn á hest.	when Godmund then came to horses.	Godmund had then come on horseback.
Þorsteinn bað þá ríða, "því að nú er ekki deigum vært".	Thorstein bid then to-ride, "because that now is not weak short".	Thorstein then bid then that they ride away, "because now is not the time for weakness".
þeir ríða til árinnar.	they rode to the-river.	They rode to the river
var þá aptr kominn hallrinn og broddrinn.	was then back coming the-marble and the-point.	Then the marble and point was coming back.

The Tale of Thorsteinn House-Power (Old Icelandic)

Old Icelandic	Literal	English
Þorsteinn segir, að Geirröður var dauður.	Thorstein said, that Geirrod was dead.	Thorstein said that Geirrod was dead.
ríða þeir nú yfir ána og þangað, sem þeir höfðu fundizt.	rode they now across the river from-there, where they had met.	They now rode across the river from there, where they had met.
þá mælti Þorsteinn:	then spoke Thorstein:	Then Thorstein spoke:
"hér munum vér nú skilja, og mun mönnum mínum mál þykkja, að ek komi til þeira".	"forces should we now separate, and should men mine the-matter think, that I come to them".	"Our forces should now separate, and my men think that I should come to them.
"far heim með mér",	"travel home with me",	"Travel home with me",
sagði Goðmundr, "og skal ek launa þér góða fylgd".	said Godmund, "and shall I repay you good following".	said Godmund, "and I shall repay you for your good help".
"síðan mun ek þess vitja",	"afterwards should I this visit",	"Afterwards I should visit",
segir Þorsteinn, "en aptr skalt þú fara með fjölmenni í Geirröðargarða.	said Thorstein, "but back shall you travel with following-men to Geirrod's-Town.	said Thorstein, "but you should travel back to Geirrod's-Town with a following of men.
er nú landið í yðru valdi".	is now the-land in your control".	Now the land is in your control".
"þú munt ráða",	"you should reckon",	"Whatever you reckon"
sagði Goðmundr, "en Óláfi konungi skaltu færa kveðju mína".	said Godmund, "then Olaf the-king shall be-brought greetings mine".	said Godmund, "then King Olaf shall be brought my greetings".
tók hann þá eitt gullker og silfrdisk og tvítugt handklæði gullofit og sendi konungi, en bað Þorstein vitja sín, og skildu með kærleikum.	took he then a golden-bowl and silver-dish and twenty handcloths gold-woven and sent the-king, and asked Thorstein visit him, and separated with friendly-terms.	He then took a golden bowl and a silver dish and twenty gold woven towels also to send to the king, and he asked Thorstein to visit him, and they separated on friendly terms.

11

en nú sér Þorsteinn, hvar Agði jarl ferr í allmiklum jötunmóð.	and now saw Thorstein, where Agdi the-earl travelling in all-mighty giant's-wrath.	And now saw Thorstein, where Earl Agdi was travelling in an almighty giant's wrath.

The Tale of Thorsteinn House-Power (Old Icelandic)

Old Icelandic	Literal	English
Þorsteinn ferr eptir honum.	Thorstein went after him.	Thorstein went after him.
sér hann þá mikinn húsabæ, er Agði átti.	saw he then great farmstead, which Agdi owned.	He then saw a great farmstead, which Agdi owned.
aldingarður var við grindhliðið, og stóð þar við ein jungfrú.	orchard was with gate, and stood there with a young-woman.	There was an orchard, and at the gate there stood a young woman.
hún var dóttir Agða og hét Goðrún.	she was daughter Agdi's and named Gudrun.	She was Agdi's daughter and was named Gudrun.
mikil var hún og fríð.	tall was she and peaceful.	She was tall and fair.
hún heilsaði föður sínum og spurði tíðenda.	she greeted father hers and asked of-news.	She greeted her father and asked him the news.
"nóg eru tíðendi",	"enough is news",	"There is news enough",
segir hann.	said he.	he said.
"Geirröður konungr er dauður, og hefir Goðmundur af Glæsisvöllum svikit oss alla og hefir leynt þar kristnum manni, og heitir sá Þorsteinn Bæjarmagn.	"Geirrod the-king is dead, and has Godmund of Glasir-Plains tricked us all and has hidden there Christian man, and named so Thorstein House-Power.	"King Geirrod is dead, and Godmund of Glasir-Plains has tricked us all and has hidden a Christian man there, and he is named Thorstein House-Power.
hann hefir ausit eldi í augu oss.	he has thrown fire in eyes ours.	He has thrown fire in our eyes.
skal ek nú drepa menn hans".	shall I now kill men his".	I shall now kill his men".
kastar hann þar niður hornunum Hvítingum og hljóp til skógar, sem hann væri galinn.	threw he there down the-horn Whitings and ran to the-forest, as-if he was mad.	There he threw down the horn called Whitings and ran to the forest as if he was mad.
Þorsteinn gekk að Goðrúnu.	Thorstein went to Gudrun.	Thorstein went to Gudrun.
hún heilsaði honum og spurði hann að nafni.	she greeted him and asked him of name.	She greeted him and asked him his name.
hann kvaðst Þorsteinn Bæjarbarn heita, hirðmaður Ólafs konungs.	he said Thorstein House-Child named, court-man Olaf's the-king.	He said he was named Thorstein House-Child, a court man of King Olaf.
"stórr mun þar inn stærsti, sem þú ert barnit",	"big must there the biggest, if you are the-child",	"His big must be the biggest, if you are the child",

The Tale of Thorsteinn House-Power (Old Icelandic)

Old Icelandic	Literal	English
sagði hún.	said she.	she said.
"viltu fara með mér",	"will-you travel with me",	"Will you travel with me",
segir Þorsteinn, "og taka við trú?"	said Thorstein, "and take with the-faith?"	said Thorstein, "and take the faith?".
"við lítit yndi á ek hér að skiljast",	"with little happiness that I here to separate",	"With little happiness here to separate from", she said,
segir hún, "því að móðir mín er dauð.	said she, "because that mother mine is dead.	"because my mother is dead.
hún var dóttir Óttars jarls af Hólmgörðum, og váru þau ólík að skapsmunum, því að faðir minn er mjög tröllaukinn, og sé ek nú, að hann er feigr.	she was daughter Ottar's the-earl of Novgorod, and were they unlike in mood-mind, as that father mine is much troll-possessed, and see I now, that he is doomed.	She was the daughter of Earl Ottar of Novgorod, and they were unlike in temperament, as my father who is troll-possessed, and I see now that he is doomed.
en ef þú vilt fylgja mér aptr hingað, þá mun ek fara með þér".	then if you will follow me back here, then shall I travel with you".	Then if you will follow back here with me, then I shall travel with you".
síðan tók hún þing sín, en Þorsteinn tók hornin Hvítinga.	afterwards took she things hers, and Thorstein took the-horn Whitings.	Afterwards she took her things, and Thorstein took the horn called Whitings.
síðan gengu þau á skóginn og sáu, hvar Agði fór.	afterwards went they into the-forest and saw, where Agdi went.	Afterwards they went into the forest and saw, where Agdi went.
hann grenjaði mjög og helt fyrir augun.	he screamed much and held before eyes.	He screamed a lot and held his hands before his eyes.
hafði það saman borið, þegar hann sá skip Þorsteins, hljóp sá verkr í þjófsaugun á honum, að hann sá eigi.	had that together borne, as-soon-as he saw ship Thorstein's, ran so pain in thief's-eyes of his, that he saw not.	That had happened together with, as soon as he saw Thorstein's ship, a pain ran in his thief's eyes, so that he could not see.
var þá komið að sólarfalli, er þau komu til skips.	was then coming to sunset, when they came to ships.	It was approaching sunset, when they came to the ships.
váru menn Þorsteins þá burt búnir, en er þeir sáu Þorstein, urðu þeir fegnir.	when men Thorstein's then away prepared, then when they saw Thorstein, became they joyful.	When Thorstein's men were preparing to journey away, then they saw Thorstein and became joyful.

The Tale of Thorsteinn House-Power (Old Icelandic)

Old Icelandic	Literal	English
sté Þorsteinn þá á skip, og sigldu burt.	stepped Thorstein then onto the-ship, and sailed away.	Thorstein stepped onto the ship, and they sailed away.
er eigi getið um ferð hans, fyrr en hann kom heim í Noreg.	is nothing told-of about the-journey his, before that he came home to Norway.	Nothing is told of his journey, before he came home to Norway.

12

þenna vetr sat Óláfur konungr í Þrándheimi.	that winter sat Olaf the-king in Trondheim.	That winter King Olaf sat at Trondheim.
Þorsteinn fann konung að Jólum og færði honum gripi þá, sem Goðmundur sendi honum, og hornin Hvítinga og marga aðra gripi.	Thorstein met the-king at Yule and brought him treasure then, which Godmund sent him, and the-horn Whitings and many other treasures.	Thorstein met the king at Yule and brought him treasure, which Godmund had sent him, and the horn called Whitings, and many other treasures.
sagði hann konungi frá ferðum sínum og sýndi honum Goðrúnu.	told he the-king from voyage his and showed him Gudrun.	He told the king of his voyages and showed him Gudrun.
konungr þakkaði honum, og lofuðu allir hans hreysti og þótti mikils um vert.	the-king thanked him, and praised all his valour and thought much about worthy.	The king thanked him, and praised all his valour and thought much of his worthiness.
síðan lét konungr skíra Goðrúnu og kenna trú.	afterwards had the-king baptised Gudrun and taught the-faith.	Afterwards the king had Gudrun baptised and taught the faith.
Þorsteinn lék svipuleik um Jólin, og þótti mönnum það skemmtan mikil.	Thorstein played the-scourge about Yule, and thought men that amusement great.	Thorstein played the scourge through Yule, and men thought it was great amusement.
Hvítingar gengu í minnum, og váru tveir menn um hvárt horn.	Whitings went in came, and were two men about each horn.	The Whitings were brought in, and two men shared each horn.
en ker það, sem Goðmundur hafði sent konungi, gekk engum af að drekka utan Þorsteini Bæjarbarni.	the vessel that, which Godmund had sent the-king, went none of of drinking except Thorstein House-Child.	The cup that Godmund had sent the king, was not drunk from except by Thorstein House-Child.
handklæðit brann eigi, þótt því væri í eld kastað, og var hreinna eptir en áður.	hand-cloth burned not, though that was in fire cast, and was cleaner after than before.	The hand-cloth did not burn, even though it was cast in fire, and was cleaner than before.

The Tale of Thorsteinn House-Power (Old Icelandic)

Old Icelandic	Literal	English
Þorsteinn talar um við konung, að hann vildi gera brullaup til Goðrúnar, en konungr veitti honum það, og var það sæmilig veizla.	Thorstein talked through with the-king, that he wished to-make wedding-proposal to Gudrun, and the-king granted him that, and was that well feast.	Thorstein talked through with the king, that he wished to make a wedding proposal to Gudrun, and the king granted him that, and was there a splendid feast.
og ina fyrstu nótt, er þau kómu í eina sæng og niður var hleypt fortjaldinu, þá brast upp þilfjöl að höfðum Þorsteins, og var þar kominn Agði jarl og ætlaði að drepa hann.	and the first night, when they came to one bed and down was cast the-curtain, then burst up decks over head Thorstein's, and was then come Agdi the-earl and intended to kill him.	And on the first night, when they came to bed together, the curtain was cast down, and then the decks over Thorstein's head burst open, and there had come Earl Agdi intending to kill him.
en þar laust í móti hita svá miklum, að hann þorði eigi inn að ganga.	but then loosed in opposition heat so great, that he dared not in to go.	But then was released so great a heat against him, that he dared not go in.
sneri hann þá í burtu.	turned he then to away.	He turned away.
þá kom konungr að og sló hann með gullbúnu refði í höfuðið, en hann steyptist niður í jörðina.	then came the-king to and struck him with gold-plated staff about head, then he fell down to the-ground.	Then the king came and struck him with a gold plated staff on the head, then he fell face down on the ground.
helt konungr vörð um nóttina, en um morguninn váru horfin hornin Hvítingar.	held the-king guard about the-night, then about morning were disappeared the-horns Whitings.	The king held guard through the night, and then in the morning the horns called Whitings had disappeared.
gekk veizlan vel fram.	went the-feast well from-there.	The feast went well from there.
sat Þorsteinn með konungi um vetrinn, og unnust þau Goðrún vel.	sat Thorstein with the-king through winter, and loved they Gudrun well.	Thorstein sat with the king through the winter, and he and Gudrun loved each other well.
um várið beiddi Þorsteinn orlofs að sigla í Austrveginn og finna Goðmund konung.	about spring asked Thorstein vacation to sail to Eastern-Lands and find Godmund the-king.	In the spring Thorstein asked for a vacation to sail to the Eastern-Lands to find King Godmund.
en konungr sagðist það eigi gera, utan hann lofaði að koma aptr.	but the-king said that not to-do, without him pledging to come back.	But the king said that he should not do it without promising to come back.
Þorsteinn hét því.	Thorstein promised accordingly.	Thorstein promised accordingly.

The Tale of Thorsteinn House-Power (Old Icelandic)

Old Icelandic	Literal	English
konungr bað hann halda trú sína vel, "og eig meira undir þér en þeim Austr þar".	the-king asked him keep faith his well, "and have more behind you than they Eastern-Lands there".	The king asked him to keep his faith well: "and have more behind you than those in the Eastern-Lands there".
skildust þeir með kærleikum, og báðu allir vel fyrir honum, því að Þorsteinn var orðinn vinsæll.	separated they with friendship, and bid all well for him, because that Thorstein was became popular.	They separated with friendship, and all bid him well, for Thorstein had become popular.
sigldi hann í Austrveg, og er eigi getið annars en sú ferð færist vel.	sailed he to Eastern-Lands, and was nothing told-of other than so travelled the-journey well.	He sailed to the Eastern-Lands, and nothing was told other than that he travelled the journey well.
kom hann á Glæsisvöllu, og fagnaði Goðmundur honum vel.	came he to Glasir-Plains, and welcomed Godmund him well.	He came to Glasir-Plains, and Godmund welcomed him well.
Þorsteinn mælti:	Thorstein spoke:	Thorstein spoke:
"hvað hafið þér frétt ór Geirröðargörðum?"	"what have you news of Geirrod's-Town?"	"What news do you have of Geirrod's-Town?"
"þangað fór ek",	"there travelled I",	"I travelled there",
segir Goðmundr, "og gáfu þeir landið í mitt vald, og ræður þar fyrir Heiðrekr Úlfhamr, sonr minn".	said Godmund, "and gave they land to me power, and rules there over Heidrek Wolf-Skin, son mine".	said Godmund, "and they gave me power over the land, and ruling over there is Heidrek Wolf-Skin, my son".
"hvar er Agði jarl?"	"what of Agdi the-earl?"	"What of Earl Agdi?"
segir Þorsteinn.	said Thorstein.	said Thorstein.
"hann lét gera sér haug, þá þér fóruð",	"he had done himself a-burial-mound, when you travelled",	"He had made himself a burial mound, when you travelled",
segir Goðmundr, "og gekk þar í með mikið fé, en þeir Jökull og Frosti drukknuðu í ánni Hemru, er þeir fóru frá veizlunni, en ek hefi nú vald yfir heraðinu á Grundum".	said Godmund, "and went there in with much wealth, but they Jokul and Frosti drowned in the-river Hemra, as they travelled from the-feast, then I have now power across the-district of Grundir".	said Godmund", and retired there with much wealth, and Jokul and Frosti drowned in the river Hemra, as they travelled from the feast, and I now have power across the district of Grundir".
"þar er nú mikið undir",	"there is now much under",	"There is now a lot under it",

The Tale of Thorsteinn House-Power (Old Icelandic)

Old Icelandic	Literal	English
segir Þorsteinn, "hverju þú vilt mér af skipta, því að mér þykkir Goðrún eiga arf allan eptir föður sinn, Agða jarl".	said Thorstein, "how you will me to give, because that to-me seems Gudrun my-wife inheritance all after father his, Agdi the-earl".	said Thorstein, "how much you wish to let me have, because it seems to me that my wife Gudrun is entitled to all the inheritance after he father, Earl Agdi".
"ef þú vilt vera minn maður",	"if you will be my man",	"If you will be my man",
sagði Goðmundr.	said Godmund.	said Godmund.
"þá muntu ekki vanda um trú mína",	"then should not custom about the-faith mine",	"Then you will not have any problems with my faith",
segir Þorsteinn.	said Thorstein.	said Thorstein.
"það vil ek",	"that will I",	"That I will",
sagði Goðmundr.	said Godmund.	said Godmund.
sídan fóru þeir til Grunda, og tók Þorsteinn heraðið undir sik.	afterwards travelled they to Grundir, and took Thorstein the-district under himself.	Afterwards they travelled to Grundir, and Thorstein took the district under himself.

13

Þorsteinn reisti bú að Gnípalundi, því að Agði jarl hafði gengið aptr og eytt bæinn.	Thorstein raised the-dwelling at Gnipalund, because that Agdi the-earl had come back and devastated the-dwelling.	Thorstein raised the house at Gnipalund, as Earl Agdi had come back and devastated the old house.
gerðist Þorsteinn höfðingi mikill.	became Thorstein a-chieftain great.	Thorstein became a great chieftain.
Goðrún fæddi sveinbarn mikið litlu síðar, og hét Brynjólfur.	Gudrun raised a-baby-boy large little since, and named Brynjolf.	Gudrun gave birth to a big baby boy, and he was named Brynjolf.
ekki var traust, að Agði jarl glettist eigi við Þorstein.	not was trusted, that Agdi the-earl playing-tricks not against Thorstein.	There was no confidence that Earl Agdi would not play-tricks against Thorstein.
eina nótt gekk Þorsteinn af sæng sinni og sá, hvar að Agði fór.	one night went Thorstein to bed his and saw, where that Agdi moving.	One night Thorstein got out of his bed and saw where Agdi was moving.

The Tale of Thorsteinn House-Power (Old Icelandic)

Old Icelandic	Literal	English
hann þorði hvergi inn í hliðin, því að kross var fyrir hverjum dyrum.	he dared neither in the the-gates, because that the-cross was before each doorway.	He dared not enter the gates, for there was a cross at every door.
Þorsteinn gekk til haugsins.	Thorstein went to burial-mound-his.	Thorstein went to the mound.
hann var opinn, og gekk hann inn og tók burt hornin Hvítinga.	it was open, and went he inside and took away the-horns Whitings.	It was open, and he went inside and took away the horns called Whitings.
þá kom Agði jarl í hauginn, en Þorsteinn hljóp út hjá honum og setti kross í dyrrnar, og laukst aptr haugrinn, og hefir ekki orðið vart við Agða síðan.	then came Agdi the-earl into the-mound, and Thorstein ran out beside him and set the-cross in the-door, and closed afterwards the-mound, and has no word was of Agdi since..	Then Earl Agdi came to the mound, but Thorstein ran out beside him and put a cross in the door, and the mound was closed, and Agdi has not been seen since.
um sumarið eptir fór Þorsteinn til Noregs og færði Óláfi konungi hornin Hvítinga.	about summer after went Thorstein to Norway and brought Olaf the-king the-horns Whitings.	The following summer Thorstein went to Norway, and brought King Olaf the horns called Whitings.
síðan fekk hann orlof og sigldi til eigna sinna.	then got he leave to sail to possessions his.	Then he took leave and sailed to his possessions.
bauð konungr honum halda vel trú sína.	asked the-king him hold well faith his.	The king commanded him to keep his faith well.
höfum vér eigi frétt síðan til Þorsteins.	have we not news since of Thorstein's.	We have not heard from Thorstein since.
en þá Óláfur konungr hvarf af Orminum Langa, hurfu hornin Hvítingar.	but when Olaf the-king disappeared from The-Serpent Long, vanished the-horns Whitings.	But when King Olaf disappeared from the Long Serpent, the horns of the Whites disappeared.
lúkum vér þar þætti Þorsteins Bæjarbarns.	end we there the-story Thorstein's House-Child.	We end there the tale of Thorstein House-Child.

Word List (Old Icelandic to English)

Word List (Old Icelandic to English)

Old Icelandic	English
A, a	
að	about, against, as, at, from, him, in, it, of, over, than, that, the, to, towards, when, which
aðra	other
aðrir	others
af	drink, from, from, of, of, off, that, to, to
afhenda	off-handed, of-hand
afklæðast	undressed
afklæddust	undressed
afl	strength
afla	provide
afli	a-forge, strength
Agða	Agdi (name), Agdi (name), Agdi's (name)
Agði	Agdi (name), Agdi (name)
akkerum	anchor
aldingarður	orchard
aldri	never, never
alla	all, all
allan	all
allar	all
allir	all, all
allmiklum	all-mighty
allr	all, all
alls	all
Allsterk	All-Strong (name)
Allsterkr	All-Strong (name)
allt	all, all
andliti	face
annan	another-thing
annarr	another, one, one, the-other
annarri	another, one
annars	other
annast	he-took-care-of
aptnaði	the-evening
aptr	afterwards, back, back, return
arf	inheritance
atgang	to-going
atgangr	to-going
atsetu	a-seat
auðið	fated
auga	eyes, eyes
augu	eyes, eyes
augum	eyes
augun	eyes
auka	extra, more
aura	ounces
ausit	thrown
austr	east, east, Eastern-Lands (place)
Austrveg	Eastern-Lands (place)
Austrveginn	Eastern-Lands (place)
Á, á	
á	a, about, a-river, at, beside, by, for, from, in, into, is, of, on, onto, that, the, then, to, was, who, with
ábyrgjast	take-care-of
áður	after, before
áliðnum	following
álna	cubits
álnar	a-yard
ána	the, the-river
ánni	the-river, the-river
árinnar	the-river, the-river
átti	had, owned
áttu	had
ávallt	always
Æ, æ	
ætla	intend, suppose
ætlaði	intended
ætlan	intentions
ætlar	intended
ættar	lineage

257

Word List (Old Icelandic to English)

Old Icelandic	English
ætti	had

B, b

Old Icelandic	English
bað	asked, bid, ordered
báðu	bid
báðum	both
bæinn	the-dwelling
Bæjarbarn	House-Child (name)
Bæjarbarni	House-Child (name)
Bæjarbarns	House-Child (name)
Bæjarmagn	House-Power (name)
bak	back, the-back
Bálagarðssíðu	Balagardsida (place)
bana	dead, death
bandvettlinga	mittens
bani	death, the-death
bar	bore, carried
barn	the-child
barni	a-baby
barnit	child, the-child
báru	carried
bárust	bore
bauð	asked, offered
beiddi	asked
beini	the-bone
beinum	the-bone
beitina	opening, the-opening
bekk	a-bench, bench
bekkinn	of-the-bench
bekkjar	bench
bekknum	that-bench, the-bench
ber	bear
bera	bear, brought
berast	bore
berði	threw
berið	bring
berizt	bear
betr	better
betra	better
betri	better
beztir	best
bíða	abide, await
biður	asked
bik	pitch

Old Icelandic	English
birti	revealed
bjálfa	Bjalfi
bjálfi	Bjalfi
bjó	lived, prepared
bjuggust	settled
blár	black
bleikum	pale
boð	an-invite
boði	breaking
bóndi	farmer
borð	table
borða	the-tables
borðinu	table
borðum	a-table, the-tables
borg	a-city
borgarinnar	the-city, the-town
borgina	the-city, the-town
borið	borne
borin	brought
borinn	carried
börn	children
brá	drew
bráðnaði	melted
bræðir	thaws
bragði	looking
brann	burned
brast	burst
braut	way
brautinni	turned-away, turning
breiða	broad
breiddu	spread
breitt	broad
breyttu	behaved
bringu	the-chest
brodd	point
broddinum	point, the-point
broddrinn	the-point
bróður	brother
brosti	burst-out-laughing
brotnaði	broke, broken
brott	away
brullaup	wedding-proposal
Brynjólfur	Brynjolf (name)
bú	the-dwelling
búa	live

Word List (Old Icelandic to English)

Old Icelandic	English
bugtinni	the-curve
búið	inlaid, prepared
búin	prepared
búk	thick-set
búnir	prepared
burt	away
burtu	away
býður	invite
byggð	settlements
byr	fair-wind
byrlaranum	the-cup-bearer

D, d

Old Icelandic	English
dag	day
Dagný	Dagny (name)
dagsins	of-the-day
datt	fell
dauð	dead
dauður	dead
degi	day
deigum	weak
deyr	dies
díki	the-moat
djúp	deep
dóttir	daughter
draga	carry, drag
drakk	drank
drap	killed
draup	dripped
dregr	drew
drekka	drink, drinking, they, to-drink
drekkir	drink
drekkr	drinks
drengr	fellow
drep	gangrene
drepa	kill
drepnir	killed
Drött	Drott (name)
drottning	the-queen
Dröttr	Drott (name)
drukkið	drank, drink, drinking, drink-to, drunk
drukkin	drunk
drukknuðu	drowned
drukku	drank
drykkju	drinking
drykkjumaður	drinking-man
drykkjuskapr	drinking
drykknum	drink
dúka	tablecloths
dúkinn	table-cloth, the-table-cloth
dúkr	table-cloth
dunur	a-din
dvelr	delays
dverg	dwarf
dvergnum	the-dwarf
dvergrinn	dwarf, the-dwarf
dvergsbarnit	the-dwarf's-boy
dýr	wild-animals
dyranna	the-door
dyrr	door, the-door
dyrrnar	the-door
dyrum	doorway

E, e

Old Icelandic	English
eða	and, but, or
ef	if
eiða	oath, oaths
eig	have
eiga	my-wife, said-of, to-own
eigi	none, not, nothing
eigna	possessions
eignir	property
eigum	own
eik	oak
eikinni	the-oak
eimyrja	embers
ein	a
eina	a, one
einhvern	some-way
einhverr	someone
einir	alone
einn	a, one
einni	a
einskis	nothing

259

Word List (Old Icelandic to English)

Old Icelandic	English
einu	in-one, one
einum	a, one
eitr	poison
eitt	a, one
ek	I
ekki	no, not, nothing
eld	fire
eldi	fire
eldist	oldest
eldrinn	the-fire
eldsskara	fire-poker
eldur	fire, the-flames
eltu	chased
en	about, and, but, on, than, that, the, then, though, when, while
endast	ending
enga	any, none
engan	no-one
engi	no, none, not
engir	no
engu	nothing
engum	no, none
enn	but, than
eptir	after, behind
er	am, and, as, be, from, have, is, of, that, then, was, when, which, who
erfi	inheritance
ergist	feebler
erninum	the-eagle
ert	are
ertu	are-you
eru	are, is, they-are, were
erum	are
eyra	ear
eyranu	ears
eyri	an-ounce-of
eytt	devastated

F, f

Old Icelandic	English
fá	get, pay
faðir	father
fæddi	raised
færa	be-brought
færði	brought, took
færir	travel
færist	the-journey
fæti	feet
fætr	feet
fagnaði	celebrated, welcomed
fagr	beautiful
fagrar	fair
fagrt	fair
fangbrögðum	to-wrestling
fann	found, met
fannst	found
far	travel
fara	go, to-travel, travel, travelled, travelling
farið	go, gone
farin	gone
fast	fastened, hard, hard
fastara	harder
fé	wealth
féfátt	lack-of-money
feginn	relieved
fegnir	joyful
feiga	doomed
feigr	doomed, fated-to-die
fekk	got, went
fela	hide
félagi	companion
fell	falling, fell
felli	wave
fellir	drops
fellu	fell
felr	fold
fengnir	get
fengu	caught
fengust	got-they
ferð	journey, the-journey, travelled, voyage
ferðum	voyage
ferr	travelling, went
fésparir	fee-sparing
festi	joined
festir	fastened

Word List (Old Icelandic to English)

Old Icelandic	English
fimleika	tricks
fingrgull	finger-gold
finna	find
finnumst	meet
fitan	fat
fjalli	mountains
fjarstætt	far-away
fjölkunnigr	skilled-in-magic
fjölmenni	following-men
fjóra	four
fjórar	four
fjörð	fjord
fjórðunga	quarters
fjórum	four
fleira	more
flestum	most
fleygir	flew-it
flokk	band, company
flokki	men
flýgr	flies
föður	father
föðurnum	to-the-father
fólk	folk
fólki	folk
föll	falling
fönn	snow
fór	moving, travelled, went
fortjaldinu	the-curtain
fóru	travelled, went
fóruð	travelled
förunautr	companion
fótrinn	leg
fótum	feet
frá	away-from, from, went-from
fram	from, from-there, to
framboðligr	be-offered
framt	provide
frár	swift
fremstir	foremost
frétt	news
fríð	peaceful
Frosta	Frosti (name)
frosti	Frosti, Frosti (name)
fugla	birds
full	drunk
Fullsterk	Full-Strong (name)
Fullsterkr	Full-Strong (name)
fullu	the-full
fúlt	foul
fundizt	met
furðuliga	exceedingly
fylgd	following
fylgdi	followed, following
fylgja	follow, following
fylgt	followed
fylldan	filled
fyllt	horn
fyrir	before, before-them, for, over
fyrr	before
fyrst	first
fyrsta	first
fyrstu	first
fyrstum	first

G, g

Old Icelandic	English
gað	got
gæfa	luck
gæfu	luck
gaf	gave
gáfu	gave
gagn	benefit
gagnvart	going-from
galdrafullt	magic-full
galinn	mad
gamalla	the-old
gamans	games
gamni	game
gamninu	the-game
gandreið	witch-ride
ganga	go, going, walk
gangandi	walking
gangi	go
gátum	opening
Gaulardal	Gaulardale (place)
gef	give
gefa	give
gefur	given

Word List (Old Icelandic to English)

Old Icelandic	English
gegnt	opposite
Geirröð	Geirrod (name)
Geirröðargarða	Geirrod's-Town (place)
Geirröðargörðum	Geirrod's-Town (place)
Geirröði	Geirrod (name), Geirrod's (name)
Geirröður	Geirrod (name)
gekk	went
gengið	come
gengr	went
gengu	went
ger	done
gera	do, done, make, to-do, to-make
gerði	did
gerðist	became
gerðu	did
gersema	precious-things
gersemar	treasured, treasures
gersemi	a-treasure, treasure, treasures
gert	made
get	guess
geta	get
getið	told-of
getr	get
geyma	retain, to-mind
gimsteinar	precious-stones
gjafirnar	the-gifts
gjarna	gladly
glaðir	glad, gladly
Glæsisvöllu	Glasir-Plains (place)
Glæsisvöllum	Glasir-Plains (place)
glerglugg	glass-window
glettist	playing-tricks
glíma	wrestle, wrestling
glímt	wrestled
glóanda	burning, glowing
glugginn	the-skylight
gneistaflaug	a-shower-of-sparks
gneistaflaugin	sparks-flying
gneistar	sparks
Gnípalundi	Gnipalund (place)
góða	good, Good (name), the-good
góði	good, Good (name)
Goðmund	Godmund (name)
Goðmundar	Godmund (name), Godmund's (name)
Goðmundi	Godmund (name)
Goðmundr	Godmund (name)
goðmundur	Godmund, Godmund (name)
góðri	luck
Goðrún	Gudrun (name)
Goðrúnar	Gudrun (name)
Goðrúnu	Gudrun (name)
góðum	good
góður	good
gólfi	the-floor
gólfit	floor, the-floor
gott	good
græð	tend-to
grafit	dug
grám	grey
granda	to-injure
greip	grabbed, gripped
grenjaði	howling, screamed
Grím	Grim (name)
Grími	Grim (name)
Grímr	Grim (name)
grindhliðið	gate
grip	grabbed
gripi	treasure, treasures
Grunda	Grundir (place)
Grundir	Grundir (place)
Grundum	Grundir (place)
guðvef	precious-cloth
guðvefjarskikkju	a-precious-cloak
gul	gold
gull	gold
gullbúnu	gold-plated
gullhnött	gold-ball
gullhring	gold-ring
gullhringa	gold-rings
gulli	gold
gullker	golden-bowl
gullkórónu	gold-crown
gullligt	gold
gullligum	gold
gullmen	gold-necklace

Word List (Old Icelandic to English)

Old Icelandic	English
gullofit	gold-woven
gullskotnum	gold-trimmed
gulr	gold, yellow
gustr	Gust

H, h

Old Icelandic	English
há	high
hæfa	hit
hægt	possible
hættu	dangerous
hafa	had, had, have, having
hafði	had
hafið	have
haft	had, have
hafvillur	open-sea
haglhríð	hailstorm
Hákon	Hakon (name)
halda	hold, keep
hálfan	half
hall	marble, piece-of-marble
hallar	hall
hallargólfi	hall-floor
hallargólfit	hall-floor
hallinn	the-marble, the-piece-of-marble
hallinum	the-marble
hallrinn	the-marble, the-piece-of-marble
háls	the-neck
hálsinum	throat
hamingju	luck
hana	he, it, she
handklæði	hand-cloths
handklæðit	hand-cloth
handsals	binding
hann	he, him, it, men
hans	him, his
harðasti	hardest
harðúðigr	hard-minded
hásæti	a-high-seat, high-seat
háski	dangerous
hátíð	festival
háttar	kinds
haug	a-burial-mound
hauginn	the-mound
haugrinn	the-mound
haugsins	burial-mound-his
heðan	from-hence
hefði	had
hefi	have
hefir	had, has, have
hefna	avenge
Heiðrekr	Heidrek (name)
heiður	honour
heill	whole
heilsaði	greeted
heim	home
heiminum	the-world
heimsliga	foolishly
heit	declared
heita	be-named, named, promised
heiti	named
heitir	called, named
heitt	hot
hel	death
heldur	rather
helt	held
helzt	held
Hemra	Hemra (place)
Hemru	Hemra (place)
henda	catch
hendi	hand
hendur	hand
hentar	suits
henti	caught
hér	forces, here
heraði	district
heraðið	the-district
heraðinu	the-district
hernaði	raiding
hest	horses
hesta	horses
hestar	horses
hestarnir	the-horses
hesti	horse
hestr	horse
hestum	horses

Word List (Old Icelandic to English)

Old Icelandic	English	Old Icelandic	English
hét	is-named, named, promised	höllinni	the-hall
heyra	hear	Hólmgörðum	Novgorod (place)
heyrir	heard	hólnum	the-mound
himni	the-sky	hömrum	a-steep-cliff
hingað	here	hönd	hand
hinir	others, the-other	höndum	hands
hirðið	take-care	honum	he, him, his, it, to-him
hirðmaður	court-man	horfin	disappeared
hirðmönnum	court-men	horn	a-horn, horn, horns
hirðprýði	court	hornin	the-horn, the-horns
hita	heat	horninu	horn, the-horn
hjá	beside	hornit	a-horn, horn, the
hjástöðu	beside-standing	hornunum	the-horn
hjó	hewed	hösvaðist	went-for
hlæjandi	smiling	Hösvi	Hosvir (name)
hlátr	laughter	Hösvir	Hosvir (name)
hlátri	laughter	hratt	pushed
hlaupa	ran	hraustr	brave
hleypr	ran	hreinna	cleaner
hleypt	cast	hreysti	bravery, valour
hliðin	the-gates	hring	a-circle, ring
hlíðir	slope	hringinn	the-ring
hljóðfæra	musical-instruments	hringnum	the-ring
hljóðfæri	musical-instruments	hringrinn	the-ring
hljóp	ran	hristi	shook
hló	laughed	hrutu	erupted
hlógu	laughed	hrysi	trembled
hluti	lot	hug	think
hlýðni	homage	hugr	thought
hlytir	to-get	huldumaður	a-hidden-man
hnakkinn	the-back-of-the-head	hulinshjálm	helm-of-invisibility
hnefann	fist	hún	she
höfði	head	hurfu	disappeared, vanished
höfðingi	a-chieftain	hús	house, the-house
höfðu	had	húsabæ	farmstead
höfðum	head	húsum	houses
höfn	the-harbour	hvað	what, who
höfuðið	head, his-head	hvaðan	from-where
höfum	have	hvar	were, what, where
hól	hill	hvarf	disappeared
holdi	flesh	hvárki	neither
hólinn	the-mound	hvárn	each
hóll	mound	hvárntveggja	either-side
höll	a-hall, the-hall	hvárt	each, whether, which
höllina	the-hall	hvárttveggja	either

264

Word List (Old Icelandic to English)

Old Icelandic	English
hvergi	neither
hverju	how
hverjum	each
hvern	everyone
hverr	anyone, each, who
hverrar	whose
hversu	how-so
hvert	each, what
hví	what, why
Hvítinga	Whitings (name)
Hvítingar	Whitings (name)
Hvítingum	Whitings (name)
hvítr	white
hvítt	white

I, i

illa	badly, ill
ilmr	sweet-smell
in	the
ina	the
indíalandi	India
inn	in, inside, the
innanborðs	aboard
inum	the
it	the, this

Í, í

í	about, all, among, at, if, in, into, it, of, on, the, to, was, with-that

J, j

jafnan	every-time
jafnstóra	equally-as-big, equally-large
jafnstórr	equally-big
Jamtaland	Jamtland (place)
jarl	earl, the-earl
jarli	the-earl, the-earl's
jarls	the-earl, the-earl's
Járnskeggja	Iron-Beard (name)
Jökli	Jokul's (name)
Jökull	Jokul (name)
Jólin	Yule (name)
Jólum	Yule (name)
jörðina	the-ground
jötnum	giants
Jötunheima	Giant-Home (place)
Jötunheimar	Giant-Land (place)
jötunmóð	giant's-wrath
jungfrú	young-woman

K, k

kærleikum	friendly-terms, friendship
kallað	called
kallaður	called
kallar	call, called
kalt	cold
kann	can, knows
kanna	explore
kapparnir	champions
Karkr	Kark (name)
kastað	cast
kastaði	cast, threw
kastar	threw
kastið	throw
kátir	merry
kaupferðir	trading-voyages
kaupferðum	trading-journeys
keiktist	bent
kem	come
kempa	warrior
kemur	came, comes
kenna	know, taught
kenndur	recognised
ker	vessel
keyrir	the-stick
kikna	bent-backwards
kinnbeinit	chin-bone
kjaptinum	mouth, the-mouth
kjaptrinn	jaw
kjós	choose
klæddu	dressed

Word List (Old Icelandic to English)

Old Icelandic	English
klæði	clothed, clothes
klæðin	clothes
klæðir	clothed
klæðsekk	sack
klæðum	clothes
kné	knees
knésbætr	the-back-of-the-knees
knettinum	the-ball
knöttinn	the-ball
knöttrinn	the-ball
kollóttan	bald-headed
Kollsveinn	Kollsvein (name), the-boy
kölluð	called
kom	came
koma	came, come, coming
komi	come
komið	coming
komin	coming
kominn	came, come, coming
komnir	come
komu	came
kómu	came
kómust	came
kona	wife
konung	the-king
konungi	king, the-king
konungnum	the-king
konungr	king, the-king
konungrinn	the-king
konungs	the-king, the-king's
konungshöll	the-king's-hall
konungsnafn	the-king's-name
konungsson	a-king's-son, the-king's-son
konur	women
köppunum	the-cups
kórónu	the-crown
köstuðu	cast
krásum	food
krefja	demand
kristinn	a-Christian, Christian
kristnum	Christian
krókstaf	crooked-staff
krókstafinn	the-crooked-stick
krókstafur	crooked-stick
kross	the-cross
krummurnar	grabbed
kumpánar	fellows
kunnáttu	skills
kunngera	to-announce, wiser
kunnigt	know
kvað	said
kvaddi	called
kvaðst	said
kveðju	greetings
kveðst	greetings, said
kveld	the-evening
kveldið	evening
kvikt	alive, living-thing
kvöld	evening
kyn	kin
kyssti	kissed

L, l

Old Icelandic	English
lá	had, laid, lay
lætr	acts, have
lagði	had, laid
lagðist	lay
lagi	thrust
lagt	left
lágu	laid
land	land, the-land
landi	the-land
landið	land, the-land
landsuðri	South-East
landsuður	the-south-east
Langa	Long (name)
langan	long
lát	have, let
láta	have, lay-out, to-have
látum	leave-it
laukst	closed
laun	to-repay
launa	repay
launað	repay
laust	loosed
leggja	grant
leiða	led
leiddur	led

Word List (Old Icelandic to English)

Old Icelandic	English
leika	play
leikinn	games, trick
leit	had
lék	played
lékst	played
lén	a-fee
lendur	landed
lengr	longer
lét	had
léti	made
létu	had
leynt	hidden
lið	assistance, the-company-of
liði	company, dislocated
líður	passed
lifði	lived
lífgjöf	life-gift
lifir	lives
liggja	lie-down
liggr	lying
líkari	like
líkast	like
listamann	a-skilled-craftsman
lítill	little, small
lítilli	little
lítilmannliga	weakly
lítinn	little
lítit	little
litlu	little
ljótan	hideous
lófa	promise
lofaði	pledging
lofuðu	praised
lög	law
logaði	blazed
logandi	ablaze
logit	a-lie
lokið	ended
löngu	long
lopti	the-air, the-sky
Lúkanus	Lucanus (name)
lúkum	end

M, m

Old Icelandic	English
má	may
maður	a-man, man
mæðast	get-tired
mæla	speak
mælir	speaks
mælt	spoke
mælti	said, spoke
mál	conversations, the-matter
máldrykkju	drinking
manna	man, men, men, men's
manni	man
manns	man
mannshöfuð	a-man's-head
mánuð	a-month
marga	many
margir	many
matr	food
matsveinar	food-servants
mátt	may
mátti	could
mátuligr	fitting
með	along, with
meðalmaður	an-average-man
meðan	as-long-as, while
mega	may
megi	may
megin	side
meira	more
menn	men, the-men
mér	I, me, to-me
mest	most, mostly
mestr	the-greatest, the-most
miðit	the-middle
miðju	the-middle
mik	me, myself
mikið	great, large, much
mikil	great, tall
mikill	great, large
mikils	much
mikinn	great, much
mikla	great
miklar	great, much
mikli	larger, largest

Word List (Old Icelandic to English)

Old Icelandic	English
miklu	much
miklum	great
millum	between
mín	me, mine, my
mína	mine
mínir	mine, my
minn	mine, my
minni	in-memory, smaller
minnum	came
mínu	mine
mínum	mine
miskunnar	mercy
missa	lose
missi	lost
mitt	me, mine
mjög	great, much
móðir	mother
móðu	large-river
móðuna	the-river
mönnum	men, the-men
morgin	morning, the-morning
morgininn	morning
morginn	morning
morgni	morning
morguninn	morning
mörkina	the-trees
mót	against, meet, to-meet
móti	against, meet, oppose, opposition, to-meet
mun	could, must, shall, should, should-be, would
mundi	could-be, should, would, would-have
mundu	must-be, would
mundum	would-be
muni	would
munni	a-mouth
munt	must-be, should
muntu	shall-you, should
munu	should, would-be
munum	should
mútur	payment
myrkr	fog

N, n

Old Icelandic	English
nær	near
næst	near, next, next-to
nætr	nights
nafn	name
nafnbætr	name-titles
nafnfesti	naming-gift
nafni	name
nam	took
nasir	nose
nát	get-hold-of, hold-of
náttúru	natured
né	nor
neðra	under
nefit	nose
nefndi	named
nefndir	named
nema	but, except
neytr	good-use
níðingr	a-coward
niðrgangs	down-going
niður	below, down
nóg	enough
nokkura	some
nokkurn	some
nokkurr	something
nokkuru	some, somewhat
nokkut	anything, some
Noreg	Norway (place)
Noregi	Norway (place)
Noregs	Norway (place)
nösunum	on-the-nose
nótt	night
nóttina	night, the-night
nú	now

O, o

Old Icelandic	English
of	of
ofan	down, over
ofmagni	to-overpower

Word List (Old Icelandic to English)

Old Icelandic	English
og	ad, also, and, filled, river, to
okkr	us
olnbogarnir	elbows
opinn	open
opt	often
orðið	word
orðinn	became
orðum	words
orkar	able-to
orkufátt	low-energy
orlof	leave
orlofs	vacation
Orminum	The-Serpent (name)
oss	ours, us

Ó, ó

Old Icelandic	English
óaflátssamr	un-indulgent
Óðinn	Odin (name)
Óðins	Odin's (name)
Óðni	Odin (name)
óðu	waded
ófarin	unfinished
ófögnuður	unhappy
ófriðar	un-peace
óhýrligr	unfriendly-looking
Óláf	Olaf (name)
Ólafi	Olaf (name)
Óláfs	Olaf's (name)
Ólafur	Olaf (name)
ólík	unlike
ólyfjan	poison
óorðna	unspoken
ór	away-from, from, of, out-of, through
óskyldara	less-should
ótal	countless
óþýður	unfriendly
Óttars	Ottar's (name)
óvæginn	ruthless
óvit	unconscious

Ö, ö

Old Icelandic	English
öðrum	one, other
öfundsjúkir	jealous
ökkla	ankles
öllum	all
öndvegit	opposite
önnur	another, one, other
örn	eagle

P, p

Old Icelandic	English
pilt	boy
piltrinn	the-boy
pjakka	prick
pjakkar	prick, pricked
prett	tricked
pungi	pouch

R, r

Old Icelandic	English
ráð	advice, counsel
ráða	advice, decide, reckon
ráðast	arranged
ræð	ruler
ræður	rules
rak	drove
ráku	drove
rann	ran
rasaði	tumbled
rauðum	red
rauður	red
rautt	red
réð	advised, ruled
réðst	moved
refði	staff
reið	riding
reiddist	rose
reiðu	ride
reis	rose
reisti	raised
reistu	raised
renna	ran
reyk	smoke

Word List (Old Icelandic to English)

Old Icelandic	English
reynt	test
ríða	ride, ride-away, riding, rode, to-ride
riðu	rode
ríður	rode
rifnaði	split
ríki	kingdom
Risaland	Giant-Land (place)
Risalandi	Giant-Land (place)
Risalands	Giant-Land (place)
ríss	rose
rjóðrinu	the-clearing
rjóður	clearing
rönd	around
röndum	stripes
röskr	brave
ruggaði	rocking
rúm	room

S, s

Old Icelandic	English
sá	saw, see, seeing, so, there
sækið	seek
sæmilig	well
sæng	bed
sæti	seat
sætis	seat
sætr	mountain-pastures
sagði	said, said, told, told
sagðist	said
sagt	told, told
saka	injury
sama	same
saman	together
sár	wound
sat	sat
sáttir	agreed
sáttu	saw-you
sáu	saw
sauða	wether's
saur	the-mud
sé	even, he-is, is, see, you
sefur	slept
seg	say
segir	said, said-to, say, told
segist	said
segja	say, tell
seint	slowly
selshöfuð	seal's-head
sem	as, as-if, if, that, whatever, where, which, who
sendi	sent
sendiferðir	missions
sendur	sent
sent	sent
sér	he, him, himself, his, saw, see, to-him, to-see
serk	shirt
serkinn	the-shirt
serkr	shirt
sét	seen
setning	the-setting
setti	set
settist	sat
sex	six
sídan	afterwards
síðan	after, afterwards, since, since., then
síðar	afterwards, since
síðum	sides
siður	the-custom
sigla	sail, sailed
sigldi	sail, sailed
sigldu	sailed
Sigurðarson	Son-of-Sigurd (name)
sik	him, himself, his, themselves
silfrdisk	silver-dish
silfrhring	silver-ring
silfri	silver
silfrkerum	silver
silfrs	silver
sín	hers, him, their, themselves
sína	his, their
sínar	his
sindraði	sparkled
sinn	his, occasion, their

Word List (Old Icelandic to English)

Old Icelandic	English
sinna	his
sinnar	his
sinni	his, this
síns	his
sínum	hers, his
sitja	sit
sitr	sat
sitt	his, sat
sjá	saw, see, to-see
sjaldsénir	rarely-seen
sjálfur	itself
sjau	seven
sjáum	see
skal	shall
skál	shall
skalf	shook
skalt	shall
skaltu	shall, shall-you
skálum	bowls
skammt	a-short-distance, short
skapsmunum	mood-mind
skarlatsklæðum	scarlet-clothing
skatta	tax
skattgildir	tributaries
skaut	shot
skeggit	beard
skemmta	amuse
skemmtan	amusement
skemmtunar	amusement, entertainment
sker	a-rock
skildi	separated
skildu	separated
skildust	separated
skilja	separate, such
skiljast	separate
skilr	separating
skinnslit	colour
skip	a-ship, ship, the-ship
skipað	directed-to
skips	ships, the-ships
skipta	give
skipuð	equipped
skíra	baptised
skjótt	swiftly

Old Icelandic	English
skóga	forests
skógar	the-forest
skóginn	the-forest, the-forests
skörina	high-seat
skorinn	cut
skuli	shall
skulu	shall, should
skuluð	should
skyldi	should
skyldu	and, would
slær	struck
slagir	artful
slegit	struck
slík	such
slíka	such
slíkan	such
slíkar	such
slikum	such
sló	struck
slógu	formed
slysalaust	accidents-without
smáleik	small-games
smáleika	small-games
smásveinn	little-boy
snarað	twisted
snaraði	flew-it, threw, turned-quickly
snekkju	a-sailboat
snemma	early, soon
sneri	turned
sniðglímu	hip-throw
snjó	snow
snjórinn	the-snow
snöruðu	threw
snúinn	twisted
sofa	seep, sleep, slept
sögðu	said
sól	the-sun
sólarfalli	sunset
sólin	sunrise
sólir	suns
sólskin	sunshine
son	son
sonr	son
sprakk	broke
spring	burst

Word List (Old Icelandic to English)

Old Icelandic	English
spurði	asked
spyrjast	was-heard
staðar	standing, to-stand
stærsti	biggest
staf	staff
stafinn	the-staff, the-stick
stafnum	stick
stakk	struck
stálbroddr	steel-point
staldraði	lingered
stall	stable
standa	stand
stangaði	stabbed
sté	stepped
stefna	directed
stein	stone
steinhús	stone-house
steinkastinu	stone-throwing
steinn	stone
sterkari	stronger
sterkastr	strongest
sterkliga	strongly
sterkr	strong
steypa	cast
steyptist	fell, knocked
steyptu	cast
stígr	climbed
stikilinn	horn-point
stiklinum	the-narrow
stóð	stood, weighed
stóðu	stood
stöðum	places
stokkinn	the-foot-board
stökkva	jumped
stóra	great
stórr	big
stórri	large
strengdi	boldly
stríðlyndur	obstinate
ströng	strong
studdi	steadied
stundu	while
stundum	awhile
styrkja	strengthen
sú	so
sumarið	summer
sundi	swimming
sundur	apart
svá	saw, so, the
svarar	answered
svarið	sworn
svartan	black
sveinar	companions, men
sveinbarn	a-baby-boy
sveinn	boy
sverja	swear
svikit	tricked
svipmikill	a-striking
sviptingar	tussle
svipuleik	the-scourge
svipuleikr	the-scourge
sýna	show
sýndar	shown
sýndi	showed
sýndist	seemed, thought
sýnis	his
synjast	refuse

T, t

Old Icelandic	English
tak	take
taka	take, took
takið	take
talar	talked
tána	toe
tánni	toe
tekið	taken
tekinn	taken
tekr	takes, took
tennr	teeth
tennrnar	teeth, the-teeth
tíðenda	news, of-news
tíðendi	news
til	for, of, to
tíma	time
tíu	ten
tjald	tents
togast	pulled
tók	received, took, tugged
tókst	took

Word List (Old Icelandic to English)

Old Icelandic	English
tóku	took
tókust	took
töldust	considered
tólf	twelve
töluðu	told
trapiza	table
traust	trusted
Trausti	Trusty (name)
trautt	scarcely
treysta	reckon, trust
treysti	trust
tröllaukinn	troll-possessed
tröllsligri	troll-like
tröllum	trolls
trú	faith, the-faith
Tryggvason	Tryggvason (name)
tuttugu	twenty
tvá	two
tvær	two
tvau	two
tveggja	two
tveir	of, two
tvítugt	twenty

Þ, þ

Old Icelandic	English
þá	them, then, when
það	it, that
þaðan	from-there
þær	there, those
þætti	seem, the-story
þakkaði	thanked, thanked
þakkar	thanked
þangað	from-there, there
þann	that, the, then
þar	here, then, then, there, they, was
þau	their, they
þegar	as-soon-as, straightaway, then, there
þeim	from-them, theirs, them, then, they
þeir	should, them, there, they
þeira	their, theirs, them, there, they, they-were
þeirar	there
þeiri	their
þekkti	knew
þenna	that
þér	to-you, you, yours
þerris	dry
þess	this
þessa	this
þessi	these, this
þessu	this
þetta	this
þíða	thaw
þik	you
þilfjöl	decks
þín	you, your
þína	yours
þínar	your
þing	assembly, things
þinn	yours
þit	you-two
þitt	your, yours
þjófsaugun	thief's-eyes
þjófshakan	thievish-chin
þjófsnefit	thieving-nose
þjóna	serve, serving
þjónar	serve
þó	though
þökkuðu	thanked
þol	endure
þorði	dared
þorir	dare, dared, daring
Þormóður	Thormod (name)
Þórs	Thor's (name)
Þorstein	Thorstein (name)
Þorsteini	Thorstein (name)
Þorsteinn	Thorstein (name)
Þorsteins	Thorstein's (name)
þótt	though
þótti	seemed, thought
þóttist	thought
þræli	servant
Þrándheimi	Trondheim (place)
þreif	grabbed
þremr	three

Word List (Old Icelandic to English)

Old Icelandic	English
þríhyrndr	three-sided
þrír	three
þrjá	three
þú	you
þung	heavy
þurfa	need
því	accordingly, as, because, it, that, then, therefore
þvílíkir	the-like
þykki	seems, think
þykkir	seems
þykkja	think, value, valued
þyngst	heaviest

U, u

Old Icelandic	English
ullu	wool
um	about, around, through
undan	away, away-from, before
undir	behind, down, under
undirheimum	under-world
undraðist	surprised
undrast	wonder
undruðust	wondered
unga	young
unnust	loved
unum	happy
upp	up
upphlaup	uproar
uppi	up
uppsprettu	up-spring
urðu	became, came
utan	except, except-for, out, out-of, outside, without
uxahnútu	ox-bone

Ú, ú

Old Icelandic	English
úlfaldi	camel
Úlfhamr	Wolf-Skin (name)
Úlfheðinn	Ulfhedin (name)
út	out
úti	out, over
útlægr	outlawed

V, v

Old Icelandic	English
vá	was
vaða	wades
væði	waded-through
vænginn	the-wing
vænsta	good
væri	should-be, was, would
vært	short
væru	were
vaf	wove
vakrliga	nimbly
vald	power
valdi	control
ván	is-expected
vanda	custom, difficulty
vanr	accustomed
vánt	difficulty
vápnaða	weaponed
var	was, were, when
vár	ours
varð	became, was
varðist	defended
vári	spring
várið	spring
varir	aware
varr	aware
vart	was
várt	ours
váru	were, when
vaskligri	braver
vatn	the-water
vatnið	the-water
vátr	water
vaxa	grow
veður	weather
veg	way
veginn	the-road
veik	turned
veit	know, known, knows

Word List (Old Icelandic to English)

Old Icelandic	English
veita	grant, to-grant
veitti	granted
veittu	grant
veizla	feast
veizlan	the-feast
veizlunni	the-feast
vel	well
velfaranda	well-faring
vér	was, we
vera	be, being, were
verða	be, become, becomes
verður	became, becomes, came
verkr	pain
vert	worth, worthy
vestri	the-west
vetr	winter
vetrinn	winter
vettlingana	mitten
við	against, by, of, to, with
víða	widely
Vík	Vik (place)
víkr	moved
vil	will, wish
vilda	wish
vildi	willed, wished, wished-to, would
vildu	wished, would
vili	wish
vilja	he-wished, wished
viljum	wish
vill	will, wished
villa	lost-way
vilt	will, wish
viltu	will-you
vín	wine
vinsæll	popular
virðing	worthy
víst	certainly
vit	know
vita	knew, know
vitja	visit
víttr	bewitched
vöknaði	became-wet
vön	want
vörð	guard
vort	ours
vöttum	gloves
vöxt	grown

Y, y

Old Icelandic	English
yðrir	your
yðru	your
yðrum	yours
yður	you
yfir	across, over
yndi	happiness
Yrjum	Yrjar (place)

Ý, ý

ýmist	either

Word List (English to Old Icelandic)

Word List (English to Old Icelandic)

English	*Old Icelandic*

A, a

English	*Old Icelandic*
a	*á, ein, eina, einn, einni, einum, eitt*
a-baby	*barni*
a-baby-boy	*sveinbarn*
a-bench	*bekk*
abide	*bíða*
ablaze	*logandi*
able-to	*orkar*
aboard	*innanborðs*
about	*á, að, en, í, um*
a-burial-mound	*haug*
accidents-without	*slysalaust*
accordingly	*því*
accustomed	*vanr*
a-chieftain	*höfðingi*
a-Christian	*kristinn*
a-circle	*hring*
a-city	*borg*
a-coward	*níðingr*
across	*yfir*
acts	*lætr*
ad	*og*
a-din	*dunur*
advice	*ráð, ráða*
advised	*réð*
a-fee	*lén*
a-forge	*afli*
after	*áður, eptir, síðan*
afterwards	*aptr, sídan, síðan, síðar*
against	*að, mót, móti, við*
Agdi (name)	*Agða, Agði*
Agdi's (name)	*Agða*
agreed	*sáttir*
a-hall	*höll*
a-hidden-man	*huldumaður*
a-high-seat	*hásæti*
a-horn	*horn, hornit*
a-king's-son	*konungsson*
a-lie	*logit*
alive	*kvikt*

English	*Old Icelandic*
all	*alla, allan, allar, allir, allr, alls, allt, í, öllum*
all-mighty	*allmiklum*
All-Strong (name)	*Allsterk, Allsterkr*
alone	*einir*
along	*með*
also	*og*
always	*ávallt*
am	*er*
a-man	*maður*
a-man's-head	*mannshöfuð*
among	*í*
a-month	*mánuð*
a-mouth	*munni*
amuse	*skemmta*
amusement	*skemmtan, skemmtunar*
an-average-man	*meðalmaður*
anchor	*akkerum*
and	*eða, en, er, og, skyldu*
an-invite	*boð*
ankles	*ökkla*
another	*annarr, annarri, önnur*
another-thing	*annan*
an-ounce-of	*eyri*
answered	*svarar*
any	*enga*
anyone	*hverr*
anything	*nokkut*
apart	*sundur*
a-precious-cloak	*guðvefjarskikkju*
are	*ert, eru, erum*
are-you	*ertu*
a-river	*á*
a-rock	*sker*
around	*rönd, um*
arranged	*ráðast*
artful	*slagir*
as	*að, er, sem, því*
a-sailboat	*snekkju*
a-seat	*atsetu*
a-ship	*skip*
a-short-distance	*skammt*
a-shower-of-sparks	*gneistaflaug*

Word List (English to Old Icelandic)

English	*Old Icelandic*	English	*Old Icelandic*
as-if	*sem*	behind	*eptir, undir*
asked	*bað, bauð, beiddi, biður, spurði*	being	*vera*
		below	*niður*
a-skilled-craftsman	*listamann*	be-named	*heita*
as-long-as	*meðan*	bench	*bekk, bekkjar*
assembly	*þing*	benefit	*gagn*
assistance	*lið*	bent	*keiktist*
as-soon-as	*þegar*	bent-backwards	*kikna*
a-steep-cliff	*hömrum*	be-offered	*framboðligr*
a-striking	*svipmikill*	beside	*á, hjá*
at	*á, að, í*	beside-standing	*hjástöðu*
a-table	*borðum*	best	*beztir*
a-treasure	*gersemi*	better	*betr, betra, betri*
avenge	*hefna*	between	*millum*
await	*bíða*	bewitched	*víttr*
aware	*varir, varr*	bid	*bað, báðu*
away	*brott, burt, burtu, undan*	big	*stórr*
		biggest	*stærsti*
away-from	*frá, ór, undan*	binding	*handsals*
awhile	*stundum*	birds	*fugla*
a-yard	*álnar*	Bjalfi	*bjálfa, bjálfi*
		black	*blár, svartan*
		blazed	*logaði*

B, b

English	*Old Icelandic*	English	*Old Icelandic*
		boldly	*strengdi*
back	*aptr, bak*	bore	*bar, bárust, berast*
badly	*illa*	borne	*borið*
Balagardsida (place)	*Bálagarðssíðu*	both	*báðum*
bald-headed	*kollóttan*	bowls	*skálum*
band	*flokk*	boy	*pilt, sveinn*
baptised	*skíra*	brave	*hraustr, röskr*
be	*er, vera, verða*	braver	*vaskligri*
bear	*ber, bera, berizt*	bravery	*hreysti*
beard	*skeggit*	breaking	*boði*
beautiful	*fagr*	bring	*berið*
be-brought	*færa*	broad	*breiða, breitt*
became	*gerðist, orðinn, urðu, varð, verður*	broke	*brotnaði, sprakk*
		broken	*brotnaði*
became-wet	*vöknaði*	brother	*bróður*
because	*því*	brought	*bera, borin, færði*
become	*verða*	Brynjolf (name)	*Brynjólfur*
becomes	*verða, verður*	burial-mound-his	*haugsins*
bed	*sæng*	burned	*brann*
before	*áður, fyrir, fyrr, undan*	burning	*glóanda*
before-them	*fyrir*	burst	*brast, spring*
behaved	*breyttu*	burst-out-laughing	*brosti*

277

Word List (English to Old Icelandic)

English	Old Icelandic
but	eða, en, enn, nema
by	á, við

C, c

English	Old Icelandic
call	kallar
called	heitir, kallað, kallaður, kallar, kölluð, kvaddi
came	kemur, kom, koma, kominn, komu, kómu, kómust, minnum, urðu, verður
camel	úlfaldi
can	kann
carried	bar, báru, borinn
carry	draga
cast	hleypt, kastað, kastaði, köstuðu, steypa, steyptu
catch	henda
caught	fengu, henti
celebrated	fagnaði
certainly	víst
champions	kapparnir
chased	eltu
child	barnit
children	börn
chin-bone	kinnbeinit
choose	kjós
Christian	kristinn, kristnum
cleaner	hreinna
clearing	rjóður
climbed	stígr
closed	laukst
clothed	klæði, klæðir
clothes	klæði, klæðin, klæðum
cold	kalt
colour	skinnslit
come	gengið, kem, koma, komi, kominn, komnir
comes	kemur
coming	koma, komið, komin, kominn
companion	félagi, förunautr
companions	sveinar
company	flokk, liði
considered	töldust
control	valdi
conversations	mál
could	mátti, mun
could-be	mundi
counsel	ráð
countless	ótal
court	hirðprýði
court-man	hirðmaður
court-men	hirðmönnum
crooked-staff	krókstaf
crooked-stick	krókstafur
cubits	álna
custom	vanda
cut	skorinn

D, d

English	Old Icelandic
Dagny (name)	Dagný
dangerous	hættu, háski
dare	þorir
dared	þorði, þorir
daring	þorir
daughter	dóttir
day	dag, degi
dead	bana, dauð, dauður
death	bana, bani, hel
decide	ráða
decks	þilfjöl
declared	heit
deep	djúp
defended	varðist
delays	dvelr
demand	krefja
devastated	eytt
did	gerði, gerðu
dies	deyr
difficulty	vanda, vánt
directed	stefna
directed-to	skipað
disappeared	horfin, hurfu, hvarf
dislocated	liði
district	heraði
do	gera

Word List (English to Old Icelandic)

English	*Old Icelandic*	English	*Old Icelandic*
done	*ger, gera*	ended	*lokið*
doomed	*feiga, feigr*	ending	*endast*
door	*dyrr*	endure	*þol*
doorway	*dyrum*	enough	*nóg*
down	*niður, ofan, undir*	entertainment	*skemmtunar*
down-going	*niðrgangs*	equally-as-big	*jafnstóra*
drag	*draga*	equally-big	*jafnstórr*
drank	*drakk, drukkið, drukku*	equally-large	*jafnstóra*
dressed	*klæddu*	equipped	*skipuð*
drew	*brá, dregr*	erupted	*hrutu*
drink	*af, drekka, drekkir, drukkið, drykknum*	even	*sé*
		evening	*kveldið, kvöld*
drinking	*drekka, drukkið, drykkju, drykkjuskapr, máldrykkju*	everyone	*hvern*
		every-time	*jafnan*
		exceedingly	*furðuliga*
drinking-man	*drykkjumaður*	except	*nema, utan*
drinks	*drekkr*	except-for	*utan*
drink-to	*drukkið*	explore	*kanna*
dripped	*draup*	extra	*auka*
drops	*fellir*	eyes	*auga, augu, augum, augun*
Drott (name)	*Drött, Dröttr*		
drove	*rak, ráku*		
drowned	*drukknuðu*		

F, f

English	*Old Icelandic*
drunk	*drukkið, drukkin, full*
dry	*þerris*
dug	*grafit*
dwarf	*dverg, dvergrinn*

E, e

English	*Old Icelandic*	English	*Old Icelandic*
each	*hvárn, hvárt, hverjum, hverr, hvert*	face	*andliti*
		fair	*fagrar, fagrt*
eagle	*örn*	fair-wind	*byr*
ear	*eyra*	faith	*trú*
earl	*jarl*	falling	*fell, föll*
early	*snemma*	far-away	*fjarstætt*
ears	*eyranu*	farmer	*bóndi*
east	*austr*	farmstead	*húsabæ*
Eastern-Lands (place)	*Austr, Austrveg, Austrveginn*	fastened	*fast, festir*
		fat	*fitan*
either	*hvárttveggja, ýmist*	fated	*auðið*
either-side	*hvárntveggja*	fated-to-die	*feigr*
elbows	*olnbogarnir*	father	*faðir, föður*
embers	*eimyrja*	feast	*veizla*
end	*lúkum*	feebler	*ergist*
		fee-sparing	*fésparir*
		feet	*fæti, fætr, fótum*
		fell	*datt, fell, fellu, steyptist*
		fellow	*drengr*
		fellows	*kumpánar*

Word List (English to Old Icelandic)

English	Old Icelandic	English	Old Icelandic
festival	hátíð		
filled	fylldan, og		
find	finna		
finger-gold	fingrgull		
fire	eld, eldi, eldur		
fire-poker	eldsskara		
first	fyrst, fyrsta, fyrstu, fyrstum		
fist	hnefann		
fitting	mátuligr		
fjord	fjörð		
flesh	holdi		
flew-it	fleygir, snaraði		
flies	flýgr		
floor	gólfit		
fog	myrkr		
fold	felr		
folk	fólk, fólki		
follow	fylgja		
followed	fylgdi, fylgt		
following	áliðnum, fylgd, fylgdi, fylgja		
following-men	fjölmenni		
food	krásum, matr		
food-servants	matsveinar		
foolishly	heimsliga		
for	á, fyrir, til		
forces	hér		
foremost	fremstir		
forests	skóga		
formed	slógu		
foul	fúlt		
found	fann, fannst		
four	fjóra, fjórar, fjórum		
friendly-terms	kærleikum		
friendship	kærleikum		
from	á, að, af, er, frá, fram, ór		
from-hence	heðan		
from-them	þeim		
from-there	fram, þaðan, þangað		
from-where	hvaðan		
Frosti	frosti		
Frosti (name)	Frosta, Frosti		
Full-Strong (name)	Fullsterk, Fullsterkr		

G, g

English	Old Icelandic
game	gamni
games	gamans, leikinn
gangrene	drep
gate	grindhliðið
Gaulardale (place)	Gaulardal
gave	gaf, gáfu
Geirrod (name)	Geirröð, Geirröði, Geirröður
Geirrod's (name)	Geirröði
Geirrod's-Town (place)	Geirröðargarða, Geirröðargörðum
get	fá, fengnir, geta, getr
get-hold-of	nát
get-tired	mæðast
Giant-Home (place)	Jötunheima
Giant-Land (place)	Jötunheimar, Risaland, Risalandi, Risalands
giants	jötnum
giant's-wrath	jötunmóð
give	gef, gefa, skipta
given	gefur
glad	glaðir
gladly	gjarna, glaðir
Glasir-Plains (place)	Glæsisvöllu, Glæsisvöllum
glass-window	glerglugg
gloves	vöttum
glowing	glóanda
Gnipalund (place)	Gnípalundi
go	fara, farið, ganga, gangi
Godmund	goðmundur
Godmund (name)	Goðmund, Goðmundar, Goðmundi, Goðmundr, Goðmundur
Godmund's (name)	Goðmundar
going	ganga
going-from	gagnvart
gold	gul, gull, gulli, gullligt, gullligum, gulr
gold-ball	gullhnött

Word List (English to Old Icelandic)

English	Old Icelandic	English	Old Icelandic
gold-crown	*gullkórónu*	hall	*hallar*
golden-bowl	*gullker*	hall-floor	*hallargólfi, hallargólfit*
gold-necklace	*gullmen*	hand	*hendi, hendur, hönd*
gold-plated	*gullbúnu*	hand-cloth	*handklæðit*
gold-ring	*gullhring*	hand-cloths	*handklæði*
gold-rings	*gullhringa*	hands	*höndum*
gold-trimmed	*gullskotnum*	happiness	*yndi*
gold-woven	*gullofit*	happy	*unum*
gone	*farið, farin*	hard	*fast*
good	*góða, góði, góðum, góður, gott, vænsta*	harder	*fastara*
		hardest	*harðasti*
Good (name)	*Góða, Góði*	hard-minded	*harðúðigr*
good-use	*neytr*	has	*hefir*
got	*fekk, gað*	have	*eig, er, hafa, hafið, haft, hefi, hefir, höfum, lætr, lát, láta*
got-they	*fengust*		
grabbed	*greip, grip, krummurnar, þreif*		
		having	*hafa*
grant	*leggja, veita, veittu*	he	*hana, hann, honum, sér*
granted	*veitti*		
great	*mikið, mikil, mikill, mikinn, mikla, miklar, miklum, mjög, stóra*	head	*höfði, höfðum, höfuðið*
		hear	*heyra*
greeted	*heilsaði*	heard	*heyrir*
greetings	*kveðju, kveðst*	heat	*hita*
grey	*grám*	heaviest	*þyngst*
Grim (name)	*Grím, Grími, Grímr*	heavy	*þung*
gripped	*greip*	Heidrek (name)	*Heiðrekr*
grow	*vaxa*	he-is	*sé*
grown	*vöxt*	held	*helt, helzt*
Grundir (place)	*Grunda, Grundir, Grundum*	helm-of-invisibility	*hulinshjálm*
		Hemra (place)	*Hemra, Hemru*
guard	*vörð*	here	*hér, hingað, þar*
Gudrun (name)	*Goðrún, Goðrúnar, Goðrúnu*	hers	*sín, sínum*
		he-took-care-of	*annast*
guess	*get*	hewed	*hjó*
Gust	*gustr*	he-wished	*vilja*
		hidden	*leynt*

H, h

English	Old Icelandic	English	Old Icelandic
		hide	*fela*
		hideous	*ljótan*
had	*ætti, átti, áttu, hafa, hafði, haft, hefði, hefir, höfðu, lá, lagði, leit, lét, létu*	high	*há*
		high-seat	*hásæti, skörina*
		hill	*hól*
		him	*að, hann, hans, honum, sér, sik, sín*
hailstorm	*haglhríð*		
Hakon (name)	*Hákon*	himself	*sér, sik*
half	*hálfan*	hip-throw	*sniðglímu*

281

Word List (English to Old Icelandic)

English	Old Icelandic	English	Old Icelandic
his	*hans, honum, sér, sik, sína, sínar, sinn, sinna, sinnar, sinni, síns, sínum, sitt, sýnis*	into	*á, í*
		invite	*býður*
		Iron-Beard (name)	*Járnskeggja*
		is	*á, er, eru, sé*
his-head	*höfuðið*	is-expected	*ván*
hit	*hæfa*	is-named	*hét*
hold	*halda*	it	*að, hana, hann, honum, í, það, því*
hold-of	*nát*		
homage	*hlýðni*	itself	*sjálfur*
home	*heim*		
honour	*heiður*		
horn	*fyllt, horn, horninu, hornit*		

J, j

English	Old Icelandic
Jamtland (place)	*Jamtaland*
jaw	*kjaptrinn*
jealous	*öfundsjúkir*
joined	*festi*
Jokul (name)	*Jökull*
Jokul's (name)	*Jökli*
journey	*ferð*
joyful	*fegnir*
jumped	*stökkva*

English	Old Icelandic
horn-point	*stikilinn*
horns	*horn*
horse	*hesti, hestr*
horses	*hest, hesta, hestar, hestum*
Hosvir (name)	*Hösvi, Hösvir*
hot	*heitt*
house	*hús*
House-Child (name)	*Bæjarbarn, Bæjarbarni, Bæjarbarns*
House-Power (name)	*Bæjarmagn*
houses	*húsum*
how	*hverju*
howling	*grenjaði*
how-so	*hversu*

K, k

English	Old Icelandic
Kark (name)	*Karkr*
keep	*halda*
kill	*drepa*
killed	*drap, drepnir*
kin	*kyn*
kinds	*háttar*
king	*konungi, konungr*
kingdom	*ríki*
kissed	*kyssti*
knees	*kné*
knew	*þekkti, vita*
knocked	*steyptist*
know	*kenna, kunnigt, veit, vit, vita*
known	*veit*
knows	*kann, veit*
Kollsvein (name)	*Kollsveinn*

I, i

English	Old Icelandic
I	*ek, mér*
if	*ef, í, sem*
ill	*illa*
in	*á, að, í, inn*
India	*indíalandi*
inheritance	*arf, erfi*
injury	*saka*
inlaid	*búið*
in-memory	*minni*
in-one	*einu*
inside	*inn*
intend	*ætla*
intended	*ætlaði, ætlar*
intentions	*ætlan*

L, l

Word List (English to Old Icelandic)

English	*Old Icelandic*
lack-of-money	*féfátt*
laid	*lá, lagði, lágu*
land	*land, landið*
landed	*lendur*
large	*mikið, mikill, stórri*
larger	*mikli*
large-river	*móðu*
largest	*mikli*
laughed	*hló, hlógu*
laughter	*hlátr, hlátri*
law	*lög*
lay	*lá, lagðist*
lay-out	*láta*
leave	*orlof*
leave-it	*látum*
led	*leiða, leiddur*
left	*lagt*
leg	*fótrinn*
less-should	*óskyldara*
let	*lát*
lie-down	*liggja*
life-gift	*lífgjöf*
like	*líkari, líkast*
lineage	*ættar*
lingered	*staldraði*
little	*lítill, lítilli, lítinn, lítit, litlu*
little-boy	*smásveinn*
live	*búa*
lived	*bjó, lifði*
lives	*lifir*
living-thing	*kvikt*
long	*langan, löngu*
Long (name)	*Langa*
longer	*lengr*
looking	*bragði*
loosed	*laust*
lose	*missa*
lost	*missi*
lost-way	*villa*
lot	*hluti*
loved	*unnust*
low-energy	*orkufátt*
Lucanus (name)	*Lúkanus*

English	*Old Icelandic*
luck	*gæfa, gæfu, góðri, hamingju*
lying	*liggr*

M, m

mad	*galinn*
made	*gert, léti*
magic-full	*galdrafullt*
make	*gera*
man	*maður, manna, manni, manns*
many	*marga, margir*
marble	*hall*
may	*má, mátt, mega, megi*
me	*mér, mik, mín, mitt*
meet	*finnumst, mót, móti*
melted	*bráðnaði*
men	*flokki, hann, manna, menn, mönnum, sveinar*
men's	*manna*
mercy	*miskunnar*
merry	*kátir*
met	*fann, fundizt*
mine	*mín, mína, mínir, minn, mínu, mínum, mitt*
missions	*sendiferðir*
mitten	*vettlingana*
mittens	*bandvettlinga*
mood-mind	*skapsmunum*
more	*auka, fleira, meira*
morning	*morgin, morgininn, morginn, morgni, morguninn*
most	*flestum, mest*
mostly	*mest*
mother	*móðir*
mound	*hóll*
mountain-pastures	*sætr*
mountains	*fjalli*
mouth	*kjaptinum*
moved	*réðst, víkr*
moving	*fór*

283

Word List (English to Old Icelandic)

English	Old Icelandic
much	*mikið, mikils, mikinn, miklar, miklu, mjög*
musical-instruments	*hljóðfæra, hljóðfæri*
must	*mun*
must-be	*mundu, munt*
my	*mín, mínir, minn*
myself	*mik*
my-wife	*eiga*

N, n

English	Old Icelandic
name	*nafn, nafni*
named	*heita, heiti, heitir, hét, nefndi, nefndir*
name-titles	*nafnbætr*
naming-gift	*nafnfesti*
natured	*náttúru*
near	*nær, næst*
need	*þurfa*
neither	*hvárki, hvergi*
never	*aldri*
news	*frétt, tíðenda, tíðendi*
next	*næst*
next-to	*næst*
night	*nótt, nóttina*
nights	*nætr*
nimbly	*vakrliga*
no	*ekki, engi, engir, engum*
none	*eigi, enga, engi, engum*
no-one	*engan*
nor	*né*
Norway (place)	*Noreg, Noregi, Noregs*
nose	*nasir, nefit*
not	*eigi, ekki, engi*
nothing	*eigi, einskis, ekki, engu*
Novgorod (place)	*Hólmgörðum*
now	*nú*

O, o

English	Old Icelandic
oak	*eik*
oath	*eiða*
oaths	*eiða*
obstinate	*stríðlyndur*
occasion	*sinn*
Odin (name)	*Óðinn, Óðni*
Odin's (name)	*Óðins*
of	*á, að, af, er, í, of, ór, til, tveir, við*
off	*af*
offered	*bauð*
off-handed	*afhenda*
of-hand	*afhenda*
of-news	*tíðenda*
often	*opt*
of-the-bench	*bekkinn*
of-the-day	*dagsins*
Olaf (name)	*Óláf, Ólafi, Ólafur*
Olaf's (name)	*Ólafs*
oldest	*eldist*
on	*á, en, í*
one	*annarr, annarri, eina, einn, einu, einum, eitt, öðrum, önnur*
on-the-nose	*nösunum*
onto	*á*
open	*opinn*
opening	*beitina, gátum*
open-sea	*hafvillur*
oppose	*móti*
opposite	*gegnt, öndvegit*
opposition	*móti*
or	*eða*
orchard	*aldingarður*
ordered	*bað*
other	*aðra, annars, öðrum, önnur*
others	*aðrir, hinir*
Ottar's (name)	*Óttars*
ounces	*aura*
ours	*oss, vár, várt, vort*
out	*út, utan, úti*
outlawed	*útlægr*
out-of	*ór, utan*
outside	*utan*
over	*að, fyrir, ofan, úti, yfir*

Word List (English to Old Icelandic)

English	*Old Icelandic*
own	*eigum*
owned	*átti*
ox-bone	*uxahnútu*

P, p

English	*Old Icelandic*
pain	*verkr*
pale	*bleikum*
passed	*líður*
pay	*fá*
payment	*mútur*
peaceful	*fríð*
piece-of-marble	*hall*
pitch	*bik*
places	*stöðum*
play	*leika*
played	*lék, lékst*
playing-tricks	*glettist*
pledging	*lofaði*
point	*brodd, broddinum*
poison	*eitr, ólyfjan*
popular	*vinsæll*
possessions	*eigna*
possible	*hægt*
pouch	*pungi*
power	*vald*
praised	*lofuðu*
precious-cloth	*guðvef*
precious-stones	*gimsteinar*
precious-things	*gersema*
prepared	*bjó, búið, búin, búnir*
prick	*pjakka, pjakkar*
pricked	*pjakkar*
promise	*lófa*
promised	*heita, hét*
property	*eignir*
provide	*afla, framt*
pulled	*togast*
pushed	*hratt*

Q, q

English	*Old Icelandic*
quarters	*fjórðunga*

R, r

English	*Old Icelandic*
raiding	*hernaði*
raised	*fæddi, reisti, reistu*
ran	*hlaupa, hleypr, hljóp, rann, renna*
rarely-seen	*sjaldsénir*
rather	*heldur*
received	*tók*
reckon	*ráða, treysta*
recognised	*kenndur*
red	*rauðum, rauður, rautt*
refuse	*synjast*
relieved	*feginn*
repay	*launa, launað*
retain	*geyma*
return	*aptr*
revealed	*birti*
ride	*reiðu, ríða*
ride-away	*ríða*
riding	*reið, ríða*
ring	*hring*
river	*og*
rocking	*ruggaði*
rode	*ríða, riðu, ríður*
room	*rúm*
rose	*reiddist, reis, ríss*
ruled	*réð*
ruler	*ræð*
rules	*ræður*
ruthless	*óvæginn*

S, s

English	*Old Icelandic*
sack	*klæðsekk*
said	*kvað, kvaðst, kveðst, mælti, sagði, sagðist, segir, segist, sögðu*
said-of	*eiga*
said-to	*segir*
sail	*sigla, sigldi*
sailed	*sigla, sigldi, sigldu*
same	*sama*

Word List (English to Old Icelandic)

English	Old Icelandic	English	Old Icelandic
sat	sat, settist, sitr, sitt	side	megin
saw	sá, sáu, sér, sjá, svá	sides	síðum
saw-you	sáttu	silver	silfri, silfrkerum, silfrs
say	seg, segir, segja	silver-dish	silfrdisk
scarcely	trautt	silver-ring	silfrhring
scarlet-clothing	skarlatsklæðum	since	síðan, síðar
screamed	grenjaði	since.	síðan
seal's-head	selshöfuð	sit	sitja
seat	sæti, sætis	six	sex
see	sá, sé, sér, sjá, sjáum	skilled-in-magic	fjölkunnigr
seeing	sá	skills	kunnáttu
seek	sækið	sleep	sofa
seem	þætti	slept	sefur, sofa
seemed	sýndist, þótti	slope	hlíðir
seems	þykki, þykkir	slowly	seint
seen	sét	small	lítill
seep	sofa	smaller	minni
sent	sendi, sendur, sent	small-games	smáleik, smáleika
separate	skilja, skiljast	smiling	hlæjandi
separated	skildi, skildu, skildust	smoke	reyk
separating	skilr	snow	fönn, snjó
servant	þræli	so	sá, sú, svá
serve	þjóna, þjónar	some	nokkura, nokkurn, nokkuru, nokkut
serving	þjóna		
set	setti	someone	einhverr
settled	bjuggust	something	nokkurr
settlements	byggð	some-way	einhvern
seven	sjau	somewhat	nokkuru
shall	mun, skal, skál, skalt, skaltu, skuli, skulu	son	son, sonr
		Son-of-Sigurd (name)	Sigurðarson
shall-you	muntu, skaltu	soon	snemma
she	hana, hún	South-East	landsuðri
ship	skip	sparkled	sindraði
ships	skips	sparks	gneistar
shirt	serk, serkr	sparks-flying	gneistaflaugin
shook	hristi, skalf	speak	mæla
short	skammt, vært	speaks	mælir
shot	skaut	split	rifnaði
should	mun, mundi, munt, muntu, munu, munum, skulu, skuluð, skyldi, þeir	spoke	mælt, mælti
		spread	breiddu
		spring	vári, várið
		stabbed	stangaði
should-be	mun, væri	stable	stall
show	sýna	staff	refði, staf
showed	sýndi	stand	standa
shown	sýndar	standing	staðar

Word List (English to Old Icelandic)

English	Old Icelandic	English	Old Icelandic
steadied	*studdi*	tall	*mikil*
steel-point	*stálbroddr*	taught	*kenna*
stepped	*sté*	tax	*skatta*
stick	*stafnum*	teeth	*tennr, tennrnar*
stone	*stein, steinn*	tell	*segja*
stone-house	*steinhús*	ten	*tíu*
stone-throwing	*steinkastinu*	tend-to	*græð*
stood	*stóð, stóðu*	tents	*tjald*
straightaway	*þegar*	test	*reynt*
strength	*afl, afli*	than	*að, en, enn*
strengthen	*styrkja*	thanked	*þakkaði, þakkar, þökkuðu*
stripes	*röndum*		
strong	*sterkr, ströng*	that	*á, að, af, en, er, sem, það, þann, þenna, því*
stronger	*sterkari*		
strongest	*sterkastr*	that-bench	*bekknum*
strongly	*sterkliga*	thaw	*þíða*
struck	*slær, slegit, sló, stakk*	thaws	*bræðir*
such	*skilja, slík, slíka, slíkan, slíkar, slikum*	the	*á, að, ána, en, hornit, í, in, ina, inn, inum, it, svá, þann*
suits	*hentar*		
summer	*sumarið*	the-air	*lopti*
sunrise	*sólin*	the-back	*bak*
suns	*sólir*	the-back-of-the-head	*hnakkinn*
sunset	*sólarfalli*	the-back-of-the-knees	*knésbætr*
sunshine	*sólskin*	the-ball	*knettinum, knöttinn, knöttrinn*
suppose	*ætla*		
surprised	*undraðist*	the-bench	*bekknum*
swear	*sverja*	the-bone	*beini, beinum*
sweet-smell	*ilmr*	the-boy	*kollsveinn, piltrinn*
swift	*frár*	the-chest	*bringu*
swiftly	*skjótt*	the-child	*barn, barnit*
swimming	*sundi*	the-city	*borgarinnar, borgina*
sworn	*svarið*	the-clearing	*rjóðrinu*
		the-company-of	*lið*

T, t

English	Old Icelandic
		the-crooked-stick	*krókstafinn*
		the-cross	*kross*
		the-crown	*kórónu*
table	*borð, borðinu, trapiza*	the-cup-bearer	*byrlaranum*
table-cloth	*dúkinn, dúkr*	the-cups	*köppunum*
tablecloths	*dúka*	the-curtain	*fortjaldinu*
take	*tak, taka, takið*	the-curve	*bugtinni*
take-care	*hirðið*	the-custom	*siður*
take-care-of	*ábyrgjast*	the-death	*bani*
taken	*tekið, tekinn*	the-district	*heraðið, heraðinu*
takes	*tekr*	the-door	*dyranna, dyrr, dyrrnar*
talked	*talar*	the-dwarf	*dvergnum, dvergrinn*

Word List (English to Old Icelandic)

English	Old Icelandic
the-dwarf's-boy	dvergsbarnit
the-dwelling	bæinn, bú
the-eagle	erninum
the-earl	jarl, jarli, jarls
the-earl's	jarli, jarls
the-evening	aptnaði, kveld
the-faith	trú
the-feast	veizlan, veizlunni
the-fire	eldrinn
the-flames	eldur
the-floor	gólfi, gólfit
the-foot-board	stokkinn
the-forest	skógar, skóginn
the-forests	skóginn
the-full	fullu
the-game	gamninu
the-gates	hliðin
the-gifts	gjafirnar
the-good	góða
the-greatest	mestr
the-ground	jörðina
the-hall	höll, höllina, höllinni
the-harbour	höfn
the-horn	hornin, horninu, hornunum
the-horns	hornin
the-horses	hestarnir
the-house	hús
their	sín, sína, sinn, þau, þeira, þeiri
theirs	þeim, þeira
the-journey	færist, ferð
the-king	konung, konungi, konungnum, konungr, konungrinn, konungs
the-king's	konungs
the-king's-hall	konungshöll
the-king's-name	konungsnafn
the-king's-son	konungsson
the-land	land, landi, landið
the-like	þvílíkir
them	þá, þeim, þeir, þeira
the-marble	hallinn, hallinum, hallrinn
the-matter	mál
the-men	menn, mönnum
the-middle	miðit, miðju
the-moat	díki
the-morning	morgin
the-most	mestr
the-mound	hauginn, haugrinn, hólinn, hólnum
the-mouth	kjaptinum
themselves	sik, sín
the-mud	saur
then	á, en, er, síðan, þá, þann, þar, þegar, þeim, því
the-narrow	stiklinum
the-neck	háls
the-night	nóttina
the-oak	eikinni
the-old	gamalla
the-opening	beitina
the-other	annarr, hinir
the-piece-of-marble	hallinn, hallrinn
the-point	broddinum, broddrinn
the-queen	drottning
there	sá, þær, þangað, þar, þegar, þeir, þeira, þeirar
therefore	því
the-ring	hringinn, hringnum, hringrinn
the-river	ána, ánni, árinnar, móðuna
the-road	veginn
the-scourge	svipuleik, svipuleikr
these	þessi
The-Serpent (name)	Orminum
the-setting	setning
the-ship	skip
the-ships	skips
the-shirt	serkinn
the-sky	himni, lopti
the-skylight	glugginn
the-snow	snjórinn
the-south-east	landsuður
the-staff	stafinn
the-stick	keyrir, stafinn
the-story	þætti
the-sun	sól
the-table-cloth	dúkinn

Word List (English to Old Icelandic)

English	Old Icelandic
the-tables	*borða, borðum*
the-teeth	*tennrnar*
the-town	*borgarinnar, borgina*
the-trees	*mörkina*
the-water	*vatn, vatnið*
the-west	*vestri*
the-wing	*vænginn*
the-world	*heiminum*
they	*drekka, þar, þau, þeim, þeir, þeira*
they-are	*eru*
they-were	*þeira*
thick-set	*búk*
thief's-eyes	*þjófsaugun*
thieving-nose	*þjófsnefit*
thievish-chin	*þjófshakan*
things	*þing*
think	*hug, þykki, þykkja*
this	*it, sinni, þess, þessa, þessi, þessu, þetta*
Thormod (name)	*Þormóður*
Thor's (name)	*Þórs*
Thorstein (name)	*Þorstein, Þorsteini, Þorsteinn*
Thorstein's (name)	*Þorsteins*
those	*þær*
though	*en, þó, þótt*
thought	*hugr, sýndist, þótti, þóttist*
three	*þremr, þrír, þrjá*
three-sided	*þríhyrndr*
threw	*berði, kastaði, kastar, snaraði, snöruðu*
throat	*hálsinum*
through	*ór, um*
throw	*kastið*
thrown	*ausit*
thrust	*lagi*
time	*tíma*
to	*á, að, af, fram, í, og, til, við*
to-announce	*kunngera*
to-do	*gera*
to-drink	*drekka*
toe	*tána, tánni*
to-get	*hlytir*
together	*saman*
to-going	*atgang, atgangr*
to-grant	*veita*
to-have	*láta*
to-him	*honum, sér*
to-injure	*granda*
told	*sagði, sagt, segir, töluðu*
told-of	*getið*
to-make	*gera*
to-me	*mér*
to-meet	*mót, móti*
to-mind	*geyma*
took	*færði, nam, taka, tekr, tók, tókst, tóku, tókust*
to-overpower	*ofmagni*
to-own	*eiga*
to-repay	*laun*
to-ride	*ríða*
to-see	*sér, sjá*
to-stand	*staðar*
to-the-father	*föðurnum*
to-travel	*fara*
towards	*að*
to-wrestling	*fangbrögðum*
to-you	*þér*
trading-journeys	*kaupferðum*
trading-voyages	*kaupferðir*
travel	*færir, far, fara*
travelled	*fara, ferð, fór, fóru, fóruð*
travelling	*fara, ferr*
treasure	*gersemi, gripi*
treasured	*gersemar*
treasures	*gersemar, gersemi, gripi*
trembled	*hrysi*
tributaries	*skattgildir*
trick	*leikinn*
tricked	*prett, svikit*
tricks	*fimleika*
troll-like	*tröllsligri*
troll-possessed	*tröllaukinn*
trolls	*tröllum*
Trondheim (place)	*Þrándheimi*
trust	*treysta, treysti*
trusted	*traust*

Word List (English to Old Icelandic)

English	Old Icelandic
Trusty (name)	Trausti
Tryggvason (name)	Tryggvason
tugged	tók
tumbled	rasaði
turned	sneri, veik
turned-away	brautinni
turned-quickly	snaraði
turning	brautinni
tussle	sviptingar
twelve	tólf
twenty	tuttugu, tvítugt
twisted	snarað, snúinn
two	tvá, tvær, tvau, tveggja, tveir

U, u

English	Old Icelandic
Ulfhedin (name)	Úlfheðinn
unconscious	óvit
under	neðra, undir
under-world	undirheimum
undressed	afklæðast, afklæddust
unfinished	ófarin
unfriendly	óþýður
unfriendly-looking	óhýrligr
unhappy	ófögnuður
un-indulgent	óaflátssamr
unlike	ólík
un-peace	ófriðar
unspoken	óorðna
up	upp, uppi
uproar	upphlaup
up-spring	uppsprettu
us	okkr, oss

V, v

English	Old Icelandic
vacation	orlofs
valour	hreysti
value	þykkja
valued	þykkja
vanished	hurfu
vessel	ker
Vik (place)	Vík
visit	vitja
voyage	ferð, ferðum

W, w

English	Old Icelandic
waded	óðu
waded-through	væði
wades	vaða
walk	ganga
walking	gangandi
want	vön
warrior	kempa
was	á, er, í, þar, vá, væri, var, varð, vart, vér
was-heard	spyrjast
water	vátr
wave	felli
way	braut, veg
we	vér
weak	deigum
weakly	lítilmannliga
wealth	fé
weaponed	vápnaða
weather	veður
wedding-proposal	brullaup
weighed	stóð
welcomed	fagnaði
well	sæmilig, vel
well-faring	velfaranda
went	fekk, ferr, fór, fóru, gekk, gengr, gengu
went-for	hösvaðist
went-from	frá
were	eru, hvar, væru, var, váru, vera
wether's	sauða
what	hvað, hvar, hvert, hví
whatever	sem
when	að, en, er, þá, var, váru
where	hvar, sem
whether	hvárt
which	að, er, hvárt, sem
while	en, meðan, stundu
white	hvítr, hvítt

Word List (English to Old Icelandic)

English	Old Icelandic	English	Old Icelandic
Whitings (name)	Hvítinga, Hvítingar, Hvítingum	yellow	gulr
who	á, er, hvað, hverr, sem	you	sé, þér, þik, þín, þú, yður
whole	heill	young	unga
whose	hverrar	young-woman	jungfrú
why	hví	your	þín, þínar, þitt, yðrir, yðru
widely	víða		
wife	kona	yours	þér, þína, þinn, þitt, yðrum
wild-animals	dýr		
will	vil, vill, vilt	you-two	þit
willed	vildi	Yrjar (place)	Yrjum
will-you	viltu	Yule (name)	Jólin, Jólum
wine	vín		
winter	vetr, vetrinn		
wiser	kunngera		
wish	vil, vilda, vili, viljum, vilt		
wished	vildi, vildu, vilja, vill		
wished-to	vildi		
witch-ride	gandreið		
with	á, með, við		
without	utan		
with-that	í		
Wolf-Skin (name)	Úlfhamr		
women	konur		
wonder	undrast		
wondered	undruðust		
wool	ullu		
word	orðið		
words	orðum		
worth	vert		
worthy	vert, virðing		
would	mun, mundi, mundu, muni, skyldu, væri, vildi, vildu		
would-be	mundum, munu		
would-have	mundi		
wound	sár		
wove	vaf		
wrestle	glíma		
wrestled	glímt		
wrestling	glíma		

Y, y

A Word Comparison of Old Norse and Old Icelandic Words

A Word Comparison of Old Norse and Old Icelandic Words

Old Norse	Old Icelandic	English
áðr	áður	after
áðr	áður	after
áðr	áður	before
aldingarðr	aldingarður	orchard
at	að	about
at	að	against
at	að	as
at	að	at
at	að	from
at	að	him
at	að	in
at	að	it
at	að	of
at	að	over
at	að	than
at	að	that
at	að	the
at	að	to
at	að	towards
at	að	when
at	að	which
auðit	auðið	fated
biðr	biður	asked
borit	borið	borne
brynjólfr	Brynjólfur	Brynjolf (name)
búit	búið	inlaid
búit	búið	prepared
býðr	býður	invite
dauðr	dauður	dead
drukkit	drukkið	drank
drukkit	drukkið	drink
drukkit	drukkið	drinking
drukkit	drukkið	drink-to
drukkit	drukkið	drunk
drykkjumaðr	drykkjumaður	drinking-man
eldr	eldur	fire
eldr	eldur	the-flames
farit	farið	gone
gat	gað	got
gefr	gefur	given
geirröðr	Geirröður	Geirrod (name)
gengit	gengið	come
getit	getið	told-of
goðmundr	goðmundur	Godmund
goðmundr	Goðmundur	Godmund (name)
góðr	góður	good
grindhliðit	grindhliðið	gate
heiðr	heiður	honour
heldr	heldur	rather
hendr	hendur	hand
heraðit	heraðið	the-district
hingat	hingað	here
hirðmaðr	hirðmaður	court-man
höfuðit	höfuðið	head
höfuðit	höfuðið	his-head
huldumaðr	huldumaður	a-hidden-man
hvat	hvað	what
hvat	hvað	who
kallaðr	kallaður	called
kallat	kallað	called
kastat	kastað	cast
kemr	kemur	came
kemr	kemur	comes
kenndr	kenndur	recognised
komit	komið	coming
krókstafr	krókstafur	crooked-stick
kveldit	kveldið	evening
landit	landið	land
landit	landið	the-land
landsuðr	landsuður	the-south-east
launat	launað	repay
leiddr	leiddur	led
lendr	lendur	landed
líðr	líður	passed
lokit	lokið	ended
maðr	maður	a-man
maðr	maður	man
meðalmaðr	meðalmaður	an-average-man
mikit	mikið	great
mikit	mikið	large

A Word Comparison of Old Norse and Old Icelandic Words

Old Norse	Old Icelandic	English
mikit	*mikið*	much
mjök	*mjög*	great
mjök	*mjög*	much
niðr	*niður*	below
niðr	*niður*	down
ófögnuðr	*ófögnuður*	unhappy
ok	*og*	ad
ok	*og*	also
ok	*og*	and
ok	*og*	filled
ok	*og*	river
ok	*og*	to
Óláfr	*Óláfur*	Olaf (name)
orðit	*orðið*	word
óþýðr	*óþýður*	unfriendly
ræðr	*ræður*	rules
rauðr	*rauður*	red
ríðr	*ríður*	rode
rjóðr	*rjóður*	clearing
sefr	*sefur*	slept
sendr	*sendur*	sent
siðr	*siður*	the-custom
sjálfr	*sjálfur*	itself
skipat	*skipað*	directed-to
snarat	*snarað*	twisted
stríðlyndr	*stríðlyndur*	obstinate
sumarit	*sumarið*	summer
sundr	*sundur*	apart
svarit	*svarið*	sworn
tekit	*tekið*	taken
þangat	*þangað*	from-there
þangat	*þangað*	there
þat	*það*	it
þat	*það*	that
þormóðr	*Þormóður*	Thormod (name)
várit	*várið*	spring
vatnit	*vatnið*	the-water
veðr	*veður*	weather
verðr	*verður*	became
verðr	*verður*	becomes
verðr	*verður*	came
yðr	*yður*	you

The Tale of Sarcastic Halli (*Old Norse*)

Old Norse	Literal	English
1	**1**	**1**
Þat er upphaf þessarrar frásagnar, at Haraldr konungr Sigurðarson réð fyrir Noregi.	It is beginning this from-saying, of Harald the-king Sigurdson ruled over Norway.	The beginning is to say that King Harald Sigurdson ruled Norway.
Þat var í þann tíma, er Magnús konungr frændi hans var andaðr.	It was in that time, that Magnus the-king's kinsman his was dead.	It was in that time that Magnus the king's kinsman was dead.
Svá er sagt, at Haraldr konungr var allra manna vitrastr ok ráðigastr;	So is said, that Harald the-king was of-all men the-wisest and well-advising;	So it is said that King Harald was the wisest of all men and of advice.
varð þat ok flest at ráði, er hann lagði til.	was it also the-most that advised, that he became to.	Also most of what he had counselled had become good.
Hann var skáld gott.	He was a-poet good.	He was a good poet
Jafnan kastaði hann háðyrðum at þeim mönnum, er honum sýndist;	Equally cast he mocking to they the-people, as he thought;	and also mocked whoever he thought to.
þoldi bann ok allra manna bezt, þótt at honum yrði kagtat klámyrðum, þá er honum var gott í skapi.	endured he also all men best, though that he was cast obscene-words, then that he was good of mood.	And when he was in a good mood, he endured most men even though obscenities were cast at him.
Hann átti þá Þóru, dóttur Þórbergs Árnasonar.	He married then Thora, daughter Thorberg's Son-of-Arni.	He was then married to Thora, daughter of Thorberg, Arni's son.
Honum þótti mikit gaman at skáldskap, ok hafði jafnan þá með sér er kveða kunnu.	He thought much delight in poetry, and had always then with him that compose could.	He took much delight in poetry and always had people about him who could compose poetry.
Þjóðólfr hét maðr;	Thjodolf was-named a-man;	There was a man named Thjodolf.
hann var íslenzkr, ok ættaðr ór Svarfaðardal, kurteiss maðr ok skáld mikit.	he was an-Icelander, and descended from Svarfadardal, polite man and poet great.	He was an Icelander whose family came from Svarfadardal, a polite man and a great poet.
Hann var með Haraldi konungi í hinum mestu kærleikum.	He was with Harald the-king in the most dear-friendship.	He had great friendship with King Harald.

The Tale of Sarcastic Halli (Old Norse)

Old Norse	Literal	English
Hann kallaði konungr höfuðskáld sitt, ok virði hann mest allra skálda.	Called the-king him chief-poet his, and worthied him most of-all poets.	The king called him his chief poet, and valued him most of all the poets.
Hann var ættsmár, ok menntr vel, öfundsjúkr við þá, er til komu.	He was family-small, and educated well, un-infatuated with then, who to came.	He was from a humble family and well educated, he was envious of newcomers.
Haraldr konungr elskaði mjök íslendinga;	Harald the-king loved much Icelanders;	King Harald loved Icelanders very much.
gaf hann til Íslands marga góða gripi, klukku góða til Þingvalla;	gave he to Iceland many good things, a-bell good for Thingvellir;	He gave many good things to Iceland, including a good bell for Thingvellir.
ok þá er hallæri þat hit mikla kom á Ísland, er ekki hefir slíkt komit annat, þá sendi hann út til Íslands fjóra knörru, hlaðna af mjöli, sinn í hveru fjórðung, ok lét flytja burt fátœka menn sem flesta af landinu.	and then when famine that the greatest came to Iceland, that not had such come another, then sent he out to Iceland four knorrs, ladened with meal, then to each fourth, and had carried brought poor men which most off the-land.	And when the greatest famine came to Iceland, which was like no other, he then sent four knorrs loaded with flour, one to each quarter, and had brought over many of the poorest men from the land.

2

Bárðr hét maðr, ok var hirðmaðr Haralds konungs.	Bard was-named a-man, and was court-man Harald's the-king's.	There was a man named Bard who was a court man of King Harald's.
Hann sigldi til Íslands, ok kom út at Gásum, ok vistaðist þar um vetrinn.	He sailed to Iceland, and came out to Gasir, and found-a-place there about winter.	He sailed to Iceland and came out to Gasir and found a place there for the winter.
Sá maðr tók sér far með honum, er Halli hét, ok var kallaðr Sneglu-Halli;	So a-man took himself passage with him, was Halli named, and was called Sarcastic-Halli;	So a man took passage with him who was named Halli, and he was called Sarcastic Halli.
hann var kallaðr skáld gott ok orðgreppr mikill.	he was called a-poet good and word-bold much.	He was a good poet and very bold with words.
Halli var hár maðr ok hálslangr, herðalítill ok handsiðr ok ljótlimaðr;	Halli was high man and long-neck, narrow-shouldered and long-armed and ugly-limbed;	Halli was a tall man with a long neck, narrow shoulders, long arms, and ill-proportioned limbs.

The Tale of Sarcastic Halli (Old Norse)

Old Norse	Literal	English
hann var ættaðr ór Fljótum.	he was descended out-of Fljot.	His descendants were from Fljot.
Þeir sigldu þegar (er þeir) váru búnir, ok höfðu langa útivist, tóku Noreg um haustit norðr við Þrándheim, við eyjar þær, er Hítrar heita, ok sigldu síðan inn til Agðaness ok lágu þar um nótt.	They sailed as-soon-as (was they) were prepared, and had long out-journey, took Norway about autumn north with Trondheim, with islands there, which Hitra named, and sailed since then to Agdanes and lay there about the-night.	They sailed as soon as they were ready and had a long passage, they reached Norway in the autumn north of Trondheim at the islands there which are called Hitra, and then sailed to Agdanes and laid up there for the night.
Enn um morgininn eftir sigldu þeir inn eftir firðinum lítinn byr;	Then about morning after sailed they then back-from the-fjord little fair-wind;	Then in the morning they sailed afterwards into the fjord with a light fair wind.
enn er þeir komu inn um Rein, sá þeir, at langskip þrjú röru innan eftir firðinum.	and when they came of about Reine, saw they, of longships three rowing in after the-fjord.	And when they came to Reine they saw three longships rowing back from the fjord.
Dreki var hit þriðja skipit.	Dragon was the third ship.	The third ship was a dragon ship.
Ok er skipin röru hjá kaupskipinu, þá gekk maðr fram ór lyftingunni á drekanum, í rauðum skarlatsklæðum, ok hafði gullhlað um enni, bæði mikill ok tiguligr.	And when the-ships rowing beside trading-ship, then got a-man from out lifting from the-dragon-ship, in red scarlet, and had gold-band about forehead, both great and dignified.	And when the ships were rowing beside the trading ship, a man came up out of the dragon ship in red scarlet with a gold band about his forehead, both great and dignified.
Þessi maðr tók til orða:	This man took to words:	This man spoke:
"Hverr stýrir skipinu eðr hvar váru þér í vetr, hvaðan ýttu þér, eðr hvar tóku þér fyrst land, eðr hvar lágu þér í nótt?"	"Who steers the-ship and where were you in winter, from-where pushed you, and where took you first land, and where laid you in the-night?"	"Who steers the ship, and where were you in winter, and where did you first take land, and where did you lay up last night?"
Þeim varð næsta orðfátt kaupmönnum, er svá var margs spurt senn.	They were next word-fallen the-trading-men, as so were many questions but.	The trading men were lost for words because there were so many questions, but
Halli svarar þá:	Halli answered then:	Halli answered them.

The Tale of Sarcastic Halli (Old Norse)

Old Norse	Literal	English
"Vér várum í vetr á Íslandi, enn ýttum af Gásum, enn Bárðr heitir stýrimaðr, enn tókum land við Hítrar, enn lágum í nótt við Agðanes?"	"We were in winter in Iceland, and pushed from Gasir, and Bard is-named steersman, and took land at Hitra, and laid about the-night at Agdanes?"	"We were in Iceland for the winter, and we pushed on from Gasir, and Bard is the name of the steersman, we took land at Hitra, and we laid up for the night at Agdanes".
Þessi maðr spurði, er reyndar var Haraldr konungr Sigurðarson:	This man asking, which actually was Harald the-king Sigurdson:	This man who was asking, was actually King Harald Sigurdson.
"Sarð hann yðr þá eigi hann Agði?"	"Wounded he you then not he Agdi?"	"Did Agdi not wound you?"
"Eigi enn þá?" sagði Halli.	"Not yet then?" said Halli.	"Not yet", said Halli.
Konungrinn brosti at, ok mælti:	The-king laughed and, also spoke:	The king laughed and also spoke:
"Er nökkurr til ráðs um, at hann muni enn síðar meir veita yðr þessa þjónustu?"	"Is something to agreement about, that he shall but afterwards more grant you this service?"	"Is there some agreement that he shall do you this service sometime later?"
"Ekki?" sagði hann Halli, "ok bar þó einn hlutr mest til þess, er vér fengum enga skömm af honum?"	"Not?" told he Halli, "and bears though one part there to this, that we travel not disgrace of him?"	Halli told him not, "and so it bears most in one part that we travel without suffering disgrace by him".
"Hvat var þat?"	"What was that?"	"What was that?"
sagði konungr.	said the-king.	said the king.
Halli vissi gerla, við hveru hann talaði.	Halli knew completely, with whom he talked.	Halli knew completely who he was talking to.
"Þat, herra?"	"That, lord?"	"That, lord",
sagði hann, "ef yðr forvitnar at vita, at hann Agði beið at þessu oss tignari manna, ok vænti yðar þangat í kveld, ok mun hann þá gjalda af höndum þessa skuld ótæpt?"	said he, "if you fore-knowing to know, that he Agdi waited for this us nobler men, and expected you from-there in the-evening, and shall he then pay of hand this debt unsettled?"	he said, "if you are curious to know, that Agdi was waiting for nobler men than us, and expected your arrival there this evening, and he shall pay you this debt fully".
"Þú munt vera orðhákr mikill?"	"You must be word-tall much?"	"You must be very brave of words",
segir konungr.	said the-king.	said the king.

The Tale of Sarcastic Halli (Old Norse)

Old Norse	Literal	English
Eigi er getit orða þeira fleiri at sinni.	Not is told words theirs more than these.	It is not told what more their words were than this.
Sigldu þeir kaupmennirnir inn til Kaupangs, ok skipuðu þar vöru upp, ok leigðu sér hús í bœnum.	Sailed they merchant-men then to Kapuang, and ships there were upped, and rented themselves a-house in town.	The merchants then sailed to Kaupang, upped their ships and rented themselves a house in town.
Fám nóttum síðar kom konungr inn aftr til bœjar, ok hafði hann farit til eyja út at skemta sér.	A-few nights afterwards came the-king then returning to the-town, and had he travelled to islands out to entertain himself.	After a few nights the king came returning to the town, as he had gone out to the islands to entertain himself.
Halli bað Bárð at fylgja sér til konungsins, ok kveðst vilja biðja hann vetrvistar;	Halli asked Bard to follow him to the-king, and said wished to-ask him winter-provisions;	Halli asked Bard to lead him to the king and said that he wished to ask him for winter lodgings.
enn Bárðr bauð honum með sér at vera.	but Bard invited him with himself to be.	But Bard invited him to stay with him.
Halli bað hann hafa þökk fyrir, enn kveðst með konunginum vilja vera, ef þess væri kostr.	Halli bid him having thanks for, but said with the-king wished to-be, if this was a-choice.	Halli thanked him but said that he wished to stay with the king if that was a choice.

3

Einn dag gekk Bárðr til konungs ok Halli með honum.	One day went Bard to the-king and Halli with him.	One day Bard went to meet the king and Halli went with him.
Bárðr kvaddi konung.	Bard greeted the-king.	Bard greeted the king.
Konungr tók vel kveðju hans, ok spurði margs af Íslandi, eðr hvárt hann hefði flutt útan nökkura íslenzka menn.	The-king received well greeting his, and asked many-things of Iceland, and whether he had brought out any Icelander men.	The king received his greeting well and asked many things of Iceland and whether he had brought any men from Iceland.
Bárðr sagðist flutt hafa einn íslenzkan mann;	Bard said brought had one Icelander man;	Bard said that he had brought one Icelander man
"ok heitir hann Halli, ok er nú hér, herra, ok vill biðja yðr vetrvistar?"	"and named he Halli, and is now here, lord, and wishes to-ask you winter-lodgings?"	"and he is named Halli, and he is now here lord, and wishes to ask you for winter lodgings".
Halli gekk þá fyrir konunginn ok kvaddi hann.	Halli went then before the-king and greeted him.	Halli then went before the king and greeted him.

The Tale of Sarcastic Halli (Old Norse)

Old Norse	Literal	English
Konungrinn tók honum vel, ok spurði, hvárt hann hefði svarat honum á firðinum, "er vér fundumst?"	The-king received him well, and asked, whether he had answered him in the-fjord, "when we met?"	The king received him well and asked whether he had answered him in the fjord "when we met".
"Sá er hinn sami?"	"So is the same?"	"I am the same",
segir Halli.	said Halli.	said Halli.
Konungrinn sagðist eigi spara mundu mat við hann, ok bað vera at búi sínu nökkuru.	The-king said not withhold would food from him, and invited to-be to estate his one-of.	The king said he would not withhold food from him and invited him to be on one of his estates.
Halli kveðst með hirðinni vilja vera, eðr leita sér annars ella.	Halli said with the-court to-be wished, or find himself another or-else.	Halli said that he wished to be at court or to find somewhere else.
Konungrinn kvað svá fara jafnan, at "mér er um kennt, ef várr vinskapr ferr eigi vel af hendi, þó at mér þykki varla svá vera.	The-king said so goes always, that "to-me is about blame, if our friendship goes not well of to-hand, though that to-me seems hardly so being.	The king said that it always goes "that I am to blame if our friendship does not go well, though that seems to me hardly to be.
Eru þér einráðir íslendingar ok ósiðblendnir.	They-are you one-decision Icelanders and un-custom-mixing.	You are single-minded, you Icelanders, and unsociable.
Nú ver, ef þú vill, ok ábyrgst þik sjálfr, hvat sem í kann gerast?"	Now be, if you wish, and responsible you yourself, what which about can be?"	Now be here if you wish, and you are responsible for yourself whatever will be".
Halli kvað svá vera skyldu, ok þakkaði konunginum.	Halli said so being would, and thanked the-king.	Halli said that it would be so, and thanked the king.
Var hann nú með hirðinni, ok líkaði hverjum manni vel til hans.	Was he now with the-court-men, and liked each man well to him.	He was now with the court men and he was liked by each of them.
Sigurðr hét sessunautr Halla, gamall hirðmaðr ok gæfr.	Sigurd was-named bench-companion Halli, old court-man and agreeable.	Halli's bench companion was named Sigurd, an old court man and agreeable.
Sá var siðr Haralds konungs, at eta einmælt;	So was the-custom Harald's the-king's, to eat one-meal;	It was Harald's custom to eat one meal a day.

The Tale of Sarcastic Halli (Old Norse)

Old Norse	Literal	English
var fyrst borin vist fyrir konung, sem vánligt var, ok var hann þá jafnan mjök mettr, er vistin kom fyrir aðra.	were first brought provisions for the-king, as expected was, and was he then usually much satisfied, when the-supply came before others.	First the food was brought before the king, as was expected, and he was usually very much satisfied when the food was brought to the others.
Enn þá er hann var mettr, klappaði hann með hnífskefti sínu á borðit, ok skyldi þá þegar ryðja borðin, ok váru margir þá hvergi nærri mettir.	But then when he was satisfied, rapped he with knife-handle his on the-table, and would then straight-away cleared tables, and were many then nowhere near satisfied.	But then when he was satisfied, he rapped his knife handle on the table, and then straight away the tables were cleared, and many people were then nowhere near satisfied.
Þat bar til eitt sinn, er konungr gekk úti um stræti ok fylgdin með honum,	It bore to once then, that the-king went out about the-street and followers with him,	It happened once that the king went out in the street with his followers, and many of them were nowhere near satisfied.
at þeir heyrðu í eitt herbergi deild mikla.	that they heard in one hostel room great.	They heard something great in an inn.
Þar váru at sútari ok járnsmiðr, ok þar næst flugust þeir á.	They were a tanner and ironsmith, and there near flew they to.	It was a tanner and an ironsmith, and they nearly flew towards eachother.
Konungrinn nam staðar ok sá á um stund.	The-king took place and saw for about awhile.	The king took his place and watched for a while.
Síðan mælti hann:	Afterwards spoke he:	Afterwards he spoke:
"Göngum burt,	"We-are-going away,	"Let us go away.
hér vil ek engan hlut at eiga;	here wish I none part to own;	I do not wish to be a part of this here,
enn þú, Þjóðólfr, yrk um þá vísu?"	but you, Thjodolf, write about then a-verse?"	but you Thjodolf write a verse about it".
"Herra?" segir hann, "eigi sómir þat, þar sem ek em kallaðr höfuðskáld yðart?"	"Lord?" said Thjodolf, "not common that, there as I am called chief-poet yours?"	"Lord", said Thjodolf, "I don't agree there, since I am called your chief poet".
Konungr svarar:	The-king answered:	The king answered:
"Þetta er meiri vandi enn þú munt ætla;	"This is more difficult than you should suppose;	"This is more difficult than you think.

The Tale of Sarcastic Halli (Old Norse)

Old Norse	Literal	English
þú skalt gera af þeim alla menn aðra en þeir eru:	you shall make of them completely men other than they are:	You shall make the men completely other than they are.
lát annan vera Sigurð Fáfnisbana, ok annan Fáfni, ok kenn þó hvárn til sinnar iðnar?"	have one be Sigurd Slayer-of-Fafnir, and another Fafnir, also know though each to his trade?"	Have one be Sigurd the Slayer of Fafnir, and another Fafnir, and also identify each one's trade".
Þjóðólfr kvað þá vísu:	Thjodolf recited then a-verse:	Thjodolf then recited a verse:
Sigurðr eggjaði sleggju snák váligrar brákar, enn skapdreki skinna skreið of leista heiði,	Sigurd urged the-hammer snake wretched breaker, but mood-dragon of-skins crawled off of-footwear the-heath,	Sigurd urged the-hammer snake wretched breaker, but mood-dragon of-skins crawled off of-footwear the-heath.
menn sásk orm, áðr ynni	people with-footwear the-serpent, before won	People with-footwear the-serpent before won
ilvegs búinn kilju nautaleðrs á naðri neflangr konungr tangar.	evil-ways prepared the-binding ox-skin of serpent long-nosed king's tongs.	evil-ways prepared the-binding, ox-skin of serpent long-nosed king's tongs.
"Þetta er vel kveðit?"	"That is well worded?"	"That is well composed",
segir konungr, "ok kveð nú aðra, ok lát þá annan vera Þór, enn annan Geirrauð jötun, ok kenn þó hvárn til sinnar iðnar.	said the-king, "and recite now another, and have now being one Thor, and another Geirrod the-giant, and know though each to their trade.	said the king, "and now recite another and have one being Thor and another Geirrod the Giant, and identify each with their trade".
Þá kvað Þjóðólfr vísu:	Then recited Thjodolf a-verse:	Then Thjodolf recited a verse:
Varp ór þrætu þorpi Þórr smiðbelgja stórra hvatt eldingum höldnum hafra kjöts at jötni; hljóðgreipum tók húðar hrökkvi-skafls ór afli glaðr við galdra smiðju Geirrauðr síu þeiri.	Threw from threatening village Thor smith-bellows great encouraged lightning held goat flesh the giant; sound-grippers (ears) took hide shaken of power glad with magic of-the-smith Geirrod sift of-them.	Threw from threatening village Thor smith-bellows great lightning held goat flesh the giant. Sound-grippers (ears) took hide shaken of power glad with magic of-the-smith Geirrod sift of-them.
"Ekki ertú ámælisverðr um þat?"	"Not are-you talked about that?"	"You are not over talked about",
sagði konungr, "at þú ert órleysingr til skáldskapar?"	said the-king, "that you are over-praised as a-poet?"	said the king, "when you are praised as a poet".

The Tale of Sarcastic Halli (Old Norse)

Old Norse	Literal	English
Ok lofuðu allir, at vel væri ort.	And praised all, to well being worded.	And all praised him on how well it had been composed.
Ekki var Halli við þetta.	Not was Halli with this.	Halli was not present with them.
Ok um kveldit, er menn sátu við drykk, kváðu þeir fyrir Halla, ok sögðu hann eigi mundu svá yrkja, þótt hann þœttist skáld mikit.	And about evening, when men sat with drink, recited they for Halli, and told him not would so compose, though he thought a-poet great.	And that evening when men sat drinking they recited the poem for Halli and told him that he could not compose such a poem even though he thought of himself as a great poet.
Halli kveðst vita, at hann orti verr enn Þjóðólfr.	Halli said knew, that he worded worse than Thjodolf.	Halli said that he knew he composed worse poetry than Thjodolf
"Enn þó mun mér firrst um fara, ef ek em eigi við staddr yrkis-efnin?"	"In-the-end shall then to-me lost about going, if I seek not with to compose?"	"in the end I shall lose if I do not try to compose a verse, and if I am not present",
segir Halli.	said Halli.	said Halli.
Þetta var þegar sagt konungi, ok snúit svá, at hann þœttist eigi minna skáld enn Þjóðólfr.	This was then told-to the-king, and turned so, that he thought not less a-poet than Thjodolf.	This was then told to the king and turned around to say that he thought himself no less of a poet than Thjodolf.
Konungr kvað honum eigi at því verða mundu, "enn vera kann, at vér fáim þetta reynt af stundu?"	The-king said him not that therefore be would, "but be can-it, that we get that tested in awhile?"	The king said that he would not be that, "but it can be that we can test him in a while".

4

Þat var einn dag, er menn sátu yfir borðum, at þar gekk inn í höllina dvergr einn, er Túta hét;	It was one day, when people were sitting at-table, that there went then into the-hall dwarf one, who Tuta named;	It was one day when people were sitting at the table that a dwarf named Tuta went into the hall.
hann var frískr at ætt.	he was Frisian by descent.	He was Frisian by descent.
Hann hafði lengi verit með Haraldi konungi.	He had long been with Harald the-king.	He had been with King Harald a long time.

The Tale of Sarcastic Halli (Old Norse)

Old Norse	Literal	English
Hann var eigi hærri enn þrevett barn, enn allra manna digrastr ok herðamestr, höfuðit mikit ok elliligt, hryggrinn eigi allskammr, enn sýlt í neðan, þar sem fœtrnir váru.	He was not higher than three-winters-old child, but of-all men thick-set and most-hardy, head great and elderly, spine not very-short, but sleek of below, there where the-legs were.	He was no taller than a child of three years old, but he was the most thick set and hardy of all men, he had a large and elderly looking head, and his back was not very short, but sleek below where his legs were.
Haraldr konungr átti brynju, þá er hann kallaði Emmu;	Harald the-king hat coat-of-mail, then which he called Emma;	King Harald had a coat of mail which he called Emma.
hann hafði látit gera hana í Miklagarði.	he had had made her in Byzantium.	He had had it made in Byzantium.
Hon var svá síð, at hon tók niðr á skó Haraldi konungi, þá er hann stóð réttr;	She was so long, that she took down to shoes Harald's the-king, then when he stood upright;	It was so long that it reached down to King Harald's shoes when he stood upright.
var hon öll tvöföld, ok svá styrk, at aldrigi festi járn á.	was she all two-fold, and so strong, that never pierced iron-weapon an.	It was all double-thickness and so strong that it was never pierced by an iron weapon.
Konungrinn hafði látit fœra dverginn í brynjuna ok setja hjálm á höfuð honum, ok gyrði hann sverði.	The-king had had sent-for the-dwarf in coat-of-mail and set helmet on head his, and equipped him a-sword.	The king had ordered the dwarf to be in the coat of mail with a helmet set on his head and equipped with a sword.
Síðan gekk hann inn í höllina, sem fyrr var ritat, ok þótti maðrinn vera undrskapaðr.	After went he in to the-hall, as before was written, and thought the-man was wonder-created.	After he went into the hall as was written before, and the man was thought to be a wonder.
Konungrinn kvaddi sér hljóðs, ok mælti:	The-king called to be-heard, and spoke:	The king called to be heard and spoke:
"Sá maðr, er kveðr um dverginn vísu, svá at mér þykki vel kveðin, þiggi af mér kníf þenna ok belti?"	"So the-man, who words about the-dwarf a-verse, so that to-me seems well worded, receives of me knife this and belt?"	"So the man who composes a verse about the dwarf, so that I think it is a good verse, will accept of me this knife and a belt",
ok lagði fram á borðit fyrir sik gripina:	and laid from to table before him the-trinkets:	and he put the trinkets on the table for him,

The Tale of Sarcastic Halli (Old Norse)

Old Norse	Literal	English
"Enn vitit þat fyrir víst, ef mér þykkir eigi vel kveðin, at hann skal hafa óþökk mína, ok missa gripanna beggja?"	"But know that for certainly, if to-me seems not well worded, that he shall have un-thanks mine, and miss the-trinkets both?"	"but know for certain that if I don't think it is a good poem, he will have my displeasure and lose the trinkets both".
Ok þegar er konungr hafði flutt erindi sitt, kveðr maðr vísu útar á bekkinn, ok var þat Sneglu-Halli:	And as-soon-as when the-king had delivered message his, recited a-man a-verse out from the-bench, and was that Sarcastic-Halli:	And as soon as the king had delivered his speech, a man recited a verse outside of the bench, and it was Sarcastic-Halli:
Fœrðr sýndisk mér frændi Frísa kyns í brynju, gengr fyr hirð í hringum	Brought seems to-me kinsman Frisian kin in chain-mail, going before the-court in circles	Brought seems to-me kinsman Frisian kin in chain-mail. Going before the-court in circles
hjálmfaldinn kúrvaldi; flœr-at eld í ári úthlaupi vanr Túta, sé'k á síðu leika sverð rúghleifa skerði.	the-helmet folded; fleeing the-fire in all-year out-running custom Tuta, see of side games sword rye-loaf cuts.	the-helmet folded. Fleeing the-fire in all-year out-running custom Tuta. See I of side games sword rye-loaf cuts.
Konungr bað fœra honum gripina:	The-king ordered brought to-him the-trinkets:	The king ordered the trinkets to be brought to him
"Ok skaltú ná hér á sannmæli, því at vísan er vel kveðin?"	"And shall-you obtain here in true-words, because it the-verse is well worded?"	"and you will find the truth here, because the verse is well recited".
Þjóðólfi fannst fátt um.	Thjodolf thought little about.	
Þat var einn dag, er konungrinn var mettr, at konungr klappaði knífi á borðit, ok bað ryðja.	It was one day, when the-king was finished-eating, that the-king struck knife on the-table, and ordered cleared.	One day when the king had finished eating he struck his knife on the table and ordered the tables to be cleared.
Þjónustumenn gerðu svá,	The-servants did so,	The servants did so.
Þá var Halli hvergi nærri mettr.	Then was Halli nowhere near satisfied.	Then Halli was nowhere near satisfied.
Tók hann þá stykki eitt af diskinum, ok helt eftir, ok kvað þetta:	Took he then piece one off the-plate, and held back, and recited this:	He then took a piece of food from the place and held it back and recited this:
Hirði ek eigi hvat Haraldr klappar, læt ek gnauða grön,	Care I not that Harald's hammering, have I gnawing moustache,	Care I not that Harald's hammering. Have I gnawing moustache.

The Tale of Sarcastic Halli (Old Norse)

Old Norse	Literal	English
geng ek fullr at sofa.	going I full to sleep.	Going I full to sleep.
Um morgininn eftir, er konungr var kominn í sæti sitt ok hirðin, gekk Halli í höllina fyrir konunginn.	About morning after, when the-king was coming to sit himself and courtiers, went Halli into the-hall before the-king.	About morning when the king had come to sit with his courtiers, Halli went into the hall and went before the king.
Hann hafði skjöld sinn ok sverð á baki sér.	He had shield his and sword about back his.	He had his shield and sword on his back.
Hann kvað vísu:	He spoke a-verse:	He spoke a verse:
Selja mun'k við sufli sverð mitt, konungr, verða, ok, rymskyndir randa, rauðan skjöld við brauði; hungrar hilmis drengi, heldr gangu vér svangir; mér dregr hrygg at hverju (Haraldr sveltir mik) belti.	Barter will of with-bread sword mine, the-king, becomes, and, quickly-cleared round, the-red shield with bread; hungry helmsman's boys, rather going are-we hungry; to-me draws the-spine that which (Harald starving me) belt.	Barter will I of with-bread sword mine, the-king, becomes, and quickly-cleared round the-red shield with bread. Hungry helmsman's boys. Rather going are-we hungry. To-me draws the-spine, that which, Harald starving me, belt.
Engu svarar konungr, ok lét sem hann heyrði eigi;	None answered the-king, and had as he heard not;	The king gave no answer and acted as though he had not heard,
enn þat vissu allir menn, at honum mislíkaði.	but though knew all people, that he mis-liked.	but all the people knew that he disliked this.
Litlu síðar var þat, at konungrinn gekk úti ok fylgdin með honum;	A-little afterwards was it, that the-king went out and followers with him;	A little while afterwards one day the king went out into the street and had his followers with him.
þar var ok Halli í för.	there was also Halli with going.	And there was also Halli going with them.
Hann snaraði fram hjá konunginum.	He rushed ahead nearby the-king.	He rushed ahead to be near the king.
Konungrinn kvað þetta:	The-king spoke this:	The king spoke this:
"Hvert stillir þú Halli?"	"Where heading you Halli?"	"Where are you heading Halli?"
Halli svarar:	Halli answered:	Halli answered:
"Hleyp'k fram at skyrkaupum?"	"running forwards to cow-buying?"	"I am running to buy a cow".

The Tale of Sarcastic Halli (Old Norse)

Old Norse	Literal	English
"Graut muntú gera láta?"	"Porridge would-you look-to have?"	"Will you look to have porridge?"
segir konungr.	said the-king.	said the king.
"Görr matr es þat, smjörvan?"	"Ready-made food is that, buttered?"	"It is a ready made meal, when buttered",
segir Halli.	said Halli.	said Halli.
Hleypr hann Halli þá upp í garðinn, ok þangat sem var eldahús;	Ran he Halli then up to garden, and from-there as was fire-house (kitchen);	Then Halli ran up to a house where there was a kitchen.
þar hafði hann látit gera graut í stórum katli, settist til ok át grautinn.	there had he had made porridge in stone-kettle and, sat to and eat the-porridge.	There he had made porridge in a stone kettle, and sat there to eat the porridge.
Konungr sér, at Halli hverfr upp í garðinn.	The-king saw, that Halli turned up-to the garden.	The king saw that Halli had gone into the house.
Hann kvaddi til Þjóðólf ok tvá menn aðra, at leita Halla.	He called to Thjodolf and two men other, to look-for Halli.	He called to Thjodolf and two other men to look for Halli.
Konungr veik ok upp í garðinn.	The-king turned also up to the-house.	The king also arrived at the house.
Þeir finna hann, þar sem hann át grautinn.	They found him, there as he ate porridge.	They found him there as he ate the porridge.
Konungr kom þá at, ok sá, hvat hann hafðist at.	The-king came then to, and saw, what Halli had to.	The king came to him and saw what Halli was doing.
Konungr var hinn reiðasti, ok spurði Halla hví hann fór af Íslandi til höfðingja, til þess at gera af sér skömm ok gabb.	The-king was the most-angry, and asked Halli if he travelled from Iceland to chieftains, to this that make of himself scandal and mockery.	The king was very angry and asked Halli if he had travelled from Iceland to visit chieftains and make scandal and mockery.
"Látit eigi svá, herra?"	"Let not so, lord?"	"Let it not be so",
segir Halli;	said Halli;	said Halli,
"jafnan sé ek yðr eigi drepa kendi við góðum sendingum?"	"always see I you not kill hands with good delivery?"	"always I see that you do not kill hands that deliver good food".

The Tale of Sarcastic Halli (Old Norse)

Old Norse	Literal	English
Halli stóð þá upp, ok kastaði niðr katlinum, ok skall við haddan.	Halli stood then up, and cast down the-kettle, and hit against the-lid.	Halli then stood up and threw down the kettle, and hit against the lid.
Þjóðólfr kvað þá þetta:	Thjodolf recited then this:	Thjodolf then recited this:
Haddan skall, enn Halli hlaut offylli grautar, hornspánu kveð'k honum hlýða betr enn prýði.	The-handle rattled, and Halli a-lot-of gluttony of-porridge, horn-spoon say to-him suits better than finery.	The-handle rattled and Halli a-lot-of gluttony of-porridge. Horn-spoon say I to-him suits better than finery.
Konungrinn gekk þá burtu ok var allreiðr,	The-king went then away and was all-angry,	The king then went away and was very angry.
ok um kveldit kom engi matr fyrir Halla, sem fyrir aðra menn.	and about evening came no food before Halli, as before other people.	And about evening there came no food for Halli as there had been for the other people.
Ok er menn höfðu snætt um stund, komu inn tveir menn, ok báru milli sín trog mikit, fullt grautar, ok með spán, ok settu fyrir Halla.	And when people had dined about awhile, came then two men, and carried between themselves trough great, full of-porridge, and with a-spoon, and set before Halli.	And when people had dined for a while, then came two men carrying between themselves a great through, full of porridge, and with a spoon set it before Halli.
Hann tók við ok át sem hann lysti, ok hætti síðan.	He took to and ate as he appetite, and stopped afterwards.	He took it and ate as much as his appetite would allow, and then stopped.
Konungr bað Halla eta meira.	The-king ordered Halli eat more.	The king ordered Halli to eat more.
Hann kveðst eigi mundu eta meira at sinni.	He said not would eat more for himself.	He said he himself would not eat any more.
Haraldr konungr brá þá sverði, ok bað Halla eta grautinn, þar til er hann spryngi af.	Harald the-king drew then a-sword, and ordered Halli eat porridge, there until that he burst of.	King Harald then drew a sword and ordered Halli to eat the porridge until he burst.
Halli kveðst eigi mundu sprengja sik á grauti, enn sagði konung ná mundu lífi sínu, ef hann væri á þat einhugi.	Halli said not would burst himself with porridge, but told the-king take could life his, if he would-be of that one-minded.	Halli said that he would not burst himself with porridge, but told the king that he could take his life if he was of a mind to do so.
Konungr sezt þá niðr ok slíðrar sverðit.	The-king sat then down and sheathed sword.	The king then sat down and sheathed his sword.

The Tale of Sarcastic Halli (Old Norse)

Old Norse	Literal	English
5	**5**	**5**
Nökkuru síðar var þat einn dag, at konungr tók disk einn af borði sínu, ok var á steiktr gríss, ok bað Tútu dverg at fœra Halla,	Somewhat later was it one day, that the-king took plate one off table his, and was it roasted pig, and ordered Tuta the-dwarf to bring Halli,	One day somewhat later, the king took a plate off his table, and on it was a roasted pig, he ordered Tuta the dwarf to bring it to Halli
"ok bið hann yrkja vísu, ef hann vill halda lífinu, ok hafa kveðit, áðr þú kemr fyrir hann, ok seg honum eigi fyrr enn þú kemr á mitt gólf?"	"and order him to-compose a-verse, if he wishes to-hold his-life, and have spoken, after you come before him, and tell him not before that you come to the-middle the-floor?"	"and order him to compose a verse if he wishes to hold his life, and recite it after you come before him, and tell him not before you are in the middle of the floor".
"Eigi em ek þess fúss?"	"Not am I this willing?"	"I am not willing to do this",
segir Túta, "því at mér líkar vel við Halla?"	said Tuta, "because that I like well with Halli?"	said Tuta, "because I like Halli".
"Sé ek",	"See I",	"I see",
segir konungr,	said the-king,	said the king,
"at þér líkar vel vísan ok þykkir góð, sú er hann orti um þik, ok muntú gerla heyra kunna.	"that you consider good verse yours that good, the-one is he worded about you, and shall-you completely hear know.	that you consider his verse good that he composed about you, and you know how to listen carefully.
Nú far burt í stað, ok ger sem ek býð?"	Now go away to the-place, and do as I command?"	Now to away and do as I command".
Túta tók við diskinum, ok gekk á mitt gólfið ok mælti:	Tuta took with the-plate, and went to the-middle of-the-floor and spoke:	Tuta now took the place and went to the middle of the floor and spoke:
"Þú, Halli, yrk vísu at boði konungs, ok haf ort, áðr ek kem fyrir þik, ef þú vill halda lífinu?"	"You, Halli, compose a-verse to order the-king's, and have worded, before I come before you, if you wish to-hold your-life?"	"You Halli are ordered by the king to compose a verse and have it composed before I come before you if you wish to hold your life".
Halli stóð þá upp, ok rétti hendr í móti diskinum, ok kvað vísu:	Halli stood then up, and extended hand to meet the-plate, and recited a-verse:	Halli then stood up and extended a hand to meet the plate and recited a verse:
Grís þá greppr at ræsi gruntrauðustum dauðan,	Pig then grasped of the-ruler deep-red death,	Pig then grasped of the-ruler deep-red death.

The Tale of Sarcastic Halli (Old Norse)

Old Norse	Literal	English
Njörðr sér börg á borði baulands fyr (sér) standa;	Njord sees the-city on the-table ring-land before (himself) standing;	Njord sees the-city on the-table ring-land before standing.
runa síður lít'k rauðar, ræð'k skjótt gera kvæði, rana hefir seggr af svíni (send heill, konungr) brenndan.	row since coloured red, speak rapidly made poem, the-trunk has said man swine (send health, king) burnt.	Row since coloured I red. Speak I rapidly made poem. The-trunk has said man swine, send health king, burnt.
Konungr mælti þá:	The-king spoke then:	The king then spoke:
"Nú skal gefa þér upp reiði mína, Halli, því at vísan er vel kveðin, svá skjótt sem til var tekit?"	"Now shall give you up anger mine, Halli, because that verse is well recited, so quickly as to was taken?"	"Now I will give up my anger for you, Halli, because the sentence is well recited as soon as it was taken".

6

Frá því er sagt einn dag, at Halli gekk fyrir konunginn, þá er hann var glaðr ok kátr.	From then is said one day, that Halli went before the-king, then as he was glad and cheerful.	From then it is said that one day Halli went before the king as he was glad and cheerful.
Þar var þá Þjóðólfr ok margt annarra manna.	There was then Thjodolf and many other people.	Then Thjodolf and many other people were there.
Halli sagðist hafa ort drápu um konunginn, ok bað sér hljóðs.	Halli said had worded drapa (poem) about the-king, and asked for-him be-heard.	Halli said that he had composed a drapa about the king and ask him for it to be heard.
Konungrinn spurði, hvárt Halli hefði nökkut kvæði fyrri ort.	The-king asked, whether Halli had anything composed before worded.	The king asked whether Halli had composed anything before.
Halli kveðst eigi hafa fyrri ort.	Halli said not had before worded.	He said he had not composed anything.
"Þat munu menn mæla?"	"It would people say?"	"Some people would say",
segir konungr, "at þú takist mikit á hendr, slík skáld sem ort hafa um mik áðr, eftir nökkurum málefnum;	said the-king, "that you take much in hand, such poets as worded have about me before, after some matters;	said the king, "that you take much in hand, as such poets have composed poems about me for various reasons.
eðr hvat sýnist þér Þjóðólfr?"	but what seems to-you Thjodolf?"	But what seems advisable to you Thjodolf?"
"Eigi kann ek, herra, at gefa yðr ráð?"	"Not can I, lord, to give you advice?"	"I can not give you advice, lord",

The Tale of Sarcastic Halli (Old Norse)

Old Norse	Literal	English
segir Þjóðólfr, "enn hitt mun hóti nær, at ek muna kunna at gefa Halla heilræði?"	said Thjodolf, "but then could not near, that I would know to teach Halli sound-advice?"	said Thjodolf, "but then I could give Halli some sound advice".
"Hvert er þat?"	"What is that?"	"What is that?"
sagði konungr.	said the-king.	said the king.
"Þat fyrst, herra, at hann ljúgi ekki at yðr?"	"That first, lord, that he lie not to you?"	"First of all that he not lie to you".
"Hvat lýgr hann nú?"	"What lies he now?"	"What does he lie about now?"
segir konungr.	said the-king.	said the king.
"Þat lýgr hann, at hann sagðist ekki kvæði ort hafa?"	"That lying he, that he said not composed words had?"	"He is lying when he says that he has not composed such words",
sagði Þjóðólfr, "enn ek segi hann ort hafa?"	said Thjodolf, "but I say he words has?"	said Thjodolf, "but I say that he has composed".
"Hvert er kvæði þat?"	"What is composed that?"	"What has he composed?",
segir konungr, "eðr um hvat er ort?"	said the-king, "and about what is worded?"	said the king, "and what is it composed about?"
Þjóðólfr svarar:	Thjodolf answered:	Thjodolf answered:
"Þat köllu vér Kollu-vísur, er hann orti um kýr, er hann gætti ut á Íslandi?"	"That call we cow-verses, which he worded about cows, that he guarded out in Iceland?"	"That which we call Cow-verses, which he composed about cows that he guarded out in Iceland".
"Er þat satt, Halli?"	"Is that true, Halli?"	"Is that true Halli?"
segir konungr.	said the-king.	said the king.
"Satt er þat?"	"True is that?"	"That is true",
segir Halli.	said Halli.	said Halli.
"Hví sagðir þú, at þú hefðir ekki kvæði ort?"	"Why said you, that you had not composed words?"	"Why did you say that you had not composed such words?"
sagði konungr.	said the-king.	said the king.

The Tale of Sarcastic Halli (Old Norse)

Old Norse	Literal	English
"Því" sagði Halli, "at lítil kvæðismynd mundi á því þykkja, ef þetta skal heyra, ok lítt mun því verða á loft haldit?"	"Because" said Halli, "that little poem-image would be therefore seemed, if it should heard, and little would therefore worth of praised held?"	"Because", said Halli, "that such a little poem would seem if heard worth little praise".
"Þat viljum vér fyrst heyra?"	"That wish we first to-hear?"	"We wish to hear that first",
segir konungr.	said the-king.	said the king.
"Skemt mun þá fleira?"	"Entertainment should then more?"	"Then there should be more than one amusement",
segir Halli.	said Halli.	said Halli.
"Hverju þá?"	"What then?"	"What then?"
segir konungr.	said the-king.	said the king.
"Kveða mun Þjóðólfr þá skulu Sorptrogs-vísur, er hann orti úti á Íslandi?"	"Recite should Thjodolf then should food-trough-verses, which he worded out in Iceland?"	"Thjodolf should then recite Food-trough-verses which he composed out in Iceland",
segir Halli, "ok er þat vel, at, Þjóðólfr leitaði á mik eða af virði fyrir mér, því at upp eru svá í mér bitar ok jaxlar, at ek kann vel at svara honum jöfnum orðum?"	said Halli, "and is that well, that, Thjodolf sought to me but disrespected before me because, that up we-are so coming that my bite and molars, that I can well to answer him even words?"	said Halli, "and it is well that Thjodolf sought to disrespect me, but because my bite and molars are up I can answer him well with words".
Konungr brosti at, ok þótti gaman at etja þeim saman.	The-king smiled at, and thought enjoyment to provoke them together.	The king smiled and thought it was enjoyable to provoke them against eachother.
"Hveru veg er kvæði þat, eðr um hvat er ort?"	"What way is composed that, and about what are words?"	"What is it composed about and what are the words?"
segir konungr.	said the-king.	said the king.
Halli svarar:	Halli answered:	Halli answered:

The Tale of Sarcastic Halli (Old Norse)

Old Norse	Literal	English
"Þat er ort um þat, er hann bar út ösku með öðrum systkinum sínum, ok þótti þá til einkis annars fœrr fyrir vitsmuna sakir, ok varð þó um at sjá, at eigi væri eldr í, svá at mein yrði at, því at hann þurfti allt vit sitt í þann tíma?"	"That is worded about that, which he bore out ashes with other siblings his, and thought then to nothing other accomplished before intellect sake, and became though about to see, that not would fire about, so that mean should that, because that he needed all wit his at that time?"	"It is composed about carrying out ashes with his other siblings, and he was thought capable of accomplishing nothing more for the sake of his intellect, and it was necessary to see that there was no fire about because he needed all his wit at that time".
Konungr spyrr ef þetta væri satt?	The-king asked if that was true	The king asked if that was true.
"Satt er þat, herra?"	"True is that, lord?"	"That is true, lord",
segir Þjóðólfr.	said Thjodolf.	said Thjodolf.
"Hví hafðir þú svá óvirðuligt verk?"	"Why had you so unworthy work?"	"Why did you have such unworthy work?"
segir konungr.	said the-king.	said the king.
"Því, herra?"	"Because, lord?"	"Because lord",
segir Þjóðólfr,	said Thjodolf,	said Thjodolf,
"at ek vilda flýta oss til leika, enn eigi váru verk á mik lagin?"	"that I wished quickly us to play, and not was work to me assigned?"	"that I wished to get us quickly out to play, and no work was assigned to me".
"Þat olli því?"	"That cause therefore?"	"It caused",
segir Halli,	said Halli,	said Halli,
"at þú þóttir eigi hafa verkmanns vit?"	"that you thought not had workman's wit?"	that you were thought not to have the sense of a worker".
"Ekki skulu þit við talast?"	"Not should you-two against speak?"	"You must not argue",
segir konungr, "enn heyra vilju vér kvæðin bæði?"	said the-king, "but hear wish we poems both?"	said the king, "but we want to hear both the poems".
Ok svá varð at vera.	And so became to be.	And so it was.
Kvað þá hvárr sitt kvæði;	Recited then each their poems;	Then each recited their poems.

The Tale of Sarcastic Halli (Old Norse)

Old Norse	Literal	English
ok er lokit var kvæðunum, mælti konungrinn:	and when concluded was the-poetry, spoke the-king:	And when the poems were finished, the king said:
"Lítit er kvæðit hvárttveggja, enda munu lítil hafa verit yrkisefnin, ok þat þó enn minna, er þú hefir ort, Þjóðólfr?"	"Little is poem each-way, ended would little have been the-themes, and is though the lesser, is you have worded, Thjodolf?"	"The poems are little on both sides, because the themes were small, and the lesser one is the one that you have composed Thjodolf".
"Svá er ok, herra?"	"So is also, lord?"	"And so it is, lord",
segir Þjóðólfr, "ok er Halli orðhvass mjök.	said Thjodolf, "and is Halli sharp-tongued much.	said Thjodolf, "and Halli is very sharp tongued.
Enn skyldara þœtti mér honum, at hefna föður síns, enn at eiga sennur við mik hér í Noregi?"	But should seems to-me of-him, to avenge father his, but that not chatter with me here in Norway?"	But I think it's more important for him to avenge his father than to have a fight with me here in Norway".
"Er þat satt, Halli?"	"Is that true, Halli?"	"Is that true Halli?"
segir konungr.	said the-king.	said the king.
"Satt er þat, herra?"	"True is that, lord?"	"That is true, lord",
segir Halli.	said He.	he said.
"Hví fórtu af Íslandi til höfðingja við þat, at þú hafðir eigi hefnt föður þíns?"	"Why went-you from Iceland to chieftains with than, that you have not avenged father yours?"	"Why did you go from Iceland to meet the chieftains when you had not avenged your father?"
segir konungr.	said the-king.	said the king.
"Því, herra?"	"Because, lord?"	"Because, lord",
"at ek var barn at aldri, þá er faðir minn var veginn, ok tóku frændr (mínir) málit, ok sættust á fyrir mína hönd.	"said Halli that I was a-child, in age when father mine was, killed and took (kinsman) the-matter, and settled it before my hand.	said Halli, "I was a child in age when my father was killed, and my cousins took the case and settled on my behalf.
Enn þat þykkir illt nafn á váru landi, at heita griðníðingr?"	But it considered ill named in our land, to call truce-breaker?"	But it is considered ill called in our land to be a truce-breaker".
Konungrinn svarar:	The-king answered:	The king answered:

313

The Tale of Sarcastic Halli (Old Norse)

Old Norse	Literal	English
"Þat er nauðsyn at ganga eigi á grið eðr sættir, ok er ór þessu allvel leyst?"	"It is necessary to go not to peace or settlements, and that from this all-well answered?"	"It is necessary to go to peace or reconciliation and this is well resolved".
"Svá hugða ek, herra?"	"So thought I, lord?"	"So I thought, lord",
segir Halli, *"enn vel má Þjóðólfr tala stórmannliga um slíka hluti, því at öngvan veit ek jafngreypiliga hefnt hafa föður síns sem hann?"*	said Halli, "and well may Thjodolf speak big-man-like about such a-thing, since that none know I equally-badly revenge had his father as he?"	said Halli, "and well may Thjodolf speak arrogantly about such a thing since no one I know has equally badly avenged his father as him".
"Víst er Þjóðólfr líklegr til, at hafa þat hraustliga gert?"	"Certainly is Thjodolf likely to, that have that boldly done?"	"Certainly Thjodolf is like to have done that boldly",
segir konungr;	said the-king;	said the king,
"eðr hvat er verkum gert um þat, at hann hafi þat framar gert enn aðrir menn?"	"but what are actions done about it, that he has that from done than other people?"	but what actions did he take unlike other people?
Þat helzt, herra?	That rather, lord?	"Rather, lord",
segir Halli, *"at hann át föðurbana sinn".*	said Halli, "that he ate his father's-killer".	said Halli, "that he ate his father's killer".
Nú œptu menn upp, ok þóttust aldrei slík undr heyrt hafa.	Now called-out people up, and thought never such wonder heard had.	Now people rose up and called out and thought they had never heard of such a wonder.
Konungrinn brosti at, ok bað menn vera hljóða.	The-king grinned at, and ordered men to-be calm.	The king grinned and ordered people to be calm.
"Ger þetta satt, er þú sagðir, Halli?"	"Does this true, that you said, Halli?"	"Do so that what you say is true Halli",
segir konungr.	said the-king.	said the king.
Halli mælti:	Halli spoke:	Halli spoke:
"Þat hygg ek, at Þórljótr héti faðir Þjóðólfs.	"That think I, that Thorljot named father Thjodolf's.	"I think that Thjodolf's father was named Thorljot.
Hann bjó í Svarfaðardal á Íslandi, ok var hann fátœkr mjök, enn átti fjölda barna.	He lived in Svarfadardal in Iceland, and was he fee-taken much, and had many children.	He lived in Svarfadardal in Iceland and he was very poor and had many children.

The Tale of Sarcastic Halli (Old Norse)

Old Norse	Literal	English
Enn þat er siðr á Íslandi á haustum, at bœndr þinga til fátœkra manna, ok var þá engi fyrri til nefndr, enn Þorljótr, faðir Þjóðólfs;	But it is a-custom in Iceland in autumn, that farmers assemble to the-poor people, and was then none before to named, than Thorljot, father Thjodolf's;	But it is a custom in Iceland in the autumn for farmers to hold meetings for poor people, and there was no one better than Thorljot, Thjodolf's father,
ok einn bóndi var svá, stórlyndr, at hann gaf honum sumargamlan kálf.	and one farmer was so, large-repaying (generous), that he gave him one-summer-old a-calf.	and one farmer was so generous that he gave him a summer-old calf.
Síðan sœkir hann kálfinn ok hafði í taumi, ok var lykkja á enda taumsins;	Then sought he the-calf and had a leash, and was noose at the-end the-leash;	Then he fetched the calf and had it on a leash and there was a loop at the end of the leash.
ok er hanu kom heim at túngarði sínum, hefr hann kálfinn upp á garðinn, ok var furðanliga hár garðrinn;	and when he came home to hayfield-wall his, had he the-calf up on the-wall, and was extremely high the-wall;	And when he came home to his yard wall he had the calf up on the wall, and it was extremely high,
þó var hærra fyrir innan, því at þar hafði verit grafit torf til garðsins.	though was higher before inside, because that there had been dug turf up-to the-wall.	but it was higher on the inside because the turf had been dug up to the wall.
Síðan ferr hann inn yfir garðinn;	Afterwards went he then over the-wall;	Then he went into the yard,
enn kálfrinn veltr út af garðinum.	but the-calf hung outside of the-wall.	but the calf tumbled out of the yard.
Enn lykkjan, er á var taums-endanum, brást um háls honum Þorljóti, ok kenndi hann eigi niðr fótum;	Then the-noose, that about was the-leash, transformed about neck his Thorljot, and felt he not down feet;	But the loop that was on the end of the leash snapped around Thorljot's neck and he didn't fall to his feet.
hekk nú sínum megin hvárr, ok váru dauðir báðir, þegar er til var komit.	hung now his side each, and were dead both, already then until who came.	Now each hung separately and both were dead by the time it was over.
Drógu börnin heim kálfinn, ok gerðu til matar, ok hygg ek, at Þjóðólfr hefði óskerðan sinn hlut af honum?"	Drew the-children home the-calf, and made into food, and think I, that Thjodolf had the-whole his share of him?"	The children brought the calf home and made it for dinner, and I think Thjodolf had his share of it intact".
"Nærri hófi mundi þat"	"Close-to reasonable should-be that"	"That would be more reasonable",
segir konungr.	said the-king.	said the king.

The Tale of Sarcastic Halli (Old Norse)

Old Norse	Literal	English
Þjóðólfr brá sverði, ok vildi höggva til Halla.	Thjodolf drew sword, and wished to-strike to Halli.	Thjodolf drew his sword and wanted to attack Halli.
Hljópu menn þá í milli þeira.	Ran men then in between them.	Men ran in between them.
Konungr kvað hvárigum hlýða skyldu, at gera öðrum mein:	The-king said neither obeying should, to do eachother harm:	The king said that neither should do eachother harm if they obeyed him.
"Leitaðir þú, Þjóðólfr, fyrr á Halla?"	"Seek you, Thjodolf, went-before to Halli?"	"Thjodolf, you went for Halli first".
Varð nú svá at vera sem konungr vildi.	Was now so as being as the-king willed.	Then it was now as the king wished.
Færði Halli drápuna, ok mæltist hon vel fyrir, ok launaði konungr honum góðum penningum.	Performed Halli the-drapa (poem), and recited it well for, and rewarded the-king him good payment.	Halli performed the drapa and it was well received, and the king paid him good money.
Leið nú á vetrinn ok var allt kyrrt.	Passed now to winter and was all peaceful.	It now passed to winter and everything was quiet.

7

Old Norse	Literal	English
Einarr er maðr nefndr, ok var kallaðr fluga.	Einar was a-man named, and was called Fly.	There was a man named Einar who was called Fly.
Hann var son Háreks ór Þjóttu.	He was son Harek's from Thjotta.	He was the son of Harek from Thjotta.
Hann var lendr maðr, ok hafði sýslu á Hálogalandi ok Finnferð af konungi, ok var nú í kærleikum miklum við konung, enn þó eldi þar jafnan ýmsu á.	He was land man, and had business in Halogaland and Finland-voyages of the-king's, and was now in friendship much with the-king, but though fire there equally about was.	He was a land owning man and had business in Halogaland and voyages to Finland, and was now in great friendship with the king, but there was always something going on there.
Einarr var óeyrðarmaðr mikill.	Einar was unreliable much.	Einar was very unreliable.
Drap hann menn, ef eigi gerðu allt, sem hann vildi, ok bœtti öngan mann.	Killed he men, if not did all, as he wished, and compensated no man.	He killed people if they didn't do everything he wanted and gave compensation to no man.
Einars var ván til hirðarinnar at jólunum.	Einar was expected to court at Yule.	Einar was expected at court during Yule.

The Tale of Sarcastic Halli (Old Norse)

Old Norse	Literal	English
Þeim Halla og Sigurði sessunaut hans varð talat til Einars.	They Halli and Sigurd bench-companion his were talking about Einar.	Halli and his bench companion Sigurd were talking about Einar.
Sagði Sigurðr Halla frá, at engi maðr þyrði at mæla í móti Einari eðr í aðra skál at leggja enn hann vildi sjálfr, ok hann bœtti eigi fé fyrir víg eðr rán.	Told Sigurd Halli from, that no man dared to speak to against Einar or that other shall to allow but he wished himself, and he compensated not payment for slaying or robbery.	Sigurd told Halli that no man dared to speak against Einar or to allow anything other than what he wished, and that he paid no compensation for slaying or robbery.
Halli svarar:	Halli answered:	Halli answered:
"Vændis höfðingjar mundu slíkir kallaðir á váru landi?"	"Wicked chieftains would such be-called in our land?"	"Such a chieftain would be called wicked in our land".
"Mæl þú varliga, félagi?"	"Speak you warily, companion?"	"Speak carefully, friend",
segir Sigurðr, "því at hann er lítilbægr at orðum, ef honum eru í móti skapi?"	said Sigurd, "because that he is little-behaving that words, if he is to against mind?"	said Sigurd, "because he doesn't mix his words if he's in a bad mood".
"Þó at þér séit allir svá hræddir?"	"Though that you look all so afraid?"	"Although you are all so afraid",
segir Halli, "at engi yðarr þori, at mæla eitt orð í móti honum, þá segi ek þér þat satt, at ek skylda kæra, ef hann gerði mér rangt, ok þess get ek, at hann bœti mér?"	said Halli, "that none of-you dare, to say one word to against him, then say I to-you this true, that I would accuse, if he did me wrong, and this get I, of him compensate me?"	said Halli, "that none of you dare to say a word against him, I tell you that I would complain if he did me wrong and I expect him to make it up to me".
"Hví þér enn öðrum?"	"Why to-you than others?"	"Why are you different from others?"
segir Sigurðr.	said Sigurd.	said Sigurd.
"Þat mundi honum sýnna?"	"That would to-him appear?"	"That shall become apparent to him",
segir Halli.	said Halli.	said Halli.
Þar til þræta þeir hér um, at Halli býðr Sigurði at veðja.	They to argued them here about, that Halli offered Sigurd to wager.	They argued amongst themselves until Halli offered to make a wager with Sigurd about it.

The Tale of Sarcastic Halli (Old Norse)

Old Norse	Literal	English
Leggr Sigurðr hér við gullhring, er stóð hálfa mörk, enn Halli leggr við höfuð sitt.	Laid Sigurd here with a-gold-ring, in place half a-mark, and Halli laid with head his.	Here, Sigurd placed a gold ring that stood at half a mark, but Halli placed his head.
Einarr kemr at jólum, ok sitr hann á hœgri hönd konungi, ok menn hans út frá honum.	Einar came at Yule, and sat he by other hand the-king's, and people his about from him.	Einar came at Yule and he sat by the king's hand with his people around him.
Var honum öll þjónusta veitt sem konungi sjálfum.	Was he all service given as the-king himself.	He was given every service as much as the king himself.
Ok jóladag, er menn váru mettir, mælti konungrinn:	And Yule-day, when people were finished-eating, spoke the-king:	And on Yule day when people had finished eating the king spoke:
"Nú viljum vér hafa fleira til gamans, enn drekka.	"Now wish we to-have more to amusement, than drinking.	"Now we wish to have more amusement than drinking.
Skaltú nú, segja oss Einarr, hvat til tíðinda hefir orðit í förum yðrum?"	Shall-you now, Einar tell Us, what to news have worded on journey yours?"	Einar, you shall now tell us what word you have of news on your journey.
Einarr svarar:	Einar answered:	Einar answered:
"Ekki kann ek þat í frásagnir at fœra, herra, þó at vér knúskim bú-Finna eðr fiskimenn?"	"Not can I that as stories to bring, lord, though that we knocked-down farmers and fishermen?"	"I don't know how to tell stories, lord, even though we knocked down some farmers and fishermen".
Konungr svarar:	The-king answered:	The king answered:
"Segit settliga, því at vér erum lítilþægir at, ok þykkir oss gaman at því öllu, þó at yðr þykki lítilsvert, er jafnan standit í stríði?"	"Tell sedately, because that we are easily-satisfied by, and seems to-us a-delight that therefore all, though that you think little, is always standing in battles?"	"Tell us calmly because we are easily satisfied by it and it all seems to us a delight even though you think it is of little worth, and as you are constantly in battles".
"Þat er þá, herra, helzt at segja?"	"It is though, lord, rather to say?"	"However, lord, I prefer to say",
segir Einarr, "at í fyrra sumar, er vér komum norðr á Mörkina, mœttum vér Íslands-fari einu, ok höfðu þeir orðit þangat sæhafa, og setit þar um vetrinn.	said Einar, "that of last summer, when we came north of The-border, met we Iceland-voyage one, and had they become from-there sea-scattered, and sat there about winter.	said Einar, "that last summer when we came north of the border we met a ship journeying from Iceland, and they had been sea-scattered and were there since winter.

The Tale of Sarcastic Halli (Old Norse)

Old Norse	Literal	English
Bar ek á hendr þeim, at þeir mundu kaup átt hafa við Finna, fyrir útan yðart lof eðr mitt;	Bore I to hand them, that they would had having traded with The-Sami, for without your permission or mine;	I put it to them that they had traded with the Sami people without your permission or mine,
enn þeir duldu ok gengu eigi við;	that the denied and went not with;	which they denied and would not agree with,
enn oss þóttu þeir ótrúligir, ok beidda ek þá rannsóknar;	but we thought them un-truthful, and asked I then a-search;	but we thought they were untruthful, and I asked to search them,
enn þeir synjuðu þverliga.	but they refused crossly.	but they flatly refused.
Ek sagða þá, at þeir skyldi hafa þat, er þeim væri verra ok makligra, ok bað ek mína menn vápnast ok leggja at þeim.	I said then, that they should have it, what for-them being worse and well-deserved, and ordered I my men armed and lay at them.	I then said that they should have what was worse and more deserved for them, and I asked my men to arm themselves and attack them.
Ek hafða fimm langskip, ok lögðu vér at á bæði borð, ok léttum eigi fyrr enn hroðit var skipit.	I had five longships, and laid we to at both boards, and let-up not before that cleared was the-ship.	I had five longships and we anchored on both sides and did not let up until the ship was cleared.
Ok einn íslenzkr maðr, er þeir kölluðu Einar, varðist svá vel, at hans maka fann ek aldrigi, ok víst var skaði at um þann mann, ok eigi hefðim vér unnit skipit, ef slíkir hefði allir verit innanborðs?"	And one Icelander man, that they called Einar, guarded so well, that he equal found I never, and certainly was harm to about that man, and not have we won the-ship, if such had all been onboard?"	And one Icelander man, that they called Einar, guarded so well that I have never found his equal, and it was certainly a loss for that man, and we would not have won the ship if such men as him had all been aboard".
"Illa gerir þú þat, Einarr"	"Badly done you it, Einar"	"You did badly, Einar",
segir konungr, "er þú drepr saklausa menn, þó at eigi geri allt sem þér líkar bezt?"	said the-king, "when you killed sake-less people, though that not did all as you liked best?"	said the king, "you kill innocent people who don't do everything you like best".
"Mun ek eigi?"	"Would I not?"	"I will not",
sagði Einarr, "sitja fyrir hættu þeiri;	said Einar, "settle for danger theirs;	said Einar, "sit before that danger.
enn mæla þat sumir menn, herra, at þér gerit eigi allt sem guðréttligast;	and say it some people, lord, that you do not all as good-rightly;	But some people say, sir, that you don't do everything in the most godly way.

The Tale of Sarcastic Halli (Old Norse)

Old Norse	Literal	English
enn þeir reyndust illa, ok fundu vér mikinn finnskrepp í skipinu?"	but they proved bad, also found we much Sami-goods in the-ship?"	But they turned out to be bad and we found a great amount of Sami goods in the ship".
Halli heyrði, hvat þeir töluðu, ok kastaði knífinum fram á borðit ok hætti at eta.	Halli heard, what they spoke, and cast knife away from the-table and stopped of eating.	Halli heard what they were talking about and threw the knife on the table and stopped eating.
Sigurðr spurði, ef hann væri sjúkr.	Sigurd asked, if he was sick.	Sigurd asked if he was sick.
Hann kvað þetta sótt verra:	He said that not was:	He said it wasn't,
"Einarr fluga sagði lát Einars bróður míns, er hann kveðst fellt hafa á kaupskipinu í fyrra sumar, ok má vera at nú gefi til, at leita eftir bótunum við hann Einar?"	"Einar Fly told-of had Einar brother mine, that he said fell had on merchant-ship in before summer, and may be that now give to, of seeking after compensation with him Einar?"	"Einar Fly told about the death of my brother Einar, who he claims to have killed on the merchant ship last summer, and it may be that he now seeks to give compensation for Einar".
"Tala ekki um, félagi?"	"Speak not about, companion?"	"Do not speak about it, companion",
segir Sigurðr;	said Sigurd;	said Sigurd,
"sá mun vænstr?"	"so would-be promising?"	that would be the most promising.
"Nei?" segir Halli, "ekki mundi hann svá við mik gera, ef hann ætti eftir mik at mæla?"	"No?" said Halli, "not would he so with me doing, if he had after me the matter?"	Halli said no, "he would not do that with me if it was my case he was dealing with".
Hljóp hann þá fram yfir borðit, gekk innar fyrir hásætit ok mælti:	Jumped he then from over table, went in before high-seat and spoke:	He then jumped over the table, and went before the high seat and spoke:
"Tíðindi sögðu þér, Einarr bóndi, það er mik akta œrit mjök í drápi Einars bróður míns, er þér sögðuzt feldan hafa á kaupskipinu í fyrra sumar.	"News announced you, Einar master, that is me taxes greatly much by the-killing Einar's brother mine, who you said killed had in merchant-ship about last summer.	"You announced news which concerns me greatly, the killing of Einar, my brother, who you said you killed in the merchant ship last summer.
Nú vil ek vita, hvárt þú vill nökkuru bœta mér Einar bróður minn?"	Now wish I to-know, whether you will some compensation to-me Einar brother mine?"	Now I wish to know if you will pay me some compensation for my brother".

The Tale of Sarcastic Halli (Old Norse)

Old Norse	Literal	English
"Hefir þú eigi spurt, at ek bœti engan mann?"	"Have you not heard, that I compensate no man?"	"Have you not heard that I compensate no one",
segir Einarr.	said Einar.	said Einar.
"Eigi er mér skylt at trúa því?"	"Not I me should to believe accordingly?"	"I was not obliged to believe",
segir Halli, "at þér væri allt illa gefit, þó at ek heyrða þat sagt?"	said Halli, "that you were all evil given, though that I heard that said?"	said Halli, "that you were all evil, though I heard it said".
"Gakk burt maðr?"	"Go away man?"	"Go away man",
segir Einarr, "annarr mun verri?"	said Einar, "otherwise should-be worse?"	said Einar, "otherwise it shall be worse".
Halli gekk at sitja.	Halli went to sit.	Halli went to sit.
Sigurðr spyrr, hvé farit hefði.	Sigurd asked, how gone had.	Sigurd asked how it had gone.
Halli svarar, ok kveðst hafa hótun fyrir fébœtr.	He answered, and said had a-threat for compensation.	He answered and said that he had been given a threat as compensation.
Sigurðr bað hann eigi oftar koma á þetta mál, ok sé laus veðjanin.	Sigurd asked him not more come that this matter, and so lost the-wager.	Sigurd ask him not to persist in this matter any more, and the wager would be lost.
Halli kvað honum vel fara:	Halli said he well went:	Halli said it had gone well,
"enn á skal koma oftar?"	"but about shall come more?"	but there is more to come.
Ok annan dag eftir gekk Halli fyrir Einar ok mælti:	And the-next day after went Halli before Einar and spoke:	And the next day Halli went before Einar and spoke:
"Þat mál vil ek vekja, Einarr, ef þú vilt nökkuru bœta mér bróður minn?"	"The matter wish I awaken, Einar, if you will some compensation to-me brother mine?"	"I wish to raise the matter with you, Einar, whether you will give me some compensation for my brother".
Einarr svarar:	Einar answered:	Einar answered:
"Þú ert seinþreyttr at, ok ef þú dregst eigi brott, þá muntú fara slíka fór sem bróðir þinn eðr verri?"	"You are persistent this, and if you draw not away, then should fare such before as brother yours or worse?"	"You are persistent in this, and if you do not back away, then it should go the same way as you brother did or worse".

The Tale of Sarcastic Halli (Old Norse)

Old Norse	Literal	English
Konungrinn bað hann eigi svá svara:	The-king ordered him not so to-answer:	The king ordered him not to answer like that,
"Ok er þat frændunum ofraun, ok veit eigi, hvers hugar hverjum lér.	"And was it kinsmen too-much, and known not, how-so minds each leaned.	and it is too-much for the kinsmen and not known how each mind goes.
Enn þú, Halli, kom eigi oftar á þetta mál, því at stœrri bokkar verða at þola honum slíkt enn þú ert?"	But you, Halli, come not again of this matter, because that greater bigger-men have-been that enduring him such than you are?"	But you, Halli, do not raise this matter again because greater and bigger men have endured such as you are".
Halli svarar:	Halli answered:	Halli answered:
"Svá mun vera verða?"	"So should be becomes?"	"So it will have to be".
Gekk hann þá til rúms síns.	Went he then to rooms his.	Then he went to his rooms.
Sigurðr fagnar honum vel, ok spurði, hvé farit hefði.	Sigurd welcomed him well, and asked, how gone had.	Sigurd welcomed him well and asked how it had gone.
Halli kveðst hafa heitan fyrir fébœtr af Einari.	Halli said had threat for compensation of Einar.	Halli said that he had received a threat for compensation from Einar.
"Þótti mér þat í hug?"	"Thought me that in mind?"	"I thought that in my mind",
segir Sigurðr, "ok sé laus veðjanin?"	said Sigurd, "and so lost the-wager?"	said Sigurd, "and so the wager is lost".
"Vel ferr þér?"	"Well go you?"	"You behave well",
segir Halli, "enn enn skal ek koma í þriðja sinn?"	said Halli, "but for shall I come to a-third occasion?"	said Halli, "but I shall raise the matter a third time".
"Gefa vil ek þér nú til hringinn?"	"Give will I you now to the-ring?"	"I will now give you the ring",
sagði Sigurðr, "at þú látir vera kyrrt, er þetta hefir þó nökkut af mér til hlotizt í fyrstu?"	said Sigurd, "that you leave be peace, as this has though somewhat of me to part the first?"	said Sigurd, "so that you will let there be peace, because I am responsible for part of this.
Halli svarar:	Halli answered:	Halli answered:

The Tale of Sarcastic Halli (Old Norse)

Old Norse	Literal	English
"Sýnir þú í þessu, hverr maðr þú ert, ok eigi má þér um kenna, hversu sem til vegar ferr;	"Show you in this, what man you are, and not may you about know, how-so as to way go;	"You show what kind of man you are and you can't be blamed no matter what happens.
enn prófa skal enn um sinn?"	but prove shall one about occasion?"	But it must be tried one more time".
Ok þegar um morgininn eftir, er konungr tók handlaugar ok Einarr fluga, gekk Halli at honum, ok kvaddi konunginn.	And early about morning after, when the-king took hand-washing and Einar Fly, went Halli to him, and greeted the-king.	And early the next morning, when the king took to washing his hands along with Einar Fly, Halli went to him and greeted the king.
Konungrinn spyrr, hvat er hann vildi.	The-king asked, what is he wanted.	The king asked what he wanted.
"Herra?"	"Lord?"	"Lord",
segir Halli, "ek vil segja yðr draum minn.	said Halli, "I wish to-tell you dream mine.	said Halli, "I wish to tell you about my dream.
Ek þóttumst vera allr maðr annarr enn ek em?"	I seemed to-be all man another than I am?"	I thought I was a completely different person than I am".
"Hvat manni þóttist þú vera?"	"What man thought you to-be?"	"Who did you think you were?"
segir konungr.	said the-king.	said the king.
"Ek þóttumst vera Þórleifr jarls skáld, enn hann Einarr fluga þótti mér vera Hákon jarl Sigurðarson, ok þóttumst ek hafa ort um hann níð, ok munda ek sumt níðit, er ek vaknaða?"	"I thought being Thorleif the-earl's the-poet, but he Einar Fly seemed to-me to-be Hakon earl Sigurdson, and thought I had worded about him slander, and remembered I some the-slander, when I awoke?"	I thought I was Thorleif the poet, but Einar Fly was Earl Hakon Sigurdson, and I thought I had written about him, and I remembered some things when I woke up".
Snöri Halli þá útar eftir höllinni, ok kvað nökkut fyrir munni sér, ok námu menn eigi orðaskil.	Turned Halli then out after the-hall, and spoke something before mouth his, and took people not words-separated.	Halli then turned around outside the palace and said something in front of his mouth and the people did not understand any of it.
Konungr mælti:	The-king spoke:	The king spoke:
"Þetta var eigi draumr annarr enn hann dregr þessi dœmi saman;	"This was not a-dream another that he drew these examples together;	"This was not a dream, and he has drawn these examples together.

The Tale of Sarcastic Halli (Old Norse)

Old Norse	Literal	English
ok svá mun fara með ykkr, sem fór með Hákoni Hlaðajarli ok Þorleifi skáldi, ok þat sama gerir Halli:	and so should go with you, as went with Hakon Earl-of-Lade and Thorleif the-poet, and that same does Halli:	And so it should go with you as it went with Earl Hakon of Lade and Thorleif the poet, and Halli is doing the same thing.
hann svífst einkis, ok megu vit sjá, at bitit hefir níðit ríkari menn enn svá sem þú ert, Einarr, sem var Hákon jarl, ok mun þat munat, meðan Norðrlönd eru byggð, ok er verri einn kviðlingr, um dýran mann kveðinn, ef munaðr verðr eftir, enn lítil fémúta;	he shrinks-from nothing, and may we see, that biting has-been the-slander richer men than so as you are, Einar, as was Hakon earl, and would-be that remembered, as-long-as Northern-lands are settled, and is worse one short-poem, if remembered becomes after, then little money-bribe about, fine men composed;	He shrinks from nothing, and we may see how slander has bitten richer men than you are, Einar, as Earl Hakon was, and it would be remembered as long as the Northern Lands are settled, one short verse about powerful men, if it becomes remembered afterwards, is worse than paying a small bribe,
ok ger svá vel ok leys hann af með nökkuru?"	and do so well and repay him of with somehow?"	and so it would do well to repay him somehow".
"Þér skulut ráðar herra?"	"You should decide lord?"	"You will decide, lord"
segir Einarr, "ok seg honum, at hann taki þrjár merkr silfrs af féhirði mínum, er ek fekk honum síðast í sjóði?"	said Einar, "and tell him, that he takes three marks of-silver of fee-servant mine, that I give him the-last in purse?"	said Einar, "and tell him that he may take three marks of silver from my fee-servant in the purse I just gave him".
Þetta var sagt Halla.	This was told Halli.	This was told to Halli.
Gekk hann at finna féhirðinn, ok sagði honum sitt erindi.	Went he to find fee-servant, and told him his errand.	He went to find the fee-servant and told him.
Hann kvað vera fjórar merkr silfrs í sjóðnum.	He said be four marks of-silver in the-purse.	He said there were four marks of silver in the purse.
Halli kveðst þrjár hafa skyldu.	Halli said three have should-be.	Halli said that he was to have three.
Halli gekk þá fyrir Einar, ok sagði honum.	Halli went then before Einar, and told him.	Halli went before Einar and said to him:
"Hafa mundir þú þat, er í var sjóðnum?"	"Have would you that, which in was the-purse?"	"Have you taken what was in the purse?",
segir Einarr.	said Einar.	said Einar.

The Tale of Sarcastic Halli (Old Norse)

Old Norse	Literal	English
"Nei?" sagði Halli, "öðruvísi muntú ná lífi mínu, enn ek verða þjófr at fé þínu, ok sá ek, at þú hafðir ætlat mér þat?"	"No?" said Halli, "other-knowing shall-you obtain life mine, than I being thief of money yours, and saw I, that you have that intended to-me?"	Halli said no, "you will have to find another way to take my life than me being a thief of your money, and I saw what you intended for me".
Ok svá, var, at Einarr hafði þat ætlat Halla, at hann mundi hafa, þat er í sjóðnum var, ok þótti honum þat nóg bana-sök.	And so, was, that Einar had it intended Halli, that he would that, which in was the-purse have, and thought him that enough death-sentence.	And so it was that Einar thought that Halli would have taken whatever was in the purse, which he thought would be enough of an offence for a death sentence.
Gekk Halli nú til sætis síns, ok sýndi Sigurði féit.	Went Halli no to seat his, and showed Sigurd the-money.	Halli went now to his seat and showed Sigurd the money.
Sigurðr tók hringinn, ok kvað Halla hafa vel til unnit.	Sigurd took the-ring, and said Halli well had to won.	Sigurd took the ring and said that Halli had won it.
Hann svarar:	He answered:	He answered:
"Eigi eru vit þá jafnir þegnar, ok tak hring þinn, ok njót manna bezt.	"Not are-we with then equal men, and take the-ring yours, and enjoy man the-best.	"We are not equally good men, keep the ring and enjoy it, best of men.
Enn þér satt at segja, þá átta ek aldrigi skylt við þenna mann, er Einarr hefir drepit, ok vilda ek vita, ef ek næða fénu af honum?"	But to-you truth to say, then related-to I never should with this man, which Einar had killed, and wished I to-know, if I neared money of him?"	But to tell you the truth, I was never related to this man which Einar killed, and I wished to know if I could obtain money from him".
"Engum manni ertú líkr at prettum?"	"No man are-you like in trickery?"	"There is no one like you in trickery",
segir Sigurðr.	said Sigurd.	said Sigurd.
Einarr fór brott eftir jólin norðr á Hálogaland.	Einar went away after Yule north to Halogaland.	Einar went away after Yule north to Halogaland.

8   8   8

Um várit eftir bað Halli konung órlofs at fara til Danmerkr í kaupferð.	About spring after asked Halli the-king vacation to travel to Denmark on trading-voyage.	In the spring, King Halli asked for leave to go to Denmark on a trading voyage.

The Tale of Sarcastic Halli (Old Norse)

Old Norse	Literal	English
Konungr bað hann fara, sem hann vildi, "ok kom aftr skjótt, því at oss þykkir gaman at þér, ok far varliga fyrir Einari flugu;	The-king bid he travel, as he wished, "and come back quickly, because that we consider fun that to-you, and travel warily because-of Einar Fly;	The king asked him to go as he wished "and come back quickly because we like you and be careful of Einar Fly.
hann mun hafa illan hug á þér, ok sjaldan veit ek honum jafnsleppt tekizt hafa"	he should have evil mind to you, and seldom know I him equally-slip taken has"	He will have a bad opinion of you and I rarely know of him slipping up".
Halli tók sér far með kaupmönnum suðr til Danmerkr, ok svá til Jótlands.	Halli took himself passage with trading-men south to Denmark, and so to Jutland.	Halli took found passage with merchants south to Denmark and then to Jutland.
Rauðr hét maðr, er þar hafði sýslu, ok réðst Halli þar til vistar.	Raud was-named a-man, who there had stewardship, and appointed Halli there to lodgings.	There was a man named Raud who had a stewardship there and appointed Halli there some lodgings.
Þat bar til eitt sinn, er hann skyldi hafa þing fjölmennt, ok er menn skyldu þar mæla lögskilum sínum, þá var svá mikit háreysti ok gap, at engi maðr mátti þar málum sínum fram koma;	It bore to one occasion, that he should have assembly followers, and that men should there matters legal-settlement theirs, then was so much commotion and gaping, that no man may there matter his from come-forward;	It happened day when he was supposed to have a large assembly and when people were supposed to discuss their legal issues there, there was so much shouting and gaping that no one was allowed to present their case there
ok fóru menn við þat heim um kveldit.	and went people with that home about evening.	and the people went home that evening.
Þat var um kveldit, er menn komu til drykkjar, at Rauðr mælti:	It was about evening, that men came to drink, that Raud spoke:	It was in the evening when people came to drink that Raud said:
"Þat væri ráðleitinn maðr, er ráð fyndi til, at fólk þetta allt þagnaði?"	"It being cunning man, who plan find to, that people these all silenced?"	"It would be a wise man who could find a way to keep all these people quiet".
Halli svarar:	Halli answered:	Halli answered:
"Þat fæ ek gert, þegar er ek vil, at hér skal hvert mannsbarn þagna?"	"That can I do, as-soon-as that I wish, that here shall each man's-son silence?"	"I can do that when I want every human being to be silent".
"Þat fær þú eigi gert landi?"	"That undertaking you not do the-land?"	"You will not get that done in this land",

The Tale of Sarcastic Halli (Old Norse)

Old Norse	Literal	English
segir Rauðr.	said Raud.	said Raud.
Um morgininn komu menn til þings, ok var nú slíkt óp ok gap sem hinn fyrra dag, ok varð engum málum skilat.	About morning came people to the-assembly, and were now such shouting and gaping as the before day, and were no matters settled.	In the morning, people came to the assembly and now there was such an uproar as the previous day and no issues were resolved.
Fóru menn við þat heim.	Went men with that home.	The men then went home.
Þá mælti Rauðr:	Then spoke Raud:	Then Raud spoke:
"Viltú veðja um Halli, hvárt þú fær hljóðit á þinginn eðr eigi?"	"Will-you wager about Halli, each you carry-out silence to the-assembly or not?"	"Will you wager, Halli, that you will get silence at the assembly or not?".
Halli kveðst þess búinn.	Halli said this settled.	Halli said this would be done.
Rauðr svarar:	Raud answered:	Raud answered:
"Legg við höfuð þitt, enn ek gullhring er stendr mörk?"	"Lay with head yours, and I gold-ring which stands one-mark?"	"Lay down your head, and I will lay down a ring which is worth one mark".
"Þat skal vera?"	"That shall be?"	"So it shall be",
segir Halli.	said Halli.	said Halli.
Um morgininn spurði Halli Rauð, ef hann vildi veðjanina halda.	About morning asked Halli Raud, if he wished wager to-hold.	In the morning, Halli asked Raud if he wanted to keep the wager.
Hann kveðst halda vilja.	He said hold wished.	He said that he wished to keep it.
Komu menn nú til þingsins, ok var nú slíkt óp eðr meira, enn hina fyrri dagana.	Came men now to the-assembly, and were not such shouting and more, than the before day.	Now people came to the assembly and there was as much shouting or more as the previous days.
Ok er menn varði sízt, hleypr Halli upp, ok œpir sem mest mátti hann:	And when people were least, ran Halli up, and cried-out as high as-might he:	And when the people were at their least, Halli ran up and shouted as loud as he could:
"Hlýði allir menn;	"Listen all people;	"Listen everyone.
mér er mikils málsþörf;	for-me is great matter;	For me this is a matter of need.

The Tale of Sarcastic Halli (Old Norse)

Old Norse	Literal	English
ek skal kæra um óðindælu mína sjálfs;	I shall discuss about puzzle mine self's;	
mér er horfin hein ok heinar-sufl, skreppa ok þar með allr skreppu-skrúði, sá er karlmanni er betra at hafa, enn at missa?"	mine is lost hone and honing-grease, bag and there with all bag-tackle, so is a-man that better to have, than to lose?"	I have lost my hone and honing grease, and my bag with all its tackle, which is better for a man to have than lose".
Allir menn þögnuðu.	All people silenced.	All the people were silent.
Sumir hugðu, at hann mundi œrr orðinn, enn sumir hugðu hann mundu tala konungs erindi nökkur.	Some thought, that he could-be awed of-words, and some thought he could-be speaking the-king's errand some.	Some people thought that he was lost for words, and some thought that he could be speaking some message from the king.
Ok er hljóð fekkst, settist Halli niðr ok tók við hringnum.	And when silence received, settled Halli down and took with the-ring.	And when there was a sound, Halli sat down and took the ring.
Enn þegar menn sáu, at þetta var ekki nema dáruskapr, þá var háreysti sem áðr, ok komst Halli á hlaupi undan, því at Rauðr vildi hafa líf hans, ok þótti þetta verit hafa hin mesta ginning.	Then as-soon-as people saw, that this was nothing but mockery, then was commotion as before, and came Halli to running out-from, because that Rauð wished to-have life his, and thought this become had the most deception.	But when people saw that this was nothing but a prank, Halli was as stubborn as before and ran away from Raud who wanted his head and thought that this was the greatest deception.
Létti hann eigi fyrr enn hann kom til Englands.	Let-up he not before that he came to England.	He did not let up until he came to England.

9

Old Norse	Literal	English
Þá réð fyrir Englandi Haraldr Guðinason.	Then ruled for England Harald Godwinson.	Then Harald Godwinson ruled England.
Halli ferr þegar á konungs fund, ok kveðst ort hafa um hann drápu, ok bað sér hljóðs.	Halli went straight-away to the-king to-meet, and said had composed about him a-drapa (poem), and asked for-him be-heard.	Halli went straight away to the king and said that he had composed a drapa about him and asked that it be heard.
Konungr lét gefa honum hljóð.	The-king had granted him a-hearing.	The king granted him a hearing.

The Tale of Sarcastic Halli (Old Norse)

Old Norse	Literal	English
Sezt nú Halli fyrir kné konungi, ok flutti fram kvæðit;	Sat now Halli before knee the-king's, and brought from the-poem;	Halli sat down before the king and recited the poem.
ok er lokit var kvæðinu, spurði konungr skáld sitt, er var með honum, hveru veg at væri kvæðit.	and when ended was the-poem, asked the-king the-poet this, that was with him, each way that being the-poem.	And when the poem was finished, the king asked his poet who was with him and what the poem was about.
Hann kveðst ætla at gott væri.	He said supposed that good was.	He said that he supposed it was good.
Konungr bauð Halla með sér at vera, enn Halli kveðst búinn vera til Noregs áðr.	The-king invited Halli with him to be, but Halli said prepared being to Norway back.	The king invited Halli to stay with him, but Halli said he has already prepared to return to Norway.
Konungr kvað þá þann veg fara mundu af hendi um kvæðislaunin "við þik, sem vér njótum kvæðisins, því at engi hróðr verðr oss at því kvæði, er engi kann.	The-king said then that way going would of hand about poem-reward "with you, as we benefit the-poem, because that none fame worthy to-us that before recited, as none knows.	The king said then that it would go the same way "in rewarding you for the poem, as we benefit from the poem, because we get no fame's worth from a poem that no one knows.
Sit nú niðr á gólfit, enn ek mun láta hella silfri í höfuð þér, ok haf þat, er í hárinu loðir, ok þykkir mér þá hvárt horfa eftir öðru, er vér skulum eigi ná at nema kvæðit?"	Sit now down on the-floor, then I will have poured silver on head yours, and have it, which in the-hairs of-your-hair, and seems to-me then each turn after the-other, that we shall not obtain to but the-poem?"	Now sit down on the floor, and I will have silver poured over your head, and keep whatever sticks to your hair, and it seems to me that it looks the same on both sides because we will not get to learn the poem".
Halli svarar:	Halli answered:	Halli answered:
"Bæði mun vera, at lítilla launa mun vert vera, enda munu ok þessi launin lítil vera.	"Both should be, that little reward should worth become, and shall this repay also little being.	"Both are small rewards due and that the rewards will be small.
Lofa munu þér, herra, at ek ganga út nauðsynja minna?"	Promise shall you, lord, that I go out needs mine?"	Will you promise me that I may go outside to attend to my needs".
"Gakk sem þú vill?"	"Go as you wish?"	"Go as you wish",
segir konungr.	said the-king.	said the king.

The Tale of Sarcastic Halli (Old Norse)

Old Norse	Literal	English
Halli gekk þar til, er skipsmiðir váru, ok bar í höfuð sér tjöru, ok skrýfði sem mest hárinu, ok gerði sem diskr væri;	Halli went there to, where ship-smiths were, and bore on head his tar, and scrawled as most hair, and made as a-plate being;	Halli walked to where the shipbuilders were and carried tar on his head and fashioned into the shape of a plate
gekk síðan inn, ok bað hella silfrinu yfir sik.	went afterwards in, and asked pour the-silver over him.	and then went back inside and asked for the silver to be poured over him.
Konungr kvað hann vera brögðóttan;	The-king said he was cunning;	The king said that he was cunning,
ok var nú heilt yfir hann, ok var þat mikit silfr, er hann fekk.	and was now rather over him, and was it much silver, that he got.	and now the silver was poured over him, and it was a lot of silver that he got.
Fór hann síðan þangað, er skip þau váru, er til Noregs ætluðu, ok váru öll burtu nema eitt, ok var þar ráðinn fjöldi manna með miklum þunga;	Went he afterwards from-there, to ship there where, that to Norway intended, and were all away except one, and was that appointed many men with much heavy-cargo;	He then went to where the ships were that were going to Norway, and they were all gone, except one that had many men with much heavy cargo.
enn Halli hafði of fjár, ok vildi gjarna í burt, því at hann hafði ekki kvæði ort um konung annat enn endileysu, ok mátti hann því eigi kenna þat.	but Halli had of fee, and wished gladly to away, because that he had not composed words about the-king other than nonsense, and may he therefore not teach it.	Halli had plenty of money and wished very much to travel away, because he had not composed words about the king other than reciting nonsense, and therefore could not teach it.
Stýrimaðr bað hann fá til ráð, at Suðrmenn gengi ór skipinu, ok kveðst þá vilja gjarna taka við honum.	Steersman bid him get to advice, that Southern-men walking out-of the-ship, and said then wished gladly take with him.	The steersman told him to find a scheme so that the southern men would leave the ship, then he would gladly take him.
Enn þá var komit at vetri.	But then was coming the winter.	But then winter was coming.
Halli var hjá þeim í herbergjum um hríð.	Halli was beside them in sleeping-quarters about awhile.	Halli stayed with them in sleeping quarters for a while.
Eina nótt lét Halli illa í svefni, ok var lengi áðr enn þeir fengu vakit hann.	One night had Halli badly in sleep, and was long before that they caught awake him.	One night, Halli felt sick in his sleep and it was a long time before they could wake him up.
Þeir spurðu, hvat hann hefði dreymt.	They asked, what he had dreamed.	They asked what he had dreamed.

The Tale of Sarcastic Halli (Old Norse)

Old Norse	Literal	English
Halli kvað lokit því, at hann mundi biðja þá fars héðan frá.	Halli said finished therefore, that he would ask then travel from-there from.	Halli said that he was finished with asking for passage from there,
"Mér þótti maðr koma at mér ógrligr, ok kvað þetta:	"To-me seemed a-man come that to-me terrible, and recited this:	It seemed to me that a terrible looking man came to me and recited this:
Hröng es, þar's hávan þöngul	Roaring is, there the harbour there	Roaring is there the harbour there
held ek siz'k fjörs selda'k sýn es,	think me about since that I life,	think me about, since that I life sold.
at sit'k at Ránar,	am-I one to Ran,	Disappeared am-I one to Ran.
sumir eru í búð með humrum;	some are in lodgings with lobsters;	Some are in lodgings with lobsters.
ljóst es lýsu at gista;	light is the-whitings with guest;	Light is the-whitings with guest.
lönd á'k út við ströndu;	lands I out from the-shore;	Lands I out from the-shore.
því sit'k bleikr í brúki,	because sit pale in use,	Because sit I pale in use.
blakkir mér þari um hnakka,	pale mine intestines about neck,	Pale mine intestines about neck,
blakkir mér þari um hnakka.	pale mine intestines about neck.	pale mine intestines about neck.
Ok er Suðrmenn vissu draum þenna, réðust þeir ór skipinu, ok þótti víss bani sinn, ef þeir fœri þar á.	And when The-southerners knew this-dream then, decided they out-of the-ship, and thought certain death theirs, if they went there in.	And when the southerners knew this dream, they got out of the ship and thought it would be their death if they went there.
Halli réðst þegar á skip, ok sagði, at þetta var prettr hans enn engi draumr.	Halli took straight-away in the-ship, and said, that this was trick his and no dream.	Halli took passage in the ship straight away, and said that it was a trick, and not a dream.
Ok tóku þeir út þegar, er þeir váru búnir, ok tóku Noreg um haustit;	And took they out from-there, were they were ready, and took Norway about autumn;	And they went out when they were ready and took to Norway in the autumn,
ok fór Halli þegar til Haralds konungs.	and went Halli then to Harald the-king.	and Halli immediately went to King Harald.
Hann tók vel við Halla, ok spurði, hvárt hann hefði ort um aðra konunga.	He received well with Halli, and asked, whether he had words about other kings.	He welcomed Halli and asked if he had written about other kings.
Halli kvað þetta:	Halli said this:	Halli said this:
"Orta ek eina um jarl?"	"Worded I one about an-earl?"	Worded I one about an earl
Þula	a-Thula (poem)	a-'thula' (poem).

The Tale of Sarcastic Halli (Old Norse)

Old Norse	Literal	English
verðr at drápu *með Dönum verri;* *föll eru fjórtán* *ok föng tíu;* *opit es ok öndvert,* *öfigt stígandi.* *Svá skal yrkja* *sá's illa kann.*	worthy that drapa (poem) with The-Danes worse; mistakes are fourteen and rhymes ten; open is and upside-down, reversed ascending. Then shall compose so badly knows.	Poorer drapa with The-Danes worse. Mistakes are fourteen and rhymes ten. Open is and upside-down, reversed ascending. Then shall compose so who badly knows.
Konungr brosti at, ok þótti honum jafnan gaman at Halla.	The-king smiled that, and thought him always entertaining of Halli.	The king smiled an thought he always found Halli entertaining.

10

Old Norse	Literal	English
Haraldr konungr fór um várit til Gulaþings;	Harald the-king went about spring to Gula-assembly;	In the spring Harald went to the Gulathing Assembly.
ok um daginn spurði konungr Halla, hversu honum yrði til kvenna um þingit.	and about the-day asked the-king Halli, how-so he became to women at the-assembly.	And one day the king asked Halli how he was with women at the assembly.
Halli svarar:	Halli answered:	Halli answered:
Gott es Gulaþing þetta: *giljum vér hverjar es viljum.*	Good is Gula-assembly this: beguile we that as we-wish.	Good is Gulathing this, beguile we that as we-wish.
Konungr fór þaðan norðr til Þrándheims.	The-king went from-there north to Trondheim.	The king went north from there to Trondheim.
Ok er þeir sigldu fyrir Stað, áttu þeir Þjóðólfr ok Halli búðarvörð at halda, ok var Halli sæsjúkr mjök, ok lá undir báti, enn Þjóðólfr varð at þjóna einn.	And when they sailed for Stad, had they Thjodolf and Halli shop-keeping to hold, and was Halli seasick much, and lay under the-ship's-boat, and Thjodolf came to serve alone.	And when they sailed for Stad, Thjodolf and Halli were assigned the cooking and serving, and Halli was very seasick and lay under the ship's boat, and Thjodolf had to serve alone.
Ok er hann bar vistina, fell hann um fót Halla, er stóð út undan bátnum.	And when he carried the-provisions, fell he about leg Halli's, which stood out under the-boat.	And when he was carrying the provisions, he fell on Halli's leg, which was standing out from under the boat.
Þjóðólfr kvað þá þetta:	Thjodolf spoke then this:	Thjodolf spoke this:
Út stendr undan báti ilfat.	Out standing under the-boat sole-bucket.	"Out standing under the-boat sole-bucket.

The Tale of Sarcastic Halli (Old Norse)

Old Norse	Literal	English
Muntú nú gilja?	Shall-you now beguile	Shall-you now beguile?"
Halli svarar:	Halli answered:	Halli answered:
Þjón geri'k þann at sveini: Þjóðólf læt'k mat sjóða.	Servant made then to this-lad: Thjodolf let food boil.	Servant made I then to this-lad, Thjodolf let I food boil.
Fór konungrinn nú leiðar sinnar, unz hann kom í Kaupang.	For the-king now on-way his, until he came to Kaupang.	The king now went on his way until he came to Kaupang.
Þóra drottning var nú með honum, ok var hon lítt til Halla;	Thora the-queen was not with him, and was she little towards Halli;	Queen Thora was now with him and she did not like Halli,
enn konungr var vel til hans, ok þótti gaman at Halla jafnan.	but the-king was well towards him, and seemed to-delight in Halli always.	but the king liked him and always delighted in Halli.
Þess er getit einn dag, at konungrinn gekk úti um stræti ok fylgdin með honum.	This is told one day, that the-king went out about the-street and followers with him.	It is said that one day the king went out into the street and his follower with him.
Halli var þar í för.	Halli was there in procession.	Halli was there in the procession.
Konungrinn hafði öxi í hendi, ok öll gullrekin, enn silfrvafit skaftit ok silfrhólkr mikill á forskeftinn, ok þar í ofan steinn góðr.	The-king had an-axe in hand, and all gold-inlaid, and silver-wound the-shaft and silver-band great in upper-shaft, and there in over a-stone good.	The king had an axe in his hand and all the shafts were gold, but the shaft was wrapped in silver, and a large silver cylinder on the foreshaft, and above it a good stone.
Þat var ágætr gripr.	It was excellent possession.	It was excellent possession.
Halli sá jafnan til öxarinnar.	Halli looked always to the-axe.	Halli kept looking towards the axe.
Konungr fann þat ok brátt, ok spurði, hvárt Halla litist vel á öxina.	The-king found that and soon, and asked, whether Halli looked well of the-axe.	The king soon found out and asked if Halla had a good look at the axe.
Honum kveðst vel á lítast.	He said well it looked.	He said it looked good.
"Hefir þú sét betri öxi?"	"Have you seen a-better axe?"	"Have you seen a-better axe?"
(segir konungr).	(said the-king).	
"Eigi ætla ek þat?" segir Halli.	"Not suppose I that?" said Halli.	"I suppose not", said Halli.

The Tale of Sarcastic Halli (Old Norse)

Old Norse	Literal	English
"Viltú láta serðast til öxarinnar?"	"Will-you allow to-get-hurt for the-axe?"	"Do you want to be hurt by the axe?"
segir konungr.	said the-king.	said the king.
"Eigi?" segir Halli;	"Not?" said Halli;	Halli said not,
"enn várkunn þykki mér yðr, at þér vilit svá selja sem þér keyptut?"	"but understandable seems to-me you, that you wish so to-sell same-as you bought?"	"but it's understandable to me that you would wish to sell it for the same as you bought it".
"Svá skal vera, Halli?"	"So shall be, Halli?"	"So it shall be Halli",
segir konungr;	said the-king;	said the king,
"tak við, ok njót manna bezt:	"take with, and enjoy man the-best:	take it with you and enjoy it, best man,
gefin var mér, enda skal svá selja?"	given was to-me, and shall so to-sell?"	it was given to me, and now shall it be given to you.
Halli þakkaði konungi.	Halli thanked the-king.	Halli thanked the king.
Um kveldit, er menn komu til drykkjar talaði drottning við konung, at þat væri undarligt	About evening, when men came to drink talked the-queen with the-king, that it was scandalous	In the evening, when the men came to drink, the queen spoke to the king that it was strange
ok eigi vel til skift, at gefa Halla þá gripi, "er varla er ótíginna manna at eiga, fyrir klámyrði sín;	and not well to exchange, to give Halli then treasure, "that hardly was un-ranking man that not, before obscene his;	and it is not a good idea to give Halli the those things to a lowly man hardly has for his obscenities,
enn þó fá sumir lítit fyrir góða þjónustu"	that then give some little before good service"	but then some people get little for good service".
Konungr kveðst því ráða vilja, hverjum hann gefi gripi sína:	The-king said therefore decided wished, each he gave possessions his:	The king said that he would decide who he would give his possessions to,
"Vil ek eigi snúa orðum Halla til hins verra, þeim er tvíræð eru"	"Wish I not return words Halli to his worst, they are ambiguous are"	for I do not wish to turn Halli's words to the worse, which are ambiguous in a bad sense".
Konungr bað kalla Halla, ok svá var gert.	The-king asked to-call Halli, and so was done.	The king asked to call Halli, and it was done.

The Tale of Sarcastic Halli (Old Norse)

Old Norse	Literal	English
Halli laut honum.	Halli bowed to-him.	Halli bowed to him.
Konungr bað Halla mæla nökkur tvíræðis-orð við Þóru drottningu:	The-king ordered Halli speak something ambiguous about Thora the-queen:	The king asked Halli to say some ambiguous words to Queen Thora
"ok vit, hversu hon þolir?"	"and know, how-so she endures?"	and know how she endures it.
Halli laut þá at Þóru ok kvað:	Halli bowed then to Thora and said:	Halli bowed then to Thora and said:
Þú ert makligust miklu, (munar stórum þat) Þóra, flenna upp at enni allt leðr Haralds reðra.	You are the-best much, (delight great that) Thora, to-extend up to brow all skin Harald's genitals.	You are the-best much, delight great that, Thora, to-extend up to brow all the skin of Harald's genitals.
"Takit hann ok drepit?"	"Take him and kill?"	"Take him and kill him",
segir drottning;	said the-queen;	said the queen.
"vil ek eigi hafa hrópyrði hans?"	"will I not have obscenities his?"	"I will not have his obscenities".
Konungr bað öngvan svá djarfan vera, at á Halla tæki hér fyrir:	The-king ordered none so daring be, that to Halli take force for:	The king ordered that no one should dare take Halli by force:
"Enn at því má gera, ef þér þykkir önnur makligri til at liggja hjá mér ok vera drottning, ok kanntú varla at heyra lof þitt".	"But that then may done, if you think another more-suitable that to lie beside me and be queen, and know-you hardly to hear praise yours".	"But then it may be done if you think another is more suitable to lie beside me and be queen, and you hardly know how to hear your praise".
Þjóðólfr skáld hafði farit til Íslands, meðan Halli var í burtu frá konungi.	Thjodolf poet had travelled to Iceland, while Halli was to away from the-king.	The poet Thjodolf had gone to Iceland while Halli was away from the king.
Þjóðólfr hafði flutt útan frá Íslandi hest góðan, ok vildi gefa konungi, ok lét Þjóðólfr leiða hestinn í konungsgarð, ok sýna konungi.	Thjodolf had brought out from Iceland a-horse good, and wished to-give the-king, and had Thjodolf lead the-horse to the-king, and showed the-king.	Thjodolf had brought a good horse from Iceland and wanted to give it to the king, and he had Thjodolf lead the horse to the king's garden and show it to the king.
Konungrinn gekk at sjá hestinn, ok var (hann) mikill ok feitr.	The-king went to see the-horse, and was (he) great and stout.	The king went to see the horse and it was big and fat.

The Tale of Sarcastic Halli (Old Norse)

Old Norse	Literal	English
Halli var þar hjá, er hestrinn hafði úti sinina.	Halli was there beside, when horse had extended-out tendon.	Halli was there when the horse extended its tendon.
Halli kvað þá:	Halli spoke then:	Halli then spoke:
Sýr er ávallt, *hefir saurigt* *allt hestr Þjóðólfs reðr* *hann es dróttins serðr.*	Sow as always, has filthy all horse Thjodolf's beam he is master wounder.	Sow as always, has filthy all horse Thjodolf's beam, he is master-wounder.
"Tví, tví?"	"Tut, tut?"	"Tut tut",
segir konungr, "hann kemr aldrigi í mína eign at þessu?"	said the-king, "he comes never in mine ownership at this?"	said the king, "he will not come into my ownership at this rate".
Halli gerðist hirðmaðr konungs ok bað sér orlofs til Íslands.	Halli became court-man the-king's and asked him vacation to Iceland.	Halli became the king's court man and asked him for leave to vacate to Iceland.
Konungr bað hann fara varlega fyrir Einari flugu.	The-king bid him travel warily because-of Einar Fly.	The king asked that he travel carefully because of Einar Fly.
Halli fór til Íslands ok bjó þar.	Halli went to Iceland and settled there.	Halli went to Iceland and settled there.
Eyddust honum penningar, ok lagðist hann í útróðr;	Spent his money, and lay he to out-rowing (fishing);	He spent his money and he took to fishing,
ok eitt sinn fekk hann andróða svá mikinn, at þeir tóku nauðliga land.	and one occasion had he difficulty so much, that they took necessarily land.	and on one occasion he had so much difficulty rowing back that they just reached land.
Ok um kveldit var borinn fyrir Halla grautr;	And about evening was brought before Halli porridge;	That evening porridge was brought before Halli,
ok er hann hafði etit nökkut lítit, hnígr hann aftrábak, ok var þá dauðr.	and as he had to-eat few bites, fell he back, and was then dead.	and when he had eaten a few bites, he fell back and was then dead.
Haraldr spurði lát tveggja hirðmanna sinna af Íslandi:	Harald learned had both court-men his from Iceland:	Harald learned of the death of both his court men from Iceland,
Bolla hins prúða ok Sneglu-Halla.	Bolli the Elegant and Sarcastic-Halli.	Bolli the Elegant, and Sarcastic Halli.
Hann svaraði svá til Bolla:	He answered so to Bolli:	He said of Bolli:

The Tale of Sarcastic Halli (Old Norse)

Old Norse	Literal	English
"Fyrir dörrum mun drengrinn hnigit hafa?"	"Before spears would the-boy fallen had?"	"The boy must have fallen to spears".
Enn til Halla segir hann svá:	And to Halli said he so:	And he said of Halli:
"Á grauti mundi greyit sprungit hafa?"	"On porridge would the-poor-thing burst have?"	"The poor thing must have burst eating porridge".
Lýk ek þar sögu Sneglu-Halla.	End I there the-story Sarcastic-Halli.	And there I end the story of Sarcastic Halli.
Brot ór Haralds-drápu *Svá lét und sik* *seggja dróttinn* *lönd öll lagin,* *liðs oddviti.*	Offence about Harald's-poem So gave up he said the-lord lands of-all the-songs company leader.	Offence about Harald's poem So gave he up said the Lord Lands of all the songs The leader of company.

Word List (Old Norse to English)

Old Norse	English
A, a	
aðra	another, other, others
aðrir	other
af	disrespected, from, from, in, man, of, of, off, with
afli	power
aftr	back, returning
aftrábak	back
Agðanes	Agdanes (place)
Agðaness	Agdanes (place)
Agði	Agdi (name), Agdi (name)
akta	taxes
aldrei	never
aldri	a-child
aldrigi	never
alla	completely
allir	all, all
allr	all, all
allra	all, of-all
allreiðr	all-angry
allskammr	very-short
allt	all, all
allvel	all-well
andaðr	dead
andróða	difficulty
annan	another, another, being, one, the-next
annarr	another, another, otherwise
annarra	other
annars	another, other
annat	another, other
at	a, am-I, and, as, at, by, by, for, for, in, in, it, of, of, said, than, that, that, the, the, this, to, to, up, was, with
Á, á	
á	about, an, at, be, by, for, from, in, it, of, on, that, to, was, with
á'k	I
ábyrgst	responsible
áðr	after, back, before
ágætr	excellent
ámælisverðr	talked
ári	all-year
Árnasonar	Son-of-Arni (name)
át	ate, ate, eat
átt	having
átta	related-to
átti	had, hat, married
áttu	had
ávallt	always
Æ, æ	
ætla	suppose, supposed
ætlat	intended, that
ætluðu	intended
ætt	descent
ættaðr	descended
ætti	had
ættsmár	family-small
B, b	
bað	asked, bid, invited, ordered
báðir	both
bæði	both
bafði	had
baki	back
bana-sök	death-sentence
bani	death
bann	he
bar	bears, bore, carried
Bárð	Bard (name)
Bárðr	Bard (name)

Word List (Old Norse to English)

Old Norse	English
barn	child, I
barna	children
báru	carried
báti	the-boat, the-ship's-boat
bátnum	the-boat
bauð	invited
bauglands	ring-land
beggja	both
beið	waited
beidda	asked
bekkinn	the-bench
belti	belt
betr	better
betra	better
betri	a-better
bezt	best, the-best
bið	order
biðja	ask, to-ask
bitar	bite
bitit	biting
bjó	lived, settled
blakkir	pale
bleikr	pale
boði	order
bœjar	the-town
bœndr	farmers
bœnum	town
bœta	compensation
bœti	compensate
bœtti	compensated
bokkar	bigger-men
Bolla	Bolli (name)
bóndi	farmer, master
borð	boards
borði	table, the-table
borðin	tables
borðit	table, the-table
borðum	at-table
börg	the-city
borin	brought
borinn	brought
börnin	the-children
bótunum	compensation
brá	drew
brákar	breaker
brást	transformed
brátt	soon
brauði	bread
brenndan	burnt
bróðir	brother
bróður	brother
brögðóttan	cunning
brosti	grinned, laughed, smiled
brot	offence
brott	away
brúki	use
brynju	chain-mail, coat-of-mail
brynjuna	coat-of-mail
búð	lodgings
búðarvörð	shop-keeping
bú-Finna	farmers
búi	estate
búinn	prepared, settled
búnir	prepared, ready
burt	away, brought
burtu	away
býð	command
býðr	offered
byggð	settled
byr	fair-wind

D, d

Old Norse	English
dag	day
dagana	day
daginn	the-day
danmerkr	Denmark, Denmark (place)
dáruskapr	mockery
dauðan	death
dauðir	dead
dauðr	dead
deild	room
digrastr	thick-set
disk	plate
diskinum	the-plate
diskr	a-plate
djarfan	daring

Word List (Old Norse to English)

Old Norse	English
dœmi	examples
Dönum	the-Danes (name)
dörrum	spears
dóttur	daughter
drap	killed
drápi	the-killing
drápu	a-drapa (poem), drapa (poem)
drápuna	the-drapa (poem)
draum	dream, this-dream
draumr	a-dream, dream
dregr	draws, drew
dregst	draw
drekanum	the-dragon-ship
dreki	dragon
drekka	drinking
drengi	boys
drengrinn	the-boy
drepa	kill
drepit	kill, killed
drepr	killed
dreymt	dreamed
drógu	drew
dróttinn	the-lord
dróttins	master
drottning	queen, the-queen
drottningu	the-queen
drykk	drink
drykkjar	drink
duldu	denied
dverg	the-dwarf
dverginn	the-dwarf
dvergr	dwarf
dýran	remembered

E, e

Old Norse	English
eða	but
eðr	and, but, or
ef	if, then
eftir	about, after, back, back-from
eggjaði	urged
eiga	not, own
eigi	not
eign	ownership
eina	one
Einar	Einar (name)
Einari	Einar (name)
Einarr	Einar (name), us
Einars	Einar (name), Einar's (name)
einhugi	one-minded
einkis	nothing
einmælt	one-meal
einn	alone, one
einráðir	one-decision
einu	one
eitt	once, one
ek	Halli (name), I, me
ekki	not, nothing
eld	the-fire
eldahús	fire-house (kitchen)
eldi	fire
eldingum	lightning
eldr	fire
ella	or-else
elliligt	elderly
elskaði	loved
em	am, seek
Emmu	Emma (name)
en	than
enda	and, ended, the-end
endileysu	nonsense
enga	not
engan	no, none
engi	no, none
Englandi	England (place)
Englands	England (place)
engu	none
engum	no
enn	and, but, fine, for, in-the-end, one, than, that, the, then, yet
enni	brow, forehead
er	age, are, as, I, in, is, that, then, to, was, were, what, when, where, which, who
erindi	errand, message
ert	are

Word List (Old Norse to English)

Old Norse	English
ertú	are-you
eru	are, are-we, is, so, they-are
erum	are
es	as, is, life
eta	eat, eating
etit	to-eat
etja	provoke
eyddust	spent
eyja	islands
eyjar	islands

F, f

Old Norse	English
fá	get, give
faðir	father, when
fæ	can
fær	carry-out, undertaking
Fáfni	Fafnir (name)
Fáfnis-bana	Slayer-of-Fafnir (name)
fagnar	welcomed
fáim	get
fám	a-few
fann	found
fannst	thought
far	go, passage, travel
fara	fare, go, goes, going, travel, went
farit	gone, travelled
fars	travel
fátœka	poor
fátœkr	fee-taken
fátœkra	the-poor
fátt	little
fé	money, payment
fébœtr	compensation
féhirði	fee-servant
féhirðinn	fee-servant
féit	the-money
feitr	stout
fekk	give, got, had
fekkst	received
félagi	companion
feldan	killed
fell	fell
fellt	fell
fémúta	composed
fengu	caught
fengum	travel
fénu	money
ferr	go, goes, went
festi	pierced
fimm	five
finna	find, found, the-Sami (name)
Finnferð	Finland-voyages (place)
finnskrepp	Sami-goods
firðinum	the-fjord
firrst	lost
fiskimenn	fishermen
fjár	fee
fjölda	many
fjöldi	many
fjölmennt	followers
fjóra	four
fjórar	four
fjórðung	fourth
fjörs	since
fjórtán	fourteen
fleira	more
fleiri	more
flenna	to-extend
flest	the-most
flesta	most
Fljótum	Fljot (place)
flœr-at	fleeing
fluga	Fly (name)
flugu	Fly (name)
flugust	flew
flutt	brought, delivered
flutti	brought
flýta	quickly
flytja	carried
föður	father, his
föðurbana	his
fœra	bring, brought, sent-for
fœrði	performed
fœrðr	brought

341

Word List (Old Norse to English)

Old Norse	English
fœri	went
fœrr	accomplished
fœtrnir	the-legs
fólk	people
föll	mistakes
föng	rhymes
fór	before, for, travelled, went
för	going, procession
forskeftinn	upper-shaft
fórtu	went-you
fóru	went
förum	journey
forvitnar	fore-knowing
fót	leg
fótum	feet
frá	from
frændi	kinsman
frændr	took
frændunum	kinsmen
fram	ahead, away, forwards, from
framar	from
frásagnar	from-saying
frásagnir	stories
Frísa	Frisian (name)
frískr	Frisian
fullr	full
fullt	full
fund	to-meet
fundu	found
fundumst	met
furðanliga	extremely
fúss	willing
fylgdin	followers
fylgja	follow
fyndi	find
fyr	before
fyrir	because-of, before, for, me, over
fyrr	before, went-before
fyrra	before, last
fyrri	before
fyrst	first
fyrstu	first

G, g

Old Norse	English
gabb	mockery
gæfr	agreeable
gætti	guarded
gaf	gave
gakk	go
galdra	magic
gamall	old
gaman	a-delight, delight, enjoyment, entertaining, fun, to-delight
gamans	amusement
ganga	go
gangu	going
gap	gaping
garðinn	garden, the-house, the-wall
garðinum	the-wall
garðrinn	the-wall
garðsins	the-wall
Gásum	Gasir (place)
gefa	give, granted, teach, to-give
gefi	gave, give
gefin	given
gefit	given
Geirrauð	Geirrod (name)
Geirrauðr	Geirrod (name)
gekk	got, went
geng	going
gengi	walking
gengr	going
gengu	went
ger	do, does
gera	do, doing, done, look-to, made, make
gerast	be
gerði	did, made
gerðist	became
gerðu	did, made
geri	did
geri'k	made
gerir	does, done
gerit	do

Word List (Old Norse to English)

Old Norse	English
gerla	completely
gert	do, done
get	get
getit	told
gilja?	beguile
giljum	beguile
ginning	deception
gista	guest
gjalda	pay
gjarna	gladly
glaðr	glad
gnauða	gnawing
góð	good
góða	good
góðan	good
góðr	good
góðum	good
gólf	the-floor
gólfið	of-the-floor
gólfit	the-floor
göngum	we-are-going
görr	ready-made
gott	good
grafit	dug
graut	porridge
grautar	of-porridge
grauti	porridge
grautinn	porridge, the-porridge
grautr	porridge
greppr	grasped
greyit	the-poor-thing
grið	peace
griðníðingr	truce-breaker
gripanna	the-trinkets
gripi	possessions, things, treasure
gripina	the-trinkets
gripr	possession
grís	pig
gríss	pig
grön	moustache
gruntrauðustum	deep-red
Guðinason	Godwinson (name)
guðréttligast	good-rightly
Gulaþing	Gula-assembly (name)
Gulaþings	Gula-assembly (name)
gullhlað	gold-band
gullhring	a-gold-ring, gold-ring
gullrekin	gold-inlaid
gyrði	equipped

H, h

Old Norse	English
haddan	the-handle, the-lid
háðyrðum	mocking
hærra	higher
hærri	higher
hætti	stopped
hættu	danger
haf	have
hafa	composed, had, has, have, having, that, to-have, traded, well
hafða	had
hafði	had
hafðir	had, have
hafðist	had
hafi	has
hafra	goat
Hákon	Hakon (name)
Hákoni	Hakon (name)
halda	hold, to-hold
haldit	held
hálfa	half
Halla	Halli (name), Halli's (name)
hallæri	famine
Halli	Halli (name), he
Hálogaland	Halogaland (place)
Hálogalandi	Halogaland (place)
háls	neck
hálslangr	long-neck
hana	her
handlaugar	hand-washing
handsiðr	long-armed
hanh	he
hann	called, Halli (name), he, him, Thjodolf (name)
hans	he, him, his

Word List (Old Norse to English)

Old Norse	English
hanu	he
hár	high
Haraldi	Harald (name), Harald's (name)
Haraldr	Harald (name), Harald's (name)
Haralds	Harald (name), Harald's (name)
Haralds-drápu	Harald's-poem
Háreks	Harek's (name)
háreysti	commotion
hárinu	hair, the-hairs
hásætit	high-seat
haustit	autumn
haustum	autumn
hávan	the harbour
héðan	from-there
hefði	had
hefðim	have
hefðir	had
hefir	had, has, has-been, have
hefna	avenge
hefnt	avenged, revenge
hefr	had
heiði	the-heath
heill	health
heilræði	sound-advice
heilt	rather
heim	home
hein	hone
heinar-sufl	honing-grease
heita	call, named
heitan	threat
heitir	is-named, named
hekk	hung
held	think
heldr	rather
hella	pour, poured
helt	held
helzt	rather
hendi	hand, to-hand
hendr	hand
hér	force, here
herbergi	hostel
herbergjum	sleeping-quarters
herðalítill	narrow-shouldered
herðamestr	most-hardy
herra	lord
hest	a-horse
hestinn	the-horse
hestr	horse
hestrinn	horse
hét	named, was-named
héti	named
heyra	hear, heard, to-hear
heyrða	heard
heyrði	heard
heyrðu	heard
heyrt	heard
hilmis	helmsman's
hin	the
hina	the
hinn	the
hins	his, the
hinum	the
hirð	the-court
hirðarinnar	court
hirði	care
hirðin	courtiers
hirðinni	the-court, the-court-men
hirðmaðr	court-man
hirðmanna	court-men
hit	the
Hítrar	Hitra (place)
hitt	then
hjá	beside, nearby
hjálm	helmet
hjálmfaldinn	the-helmet
Hlaðajarli	Earl-of-Lade (name)
hlaðna	ladened
hlaupi	running
hlaut	a-lot-of
Hleyp'k	running
hleypr	ran
hljóð	a-hearing, silence
hljóða	calm
hljóðgreipum	sound-grippers (ears)
hljóðit	silence
hljóðs	be-heard
hljóp	jumped

Word List (Old Norse to English)

Old Norse	English
hljópu	ran
hlotizt	part
hlut	part, share
hluti	a-thing
hlutr	part
hlýða	obeying, suits
hlýði	listen
hnakka	neck
hnífskefti	knife-handle
hnigit	fallen
hnígr	fell
hœgri	other
höfðingja	chieftains
höfðingjar	chieftains
höfðu	had
hófi	reasonable
höfuð	head
höfuðit	head
höfuðskáld	chief-poet
höggva	to-strike
höldnum	held
höllina	the-hall
höllinni	the-hall
hon	it, she
hönd	hand
höndum	hand
honum	he, he, him, his, his, of-him, to-him
horfa	turn
horfin	lost
hornspánu	horn-spoon
hóti	not
hótun	a-threat
hræddir	afraid
hraustliga	boldly
hríð	awhile
hring	the-ring
hringinn	the-ring
hringnum	the-ring
hringum	circles
hroðit	cleared
hróðr	fame
hrökkvi-skafls	shaken
hröng	roaring
hrópyrði	obscenities
hrygg	the-spine
hryggrinn	spine
húðar	hide
hug	mind
hugar	minds
hugða	thought
hugðu	thought
humrum	lobsters
hungrar	hungry
hús	a-house
hvaðan	from-where
hvar	where
hvárigum	neither
hvárn	each
hvárr	each
hvárt	each, whether
hvárttveggja	each-way
hvat	that, what
hvatt	encouraged
hvé	how
hverfr	turned
hvergi	nowhere
hverjar	that
hverju	what, which
hverjum	each
hverr	what, who
hvers	how-so
hversu	how-so
hvert	each, what, where
hveru	each, what, whom
hví	if, why
hygg	think

I, i

Old Norse	English
iðnar	trade
ilfat	sole-bucket
illa	bad, badly, evil
illan	evil
illt	ill
ilvegs	evil-ways
inn	in, of, then
innan	in, inside
innanborðs	onboard
innar	in

Word List (Old Norse to English)

Old Norse	English

Í, í

Old Norse	English
í	a, about, as, at, by, in, into, of, on, that, the, to, was, with
Ísland	Iceland (place)
Íslandi	Iceland (place)
Íslands	Iceland (place)
Íslands-fari	Iceland-voyage
íslendinga	Icelanders
íslendingar	Icelanders
íslenzka	Icelander
íslenzkan	Icelander
íslenzkr	an-Icelander, Icelander

J, j

Old Norse	English
jafnan	always, equally, usually
jafngreypiliga	equally-badly
jafnir	equal
jafnsleppt	equally-slip
jarl	an-earl, earl
jarls	the-earl's
járn	iron-weapon
járnsmiðr	ironsmith
jaxlar	molars
jöfnum	even
jóladag	Yule-day
jólin	Yule
jólum	Yule
jólunum	Yule
Jótlands	Jutland (place)
jötni	giant
jötun	the-giant

K, k

Old Norse	English
kæra	accuse, discuss
kærleikum	dear-friendship, friendship
kagtat	cast
kálf	a-calf
kálfinn	the-calf
kálfrinn	the-calf
kalla	to-call
kallaði	called, the-king
kallaðir	be-called
kallaðr	called
kann	can, can-it, knows
kanntú	know-you
karlmanni	a-man
kastaði	cast
katli	and
katlinum	the-kettle
kátr	cheerful
kaup	had
Kaupang	Kaupang (place)
Kaupangs	Kapuang (place)
kaupferð	trading-voyage
kaupmennirnir	merchant-men
kaupmönnum	the-trading-men, trading-men
kaupskipinu	merchant-ship, trading-ship
kem	come
kemr	came, come, comes
kendi	hands
kenn	know
kenna	know, teach
kenndi	felt
kennt	blame
keyptut	bought
kilju	the-binding
kjöts	flesh
klámyrði	obscene
klámyrðum	obscene-words
klappaði	rapped, struck
klappar	hammering
klukku	a-bell
kné	knee
kníf	knife
knífi	knife
knífinum	knife
knörru	knorrs
knúskim	knocked-down
köllu	call
kölluðu	called
Kollu-vísur	cow-verses

Word List (Old Norse to English)

Old Norse	English
kom	came, come
koma	come, come-forward
kominn	coming
komit	came, come, coming
komst	came
komu	came
komum	came
konung	the-king
konunga	kings
konungi	the-king, the-king's
konunginn	the-king
konunginum	the-king
konungr	him, king, king's, the-king, the-king's
konungrinn	the-king
konungs	the-king, the-king's
konungsgarð	the-king
konungsins	the-king
kostr	a-choice
kunna	know
kunnu	could
kurteiss	polite
kúrvaldi	folded
kvað	recited, said, spoke
kvaddi	called, greeted
kváðu	recited
kvæði	composed, poem, poems, recited
kvæðin	poems
kvæðinu	the-poem
kvæðisins	the-poem
kvæðis-launin	poem-reward
kvæðis-mynd	poem-image
kvæðit	poem, the-poem
kvæðunum	the-poetry
kveð	recite
kveð'k	say
kveða	compose, recite
kveðin	recited, worded
kveðinn	after
kveðit	spoken, worded
kveðju	greeting
kveðr	recited, words
kveðst	said
kveld	the-evening
kveldit	evening
kvenna	women
kviðlingr	short-poem
kyns	kin
kýr	cows
kyrrt	peace, peaceful

L, l

Old Norse	English
lá	lay
læt	have
læt'k	let
lagði	became, laid
lagðist	lay
lagin	assigned, songs
lágu	laid, lay
lágum	laid
land	land
landi	land, the-land
landinu	the-land
langa	long
langskip	longships
lát	had, have
láta	allow, have
látir	leave
látit	had, let
launa	reward
launaði	rewarded
launin	also
laus	lost
laut	bowed
leðr	skin
legg	lay
leggja	allow, lay
leggr	laid
leið	passed
leiða	lead
leiðar	on-way
leigðu	rented
leika	games, play
leista	of-footwear
leita	find, look-for, seeking
leitaði	sought
leitaðir	seek
lendr	land
lengi	long

347

Word List (Old Norse to English)

Old Norse	English
lér	leaned
lét	gave, had
létti	let-up
léttum	let-up
leys	repay
leyst	answered
liðs	company
líf	life
lífi	life
lífinu	his-life, your-life
liggja	lie
líkaði	liked
líkar	consider, like, liked
líklegr	likely
líkr	like
lít'k	coloured
lítast	looked
lítil	little, men
lítilla	little
lítilsvert	little
lítilþægir	easily-satisfied
lítilþægr	little-behaving
lítinn	little
litist	looked
lítit	bites, little
litlu	a-little
lítt	little
ljóst	light
ljótlimaðr	ugly-limbed
ljúgi	lie
loðir	of-your-hair
lof	permission, praise
lofa	promise
loft	praised
lofuðu	praised
lögðu	laid
lögskilum	legal-settlement
lokit	concluded, ended, finished
lönd	land, lands
lyftingunni	lifting
lýgr	lies, lying
lýk	end
lykkja	noose
lykkjan	the-noose
lysti	appetite
lýsu	the-whitings

M, m

Old Norse	English
má	may
maðr	a-man, man, the-man
maðrinn	the-man
mæl	speak
mæla	matter, matters, say, speak
mælti	spoke
mæltist	recited
Magnús	Magnus (name)
maka	equal
makligra	well-deserved
makligri	more-suitable
makligust	the-best
mál	matter
málefnum	matters
málit	the-matter
málspörf	matter
málum	matter, matters
mann	becomes, man
manna	man, men, people
manni	man
mannsbarn	man's-son
marga	many
margir	many
margs	many, many-things
margt	many
mat	food
matar	food
matr	food
mátti	as-might, may
með	with
meðan	as-long-as, while
megin	side
megu	may
mein	harm, mean
meir	more
meira	more
meiri	more
menn	men, people
menntr	educated

Word List (Old Norse to English)

Old Norse	English
mér	because, for-me, I, intended, me, mine, my, to-me
merkr	marks
mest	high, most, there
mesta	most
mestu	most
mettir	finished-eating, satisfied
mettr	finished-eating, satisfied
mik	me
mikill	great, much
mikils	great
mikinn	much
mikit	great, much
mikla	great, greatest
Miklagarði	Byzantium (place)
miklu	much
miklum	much
milli	between
mína	mine, my
mínir	kinsman
minn	father, mine
minna	less, lesser, mine
míns	mine
mínu	mine
mínum	mine
mislíkaði	mis-liked
missa	lose, miss
mitt	mine, the-middle
mjök	much
mjöli	meal
mœttum	met
mönnum	the-people
morgininn	morning
mörk	a-mark, one-mark
mörkina	the-border
móti	against, meet
mun	could, shall, should, should-be, then, will, would, would-be
mun'k	will
muna	would
munaðr	little
munar	delight
munat	remembered
munda	remembered
mundi	could-be, should-be, would
mundir	would
mundu	could, could-be, would
muni	shall
munni	mouth
munt	must, should
muntú	shall-you, should, would-you
munu	shall, would

N, n

Old Norse	English
ná	obtain, take
naðri	serpent
næða	neared
nær	near
nærri	close-to, near
næst	near
næsta	next
nafn	named
nam	took
námu	took
nauðliga	necessarily
nauðsyn	necessary
nauðsynja	needs
nautaleðrs	ox-skin
neðan	below
neflangr	long-nosed
nefndr	named
nei	no
nema	but, except
níð	slander
níðit	the-slander
niðr	down
Njörðr	Njord (name)
njót	enjoy
njótum	benefit
nóg	enough
nökkur	some, something
nökkura	any
nökkurr	something

Word List (Old Norse to English)

Old Norse	English
nökkuru	one-of, some, somehow, somewhat
nökkurum	some
nökkut	anything, few, something, somewhat
norðr	north
norðrlönd	northern-lands
Noreg	Norway (place)
Noregi	Norway (place)
Noregs	Norway (place)
nótt	night, the-night
nóttum	nights
nú	no, not, now

O, o

Old Norse	English
oddviti	leader
of	of, off
ofan	over
offylli	gluttony
ofraun	too-much
oftar	again, more
og	and
ok	also, and, killed, this, yours
olli	cause
opit	open
orð	word
orða	words
orðaskil	words-separated
orðfátt	word-fallen
orðgreppr	word-bold
orðhákr	word-tall
orðhvass	sharp-tongued
orðinn	of-words
orðit	become, worded
orðum	words
orlofs	vacation
orm	the-serpent
ort	had, worded, words
orta	worded
orti	worded
oss	tell, to-us, us, we

Ó, ó

Old Norse	English
óðindælu	puzzle
óeyrðarmaðr	unreliable
ógrligr	terrible
óp	shouting
ór	about, from, of, out, out-of
órleysingr	over-praised
órlofs	vacation
ósiðblendnir	un-custom-mixing
óskerðan	the-whole
ótæpt	unsettled
óþökk	un-thanks
ótíginna	un-ranking
ótrúligir	un-truthful
óvirðuligt	unworthy

Ö, ö

Old Norse	English
öðru	the-other
öðrum	eachother, other, others
öðruvísi	other-knowing
öfigt	reversed
öfundsjúkr	un-infatuated
öll	all, of-all
öllu	all
öndvert	upside-down
öngan	no
öngvan	none
önnur	another
ösku	ashes
öxarinnar	the-axe
öxi	an-axe, axe
öxina	the-axe

Œ, œ

Old Norse	English
œpir	cried-out
œptu	called-out
œrit	greatly
œrr	awed

Word List (Old Norse to English)

Old Norse	English

P, p

penningar	money
penningum	payment
prettr	trick
prettum	trickery
prófa	prove
prúða	Elegant (name)
prýði	finery

R, r

ráð	advice, plan
ráða	decided
ráðar	decide
ráði	advised
ráðigastr	well-advising
ráðinn	appointed
ráðleitinn	cunning
ráðs	agreement
ræð'k	speak
ræsi	the-ruler
rán	robbery
rana	the-trunk
Ránar	Ran (name)
randa	round
rangt	wrong
rannsóknar	a-search
Rauð	Raud (name)
rauðan	the-red
rauðar	red
Rauðr	Raud (name)
rauðum	red
réð	ruled
reðr	beam
reðra	genitals
réðst	appointed, took
réðust	decided
reiðasti	most-angry
reiði	anger
Rein	Reine (place)
rétti	extended
réttr	upright
reyndar	actually
reyndust	proved
reynt	tested
ríkari	richer
ritat	written
röru	rowing
rúghleifa	rye-loaf
rúms	rooms
runa	row
ryðja	cleared
rymskyndir	quickly-cleared

S, s

sá	looked, saw, so
sá's	so
sæhafa	sea-scattered
sæsjúkr	seasick
sæti	sit
sætis	seat
sættir	settlements
sættust	settled
sagða	said
sagði	said, told, told-of
sagðir	said, said
sagðist	said
sagt	said, said, told, told-to
sakir	sake
saklausa	sake-less
sama	same
saman	together
sami	same
sannmæli	true-words
sarð	wounded
sásk	with-footwear
satt	true, truth
satt?	TRUE
sátu	sat, were
sáu	saw
saurigt	filthy
sé	see, so
sé'k	see
seg	tell
seggja	said
seggr	said

Word List (Old Norse to English)

Old Norse	English
segi	say
segir	said
segit	tell
segja	Einar (name), say, to-tell
seinþreyttr	persistent
séit	look
selda'k	that
selja	barter, to-sell
sem	as, same-as, where, which
send	send
sendi	sent
sendingum	delivery
senn	but
sennur	chatter
sér	for-him, him, himself, his, saw, sees, themselves, to
serðast	to-get-hurt
serðr	wounder
sessunaut	bench-companion
sessunautr	bench-companion
sét	seen
setit	sat
setja	set
settist	sat, settled
settliga	sedately
settu	set
sezt	sat
síð	long
síðan	after, afterwards, since, then
síðar	afterwards, later
síðast	the-last
siðr	a-custom, the-custom
síðu	side
síður	since
sigldi	sailed
sigldu	sailed
Sigurð	Sigurd (name)
Sigurðarson	Sigurdson (name)
Sigurði	Sigurd (name)
Sigurðr	Sigurd (name)
sik	he, him, himself
silfr	silver
silfrhólkr	silver-band
silfri	silver
silfrinu	the-silver
silfrs	of-silver
silfrvafit	silver-wound
sín	his, themselves
sína	his
sinina	tendon
sinn	father's-killer, his, occasion, theirs, then
sinna	his
sinnar	his, their
sinni	himself, these
síns	father, his
sínu	his
sínum	his, theirs
sit	sit
sit'k	one, sit
sitja	settle, sit
sitr	sat
sitt	himself, his, their, this
síu	sift
siz'k	about
sízt	least
sjá	see
sjaldan	seldom
sjálfr	himself, yourself
sjálfs	self's
sjálfum	himself
sjóða	boil
sjóði	purse
sjóðnum	the-purse
sjúkr	sick
skaði	harm
skaftit	the-shaft
skal	shall, should
skál	shall
skáld	a-poet, poet, poets, the-poet
skálda	poets
skáldi	the-poet
skáldskap	poetry
skáldskapar	a-poet
skall	hit, rattled
skalt	shall
skaltú	shall-you

Word List (Old Norse to English)

Old Norse	English
skapdreki	mood-dragon
skapi	mind, mood
skarlatsklæðum	scarlet
skemt	entertainment
skemta	entertain
skerði	cuts
skift	exchange
skilat	settled
skinna	of-skins
skip	ship, the-ship
skipin	the-ships
skipinu	the-ship
skipit	ship, the-ship
skipsmiðir	ship-smiths
skipuðu	ships
skjöld	shield
skjótt	quickly, rapidly
skó	shoes
skömm	disgrace, scandal
skreið	crawled
skreppa	bag
skreppu-skrúði	bag-tackle
skrýfði	scrawled
skuld	debt
skulu	should
skulum	shall
skulut	should
skylda	would
skyldara	should
skyldi	should, would
skyldu	should, should-be, would
skylt	should
skyrkaupum	cow-buying
sleggju	the-hammer
slíðrar	sheathed
slík	such
slíka	such
slíkir	such
slíkt	such
smiðbelgja	smith-bellows
smiðju	of-the-smith
smjörvan	buttered
snætt	dined
snák	snake
snaraði	rushed
Sneglu-Halla	Sarcastic-Halli (name)
Sneglu-Halli	Sarcastic-Halli (name)
snöri	turned
snúa	return
snúit	turned
sœkir	sought
sofa	sleep
sögðu	announced, told
sögðuzt	said
sögu	the-story
sómir	common
son	son
Sorptrogs-vísur	food-trough-verses
sótt	not
spán	a-spoon
spara	withhold
sprengja	burst
sprungit	burst
spryngi	burst
spurði	asked, asking, learned
spurðu	asked
spurt	heard, questions
spyrr	asked
Stað	Stad (place), the-place
staðar	place
staddr	to
standa	standing
standit	standing
steiktr	roasted
steinn	a-stone
stendr	standing, stands
stígandi	ascending
stillir	heading
stóð	place, stood
stœrri	greater
stórlyndr	large-repaying (generous)
stórmannliga	big-man-like
stórra	great
stórum	great, stone-kettle
stræti	the-street
stríði	battles

Word List (Old Norse to English)

Old Norse	English
ströndu	the-shore
stund	awhile
stundu	awhile
stykki	piece
stýrimaðr	steersman
stýrir	steers
styrk	strong
sú	the-one
suðr	south
suðrmenn	southern-men, the-southerners
sufli	with-bread
sumar	summer
sumargamlan	one-summer-old
sumir	some
sumt	some
sútari	tanner
svá	coming, so, then
svangir	hungry
svara	answer, to-answer
svaraði	answered
svarar	answered
svarat	answered
Svarfaðardal	Svarfadardal (place)
svefni	sleep
sveini	this-lad
sveltir	starving
sverð	sword
sverði	a-sword, sword
sverðit	sword
svífst	shrinks-from
svíni	swine
sýlt	sleek
sýn	I
sýna	showed
sýndi	showed
sýndisk	seems
sýndist	thought
sýnir	show
sýnist	seems
synjuðu	refused
sýnna	appear
sýr	sow
sýslu	business, stewardship
systkinum	siblings

T, t

Old Norse	English
tak	take
taka	take
taki	takes
takist	take
takit	take
tala	speak, speaking
talaði	talked
talast	speak
talat	talking
tangar	tongs
taumi	leash
taums-endanum	the-leash
taumsins	the-leash
tekit	taken
tekizt	taken
tíðinda	news
tíðindi	news
tignari	nobler
tiguligr	dignified
til	about, as, for, into, that, to, towards, until, up-to
tíma	time
tíu	ten
tjöru	tar
tœki	take
tók	received, took
tóku	and, took
tókum	took
töluðu	spoke
torf	turf
trog	trough
trúa	believe
túngarði	hayfield-wall
Túta	Tuta (name)
Tútu	Tuta (name)
tvá	two
tveggja	both
tveir	two
tví	tut
tvíræð	ambiguous
tvíræðis-orð	ambiguous

Word List (Old Norse to English)

Old Norse	English
tvöföld	two-fold

Þ, þ

Old Norse	English
þá	in, now, then, though
það	that
þaðan	from-there
þær	there
þagna	silence
þagnaði	silenced
þakkaði	thanked, thanked
þangað	from-there
þangat	from-there, from-there
þann	that, that, then
þar	that, there, they, they
þar's	there
þari	intestines
þat	is, it, it, than, that, the, this, though, to-me, which
þau	there
þegar	already, as-soon-as, early, from-there, straight-away, then
þegnar	men
þeim	for-them, them, they
þeir	the, them, they
þeira	theirs, them
þeiri	of-them, theirs
þenna	then, this
þér	to-you, you, yours
þess	this
þessa	this
þessarrar	this
þessi	repay, these, this
þessu	this
þetta	it, that, these, this
þiggi	receives
þik	you
þing	assembly
þinga	assemble
þinginn	the-assembly
þingit	the-assembly
þings	the-assembly
þingsins	the-assembly

Old Norse	English
Þingvalla	Thingvellir (place)
þinn	yours
þíns	yours
þínu	yours
þit	you-two
þitt	yours
Þjóðólf	Thjodolf (name)
Þjóðólfi	Thjodolf (name)
Þjóðólfr	Thjodolf (name)
Þjóðólfs	Thjodolf's (name)
þjófr	thief
þjón	servant
þjóna	serve
þjónusta	service
þjónustu	service
þjónustumenn	the-servants
Þjóttu	Thjotta (place)
þó	shall, then, though
þœtti	seems
þœttist	thought
þögnuðu	silenced
þökk	thanks
þola	enduring
þoldi	endured
þolir	endures
þöngul	there
Þór	Thor (name)
Þóra	Thora (name)
Þórbergs	Thorberg's (name)
þori	dare
Þórleifi	Thorleif (name)
Þórleifr	Thorleif (name)
Þórljóti	Thorljot (name)
Þórljótr	Thorljot (name)
þorpi	village
Þórr	Thor (name)
Þóru	Thora (name)
þótt	though, though
þótti	seemed, thought
þóttir	thought
þóttist	thought
þóttu	thought
þóttumst	seemed, thought
þóttust	thought
þræta	argued

Word List (Old Norse to English)

Old Norse	English
þrætu	threatening
Þrándheim	Trondheim (place)
Þrándheims	Trondheim (place)
þrevett	three-winters-old
þriðja	a-third, third
þrjár	three
þrjú	three
þú	you
þula	thula (poem)
þunga	heavy-cargo
þurfti	needed
þverliga	crossly
því	accordingly, because, before, since, that, then, therefore
þykki	seems, think
þykkir	consider, considered, seems, that, think
þykkja	seemed
þyrði	dared

U, u

Old Norse	English
um	about, at, if
und	up
undan	out-from, under
undarligt	scandalous
undir	under
undr	wonder
undrskapaðr	wonder-created
unnit	won
unz	until
upp	up, upped, up-to, we-are
upphaf	beginning
ut	out

Ú, ú

Old Norse	English
út	about, out, outside
útan	out, without
útar	out
úthlaupi	out-running
úti	extended-out, out
útivist	out-journey
útróðr	out-rowing (fishing)

V, v

Old Norse	English
vændis	wicked
vænstr	promising
vænti	expected
væri	being, was, were, would, would-be
vakit	awake
vaknaða	awoke
váligrar	wretched
ván	expected
vandi	difficult
vánligt	expected
vanr	custom
vápnast	armed
var	have, mine, that, was, were, who
varð	became, came, was, were
varði	were
varðist	guarded
várit	spring
várkunn	understandable
varla	hardly
varlega	warily
varliga	warily
varp	threw
várr	our
váru	our, was, were, where
várum	were
veðja	wager
veðjanin	the-wager
veðjanina	wager
veg	way
vegar	way
veginn	was
veik	turned
veit	know, known
veita	grant
veitt	given
vekja	awaken
vel	good, had, well

Word List (Old Norse to English)

Old Norse	English
veltr	hung
ver	be
vér	are-we, we
vera	be, become, being, one, to-be, was, wished
verða	be, becomes, being, have-been, worth
verðr	money-bribe, worthy
verit	become, been
verk	work
verkmanns	workman's
verkum	actions
verr	worse
verra	was, worse, worst
verri	worse
vert	worth
vetr	winter
vetri	winter
vetrinn	winter
vetrvistar	winter-lodgings, winter-provisions
við	about, against, at, from, of, to, with
víg	slaying
vil	will, wish
vilda	wished
vildi	wanted, willed, wished
vilit	wish
vilja	to-be, wished
vilju	wish
viljum	we-wish, wish
vill	will, wish, wishes
vilt	will
viltú	will-you
vinskapr	friendship
virði	before, worthied
vísan	the-verse, verse
víss	certain
vissi	knew
vissu	knew
vist	provisions
víst	certainly
vistaðist	found-a-place
vistar	lodgings
vistin	the-supply
vistina	the-provisions
vísu	a-verse
vit	know, we, wit, with
vita	knew, know, to-know
vitit	know
vitrastr	the-wisest
vitsmuna	intellect
vöru	were

Y, y

Old Norse	English
yðar	you
yðarr	of-you
yðart	your, yours
yðr	you
yðrum	yours
yfir	over, sitting
ykkr	you
ynni	won
yrði	became, should, was
yrk	compose, write
yrkisefnin	the-themes
yrkis-efnin	compose
yrkja	compose, to-compose

Ý, ý

Old Norse	English
ýmsu	about
ýttu	pushed
ýttum	pushed

Word List (English to Old Norse)

English	Old Norse
A, a	
about	á, á, á, á, á, á, á, á, á, á'k
an	á
at	á, á, á, á, á
after	áðr, áðr, áðr, aðra
another	aðra, ætlat, ætluðu, ætt, ættaðr, ætti, ættsmár, af
Agdanes (place)	Agðanes, Agðaness
Agdi (name)	Agði, Agði
a-child	aldri
all	allir, allir, allr, allr, allra, allreiðr, allt, allt, allvel
all-angry	allreiðr
all-well	allvel
all-year	ári
a	at, at
am-I	at
and	at, at, at, at, at, at, at, at
as	at, at, at, at, at, at
ate	át, át
always	ávallt, bað
asked	bað, bað, bað, báðir, bæði
a-better	betri
ask	biðja
at-table	borðum
away	brott, brynju, brynju, brynjuna
a-plate	diskr
a-drapa (poem)	drápu
a-dream	draumr
alone	einn
am	em
age	er
are	er, er, er, er
are-you	ertú
are-we	eru, eru
a-few	fám
accomplished	fœrr
ahead	fram
agreeable	gæfr
a-delight	gaman
amusement	gamans
a-gold-ring	gullhring
autumn	haustit, haustum
avenge	hefna
avenged	hefnt
a-horse	hest
a-lot-of	hlaut
a-hearing	hljóð
a-thing	hluti
a-threat	hótun
afraid	hræddir
awhile	hríð, hringum, hroðit
a-house	hús
an-Icelander	íslenzkr
an-earl	jarl
accuse	kæra
a-calf	kálf
a-man	karlmanni, kastaði
a-bell	klukku
a-choice	kostr
assigned	lagin
allow	láta, láta
also	launin, laus
answered	leyst, liðs, líf, lífi
a-little	litlu
appetite	lysti
as-might	mátti
as-long-as	meðan
a-mark	mörk
against	móti, móti
any	nökkura
anything	nökkut
awed	œrr
again	oftar
ashes	ösku
an-axe	öxi
axe	öxi
advice	ráð
advised	ráði
appointed	ráðinn, ráðleitinn
agreement	ráðs
a-search	rannsóknar
anger	reiði

Word List (English to Old Norse)

actually	reyndar	*bite*	bitar
afterwards	síðan, síðar	*biting*	bitit
a-custom	siðr	*bigger-men*	bokkar
a-poet	skáld, skáldskapar	*Bolli (name)*	Bolla
announced	sögðu	*boards*	borð
a-spoon	spán	*brought*	borin, borinn, bótunum, brá, brákar, brauði, brenndan
asking	spurði		
a-stone	steinn		
ascending	stígandi	*breaker*	brákar
answer	svara	*bread*	brauði
a-sword	sverði	*burnt*	brenndan
appear	sýnna	*brother*	bróðir, bróður
already	þegar	*boys*	drengi
as-soon-as	þegar	*but*	eða, eðr, eðr, ef, eftir
assembly	þing	*back-from*	eftir
assemble	þinga	*brow*	enni
argued	þræta	*bring*	fœra
a-third	þriðja	*because-of*	fyrir
accordingly	því	*became*	gerðist, gerðu, gerðu, geri
ambiguous	tvíræð, tvíræðis-orð		
awake	vakit	*beguile*	gilja?, giljum
awoke	vaknaða	*beside*	hjá
armed	vápnast	*be-heard*	hljóðs
awaken	vekja	*boldly*	hraustliga
actions	verkum	*bad*	illa
a-verse	vísu	*badly*	illa
		be-called	kallaðir
		blame	kennt

B, b

		bought	keyptut
		bowed	laut
be	á, á, á, á, á	*bites*	lítit
by	á, á, á, á	*becomes*	mann, mann
back	áðr, áðr, aðra, ætlat, ætluðu	*because*	mér, mér
		Byzantium (place)	Miklagarði
before	áðr, aðra, ætlat, ætluðu, ætt, ættaðr, ætti, ættsmár, af	*between*	milli
		below	neðan
		benefit	njótum
being	annan, annarr, annarr, annars	*become*	orðit, ort, ösku
		beam	reðr
bid	bað	*barter*	selja
both	báðir, bæði, bafði, baki	*bench-companion*	sessunaut, sessunautr
bears	bar	*boil*	sjóða
bore	bar	*bag*	skreppa
Bard (name)	Bárð, Bárðr	*bag-tackle*	skreppu-skrúði
belt	belti	*buttered*	smjörvan
better	betr, betra	*burst*	sprengja, sprungit, spryngi
best	bezt		

359

Word List (English to Old Norse)

big-man-like	stórmannliga	*comes*	kemr
battles	stríði	*cow-verses*	Kollu-vísur
business	sýslu	*come-forward*	koma
believe	trúa	*coming*	kominn, komit, komit
beginning	upphaf	*could*	kunnu, kúrvaldi, kvaddi
been	verit	*compose*	kveða, kveðinn, kveðju, kveldit

C, c

		cows	kýr
		company	lids
completely	alla, allir	*consider*	líkar, líkar
carried	bar, Bárð, Bárðr	*coloured*	lít'k
child	barn	*concluded*	lokit
children	barna	*could-be*	mundi, mundu
compensation	bœta, bœti, bœtti	*close-to*	nærri
compensate	bœti	*cried-out*	œpir
compensated	bœtti	*called-out*	œptu
cunning	brögðóttan, brosti	*cause*	olli
chain-mail	brynju	*chatter*	sennur
coat-of-mail	brynju, brynjuna	*cuts*	skerði
command	býð	*crawled*	skreið
can	fæ, fær	*cow-buying*	skyrkaupum
carry-out	fær	*common*	sómir
companion	félagi	*crossly*	þverliga
composed	fémúta, fengu, fénu	*considered*	þykkir
caught	fengu	*custom*	vanr
called	hann, hann, hann, hann, hans	*certain*	víss
commotion	háreysti	*certainly*	víst
call	heita, heitir		
court	hirðarinnar		

D, d

care	hirði		
courtiers	hirðin	*descent*	ætt
court-man	hirðmaðr	*descended*	ættaðr
court-men	hirðmanna	*disrespected*	af
calm	hljóða	*dead*	andaðr, andróða, annan
chieftains	höfðingja, höfðingjar	*difficulty*	andróða
chief-poet	höfuðskáld	*death-sentence*	bana-sök
circles	hringum	*death*	bani, bann
cleared	hroðit, hróðr	*drew*	brá, brákar, brauði
cast	kagtat, kálf	*day*	dag, dagana
can-it	kann	*Denmark*	danmerkr
cheerful	kátr	*Denmark (place)*	Danmerkr
come	kem, kemr, kemr, kemr, kendi	*daring*	djarfan
came	kemr, kemr, kemr, kendi, kenn, kenna, kenndi	*daughter*	dóttur
		drapa (poem)	drápu
		dream	draum, draumr

360

Word List (English to Old Norse)

English	Old Norse
draws	dregr
draw	dregst
dragon	dreki
drinking	drekka
dreamed	dreymt
drink	drykk, drykkjar
denied	duldu
dwarf	dvergr
delivered	flutt
delight	gaman, gaman
do	ger, ger, gera, gera
does	ger, gera
doing	gera
done	gera, gera, gera
did	gerði, gerði, gerðist
deception	ginning
dug	grafit
deep-red	gruntrauðustum
danger	hættu
discuss	kæra
dear-friendship	kærleikum
down	niðr
decided	ráða, ráðar
decide	ráðar
delivery	sendingum
disgrace	skömm
debt	skuld
dined	snætt
dare	þori
dared	þyrði
dignified	tiguligr
difficult	vandi

E, e

English	Old Norse
excellent	ágætr
eat	át, átt
estate	búi
examples	dœmi
Einar (name)	Einar, Einari, Einarr, Einars, Einars
Einar's (name)	Einars
elderly	elliligt
Emma (name)	Emmu
ended	enda, Englandi
England (place)	Englandi, Englands
errand	erindi
eating	eta
extremely	furðanliga
enjoyment	gaman
entertaining	gaman
equipped	gyrði
Earl-of-Lade (name)	Hlaðajarli
each	hvárn, hvárr, hvárt, hvárttveggja, hvatt, hvé
each-way	hvárttveggja
encouraged	hvatt
evil	illa, illan
evil-ways	ilvegs
equally	jafnan
equally-badly	jafngreypiliga
equal	jafnir, jafnsleppt
equally-slip	jafnsleppt
earl	jarl
even	jöfnum
evening	kveldit
easily-satisfied	lítilþægir
end	lýk
educated	menntr
except	nema
enjoy	njót
enough	nóg
eachother	öðrum
Elegant (name)	prúða
extended	rétti
entertainment	skemt
entertain	skemta
exchange	skift
early	þegar
enduring	þola
endured	þoldi
endures	þolir
extended-out	úti
expected	vænti, væri, vakit

F, f

English	Old Norse
for	á, á, á, á'k, áðr, áðr
from	á, á, á, á'k, áðr, áðr, áðr, aðra
family-small	ættsmár
farmers	bœndr, bœta
farmer	bóndi

Word List (English to Old Norse)

English	Old Norse
fair-wind	byr
fire-house (kitchen)	eldahús
fire	eldi, eldingum
fine	enn
forehead	enni
father	faðir, fæ, fær, Fáfni
Fafnir (name)	Fáfni
found	fann, far, fara
fare	fara
fee-taken	fátœkr
fee-servant	féhirði, féhirðinn
fell	fell, fellt, fémúta
five	fimm
find	finna, finna, Finnferð
Finland-voyages (place)	Finnferð
fishermen	fiskimenn
fee	fjár
followers	fjölmennt, fjóra
four	fjóra, fjórar
fourth	fjórðung
fourteen	fjórtán
Fljot (place)	Fljótum
fleeing	flœr-at
Fly (name)	fluga, flugu
flew	flugust
fore-knowing	forvitnar
feet	fótum
forwards	fram
from-saying	frásagnar
Frisian (name)	Frísa
Frisian	frískr
full	fullr, fullt
follow	fylgja
first	fyrst, fyrstu
fun	gaman
famine	hallæri
from-there	héðan, hefði, hefðim, hefðir, hefir, hefir
force	hér
fallen	hnigit
fame	hróðr
from-where	hvaðan
friendship	kærleikum, kagtat
felt	kenndi
flesh	kjöts
folded	kúrvaldi
finished	lokit
food	mat, matar, matr
for-me	mér
finished-eating	mettir, mettr
few	nökkut
finery	prýði
filthy	saurigt
for-him	sér
father's-killer	sinn
food-trough-verses	Sorptrogs-vísur
for-them	þeim
found-a-place	vistaðist

G, g

English	Old Norse
grinned	brosti
get	fá, fá, faðir
give	fá, faðir, fæ, fær
go	far, fara, fara, fara, fara
goes	fara, fara
going	fara, farit, fátœkr, fátt, fé
gone	farit
got	fekk, fekk
guarded	gætti, gaf
gave	gaf, gakk, galdra
gaping	gap
garden	garðinn
Gasir (place)	Gásum
granted	gefa
given	gefin, gefit, Geirrauð
Geirrod (name)	Geirrauð, Geirrauðr
guest	gista
gladly	gjarna
glad	glaðr
gnawing	gnauða
good	góð, góða, góðan, góðr, góðum, gott, grafit
grasped	greppr
Godwinson (name)	Guðinason
good-rightly	guðréttligast
Gula-assembly (name)	Gulaþing, Gulaþings
gold-band	gullhlað
gold-ring	gullhring
gold-inlaid	gullrekin

Word List (English to Old Norse)

goat	hafra	high	hár, Haraldi
giant	jötni	Harald (name)	Haraldi, Haraldi, Haraldr
greeted	kvaddi	Harald's (name)	Haraldi, Haraldr, Haraldr
greeting	kveðju		
games	leika	Harald's-poem	Haralds-drápu
great	mikill, mikill, mikils, mikinn, mikit, mikit	Harek's (name)	Háreks
		hair	hárinu
greatest	mikla	high-seat	hásætit
greatly	œrit	has-been	hefir
gluttony	offylli	health	heill
genitals	reðra	home	heim
greater	stœrri	hone	hein
grant	veita	honing-grease	heinar-sufl
		hung	hekk, helt
		hand	hendi, hendr, hér, hér
		here	hér

H, h

had	ætti, ættsmár, af, af, af, af, af, aftr, aftrábak, ágætr, Agðanes, Agðaness, Agði, Agði, aldri, alla, allir, allir, allr, allr, allra	hostel	herbergi
		horse	hestr, hestrinn
		hear	heyra
		heard	heyra, heyrða, heyrði, heyrðu, heyrt, hilmis
		helmsman's	hilmis
		Hitra (place)	Hítrar
having	átt, átti	helmet	hjálm
hat	átti	head	höfuð, höfuðit
he	bann, bar, bar, bar, Bárð, Bárðr, barn, barn, barna	horn-spoon	hornspánu
		hide	húðar
		hungry	hungrar, hús
Halli (name)	ek, ek, ek, eldahús	how	hvé
his	föður, föðurbana, fœra, fœra, fœrðr, fœrr, föll, fór, fór, för, förum, forvitnar, fót, fótum, frá, frændi	how-so	hvers, hversu
		hands	kendi
		hammering	klappar
		his-life	lífinu
		harm	mein, mein
higher	hærra, hærri	himself	sér, sér, sessunaut, sessunautr, síð, síðan
have	haf, hafa, hafa, hafa, hafa, hafa, hafða, hafði, hafðir		
		hit	skall
has	hafa, hafa, hafa	heading	stillir
Hakon (name)	Hákon, Hákoni	heavy-cargo	þunga
hold	halda	hayfield-wall	túngarði
held	haldit, hálfa, Halla	hardly	varla
half	hálfa	have-been	verða
Halli's (name)	Halla		
Halogaland (place)	Hálogaland, Hálogalandi		

I, i

her	hana
hand-washing	handlaugar
him	hann, hans, hans, hans, hanu, hár

Word List (English to Old Norse)

English	Old Norse
in	á, á, á'k, áðr, áðr, áðr, aðra, ætlat, ætluðu, ætt
it	á, á'k, áðr, áðr, áðr, aðra
I	á'k, áðr, áðr, áðr, aðra, ætlat
intended	ætlat, ætluðu, ætt
invited	bað, báðir
if	ef, eftir, eftir
in-the-end	enn
is	er, erindi, erindi, ert
islands	eyja, eyjar
is-named	heitir
into	í, illa
ill	illt
inside	innan
Iceland (place)	Ísland, Íslandi, Íslands
Iceland-voyage	Íslands-fari
Icelanders	íslendinga, íslendingar
Icelander	íslenzka, íslenzkan, íslenzkr
iron-weapon	járn
ironsmith	járnsmiðr
intestines	þari
intellect	vitsmuna

J, j

journey	förum
jumped	hljóp
Jutland (place)	Jótlands

K, k

killed	drap, drápu, drápu, draum, draumr
kill	drepa, drepit
kinsman	frændi, frændunum
kinsmen	frændunum
knife-handle	hnífskefti
knows	kann
know-you	kanntú
Kaupang (place)	Kaupang
Kapuang (place)	Kaupangs
know	kenn, kenna, kenndi, kennt, keyptut, kjöts, klappar
knee	kné
knife	kníf, knífi, knífinum
knorrs	knörru
knocked-down	knúskim
kings	konunga
king	konungr
king's	konungr
kin	kyns
known	veit
knew	vissi, vissu, víst

L, l

lived	bjó
laughed	brosti
lodgings	búð, bú-Finna
lightning	eldingum
loved	elskaði
life	es, eta, eta
little	fátt, fé, fébœtr, féhirði, féhirðinn, fekk, fekk, fekk
lost	firrst, fiskimenn, fjár
leg	fót
last	fyrra
look-to	gera
long-neck	hálslangr
long-armed	handsiðr
lord	herra
ladened	hlaðna
listen	hlýði
lobsters	humrum
lay	lá, læt, læt'k, lagði, lagði
let	læt'k, lagði
laid	lagði, lagðist, lagin, lágu, lágu
land	land, landi, langa, langskip
long	langa, langskip, lát
longships	langskip
leave	látir
lead	leiða
look-for	leita
leaned	lér

364

Word List (English to Old Norse)

English	Old Norse
let-up	létti, léttum
lie	liggja, líkaði
liked	líkaði, líkar
like	líkar, líkar
likely	líklegr
looked	lítast, lítil, lítil
little-behaving	lítilþægr
light	ljóst
legal-settlement	lögskilum
lands	lönd
lifting	lyftingunni
lies	lýgr
lying	lýgr
less	minna
lesser	minna
lose	missa
long-nosed	neflangr
leader	oddviti
look	séit
later	síðar
least	sízt
learned	spurði
large-repaying (generous)	stórlyndr
leash	taumi

M, m

English	Old Norse
man	af, aftr, aftrábak, ágætr, Agðanes
married	átti
master	bóndi, borð
mockery	dáruskapr, dauðan
me	ek, eldahús, eldi, eldingum
message	erindi
money	fé, fébœtr, féhirði
many	fjölda, fjöldi, fjölmennt, fjóra, fjórar, fjórðung
more	fleira, fleiri, flesta, Fljótum, flœr-at, fluga
most	flesta, Fljótum, flœr-at, fluga
mistakes	föll
met	fundumst, furðanliga
magic	galdra
made	gera, gera, gerast, gerði
make	gera
moustache	grön
mocking	háðyrðum
most-hardy	herðamestr
mind	hug, hugar
minds	hugar
molars	jaxlar
merchant-men	kaupmennirnir
merchant-ship	kaupskipinu
men	lítil, lítilla, lítilsvert, lítilþægir
may	má, maðr, maðr
matter	mæla, mæla, Magnús, maka
matters	mæla, Magnús, maka
Magnus (name)	Magnús
more-suitable	makligri
man's-son	mannsbarn
many-things	margs
mean	mein
mine	mér, mér, merkr, mest, mest, mesta, mestu, mettir, mettr
my	mér, merkr
marks	merkr
much	mikill, mikils, mikinn, mikit, mikit, mikla
mis-liked	mislíkaði
miss	missa
meal	mjöli
morning	morgininn
meet	móti
mouth	munni
must	munt
most-angry	reiðasti
mood-dragon	skapdreki
mood	skapi
money-bribe	verðr

N, n

English	Old Norse
never	aldrei, aldrigi
not	eiga, eiga, eigi, eign, eina, einarr, einhugi
nothing	einkis, einmælt
nonsense	endileysu
no	engan, engan, engi, engi, engu, engum

Word List (English to Old Norse)

none	engan, engi, engi, engu
neck	háls, hann
named	heita, heitan, heitir, held, heldr, hella
narrow-shouldered	herðalítill
nearby	hjá
neither	hvárigum
nowhere	hvergi
noose	lykkja
neared	næða
near	nær, nærri, næst
next	næsta
necessarily	nauðliga
necessary	nauðsyn
needs	nauðsynja
Njord (name)	Njörðr
north	norðr
northern-lands	norðrlönd
Norway (place)	Noreg, Noregi, Noregs
night	nótt
nights	nóttum
now	nú, óðindælu
needed	þurfti
news	tíðinda, tíðindi
nobler	tignari

O, o

of	á, á, á, á, á, á, ábyrgst, aðra, aðra, aðrir
on	á, á
other	aðra, aðra, aðrir, ætla, ætla, ætlat, af
others	aðra, aðrir
off	af, af
of-all	allra, allskammr
one	annan, annan, annarr, annarra, annars, annat, Árnasonar, at
otherwise	annarr
ordered	bað
order	bið, biðja
offence	brot
offered	býðr
or	eðr
own	eiga
ownership	eign
one-minded	einhugi
one-meal	einmælt
one-decision	einráðir
once	eitt
or-else	ella
over	fyrir, fyrr, gamall
old	gamall
of-the-floor	gólfið
of-porridge	grautar
obeying	hlýða
of-him	honum
obscenities	hrópyrði
onboard	innanborðs
obscene	klámyrði
obscene-words	klámyrðum
on-way	leiðar
of-footwear	leista
of-your-hair	loðir
one-mark	mörk
obtain	ná
ox-skin	nautaleðrs
one-of	nökkuru
other-knowing	öðruvísi
open	opit
out	ór, ór, orð, orða, orðaskil, orðfátt
out-of	ór
of-words	orðinn
over-praised	órleysingr
of-silver	silfrs
occasion	sinn
of-skins	skinna
of-the-smith	smiðju
one-summer-old	sumargamlan
of-them	þeiri
out-from	undan
outside	út
out-running	úthlaupi
out-journey	útivist
out-rowing (fishing)	útróðr
our	várr, váru
of-you	yðarr

Word List (English to Old Norse)

P, p

power	afli
pale	blakkir, bleikr
prepared	búinn, búinn
plate	disk
provoke	etja
passage	far
poor	fátœka
payment	fé, féit
pierced	festi
performed	fœrði
people	fólk, föng, fór
procession	för
pay	gjalda
porridge	graut, grautar, grauti, grautinn
peace	grið, griðníðingr
possessions	gripi
possession	gripr
pig	grís, gríss
pour	hella
poured	hella
part	hlotizt, hlut, hlut
polite	kurteiss
poem	kvæði, kvæði
poems	kvæði, kvæði
poem-reward	kvæðis-launin
poem-image	kvæðis-mynd
peaceful	kyrrt
passed	leið
play	leika
permission	lof
praise	lof
promise	lofa
praised	loft, lofuðu
puzzle	óðindælu
prove	prófa
plan	ráð
proved	reyndust
persistent	seinþreyttr
purse	sjóði
poet	skáld
poets	skáld, skáld
poetry	skáldskap
place	staðar, staddr
piece	stykki
promising	vænstr
provisions	vist
pushed	ýttu, ýttum

Q, q

queen	drottning
quickly	flýta, fœra
quickly-cleared	rymskyndir
questions	spurt

R, r

responsible	ábyrgst
returning	aftr
related-to	átta
ring-land	bauglands
ready	búnir
room	deild
remembered	dýran, eðr, ef
received	fekkst, fengum
rhymes	föng
ready-made	görr
revenge	hefnt
rather	heilt, heita, heitan
running	hlaupi, Hleyp'k
ran	hleypr, hljóð
reasonable	hófi
roaring	hröng
rapped	klappaði
recited	kvað, kvað, kvað, kváðu, kvæði, kvæði
recite	kveð, kveð'k
reward	launa
rewarded	launaði
rented	leigðu
repay	leys, lífinu
reversed	öfigt
robbery	rán
Ran (name)	Ránar
round	randa
Raud (name)	Rauð, rauðan
red	rauðar, Rauðr
ruled	réð
Reine (place)	Rein
richer	ríkari

Word List (English to Old Norse)

rowing	röru	*spine*	hryggrinn
rye-loaf	rúghleifa	*sole-bucket*	ilfat
rooms	rúms	*struck*	klappaði
row	runa	*spoke*	kvað, kváðu, kvæði
rattled	skall	*say*	kveð'k, kveða, kveðin, kveðin
rapidly	skjótt		
rushed	snaraði	*spoken*	kveðit
return	snúa	*short-poem*	kviðlingr
roasted	steiktr	*songs*	lagin
refused	synjuðu	*skin*	leðr
receives	þiggi	*seeking*	leita
		sought	leitaði, leitaðir

S, s

suppose	ætla	*speak*	mæl, mæla, mæla, mælti, mæltist
supposed	ætla		
Son-of-Arni (name)	Árnasonar	*side*	megin, menn
said	at, at, at, at, at, at, at, at, at, at, at, átta, bað	*satisfied*	mettir, mettr
		shall	mun, mun, mun, mun, mun, mun, mun, mun'k
settled	bjó, blakkir, bleikr, boði, bœjar, bœnum	*should*	mun, mun, mun, mun, mun, mun, mun'k, muna, munat, munda, mundi
soon	brátt		
smiled	brosti		
shop-keeping	búðarvörð	*should-be*	mun, mun, mun
spears	dörrum	*shall-you*	muntú, muntú
seek	em, en	*serpent*	naðri
so	eru, eru, etit, etja, eyddust	*slander*	níð
		some	nökkur, nökkur, nökkurr, nökkuru, nökkuru
spent	eyddust		
Slayer-of-Fafnir (name)	Fáfnis-bana	*something*	nökkur, nökkurr, nökkuru
stout	feitr	*somehow*	nökkuru
Sami-goods	finnskrepp	*somewhat*	nökkuru, nökkurum
since	fjörs, flenna, flest, flýta	*shouting*	óp
		sharp-tongued	orðhvass
sent-for	fœra	*saw*	sá, sá, sá's
stories	frásagnir	*sea-scattered*	sæhafa
stopped	hætti	*seasick*	sæsjúkr
sound-advice	heilræði	*sit*	sæti, sætis, sættir, sættust
sleeping-quarters	herbergjum		
silence	hljóð, hljóðgreipum, hljóðit	*seat*	sætis
		settlements	sættir
sound-grippers (ears)	hljóðgreipum	*sake*	sakir
share	hlut	*sake-less*	saklausa
suits	hlýða	*same*	sama, saman
she	hon	*sat*	sátu, sátu, sáu, sé, sé
shaken	hrökkvi-skafls	*see*	sé, sé, sé'k
		same-as	sem

Word List (English to Old Norse)

send	send	shrinks-from	svífst
sent	sendi	swine	svíni
sees	sér	sleek	sýlt
seen	sét	showed	sýna, sýndi
set	setja, settist	seems	sýndisk, sýndist, sýnir, sýnist, synjuðu
sedately	settliga		
sailed	sigldi, sigldu	show	sýnir
Sigurd (name)	Sigurð, Sigurðarson, Sigurði	sow	sýr
		stewardship	sýslu
Sigurdson (name)	Sigurðarson	siblings	systkinum
silver	silfr, silfrhólkr	speaking	tala
silver-band	silfrhólkr	silenced	þagnaði, þakkaði
silver-wound	silfrvafit	straight-away	þegar
settle	sitja	servant	þjón
sift	síu	serve	þjóna
seldom	sjaldan	service	þjónusta, þjónustu
self's	sjálfs	seemed	þótti, þótti, þóttir
sick	sjúkr	scandalous	undarligt
scarlet	skarlatsklæðum	spring	várit
ship	skip, skip	slaying	víg
ship-smiths	skipsmiðir	sitting	yfir
ships	skipuðu		
shield	skjöld		
shoes	skó		

T, t

that	á, á, á, á, ábyrgst, aðra, aðra, aðrir, ætla, ætla, ætlat, af, af, af, af, afli, aftr, akta, aldrei, aldrigi, allra
scandal	skömm
scrawled	skrýfði
sheathed	slíðrar
such	slík, slíka, slíkir, slíkt
smith-bellows	smiðbelgja
snake	snák
Sarcastic-Halli (name)	Sneglu-Halla, Sneglu-Halli
to	á, á, á, ábyrgst, aðra, aðra, aðrir, ætla, ætla akta
sleep	sofa, sögðu
son	son
taxes	akta
talked	ámælisverðr, annan
Stad (place)	Stað
the-next	annan
standing	standa, standit, steiktr
than	at, at, at, at
stands	stendr
the	at, at, at, at, at, at, at, at, átta, bað, báti, báti
stood	stóð
stone-kettle	stórum
this	at, at, at, at, at, at, átta, bað, báti, báti, bátnum
steersman	stýrimaðr
steers	stýrir
strong	styrk
the-boat	báti, báti
south	suðr
the-ship's-boat	báti
southern-men	suðrmenn
the-bench	bekkinn
summer	sumar
the-best	bezt, bið
Svarfadardal (place)	Svarfaðardal
to-ask	biðja
		the-town	bœjar
starving	sveltir	town	bœnum
sword	sverð, sverði, sverðit	table	borði, borði

369

Word List (English to Old Norse)

English	Old Norse
the-table	borði, borðin
tables	borðin
the-city	börg
the-children	börnin
transformed	brást
the-day	daginn
thick-set	digrastr
the-plate	diskinum
the-Danes (name)	Dönum
the-killing	drápi
the-drapa (poem)	drápuna
this-dream	draum
the-dragon-ship	drekanum
the-boy	drengrinn
the-lord	dróttinn
the-queen	drottning, drottningu
the-dwarf	dverg, dverginn
then	ef, eggjaði, eiga, eiga, eigi, eign, eina, einarr, einhugi, einkis, einmælt, einn, einráðir, einu, eitt
the-fire	eld
the-end	enda
they-are	eru
to-eat	etit
thought	fannst, far, far, fara, fara, farit, fars, fátœka, fátœkra, fé, féit
travel	far, fara, fara, farit
travelled	farit, fars
the-poor	fátœkra
the-money	féit
the-Sami (name)	Finna
the-fjord	firðinum
to-extend	flenna
the-most	flest
the-legs	fœtrnir
took	frændr, frásagnir, fund, fúss, fyrir, fyrr, gamall
to-meet	fund
to-delight	gaman
the-house	garðinn
the-wall	garðinn, garðinum, garðrinn, garðsins
teach	gefa, gefa
to-give	gefa
told	getit, gjalda, gólf, gólfið
the-floor	gólf, gólfið
the-porridge	grautinn
the-poor-thing	greyit
truce-breaker	griðníðingr
the-trinkets	gripanna, gripi
things	gripi
treasure	gripi
the-handle	haddan
the-lid	haddan
to-have	hafa
traded	hafa
to-hold	halda
Thjodolf (name)	hann, hárinu, hávan, hefnt
the-hairs	hárinu
the harbour	hávan
the-heath	heiði
threat	heitan
think	held, heldr, hella, hella
to-hand	hendi
the-horse	hestinn
to-hear	heyra
the-court	hirð, hirðinni
the-court-men	hirðinni
the-helmet	hjálmfaldinn
to-strike	höggva
the-hall	höllina, höllinni
to-him	honum
turn	horfa
the-ring	hring, hringinn, hringnum
the-spine	hrygg
turned	hverfr, hvergi, hverjar, hverju
trade	iðnar
the-earl's	jarls
the-giant	jötun
the-calf	kálfinn, kálfrinn
to-call	kalla
the-king	kallaði, katlinum, kaupferð, kaupmönnum, kaupmönnum, kaupskipinu, kenna, kilju, klámyrði, klámyrðum

Word List (English to Old Norse)

English	Old Norse
the-kettle	katlinum
trading-voyage	kaupferð
the-trading-men	kaupmönnum
trading-men	kaupmönnum
trading-ship	kaupskipinu
the-binding	kilju
the-king's	konungi, konunginn, konunginum
the-poem	kvæðinu, kvæðisins, kvæðis-launin
the-poetry	kvæðunum
the-evening	kveld
the-land	landi, landinu
the-noose	lykkjan
the-whitings	lýsu
the-man	maðr, maðrinn
the-matter	málit
to-me	mér, mest
there	mest, mettir, mettr, mitt, mönnum, mörk
the-middle	mitt
the-people	mönnum
the-border	mörkina
take	ná, naðri, næða, nær, nærri, næst
the-slander	níðit
the-night	nótt
the-other	öðru
too-much	ofraun
terrible	ógrligr
the-serpent	orm
the-whole	óskerðan
tell	oss, oss, oss
to-us	oss
the-axe	öxarinnar, öxina
trick	prettr
trickery	prettum
the-ruler	ræsi
the-trunk	rana
the-red	rauðan
tested	reynt
told-of	sagði
told-to	sagt
together	saman
true-words	sannmæli
true	
truth	satt
true	
to-tell	segja
to-sell	selja
themselves	sér, sér
to-get-hurt	serðast
the-last	síðast
the-custom	siðr
the-silver	silfrinu
tendon	sinina
theirs	sinn, sinn, sinnar, sinni
their	sinnar, sinni
these	sinni, sínum, sit
the-purse	sjóðnum
the-shaft	skaftit
the-poet	skáld, skálda
the-ship	skip, skipin, skipinu
the-ships	skipin
the-hammer	sleggju
the-story	sögu
the-place	stað
the-street	stræti
the-shore	ströndu
the-one	sú
the-southerners	suðrmenn
tanner	sútari
to-answer	svara
this-lad	sveini
takes	taki
talking	talat
tongs	tangar
the-leash	taums-endanum, taumsins
taken	tekit, tekizt
though	þá, það, þær, þagna, þagnaði
thanked	þakkaði, þakkaði
they	þar, þar, þar's, þat
them	þeim, þeim, þeir
to-you	þér
the-assembly	þinginn, þingit, þings, þingsins
Thingvellir (place)	Þingvalla
Thjodolf's (name)	Þjóðólfs
thief	þjófr
the-servants	þjónustumenn
Thjotta (place)	Þjóttu
thanks	þökk
Thor (name)	Þór, Þóra

Word List (English to Old Norse)

English	Old Norse
Thora (name)	Þóra, Þórbergs
Thorberg's (name)	Þórbergs
Thorleif (name)	Þórleifi, Þórleifr
Thorljot (name)	Þórljóti, Þórljótr
threatening	þrætu
Trondheim (place)	Þrándheim, Þrándheims
three-winters-old	þrevett
third	þriðja
three	þrjár, þrjú
thula (poem)	þula
therefore	því
towards	til
time	tíma
ten	tíu
tar	tjöru
turf	torf
trough	trog
Tuta (name)	Túta, Tútu
two	tvá, tveir
tut	tví
two-fold	tvöföld
threw	varp
the-wager	veðjanin
to-be	vera, vera
the-verse	vísan
the-supply	vistin
the-provisions	vistina
to-know	vita
the-wisest	vitrastr
the-themes	yrkisefnin
to-compose	yrkja

U, u

English	Old Norse
up	at, at, at
use	brúki
urged	eggjaði
us	einarr, einhugi
undertaking	fær
upper-shaft	forskeftinn
usually	jafnan
ugly-limbed	ljótlimaðr
unreliable	óeyrðarmaðr
un-infatuated	öfundsjúkr
upside-down	öndvert
un-custom-mixing	ósiðblendnir
unsettled	ótæpt
un-thanks	óþökk
un-ranking	ótíginna
un-truthful	ótrúligir
unworthy	óvirðuligt
upright	réttr
until	til, til
up-to	til, tíma
under	undan, undarligt
upped	upp
understandable	várkunn

V, v

English	Old Norse
very-short	allskammr
vacation	orlofs, órlofs
village	þorpi
verse	vísan

W, w

English	Old Norse
was	á, á, ábyrgst, aðra, aðra, aðrir, ætla, ætla, ætlat, af, af, af
with	á, ábyrgst, aðra, aðra, aðrir, ætla, ætla
waited	beið
were	er, er, er, er, er, er, eru, eru, etit
what	er, er, er, er, er, eru
when	er, er
where	er, er, er, eru, eru
which	er, er, eru, eru
who	er, eru, eru
welcomed	fagnar
went	fara, farit, fars, fátœka, fátœkra, fé, féit
went-you	fórtu
willing	fúss
went-before	fyrr
walking	gengi
we-are-going	göngum
well	hafa, halda
was-named	hét
whether	hvárt
whom	hveru

Word List (English to Old Norse)

English	Old Norse
why	hví
worded	kveðin, kveðit, kveðit, kveðr, kveðr, kveðst
words	kveðr, kveðst, kveld, kvenna
women	kvenna
well-deserved	makligra
while	meðan
will	mun, mun, mun, mun'k, muna
would	mun, mun, mun'k, muna, munat, munda, mundi, mundi, mundir, mundu
would-be	mun, mun'k
would-you	muntú
word	orð
words-separated	orðaskil
word-fallen	orðfátt
word-bold	orðgreppr
word-tall	orðhákr
we	oss, ótæpt, óþökk
well-advising	ráðigastr
wrong	rangt
written	ritat
wounded	sarð
with-footwear	sásk
wounder	serðr
withhold	spara
with-bread	sufli
wonder	undr
wonder-created	undrskapaðr
won	unnit, unz
we-are	upp
without	útan
wicked	vændis
wretched	váligrar
warily	varlega, varliga
wager	veðja, veðjanin
way	veg, vegar
wished	vera, verða, verðr, verk
worth	verða, verðr
worthy	verðr
work	verk
workman's	verkmanns
worse	verr, verra, verra
worst	verra
winter	vetr, vetri, vetrinn
winter-lodgings	vetrvistar
winter-provisions	vetrvistar
wish	vil, vilda, vildi, vildi, vildi
wanted	vildi
willed	vildi
we-wish	viljum
wishes	vill
will-you	viltú
worthied	virði
wit	vit
write	yrk

Y, y

English	Old Norse
yet	enn
Yule-day	jóladag
Yule	jólin, jólum, jólunum
your-life	lífinu
yours	ok, öll, öndvert, öngan, öngvan, óp, opit, ór
yourself	sjálfr
you	þér, þér, þess, þessa, þessarrar, þessi
you-two	þit
your	yðart

The Tale of Sarcastic Halli (*Old Icelandic*)

Old Icelandic	Literal	English
1	**1**	**1**
Það er upphaf þessar frásagnar að Haraldur konungur Sigurðarson réð fyrir Noregi.	It is beginning this from-saying of Harald the-king Sigurdson ruled over Norway.	The beginning is to say that King Harald Sigurdson ruled Norway.
Það var í þann tíma er Magnús konungur frændi hans var andaður.	It was in that time that Magnus the-king's kinsman his was dead.	It was in that time that Magnus the king's kinsman was dead.
Svo er sagt að Haraldur konungur var allra manna vitrastur og ráðugastur.	So is said that Harald the-king was of-all men the-wisest and well-advising.	So it is said that King Harald was the wisest of all men and of advice.
Varð það og flest að ráði er hann lagði til.	Was it also the-most that advised that he became to.	Also most of what he had counselled had become good.
Hann var skáld gott	He was a-poet good	He was a good poet
og jafnan kastaði hann háðyrðum að þeim mönnum er honum sýndist.	and equally cast he mocking to they the-people as he thought.	and also mocked whoever he thought to.
Þoldi hann og allra manna best þótt að honum væri kastað klámyrðum þá er honum var gott í skapi.	Endured he also all men best though that he was cast obscene-words then that he was good of mood.	And when he was in a good mood, he endured most men even though obscenities were cast at him.
Hann átti þá Þóru dóttur Þorbergs Árnasonar.	He married then Thora daughter Thorberg's Son-of-Arni.	He was then married to Thora, daughter of Thorberg, Arni's son.
Honum þótti mikið gaman að skáldskap og hafði jafnan þá með sér er kveða kunnu.	He thought much delight in poetry and had always then with him that compose could.	He took much delight in poetry and always had people about him who could compose poetry.
Þjóðólfur hét maður.	Thjodolf was-named a-man.	There was a man named Thjodolf.
Hann var íslenskur og ættaður úr Svarfaðardal, kurteis maður og skáld mikið.	He was an-Icelander and descended from Svarfadardal, polite man and poet great.	He was an Icelander whose family came from Svarfadardal, a polite man and a great poet.

The Tale of Sarcastic Halli (Old Icelandic)

Old Icelandic	Literal	English
Hann var með Haraldi konungi í hinum mestum kærleikum.	He was with Harald the-king in the most dear-friendship.	He had great friendship with King Harald.
Kallaði konungur hann höfuðskáld sitt og virti hann mest allra skálda.	Called the-king him chief-poet his and worthied him most of-all poets.	The king called him his chief poet, and valued him most of all the poets.
Hann var ættsmár og menntur vel, öfundsjúkur við þá er til komu.	He was family-small and educated well, un-infatuated with then who to came.	He was from a humble family and well educated, he was envious of newcomers.
Haraldur konungur elskaði mjög Íslendinga.	Harald the-king loved much Icelanders.	King Harald loved Icelanders very much.
Gaf hann til Íslands marga góða hluti, klukku góða til Þingvallar.	Gave he to Iceland many good things, a-bell good for Thingvellir.	He gave many good things to Iceland, including a good bell for Thingvellir.
Og þá er hallæri það hið mikla kom á Ísland er ekki hefir slíkt komið annað þá sendi hann út til Íslands fjóra knörru hlaðna með mjöl, sinn í hvern fjórðung, og lét flytja í brott fátæka menn sem flesta af landinu.	And then when famine that the greatest came to Iceland that not had such come another then sent he out to Iceland four knorrs ladened with meal, then to each fourth, and had carried to brought poor men which most off the-land.	And when the greatest famine came to Iceland, which was like no other, he then sent four knorrs loaded with flour, one to each quarter, and had brought over many of the poorest men from the land.

2

Bárður hét maður og var hirðmaður Haralds konungs.	Bard was-named a-man and was court-man Harald's the-king's.	There was a man named Bard who was a court man of King Harald's.
Hann sigldi til Íslands og kom út að Gásum og vistaðist þar um veturinn.	He sailed to Iceland and came out to Gasir and found-a-place there about winter.	He sailed to Iceland and came out to Gasir and found a place there for the winter.
Sá maður tók sér far með honum er Halli hét og var kallaður Sneglu-Halli.	So a-man took himself passage with him was Halli named and was called Sarcastic-Halli.	So a man took passage with him who was named Halli, and he was called Sarcastic Halli.
Hann var skáld gott og orðgreppur mikill.	He was a-poet good and word-bold much.	He was a good poet and very bold with words.
Halli var hár maður og hálslangur, herðilítill og handsíður og ljótlimaður.	Halli was high man and long-neck, narrow-shouldered and long-armed and ugly-limbed.	Halli was a tall man with a long neck, narrow shoulders, long arms, and ill-proportioned limbs.

The Tale of Sarcastic Halli (Old Icelandic)

Old Icelandic	Literal	English
Hann var ættaður úr Fljótum.	He was descended out-of Fljot.	His descendants were from Fljot.
Þeir sigldu þegar þeir voru búnir og höfðu langa útivist, tóku Noreg um haustið norður við Þrándheim við eyjar þær er Hítrar heita og sigldu síðan inn til Agðaness og lágu þar um nótt.	They sailed as-soon-as they were prepared and had long out-journey, took Norway about autumn north with Trondheim with islands there which Hitra named and sailed since then to Agdanes and lay there about the-night.	They sailed as soon as they were ready and had a long passage, they reached Norway in the autumn north of Trondheim at the islands there which are called Hitra, and then sailed to Agdanes and laid up there for the night.
En um morguninn sigldu þeir inn eftir firðinum lítinn byr.	Then about morning sailed they then back-from the-fjord little fair-wind.	Then in the morning they sailed afterwards into the fjord with a light fair wind.
Og er þeir komu inn um Rein sáu þeir að langskip þrjú reru innan eftir firðinum.	And when they came of about Reine saw they of longships three rowing in after the-fjord.	And when they came to Reine they saw three longships rowing back from the fjord.
Dreki var hið þriðja skipið.	Dragon was the third ship.	The third ship was a dragon ship.
Og er skipin reru hjá kaupskipinu þá gekk maður fram úr lyftingunni á drekanum í rauðum skarlatsklæðum og hafði gullhlað um enni, bæði mikill og tigulegur.	And when the-ships rowing beside trading-ship then got a-man from out lifting from the-dragon-ship in red scarlet and had gold-band about forehead, both great and dignified.	And when the ships were rowing beside the trading ship, a man came up out of the dragon ship in red scarlet with a gold band about his forehead, both great and dignified.
Þessi maður tók til orða:	This man took to words:	This man spoke:
"Hver stýrir skipinu eða hvar voruð þér í vetur eða hvar tókuð þér fyrst land eða hvar láguð þér í nótt?"	"Who steers the-ship and where were you in winter and where took you first land and where laid you in the-night?"	"Who steers the ship, and where were you in winter, and where did you first take land, and where did you lay up last night?"
Þeim varð næsta orðfall kaupmönnum er svo var margs spurt en	They were next word-fallen the-trading-men as so were many questions but	The trading men were lost for words because there were so many questions, but
Halli svarar þá:	Halli answered then:	Halli answered them.

The Tale of Sarcastic Halli (Old Icelandic)

Old Icelandic	Literal	English
"Vér vorum í vetur á Íslandi en ýttum af Gásum en Bárður heitir stýrimaður en tókum land við Hítrar en lágum í nótt við Agðanes".	"We were in winter in Iceland and pushed from Gasum and Bard is-named steersman and took land at Hitra and laid about the-night at Agdanes".	"We were in Iceland for the winter, and we pushed on from Gasir, and Bard is the name of the steersman, we took land at Hitra, and we laid up for the night at Agdanes".
Þessi maður spurði, er reyndar var Haraldur konungur Sigurðarson:	This man asking, which actually was Harald the-king Sigurdson:	This man who was asking, was actually King Harald Sigurdson.
"Sarð hann yður ei Agði?"	"Wounded he you not Agdi	"Did Agdi not wound you?"
"Eigi enna", segir Halli.	"Not yet", said Halli.	"Not yet", said Halli.
Konungurinn brosti að og mælti:	The-king laughed and also spoke:	The king laughed and also spoke:
"Er nokkur til ráðs um að hann muni enn síðar meir veita yður þessa þjónustu?"	"Is something to agreement about that he shall but afterwards more grant you this service?"	"Is there some agreement that he shall do you this service sometime later?"
Ekki, sagði hann Halli, "og bar þó einn hlutur þar mest til þess er vér fórum enga skömm af honum".	Not, told he Halli, "and bears though one part there most to this that we travel not disgrace of him".	Halli told him not, "and so it bears most in one part that we travel without suffering disgrace by him".
"Hvað var það?"	"What was that?"	"What was that?"
segir konungur.	said the-king.	said the king.
Halli vissi gjörla við hvern hann talaði.	Halli knew completely with whom he talked.	Halli knew completely who he was talking to.
"Það herra",	"That lord",	"That, lord",
segir hann, "ef yður forvitnar að vita að hann Agði beið að þessu oss tignari manna og vætti yðvar þangað í kveld og mun hann þá gjalda af höndum þessa skuld ótæpt".	said he, "if you fore-knowing to know that he Agdi waited for this us nobler men and expected you from-there in the-evening and shall he then pay of hand this debt unsettled".	he said, "if you are curious to know, that Agdi was waiting for nobler men than us, and expected your arrival there this evening, and he shall pay you this debt fully".
"Þú munt vera orðhákur mikill",	"You must be word-tall much",	"You must be very brave of words",
segir konungur.	said the-king.	said the king.

The Tale of Sarcastic Halli (Old Icelandic)

Old Icelandic	Literal	English
Ei er getið orða þeirra fleiri að sinni.	Not is told words theirs more than these.	It is not told what more their words were than this.
Sigldu þeir kaupmennirnir inn til Kaupangs og skipuðu þar upp og leigðu sér hús í bænum.	Sailed they merchant-men then to Kapuang and ships there upped and rented themselves a-house in town.	The merchants then sailed to Kaupang, upped their ships and rented themselves a house in town.
Fám nóttum síðar kom konungur inn aftur til bæjar og hafði hann farið í eyjar út að skemmta sér.	A-few nights afterwards came the-king then returning to the-town and had he travelled to islands out to entertain himself.	After a few nights the king came returning to the town, as he had gone out to the islands to entertain himself.
Halli bað Bárð fylgja sér til konungsins og kveðst vilja biðja hann veturvistar.	Halli asked Bard follow him to the-king and said wished to-ask him winter-provisions.	Halli asked Bard to lead him to the king and said that he wished to ask him for winter lodgings.
En Bárður bauð honum með sér að vera.	But Bard invited him with himself to be.	But Bard invited him to stay with him.
Halli bað hann hafa þökk fyrir en kveðst með konunginum vilja vera ef þess væri kostur.	Halli bid him having thanks for but said with the-king wished to-be if this was a-choice.	Halli thanked him but said that he wished to stay with the king if that was a choice.

3

Einn dag gekk Bárður til konungs og Halli með honum.	One day went Bard to the-king and Halli with him.	One day Bard went to meet the king and Halli went with him.
Bárður kvaddi konung.	Bard greeted the-king.	Bard greeted the king.
Konungur tók vel kveðju hans og spurði margs af Íslandi eða hvort hann hefði flutt utan nokkra íslenska menn.	The-king received well greeting his and asked many-things of Iceland and whether he had brought out any Icelander men.	The king received his greeting well and asked many things of Iceland and whether he had brought any men from Iceland.
Bárður sagðist flutt hafa einn íslenskan mann	Bard said brought had one Icelander man	Bard said that he had brought one Icelander man
"og heitir hann Halli og er nú hér herra og vill biðja yður veturvistar".	"and named he Halli and is now here lord and wishes to-ask you winter-lodgings".	"and he is named Halli, and he is now here lord, and wishes to ask you for winter lodgings".
Halli gekk þá fyrir konunginn og kvaddi hann.	Halli went then before the-king and greeted him.	Halli then went before the king and greeted him.

The Tale of Sarcastic Halli (Old Icelandic)

Old Icelandic	Literal	English
Konungurinn tók honum vel og spurði hvort hann hefði svarað honum á firðinum "er vér fundumst".	The-king received him well and asked whether he had answered him in the-fjord "when we met".	The king received him well and asked whether he had answered him in the fjord "when we met".
"Sjá hinn sami",	"So the same",	"I am the same",
segir Halli.	said Halli.	said Halli.
Konungurinn sagðist ei spara mundu mat við hann og bað vera að búi sínu nokkru.	The-king said not withhold would food from him and invited to-be to estate his one-of.	The king said he would not withhold food from him and invited him to be on one of his estates.
Halli kveðst með hirðinni vera vilja eða leita sér annars ella.	Halli said with the-court to-be wished or find himself another or-else.	Halli said that he wished to be at court or to find somewhere else.
Konungurinn kvað svo fara jafnan "að mér er um kennt ef vor vinskapur fer ei vel af hendi þó að mér þyki varla svo vera.	The-king said so goes always "that to-me is about blame if our friendship goes not well of to-hand though that to-me seems hardly so being.	The king said that it always goes "that I am to blame if our friendship does not go well, though that seems to me hardly to be.
Eruð þér einráðir Íslendingar og ósiðblandnir.	They-are you one-decision Icelanders and un-custom-mixing.	You are single-minded, you Icelanders, and unsociable.
Nú ver ef þú vilt og ábyrgst þig sjálfur hvað sem í kann gerast".	Now be if you wish and responsible you yourself what which about can be".	Now be here if you wish, and you are responsible for yourself whatever will be".
Halli kvað svo vera skyldu og þakkaði konunginum.	Halli said so being would and thanked the-king.	Halli said that it would be so, and thanked the king.
Var hann nú með hirðinni og líkaði hverjum manni vel til hans.	Was he now with the-court-men and liked each man well to him.	He was now with the court men and he was liked by each of them.
Sigurður hét sessunautur Halla, gamall hirðmaður og gæfur.	Sigurd was-named bench-companion Halli, old court-man and agreeable.	Halli's bench companion was named Sigurd, an old court man and agreeable.
Sá var siður Haralds konungs að eta einmælt.	So was the-custom Harald's the-king's to eat one-meal.	It was Harald's custom to eat one meal a day.

The Tale of Sarcastic Halli (Old Icelandic)

Old Icelandic	Literal	English
Var fyrst borin vist fyrir konung, sem von var, og var hann þá jafnan mjög mettur er vistin kom fyrir aðra.	Were first brought provisions for the-king, as expected was, and was he then usually much satisfied when the-supply came before others.	First the food was brought before the king, as was expected, and he was usually very much satisfied when the food was brought to the others.
En þá er hann var mettur klappaði hann með hnífskafti sínu á borðið og skyldi þá þegar ryðja borðin og voru margir þá hvergi nærri mettir.	But then when he was satisfied rapped he with knife-handle his on the-table and would then straight-away cleared tables and were many then nowhere near satisfied.	But then when he was satisfied, he rapped his knife handle on the table, and then straight away the tables were cleared, and many people were then nowhere near satisfied.
Það bar við eitt sinn er konungur gekk úti um stræti og fylgdin með honum og voru margir þá hvergi nærri mettir.	It bore to once then that the-king went out about the-street and followers with him and were many then none near satisfied.	It happened once that the king went out in the street with his followers, and many of them were nowhere near satisfied.
Þeir heyrðu í eitt herbergi deild mikla.	They heard in one hostel room great.	They heard something great in an inn.
Þar voru að sútari og járnsmiður og þar næst flugust þeir á.	They were a tanner and ironsmith and there near flew they to.	It was a tanner and an ironsmith, and they nearly flew towards eachother.
Konungurinn nam staðar og sá á um stund.	The-king took place and saw for about awhile.	The king took his place and watched for a while.
Síðan mælti hann:	Afterwards spoke he:	Afterwards he spoke:
"Göngum brott.	"We-are-going away.	"Let us go away.
Hér vil eg öngvan hlut að eiga	Here wish I none part to own	I do not wish to be a part of this here,
en þú Þjóðólfur yrk um þá vísu".	but you Thjodolf write about then a-verse".	but you Thjodolf write a verse about it".
Herra, segir Þjóðólfur, "ei samir það þar sem eg er kallaður höfuðskáld yðvart".	Lord, said Thjodolf, "not common that there as I am called chief-poet yours".	"Lord", said Thjodolf, "I don't agree there, since I am called your chief poet".
Konungur svarar:	The-king answered:	The king answered:
"Þetta er meiri vandi en þú munt ætla.	"This is more difficult than you should suppose.	"This is more difficult than you think.

The Tale of Sarcastic Halli (Old Icelandic)

Old Icelandic	Literal	English
Þú skalt gera af þeim alla menn aðra en þeir eru.	You shall make of them completely men other than they are.	You shall make the men completely other than they are.
Lát annan vera Sigurð Fáfnisbana en annan Fáfni og kenn þó hvern til sinnar iðnar".	Have one be Sigurd Slayer-of-Fafnir and another Fafnir also know though each to his trade".	Have one be Sigurd the Slayer of Fafnir, and another Fafnir, and also identify each one's trade".
Þjóðólfur kvað þá vísu:	Thjodolf recited then a-verse:	Thjodolf then recited a verse:
Sigurðr eggjaði sleggju snák válegrar brákar en skapdreki skinna skreið af leista heiði. Mönnum leist ormr áðr ynni ilvegs búinn kilju, nautaleðrs á naðri neflangr konungr tangar.	Sigurd urged the-hammer snake wretched breaker, but mood-dragon of-skins crawled off of-footwear the-heath. People with-footwear the-serpent before won evil-ways prepared the-binding, ox-skin of serpent long-nosed king's tongs.	Sigurd urged the-hammer snake wretched breaker, but mood-dragon of-skins crawled off of-footwear the-heath. People with-footwear the-serpent before won evil-ways prepared the-binding, ox-skin of serpent long-nosed king's tongs.
"Þetta er vel kveðið",	"That is well worded",	"That is well composed",
segir konungur, "og kveð nú aðra og lát nú vera annan Þór en annan Geirröð jötun og kenn þó hvern til sinnar iðnar".	said the-king, "and recite now another and have now being one Thor and another Geirrod the-giant and know though each to their trade".	said the king, "and now recite another and have one being Thor and another Geirrod the Giant, and identify each with their trade".
Þá kvað Þjóðólfur vísu:	Then recited Thjodolf a-verse:	Then Thjodolf recited a verse:
Varp úr þrætu þorpi Þórr smiðbelgja stórra hvofteldingum höldnu hafra kjöts að jötni. Hljóðgreipum tók húðar hrökkviskafls af afli glaðr við galdra smiðju Geirröðr síu þeirri.	Threw from threatening village Thor smith-bellows great encouraged-lightning held goat flesh the giant. Sound-grippers (ears) took hide shaken of power glad with magic of-the-smith Geirrod sift of-them.	Threw from threatening village Thor smith-bellows great lightning held goat flesh the giant. Sound-grippers (ears) took hide shaken of power glad with magic of-the-smith Geirrod sift of-them.
"Ekki ertu mæltur um það",	"Not are-you talked about that",	"You are not over talked about",
segir konungur, "að þú ert úrleysingur til skáldskapar".	said the-king, "that you are over-praised as a-poet".	said the king, "when you are praised as a poet".

The Tale of Sarcastic Halli (Old Icelandic)

Old Icelandic	Literal	English
Og lofuðu allir að vel væri ort.	And praised all to well being worded.	And all praised him on how well it had been composed.
Ekki var Halli við þetta.	Not was Halli with this.	Halli was not present with them.
Og um kveldið er menn sátu við drykk kváðu þeir fyrir Halla og sögðu hann ei mundu svo yrkja þótt hann þættist skáld mikið.	And about evening when men sat with drink recited they for Halli and told him not would so compose though he thought a-poet great.	And that evening when men sat drinking they recited the poem for Halli and told him that he could not compose such a poem even though he thought of himself as a great poet.
Halli kveðst vita að hann orti verr en Þjóðólfur	Halli said knew that he worded worse than Thjodolf	Halli said that he knew he composed worse poetry than Thjodolf
"enda mun þá firrst um fara ef eg leita ekki við að yrkja enda sé eg ekki við",	"in-the-end shall then lost about going if I seek not with to compose and am I not with",	"in the end I shall lose if I do not try to compose a verse, and if I am not present",
segir Halli.	said Halli.	said Halli.
Þetta var þegar sagt konungi og snúið svo að hann þættist ei minna skáld en Þjóðólfur.	This was then told-to the-king and turned so that he thought not less a-poet than Thjodolf.	This was then told to the king and turned around to say that he thought himself no less of a poet than Thjodolf.
Konungur kvað honum ei að því verða mundu "en vera kann að vér fáum þetta reynt af stundu".	The-king said him not that therefore be would "but be can-it that we get that tested in awhile".	The king said that he would not be that, "but it can be that we can test him in a while".

4

Það var einn dag er menn sátu yfir borðum að þar gekk inn í höllina dvergur einn er Túta hét.	It was one day when people were sitting at-table that there went then into the-hall dwarf one who Tuta named.	It was one day when people were sitting at the table that a dwarf named Tuta went into the hall.
Hann var frískur að ætt.	He was Frisian by descent.	He was Frisian by descent.
Hann hafði lengi verið með Haraldi konungi.	He had long been with Harald the-king.	He had been with King Harald a long time.

The Tale of Sarcastic Halli (Old Icelandic)

Old Icelandic	Literal	English
Hann var ei hærri en þrevett barn en allra manna digrastur og herðimestur, höfuðið mikið og eldilegt, hryggurinn ei allskammur en sýlt í neðan þar sem fæturnir voru.	He was not higher than three-winters-old child but of-all men thick-set and most-hardy, head great and elderly, spine not very-short but sleek of below there where the-legs were.	He was no taller than a child of three years old, but he was the most thick set and hardy of all men, he had a large and elderly looking head, and his back was not very short, but sleek below where his legs were.
Haraldur konungur átti brynju þá er hann kallaði Emmu.	Harald the-king hat coat-of-mail then which he called Emma.	King Harald had a coat of mail which he called Emma.
Hann hafði látið gera hana í Miklagarði.	He had had made her in Byzantium.	He had had it made in Byzantium.
Hún var svo síð að hún tók niður á skó Haraldi konungi þá er hann stóð réttur.	She was so long that she took down to shoes Harald's the-king then when he stood upright.	It was so long that it reached down to King Harald's shoes when he stood upright.
Var hún öll tveföld og svo styrk að aldrei festi járn á.	Was she all two-fold and so strong that never pierced iron-weapon an.	It was all double-thickness and so strong that it was never pierced by an iron weapon.
Konungurinn hafði látið fara dverginn í brynjuna og setja hjálm á höfuð honum og gyrti hann sverði.	The-king had had sent-for the-dwarf in coat-of-mail and set helmet on head his and equipped him a-sword.	The king had ordered the dwarf to be in the coat of mail with a helmet set on his head and equipped with a sword.
Síðan gekk hann í höllina sem fyrr var ritað og þótti maðurinn vera undurskapaður.	After went he into the-hall as before was written and thought the-man was wonder-created.	After he went into the hall as was written before, and the man was thought to be a wonder.
Konungur kvaddi sér hljóðs og mælti:	The-king called to be-heard and spoke:	The king called to be heard and spoke:
"Sá maður er kveður um dverginn vísu svo að mér þyki vel kveðin þiggi að mér hníf þenna og belti"	"So the-man who words about the-dwarf a-verse so that to-me seems well worded receives of me knife this and belt"	"So the man who composes a verse about the dwarf, so that I think it is a good verse, will accept of me this knife and a belt",
og lagði fram á borðið fyrir sig gripina	and laid from to table before him the-trinkets,	and he put the trinkets on the table for him,

The Tale of Sarcastic Halli (Old Icelandic)

Old Icelandic	Literal	English
"en vitið það víst ef mér þykir ei vel kveðin að hann skal hafa óþökk mína en missa gripanna beggja".	"but know that certainly if to-me seems not well worded that he shall have un-thanks mine and miss the-trinkets both".	"but know for certain that if I don't think it is a good poem, he will have my displeasure and lose the trinkets both".
Og þegar er konungur hafði flutt erindi sitt kveður maður vísu utar á bekkinn og var það Sneglu-Halli:	And as-soon-as when the-king had delivered message his recited a-man a-verse out from the-bench and was that Sarcastic-Halli:	And as soon as the king had delivered his speech, a man recited a verse outside of the bench, and it was Sarcastic-Halli:
Færðr sýnist mér frændi Frísa kyns í brynju. Gengr fyrir hirð í hringum hjálmfaldinn kurfaldi. Flærat eld í ári úthlaupi vanr Túta. Sé eg á síðu leika sverð rúghleifa skerði.	Brought seems to-me kinsman Frisian kin in chain-mail. Going before the-court in circles the-helmet folded. Fleeing the-fire in all-year out-running custom Tuta. See I of side games sword rye-loaf cuts.	Brought seems to-me kinsman Frisian kin in chain-mail. Going before the-court in circles the-helmet folded. Fleeing the-fire in all-year out-running custom Tuta. See I of side games sword rye-loaf cuts.
Konungur bað færa honum gripuna	The-king ordered brought to-him the-trinkets	The king ordered the trinkets to be brought to him
"og skaltu ná hér á sannmæli því að vísan er vel kveðin".	"and shall-you obtain here in true-words because it the-verse is well worded".	"and you will find the truth here, because the verse is well recited".
Það var einn dag er konungurinn var mettur að konungur klappaði hnífi á borðið og bað ryðja.	It was one day when the-king was finished-eating that the-king struck knife on the-table and ordered cleared.	One day when the king had finished eating he struck his knife on the table and ordered the tables to be cleared.
Þjónustumenn gerðu svo.	The-servants did so.	The servants did so.
Þá var Halli hvergi nærri mettur.	Then was Halli nowhere near satisfied.	Then Halli was nowhere near satisfied.
Tók hann þá stykki eitt af diskinum og hélt eftir og kvað þetta:	Took he then piece one off the-plate and held back and recited this:	He then took a piece of food from the place and held it back and recited this:
Hirði eg ei hvað Haraldr klappar. Læt eg gnadda grön. Geng eg fullur að sofa.	Care I not that Harald's hammering. Have I gnawing moustache. Going I full to sleep.	Care I not that Harald's hammering. Have I gnawing moustache. Going I full to sleep.

The Tale of Sarcastic Halli (Old Icelandic)

Old Icelandic	Literal	English
Um morguninn eftir er konungur var kominn í sæti sitt og hirðin gekk Halli í höllina og fyrir konunginn.	About morning after when the-king was coming to sit himself and courtiers went Halli into the-hall and before the-king.	About morning when the king had come to sit with his courtiers, Halli went into the hall and went before the king.
Hann hafði skjöld sinn og sverð á baki sér.	He had shield his and sword about back his.	He had his shield and sword on his back.
Hann kvað vísu:	He spoke a-verse:	He spoke a verse:
Selja mun eg við sufli sverð mitt, konungr, verða, og rymskyndir randa rauðan skjöld við brauði. Hungrar hilmis drengi. Heldr göngum vér svangir. Mér dregr hrygg, að hvoru, Haraldr sveltir mig, belti.	Barter will I of with-bread sword mine, the-king, becomes, and quickly-cleared round the-red shield with bread. Hungry helmsman's boys. Rather going are-we hungry. To-me draws the-spine, that which, Harald starving me, belt.	Barter will I of with-bread sword mine, the-king, becomes, and quickly-cleared round the-red shield with bread. Hungry helmsman's boys. Rather going are-we hungry. To-me draws the-spine, that which, Harald starving me, belt.
Engu svarar konungur og lét sem hann heyrði ei	None answered the-king and had as he heard not	The king gave no answer and acted as though he had not heard,
en þó vissu allir menn að honum mislíkaði.	but though knew all people that he mis-liked.	but all the people knew that he disliked this.
Litlu síðar var það einn dag er konungurinn gekk úti um stræti og fylgdin með honum.	A-little afterwards was it one day that the-king went out about the-street and followers with him.	A little while afterwards one day the king went out into the street and had his followers with him.
Þar var og Halli í för.	There was also Halli with going.	And there was also Halli going with them.
Hann snaraði fram hjá konunginum.	He rushed ahead nearby the-king.	He rushed ahead to be near the king.
Konungurinn kvað þetta:	The-king spoke this:	The king spoke this:
"Hvert stillir þú Halli?"	"Where heading you Halli?"	"Where are you heading Halli?"
Halli svarar:	Halli answered:	Halli answered:
"Hleyp eg fram að kýrkaupi".	"Running I forwards to cow-buying".	"I am running to buy a cow".

The Tale of Sarcastic Halli (Old Icelandic)

Old Icelandic	Literal	English
"Graut muntu gervan láta?"	"Porridge would-you look-to have?"	"Will you look to have porridge?"
segir konungur.	said the-king.	said the king.
"Gjör matr er það, smjörvan",	"Ready-made food is that, buttered",	"It is a ready made meal, when buttered",
segir Halli.	said Halli.	said Halli.
Hleypur hann Halli þá upp í garðinn og þangað sem var eldahús.	Ran he Halli then up to garden and from-there as was fire-house (kitchen).	Then Halli ran up to a house where there was a kitchen.
Þar hafði hann látið gera graut í steinkatli og settist til og etur grautinn.	There had he had made porridge in stone-kettle and sat to and eat the-porridge.	There he had made porridge in a stone kettle, and sat there to eat the porridge.
Konungurinn sér að Halli hverfur upp í garðinn.	The-king saw that Halli turned up-to the garden.	The king saw that Halli had gone into the house.
Hann kvaddi til Þjóðólf og tvo menn aðra að leita Halla.	He called to Thjodolf and two men other to look-for Halli.	He called to Thjodolf and two other men to look for Halli.
Konungur veik og upp í garðinn.	The-king turned also up to the-house.	The king also arrived at the house.
Þeir finna hann þar sem hann át grautinn.	They found him there as he ate porridge.	They found him there as he ate the porridge.
Konungurinn kom þá að og sá hvað Halli hafðist að.	The-king came then to and saw what Halli had to.	The king came to him and saw what Halli was doing.
Konungurinn var hinn reiðasti og spurði Halla því hann fór af Íslandi til höfðingja til þess að gera af sér skömm og gabb.	The-king was the most-angry and asked Halli if he travelled from Iceland to chieftains to this that make of himself scandal and mockery.	The king was very angry and asked Halli if he had travelled from Iceland to visit chieftains and make scandal and mockery.
"Látið eigi svo herra",	"Let not so lord",	"Let it not be so",
segir Halli,	said Halli,	said Halli,
"jafnan sé eg yður ei drepa hendi við góðum sendingum".	"always see I you not kill hands with good delivery".	"always I see that you do not kill hands that deliver good food".

The Tale of Sarcastic Halli (Old Icelandic)

Old Icelandic	Literal	English
Halli stóð þá upp og kastaði niður katlinum og skall við haddan.	Halli stood then up and cast down the-kettle and hit against the-lid.	Halli then stood up and threw down the kettle, and hit against the lid.
Þjóðólfur kvað þá þetta:	Thjodolf recited then this:	Thjodolf then recited this:
Haddan skall en Halli hlaut offylli grautar. Hornspónu kveð eg honum hlýða betr en prýði.	The-handle rattled and Halli a-lot-of gluttony of-porridge. Horn-spoon say I to-him suits better than finery.	The-handle rattled and Halli a-lot-of gluttony of-porridge. Horn-spoon say I to-him suits better than finery.
Konungurinn gekk þá brottu og var allreiður.	The-king went then away and was all-angry.	The king then went away and was very angry.
Og um kveldið kom engi matur fyrir Halla sem fyrir aðra menn.	And about evening came no food before Halli as before other people.	And about evening there came no food for Halli as there had been for the other people.
Og er menn höfðu snætt um stund komu enn tveir menn og báru í milli sín trog mikið, fullt grautar, og með spón og settu fyrir Halla.	And when people had dined about awhile came then two men and carried in between themselves trough great, full of-porridge, and with a-spoon and set before Halli.	And when people had dined for a while, then came two men carrying between themselves a great through, full of porridge, and with a spoon set it before Halli.
Hann tók til og át sem hann lysti og hætti síðan.	He took to and ate as he appetite and stopped afterwards.	He took it and ate as much as his appetite would allow, and then stopped.
Konungur bað Halla eta meira.	The-king ordered Halli eat more.	The king ordered Halli to eat more.
Hann kveðst ei mundu eta meira að sinni.	He said not would eat more for himself.	He said he himself would not eat any more.
Haraldur konungur brá þá sverði og bað Halla eta grautinn þar til er hann spryngi af.	Harald the-king drew then a-sword and ordered Halli eat porridge there until that he burst of.	King Harald then drew a sword and ordered Halli to eat the porridge until he burst.
Halli kveðst ei mundu sprengja sig á grauti en segir konung ná mundu lífi sínu ef hann væri á það einhugi.	Halli said not would burst himself with porridge but told the-king take could life his if he would-be of that one-minded.	Halli said that he would not burst himself with porridge, but told the king that he could take his life if he was of a mind to do so.
Konungur sest þá niður og slíðrar sverðið.	The-king sat then down and sheathed sword.	The king then sat down and sheathed his sword.

The Tale of Sarcastic Halli (Old Icelandic)

Old Icelandic	Literal	English
5	**5**	**5**
Nokkru síðar var það einn dag að konungur tók disk einn af borði sínu og var á steiktur grís og bað Tútu dverg færa Halla	Somewhat later was it one day that the-king took plate one off table his and was it roasted pig and ordered Tuta the-dwarf bring Halli	One day somewhat later, the king took a plate off his table, and on it was a roasted pig, he ordered Tuta the dwarf to bring it to Halli
"og bið hann yrkja vísu ef hann vill halda lífinu og hafa kveðið áður þú kemur fyrir hann og seg honum ei fyrr en þú kemur á mitt gólf"	"and order him to-compose a-verse if he wishes to-hold his-life and have spoken after you come before him and tell him not before that you come to the-middle the-floor	"and order him to compose a verse if he wishes to hold his life, and recite it after you come before him, and tell him not before you are in the middle of the floor".
"Ekki er eg þess fús",	"Not am I this willing",	"I am not willing to do this",
segir Túta, "því að mér líkar vel við Halla".	said Tuta, "because that I like well with Halli".	said Tuta, "because I like Halli".
"Sé eg",	"See I",	"I see",
sagði konungur,	said the-king,	said the king,
"að þér þykir góð vísan sú er hann orti um þig og muntu gjörla heyra kunna.	"that you consider good verse yours that he worded about you and shall-you completely hear know.	that you consider his verse good that he composed about you, and you know how to listen carefully.
Nú far í burt í stað og ger sem eg býð".	Now go to away to the-place and do as I command".	Now to away and do as I command".
Túta tók nú við diskinum og gekk á mitt gólfið og mælti:	Tuta took now with the-plate and went to the-middle of-the-floor and spoke:	Tuta now took the place and went to the middle of the floor and spoke:
"Þú Halli yrk vísu að boði konungs og haf ort áður eg kem fyrir þig ef þú vilt halda lífinu".	"You Halli compose a-verse to order the-king's and have worded before I come before you if you wish to-hold your-life".	"You Halli are ordered by the king to compose a verse and have it composed before I come before you if you wish to hold your life".
Halli stóð þá upp og rétti hendur í móti diskinum og kvað vísu:	Halli stood then up and extended hand to meet the-plate and recited a-verse:	Halli then stood up and extended a hand to meet the plate and recited a verse:
Grís þá greppr að ræsi gruntrauðustum dauðan.	Pig then grasped of the-ruler deep-red death.	Pig then grasped of the-ruler deep-red death.

The Tale of Sarcastic Halli (Old Icelandic)

Old Icelandic	Literal	English
Njörðr sér börg á borði bauglands fyrir standa. Runa síðr lít eg rauðar. Ræð eg skjótt gera kvæði. Rana hefir seggr af svíni, send heill konungr, brenndan.	Njord sees the-city on the-table ring-land before standing. Row since coloured I red. Speak I rapidly made poem. The-trunk has said man swine, send health king, burnt.	Njord sees the-city on the-table ring-land before standing. Row since coloured I red. Speak I rapidly made poem. The-trunk has said man swine, send health king, burnt.
Konungur mælti þá:	The-king spoke then:	The king then spoke:
"Nú skal gefa þér upp reiði mína Halli því að vísan er vel kveðin svo skjótt sem til var tekið".	"Now shall give you up anger mine Halli because that verse is well recited so quickly as to was taken".	"Now I will give up my anger for you, Halli, because the sentence is well recited as soon as it was taken".

6

Frá því er sagt einn dag að Halli gekk fyrir konunginn þá er hann var glaður og kátur.	From then is said one day that Halli went before the-king then as he was glad and cheerful.	From then it is said that one day Halli went before the king as he was glad and cheerful.
Þar var þá Þjóðólfur og margt annarra manna.	There was then Thjodolf and many other people.	Then Thjodolf and many other people were there.
Halli sagðist hafa ort drápu um konunginn og bað sér hljóðs.	Halli said had worded drapa about the-king and asked for-him be-heard.	Halli said that he had composed a drapa about the king and ask him for it to be heard.
Konungurinn spurði hvort Halli hefði nokkuð kvæði fyrri ort.	The-king asked whether Halli had anything composed before worded.	The king asked whether Halli had composed anything before.
Halli kveðst ekki hafa ort.	Halli said not had worded.	He said he had not composed anything.
"Það munu sumir menn mæla",	"It would some people say",	"Some people would say",
segir konungur, "að þú takist mikið á hendur, slík skáld sem ort hafa um mig áður eftir nokkrum málefnum.	said the-king, "that you take much in hand, such poets as worded have about me before after some matters.	said the king, "that you take much in hand, as such poets have composed poems about me for various reasons.
Eða hvað sýnist þér ráð Þjóðólfur?"	But what seems to-you advisable Thjodolf?"	But what seems advisable to you Thjodolf?"
"Ekki kann eg herra að gefa yður ráð",	"Not can I lord to give you advice",	"I can not give you advice, lord",

The Tale of Sarcastic Halli (Old Icelandic)

Old Icelandic	Literal	English
segir Þjóðólfur, "en hitt mun hóti nær að eg mun kunna að kenna Halla heilræði".	said Thjodolf, "but then could not near that I would know to teach Halli sound-advice".	said Thjodolf, "but then I could give Halli some sound advice".
"Hvert er það?"	"What is that?"	"What is that?"
segir konungur.	said the-king.	said the king.
"Það fyrst herra að hann ljúgi ekki að yður".	"That first lord that he lie not to you".	"First of all that he not lie to you".
"Hvað lýgur hann nú?"	"What lies he now?"	"What does he lie about now?"
segir konungur.	said the-king.	said the king.
"Það lýgur hann að hann sagðist ekki kvæði ort hafa",	"That lying he that he said not composed words had",	"He is lying when he says that he has not composed such words",
segir Þjóðólfur, "en eg segi hann ort hafa".	said Thjodolf, "but I say he words has".	said Thjodolf, "but I say that he has composed".
"Hvert er kvæði það",	"What is composed that",	"What has he composed?",
segir konungur, "eða um hvað er ort?"	said the-king, "and about what is worded?"	said the king, "and what is it composed about?"
Þjóðólfur svarar:	Thjodolf answered:	Thjodolf answered:
"Það köllum vér Kolluvísur er hann orti um kýr er hann gætti út á Íslandi".	"That call we Cow-verses which he worded about cows that he guarded out in Iceland".	"That which we call Cow-verses, which he composed about cows that he guarded out in Iceland".
"Er það satt Halli?"	"Is that true Halli?"	"Is that true Halli?"
segir konungur.	said the-king.	said the king.
"Satt er það",	"True is that",	"That is true",
segir Halli.	said Halli.	said Halli.
"Því sagðir þú að þú hefðir ekki kvæði ort?"	"Why said you that you had not composed words?"	"Why did you say that you had not composed such words?"
segir konungur.	said the-king.	said the king.

The Tale of Sarcastic Halli (Old Icelandic)

Old Icelandic	Literal	English
"Því", segir Halli, "að lítil kvæðismynd mundi á því þykja ef þetta skal heyra og lítt mun því verða á loft haldið".	"Because", said Halli, "that little poem-image would be therefore seemed if it should heard and little would therefore worth of praised held".	"Because", said Halli, "that such a little poem would seem if heard worth little praise".
"Það viljum vér fyrst heyra",	"That wish we first to-hear",	"We wish to hear that first",
segir konungur.	said the-king.	said the king.
"Skemmt mun þá fleira",	"Entertainment should then more",	"Then there should be more than one amusement",
segir Halli.	said Halli.	said Halli.
"Hverju þá?"	"What then?"	"What then?"
segir konungur.	said the-king.	said the king.
"Kveða mun Þjóðólfur þá skulu Soðtrogsvísur er hann orti út á Íslandi",	"Recite should Thjodolf then should Food-trough-verses which he worded out in Iceland",	"Thjodolf should then recite Food-trough-verses which he composed out in Iceland",
segir Halli, "og er það vel að Þjóðólfur leitaði á mig eða afvirti fyrir mér því að upp eru svo komnir í mér bitar og jaxlar að eg kann vel að svara honum jöfnum orðum".	said Halli, "and is that well that Thjodolf sought to me but disrespected before me because that up we-are so coming that my bite and molars that I can well to answer him even words".	said Halli, "and it is well that Thjodolf sought to disrespect me, but because my bite and molars are up I can answer him well with words".
Konungur brosti að og þótti honum gaman að etja þeim saman.	The-king smiled at and thought he enjoyment to provoke them together.	The king smiled and thought it was enjoyable to provoke them against eachother.
"Hvern veg er kvæði það eða um hvað er ort?"	"What way is composed that and about what are words?"	"What is it composed about and what are the words?"
segir konungur.	said the-king.	said the king.
Halli svarar:	Halli answered:	Halli answered:

The Tale of Sarcastic Halli (Old Icelandic)

Old Icelandic	Literal	English
"Það er ort um það er hann bar út ösku með öðrum systkinum sínum og þótti þá til einkis annars fær fyrir vitsmuna sakir og varð þó um að sjá að ei væri eldur í því að hann þurfti allt vit sitt í þann tíma".	"That is worded about that which he bore out ashes with other siblings his and thought then to nothing other accomplished before intellect sake and became though about to see that not would fire about because that he needed all wit his at that time".	"It is composed about carrying out ashes with his other siblings, and he was thought capable of accomplishing nothing more for the sake of his intellect, and it was necessary to see that there was no fire about because he needed all his wit at that time".
Konungur spyr ef þetta væri satt.	The-king asked if that was true.	The king asked if that was true.
"Satt er það herra",	"True is that lord",	"That is true, lord",
segir Þjóðólfur.	said Thjodolf.	said Thjodolf.
"Því hafðir þú svo óvirðulegt verk?"	"Why had you so unworthy work?"	"Why did you have such unworthy work?"
segir konungur.	said the-king.	said the king.
"Því herra",	"Because lord",	"Because lord",
segir Þjóðólfur,	said Thjodolf,	said Thjodolf,
"að eg vildi flýta oss til leika en ekki voru verk á mig lagin".	"that I wished quickly us to play and not was work to me assigned".	"that I wished to get us quickly out to play, and no work was assigned to me".
"Það olli því",	"That cause therefore",	"It caused",
segir Halli,	said Halli,	said Halli,
"að þú þóttir ei hafa verkmanns vit".	"that you thought not had workman's wit".	that you were thought not to have the sense of a worker".
"Ekki skuluð þið við talast",	"Not should you-two against speak",	"You must not argue",
segir konungur, "en heyra viljum vér kvæðin bæði".	said the-king, "but hear wish we poems both".	said the king, "but we want to hear both the poems".
Og svo varð að vera.	And so became to be.	And so it was.
Kvað þá hvor sitt kvæði.	Recited then each their poems.	Then each recited their poems.
Og er lokið var kvæðunum mælti konungurinn:	And when concluded was the-poetry spoke the-king:	And when the poems were finished, the king said:

The Tale of Sarcastic Halli (Old Icelandic)

Old Icelandic	Literal	English
"Lítið er kvæðið hvorttveggja enda munu lítil hafa verið yrkisefnin og er það þó enn minna er þú hefir ort Þjóðólfur".	"Little is poem each-way ended would little have been the-themes and is that though the lesser is you have worded Thjodolf".	"The poems are little on both sides, because the themes were small, and the lesser one is the one that you have composed Thjodolf".
"Svo er og herra",	"So is also lord",	"And so it is, lord",
segir Þjóðólfur, "og er Halli orðhvass mjög.	said Thjodolf, "and is Halli sharp-tongued much.	said Thjodolf, "and Halli is very sharp tongued.
En skyldara þætti mér honum að hefna föður síns en eiga sennur við mig hér í Noregi".	But should seems to-me of-him to avenge father his but not chatter with me here in Norway".	But I think it's more important for him to avenge his father than to have a fight with me here in Norway".
"Er það satt Halli?"	"Is that true Halli?"	"Is that true Halli?"
segir konungur.	said the-king.	said the king.
"Satt er það herra",	"True is that lord",	"That is true, lord",
segir hann.	said he.	he said.
"Hví fórstu af Íslandi til höfðingja við það að þú hafðir eigi hefnt föður þíns?"	"Why went-you from Iceland to chieftains with than that you have not avenged father yours?"	"Why did you go from Iceland to meet the chieftains when you had not avenged your father?"
segir konungur.	said the-king.	said the king.
"Því herra",	"Because lord",	"Because, lord",
segir Halli, "að eg var barn að aldri er faðir minn var veginn og tóku frændur málið og sættust á fyrir mína hönd.	said Halli, "that I was a-child in age when father mine was killed and took kinsman the-matter and settled it before my hand.	said Halli, "I was a child in age when my father was killed, and my cousins took the case and settled on my behalf.
En það þykir illt nafn á voru landi að heita griðníðingur".	But it considered ill named in our land to call truce-breaker".	But it is considered ill called in our land to be a truce-breaker".
Konungurinn svarar:	The-king answered:	The king answered:
"Það er nauðsyn að ganga ei á grið eða sættir og er úr þessu allvel leyst".	"It is necessary to go not to peace or settlements and that from this all-well answered".	"It is necessary to go to peace or reconciliation and this is well resolved".

The Tale of Sarcastic Halli (Old Icelandic)

Old Icelandic	Literal	English
"Svo hugði eg herra",	"So thought I lord",	"So I thought, lord",
segir Halli, "en vel má Þjóðólfur tala stórmannlega um slíka hluti því að öngvan veit eg jafngreypilega hefnt hafa síns föður sem hann".	said Halli, "and well may Thjodolf speak big-man-like about such a-thing since that none know I equally-badly revenge had his father as he".	said Halli, "and well may Thjodolf speak arrogantly about such a thing since no one I know has equally badly avenged his father as him".
"Víst er Þjóðólfur líklegur til að hafa það hraustlega gert",	"Certainly is Thjodolf likely to that have that boldly done",	"Certainly Thjodolf is like to have done that boldly",
segir konungur,	said the-king,	said the king,
"eða hvað verkum gert um það að hann hafi það framar gert en aðrir menn?"	"but what actions done about it that he has that from done than other people?"	but what actions did he take unlike other people?
"Það helst herra",	"That rather lord",	"Rather, lord",
segir Halli, "að hann át sinn föðurbana".	said Halli, "that he ate his father's-killer.	said Halli, "that he ate his father's killer".
Nú æptu menn upp og þóttust aldrei slík undur heyrt hafa.	Now called-out people up and thought never such wonder heard had.	Now people rose up and called out and thought they had never heard of such a wonder.
Konungurinn brosti að og bað menn vera hljóða.	The-king grinned at and ordered men to-be calm.	The king grinned and ordered people to be calm.
"Ger þetta satt er þú segir Halli",	"Does this true that you said Halli",	"Do so that what you say is true Halli",
segir konungur.	said the-king.	said the king.
Halli mælti:	Halli spoke:	Halli spoke:
"Það hygg eg að Þorljótur héti faðir Þjóðólfs.	"That think I that Thorljot named father Thjodolf's.	"I think that Thjodolf's father was named Thorljot.
Hann bjó í Svarfaðardal á Íslandi og var hann fátækur mjög en átti fjölda barna.	He lived in Svarfadardal in Iceland and was he fee-taken much and had many children.	He lived in Svarfadardal in Iceland and he was very poor and had many children.

The Tale of Sarcastic Halli (Old Icelandic)

Old Icelandic	Literal	English
En það er siður á Íslandi á haustum að bændur þinga til fátækra manna og var þá engi fyrri til nefndur en Þorljótur faðir Þjóðólfs	But it is a-custom in Iceland in autumn that farmers assemble to the-poor people and was then none before to named than Thorljot father Thjodolf's	But it is a custom in Iceland in the autumn for farmers to hold meetings for poor people, and there was no one better than Thorljot, Thjodolf's father,
og einn bóndi var svo stórlyndur að honum gaf sumargamlan kálf.	and one farmer was so large-repaying (generous) that he gave one-summer-old a-calf.	and one farmer was so generous that he gave him a summer-old calf.
Síðan sækir hann kálfinn og hafði á taum og var lykkja á enda taumsins.	Then sought he the-calf and had a leash and was noose at the-end the-leash.	Then he fetched the calf and had it on a leash and there was a loop at the end of the leash.
Og er hann kemur heim að túngarði sínum hefur hann kálfinn upp á garðinn og var furðulega hár garðurinn en	And when he came home to hayfield-wall his had he the-calf up on the-wall and was extremely high the-wall but	And when he came home to his yard wall he had the calf up on the wall, and it was extremely high,
þó var hærra fyrir innan því að þar hafði verið grafið torf til garðsins.	though was higher before inside because that there had been dug turf up-to the-wall.	but it was higher on the inside because the turf had been dug up to the wall.
Síðan fer hann inn yfir garðinn	Afterwards went he then over the-wall	Then he went into the yard,
en kálfurinn veltur út af garðinum.	but the-calf hung outside of the-wall.	but the calf tumbled out of the yard.
En lykkjan er á var taumsendanum brást um háls honum Þorljóti og kenndi hann ei niður fótum.	Then the-noose that about was the-leash transformed about neck his Thorljot and felt he not down feet.	But the loop that was on the end of the leash snapped around Thorljot's neck and he didn't fall to his feet.
Hékk nú sínumegin hvor og voru dauðir báðir er til var komið.	Hung now on-his-side each and were dead both then until who came.	Now each hung separately and both were dead by the time it was over.
Drógu börnin heim kálfinn og gerðu til matar og hygg eg að Þjóðólfur hefði óskert sinn hlut af honum".	Drew the-children home the-calf and made into food and think I that Thjodolf had the-whole his share of him".	The children brought the calf home and made it for dinner, and I think Thjodolf had his share of it intact".
"Nærri hófi mundi það",	"Close-to reasonable should-be that",	"That would be more reasonable",
segir konungur.	said the-king.	said the king.

The Tale of Sarcastic Halli (Old Icelandic)

Old Icelandic	Literal	English
Þjóðólfur brá sverði og vildi höggva til Halla.	Thjodolf drew sword and wished to-strike to Halli.	Thjodolf drew his sword and wanted to attack Halli.
Hljópu menn þá í milli þeirra.	Ran men then in between them.	Men ran in between them.
Konungur kvað hvorigum hlýða skyldu að gera öðrum mein:	The-king said neither obeying should to do eachother harm:	The king said that neither should do eachother harm if they obeyed him.
"Leitaðir þú Þjóðólfur fyrri á Halla".	"Seek you Thjodolf went-before to Halli".	"Thjodolf, you went for Halli first".
Varð nú svo að vera sem konungur vildi.	Was now so as being as the-king willed.	Then it was now as the king wished.
Færði Halli drápuna og mæltist hún vel fyrir og launaði konungur honum góðum peningum.	Performed Halli the-drapa (poem) and recited it well for and rewarded the-king him good payment.	Halli performed the drapa and it was well received, and the king paid him good money.
Leið nú á veturinn og var allt kyrrt.	Passed now to winter and was all peaceful.	It now passed to winter and everything was quiet.

7

Einar var maður nefndur og var kallaður fluga.	Einar was a-man named and was called Fly.	There was a man named Einar who was called Fly.
Hann var son Háreks úr Þjóttu.	He was son Harek's from Thjotta.	He was the son of Harek from Thjotta.
Hann var lendur maður og hafði sýslu á Hálogalandi og finnferð af konungi og var nú í kærleikum miklum við konung en þó eldi þar jafnan ýmsu á.	He was land man and had business in Halogaland and Finland-voyages of the-king's and was now in friendship much with the-king but though fire there equally about was.	He was a land owning man and had business in Halogaland and voyages to Finland, and was now in great friendship with the king, but there was always something going on there.
Einar var óeinarðarmaður mikill.	Einar was unreliable much.	Einar was very unreliable.
Drap hann menn ef ei gerðu allt sem hann vildi og bætti öngvan mann.	Killed he men if not did all as he wished and compensated no man.	He killed people if they didn't do everything he wanted and gave compensation to no man.
Einars var von til hirðarinnar að jólunum.	Einar was expected to court at Yule.	Einar was expected at court during Yule.

The Tale of Sarcastic Halli (Old Icelandic)

Old Icelandic	Literal	English
Þeim Halla og Sigurði sessunaut hans varð talað til Einars.	They Halli and Sigurd bench-companion his were talking about Einar.	Halli and his bench companion Sigurd were talking about Einar.
Sagði Sigurður Halla frá að engi maður þorði að mæla í móti Einari eða í aðra skál að leggja en hann vildi og hann bætti ekki fé fyrir víg eða rán.	Told Sigurd Halli from that no man dared to speak to against Einar or that other shall to allow but he wished and he compensated not payment for slaying or robbery.	Sigurd told Halli that no man dared to speak against Einar or to allow anything other than what he wished, and that he paid no compensation for slaying or robbery.
Halli svarar:	Halli answered:	Halli answered:
"Vændishöfðingjar mundu slíkt kallaðir á voru landi".	"Wicked-chieftain would such be-called in our land".	"Such a chieftain would be called wicked in our land".
"Mæl þú varlega félagi",	"Speak you warily companion",	"Speak carefully, friend",
segir Sigurður, "því að hann er lítilþægur að orðum ef honum er í móti skapi".	said Sigurd, "because that he is little-behaving that words if he is to against mind".	said Sigurd, "because he doesn't mix his words if he's in a bad mood".
"Þó að þér séuð allir svo hræddir",	"Though that you look all so afraid",	"Although you are all so afraid",
segir Halli, "að enginn yðvar þori að mæla eitt orð í móti honum þá segi eg þér það að eg skyldi kæra ef hann gerði mér rangt og þess get eg að hann bæti mér".	said Halli, "that none of-you dare to say one word to against him then say I to-you this that I would accuse if he did me wrong and this get I of him compensate me".	said Halli, "that none of you dare to say a word against him, I tell you that I would complain if he did me wrong and I expect him to make it up to me".
"Hví þér en öðrum?"	"Why to-you than others?"	"Why are you different from others?"
segir Sigurður.	said Sigurd.	said Sigurd.
"Það mundi honum sýnast",	"That would to-him appear",	"That shall become apparent to him",
segir Halli.	said Halli.	said Halli.
Þar til þræta þeir hér um að Halli býður Sigurði að veðja hér um.	They to argued them here about that Halli offered Sigurd to wager here about.	They argued amongst themselves until Halli offered to make a wager with Sigurd about it.

The Tale of Sarcastic Halli (Old Icelandic)

Old Icelandic	Literal	English
Leggur Sigurður hér við gullhring er stóð hálfa mörk en Halli leggur við höfuð sitt.	Laid Sigurd here with a-gold-ring in place half a-mark and Halli laid with head his.	Here, Sigurd placed a gold ring that stood at half a mark, but Halli placed his head.
Einar kemur að jólunum og situr hann á aðra hönd konungi og menn hans út frá honum.	Einar came at Yule and sat he by other hand the-king's and people his about from him.	Einar came at Yule and he sat by the king's hand with his people around him.
Var honum öll þjónusta veitt sem konungi sjálfum.	Was he all service given as the-king himself.	He was given every service as much as the king himself.
Og jóladag er menn voru mettir mælti konungurinn:	And Yule-day when people were finished-eating spoke the-king:	And on Yule day when people had finished eating the king spoke:
"Nú viljum vér hafa fleira til gamans en drekka.	"Now wish we to-have more to amusement than drinking.	"Now we wish to have more amusement than drinking.
Skaltu nú Einar segja oss hvað til tíðinda hefir orðið í förum yðrum".	Shall-you now Einar tell us what to news have worded on journey yours".	Einar, you shall now tell us what word you have of news on your journey.
Einar svarar:	Einar answered:	Einar answered:
"Ekki kann eg það í frásagnir að færa herra þó að vér hnúskum búfinna eða fiskimenn".	"Not can I that as stories to bring lord though that we knocked-down farmers and fishermen".	"I don't know how to tell stories, lord, even though we knocked down some farmers and fishermen".
Konungur svarar:	The-king answered:	The king answered:
"Segið settlega því að vér erum lítilþægir að og þykir oss gaman að því öllu þó að yður þyki lítils vert er jafnan staðið í stríði".	"Tell sedately because that we are easily-satisfied by and seems to-us a-delight that therefore all though that you think little worth is always standing in battles".	"Tell us calmly because we are easily satisfied by it and it all seems to us a delight even though you think it is of little worth, and as you are constantly in battles".
"Það er þó herra helst að segja",	"It is though lord rather to say",	"However, lord, I prefer to say",
segir Einar, "að í fyrra sumar er vér komum norður á Mörkina mættum vér Íslandsfari einu og höfðu þeir orðið þangað sæhafa og setið þar um veturinn.	said Einar, "that of last summer when we came north of The-border met we Iceland-voyage one and had they become from-there sea-scattered and sat there about winter.	said Einar, "that last summer when we came north of the border we met a ship journeying from Iceland, and they had been sea-scattered and were there since winter.

The Tale of Sarcastic Halli (Old Icelandic)

Old Icelandic	Literal	English
Bar eg á hendur þeim að þeir mundu átt hafa kaup við Finna fyrir utan yðvart lof eða mitt	Bore I to hand them that they would had having traded with The-Sami for without your permission or mine	I put it to them that they had traded with the Sami people without your permission or mine,
en þeir duldu og gengu ei við	that the denied and went not with	which they denied and would not agree with,
en oss þóttu þeir ótrúlegir og beiddi eg þá rannsóknar	but we thought them un-truthful and asked I then a-search	but we thought they were untruthful, and I asked to search them,
en þeir synjuðu þverlega.	but they refused crossly.	but they flatly refused.
Eg sagði það þá að þeir skyldu hafa það er þeim væri verra og maklegra og bað eg mína menn vopnast og leggja að þeim.	I said that then that they should have it what for-them being worse and well-deserved and ordered I my men armed and lay at them.	I then said that they should have what was worse and more deserved for them, and I asked my men to arm themselves and attack them.
Eg hafði fimm langskip og lögðum vér að á bæði borð og léttum ei fyrr en hroðið var skipið.	I had five longships and laid we to at both boards and let-up not before that cleared was the-ship.	I had five longships and we anchored on both sides and did not let up until the ship was cleared.
Og einn íslenskur maður er þeir kölluðu Einar varðist svo vel að hans maka fann eg aldrei og víst var skaði að um þann mann og ei hefðum vér unnið skipið ef slíkir hefðu allir verið innanborðs".	And one Icelander man that they called Einar guarded so well that he equal found I never and certainly was harm to about that man and not have we won the-ship if such had all been onboard".	And one Icelander man, that they called Einar, guarded so well that I have never found his equal, and it was certainly a loss for that man, and we would not have won the ship if such men as him had all been aboard".
"Illa gerðir þú það Einar",	"Badly done you it Einar",	"You did badly, Einar",
segir konungur, "er þú drepur saklausa menn þó að ei geri allt sem þér líkar best".	said the-king, "when you killed sake-less people though that not did all as you liked best".	said the king, "you kill innocent people who don't do everything you like best".
"Mun eg ei",	"Would I not",	"I will not",
segir Einar, "sitja fyrir hættu þeirri.	said Einar, "settle for danger theirs.	said Einar, "sit before that danger.
En mæla það sumir menn herra að þér gerið ei allt sem guðréttilegast.	And say it some people lord that you do not all as good-rightly.	But some people say, sir, that you don't do everything in the most godly way.

The Tale of Sarcastic Halli (Old Icelandic)

Old Icelandic	Literal	English
En þeir reyndust illa og fundum vér mikinn finnskrepp í skipinu".	But they proved bad also found we much Sami-goods in the-ship".	But they turned out to be bad and we found a great amount of Sami goods in the ship".
Halli heyrði hvað þeir töluðu og kastaði hnífinum fram á borðið og hætti að eta.	Halli heard what they spoke and cast knife away from the-table and stopped of eating.	Halli heard what they were talking about and threw the knife on the table and stopped eating.
Sigurður spurði ef hann væri sjúkur.	Sigurd asked if he was sick.	Sigurd asked if he was sick.
Hann kvað það ei vera	He said that not was	He said it wasn't,
en kvað þetta þó sótt verra:	but said this though sickness worse:	but he said this was even worse:
"Einar fluga sagði lát Einars bróður míns er hann kveðst fellt hafa á kaupskipinu í fyrra sumar og má vera að nú gefi til að leita eftir bótunum við hann Einar".	"Einar Fly told-of had Einar brother mine that he said fell had on merchant-ship in before summer and may be that now give to of seeking after compensation with him Einar".	"Einar Fly told about the death of my brother Einar, who he claims to have killed on the merchant ship last summer, and it may be that he now seeks to give compensation for Einar".
"Tala ekki um félagi",	"Speak not about companion",	"Do not speak about it, companion",
segir Sigurður,	said Sigurd,	said Sigurd,
"sá mun vænstur".	"so would-be promising".	that would be the most promising.
Nei, sagði Halli, "ekki mundi hann svo við mig gera ef hann ætti eftir mig að mæla".	No, said Halli, "not would he so with me doing if he had after me the matter".	Halli said no, "he would not do that with me if it was my case he was dealing with".
Hljóp hann þá fram yfir borðið, gekk innar fyrir hásætið og mælti:	Jumped he then from over table, went in before high-seat and spoke:	He then jumped over the table, and went before the high seat and spoke:
"Tíðindi sögðuð þér Einar bóndi, þau mér akta ærið mjög, í drápi Einars bróður míns er þér sögðust felldan hafa á kaupskipinu í fyrra sumar.	"News announced you Einar master, that me taxes greatly much, by the-killing Einar's brother mine who you said killed had in merchant-ship about last summer.	"You announced news which concerns me greatly, the killing of Einar, my brother, who you said you killed in the merchant ship last summer.

The Tale of Sarcastic Halli (Old Icelandic)

Old Icelandic	Literal	English
Nú vil eg vita hvort þú vilt nokkru bæta mér Einar bróður minn".	Now wish I to-know whether you will some compensation to-me Einar brother mine".	Now I wish to know if you will pay me some compensation for my brother".
"Hefir þú ei spurt að eg bæti engan mann?"	"Have you not heard that I compensate no man?"	"Have you not heard that I compensate no one",
segir Einar.	said Einar.	said Einar.
"Eigi er mér skylt að trúa því",	"Not I me should to believe accordingly",	"I was not obliged to believe",
segir Halli, "að þér væri allt illa gefið þó að eg heyrði það sagt".	said Halli, "that you were all evil given though that I heard that said".	said Halli, "that you were all evil, though I heard it said".
"Gakk burt maður",	"Go away man",	"Go away man",
segir Einar, "annar mun verri".	said Einar, "otherwise should-be worse".	said Einar, "otherwise it shall be worse".
Halli gekk að sitja.	Halli went to sit.	Halli went to sit.
Sigurður spyr hve farist hefði.	Sigurd asked how gone had.	Sigurd asked how it had gone.
Hann svarar og kveðst hafa hótun fyrir fébætur.	He answered and said had a-threat for compensation.	He answered and said that he had been given a threat as compensation.
Sigurður bað hann ei oftar koma á þetta mál og sé laus veðjanin.	Sigurd asked him not more come that this matter and so lost the-wager.	Sigurd ask him not to persist in this matter any more, and the wager would be lost.
Halli kvað honum vel fara	Halli said he well went	Halli said it had gone well,
"en á skal koma oftar".	"but about shall come more".	but there is more to come.
Og annan dag eftir gekk Halli fyrir Einar og mælti:	And the-next day after went Halli before Einar and spoke:	And the next day Halli went before Einar and spoke:
"Það mál vil eg vekja Einar ef þú vilt nokkru bæta mér bróður minn".	"The matter wish I awaken Einar if you will some compensation to-me brother mine".	"I wish to raise the matter with you, Einar, whether you will give me some compensation for my brother".
Einar svarar:	Einar answered:	Einar answered:

The Tale of Sarcastic Halli (Old Icelandic)

Old Icelandic	Literal	English
"Þú ert seinþreyttur að og ef þú dregst ei brott þá muntu fara slíka för sem bróðir þinn eða verri".	"You are persistent this and if you draw not away then should fare such before as brother yours or worse".	"You are persistent in this, and if you do not back away, then it should go the same way as you brother did or worse".
Konungurinn bað hann ei svo svara	The-king ordered him not so to-answer	The king ordered him not to answer like that,
"og er það frændunum ofraun og veit ei hvers hugar hverjum lér.	"and was it kinsmen too-much and known not how-so minds each leaned.	and it is too-much for the kinsmen and not known how each mind goes.
En þú Halli kom ei aftur á þetta mál því að stærri bokkar verða að þola honum slíkt en þú ert".	But you Halli come not again of this matter because that greater bigger-men have-been that enduring him such than you are".	But you, Halli, do not raise this matter again because greater and bigger men have endured such as you are".
Halli svarar:	Halli answered:	Halli answered:
"Svo mun vera verða".	"So should be becomes".	"So it will have to be".
Gekk hann þá til rúms síns.	Went he then to rooms his.	Then he went to his rooms.
Sigurður fagnar honum vel og spurði hve farist hafði.	Sigurd welcomed him well and asked how gone had.	Sigurd welcomed him well and asked how it had gone.
Halli kveðst hafa heitan fyrir fébætur af Einari.	Halli said had threat for compensation of Einar.	Halli said that he had received a threat for compensation from Einar.
"Þótti mér það í hug",	"Thought me that in mind",	"I thought that in my mind",
segir Sigurður, "og sé laus veðjanin".	said Sigurd, "and so lost the-wager".	said Sigurd, "and so the wager is lost".
"Vel fer þér",	"Well go you",	"You behave well",
segir Halli, "en á skal eg koma þriðja sinn".	said Halli, "but for shall I come a-third occasion".	said Halli, "but I shall raise the matter a third time".
"Gefa vil eg þér nú til hringinn",	"Give will I you now to the-ring",	"I will now give you the ring",
sagði Sigurður, "að þú látir vera kyrrt er þetta hefir þó nokkuð af mér til hlotist í fyrstu".	said Sigurd, "that you leave be peace as this has though somewhat of me to part the first".	said Sigurd, "so that you will let there be peace, because I am responsible for part of this.

The Tale of Sarcastic Halli (Old Icelandic)

Old Icelandic	Literal	English
Halli svarar:	Halli answered:	Halli answered:
"Sýnir þú hver maður þú ert og ekki má þér um kenna hversu sem til vegar fer.	"Show you what man you are and not may you about know how-so as to way go.	"You show what kind of man you are and you can't be blamed no matter what happens.
En prófa skal enn um sinn".	But prove shall one about occasion".	But it must be tried one more time".
Og þegar um morguninn er konungur tók handlaugar og Einar fluga gekk Halli að honum og kvaddi konunginn.	And early about morning when the-king took hand-washing and Einar Fly went Halli to him and greeted the-king.	And early the next morning, when the king took to washing his hands along with Einar Fly, Halli went to him and greeted the king.
Konungurinn spyr hvað hann vildi.	The-king asked what he wanted.	The king asked what he wanted.
Herra,	"Lord",	"Lord",
segir Halli, "eg vil segja yður draum minn.	said Halli, "I wish to-tell you dream mine.	said Halli, "I wish to tell you about my dream.
Eg þóttist vera allur maður annar en eg er".	I seemed to-be all man another than I am".	I thought I was a completely different person than I am".
"Hvað manni þóttist þú vera?"	"What man thought you to-be?"	"Who did you think you were?"
segir konungur.	said the-king.	said the king.
"Eg þóttist vera Þorleifur skáld en hann Einar fluga þótti mér vera Hákon jarl Sigurðarson og þóttist eg hafa ort um hann níð og mundi eg sumt níðið er eg vaknaði".	"I thought being Thorleif the-poet but he Einar Fly seemed to-me to-be Hakon earl Sigurdson and thought I had worded about him slander and remembered I some the-slander when I awoke".	I thought I was Thorleif the poet, but Einar Fly was Earl Hakon Sigurdson, and I thought I had written about him, and I remembered some things when I woke up".
Sneri Halli þá utar eftir höllunni og kvað nokkuð fyrir munni sér og námu menn ei orðaskil.	Turned Halli then out after the-hall and spoke something before mouth his and took people not words-separated.	Halli then turned around outside the palace and said something in front of his mouth and the people did not understand any of it.
Konungur mælti:	The-king spoke:	The king spoke:

The Tale of Sarcastic Halli (Old Icelandic)

Old Icelandic	Literal	English
"Þetta var ekki draumur annar en hann dregur þessi dæmi saman.	"This was not a-dream another that he drew these examples together.	"This was not a dream, and he has drawn these examples together.
Og svo mun fara með ykkur sem fór með þeim Hákoni Hlaðajarli og Þorleifi skáldi og það sama gerir Halli.	And so should go with you as went with they Hakon Earl-of-Lade and Thorleif the-poet and that same does Halli.	And so it should go with you as it went with Earl Hakon of Lade and Thorleif the poet, and Halli is doing the same thing.
Hann svífst einkis og megum við sjá að bitið hefir níðið ríkari menn en svo sem þú ert Einar, sem var Hákon jarl, og mun það munað meðan Norðurlönd eru byggð og er verri einn kviðlingur, ef munaður verður eftir, en lítil fémúta, um dýran mann kveðinn	He shrinks-from nothing and may we see that biting has-been the-slander richer men than so as you are Einar, as was Hakon earl, and would-be that remembered as-long-as Northern-lands are settled and is worse one short-poem, if remembered becomes after, then little money-bribe, about fine men composed	He shrinks from nothing, and we may see how slander has bitten richer men than you are, Einar, as Earl Hakon was, and it would be remembered as long as the Northern Lands are settled, one short verse about powerful men, if it becomes remembered afterwards, is worse than paying a small bribe,
og ger svo vel og leys hann af með nokkru".	and do so well and repay him of with somehow".	and so it would do well to repay him somehow".
"Þér skuluð ráða herra",	"You should decide lord",	"You will decide, lord"
segir Einar, "og seg honum að hann taki þrjár merkur silfurs af féhirði mínum er eg fékk honum síðast í sjóði".	said Einar, "and tell him that he takes three marks of-silver of fee-servant mine that I give him the-last in purse".	said Einar, "and tell him that he may take three marks of silver from my fee-servant in the purse I just gave him".
Þetta var sagt Halla.	This was told Halli.	This was told to Halli.
Gekk hann að finna féhirðinn og sagði honum.	Went he to find fee-servant and told him.	He went to find the fee-servant and told him.
Hann kvað vera fjórar merkur silfurs í sjóðnum.	He said be four marks of-silver in the-purse.	He said there were four marks of silver in the purse.
Halli kveðst þrjár hafa skyldu.	Halli said three have should-be.	Halli said that he was to have three.
Halli gekk þá fyrir Einar og sagði honum.	Halli went then before Einar and told him.	Halli went before Einar and said to him:
"Hafa mundir þú það er í var sjóðnum",	"Have would you that which in was the-purse",	"Have you taken what was in the purse?",
segir Einar.	said Einar.	said Einar.

The Tale of Sarcastic Halli (Old Icelandic)

Old Icelandic	Literal	English
Nei, sagði Halli, "öðruvís skaltu ná lífi mínu en eg verði þjófur af fé þínu og sá eg að þú hafðir það ætlað mér".	No, said Halli, "other-knowing shall-you obtain life mine than I being thief of money yours and saw I that you have that intended to-me".	Halli said no, "you will have to find another way to take my life than me being a thief of your money, and I saw what you intended for me".
Og svo var að Einar hafði það ætlað Halla að hann mundi það er í var sjóðnum hafa og þótti honum það nóg banasök.	And so was that Einar had it intended Halli that he would that which in was the-purse have and thought him that enough death-sentence.	And so it was that Einar thought that Halli would have taken whatever was in the purse, which he thought would be enough of an offence for a death sentence.
Gekk Halli nú til sætis síns og sýndi Sigurði féð.	Went Halli no to seat his and showed Sigurd the-money.	Halli went now to his seat and showed Sigurd the money.
Sigurður tók hringinn og kvað Halla vel hafa til unnið.	Sigurd took the-ring and said Halli well had to won.	Sigurd took the ring and said that Halli had won it.
Hann svarar:	He answered:	He answered:
"Eigi erum við þá jafnir þegnar og tak hring þinn og njót manna best.	"Not are-we with then equal men and take the-ring yours and enjoy man the-best.	"We are not equally good men, keep the ring and enjoy it, best of men.
En þér satt að segja þá átti eg aldrei skylt við þenna mann er Einar hefir drepið og vildi eg vita ef eg næði fénu af honum".	But to-you truth to say then related-to I never should with this man which Einar had killed and wished I to-know if I neared money of him".	But to tell you the truth, I was never related to this man which Einar killed, and I wished to know if I could obtain money from him".
"Engum manni ertu líkur að prettum",	"No man are-you like in trickery",	"There is no one like you in trickery",
segir Sigurður.	said Sigurd.	said Sigurd.
Einar fór brott eftir jólin norður á Hálogaland.	Einar went away after Yule north to Halogaland.	Einar went away after Yule north to Halogaland.

8

Um vorið bað Halli konung orlofs að fara til Danmerkur í kaupferð.	About spring asked Halli the-king vacation to travel to Denmark on trading-voyage.	In the spring, King Halli asked for leave to go to Denmark on a trading voyage.

The Tale of Sarcastic Halli (Old Icelandic)

Old Icelandic	Literal	English
Konungur bað hann fara sem hann vildi "og kom aftur skjótt því oss þykir gaman að þér og far varlega fyrir Einari flugu.	The-king bid he travel as he wished "and come back quickly because we consider fun that to-you and travel warily because-of Einar Fly.	The king asked him to go as he wished "and come back quickly because we like you and be careful of Einar Fly.
Hann mun hafa illan hug á þér og sjaldan veit eg honum jafnsleppt tekist hafa".	He should have evil mind to you and seldom know I him equally-slip taken has".	He will have a bad opinion of you and I rarely know of him slipping up".
Halli tók sér far með kaupmönnum suður til Danmerkur og svo til Jótlands.	Halli took himself passage with trading-men south to Denmark and so to Jutland.	Halli took found passage with merchants south to Denmark and then to Jutland.
Rauður hét maður er þar hafði sýslu og réðst Halli þar til vistar.	Raud was-named a-man who there had stewardship and appointed Halli there to lodgings.	There was a man named Raud who had a stewardship there and appointed Halli there some lodgings.
Það bar til eitt sinn er hann skyldi hafa þing fjölmennt og er menn skyldu þar mæla lögskilum sínum þá var svo mikið háreysti og gap að engi maður mátti þar málum sínum fram koma	It bore to one occasion that he should have assembly followers and that men should there matters legal-settlement theirs then was so much commotion and gaping that no man may there matter his from come-forward	It happened day when he was supposed to have a large assembly and when people were supposed to discuss their legal issues there, there was so much shouting and gaping that no one was allowed to present their case there
og fóru menn við það heim um kveldið.	and went people with that home about evening.	and the people went home that evening.
Það var um kveldið er menn komu til drykkjar að Rauður mælti:	It was about evening that men came to drink that Raud spoke:	It was in the evening when people came to drink that Raud said:
"Það væri ráðleitinn maður er ráð fyndi til að fólk þetta allt þagnaði".	"It being cunning man who plan find to that people these all silenced".	"It would be a wise man who could find a way to keep all these people quiet".
Halli svarar:	Halli answered:	Halli answered:
"Það fæ eg gert þegar eg vil að hér skal hvert mannsbarn þagna".	"That can I do as-soon-as I wish that here shall each man's-son silence".	"I can do that when I want every human being to be silent".
"Það færð þú ei gert landi",	"That undertaking you not do the-land",	"You will not get that done in this land",
segir Rauður.	said Raud.	said Raud.

The Tale of Sarcastic Halli (Old Icelandic)

Old Icelandic	Literal	English
Um morguninn komu menn til þings og var nú slíkt óp og gap sem hinn fyrra dag og varð öngum málum skilað.	About morning came people to the-assembly and were now such shouting and gaping as the before day and were no matters settled.	In the morning, people came to the assembly and now there was such an uproar as the previous day and no issues were resolved.
Fóru menn við það heim.	Went men with that home.	The men then went home.
Þá mælti Rauður:	Then spoke Raud:	Then Raud spoke:
"Viltu veðja um Halli hvort þú færð hljóðið á þinginu eða ei?"	"Will-you wager about Halli each you carry-out silence to the-assembly or not?"	"Will you wager, Halli, that you will get silence at the assembly or not?".
Halli kveðst þess búinn.	Halli said this settled.	Halli said this would be done.
Rauður svarar:	Raud answered:	Raud answered:
"Legg við höfuð þitt en eg gullhring er stendur mörk".	"Lay with head yours and I gold-ring which stands one-mark".	"Lay down your head, and I will lay down a ring which is worth one mark".
"Það skal vera",	"That shall be",	"So it shall be",
segir Halli.	said Halli.	said Halli.
Um morguninn spurði Halli Rauð ef hann vildi veðjanina halda.	About morning asked Halli Raud if he wished wager to-hold.	In the morning, Halli asked Raud if he wanted to keep the wager.
Hann kveðst halda vilja.	He said hold wished.	He said that he wished to keep it.
Komu menn nú til þingsins og var nú slíkt óp eða meira sem hina fyrri dagana.	Came men now to the-assembly and were not such shouting and more than the before day.	Now people came to the assembly and there was as much shouting or more as the previous days.
Og er menn varði síst hleypur Halli upp og æpir sem hæst mátti hann:	And when people were least ran Halli up and cried-out as high as-might he:	And when the people were at their least, Halli ran up and shouted as loud as he could:
"Hlýði allir menn.	"Listen all people.	"Listen everyone.
Mér er máls þörf.	For-me is matter of-need.	For me this is a matter of need.

The Tale of Sarcastic Halli (Old Icelandic)

Old Icelandic	Literal	English
Mér er horfin hein og heinasmjör, skreppa og þar með allur skreppuskrúði sá er karlmanni er betra að hafa en að missa".	Mine is lost hone and honing-grease, bag and there with all bag-tackle so is a-man that better to have than to lose".	I have lost my hone and honing grease, and my bag with all its tackle, which is better for a man to have than lose".
Allir menn þögnuðu.	All people silenced.	All the people were silent.
Sumir hugðu að hann mundi ær orðinn en sumir hugðu að hann mundi tala konungs erindi nokkur.	Some thought that he could-be awed of-words and some thought that he could-be speaking the-king's errand some.	Some people thought that he was lost for words, and some thought that he could be speaking some message from the king.
Og er hljóð fékkst settist Halli niður og tók við hringinum.	And when silence received settled Halli down and took with the-ring.	And when there was a sound, Halli sat down and took the ring.
En þegar menn sáu að þetta var ekki nema dáruskapur þá var háreysti sem áður og komst Halli á hlaupi undan því að Rauður vildi hafa líf hans og þótti þetta verið hafa hin mesta ginning.	Then as-soon-as people saw that this was nothing but mockery then was commotion as before and came Halli to running out-from because that Raud wished to-have life his and thought this become had the most deception.	But when people saw that this was nothing but a prank, Halli was as stubborn as before and ran away from Raud who wanted his head and thought that this was the greatest deception.
Létti hann eigi fyrr en hann kom til Englands.	Let-up he not before that he came to England.	He did not let up until he came to England.

9

Þá réð fyrir Englandi Haraldur Guðinason.	Then ruled for England Harald Godwinson.	Then Harald Godwinson ruled England.
Halli fer þegar á konungs fund og kveðst hafa ort um hann drápu og bað sér hljóðs.	Halli went straight-away to the-king to-meet and said had composed about him a-drapa (poem) and asked for-him be-heard.	Halli went straight away to the king and said that he had composed a drapa about him and asked that it be heard.
Konungur lét gefa honum hljóð.	The-king had granted him a-hearing.	The king granted him a hearing.
Sest Halli fyrir kné konungi og flutti fram kvæðið.	Sat Halli before knee the-king's and brought from the-poem.	Halli sat down before the king and recited the poem.

The Tale of Sarcastic Halli (Old Icelandic)

Old Icelandic	Literal	English
Og er lokið var kvæðinu spurði konungur skáld sitt er var með honum hvern veg væri kvæðið.	And when ended was the-poem asked the-king the-poet this that was with him each way being the-poem.	And when the poem was finished, the king asked his poet who was with him and what the poem was about.
Hann kveðst ætla að gott væri.	He said supposed that good was.	He said that he supposed it was good.
Konungur bauð Halla með sér að vera en Halli kveðst búinn vera til Noregs áður.	The-king invited Halli with him to be but Halli said prepared being to Norway back.	The king invited Halli to stay with him, but Halli said he has already prepared to return to Norway.
Konungur kvað þá þann veg fara mundu af hendi "um kvæðislaun við þig sem vér njótum kvæðisins því að enginn hróður verður oss að því kvæði er enginn kann.	The-king said then that way going would of hand "about poem-reward with you as we benefit the-poem because that none fame worthy to-us that before recited as none knows.	The king said then that it would go the same way "in rewarding you for the poem, as we benefit from the poem, because we get no fame's worth from a poem that no one knows.
Sit nú niður á gólfið en eg mun láta hella silfri í höfuð þér og haf þá það er í hárinu loðir og þykir mér þá hvort horfa eftir öðru er vér skulum eigi ná að nema kvæðið".	Sit now down on the-floor then I will have poured silver on head yours and have then it which in the-hairs of-your-hair and seems to-me then each turn after the-other that we shall not obtain to but the-poem".	Now sit down on the floor, and I will have silver poured over your head, and keep whatever sticks to your hair, and it seems to me that it looks the same on both sides because we will not get to learn the poem".
Halli svarar:	Halli answered:	Halli answered:
"Bæði mun vera að lítilla launa mun vert vera enda munu þessi launin og lítil vera.	"Both should be that little reward should worth become and shall this repay also little being.	"Both are small rewards due and that the rewards will be small.
Lofa munuð þér herra að eg gangi út nauðsynja minna".	Promise shall you lord that I go out needs mine".	Will you promise me that I may go outside to attend to my needs".
"Gakk sem þú vilt",	"Go as you wish",	"Go as you wish",
segir konungur.	said the-king.	said the king.
Halli gekk þar til er skipsmiðir voru og bar í höfuð sér tjöru og gerði sem diskur væri	Halli went there to where ship-smiths were and bore on head his tar and made as a-plate being	Halli walked to where the shipbuilders were and carried tar on his head and fashioned into the shape of a plate

The Tale of Sarcastic Halli (Old Icelandic)

Old Icelandic	Literal	English
og gekk síðan inn og bað hella silfrinu yfir sig.	and went afterwards in and asked pour the-silver over him.	and then went back inside and asked for the silver to be poured over him.
Konungur kvað hann vera brögðóttan	The-king said he was cunning	The king said that he was cunning,
og var nú hellt yfir hann og var það mikið silfur er hann fékk.	and was now rather over him and was it much silver that he got.	and now the silver was poured over him, and it was a lot of silver that he got.
Fór hann síðan þangað er skip þau voru er til Noregs ætluðu og voru öll burtu nema eitt og var þar ráðinn fjöldi manna með miklum þunga.	Went he afterwards from-there to ship there where that to Norway intended and were all away except one and was that appointed many men with much heavy-cargo.	He then went to where the ships were that were going to Norway, and they were all gone, except one that had many men with much heavy cargo.
En Halli hafði of fjár og vildi gjarna í burt því að hann hafði ekki kvæði ort um konung annað en kveðið endilausu og mátti hann því ekki kenna það.	But Halli had of fee and wished gladly to away because that he had not composed words about the-king other than reciting nonsense and may he therefore not teach it.	Halli had plenty of money and wished very much to travel away, because he had not composed words about the king other than reciting nonsense, and therefore could not teach it.
Stýrimaður bað hann fá til ráð að suðurmenn gengju úr skipinu og kveðst þá vilja gjarna taka við honum.	Steersman bid him get to advice that southern-men walking out-of the-ship and said then wished gladly take with him.	The steersman told him to find a scheme so that the southern men would leave the ship, then he would gladly take him.
En þá var komið að vetri.	But then was coming the winter.	But then winter was coming.
Halli var hjá þeim í herbergjum um hríð.	Halli was beside them in sleeping-quarters about awhile.	Halli stayed with them in sleeping quarters for a while.
Eina nótt lét Halli illa í svefni og var lengi áður þeir fengu vakið hann.	One night had Halli badly in sleep and was long before they caught awake him.	One night, Halli felt sick in his sleep and it was a long time before they could wake him up.
Þeir spurðu hvað hann hefði dreymt.	They asked what he had dreamed.	They asked what he had dreamed.
Halli kvað lokið því að hann mundi biðja þá fars héðan frá,	Halli said finished therefore that he would ask then travel from-there from,	Halli said that he was finished with asking for passage from there,

The Tale of Sarcastic Halli (Old Icelandic)

Old Icelandic	Literal	English
"mér þótti maður koma að mér ógurlegur og kvað þetta:"	"to-me seemed a-man come that to-me terrible and recited this:	It seemed to me that a terrible looking man came to me and recited this:
Hröng er þars hafnan þöngul	Roaring is there the harbour there	Roaring is there the harbour there
held eg um, síð er eg fjör seldag.	think me about, since that I life sold.	think me about, since that I life sold.
Hverft er sitk að Ránar.	Disappeared am-I one to Ran.	Disappeared am-I one to Ran.
Sumir eru í búð með humrum.	Some are in lodgings with lobsters.	Some are in lodgings with lobsters.
Ljóst er lýsu að gista.	Light is the-whitings with guest.	Light is the-whitings with guest.
Lendi eg út við ströndu.	Lands I out from the-shore.	Lands I out from the-shore.
Því sit eg bleikr í brúki.	Because sit I pale in use.	Because sit I pale in use.
Blakir mér þarmr um hnakka,	Pale mine intestines about neck,	Pale mine intestines about neck,
blakir mér fyrir þínum hnakka.	pale mine intestines about neck.	pale mine intestines about neck.
Og er suðurmenn vissu draum þenna réðust þeir úr skipinu og þótti bani sinn ef þeir færu þar í.	And when the-southerners knew this-dream then decided they out-of the-ship and thought death theirs if they went there in.	And when the southerners knew this dream, they got out of the ship and thought it would be their death if they went there.
Halli réðst þegar í skip og sagði að þetta var prettur hans en engi draumur.	Halli took straight-away in the-ship and said that this was trick his and no dream.	Halli took passage in the ship straight away, and said that it was a trick, and not a dream.
Og tóku þeir út þegar þeir voru búnir og tóku Noreg um haustið	And took they out from-there they were ready and took Norway about autumn	And they went out when they were ready and took to Norway in the autumn,
og fór Halli þegar til Haralds konungs.	and went Halli then to Harald the-king.	and Halli immediately went to King Harald.
Hann tók vel við Halla og spurði hvort hann hefði þá ort um aðra konunga.	He received well with Halli and asked whether he had then words about other kings.	He welcomed Halli and asked if he had written about other kings.
Halli kvað þetta:	Halli said this:	Halli said this:
Orti eg eina um jarl	"Worded I one about an-earl	Worded I one about an earl
þulu.	a-thula (poem).	a-'thula' (poem).
Verðrat drápa	Worthy-that drapa (poem)	Poorer drapa
með Dönum verri.	with The-Danes worse.	with The-Danes worse.

The Tale of Sarcastic Halli (Old Icelandic)

Old Icelandic	Literal	English
Föll eru fjórtán og föng tíu. Opið er og öndvert, öfugt stígandi. Svo skal yrkja sá er illa kann.	Mistakes are fourteen and rhymes ten. Open is and upside-down, reversed ascending. Then shall compose so who badly knows.	Mistakes are fourteen and rhymes ten. Open is and upside-down, reversed ascending. Then shall compose so who badly knows.
Konungur brosti að og þótti honum jafnan gaman að Halla.	The-king smiled that and thought him always entertaining of Halli.	The king smiled an thought he always found Halli entertaining.

10

Haraldur konungur fór um vorið til Gulaþings.	Harald the-king went about spring to Gula-assembly.	In the spring Harald went to the Gulathing Assembly.
Og um daginn spurði konungur Halla hversu honum yrði til kvenna um þingið.	And about the-day asked the-king Halli how-so he became to women at the-assembly.	And one day the king asked Halli how he was with women at the assembly.
Halli svarar:	Halli answered:	Halli answered:
Gott er Gulaþing þetta, giljum við hvað er viljum.	Good is Gula-assembly this, beguile we that as we-wish.	Good is Gulathing this, beguile we that as we-wish.
Konungurinn fór þaðan norður til Þrándheims.	The-king went from-there north to Trondheim.	The king went north from there to Trondheim.
Og er þeir sigldu fyrir Stað áttu þeir Þjóðólfur og Halli búðarvörð að halda og var Halli sæsjúkur mjög og lá undir báti en Þjóðólfur varð að þjóna einn.	And when they sailed for Stad had they Thjodolf and Halli shop-keeping to hold and was Halli seasick much and lay under the-ship's-boat and Thjodolf came to serve alone.	And when they sailed for Stad, Thjodolf and Halli were assigned the cooking and serving, and Halli was very seasick and lay under the ship's boat, and Thjodolf had to serve alone.
Og er hann bar vistina féll hann um fót Halla er stóð út undan bátinum.	And when he carried the-provisions fell he about leg Halli's which stood out under the-boat.	And when he was carrying the provisions, he fell on Halli's leg, which was standing out from under the boat.
Þjóðólfur kvað þetta:	Thjodolf spoke this:	Thjodolf spoke this:
Út stendr undan báti ilfat. Muntu nú gilja?	Out standing under the-boat sole-bucket. Shall-you now beguile?	"Out standing under the-boat sole-bucket. Shall-you now beguile?"

The Tale of Sarcastic Halli (Old Icelandic)

Old Icelandic	Literal	English
Halli svarar:	Halli answered:	Halli answered:
Þjón geri eg þann að sveini, Þjóðólf læt eg mat sjóða.	Servant made I then to this-lad, Thjodolf let I food boil.	Servant made I then to this-lad, Thjodolf let I food boil.
Fór konungurinn nú leiðar sinnar uns hann kom í Kaupangur.	For the-king now on-way his until he came to Kaupang.	The king now went on his way until he came to Kaupang.
Þóra drottning var nú með honum og var hún lítt til Halla	Thora the-queen was not with him and was she little towards Halli	Queen Thora was now with him and she did not like Halli,
en konungur var vel til hans og þótti gaman að Halla jafnan.	but the-king was well towards him and seemed to-delight in Halli always.	but the king liked him and always delighted in Halli.
Þess er getið einn dag að konungurinn gekk út um stræti og fylgdin með honum.	This is told one day that the-king went out about the-street and followers with him.	It is said that one day the king went out into the street and his follower with him.
Halli var þar í för.	Halli was there in procession.	Halli was there in the procession.
Konungurinn hafði öxi í hendi og öll gullrekin en silfurvafið skaftið og silfurhólkur mikill á forskeftinu og þar í ofan steinn góður.	The-king had an-axe in hand and all gold-inlaid and silver-wound the-shaft and silver-band great in upper-shaft and there in over a-stone good.	The king had an axe in his hand and all the shafts were gold, but the shaft was wrapped in silver, and a large silver cylinder on the foreshaft, and above it a good stone.
Það var ágætur gripur.	It was excellent possession.	It was excellent possession.
Halli sá jafnan til öxarinnar.	Halli looked always to the-axe.	Halli kept looking towards the axe.
Konungur fann það brátt og spurði hvort Halla litist vel á öxina.	The-king found that soon and asked whether Halli looked well of the-axe.	The king soon found out and asked if Halla had a good look at the axe.
Honum kveðst vel á lítast.	He said well it looked.	He said it looked good.
"Hefir þú séð betri öxi?"	"Have you seen a-better axe?"	"Have you seen a-better axe?"
"Eigi ætla eg", segir Halli.	"Not suppose I", said Halli.	"I suppose not", said Halli.

The Tale of Sarcastic Halli (Old Icelandic)

Old Icelandic	Literal	English
"Viltu láta serðast til öxarinnar?"	"Will-you allow to-get-hurt for the-axe?"	"Do you want to be hurt by the axe?"
segir konungur.	said the-king.	said the king.
Eigi, segir Halli,	Not, said Halli,	Halli said not,
"en vorkunn þykir mér yður að þér viljið svo selja sem þér keyptuð".	"but understandable seems to-me you that you wish so to-sell same-as you bought".	"but it's understandable to me that you would wish to sell it for the same as you bought it".
"Svo skal vera Halli",	"So shall be Halli",	"So it shall be Halli",
segir konungur,	said the-king,	said the king,
"tak með og njót manna best,	"take with and enjoy man the-best,	take it with you and enjoy it, best man,
gefin var mér enda skal svo selja".	given was to-me and shall so to-sell".	it was given to me, and now shall it be given to you.
Halli þakkaði konungi.	Halli thanked the-king.	Halli thanked the king.
Um kveldið er menn komu til drykkjar talaði drottning við konung að það væri undarlegt	About evening when men came to drink talked the-queen with the-king that it was scandalous	In the evening, when the men came to drink, the queen spoke to the king that it was strange
"og ei vel til skipt að gefa Halla þá gripi er varla er ótiginna manna eiga fyrir klámyrði sín	"and not well to exchange to give Halli then treasure that hardly was un-ranking man not before obscene his	and it is not a good idea to give Halli the those things to a lowly man hardly has for his obscenities,
en þá fá sumir lítið fyrir góða þjónustu".	that then give some little before good service".	but then some people get little for good service".
Konungur kveðst því ráða vilja hverjum hann gæfi gripi sína,	The-king said therefore decided wished each he gave possessions his,	The king said that he would decide who he would give his possessions to,
"vil eg ei snúa orðum Halla til hins verra þeim er tvíræði eru".	"wish I not return words Halli to his worst they are ambiguous are".	for I do not wish to turn Halli's words to the worse, which are ambiguous in a bad sense".
Konungur bað kalla Halla og svo var gert.	The-king asked to-call Halli and so was done.	The king asked to call Halli, and it was done.
Halli laut honum.	Halli bowed to-him.	Halli bowed to him.

The Tale of Sarcastic Halli (Old Icelandic)

Old Icelandic	Literal	English
Konungur bað Halla mæla nokkur tvíræðisorð við Þóru drottningu	The-king ordered Halli speak something ambiguous about Thora the-queen	The king asked Halli to say some ambiguous words to Queen Thora
"og vit hversu hún þolir".	"and know how-so she endures".	and know how she endures it.
Halli laut þá að Þóru og kvað:	Halli bowed then to Thora and said:	Halli bowed then to Thora and said:
Þú ert maklegust miklu, munar stórum það, Þóra, flenna upp að enni allt leðr Haralds reðri.	You are the-best much, delight great that, Thora, to-extend up to brow all skin Harald's genitals.	You are the-best much, delight great that, Thora, to-extend up to brow all the skin of Harald's genitals.
"Takið hann og drepið",	"Take him and kill",	"Take him and kill him",
segir drottning.	said the-queen.	said the queen.
"Vil eg eigi hafa hrópyrði hans".	"Will I not have obscenities his".	"I will not have his obscenities".
Konungur bað öngvan svo djarfan vera að á Halla tæki hér fyrir:	The-king ordered none so daring be that to Halli take force for:	The king ordered that no one should dare take Halli by force:
"En að því má gera ef þér þykir önnur maklegri til að liggja hjá mér og vera drottning og kanntu varla að heyra lof þitt".	"But that then may done if you think another more-suitable that to lie beside me and be queen and know-you hardly to hear praise yours".	"But then it may be done if you think another is more suitable to lie beside me and be queen, and you hardly know how to hear your praise".
Þjóðólfur skáld hafði farið til Íslands meðan Halli var í burtu frá konungi.	Thjodolf poet had travelled to Iceland while Halli was to away from the-king.	The poet Thjodolf had gone to Iceland while Halli was away from the king.
Þjóðólfur hafði flutt utan af Íslandi hest góðan og vildi gefa konungi og lét Þjóðólfur leiða hestinn í konungsgarð og sýna konungi.	Thjodolf had brought out from Iceland a-horse good and wished to-give the-king and had Thjodolf lead the-horse to the-king and showed the-king.	Thjodolf had brought a good horse from Iceland and wanted to give it to the king, and he had Thjodolf lead the horse to the king's garden and show it to the king.
Konungurinn gekk að sjá hestinn og var mikill og feitur.	The-king went to see the-horse and was great and stout.	The king went to see the horse and it was big and fat.

The Tale of Sarcastic Halli (Old Icelandic)

Old Icelandic	Literal	English
Halli var þar hjá er hesturinn hafði úti sinina.	Halli was there beside when horse had extended-out tendon.	Halli was there when the horse extended its tendon.
Halli kvað þá:	Halli spoke then:	Halli then spoke:
Sýr er ávallt, hefir saurugt allt hestr Þjóðólfs erðr, hann er drottinserðr.	Sow as always, has filthy all horse Thjodolf's beam, he is master-wounder.	Sow as always, has filthy all horse Thjodolf's beam, he is master-wounder.
"Tví, tví",	"Tut, tut",	"Tut tut",
segir konungur, "hann kemur aldrei í mína eigu að þessu".	said the-king, "he comes never in mine ownership at this".	said the king, "he will not come into my ownership at this rate".
Halli gerðist hirðmaður konungs og bað sér orlofs til Íslands.	Halli became court-man the-king's and asked him vacation to Iceland.	Halli became the king's court man and asked him for leave to vacate to Iceland.
Konungur bað hann fara varlega fyrir Einar flugu.	The-king bid him travel warily because-of Einar Fly.	The king asked that he travel carefully because of Einar Fly.
Halli fór til Íslands og bjó þar.	Halli went to Iceland and settled there.	Halli went to Iceland and settled there.
Eyddust honum peningar og lagðist hann í útróður	Spent his money and lay he to out-rowing (fishing)	He spent his money and he took to fishing,
og eitt sinn fékk hann andróða svo mikinn að þeir tóku nauðulega land.	and one occasion had he difficulty so much that they took necessarily land.	and on one occasion he had so much difficulty rowing back that they just reached land.
Og um kveldið var borinn fyrir Halla grautur	And about evening was brought before Halli porridge	That evening porridge was brought before Halli,
og er hann hafði etið fá bita hnígur hann aftur og var þá dauður.	and as he had to-eat few bites fell he back and was then dead.	and when he had eaten a few bites, he fell back and was then dead.
Haraldur spurði lát tveggja hirðmanna sinna af Íslandi,	Harald learned had both court-men his from Iceland,	Harald learned of the death of both his court men from Iceland,
Bolla hins prúða og Sneglu-Halla.	Bolli the Elegant and Sarcastic-Halli.	Bolli the Elegant, and Sarcastic Halli.
Hann svaraði svo til Bolla:	He answered so to Bolli:	He said of Bolli:

The Tale of Sarcastic Halli (Old Icelandic)

Old Icelandic	Literal	English
"Fyrir dörrum mun drengurinn hnigið hafa".	"Before spears would the-boy fallen had".	"The boy must have fallen to spears".
En til Halla sagði hann svo:	And to Halli said he so:	And he said of Halli:
"Á grauti mundi greyið sprungið hafa".	"On porridge would the-poor-thing burst have".	"The poor thing must have burst eating porridge".
Lýk eg þar sögu frá Sneglu-Halla.	End I there the-story from Sarcastic-Halli.	And there I end the story of Sarcastic Halli.

Word List (Old Icelandic to English)

Old Icelandic	English

A, a

að	a, and, as, at, by, for, in, it, of, than, that, the, this, to, with
aðra	another, other, others
aðrir	other
af	from, from, in, man, of, of, off
afli	power
aftur	again, back, returning
afvirti	disrespected
Agðanes	Agdanes (place)
Agðaness	Agdanes (place)
Agði	Agdi (name), Agdi (name)
akta	taxes
aldrei	never, never
aldri	age
alla	completely
allir	all, all
allra	all, of-all, of-all
allreiður	all-angry
allskammur	very-short
allt	all
allur	all
allvel	all-well
andaður	dead
andróða	difficulty
annað	another, other
annan	another, one, the-next
annar	another, another, otherwise
annarra	other
annars	another, other

Á, á

á	a, about, an, at, be, by, for, from, in, it, of, on, that, to, was, with
ábyrgst	responsible
áðr	before
áður	after, back, before
ágætur	excellent
ári	all-year
Árnasonar	Son-of-Arni (name)
át	ate, ate
átt	had
átti	had, hat, married, related-to
áttu	had
ávallt	always

Æ, æ

æpir	cried-out
æptu	called-out
ær	awed
ærið	greatly
ætla	suppose, suppose, supposed
ætlað	intended
ætluðu	intended
ætt	descent
ættaður	descended
ætti	had
ættsmár	family-small

B, b

bað	asked, bid, invited, ordered
báðir	both
bæði	both
bæjar	the-town
bændur	farmers
bænum	town
bæta	compensation
bæti	compensate
bætti	compensated
baki	back
banasök	death-sentence
bani	death

418

Word List (Old Icelandic to English)

Old Icelandic	English	*Old Icelandic*	English
bar	bears, bore, carried	*brauði*	bread
Bárð	Bard (name)	*brenndan*	burnt
Bárður	Bard (name)	*bróðir*	brother
barn	a-child, child	*bróður*	brother
barna	children	*brögðóttan*	cunning
báru	carried	*brosti*	grinned, laughed, smiled
báti	the-boat, the-ship's-boat	*brott*	away, brought
bátinum	the-boat	*brottu*	away
bauð	invited	*brúki*	use
bauglands	ring-land	*brynju*	chain-mail, coat-of-mail
beggja	both	*brynjuna*	coat-of-mail
beið	waited	*búð*	lodgings
beiddi	asked	*búðarvörð*	shop-keeping
bekkinn	the-bench	*búfinna*	farmers
belti	belt	*búi*	estate
best	best, the-best	*búinn*	prepared, settled
betr	better	*búnir*	prepared, ready
betra	better	*burt*	away
betri	a-better	*burtu*	away
bið	order	*býð*	command
biðja	ask, to-ask	*býður*	offered
bita	bites	*byggð*	settled
bitar	bite	*byr*	fair-wind
bitið	biting		
bjó	lived, settled		
blakir	pale		
bleikr	pale		
boði	order		
bokkar	bigger-men		
Bolla	Bolli (name)		
bóndi	farmer, master		
borð	boards		
borði	table, the-table		
borðið	table, the-table		
borðin	tables		
borðum	at-table		
börg	the-city		
borin	brought		
borinn	brought		
börnin	the-children		
bótunum	compensation		
brá	drew		
brákar	breaker		
brást	transformed		
brátt	soon		

D, d

Old Icelandic	English
dæmi	examples
dag	day
dagana	day
daginn	the-day
Danmerkur	Denmark (place)
dáruskapur	mockery
dauðan	death
dauðir	dead
dauður	dead
deild	room
digrastur	thick-set
disk	plate
diskinum	the-plate
diskur	a-plate
djarfan	daring
dönum	the-Danes (name)
dörrum	spears

Word List (Old Icelandic to English)

Old Icelandic	English
dóttur	daughter
drap	killed
drápa	drapa (poem)
drápi	the-killing
drápu	a-drapa (poem), drapa
drápuna	the-drapa (poem)
draum	dream, this-dream
draumur	a-dream, dream
dregr	draws
dregst	draw
dregur	drew
drekanum	the-dragon-ship
dreki	dragon
drekka	drinking
drengi	boys
drengurinn	the-boy
drepa	kill
drepið	kill, killed
drepur	killed
dreymt	dreamed
drógu	drew
drottinserðr	master-wounder
drottning	queen, the-queen
drottningu	the-queen
drykk	drink
drykkjar	drink
duldu	denied
dverg	the-dwarf
dverginn	the-dwarf
dvergur	dwarf
dýran	fine

E, e

Old Icelandic	English
eða	and, but, or
ef	if
eftir	after, back, back-from
eg	I, me
eggjaði	urged
ei	not
eiga	not, own
eigi	not
eigu	ownership
eina	one
Einar	Einar (name)
Einari	Einar (name)
Einars	Einar (name), Einar's (name)
einhugi	one-minded
einkis	nothing
einmælt	one-meal
einn	alone, one
einráðir	one-decision
einu	one
eitt	once, one
ekki	not, nothing
eld	the-fire
eldahús	fire-house (kitchen)
eldi	fire
eldilegt	elderly
eldur	fire
ella	or-else
elskaði	loved
Emmu	Emma (name)
en	and, but, than, that, then
enda	and, ended, in-the-end, the-end
endilausu	nonsense
enga	not
engan	no
engi	no, none
enginn	none
Englandi	England (place)
Englands	England (place)
engu	none
engum	no
enn	but, one, the, then
enna	yet
enni	brow, forehead
er	am, am-I, are, as, I, in, is, that, then, to, was, what, when, where, which, who
erðr	beam
erindi	errand, message
ert	are
ertu	are-you
eru	are, we-are

Word List (Old Icelandic to English)

Old Icelandic	English
eruð	they-are
erum	are, are-we
eta	eat, eating
etið	to-eat
etja	provoke
etur	eat
eyddust	spent
eyjar	islands

F, f

Old Icelandic	English
fá	few, get, give
faðir	father
fæ	can
fær	accomplished
færa	bring, brought
færð	carry-out, undertaking
færði	performed
færðr	brought
færu	went
fæturnir	the-legs
Fáfni	Fafnir (name)
Fáfnisbana	Slayer-of-Fafnir (name)
fagnar	welcomed
fám	a-few
fann	found
far	go, passage, travel
fara	fare, go, goes, going, sent-for, travel, went
farið	travelled
farist	gone
fars	travel
fátæka	poor
fátækra	the-poor
fátækur	fee-taken
fáum	get
fé	money, payment
fébætur	compensation
féð	the-money
féhirði	fee-servant
féhirðinn	fee-servant
feitur	stout
fékk	give, got, had
fékkst	received
félagi	companion
féll	fell
felldan	killed
fellt	fell
fémúta	money-bribe
fengu	caught
fénu	money
fer	go, goes, went
festi	pierced
fimm	five
finna	find, found, the-Sami (name)
finnferð	Finland-voyages (place)
finnskrepp	Sami-goods
firðinum	the-fjord
firrst	lost
fiskimenn	fishermen
fjár	fee
fjölda	many
fjöldi	many
fjölmennt	followers
fjör	life
fjóra	four
fjórar	four
fjórðung	fourth
fjórtán	fourteen
flærat	fleeing
fleira	more
fleiri	more
flenna	to-extend
flest	the-most
flesta	most
Fljótum	Fljot (place)
Fluga	Fly (name)
Flugu	Fly (name)
flugust	flew
flutt	brought, delivered
flutti	brought
flýta	quickly
flytja	carried
föður	father
föðurbana	father's-killer
fólk	people
föll	mistakes

421

Word List (Old Icelandic to English)

Old Icelandic	English
föng	rhymes
fór	for, travelled, went
för	before, going, procession
forskeftinu	upper-shaft
fórstu	went-you
fóru	went
fórum	travel
förum	journey
forvitnar	fore-knowing
fót	leg
fótum	feet
frá	from
frændi	kinsman
frændunum	kinsmen
frændur	kinsman
fram	ahead, away, forwards, from
framar	from
frásagnar	from-saying
frásagnir	stories
frísa	Frisian (name)
frískur	Frisian
fullt	full
fullur	full
fund	to-meet
fundum	found
fundumst	met
furðulega	extremely
fús	willing
fylgdin	followers
fylgja	follow
fyndi	find
fyrir	because-of, before, for, intestines, over
fyrr	before
fyrra	before, last
fyrri	before, went-before
fyrst	first
fyrstu	first

G, g

Old Icelandic	English
gabb	mockery
gæfi	gave
gæfur	agreeable
gætti	guarded
gaf	gave
gakk	go
galdra	magic
gamall	old
gaman	a-delight, delight, enjoyment, entertaining, fun, to-delight
gamans	amusement
ganga	go
gangi	go
gap	gaping
garðinn	garden, the-house, the-wall
garðinum	the-wall
garðsins	the-wall
garðurinn	the-wall
Gásum	Gasir (place)
gefa	give, granted, to-give
gefi	give
gefið	given
gefin	given
Geirröð	Geirrod (name)
Geirröðr	Geirrod (name)
gekk	got, went
geng	going
gengju	walking
gengr	going
gengu	went
ger	do, does
gera	do, doing, done, made, make
gerast	be
gerði	did, made
gerðir	done
gerðist	became
gerðu	did, made
geri	did, made
gerið	do
gerir	does
gert	do, done
gervan	look-to
get	get
getið	told

Word List (Old Icelandic to English)

Old Icelandic	English
gilja	beguile
giljum	beguile
ginning	deception
gista	guest
gjalda	pay
gjarna	gladly
gjör	ready-made
gjörla	completely
glaðr	glad
glaður	glad
gnadda	gnawing
góð	good
góða	good
góðan	good
góðum	good
góður	good
gólf	the-floor
gólfið	of-the-floor, the-floor
göngum	going, we-are-going
gott	good
grafið	dug
graut	porridge
grautar	of-porridge
grauti	porridge
grautinn	porridge, the-porridge
grautur	porridge
greppr	grasped
greyið	the-poor-thing
grið	peace
griðníðingur	truce-breaker
gripanna	the-trinkets
gripi	possessions, treasure
gripina	the-trinkets
gripuna	the-trinkets
gripur	possession
grís	pig
grön	moustache
gruntrauðustum	deep-red
Guðinason	Godwinson (name)
guðréttilegast	good-rightly
gulaþing	Gula-assembly (name)
gulaþings	Gula-assembly (name)
gullhlað	gold-band
gullhring	a-gold-ring, gold-ring
gullrekin	gold-inlaid
gyrti	equipped

H, h

Old Icelandic	English
haddan	the-handle, the-lid
háðyrðum	mocking
hærra	higher
hærri	higher
hæst	high
hætti	stopped
hættu	danger
haf	have
hafa	had, has, have, having, to-have
hafði	had
hafðir	had, have
hafðist	had
hafi	has
hafnan	the harbour
hafra	goat
Hákon	Hakon (name)
Hákoni	Hakon (name)
halda	hold, to-hold
haldið	held
hálfa	half
Halla	Halli (name), Halli's (name)
hallæri	famine
Halli	Halli (name)
Hálogaland	Halogaland (place)
Hálogalandi	Halogaland (place)
háls	neck
hálslangur	long-neck
hana	her
handlaugar	hand-washing
handsíður	long-armed
hann	he, him
hans	he, him, his
hár	high
Haraldi	Harald (name), Harald's (name)

Word List (Old Icelandic to English)

Old Icelandic	English
haraldr	Harald (name), Harald's (name)
Haralds	Harald (name), Harald's (name)
Haraldur	Harald (name)
Háreks	Harek's (name)
háreysti	commotion
hárinu	the-hairs
hásætið	high-seat
haustið	autumn
haustum	autumn
héðan	from-there
hefði	had
hefðir	had
hefðu	had
hefðum	have
hefir	had, has, has-been, have
hefna	avenge
hefnt	avenged, revenge
hefur	had
heiði	the-heath
heill	health
heilræði	sound-advice
heim	home
hein	hone
heinasmjör	honing-grease
heita	call, named
heitan	threat
heitir	is-named, named
hékk	hung
held	think
heldr	rather
hella	pour, poured
hellt	rather
helst	rather
hélt	held
hendi	hand, hands, to-hand
hendur	hand
hér	force, here
herbergi	hostel
herbergjum	sleeping-quarters
herðilítill	narrow-shouldered
herðimestur	most-hardy
herra	lord
hest	a-horse
hestinn	the-horse
hestr	horse
hesturinn	horse
hét	named, was-named
héti	named
heyra	hear, heard, to-hear
heyrði	heard
heyrðu	heard
heyrt	heard
hið	the
hilmis	helmsman's
hin	the
hina	the
hinn	the
hins	his, the
hinum	the
hirð	the-court
hirðarinnar	court
hirði	care
hirðin	courtiers
hirðinni	the-court, the-court-men
hirðmaður	court-man
hirðmanna	court-men
Hítrar	Hitra (place)
hitt	then
hjá	beside, nearby
hjálm	helmet
hjálmfaldinn	the-helmet
Hlaðajarli	Earl-of-Lade (name)
hlaðna	ladened
hlaupi	running
hlaut	a-lot-of
hleyp	running
hleypur	ran
hljóð	a-hearing, silence
hljóða	calm
hljóðgreipum	sound-grippers (ears)
hljóðið	silence
hljóðs	be-heard
hljóp	jumped
hljópu	ran
hlotist	part
hlut	part, share
hluti	a-thing, things

424

Word List (Old Icelandic to English)

Old Icelandic	English
hlutur	part
hlýða	obeying, suits
hlýði	listen
hnakka	neck
hníf	knife
hnífi	knife
hnífinum	knife
hnífskafti	knife-handle
hnigið	fallen
hnígur	fell
hnúskum	knocked-down
höfðingja	chieftains
höfðu	had
hófi	reasonable
höfuð	head
höfuðið	head
höfuðskáld	chief-poet
höggva	to-strike
höldnu	held
höllina	the-hall
höllunni	the-hall
hönd	hand
höndum	hand
honum	he, him, his, of-him, to-him
horfa	turn
horfin	lost
hornspónu	horn-spoon
hóti	not
hótun	a-threat
hræddir	afraid
hraustlega	boldly
hríð	awhile
hring	the-ring
hringinn	the-ring
hringinum	the-ring
hringum	circles
hroðið	cleared
hróður	fame
hrökkviskafls	shaken
hröng	roaring
hrópyrði	obscenities
hrygg	the-spine
hryggurinn	spine
húðar	hide
hug	mind
hugar	minds
hugði	thought
hugðu	thought
humrum	lobsters
hún	it, she
hungrar	hungry
hús	a-house
hvað	that, what
hvar	where
hve	how
hver	what, who
hverft	disappeared
hverfur	turned
hvergi	none, nowhere
hverju	what
hverjum	each
hvern	each, what, whom
hvers	how-so
hversu	how-so
hvert	each, what, where
hví	why
hvofteldingum	encouraged-lightning
hvor	each
hvorigum	neither
hvort	each, whether
hvorttveggja	each-way
hvoru	which
hygg	think

I, i

iðnar	trade
ilfat	sole-bucket
illa	bad, badly, evil
illan	evil
illt	ill
ilvegs	evil-ways
inn	in, of, then
innan	in, inside
innanborðs	onboard
innar	in

Í, í

Word List (Old Icelandic to English)

Old Icelandic	English
í	about, as, at, by, in, into, of, on, that, the, to, with
Ísland	Iceland (place)
Íslandi	Iceland (place)
Íslands	Iceland (place)
íslandsfari	Iceland-voyage
íslendinga	Icelanders
íslendingar	Icelanders
íslenska	Icelander
íslenskan	Icelander
íslenskur	an-Icelander, Icelander

J, j

Old Icelandic	English
jafnan	always, equally, usually
jafngreypilega	equally-badly
jafnir	equal
jafnsleppt	equally-slip
jarl	an-earl, earl
járn	iron-weapon
járnsmiður	ironsmith
jaxlar	molars
jöfnum	even
jóladag	Yule-day
jólin	Yule
jólunum	Yule
Jótlands	Jutland (place)
jötni	giant
jötun	the-giant

K, k

Old Icelandic	English
kæra	accuse
kærleikum	dear-friendship, friendship
kálf	a-calf
kálfinn	the-calf
kálfurinn	the-calf
kalla	to-call
kallaði	called
kallaðir	be-called
kallaður	called
kann	can, can-it, knows
kanntu	know-you
karlmanni	a-man
kastað	cast
kastaði	cast
katlinum	the-kettle
kátur	cheerful
kaup	traded
Kaupangs	Kapuang (place)
Kaupangur	Kaupang (place)
kaupferð	trading-voyage
kaupmennirnir	merchant-men
kaupmönnum	the-trading-men, trading-men
kaupskipinu	merchant-ship, trading-ship
kem	come
kemur	came, come, comes
kenn	know
kenna	know, teach
kenndi	felt
kennt	blame
keyptuð	bought
kilju	the-binding
kjöts	flesh
klámyrði	obscene
klámyrðum	obscene-words
klappaði	rapped, struck
klappar	hammering
klukku	a-bell
kné	knee
knörru	knorrs
kölluðu	called
köllum	call
kolluvísur	cow-verses
kom	came, come
koma	come, come-forward
komið	came, come, coming
kominn	coming
komnir	coming
komst	came
komu	came
komum	came
konung	the-king
konunga	kings
konungi	the-king, the-king's

Word List (Old Icelandic to English)

Old Icelandic	English	*Old Icelandic*	English
konunginn	the-king	lá	lay
konunginum	the-king	læt	have, let
konungr	king, king's, the-king	lagði	became, laid
konungs	the-king, the-king's	lagðist	lay
konungsgarð	the-king	lagin	assigned
konungsins	the-king	lágu	lay
konungur	the-king, the-king's	láguð	laid
konungurinn	the-king	lágum	laid
kostur	a-choice	land	land
kunna	know	landi	land, the-land
kunnu	could	landinu	the-land
kurfaldi	folded	langa	long
kurteis	polite	langskip	longships
kvað	recited, said, spoke	lát	had, have, have
kvaddi	called, greeted	láta	allow, have
kváðu	recited	látið	had, let
kvæði	composed, poem, poems, recited	látir	leave
		launa	reward
kvæðið	poem, the-poem	launaði	rewarded
kvæðin	poems	launin	repay
kvæðinu	the-poem	laus	lost
kvæðisins	the-poem	laut	bowed
kvæðislaun	poem-reward	leðr	skin
kvæðismynd	poem-image	legg	lay
kvæðunum	the-poetry	leggja	allow, lay
kveð	recite, say	leggur	laid
kveða	compose, recite	leið	passed
kveðið	reciting, spoken, worded	leiða	lead
		leiðar	on-way
kveðin	recited, worded	leigðu	rented
kveðinn	composed	leika	games, play
kveðju	greeting	leist	with-footwear
kveðst	said	leista	of-footwear
kveður	recited, words	leita	find, look-for, seek, seeking
kveld	the-evening		
kveldið	evening	leitaði	sought
kvenna	women	leitaðir	seek
kviðlingur	short-poem	lendi	lands
kyns	kin	lendur	land
kýr	cows	lengi	long
kýrkaupi	cow-buying	lér	leaned
kyrrt	peace, peaceful	lét	had
		létti	let-up
		léttum	let-up

L, l

leys	repay
leyst	answered

Word List (Old Icelandic to English)

Old Icelandic	English
líf	life
lífi	life
lífinu	his-life, your-life
liggja	lie
líkaði	liked
líkar	like, liked
líklegur	likely
líkur	like
lít	coloured
lítast	looked
lítið	little
lítil	little
lítilla	little
lítils	little
lítilþægir	easily-satisfied
lítilþægur	little-behaving
lítinn	little
litist	looked
litlu	a-little
lítt	little
ljóst	light
ljótlimaður	ugly-limbed
ljúgi	lie
loðir	of-your-hair
lof	permission, praise
lofa	promise
loft	praised
lofuðu	praised
lögðum	laid
lögskilum	legal-settlement
lokið	concluded, ended, finished
lyftingunni	lifting
lýgur	lies, lying
lýk	end
lykkja	noose
lykkjan	the-noose
lysti	appetite
lýsu	the-whitings

M, m

Old Icelandic	English
má	may
maður	a-man, man, the-man
maðurinn	the-man
mæl	speak
mæla	matter, matters, say, speak
mælti	spoke
mæltist	recited
mæltur	talked
mættum	met
Magnús	Magnus (name)
maka	equal
maklegra	well-deserved
maklegri	more-suitable
maklegust	the-best
mál	matter
málefnum	matters
málið	the-matter
máls	matter
málum	matter, matters
mann	man, men
manna	man, men, people
manni	man
mannsbarn	man's-son
marga	many
margir	many
margs	many, many-things
margt	many
mat	food
matar	food
matr	food
mátti	as-might, may
matur	food
með	with
meðan	as-long-as, while
megum	may
mein	harm
meir	more
meira	more
meiri	more
menn	men, people
menntur	educated
mér	for-me, I, me, mine, my, to-me
merkur	marks
mest	most
mesta	most
mestum	most

Word List (Old Icelandic to English)

Old Icelandic	English
mettir	finished-eating, satisfied
mettur	finished-eating, satisfied
mig	me
mikið	great, much
mikill	great, much
mikinn	much
mikla	great, greatest
miklagarði	Byzantium (place)
miklu	much
miklum	much
milli	between
mína	mine, my
minn	mine
minna	less, lesser, mine
míns	mine
mínu	mine
mínum	mine
mislíkaði	mis-liked
missa	lose, miss
mitt	mine, the-middle
mjög	much
mjöl	meal
mönnum	people, the-people
morguninn	morning
mörk	a-mark, one-mark
mörkina	the-border
móti	against, meet
mun	could, shall, should, should-be, will, would, would-be
munað	remembered
munaður	remembered
munar	delight
mundi	could-be, remembered, should-be, would
mundir	would
mundu	could, would
muni	shall
munni	mouth
munt	must, should
muntu	shall-you, should, would-you
munu	shall, would
munuð	shall

N, n

Old Icelandic	English
ná	obtain, take
naðri	serpent
næði	neared
nær	near
nærri	close-to, near
næst	near
næsta	next
nafn	named
nam	took
námu	took
nauðsyn	necessary
nauðsynja	needs
nauðulega	necessarily
nautaleðrs	ox-skin
neðan	below
neflangr	long-nosed
nefndur	named
nei	no
nema	but, except
níð	slander
níðið	the-slander
niður	down
Njörðr	Njord (name)
njót	enjoy
njótum	benefit
nóg	enough
nokkra	any
nokkru	one-of, some, somehow, somewhat
nokkrum	some
nokkuð	anything, something, somewhat
nokkur	some, something
norður	north
norðurlönd	northern-lands
Noreg	Norway (place)
Noregi	Norway (place)
Noregs	Norway (place)
nótt	night, the-night
nóttum	nights
nú	no, not, now

Word List (Old Icelandic to English)

Old Icelandic	English

O, o

Old Icelandic	English
of	of
ofan	over
offylli	gluttony
ofraun	too-much
oftar	more
og	also, and
olli	cause
opið	open
orð	word
orða	words
orðaskil	words-separated
orðfall	word-fallen
orðgreppur	word-bold
orðhákur	word-tall
orðhvass	sharp-tongued
orðið	become, worded
orðinn	of-words
orðum	words
orlofs	vacation
ormr	the-serpent
ort	composed, worded, words
orti	worded
oss	to-us, us, we

Ó, ó

Old Icelandic	English
óeinarðarmaður	unreliable
ógurlegur	terrible
óp	shouting
ósiðblandnir	un-custom-mixing
óskert	the-whole
ótæpt	unsettled
óþökk	un-thanks
ótiginna	un-ranking
ótrúlegir	un-truthful
óvirðulegt	unworthy

Ö, ö

Old Icelandic	English
öðru	the-other
öðrum	eachother, other, others
öðruvís	other-knowing
öfugt	reversed
öfundsjúkur	un-infatuated
öll	all
öllu	all
öndvert	upside-down
öngum	no
öngvan	no, none
önnur	another
ösku	ashes
öxarinnar	the-axe
öxi	an-axe, axe
öxina	the-axe

P, p

Old Icelandic	English
peningar	money
peningum	payment
prettum	trickery
prettur	trick
prófa	prove
Prúða	Elegant (name)
prýði	finery

R, r

Old Icelandic	English
ráð	advice, advisable, plan
ráða	decide, decided
ráði	advised
ráðinn	appointed
ráðleitinn	cunning
ráðs	agreement
ráðugastur	well-advising
ræð	speak
ræsi	the-ruler
rán	robbery
rana	the-trunk
Ránar	Ran (name)
randa	round
rangt	wrong
rannsóknar	a-search

Word List (Old Icelandic to English)

Old Icelandic	English
Rauð	Raud (name)
rauðan	the-red
rauðar	red
rauðum	red
Rauður	Raud (name)
réð	ruled
reðri	genitals
réðst	appointed, took
réðust	decided
reiðasti	most-angry
reiði	anger
Rein	Reine (place)
reru	rowing
rétti	extended
réttur	upright
reyndar	actually
reyndust	proved
reynt	tested
ríkari	richer
ritað	written
rúghleifa	rye-loaf
rúms	rooms
runa	row
ryðja	cleared
rymskyndir	quickly-cleared

S, s

Old Icelandic	English
sá	looked, saw, so
sæhafa	sea-scattered
sækir	sought
sæsjúkur	seasick
sæti	sit
sætis	seat
sættir	settlements
sættust	settled
sagði	said, said, told, told-of
sagðir	said
sagðist	said
sagt	said, said, told, told-to
sakir	sake
saklausa	sake-less
sama	same
saman	together
sami	same
samir	common
sannmæli	true-words
sarð	wounded
satt	true, truth
sátu	sat, were
sáu	saw
saurugt	filthy
sé	am, see, so
séð	seen
seen	so
seg	tell
seggr	said
segi	say
segið	tell
segir	said, told
segja	say, tell, to-tell
seinþreyttur	persistent
seldag	sold
selja	barter, to-sell
sem	as, same-as, than, where, which
send	send
sendi	sent
sendingum	delivery
sennur	chatter
sér	for-him, him, himself, his, saw, sees, themselves, to
serðast	to-get-hurt
sessunaut	bench-companion
sessunautur	bench-companion
sest	sat
setið	sat
setja	set
sest	sat, settled
settist	sat, settled
settlega	sedately
settu	set
séuð	look
síð	long, since
síðan	after, afterwards, since, then
síðar	afterwards, later
síðast	the-last
síðr	since

Word List (Old Icelandic to English)

Old Icelandic	English
síðu	side
siður	a-custom, the-custom
sig	him, himself
sigldi	sailed
sigldu	sailed
Sigurð	Sigurd (name)
Sigurðarson	Sigurdson (name)
Sigurði	Sigurd (name)
Sigurðr	Sigurd (name)
Sigurður	Sigurd (name)
silfri	silver
silfrinu	the-silver
silfur	silver
silfurhólkur	silver-band
silfurs	of-silver
silfurvafið	silver-wound
sín	his, themselves
sína	his
sinina	tendon
sinn	his, occasion, theirs, then
sinna	his
sinnar	his, their
sinni	himself, these
síns	his
sínu	his
sínum	his, theirs
sínumegin	on-his-side
síst	least
sit	sit
sitja	settle, sit
sitk	one
sitt	himself, his, their, this
situr	sat
síu	sift
sjá	see
sjaldan	seldom
sjálfum	himself
sjálfur	yourself
sjóða	boil
sjóði	purse
sjóðnum	the-purse
sjúkur	sick
skaði	harm
skaftið	the-shaft
skal	shall, should
skál	shall
skáld	a-poet, poet, poets, the-poet
skálda	poets
skáldi	the-poet
skáldskap	poetry
skáldskapar	a-poet
skall	hit, rattled
skalt	shall
skaltu	shall-you
skapdreki	mood-dragon
skapi	mind, mood
skarlatsklæðum	scarlet
skemmt	entertainment
skemmta	entertain
skerði	cuts
skilað	settled
skinna	of-skins
skip	ship, the-ship
skipið	ship, the-ship
skipin	the-ships
skipinu	the-ship
skipsmiðir	ship-smiths
skipt	exchange
skipuðu	ships
skjöld	shield
skjótt	quickly, rapidly
skó	shoes
skömm	disgrace, scandal
skreið	crawled
skreppa	bag
skreppuskrúði	bag-tackle
skuld	debt
skulu	should
skuluð	should
skulum	shall
skyldara	should
skyldi	should, would
skyldu	should, should-be, would
skylt	should
sleggju	the-hammer
slíðrar	sheathed
slík	such

Word List (Old Icelandic to English)

Old Icelandic	English
slíka	such
slíkir	such
slíkt	such
smiðbelgja	smith-bellows
smiðju	of-the-smith
smjörvan	buttered
snætt	dined
snák	snake
snaraði	rushed
Sneglu-Halla	Sarcastic-Halli (name)
Sneglu-Halli	Sarcastic-Halli (name)
sneri	turned
snúa	return
snúið	turned
soðtrogsvísur	food-trough-verses
sofa	sleep
sögðu	told
sögðuð	announced
sögðust	said
sögu	the-story
son	son
sótt	sickness
spara	withhold
spón	a-spoon
sprengja	burst
sprungið	burst
spryngi	burst
spurði	asked, asking, learned
spurðu	asked
spurt	heard, questions
spyr	asked
Stað	Stad (place), the-place
staðar	place
stærri	greater
standa	standing
standið	standing
steiktur	roasted
steinkatli	stone-kettle
steinn	a-stone
stendr	standing
stendur	stands
stígandi	ascending
stillir	heading
stóð	place, stood
stórlyndur	large-repaying (generous)
stórmannlega	big-man-like
stórra	great
stórum	great
stræti	the-street
stríði	battles
ströndu	the-shore
stund	awhile
stund	awhile
stundu	awhile
stykki	piece
stýrimaður	steersman
stýrir	steers
styrk	strong
sú	yours
suður	south
suðurmenn	southern-men, the-southerners
sufli	with-bread
sumar	summer
sumargamlan	one-summer-old
sumir	some
sumt	some
sútari	tanner
svangir	hungry
svara	answer, to-answer
svarað	answered
svaraði	answered
svarar	answered
Svarfaðardal	Svarfadardal (place)
svefni	sleep
sveini	this-lad
sveltir	starving
sverð	sword
sverði	a-sword, sword
sverðið	sword
svífst	shrinks-from
svíni	swine
svo	so, then
sýlt	sleek
sýna	showed
sýnast	appear
sýndi	showed

433

Word List (Old Icelandic to English)

Old Icelandic	English
sýndist	thought
sýnir	show
sýnist	seems
synjuðu	refused
sýr	sow
sýslu	business, stewardship
systkinum	siblings

T, t

Old Icelandic	English
tæki	take
tak	take
taka	take
taki	takes
takið	take
takist	take
tala	speak, speaking
talað	talking
talaði	talked
talast	speak
tangar	tongs
taum	leash
taumsendanum	the-leash
taumsins	the-leash
tekið	taken
tekist	taken
tíðinda	news
tíðindi	news
tignari	nobler
tigulegur	dignified
til	about, as, for, into, that, to, towards, until, up-to
tíma	time
tíu	ten
tjöru	tar
tók	received, took
tóku	took
tókuð	took
tókum	took
töluðu	spoke
torf	turf
trog	trough
trúa	believe
túngarði	hayfield-wall
Túta	Tuta (name)
Tútu	Tuta (name)
tveföld	two-fold
tveggja	both
tveir	two
tví	tut
tvíræði	ambiguous
tvíræðisorð	ambiguous
tvo	two

Þ, þ

Old Icelandic	English
þá	then
það	it, than, that, the, this
þaðan	from-there
þær	there
þætti	seems
þættist	thought
þagna	silence
þagnaði	silenced
þakkaði	thanked
þangað	from-there
þann	that, then
þar	that, there, they, they
þarmr	intestines
þars	there
þau	that, there
þegar	as-soon-as, early, from-there, straight-away, then
þegnar	men
þeim	for-them, them, they
þeir	the, them, they
þeirra	theirs, them
þeirri	of-them, theirs
þenna	then, this
þér	to-you, you, yours
þess	this
þessa	this
þessar	this
þessi	these, this
þessu	this
þetta	it, that, these, this
þið	you-two

Word List (Old Icelandic to English)

Old Icelandic	English
þig	you
þiggi	receives
þing	assembly
þinga	assemble
þingið	the-assembly
þinginu	the-assembly
þings	the-assembly
þingsins	the-assembly
Þingvallar	Thingvellir (place)
þinn	yours
þíns	yours
þínu	yours
þínum	about
þitt	yours
Þjóðólf	Thjodolf (name)
Þjóðólfs	Thjodolf's (name)
Þjóðólfur	Thjodolf (name)
þjófur	thief
þjón	servant
þjóna	serve
þjónusta	service
þjónustu	service
þjónustumenn	the-servants
Þjóttu	Thjotta (place)
þó	though
þögnuðu	silenced
þökk	thanks
þola	enduring
þoldi	endured
þolir	endures
þöngul	there
Þór	Thor (name)
Þóra	Thora (name)
Þorbergs	Thorberg's (name)
þorði	dared
þörf	of-need
þori	dare
Þorleifi	Thorleif (name)
Þorleifur	Thorleif (name)
Þorljóti	Thorljot (name)
Þorljótur	Thorljot (name)
þorpi	village
Þórr	Thor (name)
Þóru	Thora (name)
þótt	though
þótti	seemed, thought
þóttir	thought
þóttist	seemed, thought
þóttu	thought
þóttust	thought
þræta	argued
þrætu	threatening
Þrándheim	Trondheim (place)
Þrándheims	Trondheim (place)
þrevett	three-winters-old
þriðja	a-third, third
þrjár	three
þrjú	three
þú	you
þulu	thula (poem)
þunga	heavy-cargo
þurfti	needed
þverlega	crossly
því	accordingly, because, before, if, since, then, therefore, why
þyki	seems, think
þykir	consider, considered, seems, think
þykja	seemed

U, u

Old Icelandic	English
um	about, at
undan	out-from, under
undarlegt	scandalous
undir	under
undur	wonder
undurskapaður	wonder-created
unnið	won
uns	until
upp	up, upped, up-to
upphaf	beginning
utan	out, without
utar	out

Ú, ú

Word List (Old Icelandic to English)

Old Icelandic	English
úr	from, out, out-of
úrleysingur	over-praised
út	about, out, outside
úthlaupi	out-running
úti	extended-out, out
útivist	out-journey
útróður	out-rowing (fishing)

V, v

Old Icelandic	English
vændishöfðingjar	wicked-chieftain
vænstur	promising
væri	being, was, were, would, would-be
vætti	expected
vakið	awake
vaknaði	awoke
válegrar	wretched
vandi	difficult
vanr	custom
var	was, were, who
varð	became, came, was, were
varði	were
varðist	guarded
varla	hardly
varlega	warily
varp	threw
veðja	wager
veðjanin	the-wager
veðjanina	wager
veg	way
vegar	way
veginn	killed
veik	turned
veit	know, known
veita	grant
veitt	given
vekja	awaken
vel	well
veltur	hung
ver	be
vér	are-we, we
vera	be, become, being, to-be, was
verða	be, becomes, have-been, worth
verði	being
verðrat	worthy-that
verður	becomes, worthy
verið	become, been
verk	work
verkmanns	workman's
verkum	actions
verr	worse
verra	worse, worst
verri	worse
vert	worth
vetri	winter
vetur	winter
veturinn	winter
veturvistar	winter-lodgings, winter-provisions
við	about, against, at, from, of, to, we, with
víg	slaying
vil	will, wish
vildi	wanted, willed, wished
vilja	wished
viljið	wish
viljum	we-wish, wish
vill	wishes
vilt	will, wish
viltu	will-you
vinskapur	friendship
virti	worthied
vísan	the-verse, verse
vissi	knew
vissu	knew
vist	provisions
víst	certainly
vistaðist	found-a-place
vistar	lodgings
vistin	the-supply
vistina	the-provisions
vísu	a-verse
vit	know, wit
vita	knew, know, to-know
vitið	know
vitrastur	the-wisest

Word List (Old Icelandic to English)

Old Icelandic	English
vitsmuna	intellect
von	expected
vopnast	armed
vor	our
vorið	spring
vorkunn	understandable
voru	our, was, were, where
voruð	were
vorum	were

Y, y

yðrum	yours
yður	you
yðvar	of-you, you
yðvart	your, yours
yfir	over, sitting
ykkur	you
ynni	won
yrði	became
yrk	compose, write
yrkisefnin	the-themes
yrkja	compose, to-compose

Ý, ý

ýmsu	about
ýttum	pushed

Word List (English to Old Icelandic)

Word List (English to Old Icelandic)

English	Old Icelandic	English	Old Icelandic

A, a

English	Old Icelandic
a	á, á
about	á, á, á, á, á, á, á, á
an	á
at	á, á, á, á, á
and	að, að, að, að, að
as	að, að, að, að, að
another	aðra, áður, áður, áður, æpir, æptu, ær
after	áður, áður, áður
awed	ær
again	aftur
Agdanes (place)	Agðanes, Agðaness
Agdi (name)	Agði, Agði
age	aldri
all	allir, allir, allra, allreiður, allt, allur, allvel
all-angry	allreiður
all-well	allvel
all-year	ári
ate	át, át
always	ávallt, bað
asked	bað, bað, bað, báðir, bæði
a-child	barn
a-better	betri
ask	biðja
at-table	borðum
away	brott, brott, brottu, brynju, brynju
a-plate	diskur
a-drapa (poem)	drápu
a-dream	draumur
alone	einn
am	er, er
am-I	er
are	er, er, er, er
are-you	ertu
are-we	erum, eta
accomplished	fær
a-few	fám
ahead	fram
agreeable	gæfur
a-delight	gaman
amusement	gamans
a-gold-ring	gullhring
autumn	haustið, haustum
avenge	hefna
avenged	hefnt
a-horse	hest
a-lot-of	hlaut
a-hearing	hljóð
a-thing	hluti
a-threat	hótun
afraid	hræddir
awhile	hríð, hringum, hroðið, hróður
a-house	hús
an-Icelander	íslenskur
an-earl	jarl
accuse	kæra
a-calf	kálf
a-man	karlmanni, kastað
a-bell	klukku
a-choice	kostur
assigned	lagin
allow	láta, láta
answered	leyst, líf, lífi, lífinu
a-little	litlu
appetite	lysti
as-might	mátti
as-long-as	meðan
a-mark	mörk
against	móti, móti
any	nokkra
anything	nokkuð
also	og
ashes	ösku
an-axe	öxi
axe	öxi
advice	ráð
advisable	ráð
advised	ráði
appointed	ráðinn, ráðleitinn
agreement	ráðs
a-search	rannsóknar

Word List (English to Old Icelandic)

English	*Old Icelandic*	*English*	*Old Icelandic*
anger	reiði	biting	bitið
actually	reyndar	bigger-men	bokkar
afterwards	síðan, síðar	Bolli (name)	Bolla
a-custom	siður	boards	borð
a-poet	skáld, skáldskapar	brought	borin, borinn, bótunum, brá, brákar, brauði, brenndan
announced	sögðuð		
a-spoon	spón		
asking	spurði	breaker	brákar
a-stone	steinn	bread	brauði
ascending	stígandi	burnt	brenndan
answer	svara	brother	bróðir, bróður
a-sword	sverði	boys	drengi
appear	sýnast	but	eða, ef, eftir, eftir
as-soon-as	þegar	back-from	eftir
assembly	þing	brow	enni
assemble	þinga	beam	erðr
argued	þræta	bring	færa
a-third	þriðja	because-of	fyrir
accordingly	því	became	gerðist, gerðu, gerðu, geri
ambiguous	tvíræði, tvíræðisorð		
awake	vakið	beguile	gilja, giljum
awoke	vaknaði	beside	hjá
awaken	vekja	be-heard	hljóðs
actions	verkum	boldly	hraustlega
a-verse	vísu	bad	illa
armed	vopnast	badly	illa
		be-called	kallaðir
		blame	kennt

B, b

English	*Old Icelandic*	*English*	*Old Icelandic*
		bought	keyptuð
		bowed	laut
be	á, á, á, á, á	Byzantium (place)	miklagarði
by	á, á, á	between	milli
before	áðr, aðra, áður, áður, áður, æpir, æptu, ær	below	neðan
		benefit	njótum
back	áður, áður, æpir, æptu	become	orðið, ort, ösku
bid	bað	barter	selja
both	báðir, bæði, bændur, bæta	bench-companion	sessunaut, sessunautur
bears	bar	boil	sjóða
bore	bar	bag	skreppa
Bard (name)	Bárð, Bárður	bag-tackle	skreppuskrúði
belt	belti	buttered	smjörvan
best	best	burst	sprengja, sprungið, spryngi
better	betr, betra		
bites	bita	big-man-like	stórmannlega
bite	bitar	battles	stríði

439

Word List (English to Old Icelandic)

English	Old Icelandic
business	sýslu
because	því
believe	trúa
beginning	upphaf
being	væri, vætti, vakið
becomes	verða, verða
been	verið

C, c

English	Old Icelandic
cried-out	æpir
called-out	æptu
completely	alla, allir
compensation	bæta, bæti, bætti
compensate	bæti
compensated	bætti
carried	bar, Bárð, Bárður
child	barn
children	barna
cunning	brögðóttan, brosti
chain-mail	brynju
coat-of-mail	brynju, brynjuna
command	býð
can	fæ, fær
carry-out	færð
companion	félagi
caught	fengu
commotion	háreysti
call	heita, heitir
court	hirðarinnar
care	hirði
courtiers	hirðin
court-man	hirðmaður
court-men	hirðmanna
calm	hljóða
chieftains	höfðingja
chief-poet	höfuðskáld
circles	hringum
cleared	hroðið, hróður
called	kallaði, kallaðir, kallaður, kann
can-it	kann
cast	kastað, kastaði
cheerful	kátur
come	kem, kemur, kemur, kemur, kenn
came	kemur, kemur, kemur, kenn, kenna, kenndi, kennt
comes	kemur
cow-verses	kolluvísur
come-forward	koma
coming	komið, kominn, komnir
could	kunnu, kurfaldi, kvaddi
composed	kvæði, kveða, kveðinn
compose	kveða, kveðinn, kveðju
cows	kýr
cow-buying	kýrkaupi
coloured	lít
concluded	lokið
could-be	mundi
close-to	nærri
cause	olli
common	samir
chatter	sennur
cuts	skerði
crawled	skreið
crossly	þverlega
consider	þykir
considered	þykir
custom	vanr
certainly	víst

D, d

English	Old Icelandic
descent	ætt
descended	ættaður
disrespected	afvirti
dead	andaður, andróða, annað
difficulty	andróða
death-sentence	banasök
death	bani, bar
drew	brá, brákar, brauði
day	dag, dagana
Denmark (place)	Danmerkur
daring	djarfan
daughter	dóttur
drapa (poem)	drápa

Word List (English to Old Icelandic)

English	Old Icelandic
drapa	drápu
dream	draum, draumur
draws	dregr
draw	dregst
dragon	dreki
drinking	drekka
dreamed	dreymt
drink	drykk, drykkjar
denied	duldu
dwarf	dvergur
delivered	flutt
delight	gaman, gaman
do	ger, ger, gera, gera
does	ger, gera
doing	gera
done	gera, gera, gera
did	gerði, gerði, gerðir
deception	ginning
dug	grafið
deep-red	gruntrauðustum
danger	hættu
disappeared	hverft
dear-friendship	kærleikum
down	niður
decide	ráða
decided	ráða, ráði
delivery	sendingum
disgrace	skömm
debt	skuld
dined	snætt
dared	þorði
dare	þori
dignified	tigulegur
difficult	vandi

E, e

English	Old Icelandic
excellent	ágætur
estate	búi
examples	dæmi
Einar (name)	Einar, Einari, Einars
Einar's (name)	Einars
elderly	eldilegt
Emma (name)	Emmu
ended	enda, enda
England (place)	Englandi, Englands
errand	erindi
eat	eta, eta
eating	eta
extremely	furðulega
enjoyment	gaman
entertaining	gaman
equipped	gyrti
Earl-of-Lade (name)	Hlaðajarli
each	hverjum, hvern, hvers, hversu, hvert
encouraged-lightning	hvofteldingum
each-way	hvorttveggja
evil	illa, illan
evil-ways	ilvegs
equally	jafnan
equally-badly	jafngreypilega
equal	jafnir, jafnsleppt
equally-slip	jafnsleppt
earl	jarl
even	jöfnum
evening	kveldið
easily-satisfied	lítilþægir
end	lýk
educated	menntur
except	nema
enjoy	njót
enough	nóg
eachother	öðrum
Elegant (name)	Prúða
extended	rétti
entertainment	skemmt
entertain	skemmta
exchange	skipt
early	þegar
enduring	þola
endured	þoldi
endures	þolir
extended-out	úti
expected	vætti, vakið

F, f

English	Old Icelandic
for	á, á, á, á, að

Word List (English to Old Icelandic)

English	Old Icelandic
from	á, á, á, að, að, að, að, að
family-small	ættsmár
farmers	bændur, bæta
farmer	bóndi
fair-wind	byr
fine	dýran
fire-house (kitchen)	eldahús
fire	eldi, eldilegt
forehead	enni
few	fá
father	faðir, fæ
Fafnir (name)	Fáfni
found	fann, far, fara
fare	fara
fee-taken	fátækur
fee-servant	féhirði, féhirðinn
fell	féll, felldan, fellt
five	fimm
find	finna, finna, finnferð
Finland-voyages (place)	finnferð
fishermen	fiskimenn
fee	fjár
followers	fjölmennt, fjör
four	fjóra, fjórar
fourth	fjórðung
fourteen	fjórtán
fleeing	flærat
Fljot (place)	Fljótum
Fly (name)	Fluga, Flugu
flew	flugust
father's-killer	föðurbana
fore-knowing	forvitnar
feet	fótum
forwards	fram
from-saying	frásagnar
Frisian (name)	frísa
Frisian	frískur
full	fullt, fullur
follow	fylgja
first	fyrst, fyrstu
fun	gaman
famine	hallæri
from-there	héðan, hefði, hefðir, hefðu
force	hér
fallen	hnigið
fame	hróður
friendship	kærleikum, kálf
felt	kenndi
flesh	kjöts
folded	kurfaldi
finished	lokið
food	mat, matar, matr, mátti
for-me	mér
finished-eating	mettir, mettur
finery	prýði
filthy	saurugt
for-him	sér
food-trough-verses	soðtrogsvísur
for-them	þeim
found-a-place	vistaðist

G, g

English	Old Icelandic
greatly	ærið
grinned	brosti
get	fá, fá, faðir
give	fá, faðir, fæ, fær
go	far, fara, fara, fara, fara, farist
goes	fara, fara
going	fara, farist, fátækur, fáum, fé
gone	farist
got	fékk, fékk
gave	gæfi, gæfur
guarded	gætti, gaf
gaping	gap
garden	garðinn
Gasir (place)	Gásum
granted	gefa
given	gefið, gefin, Geirröð
Geirrod (name)	Geirröð, Geirröðr
guest	gista
gladly	gjarna
glad	glaðr, glaðuř
gnawing	gnadda

442

Word List (English to Old Icelandic)

English	Old Icelandic
good	góð, góða, góðan, góðum, góður, göngum
grasped	greppr
Godwinson (name)	Guðinason
good-rightly	guðréttilegast
Gula-assembly (name)	gulaþing, gulaþings
gold-band	gullhlað
gold-ring	gullhring
gold-inlaid	gullrekin
goat	hafra
giant	jötni
greeted	kvaddi
greeting	kveðju
games	leika
great	mikið, mikið, mikill, mikill, mikinn
greatest	mikla
gluttony	offylli
genitals	reðri
greater	stærri
grant	veita

H, h

English	Old Icelandic
had	ætti, ættsmár, af, af, af, af, aftur, aftur, afvirti, ágætur, Agðanes, Agðaness, Agði, Agði, aldri, alla, allir, allir
hat	átti
higher	hærra, hærri
high	hæst, hættu
have	haf, hafa, hafa, hafa, hafa, hafði, hafðir, hafðir, hafðist
has	hafa, hafa, hafa
having	hafa
Hakon (name)	Hákon, Hákoni
hold	halda
held	haldið, hálfa, Halla
half	hálfa
Halli (name)	Halla, Halla
Halli's (name)	Halla

English	Old Icelandic
Halogaland (place)	Hálogaland, Hálogalandi
her	hana
hand-washing	handlaugar
he	hann, hann, hans
him	hann, hans, hans, hans, hár
his	hans, hár, Haraldi, Haraldi, haraldr, Haraldr, Haralds, Haralds, Haraldur, Háreks, háreysti, hásætið, haustið
Harald (name)	Haraldi, Haraldi, haraldr, Haraldr
Harald's (name)	Haraldi, haraldr, Haraldr
Harek's (name)	Háreks
high-seat	hásætið
has-been	hefir
health	heill
home	heim
hone	hein
honing-grease	heinasmjör
hung	hékk, hélt
hand	hendi, hendi, hendur, hér
hands	hendi
here	hér
hostel	herbergi
horse	hestr, hesturinn
hear	heyra
heard	heyra, heyrði, heyrðu, heyrt, hilmis
helmsman's	hilmis
Hitra (place)	Hítrar
helmet	hjálm
head	höfuð, höfuðið
horn-spoon	hornspónu
hide	húðar
hungry	hungrar, hús
how	hve
how-so	hvers, hversu
hammering	klappar
his-life	lífinu
harm	mein, meir

443

Word List (English to Old Icelandic)

English	Old Icelandic
himself	sér, sér, sessunaut, sessunautur, séuð
hit	skall
heading	stillir
heavy-cargo	þunga
hayfield-wall	túngarði
hardly	varla
have-been	verða

I, i

English	Old Icelandic
in	á, á, að, að, að, að, að, að
it	á, að, að, að, að
intended	ætlað, ætluðu
invited	bað, báðir
if	ef, eftir
I	eg, eg, Einar
in-the-end	enda
is	er
islands	eyjar
intestines	fyrir, fyrr
is-named	heitir
into	í, illa
ill	illt
inside	innan
Iceland (place)	Ísland, Íslandi, Íslands
Iceland-voyage	íslandsfari
Icelanders	íslendinga, íslendingar
Icelander	íslenska, íslenskan, íslenskur
iron-weapon	járn
ironsmith	járnsmiður
intellect	vitsmuna

J, j

English	Old Icelandic
journey	förum
jumped	hljóp
Jutland (place)	Jótlands

K, k

English	Old Icelandic
killed	drap, drápa, drápu, drápu, draum
kill	drepa, drepið
kinsman	frændi, frændunum
kinsmen	frændunum
knife	hníf, hnífi, hnífinum
knife-handle	hnífskafti
knocked-down	hnúskum
knows	kann
know-you	kanntu
Kapuang (place)	Kaupangs
Kaupang (place)	Kaupangur
know	kenn, kenna, kenndi, kennt, keyptuð, kjöts, klappar
knee	kné
knorrs	knörru
kings	konunga
king	konungr
king's	konungr
kin	kyns
known	veit
knew	vissi, vissu, víst

L, l

English	Old Icelandic
lived	bjó
laughed	brosti
lodgings	búð, búfinna
loved	elskaði
lost	firrst, fiskimenn, fjár
life	fjör, fjóra, fjórar
leg	fót
last	fyrra
look-to	gervan
long-neck	hálslangur
long-armed	handsíður
lord	herra
ladened	hlaðna
listen	hlýði
lobsters	humrum
lay	lá, læt, læt, lagði, lagði
let	læt, lagði
laid	lagði, lagðist, lagin, lágu, láguð

Word List (English to Old Icelandic)

English	Old Icelandic
land	land, landi, langa
long	langa, langskip, lát
longships	langskip
leave	látir
lead	leiða
look-for	leita
lands	lendi
leaned	lér
let-up	létti, léttum
lie	liggja, líkaði
liked	líkaði, líkar
like	líkar, líkar
likely	líklegur
looked	lítast, lítið, lítil
little	lítið, lítil, lítilla, lítils, lítilþægir, lítilþægur
little-behaving	lítilþægur
light	ljóst
legal-settlement	lögskilum
lifting	lyftingunni
lies	lýgur
lying	lýgur
less	minna
lesser	minna
lose	missa
long-nosed	neflangr
look	séuð
later	síðar
least	síst
learned	spurði
large-repaying (generous)	stórlyndur
leash	taum

M, m

English	Old Icelandic
man	af, aftur, aftur, afvirti, ágætur
married	átti
master	bóndi
mockery	dáruskapur, dauðan
master-wounder	drottinserðr
me	eg, Einar, Einari
message	erindi
money	fé, fébætur, féhirði
money-bribe	fémúta
many	fjölda, fjöldi, fjölmennt, fjör, fjóra, fjórar
more	fleira, fleiri, flesta, Fljótum, Fluga, Flugu
most	flesta, Fljótum, Fluga, Flugu
mistakes	föll
met	fundumst, furðulega
magic	galdra
made	gera, gera, gerast, gerði
make	gera
moustache	grön
mocking	háðyrðum
most-hardy	herðimestur
mind	hug, hugar
minds	hugar
molars	jaxlar
merchant-men	kaupmennirnir
merchant-ship	kaupskipinu
may	má, maður, maður
matter	mæla, mæla, mættum, Magnús
matters	mæla, mættum, Magnús
Magnus (name)	Magnús
more-suitable	maklegri
men	mann, manna, manna, manni
man's-son	mannsbarn
many-things	margs
mine	mér, mér, merkur, mest, mesta, mestum, mettir, mettur
my	mér, merkur
marks	merkur
much	mikið, mikill, mikill, mikinn, mikla, mikla
mis-liked	mislíkaði
miss	missa
meal	mjöl
morning	morguninn
meet	móti
mouth	munni
must	munt
most-angry	reiðasti

Word List (English to Old Icelandic)

English	Old Icelandic
mood-dragon	skapdreki
mood	skapi

N, n

English	Old Icelandic
never	aldrei, aldrei
not	ei, eiga, eiga, eigi, eigu, eina, einhugi
nothing	einkis, einmælt
nonsense	endilausu
no	engan, engi, engi, enginn, engu, engum, enn
none	engi, enginn, engu, engum, enn
neck	háls, hárinu
named	heita, heitan, heitir, held, heldr, hella
narrow-shouldered	herðilítill
nearby	hjá
nowhere	hvergi
neither	hvorigum
noose	lykkja
neared	næði
near	nær, nærri, næst
next	næsta
necessary	nauðsyn
needs	nauðsynja
necessarily	nauðulega
Njord (name)	Njörðr
north	norður
northern-lands	norðurlönd
Norway (place)	Noreg, Noregi, Noregs
night	nótt
nights	nóttum
now	nú
needed	þurfti
news	tíðinda, tíðindi
nobler	tignari

O, o

English	Old Icelandic
of	á, á, á, á, á, á, ábyrgst, að
on	á, á
other	aðra, aðra, aðrir, ætla, ætla, ætla
others	aðra, aðrir
off	af
of-all	allra, allra
one	annan, annan, annar, annarra, annars, Árnasonar, átti
otherwise	annar
ordered	bað
order	bið, biðja
offered	býður
or	eða
own	eiga
ownership	eigu
one-minded	einhugi
one-meal	einmælt
one-decision	einráðir
once	eitt
or-else	ella
over	fyrir, fyrri, gamall
old	gamall
of-the-floor	gólfið
of-porridge	grautar
obeying	hlýða
of-him	honum
obscenities	hrópyrði
onboard	innanborðs
obscene	klámyrði
obscene-words	klámyrðum
on-way	leiðar
of-footwear	leista
of-your-hair	loðir
one-mark	mörk
obtain	ná
ox-skin	nautaleðrs
one-of	nokkru
other-knowing	öðruvís
open	opið
of-words	orðinn
of-silver	silfurs
occasion	sinn
on-his-side	sínumegin

Word List (English to Old Icelandic)

English	Old Icelandic
of-skins	skinna
of-the-smith	smiðju
one-summer-old	sumargamlan
of-them	þeirri
of-need	þörf
out-from	undan
out	úr, úr, úrleysingur, út, út
out-of	úr
over-praised	úrleysingur
outside	út
out-running	úthlaupi
out-journey	útivist
out-rowing (fishing)	útróður
our	vor, vorið
of-you	yðvar

P, p

English	Old Icelandic
power	afli
pale	blakir, bleikr
prepared	búinn, búinn
plate	disk
provoke	etja
performed	færði
passage	far
poor	fátæka
payment	fé, féð
pierced	festi
people	fólk, föng, fór, fór
procession	för
pay	gjalda
porridge	graut, grautar, grauti, grautinn
peace	grið, griðníðingur
possessions	gripi
possession	gripur
pig	grís
pour	hella
poured	hella
part	hlotist, hlut, hlut
polite	kurteis
poem	kvæði, kvæði
poems	kvæði, kvæði
poem-reward	kvæðislaun
poem-image	kvæðismynd
peaceful	kyrrt
passed	leið
play	leika
permission	lof
praise	lof
promise	lofa
praised	loft, lofuðu
prove	prófa
plan	ráð
proved	reyndust
persistent	seinþreyttur
purse	sjóði
poet	skáld
poets	skáld, skáld
poetry	skáldskap
place	staðar, standa
piece	stykki
promising	vænstur
provisions	vist
pushed	ýttum

Q, q

English	Old Icelandic
queen	drottning
quickly	flýta, fólk
quickly-cleared	rymskyndir
questions	spurt

R, r

English	Old Icelandic
responsible	ábyrgst
returning	aftur
related-to	átti
ring-land	bauglands
ready	búnir
room	deild
received	fékkst, fer
rhymes	föng
ready-made	gjör
revenge	hefnt
rather	heldr, hella, hella
running	hlaupi, hleyp
ran	hleypur, hljóð

Word List (English to Old Icelandic)

English	Old Icelandic
reasonable	hófi
roaring	hröng
rapped	klappaði
recited	kvað, kvað, kvað, kváðu, kvæði, kvæði
recite	kveð, kveð
reciting	kveðið
reward	launa
rewarded	launaði
repay	launin, leðr
rented	leigðu
remembered	munað, munaður, mundi
reversed	öfugt
robbery	rán
Ran (name)	Ránar
round	randa
Raud (name)	Rauð, rauðan
red	rauðar, rauðum
ruled	réð
Reine (place)	Rein
rowing	reru
richer	ríkari
rye-loaf	rúghleifa
rooms	rúms
row	runa
rattled	skall
rapidly	skjótt
rushed	snaraði
return	snúa
roasted	steiktur
refused	synjuðu
receives	þiggi

S, s

English	Old Icelandic
suppose	ætla, ætla
supposed	ætla
Son-of-Arni (name)	Árnasonar
settled	bjó, blakir, bleikr, boði, borði, borði
soon	brátt
smiled	brosti
shop-keeping	búðarvörð
spears	dörrum
spent	eyddust
Slayer-of-Fafnir (name)	Fáfnisbana
sent-for	fara
stout	feitur
Sami-goods	finnskrepp
stories	frásagnir
stopped	hætti
sound-advice	heilræði
sleeping-quarters	herbergjum
silence	hljóð, hljóðgreipum, hljóðið
sound-grippers (ears)	hljóðgreipum
share	hlut
suits	hlýða
shaken	hrökkviskafls
spine	hryggurinn
she	hún
sole-bucket	ilfat
struck	klappaði
said	kvað, kvað, kváðu, kvæði, kvæði, kvæði, kvæðið, kvæðið, kvæðin, kvæðinu, kvæðisins
spoke	kvað, kváðu, kvæði
say	kveð, kveða, kveðið, kveðið
spoken	kveðið
short-poem	kviðlingur
skin	leðr
seek	leita, leita
seeking	leita
sought	leitaði, leitaðir
speak	mæl, mæla, mæla, mælti, mæltist
satisfied	mettir, mettur
shall	mun, mun, mun, mun, mun, mun, munað, munaður
should	mun, mun, mun, mun, mun, munað, munaður, mundi, mundi, mundi
should-be	mun, mun, mun
shall-you	muntu, muntu
serpent	naðri

Word List (English to Old Icelandic)

English	Old Icelandic
slander	níð
some	nokkru, nokkru, nokkru, nokkrum, nokkuð
somehow	nokkru
somewhat	nokkru, nokkrum
something	nokkuð, nokkuð
shouting	óp
sharp-tongued	orðhvass
saw	sá, sá, sæhafa
so	sá, sæhafa, sækir, sæsjúkur
sea-scattered	sæhafa
seasick	sæsjúkur
sit	sæti, sætis, sættir
seat	sætis
settlements	sættir
sake	sakir
sake-less	saklausa
same	sama, saman
sat	sátu, sátu, sáu, sé, sé
see	sé, sé
seen	séð
sold	seldag
same-as	sem
send	send
sent	sendi
sees	sér
set	setja, settist
sedately	settlega
since	síð, síðan, síðan, síðast
side	síðu
sailed	sigldi, sigldu
Sigurd (name)	Sigurð, Sigurðarson, Sigurði, Sigurðr
Sigurdson (name)	Sigurðarson
silver	silfri, silfrinu
silver-band	silfurhólkur
silver-wound	silfurvafið
settle	sitja
sift	síu
seldom	sjaldan
sick	sjúkur
scarlet	skarlatsklæðum
ship	skip, skip
ship-smiths	skipsmiðir
ships	skipuðu
shield	skjöld
shoes	skó
scandal	skömm
sheathed	slíðrar
such	slík, slíka, slíkir, slíkt
smith-bellows	smiðbelgja
snake	snák
Sarcastic-Halli (name)	Sneglu-Halla, Sneglu-Halli
sleep	sofa, sögðu
son	son
sickness	sótt
Stad (place)	Stað
standing	standa, standið, steiktur
stone-kettle	steinkatli
stands	stendur
stood	stóð
steersman	stýrimaður
steers	stýrir
strong	styrk
south	suður
southern-men	suðurmenn
summer	sumar
Svarfadardal (place)	Svarfaðardal
starving	sveltir
sword	sverð, sverði, sverðið
shrinks-from	svífst
swine	svíni
sleek	sýlt
showed	sýna, sýndi
show	sýnir
seems	sýnist, synjuðu, sýr, sýslu
sow	sýr
stewardship	sýslu
siblings	systkinum
speaking	tala
silenced	þagnaði, þakkaði
straight-away	þegar
servant	þjón
serve	þjóna
service	þjónusta, þjónustu
seemed	þótti, þótti, þóttir

Word List (English to Old Icelandic)

English	Old Icelandic	English	Old Icelandic
scandalous	undarlegt	then	en, enda, endilausu, enga, engan, engi, engi, enginn, engu, engum, enn, enn, enn
slaying	víg		
spring	vorið		
sitting	yfir		
		the-end	enda
		they-are	eruð
		to-eat	etið
		the-legs	fæturnir

T, t

English	Old Icelandic	English	Old Icelandic
that	á, á, á, á, ábyrgst, að, að, að, að, að, að, að	travel	far, fara, fara, fara
		travelled	farið, fars
to	á, á, á, ábyrgst, að, að, að	the-poor	fátækra
		the-money	féð
than	að, að, að, að	the-Sami (name)	finna
the	að, að, að, að, aðra, aðra, aðrir, ætla, ætla, ætla, af	the-fjord	firðinum
		to-extend	flenna
		the-most	flest
this	að, að, að, aðra, aðra, aðrir, ætla, ætla, ætla, af	to-meet	fund
		to-delight	gaman
		the-house	garðinn
taxes	akta	the-wall	garðinn, garðinum, garðsins, garðurinn
the-next	annan		
the-town	bæjar		
town	bænum	to-give	gefa
the-boat	báti, báti	told	getið, gjalda, gjör, gólf, gólfið
the-ship's-boat	báti		
the-bench	bekkinn	the-floor	gólf, gólfið
the-best	best, bið	the-porridge	grautinn
to-ask	biðja	the-poor-thing	greyið
table	borði, borði	truce-breaker	griðníðingur
the-table	borði, borðið	the-trinkets	gripanna, gripi, gripi
tables	borðin	treasure	gripi
the-city	börg	the-handle	haddan
the-children	börnin	the-lid	haddan
transformed	brást	to-have	hafa
the-day	daginn	the harbour	hafnan
thick-set	digrastur	to-hold	halda
the-plate	diskinum	the-hairs	hárinu
the-Danes (name)	dönum	the-heath	heiði
the-killing	drápi	threat	heitan
the-drapa (poem)	drápuna	think	held, heldr, hella, hella
this-dream	draum	to-hand	hendi
the-dragon-ship	drekanum	the-horse	hestinn
the-boy	drengurinn	to-hear	heyra
the-queen	drottning, drottningu	the-court	hirð, hirðinni
the-dwarf	dverg, dverginn	the-court-men	hirðinni
the-fire	eld	the-helmet	hjálmfaldinn
		things	hluti

Word List (English to Old Icelandic)

English	Old Icelandic
to-strike	höggva
the-hall	höllina, höllunni
to-him	honum
turn	horfa
the-ring	hring, hringinn, hringinum
the-spine	hrygg
thought	hugði, hugðu, hún, hvað, hvað, hvar, hver, hver, hverfur
turned	hverfur, hvergi, hvergi, hverju
trade	iðnar
the-giant	jötun
the-calf	kálfinn, kálfurinn
to-call	kalla
the-kettle	katlinum
traded	kaup
trading-voyage	kaupferð
the-trading-men	kaupmönnum
trading-men	kaupmönnum
trading-ship	kaupskipinu
teach	kenna
the-binding	kilju
the-king	konung, konungi, konungi, konunginn, konunginum, konungr, konungs, konungs, konungsgarð, konungsins
the-king's	konungi, konunginn, konunginum
the-poem	kvæðið, kvæðin, kvæðinu
the-poetry	kvæðunum
the-evening	kveld
the-land	landi, landinu
the-noose	lykkjan
the-whitings	lýsu
the-man	maður, maðurinn
talked	mæltur, maklegra
the-matter	málið
to-me	mér
the-middle	mitt
the-people	mönnum
the-border	mörkina
take	ná, naðri, næði, nær, nærri, næst
took	nam, námu, nauðsyn, nauðsynja, nauðulega, nautaleðrs, nefndur
the-slander	níðið
the-night	nótt
the-other	öðru
too-much	ofraun
terrible	ógurlegur
the-serpent	ormr
the-whole	óskert
to-us	oss
the-axe	öxarinnar, öxina
trickery	prettum
trick	prettur
the-ruler	ræsi
the-trunk	rana
the-red	rauðan
tested	reynt
told-of	sagði
told-to	sagt
together	saman
true-words	sannmæli
true	
truth	satt
tell	seg, seggr, segi
to-tell	segja
to-sell	selja
themselves	sér, sér
to-get-hurt	serðast
the-last	síðast
the-custom	siður
the-silver	silfrinu
tendon	sinina
theirs	sinn, sinn, sinnar, sinni
their	sinnar, sinni
these	sinni, sínum, sínumegin
the-purse	sjóðnum
the-shaft	skaftið
the-poet	skáld, skálda
the-ship	skip, skipið, skipið
the-ships	skipin
the-hammer	sleggju
the-story	sögu

Word List (English to Old Icelandic)

English	Old Icelandic
the-place	stað
the-street	stræti
the-shore	ströndu
the-southerners	suðurmenn
tanner	sútari
to-answer	svara
this-lad	sveini
takes	taki
talking	talað
tongs	tangar
the-leash	taumsendanum, taumsins
taken	tekið, tekist
there	þær, þætti, þættist, þagna, þagnaði
thanked	þakkaði
they	þar, þar, þars, þau
them	þeim, þeim, þeir
to-you	þér
the-assembly	þingið, þinginu, þings, þingsins
Thingvellir (place)	Þingvallar
Thjodolf (name)	Þjóðólf, Þjóðólfs
Thjodolf's (name)	Þjóðólfs
thief	þjófur
the-servants	þjónustumenn
Thjotta (place)	Þjóttu
though	þó, þögnuðu
thanks	þökk
Thor (name)	Þór, Þóra
Thora (name)	Þóra, Þorbergs
Thorberg's (name)	Þorbergs
Thorleif (name)	Þorleifi, Þorleifur
Thorljot (name)	Þorljóti, Þorljótur
threatening	þrætu
Trondheim (place)	Þrándheim, Þrándheims
three-winters-old	þrevett
third	þriðja
three	þrjár, þrjú
thula (poem)	þulu
therefore	því
towards	til
time	tíma
ten	tíu
tar	tjöru

English	Old Icelandic
turf	torf
trough	trog
Tuta (name)	Túta, Tútu
two-fold	tveföld
two	tveir, tví
tut	tví
threw	varp
the-wager	veðjanin
to-be	vera
the-verse	vísan
the-supply	vistin
the-provisions	vistina
to-know	vita
the-wisest	vitrastur
the-themes	yrkisefnin
to-compose	yrkja

U, u

use	brúki
urged	eggjaði
undertaking	færð
upper-shaft	forskeftinu
usually	jafnan
ugly-limbed	ljótlimaður
unreliable	óeinarðarmaður
un-infatuated	öfundsjúkur
upside-down	öndvert
un-custom-mixing	ósiðblandnir
us	oss
unsettled	ótæpt
un-thanks	óþökk
un-ranking	ótiginna
un-truthful	ótrúlegir
unworthy	óvirðulegt
upright	réttur
until	til, til
up-to	til, tíma
under	undan, undarlegt
up	upp
upped	upp
understandable	vorkunn

V, v

Word List (English to Old Icelandic)

English	Old Icelandic
very-short	allskammur
vacation	orlofs
village	þorpi
verse	vísan

W, w

English	Old Icelandic
was	á, á, ábyrgst, að, að, að, að
with	á, ábyrgst, að, að, að
waited	beið
what	er, er, er, er, er, eru
when	er
where	er, er, er, eru, eruð
which	er, er, eru
who	er, eru, eruð
we-are	eru
went	færu, fæturnir, Fáfnisbana, fagnar, far, far, fara
welcomed	fagnar
went-you	fórstu
willing	fús
went-before	fyrri
walking	gengju
we-are-going	göngum
was-named	hét
whom	hvern
why	hví, hvorigum
whether	hvort
worded	kveðið, kveðin, kveðin, kveðst, kveður
words	kveður, kveld, kvenna, kviðlingur
women	kvenna
with-footwear	leist
well-deserved	maklegra
while	meðan
will	mun, mun, mun
would	mun, mun, munað, munaður, mundi, mundi, mundi, mundir
would-be	mun, munað
would-you	muntu
word	orð
words-separated	orðaskil
word-fallen	orðfall
word-bold	orðgreppur
word-tall	orðhákur
we	oss, ótæpt, óþökk
well-advising	ráðugastur
wrong	rangt
written	ritað
wounded	sarð
were	sátu, sáu, sé, sé, séð, seen, seg, seggr
withhold	spara
with-bread	sufli
wonder	undur
wonder-created	undurskapaður
won	unnið, uns
without	utan
wicked-chieftain	vændishöfðingjar
wretched	válegrar
warily	varlega
wager	veðja, veðjanin
way	veg, vegar
well	vel
worth	verða, verðrat
worthy-that	verðrat
worthy	verður
work	verk
workman's	verkmanns
worse	verr, verra, verra
worst	verra
winter	vetri, vetur, veturinn
winter-lodgings	veturvistar
winter-provisions	veturvistar
wish	vil, vildi, vildi, vildi
wanted	vildi
willed	vildi
wished	vildi, vilja
we-wish	viljum
wishes	vill
will-you	viltu
worthied	virti
wit	vit
write	yrk

Y, y

Word List (English to Old Icelandic)

English	Old Icelandic
yet	enna
Yule-day	jóladag
Yule	jólin, jólunum
your-life	lífinu
yourself	sjálfur
yours	sú, suður, suðurmenn, suðurmenn, sufli, sumar, sumargamlan, sumir
you	þér, þér, þess, þessa, þessar, þessi
you-two	þið
your	yðvart

A Word Comparison of Old Norse and Old Icelandic Words

A Word Comparison of Old Norse and Old Icelandic Words

Old Norse	Old Icelandic	English
áðr	áður	after
áðr	áður	back
áðr	áður	before
ætlat	ætlað	intended
ættaðr	ættaður	descended
aftr	aftur	back
aftr	aftur	returning
ágætr	ágætur	excellent
aldrigi	aldrei	never
allr	allur	all
allreiðr	allreiður	all-angry
allskammr	allskammur	very-short
andaðr	andaður	dead
annarr	annar	another
annarr	annar	otherwise
annat	annað	another
annat	annað	other
at	að	a
at	að	and
at	að	as
at	að	at
at	að	by
at	að	for
at	að	in
at	að	it
at	að	of
at	að	than
at	að	that
at	að	the
at	að	this
at	að	to
at	að	with
átta	átti	related-to
bana-sök	banasök	death-sentence
Bárðr	Bárður	Bard (name)
bátnum	bátinum	the-boat
beidda	beiddi	asked
bezt	best	best
bezt	best	the-best
bitit	bitið	biting

Old Norse	Old Icelandic	English
blakkir	blakir	pale
bœjar	bæjar	the-town
bœndr	bændur	farmers
bœnum	bænum	town
bœta	bæta	compensation
bœti	bæti	compensate
bœtti	bætti	compensated
borðit	borðið	table
borðit	borðið	the-table
bú-Finna	búfinna	farmers
burt	brott	away
burt	brott	brought
burtu	brottu	away
býðr	býður	offered
Danmerkr	Danmerkur	Denmark (place)
dáruskapr	dáruskapur	mockery
dauðr	dauður	dead
digrastr	digrastur	thick-set
diskr	diskur	a-plate
dœmi	dæmi	examples
drápu	drápa	drapa (poem)
draumr	draumur	a-dream
draumr	draumur	dream
dregr	dregur	drew
drengrinn	drengurinn	the-boy
drepit	drepið	kill
drepit	drepið	killed
drepr	drepur	killed
dvergr	dvergur	dwarf
eðr	eða	and
eðr	eða	but
eðr	eða	or
eigi	ei	not
eigi	ekki	not
eign	eigu	ownership
Einari	Einar	Einar (name)
Einarr	Einar	Einar (name)
ek	eg	I
ek	eg	me
eldr	eldur	fire

A Word Comparison of Old Norse and Old Icelandic Words

Old Norse	Old Icelandic	English
elliligt	eldilegt	elderly
endileysu	endilausu	nonsense
engan	öngvan	none
engi	enginn	none
engum	öngum	no
enn	en	and
enn	en	but
enn	en	than
enn	en	that
enn	en	then
ertú	ertu	are-you
eru	er	is
eru	eruð	they-are
eru	erum	are-we
etit	etið	to-eat
eyja	eyjar	islands
fær	færð	carry-out
fær	færð	undertaking
Fáfnis-bana	Fáfnisbana	Slayer-of-Fafnir (name)
fáim	fáum	get
farit	farið	travelled
farit	farist	gone
fátœka	fátæka	poor
fátœkr	fátækur	fee-taken
fátœkra	fátækra	the-poor
fébœtr	fébætur	compensation
féit	féð	the-money
feitr	feitur	stout
fekk	fékk	give
fekk	fékk	got
fekk	fékk	had
fekkst	fékkst	received
feldan	felldan	killed
fell	féll	fell
ferr	fer	go
ferr	fer	goes
ferr	fer	went
flœr-at	flærat	fleeing
fœra	færa	bring
fœra	færa	brought
fœra	fara	sent-for
fœrði	færði	performed
fœrðr	færðr	brought
fœri	færu	went
fœrr	fær	accomplished
fœtrnir	fæturnir	the-legs
fór	för	before
forskeftinn	forskeftinu	upper-shaft
fórtu	fórstu	went-you
frískr	frískur	Frisian
fullr	fullur	full
fundu	fundum	found
furðanliga	furðulega	extremely
fúss	fús	willing
fyr	fyrir	before
fyrr	fyrri	went-before
gæfr	gæfur	agreeable
ganga	gangi	go
gangu	göngum	going
garðrinn	garðurinn	the-wall
gefi	gæfi	gave
gefit	gefið	given
Geirrauð	Geirröð	Geirrod (name)
Geirrauðr	Geirröðr	Geirrod (name)
gengi	gengju	walking
gera	gervan	look-to
gerir	gerðir	done
gerit	gerið	do
gerla	gjörla	completely
getit	getið	told
glaðr	glaður	glad
gnauða	gnadda	gnawing
góðr	góður	good
gólfit	gólfið	the-floor
görr	gjör	ready-made
grafit	grafið	dug
grautr	grautur	porridge
greyit	greyið	the-poor-thing
griðníðingr	griðníðingur	truce-breaker
gripina	gripuna	the-trinkets
gripr	gripur	possession
gríss	grís	pig
guðréttligast	guðréttilegast	good-rightly

A Word Comparison of Old Norse and Old Icelandic Words

Old Norse	Old Icelandic	English
gyrði	gyrti	equipped
hafða	hafði	had
haldit	haldið	held
hálslangr	hálslangur	long-neck
handsiðr	handsíður	long-armed
hanh	hann	he
hann	honum	he
hanu	hann	he
Haraldr	Haraldur	Harald (name)
hásætit	hásætið	high-seat
haustit	haustið	autumn
hávan	hafnan	the harbour
hefði	hafði	had
hefði	hefðu	had
hefðim	hefðum	have
hefr	hefur	had
heilt	hellt	rather
hekk	hékk	hung
helt	hélt	held
helzt	helst	rather
hendr	hendur	hand
herðalítill	herðilítill	narrow-shouldered
herðamestr	herðimestur	most-hardy
hestrinn	hesturinn	horse
heyrða	heyrði	heard
hirðmaðr	hirðmaður	court-man
hit	hið	the
hleypr	hleypur	ran
hljóðit	hljóðið	silence
hlotizt	hlotist	part
hlutr	hlutur	part
hnífskefti	hnífskafti	knife-handle
hnigit	hnigið	fallen
hnígr	hnígur	fell
höfuðit	höfuðið	head
höldnum	höldnu	held
höllinni	höllunni	the-hall
hon	hún	it
hon	hún	she
hornspánu	hornspónu	horn-spoon
hraustliga	hraustlega	boldly
hringnum	hringinum	the-ring
hroðit	hroðið	cleared
hróðr	hróður	fame
hrökkvi-skafls	hrökkviskafls	shaken
hryggrinn	hryggurinn	spine
hugða	hugði	thought
hvárigum	hvorigum	neither
hvárn	hvern	each
hvárr	hvor	each
hvárt	hvort	each
hvárt	hvort	whether
hvárttveggja	hvorttveggja	each-way
hvat	hvað	that
hvat	hvað	what
hvé	hve	how
hverfr	hverfur	turned
hverjar	hvað	that
hverju	hvoru	which
hverr	hver	what
hverr	hver	who
hveru	hvern	each
hveru	hvern	what
hveru	hvern	whom
hví	því	if
hví	því	why
Íslands-fari	íslandsfari	Iceland-voyage
íslenzka	íslenska	Icelander
íslenzkan	íslenskan	Icelander
íslenzkr	íslenskur	an-Icelander
íslenzkr	íslenskur	Icelander
jafngreypiliga	jafngreypilega	equally-badly
járnsmiðr	járnsmiður	ironsmith
jólum	jólunum	Yule
kagtat	kastað	cast
kálfrinn	kálfurinn	the-calf
kallaði	konungur	the-king
kallaðr	kallaður	called
kanntú	kanntu	know-you
kátr	kátur	cheerful
Kaupang	Kaupangur	Kaupang (place)
kemr	kemur	came

A Word Comparison of Old Norse and Old Icelandic Words

Old Norse	Old Icelandic	English	Old Norse	Old Icelandic	English
kemr	kemur	come	lögðu	lögðum	laid
kemr	kemur	comes	lokit	lokið	concluded
kendi	hendi	hands	lokit	lokið	ended
keyptut	keyptuð	bought	lokit	lokið	finished
kníf	hníf	knife	lönd	lendi	lands
knífi	hnífi	knife	lýgr	lýgur	lies
knífinum	hnífinum	knife	lýgr	lýgur	lying
knúskim	hnúskum	knocked-down	maðr	maður	a-man
			maðr	maður	man
köllu	köllum	call	maðr	maður	the-man
Kollu-vísur	kolluvísur	cow-verses	maðrinn	maðurinn	the-man
kom	kemur	came	makligra	maklegra	well-deserved
komit	komið	came	makligri	maklegri	more-suitable
komit	komið	come	makligust	maklegust	the-best
komit	komið	coming	málit	málið	the-matter
konungr	konungur	the-king	málsþörf	máls	matter
konungr	konungur	the-king's	matr	matur	food
konungr	konungurinn	the-king	megu	megum	may
konungrinn	konungur	the-king	menn	mönnum	people
konungrinn	konungurinn	the-king	menntr	menntur	educated
kostr	kostur	a-choice	merkr	merkur	marks
kurteiss	kurteis	polite	mestu	mestum	most
kúrvaldi	kurfaldi	folded	mettr	mettur	finished-eating
kvæðis-launin	kvæðislaun	poem-reward			
kvæðis-mynd	kvæðismynd	poem-image	mettr	mettur	satisfied
kvæðit	kvæðið	poem	mik	mér	me
kvæðit	kvæðið	the-poem	mik	mig	me
kveðit	kveðið	spoken	mikit	mikið	great
kveðit	kveðið	worded	mikit	mikið	much
kveðr	kveður	recited	mjök	mjög	much
kveðr	kveður	words	mjöli	mjöl	meal
kveldit	kveldið	evening	mœttum	mættum	met
kviðlingr	kviðlingur	short-poem	morgininn	morguninn	morning
lágu	láguð	laid	mun'k	mun	will
látit	látið	had	muna	mun	would
látit	látið	let	munat	munað	remembered
leggr	leggur	laid	munda	mundi	remembered
lendr	lendur	land	mundu	mundi	could-be
líklegr	líklegur	likely	muntú	muntu	shall-you
líkr	líkur	like	muntú	muntu	should
lítilþægr	lítilþægur	little-behaving	muntú	muntu	would-you
lítit	lítið	little	munu	munuð	shall
ljótlimaðr	ljótlimaður	ugly-limbed	næða	næði	neared

458

A Word Comparison of Old Norse and Old Icelandic Words

Old Norse	Old Icelandic	English
nauðliga	nauðulega	necessarily
nefndr	nefndur	named
níðit	níðið	the-slander
niðr	niður	down
nökkur	nokkur	some
nökkur	nokkur	something
nökkura	nokkra	any
nökkurr	nokkur	something
nökkuru	nokkru	one-of
nökkuru	nokkru	some
nökkuru	nokkru	somehow
nökkuru	nokkru	somewhat
nökkurum	nokkrum	some
nökkut	nokkuð	anything
nökkut	nokkuð	something
nökkut	nokkuð	somewhat
norðr	norður	north
norðrlönd	norðurlönd	northern-lands
öðruvísi	öðruvís	other-knowing
œpir	æpir	cried-out
œptu	æptu	called-out
œrit	ærið	greatly
œrr	ær	awed
óeyrðarmaðr	óeinarðarmaður	unreliable
of	af	off
öfigt	öfugt	reversed
oftar	aftur	again
öfundsjúkr	öfundsjúkur	un-infatuated
ógrligr	ógurlegur	terrible
ok	og	also
ok	og	and
öngan	öngvan	no
opit	opið	open
orðfátt	orðfall	word-fallen
orðgreppr	orðgreppur	word-bold
orðhákr	orðhákur	word-tall
orðit	orðið	become
orðit	orðið	worded
órleysingr	úrleysingur	over-praised
órlofs	orlofs	vacation
orm	ormr	the-serpent
orta	orti	worded
ósiðblendnir	ósiðblandnir	un-custom-mixing
óskerðan	óskert	the-whole
ótíginna	ótiginna	un-ranking
ótrúligir	ótrúlegir	un-truthful
óvirðuligt	óvirðulegt	unworthy
penningar	peningar	money
penningum	peningum	payment
prettr	prettur	trick
ráðar	ráða	decide
ráðigastr	ráðugastur	well-advising
ræð'k	ræð	speak
Rauðr	Rauður	Raud (name)
reðra	reðri	genitals
réttr	réttur	upright
ritat	ritað	written
röru	reru	rowing
sá	sáu	saw
sá	seen	so
sá's	sá	so
sæsjúkr	sæsjúkur	seasick
sagða	sagði	said
sagði	segir	said
sagði	segir	told
sagðir	segir	said
satt?	satt	true
saurigt	saurugt	filthy
sé'k	sé	see
segir	sagði	said
segit	segið	tell
seinþreyttr	seinþreyttur	persistent
séit	séuð	look
sessunautr	sessunautur	bench-companion
sét	séð	seen
setit	setið	sat
settliga	settlega	sedately
sezt	sest	sat
siðr	siður	a-custom
siðr	siður	the-custom
síður	síðr	since
Sigurðr	Sigurður	Sigurd (name)

A Word Comparison of Old Norse and Old Icelandic Words

Old Norse	Old Icelandic	English
sik	sig	him
sik	sig	himself
silfr	silfur	silver
silfrhólkr	silfurhólkur	silver-band
silfrs	silfurs	of-silver
silfrvafit	silfurvafið	silver-wound
sit'k	sit	sit
sit'k	sitk	one
sitr	situr	sat
sízt	síst	least
sjálfr	sjálfur	yourself
sjúkr	sjúkur	sick
skaftit	skaftið	the-shaft
skaltú	skaltu	shall-you
skemt	skemmt	entertainment
skemta	skemmta	entertain
skift	skipt	exchange
skilat	skilað	settled
skipit	skipið	ship
skipit	skipið	the-ship
skreppuskrúði	skreppuskrúði	bag-tackle
skulu	skuluð	should
skulut	skuluð	should
skylda	skyldi	would
skyldi	skyldu	should
slíkir	slíkt	such
snöri	sneri	turned
snúit	snúið	turned
sœkir	sækir	sought
sögðu	sögðuð	announced
sögðuzt	sögðust	said
sómir	samir	common
Sorptrogsvísur	soðtrogsvísur	food-trough-verses
spán	spón	a-spoon
sprungit	sprungið	burst
spyrr	spyr	asked
standit	standið	standing
steiktr	steiktur	roasted
stendr	stendur	stands
stœrri	stærri	greater
stórlyndr	stórlyndur	large-repaying (generous)
stórmannliga	stórmannlega	big-man-like
stórum	steinkatli	stone-kettle
stund	stund	awhile
stýrimaðr	stýrimaður	steersman
suðr	suður	south
suðrmenn	suðurmenn	southern-men
suðrmenn	suðurmenn	the-southerners
svá	svo	so
svá	svo	then
svarat	svarað	answered
sverðit	sverðið	sword
sýndisk	sýnist	seems
sýnna	sýnast	appear
takit	takið	take
talat	talað	talking
taumi	taum	leash
taumsendanum	taumsendanum	the-leash
tekit	tekið	taken
tekizt	tekist	taken
þá	þó	though
það	þau	that
þangat	þangað	from-there
þar's	þars	there
þari	þarmr	intestines
þat	það	it
þat	það	than
þat	það	that
þat	það	the
þat	það	this
þat	þó	though
þeira	þeirra	theirs
þeira	þeirra	them
þeiri	þeirri	of-them
þeiri	þeirri	theirs
þessarrar	þessar	this
þetta	það	that
þik	þig	you
þinginn	þinginu	the-assembly
þingit	þingið	the-assembly

A Word Comparison of Old Norse and Old Icelandic Words

Old Norse	Old Icelandic	English
Þingvalla	Þingvallar	Thingvellir (place)
þit	þið	you-two
Þjóðólfr	Þjóðólfur	Thjodolf (name)
þjófr	þjófur	thief
þó	þá	then
þœtti	þætti	seems
þœttist	þættist	thought
Þórbergs	Þorbergs	Thorberg's (name)
Þórleifi	Þorleifi	Thorleif (name)
Þórleifr	Þorleifur	Thorleif (name)
Þórljóti	Þorljóti	Thorljot (name)
Þórljótr	Þorljótur	Thorljot (name)
þóttumst	þóttist	seemed
þóttumst	þóttist	thought
þula	þulu	thula (poem)
þverliga	þverlega	crossly
þykki	þyki	seems
þykki	þyki	think
þykki	þykir	seems
þykkir	þykir	consider
þykkir	þykir	considered
þykkir	þykir	seems
þykkir	þykir	think
þykkja	þykja	seemed
þyrði	þorði	dared
tiguligr	tigulegur	dignified
tœki	tæki	take
tóku	tókuð	took
tvá	tvo	two
tvíræð	tvíræði	ambiguous
tvíræðis-orð	tvíræðisorð	ambiguous
tvöföld	tveföld	two-fold
undarligt	undarlegt	scandalous
undr	undur	wonder
undrskapaðr	undurskapaður	wonder-created
unnit	unnið	won
unz	uns	until
ut	út	out
útan	utan	out
útan	utan	without
útar	utar	out
úti	út	out
útróðr	útróður	out-rowing (fishing)
vænstr	vænstur	promising
vænti	vætti	expected
vakit	vakið	awake
vaknaða	vaknaði	awoke
váligrar	válegrar	wretched
ván	von	expected
vánligt	von	expected
vápnast	vopnast	armed
várit	vorið	spring
várkunn	vorkunn	understandable
varliga	varlega	warily
várr	vor	our
váru	voru	our
váru	voru	was
váru	voru	were
váru	voru	where
váru	voruð	were
várum	vorum	were
veginn	var	was
veltr	veltur	hung
vér	við	we
vera	vilja	wished
verða	verði	being
verðr	verður	worthy
verit	verið	become
verit	verið	been
verra	vera	was
vetr	vetur	winter
vetrinn	veturinn	winter
vetrvistar	veturvistar	winter-lodgings
vetrvistar	veturvistar	winter-provisions
vilda	vildi	wished
vilit	viljið	wish
vilja	vera	to-be

A Word Comparison of Old Norse and Old Icelandic Words

Old Norse	Old Icelandic	English
vilju	viljum	wish
vill	vilt	will
vill	vilt	wish
viltú	viltu	will-you
vinskapr	vinskapur	friendship
virði	virti	worthied
vit	við	we
vit	við	with
vitit	vitið	know
vitrastr	vitrastur	the-wisest
yðar	yðvar	you
yðarr	yðvar	of-you
yðart	yðvart	your
yðart	yðvart	yours
yðr	yður	you
ykkr	ykkur	you

www.ingramcontent.com/pod-product-compliance
Lightning Source LLC
Chambersburg PA
CBHW051358070526
44584CB00023B/3205